D1590916

Steadfast in the Faith

Steadfast in the Faith

The Life of Patrick Cardinal O'Boyle

Morris J. MacGregor

Library St. Vincent de Paul
10701 S. Military Trail
Boynton Beach, Fl 33436

The Catholic University of America Press
Washington, D.C.

Copyright © 2006

The Catholic University of America Press

All rights reserved

The paper used in this publication meets the minimum requirements of American
National Standards for Information Science—Permanence of Paper for Printed Library Materials, ANSI z39.48-1984.

∞

Library of Congress Cataloging-in-Publication Data

MacGregor, Morris J., 1931–

    Steadfast in the faith : the life of Patrick Cardinal O'Boyle / Morris J. MacGregor.— 1st ed.

      p. cm.

    Includes bibliographical references and index.

    ISBN-13: 978-0-8132-1428-3 (hardcover : alk. paper)

    ISBN-10: 0-8132-1428-9 (hardcover : alk. paper)

    ISBN-13: 978-0-8132-1429-0 (pbk. : alk. paper)

    ISBN-10: 0-8132-1429-7 (pbk. : alk. paper)

    1. O'Boyle, Patrick, 1896–1987.   2. Cardinals—United States—Biography.

I. Title.

    x4705.0167M33 2006

    282´.092—dc22

                                 2005003942

Contents

List of Illustrations   vii
Preface   ix

1. A Scranton Childhood   1
2. A Curate's Education   21
3. Catholic Charities   42
4. Other Duties as Assigned   68
5. An Organization Man   84
6. Pomp and Circumstance   117
7. Learning on the Job   136
8. Fighting Jim Crow   166
9. A Capital Pulpit   198
10. The Measure of the Man   227
11. Vatican II   256
12. A Fretful Shepherd   273
13. A Civil Rights Crusader   304
14. *State in Fide*   335
15. "What'll They Think of Next?"   373
16. Finale   395

Bibliography   405
Index   413

Illustrations

Patrick Cardinal O'Boyle, frontispiece

The O'Boyle Homestead, County Sligo   2

Mary Muldoon O'Boyle   14

Father O'Boyle   30

A New Archbishop   119

Installation in St. Matthew's Cathedral   133

John F. Kennedy Addresses the John Carroll Society   157

A Christmas Party   158

"Cinderblock O'Boyle"   160

At Camp Florence   184

O'Boyle with Chief Justice Earl Warren and
Speaker of the House John W. McCormack   188

A Friend of Organized Labor   217

At the Presidential Rostrum   253

Campus Protest   297

Chancellor O'Boyle Announces Curran's Reinstatement   301

The Red Hat   306

Crusader for Social Justice   313

The March on Washington, 1963   315

Recognition for a Community Activist   329

Resurrection City 333

Defending *Humanae Vitae* 356

Meeting the Press 359

Pro-Life Champion 389

In Retirement 391

Courtesy of the *Catholic Standard* (pp. 14, 30, 119, 133, 158, 188, 389, 391); courtesy of the Archdiocese of Washington (cover and frontispice, pp. 157, 160, 217, 253, 301, 306, 315, 329, 333); courtesy of the author (p. 184). Many of these photographs were the work of Johnny DiJoseph.

Copyright by *Washington Post;* reprinted by permission of the District of Columbia Public Library (pp. 297, 313, 356, 359); photograph by Timothy E. Cleary (p. 2).

Preface

This book tells the story of an American cardinal's long and eventful life. It is also a tale of three cities—Scranton, New York, and Washington—and how each helped shape the ideas and attitudes of the first resident archbishop of Washington. Finally, the book investigates some of the major issues that confronted the American Church in the twentieth century. Cardinal O'Boyle's varied assignments placed him at the epicenters of these controversies.

For example, the cardinal played a part in the modernization of Catholic social services and the debate over their relation to secular society. In the World War II era, he not only organized and directed the American Church's relief program for refugees and victims of war but was also in the forefront of those who demanded that the government accord private agencies a prominent role in this important work. His campaign against racial discrimination in Washington predated the appearance of the civil rights movement, just as his racial policies propelled many Catholics into applying the Church's social teachings to the fight for racial justice. Less noticed, during the Second Vatican Council he pressed for a declaration on racial justice and firmly supported those who fought for a declaration on religious freedom. In his later years his unbending support of papal authority, especially as expressed in the encyclical on birth control, made him, unwittingly, a symbol of intransigence in the post-conciliar Church.

To explain O'Boyle's involvement in these complex issues it has been necessary to describe their genesis and development. By the same token, although what follows is a biography and not a history of an archdiocese, it has been impossible to separate completely the two disciplines. To explain adequately Cardinal O'Boyle's ideas of administration and reform it has been necessary to give a detailed account of how the Archdiocese of Washington worked during his years in charge.

Of particular concern to the biographer, the cardinal left no organized record of his career. Unlike the carefully arranged correspondence, diaries, speeches, and the like of such colleagues as Cardinals Mooney and Spellman, O'Boyle appeared sublimely indifferent to the regard of future generations. The O'Boyle papers in Washington's archdiocesan archives fit easily into two file drawers, although the small collection does include a useful series of draft notes for a projected memoir. This paucity of material forced the researcher to cast a wide net for notice of the cardinal and his ideas in the papers of colleagues and records of scores of institutions. It also meant relying to a greater extent than desired on newspapers, interviews, and other secondary sources for the cardinal's own words.

Such a task depends on the interest and generosity of many people. I must thank those who led me to the records that have survived. The Rev. Mr. Bernard Bernier, the archivist of the Washington archdiocese, not only provided access to the records of the O'Boyle years but also gave me sound guidance on how the Church in Washington works. Michael Kneis, archivist of the University of Scranton, Marian Yevics of the Lackawanna Historical Society, Mrs. Cecile B. Champagne, a private researcher, and Sister Gilmary Speirs, I.H.M., at Marywood College, found important materials concerning the cardinal's years in Pennsylvania. I am grateful too for information about his family provided by his relatives Anthony and Margaret Muldoon, Sharon Loftus, and Kathleen O'Boyle Fay.

The archives of the Archdiocese of New York proved of little help, but that lack was more than compensated for by the generous response of three priest-historians of that archdiocese, Msgr. Thomas J. Shelley and Fathers Thomas Lynch and George A. Hoehmann, as well as records manager Laura Chmielewski. Msgr. William J. Toohy of New York's Catholic Charities, Stephen Rynn, director of the Mission of the Immaculate Virgin, and Laurence Bourassa at Catholic Relief Services also provided useful information covering O'Boyle's New York years. Roman Godzak located O'Boyle's letters in the Archdiocese of Detroit archives. Closer to home, Richard L. Schmidt and James F. Anthony, archivists of St. Matthew's Cathedral, generously opened their files to me. Geraldine Rohling, archivist at the National Shrine of the Immaculate Conception, provided valuable comments on O'Boyle's role in the construction of the Shrine. Editor Mark Zimmerman generously made the considerable resources of the *Catholic Standard* available for this project. The archives of the Catholic University of America contain a number of collections important to O'Boyle's career, and I am grateful to archivist W. John Shepherd and director Timothy J.

Meagher for their insights and guidance. I am also indebted to the archivists at the United States Conference of Catholic Bishops and Georgetown University for their help.

Four researchers provided special assistance. Eileen McConnell and John O'Brien introduced me to the world of nineteenth-century Ireland and the home counties of the O'Boyles and the Muldoons. Father Rory Conley, the archdiocesan historian in Washington, generously gave me the many interviews he conducted with O'Boyle associates. Similarly, Msgr. Francis J. Weber shared with me his personal interview with Cardinal O'Boyle.

A quartet of monsignors, W. Louis Quinn, William J. Awalt, Michael DiTeccia Farina, and the late Robert O. McMain, all worked for the cardinal and all read and commented on parts of the manuscript. I am particularly indebted to Msgr. Farina, who also expedited the collection of materials and the production of the book. I turned to Archbishop John F. Donoghue and Father Raymond Kemp, both intimately involved in the *Humanae Vitae* controversy, to read and comment on my account. Dr. Kristine LaLonde and Msgr. Joseph A. Ranieri also reviewed chapters that fall within their areas of expertise. I must acknowledge my special debt to Msgr. Robert Trisco, the eminent historian and editor of the *Catholic Historical Review,* who once again has reviewed and critiqued one of my manuscripts. My greatest debt is to my old friend Father Paul F. Liston, who dutifully, diligently, and, I hope, enthusiastically read every page, lending both his editorial skills and sage advice to the manuscript.

This is the third book of mine that the expert staff of the Catholic University of America Press has prepared for publication. My esteem and gratitude for the skill of my editors, Susan Needham Barnes and Ellen K. Coughlin, and the artistry of the book's designer, Joyce Kachergis, continue to grow.

October 11, 2004   *Morris J. MacGregor*

Steadfast in the Faith

CHAPTER 1

A Scranton Childhood

Patrick Aloysius O'Boyle, the son of Irish immigrants, was born on July 18, 1896, in Scranton, Pennsylvania. If there was little gayety and much hardship for newcomers to Scranton in that storied decade, many of their children nevertheless developed an enduring affection for and loyalty to the city. So it was with the future prelate. Although Patrick O'Boyle would remain a resident for just the first twenty years of a long life, he would ever be drawn to Scranton and its people. For many decades, even into his final years, any break in his schedule inevitably meant a return to the quiet shores of his beloved Moosic Lake, a favored vacation spot for nearby Scranton, and extended visits with relatives and friends and to those local Catholic institutions that had sustained him in his youth.

Such loyalty was not without effect. It could be safely concluded, in turn, that Scranton and its people molded Patrick O'Boyle's philosophy of life in very specific ways. The simple faith practiced by his relatives formed his own uncomplicated spirituality, just as the rich mix of economic classes and ethnic groups in his neighborhood gave him a lifelong egalitarian outlook, genuine interest in religious freedom, and skepticism toward rank and privilege. Above all, Scranton influenced O'Boyle's social philosophy, developing in him a progressive economic and racial outlook that would affect many Americans in the decades to come. The city, with thousands of struggling immigrants working in its coalfields and nascent industries, was near the center of the intense economic turmoil racking the nation in the early twentieth century. The strivings of this heterogeneous proletariat, typified by the challenges faced by his own relatives, clearly absorbed the young O'Boyle's interest. With the

The O'Boyle Homestead, County Sligo. Patrick's father, Michael O'Boyle, grew up in this stone cottage, today a storage shed on the O'Boyle farm.

stubborn if sometimes irritating steadfastness that would characterize all that he did in life, he would loyally apply the lessons learned in Scranton on the wider stage to which he was called.

An Irish Heritage

Several of Cardinal O'Boyle's close associates have commented on his peculiar accent, which somehow melded the flat tones of the Appalachian highlands with a hint of the inflection of west Ireland. One close friend claimed that even a brief telephone conversation with O'Boyle would cause him to speak with a brogue for the rest of the day. Small wonder, considering the fact that Patrick was reared in a house full of recent Irish immigrants. Indeed, as a child he could count at least a dozen aunts, uncles, and more-distant relatives in permanent or temporary residence. His father found the men jobs in the mills and the women sought work as domestics in the homes of Scranton's wealthy.[1]

1. O'Boyle, Notes, pt. 1. During a four-month period in 1979 Cardinal O'Boyle dictated a series of notes briefly covering events in his life up to 1948, the first step in a memoir project later abandoned. This manuscript is filed in the Archives of the Archdiocese of Washington (hereafter AAW). The cardinal's brogue has been the subject of discussion by colleagues. See, for example, the McArdle and Gillen intvs. [For pertinent information on all interviews cited in this volume, see heading in the bibliography.]

His father, Michael O'Boyle, was himself new to America. He was born in 1860, the fourth and last child of Michael and Mary McHugh O'Boyle, a farming couple in the townland of Cabragh, three miles from Coolaney, a small market community near the center of County Sligo. Situated in the highlands of Sligo's Ox Mountains, Cabragh is a beautiful if unforgiving place for small farmers. The O'Boyles leased two plots totaling some six acres assessed at a modest four pounds, 10 shillings.[2] Here they eked out a precarious living on their stony acres with its garden plot and hilly pasture. Their cottage was a modest three-room affair with a gaping fireplace, thatched roof, and a few tiny windows (local tax assessment was set in part by the number of windows in the cottage).[3] Like other mid-century farm lads, Michael and his older brothers, Patrick and Neil, did their full share of the work, including the taxing chore of scything their hilly meadows for winterfeed and cutting turf in a nearby bog.

The family attended St. Joseph's Chapel in the Rockfield section of Coolaney, a long donkey ride over a mountain road made perilous in Sligo winters. With hedgerow schools and prohibitions against the education of Catholics now past, the children walked across the fields and forded a river (often barefooted, family lore has it) to the Cappagh National School. Michael was one of less than fifty pupils in the one-room building.[4] Nevertheless, in an era when schooling remained a sometime thing and illiteracy all too common, Michael O'Boyle received a full grammar-school education.

Like most of Ireland, rural Sligo suffered greatly during the potato famine of 1846–49 and again when the crop failed in 1860–62. Death and immigration caused an astounding drop in population. Whole townlands, especially in the remote mountain areas, were almost emptied of people. Michael remained in Cabragh through his early manhood, but there was little future for a third son. One brother, Neil, had already emigrated, while Patrick and sister Margaret had married and were starting their families. The 1880s were a time of severe depression and more crop failures. In 1889 Michael purchased passage at Coleman's Shop in Coolaney and, like so many others, set sail for a new life in a new world. He joined Neil on a farm outside New York City, eventually settling in Bedford

2. Richard Griffith, "Parish of Killoran," *General Valuation of Rateable Property in Ireland* (Dublin, 1847). The genealogical information in this chapter is based on the research of Eileen McConnell, a noted authority on Irish genealogy. Her report, with its many appended documents, is filed in AAW. The following description of the O'Boyle property and life in Cabragh in the nineteenth century is based on ltr., Patrick O'Boyle to author, 11 Nov 1999. A cousin of the cardinal, Patrick O'Boyle is the present owner of the family farm in County Sligo.

3. Description of the cottage as found in the census of Ireland taken in 1901.

4. Henry intv. Ignatius Henry is the principal of what is now called Rockfield Normal School.

Station, then a small farming community in Westchester County.[5] Although they were born just forty miles apart, it seems certain that Michael O'Boyle was fated to meet Mary Muldoon, not in County Sligo, but on the crowded west side of New York City.

Mary Muldoon was born on December 10, 1855, the second of twelve children of Patrick and Mary Carroll Muldoon in the townland of Corimla South in the parish of Kilmoremoy. Although the Muldoons would always consider themselves Mayo people (indeed, successive generations of the family's Irish setters were always named "Mayo"), their birthplace, until a boundary adjustment in 1898, was actually located in the far western reaches of Sligo.

Like the O'Boyles, the Muldoons struggled to support their family on a small farm. Patrick Muldoon leased a cottage with an outbuilding and thirteen acres.[6] Although a larger house and more acreage than the O'Boyle's, the Muldoon holdings were valued at a little less than six pounds in 1851, reflecting the hardscrabble economy of Corimla. Describing the region at the time of Mary Muldoon's birth, one writer succinctly observed, "There is much bog, and agriculture is in a very backward state."[7] The effect of the famine varied in the four Irish provinces, but the West Country suffered most. A dramatic thirty percent drop in population at mid-century underscored the plight of trade and agriculture in a region where economic conditions for the next century were summed up in the oft-heard, poignant phrase, "County Mayo, God help them!"

Unlike the more rurally situated O'Boyles, the Muldoons lived a short distance from the Moy River and bustling Ballina, Mayo's major port city. Their religious life centered on the Ardnaree section of town where Mary was baptized in

---

5. Muldoon and Donoghue intvs. Anthony and Margaret Muldoon are the cardinal's closest living relatives and the source of much of the information about the family cited in this chapter. Natives of Scranton, the Muldoons maintained close ties with the cardinal and his mother. Archbishop John F. Donoghue was O'Boyle's secretary, chancellor, and auxiliary bishop and lived with the cardinal for many years prior to Donoghue's appointment as bishop of Charlotte, North Carolina. Unless otherwise noted, these comprehensive interviews, along with O'Boyle's Notes and a fragment of an interview the cardinal gave a group of seminarians, students of Msgr. Michael Roche at Mount St. Mary's College, are the source of personal information about the O'Boyle family in this chapter. Little is known about Neil (sometimes rendered Neal) O'Boyle. In Michael O'Boyle's obituary Neil is listed as his brother, residing in New York City (*Scranton Times,*7 Jan 1907).

6. Griffith, "Parish of Kilmoremoy." Muldoon is identified as Patrick senior, to distinguish him from a Patrick junior, which in the Irish manner of those times did not necessarily mean father and son, as in this case.

7. Samuel Lewis, *A Topographical Dictionary of Ireland,* 2nd ed. (London: S. Lewis and Co., 1847). See also Ruth D. Edwards, *Historical Atlas of Irish History* (London: Methuen and Co., 1973), and Crossmolina Historical and Archeological Society, *Crossmolina Parish: An Historical Survey* (Crossmolina, County Mayo: n.d., c. 1984).

what was their parish church, the imposing if uncompleted St. Muredach's Cathedral. For the Muldoons of Mary's generation marginal farming meant unrelenting physical labor with little time for school. In an area that still counted a high rate of illiteracy, Patrick Muldoon signed the 1901 Irish census with an "X, his mark." All the Muldoon children, however, learned to read and write, although the older siblings, certainly, never had as much formal education as Michael O'Boyle enjoyed. Later in Scranton, the hardships endured by these rural families in the old country would be the stuff of countless dining-room discussions, and young Patrick absorbed the stories of the many relatives who shared his boyhood home.

Like so many other Irish families, the Muldoon children decided that emigration was their only option. (All but one of Mary's surviving brothers and sisters would eventually be reunited with her and her widowed mother in Scranton.) Brothers James and Anthony emigrated first, and by 1879 Patrick and John were about to join them in Scranton where a cousin operated a prosperous stone yard and where mill jobs were available. Mary, the oldest girl, had a different goal. Her cousin and best friend, Anne Carroll, had established herself in Manhattan as an independent, self-advertised dressmaker for leading department stores. Mary decided to seek her fortune in New York City, and in 1879 she too left Ireland to settle with her cousin at 200 West 89th Street. Family tradition claims that Mary found work as a laundress and later, with Anne Carroll's help, in one of the city's many clothing factories, but in truth nothing is known for sure about her adventures in New York before her marriage fourteen years later. Cardinal O'Boyle once offered a tantalizing glimpse when he noted that what meant most to him about his ordination as a bishop in St. Patrick's Cathedral was the awareness that, like so many Irish working girls who helped build that mighty church, his mother as a young newcomer to America had worshipped in the cathedral on Fifth Avenue.[8]

What is known of Mary Muldoon's experience in those years puts her squarely in the mainstream of Irish female immigrants. Most of these women originated in Ireland's rural West or South and became manual laborers or domestics in America's big cities. They arrived in the United States, "not as depressed survivors of famine, but in the main they made the journey with optimism," believing that they would soon better their status. More so than other immigrant groups, they stayed single or married late in life. But far from a leap into a great unknown, they arrived in America possessed of a network of relatives who pre-

8. O'Boyle, Notes, pt. 1.

ceded them, links in a chain of migration that persisted among the Irish for generations.[9]

Mary Muldoon married Michael O'Boyle in Blessed Sacrament Church, Anne Carroll's parish on West 71st Street, on December 3, 1893. The bride's brother James and a cousin, Ellen Muldoon, came in from Scranton to serve as witnesses. Even in an era when birth dates were not always precisely known, Mary Muldoon stretched credulity when she gave her age as twenty-nine. In fact she was just two weeks shy of her thirty-eighth birthday, five years her groom's senior.

Life in Working-Class Scranton, 1894–1911

The couple soon moved to Scranton, where Michael hired on as a laborer in a steel mill. The newlyweds moved in with Mary's brothers James and Anthony. Reflecting the prosperity of the stone business, the Muldoon brothers had recently built a nine-room stucco house on a lot purchased by James at 1359 Penn Avenue in the Green Ridge section of the city. Here Mary O'Boyle became homemaker for the clan, and here, in May 1895, the O'Boyles celebrated the birth of their daughter, Mary. As happened all too often in those days, the anxious parents watched over a sickly infant who, suffering convulsions, died just two weeks after her birth.

Their sadness must have been eased somewhat by the news at year's end that Mary was again pregnant. Their son, Patrick—Aloysius was a later addition—was christened on July 20, 1896, two days after his birth, at St. Paul's Church. Uncle Patrick Muldoon and his young fiancee served as sponsors. Close friends would always call the cardinal Rick, but in the family he was Patrick. Only to a select few, including his mother, was he Pat, a nickname he claimed to dislike. (When later a family asked permission to name their son after the cardinal, he agreed, so long as they promised never to call the child Pat.)[10]

With Michael advancing in his job at the mill and all the uncles employed, the family was enjoying an unexpected level of prosperity, certainly enough to pay the fare for Mary and young Patrick to visit Ballina in 1899. The duration and purpose of this visit remain a puzzle; perhaps it involved a family crisis in Ire-

9. Hasia Diner, *Erin's Daughters in America: Irish Immigrant Women in Nineteenth Century America* (Baltimore: The Johns Hopkins University Press, 1983), pp. 37–50 (quote from p. 42), and Roger Daniels, *Coming to America: A History of Immigration and Ethnicity in American Life* (New York: Harper Perennial, 1990), p. 130.

10. McArdle intv. On the nickname Rick, see ltr., Msgr. Francis J. Weber to author, 5 Feb 1997, copy in AAW.

land, perhaps it only fulfilled the simple wish of a daughter to show her parents their American grandchild. At any rate, the two returned on the SS *Oceanic* in October, accompanied by one of Michael's nieces, Winifred O'Boyle.[11]

The house in which young Patrick spent most of his boyhood was located in Scranton's thirteenth ward, a mostly working-class neighborhood more than a mile from the city center. Here modest dwellings crowded cheek by jowl with light industries. Within a two-block radius of the O'Boyle home, for example, could be found a prosperous lamp manufacturer, several breweries and textile mills, and the county jail. One block south on Penn Avenue was cousin Patrick Muldoon's stone yard, where James and Anthony worked as cutters. Bordering the ward on the southwest was one of the city's major steel mills, and equidistant to the north along Green Ridge Street were located the imposing residences of some of the city's most prosperous families. Closer to home, the corner of Penn and Marion Street served as the center of young Patrick's social life. Here was Sanderson Park, an open green space that provided ball fields and play areas for the neighboring children along with picnic grounds and a freshwater spring that attracted local families. Across the street stood St. Paul's Church. Built in 1890 to replace an old wooden structure, the new church boasted a parish hall on the lower level and a complete grade school on a second and third floor above the sanctuary. The school, opened by the Sisters of the Immaculate Heart of Mary in 1892, was later enlarged to include a high school division.

In 1900 Green Ridge was one of the newer sections of a fast-growing city of 100,000. Its mostly working-class people liked to claim that Scranton was the anthracite (hard coal) capital of the world, and indeed thousands of its residents, including many young children, toiled in often appalling conditions in the mines and coal breakers that dominated the region. Until early in the twentieth century, when ore became scarce, Scranton was also a major steel-making center. It was equally famous for its rail car industry and its silk and fancy textile mills.[12]

For the area's quarter million Catholics, religious life centered on St. Peter's Cathedral, the seat of a diocese created in 1868 when the See of Philadelphia was divided by Pope Pius IX at the recommendation of the Second Plenary Council.

11. New York Passenger Lists, 12 Oct 1899, vol. 146, p. 29. The *Oceanic* with Mary and young Patrick aboard arrived in New York from Queenstown on October 12.

12. Descriptions of Scranton at the turn of the century abound. For an early version, see "Resources and Future of Scranton," *Scranton Board of Trade Journal* (Oct 1915), pp. 14–27. John Beck, *Never Before in History: The Story of Scranton* (Northridge, Calif.: Windsor Publications, 1986), provides a recent survey. For the history of the O'Boyle parish, see *St. Paul Church Centennial Jubilee Book* (Scranton, 1987).

In addition to orphanages and scores of parochial schools, Catholics supported St. Thomas College and Mount St. Mary's Seminary, schools that would evolve into today's University of Scranton and Marywood College. A period of impressive growth for the diocese, the turn of the century was also a traumatic time marked by internecine strife and schism. To serve the numerous immigrants from eastern and southern Europe in their native languages and according to their native customs, the diocese encouraged the rapid growth of so-called national parishes. In a desperate attempt to man these parishes, bishops sometimes accepted immigrant priests and seminarians with little or no information on their previous training or status in their home dioceses. For the most part these new pastors served to advance religion, but in a few cases the exceptional demands for independent action by trustees appointed by immigrant congregations headed by maverick priests led to complex disciplinary and jurisdictional problems.[13]

The most extreme of these upheavals occurred in 1896 at Sacred Hearts of Jesus and Mary (Polish) parish. Before it was over a portion of the congregation, led by its charismatic pastor, Francis Hodur, formed an independent parish. When efforts at reconciliation proved ineffective, an excommunicated Hodur organized the Polish National Catholic Church and served as its first bishop.[14] If these events had little practical effect on life in old, predominately Irish parishes like St. Paul's, they would nevertheless have a subtle influence on Patrick O'Boyle's future in the Church. The existence of so many national parishes in his hometown provided him with early exposure to the rich and rapidly growing multiethnic nature of American Catholicism. O'Boyle would have no need to learn later, as would many of his Irish-American contemporaries, the importance of accepting such diversity while remaining wary of ethnic exclusivity.

By 1900 Michael O'Boyle had been promoted from general laborer in the iron mills and was now a heater, a category of skilled worker. Along with the rollers and roughers, he manually moved the molten metal as it passed through the furnaces. In an era when steel companies were automating many operations and thereby downgrading much of their work force, these experienced men would, for a few more decades at least, remain in premium jobs. O'Boyle and his brother-in-law Patrick Muldoon were among the heaters hired for the new rolling mill of the Scranton Bolt and Nut Company when it opened in 1900. De-

13. John P. Gallagher, *A Century of History: The Diocese of Scranton: 1868-1968* (Scranton, 1968), pp. 154-223.
14. Gallagher, *A Century of History*, pp. 222-45. See also James B. Earley's especially informative *Envisioning Faith: The Pictorial History of the Diocese of Scranton* (Devon, Pa.: William T. Cooke Publishing, 1993), pp. 109-21.

spite the general downturn in the region's steel industry, the new company quickly expanded as its production of refined bar iron, nuts, bolts, and spikes sold well. In coming years its huge plant with special rail spurs would come to dominate a bend in the Lackawanna River a mile from the O'Boyle home.[15] Heaters generally had some say in the hiring of their work crews, and in the next few years Michael O'Boyle and Patrick Muldoon were able to secure jobs in the mill for John and Stephen Muldoon, who had arrived in America in 1900.

Although relatively secure and better paid than laborers, the heaters endured near brutal working conditions. To meet production schedules in an improved economy at the turn of the century, the furnaces were continually fired up. The production line was often in operation ten to twelve hours a day, seven days a week; some heaters were required to report at three in the morning to maintain the furnaces at the ready. Cardinal O'Boyle would later recall the successful fight the steelworkers waged for shorter workweeks, but in fact such victories were temporary.[16] Nor was there improvement in pay. In flush times these specialists could on occasion earn over $100 in a seven-day week, but at the turn of the century pay still averaged little more than fifty cents an hour, barely sufficient to support a family in some degree of security.

Efforts to ameliorate conditions in the industry's workforce were at low ebb in 1900. The Amalgamated Association had won recognition in many steel companies in previous decades, but its defeat in the infamous Homestead Strike of 1892 in effect broke the union. The challenge to the status quo forcefully posed by Scranton's great labor leader Terrence Powderly and the Knights of Labor a generation before still influenced the struggling workers of the region. Yet in Scranton as in other industrial regions east of the Alleghenies the unions had never been effectively organized, even though many workers strongly resented their treatment and strongly sympathized with the unions.[17]

The O'Boyle-Muldoon clan was an ardent union household. A family photo from that era shows young Patrick O'Boyle, wearing an ironworker's union cap and carrying an American flag, preparing to march with his Uncle Stephen in a

15. "Scranton Bolt and Nut Company," *Scranton Board of Trade Journal* (Nov 1914), pp. 34 and 38. On the duties of a heater in a steel mill, see David Brody, *Steelworkers in America: The Nonunion Era* (Cambridge, Mass.: Harvard University Press, 1960), pp. 31–32, and John A. Fitch, *The Steel Workers* (New York: Charities Publishing Committee, 1910) [reprinted by the University of Pittsburgh Press, 1989], pp. 32–37 and 49–50.

16. As reported by Archbishop Philip M. Hannan in the *Catholic Standard* [hereafter *CS*], 13 Aug 1987.

17. Brody, *Steelworkers in America*, pp. 36–51, provides a comprehensive picture of the plight of steelworkers in Pennsylvania in this era.

labor parade. Talk around the family dinner table often dwelt on the plight of the workers, especially the poor working conditions, barely adequate wages, and lack of pensions and benefits. Patrick O'Boyle would later recall steelworkers, friends of his father, visiting their home when much of the talk centered on the bitter and sometimes violent struggle of working people to organize and demand justice from industries that sought with the considerable means at their disposal to crush unions. The recent victory of John Mitchell, leader of the United Mine Workers and the hero of workers in all the industries, gave them hope.

Flush with victories in 1900 over the soft coal industry in the Midwest, Mitchell decided to organize the anthracite coalfields of Pennsylvania. Scranton was at the center of the hard coal industry. Not only was anthracite mining particularly difficult and hazardous, it was also low paying since to keep wages down the operators lured desperate immigrants willing to work for a pittance into the mines. Few of the miners belonged to the union, but a brief and modestly successful walkout in 1900 induced many of them, including the European newcomers, to join and prompted Mitchell two years later to demand better wages and working conditions for the hard coal industry. When the operators rejected arbitration, the great coal strike began.[18]

The miners stood firm in the face of increasing threats and blandishments as the shutdown reached its fifth month. With the specter of winter shortages looming, President Theodore Roosevelt sensed a rising public anger and even a demand for a government takeover of the industry. In what labor historians mark as the government's transformation from its usual role as strikebreaker to its modern position as labor arbitrator, Roosevelt and his assistants twisted arms. The strike then ended in what was generally recognized as a victory for unionism.

In all of this the Catholic Church played a significant role. The presidential commission that arbitrated the settlement included, at Mitchell's insistence, a Catholic prelate, the outspoken bishop of Peoria, John Lancaster Spalding. Far more important to the workers' victory was the part played by Father John Curran and Scranton's bishop, Michael J. Hoban. In his youth Curran had worked as a breaker boy, bending to the unrelenting toil of separating the pieces of slate from the coal. He was a passionate advocate of the miners' cause and one of John Mitchell's trusted advisers during the conflict. His search for a workable solution

18. This account of the 1902 strike is based on Jonathan Grossman, "The Coal Strike of 1902—Turning Point in U.S. Policy," *Monthly Labor Review* (Oct 1975), pp. 21–28, and Susan E. Wilson, "President Theodore Roosevelt's Role in the Anthracite Coal Strike of 1902," *Labor's Heritage* (Jan 1991), pp. 4–23.

to the strike won the admiration of President Roosevelt, who became his lasting friend.[19]

Roosevelt also valued the friendship of Bishop Hoban, who figured importantly in the protracted negotiations as a newsworthy champion of collective bargaining. Hoban represented an emerging class of Catholic leaders who had come to understand the responsibility of the hierarchy for the social welfare of the worker. He publicly supported the unions and lent his prestige to their organizing efforts. At the same time he called on members to avoid radicalism "above all things." He urged one group to unite with fellow workers, "not to injure your employers, but, while maintaining and furthering your own welfare, to promote that of those in whose employment you are." He strongly endorsed John Mitchell's contention that fair pay and decent working conditions supported by strong labor legislation were essentials in the formation of a wage earner's spiritual life.[20] His open support for these principles helped sustain the miners, most of whom were Catholics, during their long siege of unemployment.

John Mitchell became the idol of all workers, nowhere more so than in Scranton, which celebrated an annual Mitchell Day when the mines and factories shut down so that the workers could parade and listen to speeches extolling his victories and explaining his philosophy. It was perhaps ironic that this Midwestern Protestant (Mitchell would finally enter the Catholic Church in 1908) had become a primary exponent of the Church's teachings on Labor as exemplified by Pope Leo XIII's recent encyclical *Rerum Novarum*. Mitchell's speeches, one historian has pointed out, contained the philosophy and at times the exact wording of the encyclical.[21] It was from Mitchell that laborers like Michael O'Boyle learned to associate their ongoing struggle in the workplace with a Church that demanded both respect for the inviolability of private property and the right to fair wages, decent working conditions, a day of rest, and the abolition of child labor.

Mitchell was held in great esteem in the O'Boyle household, and clearly,

19. Gallagher's *A Century of History,* pp. 307–8, and Earley's *Envisioning Faith,* pp. 173–79, provide useful summaries of the role of Catholic leaders in the strike.

20. Agnes Joy, "John Mitchell and Religious Leaders of the Period 1900–1910" (MA Thesis, The Catholic University of America, 1954), pp. 8, 33–35, and 119–22. The quotation is from Hoban's speech before the Retail Clerks' Protective Association as reproduced in *United Mine Workers Journal,* 9 May 1907.

21. Joy, "John Mitchell and Religious Leaders of the Period," p. 92. On typical Scranton receptions for John Mitchell, see, for example, *Scranton Times,* 30 Oct 1903, and *United Mine Workers Journal,* 31 Oct 1907.

young Patrick shared the family's enthusiasm.[22] He later recalled playing hooky from school—probably during Mitchell's appearance at the UMW convention in Scranton on October 21, 1908—to hear the charismatic leader address a miners' rally.[23] His truancy earned Patrick punishment from his teacher at St. Paul's. In telling the story a half-century later to AFL-CIO leaders, O'Boyle concluded that the sister's response to his adventure taught him that the Church in those days lacked any real interest in Labor's cause. Given the very public association of Bishop Hoban, Father Curran, and other pastors in the diocese with the miners, however, O'Boyle's report of his teacher's reaction was most likely apocryphal— a punch line meant to underscore his family's loyalty to unionism rather than any opposition from the Church.[24]

In short, Scranton was a union stronghold in those days, in thrall to John Mitchell, union's preeminent leader. The O'Boyle-Muldoon family was part of this staunch labor tradition. As a young boy Patrick, the household's only child, sat in on its Sunday evenings when the men and their friends from the mills and the cutters from the stone yards gathered to play cards and talk about union issues. Their respect for the labor leader was obvious as they exchanged stories about the latest effort to crush union organizing and the sometime violent struggles that ensued. Patrick came to see his father and uncles as abused victims, an attitude that engendered a lifelong gratitude to organized labor. The small victories won by the working men were a lesson he took to heart, indicating a source of his strong championship of unionism in later years and his frequent references to the labor movement in the Scranton of his youth.[25]

Other memories of a Scranton boyhood lingered. On Christian piety, for example, O'Boyle often made a point of his parents' faithful observance of "what-

22. The United Mine Workers later claimed that the cardinal was the son of a UMW member (see *Labor: A Weekly Newspaper,* 17 Jan 1948). No documentation for this statement can be found beyond the fact that one M. J. O'Boyle served as a representative of District 9 at the UMW Convention in Scranton in June 1903. (See ltr., Debra Placky, Labor Archives, Pennsylvania State University, to author, 9 Feb 2000, copy in AAW.) Michael O'Boyle never used a middle name. While workingmen other than coal miners joined the successful union in those times, it seems unlikely that Michael O'Boyle was among them.

23. *United Mine Workers Journal,* 1 Feb 1948.

24. O'Boyle's truancy has been frequently commented upon. See, for example, Higgins and Donoghue intvs. For a description of Mitchell's reception at the 1908 convention, which was held at Scranton's St. Thomas College, and a reproduction of his speech on that day, see *United Mine Workers Journal,* 22 Oct 1908.

25. Many of O'Boyle's colleagues made a direct connection between his pro-union policies in Washington and his family's experiences in Scranton. See, for example, Duffy, Arthur, and Higgins intvs. See also Bishop Thomas Lyons' homily at O'Boyle's funeral Mass, 14 Aug 1987.

ever the Church said." They frequented the sacraments and attended the annual parish missions. Pictures of the Holy Family adorned the walls of their home, along with a plaque that implored "God Bless Our Home." Commenting on that plaque during his retirement, an elderly O'Boyle recalled wistfully, "You don't see many of these any more."[26] Patrick became an altar boy at age eight. A frequent attendee at daily Mass, he was often called upon to substitute for missing servers. The priests and sisters at St. Paul's deeply impressed him as a child, especially the formidable pastor, Father P. J. McManus, who was a very real presence to the schoolchildren. It was McManus who would interrupt Patrick as he delivered newspapers along Penn Avenue and insist that the boy step into church to pray the rosary with him. Anxious to get his papers distributed on time, Patrick would recite the responses at breakneck speed, a practical move cheerfully accepted by the pragmatic pastor.

The Green Ridge neighborhood was home to immigrants of many religious backgrounds from all over Europe. Any antagonisms generated by ethnic differences were muted in the need to unite against a common foe, the city's anti-foreign and especially anti-Catholic bigots. Even in some of the mines, workers were met by signs proclaiming that if Irish or if Italian, or more broadly "If Catholic," one should not apply. At the same time O'Boyle remembered the irenic atmosphere in Green Ridge, where all the newcomers mingled freely. His closest boyhood friend was Charlie Whalen, son of his Presbyterian neighbors and his boon companion on the ball field. A ball field, O'Boyle later admitted, was any vacant property the children, "in a slightly Communistic fashion," commandeered oblivious to the owner's rights.[27]

Although an only child and the center of attention in a large family of doting aunts and uncles, Patrick O'Boyle would later claim that he had escaped "the psychiatric [*sic*] implications that some people attribute to that [state]."[28] He early on developed a strong work ethic instilled by his strict mother. Aunt Mary, her nephews agreed, ruled the home on Penn Avenue, and Patrick learned early that homework and chores preceded baseball. Although accurate, his memory of childhood took on a Horatio Alger sheen when he recalled for Washington audiences how wearing patched clothes was a badge of honor and how grateful he was when his father gave him a dime to spend from the money he earned as a paperboy. "We didn't know we were poor," he later confessed to a distinguished

26. As quoted in the *Washington Post* [hereafter *WP*], 21 May 1971.
27. As quoted in Mount St. Mary's intv.
28. As quoted in Mount St. Mary's intv.

Mary Muldoon O'Boyle. An undated photograph.

Washington audience. "We were happy and, in a sense, we weren't poor." Then he recited for them the immigrant's anthem: "We had the chance to work and a chance to move up the ladder."[29]

His relatives were all working toward a better life. In 1900 Mary's brother Stephen and sister Katie joined the group on Penn Avenue, and Stephen became the seventh man in the family to find work in the foundry. During regular operations the men walked to work before 6:00 a.m., carrying lunches prepared by Mary; they returned some ten hours later, after a stop at the corner saloon for the

29. O'Boyle, "The Christian in Today's World," an address delivered to the John Carroll Society, 20 Oct 1968, copy in AAW.

pail of beer that would accompany dinner. Working with dangerous machinery in temperatures that often exceeded 100 degrees on the mill floor before walking home in Scranton's frigid winters hardly sounds conducive to good health, but actually the mill workers fared better than their relatives in the stone yard. Cutters in those days were notoriously susceptible to tuberculosis, and both Tony and James Muldoon succumbed early to that disease.

Katie, like sisters Annie and Barbara, found employment as a domestic "up on the hill," as the locals referred to the mansions of the city's wealthy. The immigration story was completed in 1905 when Stephen returned to Ballina to bring back his recently widowed mother, Mary Carroll Muldoon, the family matriarch. By now Mary O'Boyle might be forgiven for thinking she was operating a hotel. Her mother and brother took the places of brothers Patrick and John, who had left to marry. Patrick Muldoon would eventually live on Capouse Avenue directly behind the family home, allowing Mary to visit with her sister-in-law over the backyard fence. Stephen Muldoon also married soon after returning from Ireland, taking wife Margaret and his mother to nearby Dunmore. These moves were preamble to Mary's second tragic loss. On January 5, 1907, Michael O'Boyle died of influenza and pneumonia. He was forty-six years old, his son Patrick ten and a half.

To a family barely making it in 1907, the death of a major wage earner produced an immediate economic crisis. Mary O'Boyle responded by entering the work force, at first in one of the large downtown laundries where she earned a dollar a day and later as a machine operator in a textile mill that manufactured women's clothing. This latter employment helped maintain the family's keen interest in the ongoing labor turmoil in America. The textile mills in the region had just ended a protracted period of unrest as workers, mostly young women and children, had demanded higher pay and reduced hours. With the help of the United Mine Workers they won a modest victory in 1901, and, at the instigation of the AFL's United Textile Workers negotiated a settlement with the owners in 1907. During the years of Mary O'Boyle's employment the mills were filled with talk of union goals,[30] and once again the house on Penn Avenue echoed with talk about the achievements of organized labor, which directly affected the welfare of the O'Boyles.

For his part Patrick added a second paper route to his daily chores. A self-proclaimed "big-time operator," he served 200 customers daily. He also man-

30. On union activities in the Scranton mills, see Bonnie Stepenoff, " 'Papa on Parade': Pennsylvania Coal Miners' Daughters and the Silk Worker Strike of 1913," *Labor's Heritage* (Winter 1996), pp. 4–21. Mary O'Boyle was listed as a machine operator in the Scranton Directory of 1910.

aged to continue in school, where his marks, especially in mathematics and debating, remained high. But it was not to last. In an economy move Uncle Jim converted the house into a duplex and sold half the property, but his health, almost certainly affected by twenty years working as a stonecutter, was not good. He was unemployed for at least three months during 1909 and was reduced to working mostly odd jobs thereafter. Patrick managed to stay in school until June 1910, but then dropped out to seek full-time work.[31] Hired by the Bradstreet Company (forerunner of today's Dunn and Bradstreet), he served as messenger, filing clerk, and general factotum for the local superintendent, V. Paul Meekins. "I thought I was a big shot," he later remarked about an eight-to-five job (with an hour lunch break) that earned him $3 a week.[32]

College Days

Any dreams Patrick may have entertained about a future in business or finance were rudely interrupted one summer day in 1911 when Mr. Meekins informed him that he was to be let go. The startled teenager learned that while he was out delivering messages his boss had been visited by Father Connel McHugh, the new assistant at St. Paul's. McHugh had demanded that Patrick be discharged so that he could return to school. The surprised young financier rushed home to have the news confirmed by his mother. She had been offered a good job and a home for them both in Dunmore Borough, Scranton's northern suburb.

In the past the proud widow had rejected offers of aid from the St. Vincent de Paul Society. She was grateful, she had told Father McHugh, a fellow immigrant, for the parish's concern, but what she really needed was steady work. The resourceful McHugh returned a week later with an offer "that will help you and Patrick."[33] Two priest-teachers were looking for a live-in housekeeper for their home at 1427 College Street in Dunmore, near Mount St. Mary's Seminary, a Catholic girls' school. Father Joseph A. Boyle was a professor of philosophy and Latin at St. Thomas. He planned to share the house with Father Thomas J.

31. That Patrick completed the tenth grade, as asserted in some accounts, is unlikely. It is certain that he left St. Paul's in 1910, and even granting that he may have begun school at age five, he could not have completed ten grades unless he skipped one. No account suggests that possibility. O'Boyle himself recalled that he left school at age fifteen, but that figure does not compute with the fully documented dates of his years in college.

32. As quoted in Mount St. Mary's intv. The division of the house, along with information about James Muldoon's work status, was recorded in the 1910 census.

33. O'Boyle, Notes, pt. 1.

McHugh, who was to become chaplain at the girl's school as well as professor of religion and Greek at St. Thomas. Mary O'Boyle accepted their offer, and quickly returned to her familiar role of housemother for a group of men. Patrick's obligations were limited to light chores around the house and yard while preparing for his return to the classroom.

The house on College Street to which the O'Boyles moved in the summer of 1911 was a modest affair at the southern edge of the girl's seminary. The campus, which contained the motherhouse and novitiate of the Immaculate Heart of Mary sisters and a large high school with some residential students, occupied several acres in a suburb that had retained its old rural flavor. Even in 1911, however, Mother Cyril Conroy, the congregation's superior, was planning to transform the school into a full-fledged college. Her goal would be realized in 1915 when Marywood College, the fifth institution of higher learning for Catholic women in the United States, welcomed the thirty-four members of its first freshman class.[34] An association begun at St. Paul's and strengthened during his college days on Marywood's campus insured Patrick O'Boyle's closeness to the Immaculate Heart of Mary sisters that lasted a lifetime.

The O'Boyles settled into the little house that would be home for Patrick for most of the next decade, first as he commuted to St. Thomas down Wyoming Avenue on the Green Ridge Trolley and, later, when he returned during his seminary's summer vacations. When searching for influences on the boy's vocation, it is well to remember that during this period he lived in what was essentially a rectory. At the head of the household were two young, energetic priest-scholars, through whom Patrick gained firsthand knowledge of priestly life.

Apparently no thought was given to Patrick's going back to St. Paul's school. That summer he crammed for the examinations that would allow him to enter St. Thomas' prep division. Boyle and McHugh both advised the boy to take the exam for the school's equivalent of the eleventh grade, but Patrick rejected their conservative approach and took the test for the twelfth-grade level. He passed, and was thus eligible at the age of fifteen to enroll in the prep school's senior class. The source of financing this prep school and college education is not clear. Certainly young Patrick, who worked in the textile mills and on farms during summers, paid a share, but the bulk of the modest tuition appears to have been arranged by the family's sponsor, Father Connel McHugh.[35]

34. Margaret Yarina, *Marywood College, The First Seventy-Five Years: A Retrospective* (Scranton, 1990), pp. 11–14, 27–28.

35. A reduction in fees by the college or direct payments by McHugh or St. Paul's parish are

The school in which Patrick O'Boyle matriculated in 1911 had been founded twenty-three years earlier as a diocesan institution, operated for brief periods by the secular clergy and the Xaverian Brothers before coming under the care of the Brothers of the Christian Schools in 1897. St. Thomas would not be incorporated as a college with degree-granting privileges until 1925. During O'Boyle's time the school was organized into three departments—collegiate, commercial, and high school—and a night-school division. Occupying a large building affectionately dubbed "Old Main" near St. Peter's Cathedral, St. Thomas operated much like one of today's junior colleges. Students preparing for careers in commerce or the medical sciences would leave after two years to enter the business world or enroll elsewhere for specialized training. Students in the collegiate division were offered the option of completing a junior and senior year, thereby earning a bachelor's degree from St. John's College, an accredited Christian Brothers institution in Washington, D.C.[36] Further complicating academic arrangements during O'Boyle's student days at St. Thomas was the fact that diocesan priests were employed to teach some of the classes, thus the presence of diocesan priests like Fathers McHugh and Boyle on a Christian Brother faculty.

Patrick's lengthy absence from school had little effect on his grades. He finished prep school second in a class of thirty-six students. Mastering a solid academic curriculum, he showed weakness only in his brush with elementary German.[37] He graduated from high school on June 17, 1912, the first in his family to achieve that academic distinction. The occasion was marked with much festivity at Old Main, but the pleasure of friends and relatives was marred by the news that Uncle James Muldoon had succumbed that very evening in his long struggle with tuberculosis.[38] Muldoon died intestate, and his possessions, consisting of

other possibilities. The student registration book at St. Thomas College [filed in the Archives of the University of Scranton (hereafter AUS)] has in the entry for student O'Boyle a note concerning tuition that reads: "See Fr. McHugh." Since Thomas McHugh was not yet associated with the school, it is assumed that the note refers to Connel McHugh.

36. The early history of St. Thomas College was surveyed in two unpublished manuscripts: Francis E. Fitzgerald (college librarian), "St. Thomas College," n.d. (c. 1927), and Thomas Murphy (associate editor, *Scranton Times*), "St. Thomas College," Nov 1931. See also advertisement in *The Aquinas*, vol. 1, no. 1 (Jan 1916). Copies of all in AUS.

37. Lists of all students, the courses they took, textbooks used, and grades achieved are preserved in AUS and unless otherwise noted are the source of the following paragraphs.

38. *Scranton Times*, 17 and 18 Jun 1912. It is likely that James Muldoon had sought relief at the West Mountain Sanitarium, a charitable institution operated by the Scranton Society for the Prevention and Cure of Tuberculosis, which would explain his absence from his home on Penn Avenue when his sister and nephew moved to College Street in 1911. See ltr., Marian Yevics, Lackawanna Historical Society, to author, 20 Feb 2001, copy in AAW.

the Penn Avenue house and its contents, valued at $3,500, were divided among his mother and seven brothers and sisters, all now living in Scranton. His sister Katie, now Mrs. Robert Parks, and her family would reside in the old house until its disposal in a sheriff's foreclosure in 1919.[39] In some ways Uncle Jim's death and the breakup of the home on Penn Avenue mark a transition in Patrick O'Boyle's life, a psychological shift from Scranton's immigrant working class to the calmer scholarly-clerical atmosphere of College Street.

O'Boyle proved to be a diligent and disciplined collegian. His concentration on the serious task of receiving a liberal arts education prompted his classmates to dub him "the hermit." There is no evidence that he participated in organized sports or indulged in extracurricular fun. He was, on the other hand, a star member of the St. Thomas debating team and served as class librarian, although this latter responsibility may not have engaged his full attention since his classmates recommended that, for his services in that post, he be awarded a wooden medal at graduation. He was also alumni editor of *The Aquinas,* a monthly magazine begun by the students in 1916. The class poem satirized him in a short stanza:

> The next in order, P. O'Boyle, the grouch,
> But when it comes to arguing he's there,
> Pasquale, the Hermit, him we call,
> His eyes are bright, and red the shade of his hair.

O'Boyle's disciplined childhood in a struggling immigrant family combined with his quick mind to help him achieve scholarly distinction. He led his class in every year but one, when his close rival and friend Henry T. Klonowski bested him. Cited for his nearly perfect grades in Greek and Latin, and praised for his oratorical gifts, he beat out Klonowski to become valedictorian of the Class of 1916, whose fifteen graduates would later count among their number six priests, including two bishops, three physicians, including the state's director of public health, a university professor, an attorney, and a pharmacist.[40]

Among the features of *The Aquinas* were essays prepared by students and alumni. The June 1916 issue carried O'Boyle's study of St. Columbanus, the sixth-century monk so revered by the Irish. This 1,600-word essay by the twenty-year-old college student is the first extant sample of O'Boyle's writing. In style and philosophical approach it plainly adumbrates much of the man's liter-

---

39. Lackawanna County Register of Wills, Letters of Administration, 23 Sep 1912, and Lackawanna County Deed Book 293 (p. 358), 24 Jan 1919.

40. *The Aquinas* 1 (Jun 1916) (source of quote) and 15 (Dec 1947).

ary output during the next sixty years. In clear but spare paragraphs, he supported the claim that Columbanus was one of the fathers of modern culture, arguing
with considerable evidence against those who labeled the Middle Ages dark and
marked the Reformation as the beginning of the modern era.[41]

Bishop Hoban presided over graduation on June 13, 1916. Sharing the stage
with him was O'Boyle, the valedictorian, and his housemate Father Joseph
Boyle, "Professor of Higher Latin" and honored speaker of the evening. The social highlight of graduation followed the next evening when the senior class
sponsored a formal dance at the Hotel Casey. Recent issues of *The Aquinas* had
featured notices about this important event, pleading for perfect attendance "for
the good of the student body." The fifteen members of the senior class were reportedly taking dancing lessons in preparation for the occasion. As alumni editor, O'Boyle had joined in the appeal for attendance and probably out of loyalty
to his classmates endured the dancing lessons. One who knew him best in later
years, however, has suggested that the very unmusical, uncoordinated, and unro-
mantic O'Boyle, his mind already on a different future, probably did attend the
dance with a female partner, but out of loyalty to his classmates, attended in
some non-participatory capacity such as greeter.

Patrick O'Boyle would soon be enduring the joshing of New York colleagues
who labeled him a provincial with an odd accent, "from a small college in a small
town."[42] The characterization was accurate, but its authors missed the greater
truth behind O'Boyle's childhood. It was a time filled with tales of suffering and
injustice endured by farmers in famine-haunted Ireland and exploited workers in
Pennsylvania's mines and mills. In short, the laboring-class tradition, so strong
in Scranton's immigrant groups at the turn of the century and exemplified by the
experiences of his close-knit family, would inform his later life. The camaraderie
among workers fighting for justice provided the context in which O'Boyle developed a social viewpoint that would make him a noteworthy champion of labor
and racial reform. At the same time the close attention received from an extended
immigrant family, priests, and teachers and the struggle to prove himself worthy
of their confidence nurtured in the young man a strong spirituality, work ethic,
and thirst for knowledge that would lead him in coming years to meet challenges
with increasing confidence and success.

41. *The Aquinas* 1 (Jun 1916), pp. 57–59.
42. Rev. Edwin Ryan, professor at Dunwoodie Seminary, as quoted in O'Boyle, Notes, pt. 3.
Variations of this remark can be found in other parts of O'Boyle's notes and in biographies of his
classmates.

CHAPTER 2

A Curate's Education

If provincial Scranton with its strong immigrant working-class ethic molded Patrick O'Boyle's progressive social philosophy, it was cosmopolitan New York that was largely responsible for his conservative theological outlook and strong respect for law and discipline. O'Boyle would prepare for the priesthood and labor for a quarter-century in increasingly complex executive posts in the Archdiocese of New York. Although in the process this particular provincial never evolved into the sophisticated cosmopolite, in many other ways he would become a thorough New Yorker. The brash, no-nonsense approach to getting things done commonly associated with that great metropolis became part of his personality. The mindset of those who governed the Church in New York became his lodestar. To the exasperation of some of his close subordinates in Washington, he brought with him to the capital a firm belief that New York offered the perfect model for how things should be, not only in mundane organizational matters, but especially in larger questions involving authority and discipline.[1]

On moral and theological issues O'Boyle reflected the traditional seminary education of those times, which tended to view things in stark black-and-white terms. Trained during an intellectually fallow period in the archdiocese's educational history, his theological horizons were defined by a rote-learned neo-Scholasticism embraced by leaders who resisted the new historical approach to religious studies that was to flower among the coming generation of Church scholars. Like many of his con-

---

1. Several of those who worked with O'Boyle made this observation. See especially Arthur and Quinn intvs.

temporaries, O'Boyle would forever remain removed from the ideas and methods of theological progressives.

The self-described country boy's experiences in New York produced a priest with rare executive ability, yet one with a markedly traditionalist approach to theology and a punctilious regard for rules great and small.

Dunwoodie, 1916–1921

Shortly after graduation from St. Thomas, O'Boyle sought an appointment with Bishop Hoban to discuss his studying for the priesthood. Cardinal O'Boyle made little note of this momentous decision in later years. Not to gainsay the working of the Holy Spirit, a call to Holy Orders usually results from the conjunction of a natural piety with the inspiration of a priestly model. In young Patrick's case he confessed to a strong spirituality nurtured in a devout family and manifested by frequent attendance at daily Mass from an early age.[2] Although he had apparently enjoyed his sixteen-month foray into the world of commerce and was upset when he lost his job, the subsequent influence of the priest-professors with whom he lived during his college years undoubtedly helped direct his thinking about a vocation. Nor to be overlooked was his strong admiration for Father Connel McHugh, the parish priest who continued to take an active interest in the fatherless boy's development.

The interview with Bishop Hoban did not go well. He had all the English-speaking priests he needed, he explained, and was limiting himself at present to recruiting men qualified to preach and teach in the languages of his many immigrant congregations. While a classmate like Polish-speaking Henry Klonowski was immediately welcomed as a candidate (Klonowski would eventually study at the prestigious North American College in Rome), O'Boyle met a different reception. The bishop proposed that he attend some unspecified seminary for three years at his own expense, after which Hoban would reconsider his application. O'Boyle explained that he could not afford such a venture and asked permission to apply elsewhere. Hoban readily agreed that O'Boyle could go wherever he pleased. Once again, Connel McHugh directly intervened. In contrast to the indifferent bishop, he arranged for Patrick to join four other St. Thomas graduates for a trip to New York on the Fourth of July, where they would take the entrance examination for the diocesan seminary in Brooklyn.

2. O'Boyle, Notes, pts. 1–3. Unless otherwise indicated, the personal information and anecdotes in this section are derived from this source.

The timing of the New York expedition created a problem for O'Boyle, who had recently landed a summer job as motorman/conductor of the open-air trolley at nearby Moosic Lake. For five cents tourists took the three-mile ride to a wooded park at the end of the lake, where its waters fell over a series of picturesque cataracts. It was a good job that earned the motorman a dollar a day and free transportation from Dunmore for not very strenuous work. After collecting tickets and piloting the little four-wheel trolley to its terminal, O'Boyle would hide his throttle under a nearby bush (to frustrate any maverick's attempt to hijack the car) and lead the party down to the glen. That still left plenty of time for reading and studying before the return trip.[3] Patrick was able to persuade his Catholic boss to let him find a substitute for the busy Fourth holiday, but in the end the other students backed out and the seminary cancelled the exam.

The indefatigable McHugh then arranged a private entrance examination for O'Boyle at St. Joseph's Seminary in Yonkers, New York. At the same time he urged the would-be seminarian to bone up on his Greek and Latin, drawing a picture of the high standards of some of the examiners, particularly the rigorous classicist, Rev. Dr. Edwin J. Ryan. Consequently during the next month passengers on the Moosic trolley witnessed the strange sight of their motorman pouring over Greek and Latin texts in preparation for a possible meeting with the scholarly paragon in Yonkers.

It must have been with considerable trepidation that the young aspirant learned on the fateful morning that, its being vacation time and many professors away, the only examiner on hand was Father Ryan. Without preamble Ryan handed Patrick a copy of the New Testament in Greek and ordered him to read aloud and translate. After only a few sentences Ryan called a halt and asked a startled O'Boyle to name his teacher. Learning that it was the American-trained Thomas McHugh, Ryan marveled at how a student "from a small town and a small college" spoke his Greek phrases with a pure Oxford accent. Hearing such elegant diction in a Scranton boy seemed to settle matters for anglophile Ryan, who had visited England and thereafter sported an English accent. Without further ado O'Boyle was accepted as a seminarian and candidate for the priesthood in the Archdiocese of New York.

O'Boyle's matriculation at St. Joseph's gave him his first brush with the vaunted bureaucratic efficiency of big-city institutions. The school year was

3. For a colorful description of Moosic Lake and its Toonerville Trolley, see *Scranton Times,* 24 Nov 1981 and 11 Feb 1982.

scheduled to begin on September 7. It was the young man's first time away from home. Yet he arrived in Yonkers after a round of family gatherings and farewell parties only to learn that school opening would be postponed several weeks because of an influenza outbreak in the area. No one had bothered to inform the out-of-town students, and the quick round trip to Scranton found him facing friends again just hours after their warm sendoff. An embarrassed O'Boyle had to endure much good-natured joshing, especially from the priests on College Street, who greeted him with "Well, you didn't last very long after all."

When the seminary finally opened several weeks later O'Boyle experienced another frustrating breakdown in communication. The recent surge in enrollment, due largely to the number of applicants among the graduates of Cathedral College, the archdiocese's new preparatory school, meant that junior seminarians shared quarters. O'Boyle drew as roommate Joseph Cotter, a graduate of Fordham who had been star center of that school's football team. Their first challenge was the philosophy placement examination. A standard seminary education consisted of one or two years studying philosophy and related subjects followed by four years of theology. O'Boyle and Cotter were led to understand that a special examination would be administered to all newcomers to the archdiocesan seminary system to determine those eligible for the shorter, five-year program. For once O'Boyle ignored seminary rules concerning lights-out when he and Cotter spent a sleepless night cramming for the test. Only when they reported bleary-eyed for the examination did they learn that all college graduates were automatically placed in the shorter program.

The school O'Boyle entered in 1916, familiarly called Dunwoodie after the popular name of its Yonkers neighborhood overlooking the Hudson River, was beginning its twentieth year as the major seminary of the Archdiocese of New York. Founded by Archbishop Michael Corrigan, it had in its first decade achieved many of that formidable prelate's ambitious goals. Thanks to the intellectual distinction of its faculty and Corrigan's own far-sighted building program, Dunwoodie became, in historian John Tracy Ellis' estimate, second only to the Catholic University of America as the center of Catholic intellectual life in the United States. On its impressive campus an ever-growing student body was mentally challenged, spiritually uplifted, and physically well cared for. Unfortunately, such eminence proved short-lived. By the time O'Boyle enrolled, the school was well into a long decline during which, historian Thomas Shelley has concluded with impressive supporting evidence, Dunwoodie graduates "were shortchanged intellectually and spiritually." By 1922 living conditions had deteri-

orated and intellectual life atrophied to such an extent that the seminary was reduced to a state "comparable to the worst days" of its nineteenth-century predecessor.[4]

Reasons for this dramatic reversal are easy to deduce. Corrigan had given
control of the seminary to a group of progressive American Sulpicians, and not
without some misgivings supported their educational innovations, especially
those introduced by the second rector, Edward Dyer. Dyer and his well-trained
faculty were eager to modernize seminary education and to that end instituted a
series of reforms that emphasized the study of Church history and Scripture and
the latest developments in the study of theology. Dunwoodie's flowering, typified by the success of its scholarly periodical, the *New York Review,* was but one
aspect of a modest revival in American Catholic intellectual life inspired by new
Catholic scholarship in Europe. Yet if welcomed by many scholars, including
Dunwoodie's faculty, it was condemned by some powerful Church leaders, traditionalists who saw in the new learning a threat to orthodoxy. A cold war ensued between the so-called Modernists and the defenders of orthodoxy, a war
that ended in 1907 when Pope Pius X condemned Modernism in his encyclical
Pascendi Dominici Gregis. With old scores to settle, powerful Church traditionalists used the papal condemnation to silence not only more radical exponents of
the new scholarship, but any teaching that from their reactionary viewpoint
smacked of criticism of orthodoxy. Some of the new intellectual leaders were si-
lenced outright; others ran for cover when bishops who had formerly encouraged their work timidly withheld support.

The crisis over Modernism caused an abrupt volte-face at Dunwoodie. The
New York Review ceased publication. In 1909 Archbishop John Farley, Corrigan's successor, dismissed the scholarly rector, James Driscoll.[5] Outstanding
scholars like Francis E. Gigot and Gabriel Oussani, suspected of Modernism,
abandoned their serious writing. Even young teachers like Edwin Ryan and John
Mitty, the future archbishop of San Francisco, were tarred with the Modernist
brush. Luckily for him, the charismatic Francis P. Duffy, the nationally famous
chaplain of New York's 69th Infantry in World War I, had departed the faculty in

4. Thomas J. Shelley, *Dunwoodie: The History of St. Joseph's Seminary Yonkers, New York*
(Westminster, Md.: Christian Classics, 1993), pp. 129, 172 (second quote), and 195 (first quote). Unless otherwise noted, the following paragraphs on Dunwoodie are based on Shelley's comprehensive work.

5. The Sulpicians had relinquished control of the seminary in 1906, when five Sulpicians on its
faculty, including Driscoll, sought incardination in the New York archdiocese at the invitation of
Archbishop Farley.

1912, for he too came under suspicion. On all sides teachers exercised extreme caution lest they suffer the fate of Driscoll and others condemned by the vigilantes in Rome or in American chanceries.[6] In place of the intellectual ferment of previous years, the seminary assumed a pseudo-intellectual atmosphere. Lectures and recitations in all theological classes were, under orders of the archbishop, given in Latin. The result was, in historian Shelley's words, "an emphasis on rote memorization and a mind-numbing sterility that were the antithesis of the educational reform introduced into American seminaries forty years earlier."

True, O'Boyle and his classmates were exposed to first-rate scholars like Gigot and Oussani, but these men were now guarded in the extreme. For the most part O'Boyle was subjected to some spectacularly inadequate teachers, a neglected library, a largely self-directed spirituality, and revised rules that led to a general retreat within the walls of the seminary. No reading was required beyond assignments in old textbooks. Instead great emphasis was placed on character formation, which extolled as priestly models those who had exhibited "courage, heroism, patriotism, discipline, obedience, and loyalty to the 'corps.'"[7] George A. Kelly, a famed New York priest and graduate of Dunwoodie in its dark years, concluded optimistically that the seminary taught men how to live in a system and how to beat the system.[8] Viewed more critically, the Dunwoodie of O'Boyle's era, like most American seminaries of the time, could be said to have emphasized individualistic piety and a stern moral outlook enhanced by rote memorization of theological texts in a rule-bound regimen.

The task of molding these "soldiers of Christ" was appropriately given to a military man. During O'Boyle's seminary days the rector was Msgr. John P. Chidwick, who had replaced the ousted Driscoll in 1909. Chidwick, most recently the chaplain of the New York City Police Department, was best known for his years as a naval chaplain, particularly for his heroic service on the battleship *Maine* at the time that vessel sank in Havana harbor on the eve of the Spanish-American War in 1898. No scholar, Chidwick was an unpretentious gentleman of the old school who introduced a strong air of military discipline and protocol along with a strongly stressed respect for institutional authority, in effect a return to the monastic atmosphere of earlier American seminaries. Although consid-

6. Thomas Lynch, "Above All Things the Truth: John P. Monaghan and the Church of New York," *Dunwoodie Review* 16 (1992–93), p. 115.

7. Michael V. Gannon, "Before and After Modernism: The Intellectual Isolation of the American Priest," *The Catholic Priest in the United States: Historical Investigations* (Collegeville, Minn.: St. John's University Press, 1971), pp. 355–56 (quote from latter page).

8. George A. Kelly, *Inside My Father's House* (New York: Doubleday & Co., 1989), p. 11.

ered the obedient executive by those determined to rid the seminary of its dangerous theological and disciplinary tendencies, Chidwick proved to be a feisty opponent of the parsimony that was, by the time of O'Boyle's graduation, endangering the health of the students because of poor diet, excessive cold, and unsanitary living conditions. Losing his appeals to an indifferent archbishop, Chidwick would resign in 1922. While in charge, however, he insisted on a carefully structured academic discipline that produced, in biographer Francis Weber's estimate, men "trained to be cultured gentlemen—orthodox in doctrine, careful in speech, literate in tastes and courteous in demeanor."[9]

Unlike some of his classmates, O'Boyle did not find the carefully structured regime unduly rigid. Used to hard work and a paperboy's early hours, he had no problem with the 5:30 wake-up call, although even he considered some of the many rules "very difficult."[10] He particularly bridled at the total ban on smoking, the lengthy periods of silence, and the prohibition against socializing with classmates in their rooms. He also complained about the truncated Wednesday holiday, which early in his student days had been squashed to an afternoon mainly devoted to local hospital visits, with a strictly enforced return to Dunwoodie by six o'clock.

The disciplined structure of seminary life still allowed for extracurricular activities. O'Boyle, by now a veteran debater, was a strong supporter of Dunwoodie's literary and sociological societies, where topics of current interest were discussed. The Literary Society met on Sunday afternoons. O'Boyle particularly relished one session at which an august deacon dared to criticize the efforts of those Irishmen who were rebelling against their English masters. O'Boyle found a life-long friend in a junior seminarian, James B. O'Reilly, who fiercely debated this proposition, citing Professor Oussani as his authority. O'Reilly brought down the house when he ended his remarks with the fervent plea that the deacon "will never make such an ass of himself in public again."

Sports were encouraged at Dunwoodie, but whether O'Boyle ever played on the school's baseball team is uncertain. It is certain, however, that he never gained membership in the school's well-regarded choir. Tone-deaf, he was advised by one faculty member, "Rick, don't ever sing, just mouth the words."[11]

9. Francis J. Weber, *His Eminence of Los Angeles: James Francis Cardinal McIntyre,* vol. 1 (Mission Hills, Calif.: St. Francis Historical Society, 1997), p. 11.

10. O'Boyle, Notes, pt. 2, is the source for this and other O'Boyle comments about seminary life in this section.

11. As quoted in the McArdle intv. See also Arthur J. Scanlan, *St. Joseph's Seminary Dunwoodie, New York, 1896–1921* (New York: The United States Catholic Historical Society, 1922). Scanlan's

Fortunately for the future cardinal, neither seminarians nor bishops are subject to examination in the field of music.

The daily routine was interrupted by term examinations immediately before Christmas. Seminarians were allowed brief home holidays during the Christmas and Easter seasons, with the long summer vacation beginning in the third week of June.[12] O'Boyle used summer vacations to earn at least part of his seminary tuition, which by his time probably exceeded the $230 per year set by Archbishop Corrigan in 1902. Part of this expense could be postponed, and O'Boyle, like many other candidates from hard-pressed families, could arrange to delay payment of as much as one-half of his seminary expenses until after ordination.

During his first days at Dunwoodie O'Boyle met a classmate who would not only become an enduring friend but would exert a major influence on some of his subsequent assignments in New York. James Francis McIntyre had left a promising career on Wall Street to enter Dunwoodie. His financial talents would lead to his rapid elevation to a position of power in the archdiocese, but in 1916 he was O'Boyle's exceptionally serious, hard-working next-door neighbor, who could not resist poking fun at a Scranton accent. At age thirty-two "Slats" McIntyre was the old man of the class, who regarded the others as boys in need of his mature influence. Untutored in the classics, he received help from O'Boyle in his Latin translations. In turn, McIntyre took a special interest in one he considered a culturally deprived country boy.

McIntyre devoted their five years together to educating O'Boyle in the mores of the big city and making sure that the loner from far-off Pennsylvania spent Thanksgiving and other brief holidays with the McIntyre clan. O'Boyle was always included in the circle when McIntyre's aunt and uncle hosted warm-weather picnics. It was on the way to one of these family outings in Westchester County that O'Boyle, arguing the relative merits of the current crop of political notables, declared his strong support for Robert M. LaFollette, the charismatic Wisconsin Progressive. His declaration so shocked the politically conservative McIntyre that he threatened to throw O'Boyle out of the car. It was done in a joking manner, O'Boyle recalled, but the incident served to demonstrate just how two friends who shared an extremely traditional theological viewpoint could differ so markedly on political matters.[13] This curious anomaly would become even

uncritical chronology of the details of seminary life serves as a useful supplement to Shelley's comprehensive account and is the source for some of the details in this section.

12. Francis Duffy, the famed chaplain of the Fighting 69th and a former Dunwoodie professor, provided an exceptionally detailed account of the seminarian's life in a separate chapter, "Life at Dunwoodie," published as part of Scanlan's history.

13. O'Boyle recounted this incident in his intv. with Francis Weber, 13 Apr 1983, copy in AAW.

more marked after these two classmates were elevated to the College of Cardinals, a rare coincidence in the history of the Church.

O'Boyle was respectful of his learned teachers, but not at the expense of his personal dignity. One of his first classes was a history lecture by the aforementioned Dr. Ryan. In the midst of a lengthy discourse on the Visigoth invasion of Rome, Ryan suddenly called on "Mr. O'Boyle" to "wake up and tell me what I have been talking about." Before going on to expound at length on a subject that he had absorbed well at St. Thomas, O'Boyle insisted on setting the record straight, informing Ryan that he had not been sleeping. That worthy appeared to back down by quickly adding "never mind about all that." O'Boyle's satisfaction at this outcome was somewhat tempered by a more experienced seminarian, who offered him some practical advice after class: "When a professor says you're sleeping, don't argue with him or you won't be here very long." O'Boyle may have heeded this warning at Dunwoodie, but there is little evidence that it was adopted as a lifelong maxim.

America joined the world at war during O'Boyle's second year at Dunwoodie. Enthusiastic support for the war effort found seminarians working on nearby farms during the school year and hiring on for war-related work during summer vacations. They took turns waiting on table in the refectory, freeing the staff for war work. They closely followed the exploits of American forces and, when the bells rang marking the armistice, they organized a local victory parade before riding into Manhattan to join in the city's grand celebration. O'Boyle was in the audience that heard Father Francis Duffy's spellbinding talk about the exploits of the American units on the western front and the responsibilities of the military chaplain. O'Boyle's hearty constitution stood him in good stead when the great postwar influenza epidemic reached Dunwoodie. On the whole the seminary was blest. Although almost half the student body was felled, only one seminarian and one school official died in the epidemic that killed more Americans than the war.

O'Boyle's last years at Dunwoodie coincided not only with a period of "intellectual emasculation" (Msgr. Shelley's words) and a notable deterioration in physical conditions in the seminary itself, but also an increased curtailment of student activities.[14] Although O'Boyle could not help being affected by these larger issues, his later comments betray no negative reaction to the level of teaching or restrictions in student activities. Rather, he focused on the growing cohe-

14. On increased restrictions on seminarians and physical conditions at Dunwoodie in the World War I era, see Shelley, *Dunwoodie*, pp. 184 (source of quote) through 190.

Father O'Boyle, shortly after his ordination in 1921.

siveness of his classmates. Numbering sixty-six students in 1916, they could count just forty-two deacons at the long retreat that preceded ordination on May 21, 1921.[15] On that day Mary O'Boyle, now sixty-five years old, along with relatives and friends watched as the new archbishop, Patrick Hayes, imposed hands upon her son. In accordance with a time-honored tradition, the mother of the newly ordained priest knelt to receive his first blessing. In the afternoon Patrick joined the Scranton contingent for the train trip back to his hometown, where he celebrated his first Mass the next day, Trinity Sunday, at St. Paul's. His brief vacation at home ended when word arrived: Father O'Boyle was to report on June 11, 1921, for duty at St. Columba's parish on Manhattan's West 25th Street.

St. Columba's, 1921–1926

The vast metropolis that constituted the five boroughs of New York was actually a bewildering collection of neighborhoods, each with its particular ethnic and economic character. In 1921 St. Columba's covered the northern half of Manhattan's Chelsea district, a generally impoverished neighborhood on the West Side just south of the notorious Hell's Kitchen. Its congregation consisted mostly of first- and second-generation Irish, remnants of a much larger Irish population that had dominated Hell's Kitchen, Chelsea, and Greenwich Village in the late nineteenth century before graduating to better surroundings. Also included in St. Columba's congregation was a scattering of German- and Italian-Americans.[16] Like its fabled neighbor to the north, Chelsea endured the many problems associated with New York tenement life. Its small factories and scattering of middle-class establishments survived from a more prestigious past and imparted a pleasing ambiance to some of its streets, but neighborhood life was dominated by the region's major employer, the Hudson River piers. There, dangerous working conditions and suppressed wages combined with open corruption and widespread criminality to plague the neighborhood. These conditions, which would continue into recent decades, were vividly portrayed by Hollywood in *On the Waterfront*.

Chelsea possessed other characteristics personified in some of its major landmarks. The fading elegance of the Chelsea Hotel on the district's major commercial street reminded residents of the area's former dominance in New York's en-

15. O'Boyle always recalled forty-four graduates in the Class of 1921, but seminary records list forty-two members, all but three destined for the Archdiocese of New York.

16. Marion R. Casey, "'From the East Side to the Seaside': Irish Americans on the Move in New York City," in *The New York Irish,* ed. Ronald H. Bayor and Timothy J. Meagher (Baltimore: Johns Hopkins University Press, 1996), pp. 399–400.

tertainment industry and of the many literary figures who lived among them. The General Theological Seminary occupied a whole city block, its huge Gothic buildings representing the still-potent Protestant presence in what had become a largely Catholic district. The National Biscuit Company on West 14th Street, the largest factory in the district, gave employment to thousands of local residents and represented the many business, large and small, that still dominated the neighborhood. Finally, the settlement house called the Hudson Guild, on West 27th Street, through its teachers, social workers, and counsellors, gave hope and a helping hand to thousands of local families. John L. Elliot, who founded the guild in 1895, was closely associated with the Ethical Culturists, and he and his social agency were regarded with great suspicion by most Catholic clergymen who, influenced by their own ghetto mentality, condemned the Hudson Guild as irreligious and Communist.[17]

Chelsea of the 1920s and 1930s was described as a "conservative Irish Catholic Community," but in fact many of the Irish and German Catholics who had crowded the neighborhood in earlier decades had risen economically and, befitting their new status, sought better housing in Morningside Heights and north of Central Park. Some had even emigrated to upscale areas like the Bronx, Queens, and Westchester County.[18] Those remaining were, in O'Boyle's words, "good, God-fearing, hard working persons on the fringe of real poverty."

As a Scranton native, the newly minted Father O'Boyle would find much that was familiar but much more that was startlingly different in this neighborhood. He would certainly feel at home in the small-town atmosphere that, even in the midst of a great city, a neighborhood like Chelsea imparted in the 1920s. The predominance of Irish Catholics in a community of largely first- and second-generation Americans was similar to his hometown, where factories and small businesses also jostled in streets with the modest homes of the workers. Nothing in his experience, however, would have prepared him for the "fringes of real poverty" he reported about his new home, a poverty enhanced by the unfair and corrupt labor practices of the dock bosses. In Scranton John Mitchell and other labor leaders had carved out a new philosophy of workers' rights. In contrast, organized labor in New York was reluctant to work with the new immigrants, and so the Irish longshoremen were victims of a vicious hiring system that demanded

17. Jeff Kisseloff, *You Must Remember This: an Oral History of Manhattan from the 1890s to World War II* (New York: Schocken Books, 1989), pp. 477–527. This survey of Chelsea in the 1920s is based on Kisseloff and on *The WPA Guide to New York City* (New York: Random House, 1939, republished in 1992 by the New Press), pp. 151–55.

18. Casey, "'From the East Side to the Seaside,'" p. 401.

they kick back a portion of their paltry wages as a condition of employment.[19] In Chelsea, education most likely came not from classrooms but from its mean streets, where, in sociologist Jeff Kisseloff's words, "the demons of poverty, sickness, starvation, alcoholism, and violence" dominated.[20]

Local parishes did what they could to alleviate the suffering through their St. Vincent de Paul Societies, but substantial relief came from the local political bosses. Tammany Hall, the city's venerable Democratic organization, operated offices—the so-called clubhouses—in each district of Manhattan. The district leader would appear every weeknight to learn firsthand from his precinct captains and the neighbors themselves the needs of families in his jurisdiction. It went without saying that Tammany's largesse was in exchange for votes. Until the advent of the New Deal's vast social programs in the 1930s and the sophisticated organization of Catholic Charities at about the same time, Tammany Hall, with all its inadequacies and obvious political chicanery, provided help for many of the impoverished. O'Boyle recognized the political system for the good it did and enthusiastically supported leaders like Al Smith who sought to reform it. (For years a portrait of Al Smith would grace O'Boyle's Washington office.)

St. Columba's church and rectory ran along the north side of West 25th Street between Eighth and Ninth Avenues. Named in honor of the sixth-century Irish saint, the parish had been established in 1845 to serve the first wave of Irish immigrants who settled in Chelsea, then a community of English and Scots-Irish Protestants. Resentment against the immigrants was fueled mainly by economic rivalry, but anti-foreign and anti-Catholic sentiments were also involved. St. Columba's congregation endured threats of mayhem from the Know-Nothings, then wielding considerable power in the city. The *New York Times* postulated that the West 25th Street firehouse, one of New York's oldest, was located near the church because of the threat of arson. In later years the congregation witnessed a bloody riot that occurred when the city's Orangemen's parade was blocked on Eighth Avenue by masses of local Irish residents.[21] By 1921 this deadly confrontation was but a memory, and local Protestant and Catholic leaders successfully united to work on projects for neighborhood betterment. Yet scars remained; the now numerically dominant immigrants and their children still exhibited that us-against-them attitude that undergirded the Catholic ghetto mentality.

19. Melvyn Dubofsky, "Organized Labor and the Immigrant in New York City, 1900–1918," *Labor History* 2 (1961): pp. 182–201.
20. Kisseloff, *You Must Remember This,* p. 478.
21. *New York Times* [hereafter *NYT*], 7 Jun 1925.

These second-generation Americans tended to cling to the safety and comfort of their Catholic ghettos. The parish, along with its school and many societies and associations, stood at the center of things. This tendency toward exclusiveness had produced a kind of "womb to tomb" Catholicism that emphasized Catholic interests and loyalty to Catholic organizations at the expense of assimilation. Parish priests like young Father O'Boyle faced a difficult challenge. Themselves victims of this same Catholic ghetto mentality, they were expected to lead their people into the American mainstream.

Father O'Boyle's first Sunday "on duty," June 12, 1921, was carefully described in the only letter to his mother that has survived.[22] Declaring himself "very happy now that I'm doing the Lord's work and hope and pray that everyday will be as fruitful as I hope this day was," he went on to list his schedule of duties. He had distributed Communion and taken up the special collection at the nine o'clock Mass; said the ten o'clock Mass, where he preached a "short sermon"; and after breakfast served as subdeacon at the solemn high Mass at eleven. After the big dinner at four o'clock he reported for baptisms, but no one showed up. "They must have heard I would be on and were afraid to take a chance," he reported. The day ended with O'Boyle presiding at a holy hour for the Holy Name Society, the principal parish organization for men. Lest Mary O'Boyle worry that her son's schedule was too heavy, Patrick assured her that he was on duty only every third Sunday and two days during the week. He was even looking forward to a Scranton vacation later in the summer. He also wanted his mother to know that he was already "in good with the girls who have charge of the eats." Returning from hearing confessions on Saturday night, he found they had left him crackers and milk. All this demonstrated, he concluded, that he was working in a well-organized parish.

Credit for the smooth operation of St. Columba's went to Msgr. William A. Thornton, pastor since 1908. In an era when pastors of urban parishes ruled with unquestioned and often arbitrary authority over usually docile assistants and congregations, O'Boyle was truly blest, as he put it, to serve under a devout and judicious guide.[23] Like O'Boyle a first-generation Irish-American, Thornton was born in Chelsea during the Civil War. After serving as assistant at St. Gabriel's Church on the East Side and a stint as superintendent of Catholic

22. Ltr., O'Boyle to "Dear Mother," 21 Jun 1921, original in AAW.

23. O'Boyle, Notes, pt. 3. For an amusing but all too accurate description of big-city pastors in the 1920s, see Thomas Shelley, *Paul J. Hallinan: First Archbishop of Atlanta* (Wilmington, Del.: Michael Glazier, Inc., 1989), p. 25.

schools, he was made pastor of the church in which he had been baptized. O'Boyle was particularly impressed by Thornton's special devotion to the poor of his tough and tormented neighborhood. On a more personal level, he was grateful that the judicious Thornton quietly overlooked his sometimes brash behavior, which might well have been reported to the chancery by a less charitable pastor.

O'Boyle never detailed the nature of his so-called brash behavior, but in that innocent age it might have been no more severe than his set-to with the formidable parish housekeeper, who took flaming exception to the young assistant's complaints about the stale and bitter coffee served to those returning from late Masses. To calm the situation, Thornton claimed he was the originator of the complaint and ordered fresh coffee prepared after each Mass.[24] Nor were Thornton's gentle lessons in priestly humility lost on O'Boyle. On one occasion Thornton took his assistant with him on a visit to the motherhouse of the Sisters of Charity, where O'Boyle sat in on Thornton's interview with the mother superior. In the course of the discussion Thornton asked her what had happened to the archbishop's portrait that had once hung prominently in the convent parlor. He accepted the superior's claim that it had been removed for repairs, but on the way home he told O'Boyle, "Now, Father, there is a lesson for you. You see, I believe there was no more room, and they just moved the portrait either up to the attic or down to the basement. It only shows how vain we can be and what a short time it all lasts."[25]

Thanks to Thornton, St. Columba's had a large modern school, divided, as was typical in those days, into separate sections for boys and girls. Large enough to welcome all those seeking admission, the school had only eight grades. After graduation at age fourteen the few boys who could afford it went on to public high schools while most went to work. Believing that the Church lost all influence over these graduates, Thornton asked O'Boyle to attempt to make some contact with the teenagers. He wanted to form a St. Joseph's Society along the lines of the one he had started at St. Gabriel's many years before. The subsequent success of St. Columba's St. Joseph Society provides an early glimpse of O'Boyle's gift for organization. After agreeing to take on the job, he visited every family in the parish with boys between ages fourteen and nineteen. He was well received, he reported, except by one fairly well-to-do matron who claimed that

24. William S. Abell, ed., *Patrick Cardinal O'Boyle As His Friends Knew Him* (Washington, D.C., 1986), p. 3.

25. Quoted in O'Boyle, Notes, pt. 3.

her son had no need for such a society. (She changed her tune when O'Boyle later had to vouch for her errant son when he ran afoul the police.) Some 300 boys answered the pastor's invitation to attend the Mass marking the foundation of the group.

Although Thornton was obviously pleased by the turnout, he was less supportive of what he considered his assistant's racy proposals. For example, he was adamantly opposed to O'Boyle's suggestion that the parish sponsor dances in the school hall for the young people. Only after O'Boyle assured the gentle puritan that he himself would be present during every minute of the heavily chaperoned dances did Thornton agree. As a further safeguard against improprieties, O'Boyle appointed a special committee to monitor the dancers. If any were found "dancing in a way that was not to be tolerated," the monitors would issue a warning. If a second warning was required, the couple would be expelled.

Policing teenagers' raging hormones proved easy compared to the daunting task of entertaining their elders. The success of the dances for the juniors led to O'Boyle's assignment as director of the parish's annual reception at the Palm Garden, a well-known local nightspot. O'Boyle spent many dreadful hours soliciting advertisements for the event from local businesses and canvassing New York agents for vaudeville acts to entertain the guests. Nothing in these unpleasant duties, however, compared with the task of selecting the parish couple to lead the grand march. Each year many competed for the honor. To resolve the heated disputes that ensued would probably have tested a Solomon. It certainly provided a valuable lesson for a future prelate.

The parish sports program was another matter. O'Boyle was anxious to enroll St. Columba's teenagers in Catholic Charities' newly established baseball league. The parish team made its debut in 1923 and promptly landed in the league basement. The boys' performance earned O'Boyle a visit from William Cavanagh, Tammany Hall's district leader, who explained that St. Columba's place in the league's cellar was intolerable. He asked if O'Boyle would accept the free services of a professional coach. A delighted parish watched its team quickly turn around as O'Boyle quietly overlooked the fact that the new coach had larded the team with some young college athletes. Using the venerable Chelsea Park as home field, St. Columba's captured the league championship in its second year. Parishioners rejoiced in the victory, none more so than Tammany's representative.

The fame of St. Columba's team spread throughout the archdiocese and prompted Father Edward J. Higgins, once an assistant at St. Columba's and now pastor at Assumption parish in far-off Peekskill, to challenge the champions. It took fourteen buses and many taxis to transport all the enthusiastic supporters, along with the trophies they were donating to the event, to the site of the Peekskill contest. O'Boyle later ruefully admitted that his team had recruited a star Yale player to substitute at third base. But even after St. Columba's whipped the opposition, the upstaters cheerfully hosted a dinner for their many guests. Msgr. Thornton thought that the parish should invite Higgins and his team to a rematch at Chelsea Park. Getting into the swing of things, that usually reserved gentleman urged the congregation to put out flags of welcome and host a lunch and dinner.

Not to be outdone, O'Boyle invited the clergy from all the surrounding parishes and arranged for a parade from the church to Chelsea Park led by the fifty-man band of the National Biscuit Company. Even the ethical culturists at the Hudson Guild caught the spirit, hoisting a great banner welcoming Father Higgins and the Peekskill guests. Viewing the throng assembled for the march, a by-now thoroughly anxious pastor asked if O'Boyle had a permit for the event. At that point the Tammany Hall representative stepped in to assure Thornton that all had been taken care of. After the parade some six thousand fans settled down to watch the battle. Seeing the crowd, Thornton confessed that he had never been involved in such a thing before and asked O'Boyle whatever would the people think. O'Boyle quickly assured his boss: "They will love you for it."

O'Boyle had decided that, since St. Columba's was host and had already won the trophy, it should not be so eager to defeat the Peekskill team a second time. The coach agreed to use his second-best pitcher. All went as planned until the fourth inning, when Father Higgins, who had doffed his coat and Roman collar to coach at third base, rejoiced in his team's four-run lead by yelling across the diamond, "Paddy, old boy, today we are beating you and we are going to beat you good."[26] This taunt, O'Boyle admitted, roused his Irish pride, and he signaled the coach to put in their best pitcher. St. Columba's won the game, to the satisfaction of local fans.

The Charity Appeals

The young assistant would remain at St. Columba's for five years, performing the varied and often routine duties that usually fell to curates in an urban, working-class neighborhood. Yet as early as 1923 archdiocesan officials had tak-

---

26. Quoted in O'Boyle, Notes, pt. 4.

en notice of O'Boyle, setting in motion a redirection of his priestly career. It began when Catholic Charities, the institution that coordinated all the archdiocese's charitable institutions and agencies, asked him to manage St. Columba's participation in its annual appeal.

The charity appeal in 1923 was a continuation of what had become an annual drive for the support of the new Catholic Charities organization begun with considerable fanfare by then-Archbishop Hayes in 1920. Auxiliary Bishop John J. Dunn was overall director of these collections managed by a committee of two hundred laymen that sought to identify 100,000 well-heeled New Yorkers who could donate major sums. Although large donations were gratefully accepted, Hayes wanted emphasis placed on ordinary parishioners to donate what they could spare on a yearly basis. To that end each parish conducted a neighborhood drive directed by a clerical and a lay leader working in tandem. Originally planned as a biannual event, the great success of the 1920 appeal ($917,000 was collected in two months) convinced Hayes it should become an annual event in every parish.[27] Under O'Boyle's direction a phalanx of volunteers spread across the parish, visiting every Catholic home. Their effort resulted in St. Columba's raising an unprecedented $8,000, to the delight of Msgr. Thornton and the amazement of the director of Catholic Charities.[28]

As punishment for his good deed, O'Boyle was appointed district manager of the 1924 appeal, supervising the drive in the ten parishes located between 14th and 42nd Streets on the West Side. Not all the autocratic pastors were pleased with what they considered the chancery's interference in their affairs, and their resistance sorely tried the young manager. Nevertheless the 1924 drive again bettered previous totals. St. Columba's itself, with considerable assistance from Msgr. Thornton, who joined in the home solicitations, raised $9,000. Tapped again in 1925, O'Boyle was named assistant to Father Edward Hayes, who directed the parish appeal for the whole archdiocese. O'Boyle was relieved of all parish duties except Masses and confessions and spent eight weeks visiting scores of parishes across the archdiocese, acquainting himself for the first time

27. Sister Mary Margretta Shea, "Patrick Cardinal Hayes and the Catholic Charities in New York City" (PhD dissertation, New York University, 1966), pp. 187–204, 229, and 258. See also Florence D. Cohalan, *A Popular History of the Archdiocese of New York* (Yonkers, N.Y.: United States Catholic Historical Society, 1983), p. 225.

28. The 1923 appeal netted nearly $853,000. See Office of Catholic Charities, "Building for the Future," 25 Mar 1924. Each year Catholic Charities issued a report breaking down the receipts, expenditures, and appropriations associated with the annual appeals. All are available in the Office of Catholic Charities, Archdiocese of New York.

with many of the men who managed the Church at the parish level. He also got to rub shoulders with many clerical and lay leaders, especially at the grand banquet where both Cardinal Hayes and Governor Al Smith addressed the directors and managers of the appeal. In all, O'Boyle admitted, he enjoyed the work, which he found interesting and "most educational."[29]

One morning he came upon the director, Father Hayes, in a funk because he believed himself in serious trouble over a telegram he had sent overnight to all the pastors in the archdiocese, warning them that the appeal was lagging and urging them to put forth a greater effort. He had sent the message out over Bishop Dunn's name, but without Dunn's approval, and now the bishop was calling Hayes on the carpet. O'Boyle promptly dismissed Hayes' worries, using reasoning that would guide his own often-impetuous actions in the years to come: superiors will respect you if you are willing to stand up to adversity and unreasonable criticism, especially if you always act in a way that you think best for the archdiocese.

This philosophy proved correct for the shaken Hayes, for a year later Bishop Dunn invited him along on a world cruise. The catch was that Msgr. Robert Keegan, the head of Catholic Charities, would agree to Hayes' long vacation only if Father O'Boyle could run the diocesan appeal in 1926. Thornton agreed to spare him, and so O'Boyle spent months attending to all the details of the drive. More dauntingly, he had to address the appeal directors, including many senior priests, on what they must do to raise the necessary funds. He needn't have worried. The 1926 appeal raised over $1 million for Catholic Charities.

By now O'Boyle was used to phone calls from Catholic Charities, but one he received shortly after completion of the 1926 drive was different. Msgr. Keegan invited him in for "a little chat," during which he explained that Father Samuel Ludlow, the founder of the Catholic Guardian Society, the unit in Catholic Charities dedicated to the supplemental care of teenage orphans and foster children, was retiring. Keegan wanted O'Boyle to succeed Ludlow. Much to Keegan's chagrin, O'Boyle took literally his order to keep their discussion secret, so it was some time before Msgr. Thornton was consulted on the proposal. O'Boyle, who was quite content with his life at St. Columba's and especially his relations with its fatherly pastor, was ambivalent about the offer. Thornton, on the other hand, while regretting the loss of his hard-working assistant, told O'Boyle, "The fact that you have been asked prompts me to say I think you should do it."

29. O'Boyle, Notes, pt. 4. Unless otherwise noted, this is the source of the following paragraphs on O'Boyle's initial association with Catholic Charities.

A flurry of activity followed, including an audience with Cardinal Hayes, who assured O'Boyle of his own special interest in homeless children and reminded the new director of the seriousness of his responsibilities. Arrangements were made for O'Boyle to live at the Church of the Holy Innocents, Father Ludlow's parish, on West 37th Street near Broadway. Located in the heart of the business district, Holy Innocents was a parish with few parishioners but many worshippers. The new tenant would be expected to say the 7:00 a.m. Mass and help with the confessions that occupied the priests many hours a day.

O'Boyle described leaving St. Columba's as a wrenching experience. He had come to feel quite at home in the old neighborhood where he had learned first-hand about the problems besetting the urban working poor and how prominently the Church's social teachings figured in its salvific work. If his experiences with the parishioners in Chelsea confirmed an understanding of the Church's social role first learned growing up in a blue-collar Scranton family, his association with his first and only pastor underscored lessons learned at Dunwoodie about the proper role of a priest.

The fatherless O'Boyle claimed that Msgr. Thornton had become a father to him, and he clearly meant to model his own priesthood on his gentle, understanding superior. Subtle theological issues were not of great concern to Thornton, who instead exemplified by his own actions the need for unquestioning loyalty to one's superiors. Usually a calm and judicious man, there were situations that could rouse his concern, such as any actions by priests that might give scandal or cause people to question the Church's constancy. How the most unsophisticated member of his congregation understood the Church's teachings was also of primary importance to him. O'Boyle would still be quoting Msgr. Thornton and telling Thornton anecdotes to his subordinates a half-century later. His habit of always approaching proposals from subordinates by first questioning how the change would be understood by the people in the pews had its antecedent in Thornton's teaching, and many of his actions in later years underscored the influence of his perceptive, gentlemanly pastor.[30] In turn, Thornton saw in O'Boyle the Church's future. When the young priest came to say goodbye and ask for his blessing, Thornton said, "Father, some day I think you will be a bishop."

Becoming a bishop was probably the last thing on O'Boyle's mind when, brooding about leaving the warm and protecting aura of his first rectory and up-

---

30. See Higgins and Hannan intvs. concerning O'Boyle's life-long apprehension over the reaction of the unsophisticated parishioner to decisions by the archbishop.

set about embarking on a new venture for which he had no training, he knocked on the door of his new home on West 37th Street. His knock was answered by the only assistant priest on duty, who said matter-of-factly: "You are welcome. Keep moving until you hit the top floor, and there you'll find a room in the front which is yours."

In an effort to combat the loneliness, he returned to St. Columba's for lunch the next day, only to be greeted by his ex-pastor with "I thought you left here."

CHAPTER 3

~𝕸

Catholic Charities

With the exception of his wartime duty as director of the bishops' overseas relief program, Patrick O'Boyle would spend the years from 1926 to 1948 working in the New York archdiocese's mammoth charities network. The years at Catholic Charities, especially those periods that put the fatherless O'Boyle in close contact with some of New York's neediest children, were among the happiest and most fulfilling in his life. Beyond the personal pleasure derived from working with orphans and foster children was the professional satisfaction gleaned from involvement in an exciting period in the nation's social history. Social service as an academic discipline came into its own in the decades after World War I, and New York's Catholic Charities was in the vanguard of those organizations reforming their welfare programs in light of modern scholarship.

Not only a period of modernization, the 1920s and 1930s were also times when private charities, particularly those controlled by religious groups, were moving into a new partnership with federal and state agencies as government expanded its role in the dispensation of welfare. An administrator with formal training in the social sciences, O'Boyle assumed in those decades increasingly important and complex duties. These not only involved him in modernizing the archdiocese's childcare agencies, but also, after the Great Depression gathered force, in defending the Church's welfare role vis-à-vis New York State's welfare offices and the federal agencies created by New Deal legislation. This work would bring O'Boyle into close contact with many social work professionals as well as key leaders in church and state, both at the local and national level. Their collaborations and conflicts would reveal much about his capacity to deal with notable men and women of vastly different experiences and beliefs.

Catholic welfare would also test his mettle as an effective supervisor. During these decades he would direct the work of hundreds of lay and religious social service professionals as they undertook the difficult task of modernizing their institutions. Most of all, the New York years would expose O'Boyle to two superiors, the irascible czar of Catholic Charities, Msgr. Robert F. Keegan, and that dynamic and demanding prelate Francis Cardinal Spellman. If these men came to admire O'Boyle for his hard work and principled and stubborn stands when under attack from superior or subordinate, he probably in turn assimilated some of their autocratic and meticulous management techniques. What is certain, these two mentors had much to do with the transformation of the diffident curate of 1926 into the assured archdiocesan consultant of 1948, and prepared him for his role in Washington.

The Children's Guardian

When O'Boyle assumed directorship of the Catholic Guardian Society in 1926, the Church in New York had been deeply involved in welfare work for over a century. Christian response to the needs of the immigrant poor, especially orphans and dependent children, combined with a fear of Protestant proselytization, stimulated Catholics to sponsor a myriad of agencies and institutions dedicated to childcare, the sick and homeless, aged, and handicapped. By the time Father Ludlow established the Guardian Society in 1913 for the support and oversight of children recently released from orphanages and foster care, the archdiocese recognized more than 122 charitable institutions sponsored, for the most part, by religious orders or parish priests.

Inevitable in such a large-scale enterprise lacking central control, this charitable work suffered considerable duplication in mission and a corresponding failure to address some needs, all at the cost of easily defined inefficiency and waste.[1] Public support for this work proved woefully inadequate, so the perpetually strapped institutions turned to charitable Catholics to keep going. The largest organized sources were the St. Vincent de Paul Society and the Ladies of

1. The following paragraphs on the antecedents of Catholic Charities in New York are based on Shea, "Patrick Cardinal Hayes and the Catholic Charities in New York City," pp. 1–157, and the skillful summary in Cohalan's *A Popular History of the Archdiocese of New York*, pp. 199–207. For additional information on this early period, see Dorothy M. Brown and Elizabeth McKeown, *The Poor Belong to Us: Catholic Charities and American Welfare* (Cambridge. Mass.: Harvard University Press, 1997), especially pp. 13–50.

Charity, but, at best, support for Catholic orphanages and the rest was loosely organized as most institutions solicited funds from their own jealously guarded cadre of donors. Cardinal Farley recognized the pressing need to coordinate the work and solicitation efforts of all these institutions. At the same time he knew that any attempt at regulation must not come at the cost of harming the initiative and jealous loyalty of those who operated and supported the many agencies.

The major impetus for change came from what was widely perceived as an attack on the Church's charitable institutions. As paltry as it was, the state subsidy was vital to agencies operated by religious denominations who resisted periodic efforts to reduce or eliminate it. Some reformers, believing that all such agencies should be state-run, opposed public subsidies in principle. The anti-Catholic element simply wanted to deny public aid to any institution administered by the Church. At the same time, a reformist mayor, John Purroy Mitchel, sought to reduce subsidies as a way to trim the municipal budget. To that end he appointed a commission to investigate the city's private charitable agencies. Its critical report led, after considerable political maneuvering, to a state-appointed investigation in 1916 under the direction of Charles A. Strong.

The Strong Commission set in motion the kind of political donnybrook that New Yorkers seemed to relish. The public was treated to lurid headlines trumpeting alleged abuses in many Catholic institutions. Sordid accounts circulated about orphans lapping up soup from greasy pails later used to feed the pigs and about how 100 boys were forced to use the same toothbrush. Excessive corporal punishment and forced child labor completed a fanciful picture of neglect and mistreatment.[2] Exaggerated and often false testimony led to an impassioned counterattack from Catholics and a resounding defeat for the mayor. The controversy finally died down after the charitable agencies under investigation were exonerated.

Yet while continuation of the vital state subsidies was assured and the lurid charges faded from public consciousness, the investigations had a lasting effect on Church leaders and fueled their determination to reorganize their charitable efforts. To the obvious need for greater efficiency was now added the shadow of public scandal. None was more determined to change the way charity was organized than Patrick J. Hayes, who had played a role in the 1916 controversy and

---

2. Brown and McKeown, *The Poor Belong to Us,* pp. 13–50, puts the controversy in context. See also Neil A. Kelly, " 'Orphans and Pigs Fed from the Same Bowl': Catholics and the New York Charities Controversy of 1916" (MA thesis, St. Joseph's Seminary, 1991), for a useful, detailed account of the Strong Commission and its aftermath.

who in 1919 succeeded Cardinal Farley as archbishop. Foremost, he wanted to create a single powerful voice that might effectively claim from the government the financial support rightly due the archdiocese for its work with the poor. He began by recruiting professional help. He had his friend Father William J. Kerby, head of Catholic University's sociology department plan a comprehensive survey of the archdiocese's charity resources. He appointed Robert F. Keegan, a graduate of Catholic University and the New York School of Social Work, his secretary for charities and director of the 1919 survey, and Father Bryan J. McEntegart, also trained in social work, a member of the survey team. These two priests would figure centrally in all the reorganization and reform that followed.

The survey completed, Cardinal Hayes lost no time in inaugurating change. He established a Committee of the Laity that would begin the fund-raising drive that had so involved Father O'Boyle. In January 1920 he created the Catholic Charities of the Archdiocese of New York as a central coordinating office uniting all his charitable institutions. Keegan, as director, divided the new organization into six divisions—among them relief services and childcare—to which the various agencies would report. Father McEntegart, for example, headed the Division of Children, which centralized the work of all the orphanages, the Home Bureau, and the after-care agencies. Although Hayes and the new director declared that the various charities would operate autonomously, it was obvious just how limited that autonomy would be when they ruled that any changes in policy or organization required approval from Catholic Charities. As the new director of the Guardian Society, for example, O'Boyle routinely reported to that agency's independent board of directors, but in fact he served under the direct supervision of Keegan and McEntegart.

When O'Boyle joined as director in 1926, the Catholic Guardian Society had become an important element in the post-institutional care of thousands of dependent and neglected children.[3] The concept of foster care was just beginning to be developed, and the state routinely committed both dependent and neglected children to religious institutions. Most of these children were discharged from the orphanages and other agencies when parents or other relations were again able to support them. The rest, the true orphans and the neglected refugees from dysfunctional homes, remained until age sixteen (later raised to

3. For an account of the society before O'Boyle's appointment, see Anne Marie McLoughlin, "The Catholic Guardian Society of the Archdiocese of New York: Its Origin and Development (1902–1945)" (MA dissertation, Fordham University, 1947), pp. 18–33. See also *Catholic News,* 27 Jan 1931.

eighteen) in institutions. These children especially were in need of further care and supervision as they struggled to approach adulthood and independent living. At the same time the children who were returned, at whatever age, to their parents or relatives needed to be guaranteed a decent and caring home. In 1926 the Guardian Society was supervising the care of more than five thousand children, 75 percent of them living with relatives, the rest in boarding houses, Guardian-operated shelters, or foster homes as wards of the society. The society's fieldworkers investigated such homes and boarding houses and operated an employment bureau for the older teenagers. All this work was performed by fewer than thirty employees in 1926, financed for the most part by Catholic Charities from funds realized in the sale of the old Catholic Orphan Asylum in downtown Manhattan.[4]

Revealing a cautious streak, Father O'Boyle carefully reviewed the society's resources before deciding that reorganization was in order. He divided its operations into three divisions. The home-care division supervised the 4,546 children discharged to parents and relations. Operating in twelve geographical districts, the division's fieldworkers visited each home quarterly and, in the case of young students, discussed their progress with their teachers. Separate divisions for boys and girls were created to care for those 750 teenagers who had been discharged by the orphanages directly to the society. Each of the divisions operated a small employment agency and used its fieldworkers to inspect boarding houses, places of employment, hospitals, and recreational centers. The three divisions operated on a budget of $38,000 during the first year the reorganization was in effect. During the prosperous years of the late 1920s, the number of children and the budget would decrease slightly (down to 4,092 children in January 1929), only to rise precipitately as the Depression hit New York's working families.[5]

Professionalism and centralization of the Church's welfare organizations were enduring themes of reforms undertaken in the 1920s. At the Guardian Society O'Boyle strongly encouraged his supervisors and fieldworkers to take courses at one of New York's universities. Others received special on-the-job training as the society adopted the casework method of operation. He also hired a full-time psy-

4. *Report of the Catholic Charities of the Archdiocese of New York, 1926*, pp. 39–40; Minutes of the Board of Trustees, Catholic Charities of the Archdiocese of New York, 3 Dec 1928. Both in the archives of Catholic Charities of the Archdiocese of New York (hereafter ACCANY). See also McLoughlin, "The Catholic Guardian Society," pp. 31–32.

5. Minutes of Board of Trustees, Catholic Charities of the Archdiocese of New York, 2 Dec 1926, 16 Dec 1927, and 3 Dec 1928. All in ACCANY.

chologist to care for those children with special educational needs. Signifying the developing centralization of Catholic welfare, he moved the Guardian Society's offices from its old home on West 37th Street to the Catholic Charities building on Madison Avenue.

O'Boyle's direct responsibility for the Guardian Society would continue until 1933. After being named McEntegart's acting assistant in 1930, however, he became increasingly involved during his superior's frequent absences in the overall operation of the Division of Children. The reduction in his time at the Guardian Society fooled no one. Clearly O'Boyle was a manager willing to delegate to trusted subordinates, yet every staff member was keenly aware of who argued for resources from public agencies, defended the society's budget at Catholic Charities, organized training programs for the staff, and solicited local businessmen for job opportunities for the teenagers.[6]

In time O'Boyle found himself serving as a sort of inspector general of all Catholic institutions for children in the city. His sympathetic approach combined with a diffident Irish charm was useful in dealing with the directors of the various agencies, some of whom continued to resist what they considered interference by this new archdiocesan office. At McEntegart's direction, for example, O'Boyle made a survey of the programs of the New York Foundling Hospital. In over sixty years of dedicated work the Sisters of Charity had cared for thousands of newborns and offered shelter to new mothers with no questions asked. Their critics, however, pointed to deficiencies in administration, health care of the infants, and attention to the children after discharge.[7] The critics wanted more trained social workers employed and closer collaboration established with the other bureaus in Catholic Charities.

McEntegart wanted O'Boyle to investigate these charges and propose any necessary reforms, but he also wanted to protect the feelings of the women who had guided this premier institution for so many years. Ever the diplomat, O'Boyle made it a point to meet with the sister superintendent on a biweekly basis, seeking her opinion and advice on his proposed reforms of the hospital's procedures. For more than a year he worked with an increasingly enthusiastic Sister Monica on acquiring professional caseworkers and revising the institution's records system. In place of a simple card file containing the records of the hundreds of orphans and foundlings, a separate casework folder for each child

---

6. O'Boyle provided a brief glimpse of his duties in the Guardian Society in his Notes, pt. 5.

7. Especially critical were the surveys performed for the archdiocese by the NCWC's Rose McHugh in 1926 and 1927. See Brown and McKeown, pp. 95–96 and 112–113.

was created with a complete dossier including detailed family history, medical reports, and treatment records. Commonplace today, this elaborate accounting system represented a breakthrough in Catholic child welfare institutions in the early 1930s and, in the case of the Foundling Hospital, produced immediate dividends.

Shortly after his inauguration in 1933, reform mayor Fiorello LaGuardia decided to inspect some prominent city charities. Without warning he invited McEntegart and O'Boyle to accompany him, and only when heading uptown in the mayoral limousine did they learn that the Foundling Hospital was their objective. After touring the premises as well as consulting one of the new case records, which clearly proved the complaints the mayor had received were groundless, LaGuardia congratulated the sister superintendent for her efficient operation. A quiet witness to the event, O'Boyle nevertheless admitted his frank pride in accomplishing the hospital's reorganization.[8]

O'Boyle's tact and self-effacement were attributes conspicuously absent in the head of Catholic Charities. Robert Keegan was, O'Boyle later pointed out, a "very effective" director, but one who "at times was difficult to understand and to get along with." In fact the dynamic leader of Catholic Charities was famous throughout the archdiocese for his blistering temper and hypercritical attitude toward subordinates. Oblivious to the feelings of city officials, but especially sensitive to his own public image, he could be quick to blame any subordinate when public statements prepared for him somehow went awry. He expected his staff to protect him. As he told one assistant, "Get this straight: even when I want to make a damned fool of myself, it's your job to see that I don't."[9]

At the same time Keegan's executive abilities and leadership qualities were recognized by public officials and professional colleagues, all of whom looked to him for guidance. O'Boyle had no trouble working under a man whose concept of the Church's welfare programs and charity organization would serve as a model for the American Church for generations. Actually, O'Boyle was fascinated by this boss and his management techniques; in later years he would regale his own subordinates with stories about the fiery monsignor.[10] For his part Keegan appreciated O'Boyle's ability to relate easily to people of all ranks. Consequently, the young priest frequently found himself called upon to calm the frayed tempers of those agency heads who resented or ignored directions from Keegan,

8. The tour of the Foundling Hospital is described in O'Boyle, Notes, pt. 6.

9. As quoted in O'Boyle, Notes, pt. 5.

10. See, for example, Higgins and Arthur intvs. For a popular assessment of Keegan's contribution, see *Report of the Board of Catholic Charities of the Archdiocese of New York, 1947*, ACCANY.

whom they considered a bumptious upstart. One of these was the head of the Mission of the Immaculate Virgin, the vast childcare institution on Staten Island. Like Keegan, Msgr. Mallick J. Fitzpatrick was a law unto himself. He had never approved of Catholic Charities and wanted no part of the organization. When troubles arose at the Mission, he would simply bypass Keegan and the Division of Children and appeal directly to Cardinal Hayes, who happened to be an old seminary classmate. This posed a clear threat to the new charities organization, and an exasperated Keegan assigned O'Boyle the task of solving the impasse between the orphanage and Catholic Charities.

O'Boyle initiated a series of informal meetings with Fitzpatrick, meetings in which business seemed to take a back seat to social chitchat. Fitzpatrick always offered his guest lunch, but only after a pre-meal scotch served in the bathroom—a practice left over from Prohibition times. Only when these important activities were concluding was business discussed. Invariably, O'Boyle would report a satisfactory solution to the current problem at the orphanage, without mentioning that he had achieved it while sitting on the rim of a bathtub. Pleased with the results, Keegan never seemed to learn O'Boyle's key to success.

During these years O'Boyle continued to live at Holy Innocents Church, where he was included in the roster of daily Masses and confessions. Keegan insisted that he have a regular day off as well as an annual vacation, so once a week O'Boyle joined clerical pals for relaxation—often at a professional ballgame or a round of golf, a sport he took up during these years. He continued to enjoy family visits with his old classmate, Frank McIntyre, since 1923 the vice-chancellor of the archdiocese, but any longer break found him back in Scranton with his mother and aunts and uncles. Mary O'Boyle had, since retiring from her housekeeping job, lived in a separate apartment at her brother Patrick's house. She was always ready to accept her son's invitations to join him on short trips to the resorts around Mount Pocono, but stubbornly resisted his efforts to get her interested in her health. He finally insisted that she have a medical examination and was amused at her outrage over the "indecency" of the affair. In fact after a life of hard work, Mary O'Boyle's heart had begun to fail, and on February 25, 1930, she died. Many of Patrick's priestly colleagues, including Frank McIntyre, were in the sanctuary at St. Paul's when he celebrated her requiem.[11]

11. Mary O'Boyle was buried in St. Catherine's Cemetery, Moscow, Pa. Years later O'Boyle had her body reinterred with those of her husband and daughter at Scranton's Cathedral Cemetery. The close bond between mother and son has been commented on by several of the cardinal's colleagues. See especially Donoghue, Muldoon, and Hannan intvs. Archbishop Hannan is the source for the story about Mary O'Boyle's reaction to a medical examination.

In Academe's Groves, 1927–1934

Shortly after O'Boyle joined Catholic Charities, Msgr. Keegan issued the new director of the Guardian Society a challenge: "If you are really interested in child welfare work, you ought to go all the way and attend the New York School." Keegan proposed that, when O'Boyle completed the program, Catholic Charities would appoint him its liaison to a psychiatric clinic for children Keegan planned to establish. "If the clinic is a success," Keegan concluded, "I will take the credit, and if it is a failure, we will blame it on you."[12]

Both Keegan and McEntegart were graduates of the prestigious New York School of Social Work, which, by the early 1920s, had become a two-year graduate program affiliated with Columbia University.[13] Employing important academics and experienced social workers, the school was a leader in the rapidly evolving profession. In the years before O'Boyle's enrollment in 1927, the school's curriculum began to reflect a tension arising over changes in the casework method of social work. Favored by both private charities and public relief agencies, this method, developed in the World War I era, stressed an individualistic approach to welfare cases, but one that continued to emphasize the role of environment in creating the injustices and abuses that led to poverty, a philosophy that had become the cornerstone of Catholic social work.[14]

Inspired by the academics on the staff, a new trend in the casework method gained popularity at the New York School during O'Boyle's years as a student. More emphasis was given to mental hygiene, the use of psychology and psychiatry, and the development of a therapeutic relationship between social worker and client, with a corresponding de-emphasis on the study of poverty's root causes. As a result, the trained psychiatric social worker quickly captured the premier position on the staff at the expense of the sociologist. Church leaders, ever suspicious of Freudian determinism and strong supporters of social reform movements, were leery of the new emphasis. But as Cardinal Hayes put it when he ordered Keegan and McEntegart to attend the New York School, "We have been criticized for our institutions. This is a new school . . . and is considered one of

12. As quoted in O'Boyle, Notes, pt. 6.

13. In 1940 the school became a graduate school of Columbia University. On the origins and history of the school during O'Boyle's student days, see Elizabeth G. Meier, *A History of the New York School of Social Work* (New York: Columbia University Press, 1954), and Saul Bernstein, et al., *The New York School of Social Work, 1898–1941* (New York: Institute of Welfare Research, Community Service Society of New York, 1942). The following paragraphs are based on these works.

14. Brown and McKeown, *The Poor Belong to Us,* pp. 73–78, provides a skillful analysis of Catholic reaction to and adoption of the new trends in social work.

the leading schools of social work in the country. Let us find out what they have that we should have. You don't have to accept everything."[15]

In time Catholic Charities came to accept the school's new definition of the casework method in its individual and family counseling, so that each client represented a unique case and the new sciences applied in diagnosing problems and proposing solutions. It never, however, abandoned its crusade against the abuses and injustices suffered by the poor. Student O'Boyle reflected this balance. While he studied the new approaches diligently and spent many months doing fieldwork in psychiatric social work, he was one professional social worker who never abandoned his dedication to the general reform of society. His interest in labor reform, stimulated by conditions in Scranton and Manhattan's West Side, and the practical social reforms instituted by Catholic Charities during the Depression molded him into a forceful advocate for change in the social order.

As at Dunwoodie, the never-shy student was quick to defend his position or correct an instructor whom he believed had wronged him. This was particularly true at the New York School, where a number of the professors were indifferent at best or even hostile to the Church. Not for O'Boyle the cliché "you go along to get along." For him such a course of action was tantamount to denying the Faith. He was always ready to argue that the Church's belief in the dignity of the individual enriched social services and minimized the danger of treating people simply as cases and statistics. If he did not win agreement from some professors, he won respect.[16]

One of his first confrontations occurred in a mental hygiene (psychiatry) class taught by Dr. Marion E. Kenworthy. The whole class was expected to review and appraise the same case, and one week Kenworthy assigned a case involving a priest accused of misconduct with an orphaned girl. Although some of his fellow Catholic students advised him to ignore the situation, O'Boyle would have none of it. Rising in class, he asked if the case against the priest had even been verified. When Kenworthy admitted that she did not know, O'Boyle reminded her that the school's casework method demanded a verified record. Before stalking out of class, he concluded "my superiors are wasting their money in sending me here." The concerned school director, Dr. Porter Lee, invited O'Boyle to lunch to discuss the confrontation, which had become the talk of the school. O'Boyle assured Lee, a scholar he highly respected, that he planned to remain in school and

15. As quoted in O'Boyle, Notes, pt. 5.

16. Bishop Thomas Lyons made this a major point in his eulogy of Cardinal O'Boyle in 1987 (copy in AAW). O'Boyle's *Notes* report in considerable detail his confrontations with the faculty of the New York School and are the source for the following paragraphs.

in Kenworthy's class, but that he would not apologize and only hoped that "what I did will be a lesson to her and others who are teaching here." Kenworthy obviously took the measure of the man, and when O'Boyle objected to an assigned book review on the grounds that he could not accept the author's philosophy, she declared his remarks a sufficient fulfillment of the requirement. O'Boyle had not acted capriciously. Before airing his objections to Flugel's *Psychoanalytic Study of the Family,* he had returned to Scranton to consult his expert friend Henry Klonowski and studied the volume with the help of the noted Catholic physician Dr. Frank Moore.

Some of O'Boyle's disagreements had their comic overtones. The professor of social philosophy was the noted criminologist and onetime warden of Sing Sing prison Dr. George W. Kirchwey. Unlike the other teachers, Kirchwey insisted on addressing O'Boyle, clad in his Roman collar, as "mister," a title O'Boyle echoed when addressing the eminent doctor. Discussing criminal behavior one day, Kirchwey informed the class that Thomas Aquinas taught and believed in vindictive punishment and asked "Mr." O'Boyle for his opinion. O'Boyle questioned the proposition, but promised to research the matter and report at the next class.

As promised, O'Boyle offered at the next session to give St. Thomas' views—in either English or Latin. The offer was ignored, but O'Boyle proceeded to play an old trick from his debating days, asking the gullible professor a series of questions. Noting his full-time job in Catholic Charities, he asked Kirchwey what would happen if he missed an assigned book review. Kirchwey promised that no penalty would ensue and the requirement would be overlooked. But what, O'Boyle persisted, would be the consequence if two, or three, or more assignments were missed? He would be reported to the dean was the reply. Would that, O'Boyle asked, constitute vindictive punishment? Kirchwey laughingly conceded the point, and thereafter it was "Father" O'Boyle and "Doctor" Kirchwey.

Such incidents were not typical of O'Boyle's student days. For the most part he found the teachers sympathetic to his rapidly forming ideas about the care of dependent children and usually agreed with them on larger sociological questions. In the case of Professor of Social Philosophy Eduard C. Lindeman, for example, O'Boyle found much to admire in his writings on democracy and the growth of American cultural values that affirmed the principle that only good means produced good ends. (In later years he would send summaries of Lindeman's speeches to his colleagues in the National Conference of Catholic Charities.)[17] Yet even with the admired Lindeman, O'Boyle "as usual," he later admitted, had his differences, differences he was never reluctant to express. But when another student approached him with a plan to ambush Lindeman, O'Boyle demurred out of his respect for authority as represented by the teacher.

Part of the New York School curriculum was three months' fieldwork in the Bureau of Child Guidance. Opened in 1922, this special clinic was financed by the Commonwealth Fund for Prevention of Delinquency and provided a strong impetus for the use of psychiatric concepts that had begun to permeate the school's courses. O'Boyle admitted that at first he felt like a fish out of water, surrounded as he was by twenty Smith College graduates studying psychiatric social work. But he quickly adjusted and became popular with some of the families of his young "clients." He also claimed to have received special attention from the staff, including its physician-director, who urged him to become a psychiatrist. O'Boyle may have been grateful for the implied compliment, but he did not take too kindly to the director, a fellow Scrantonian, who once confessed that he never boasted about his roots because Scranton "is a dirty town."

With course and fieldwork requirements met, O'Boyle began thesis preparation on a part-time schedule. He planned an ambitious comparative study of five childcare agencies, three in Manhattan and two in Boston. He was well received at all these institutions and produced what he proudly described as the longest thesis produced to that time at the school. "A Comparison of Five Child Care Institutions" boasted a thirty-page conclusion. Stubborn to the end, O'Boyle agreed to prepare a shorter conclusion as recommended by his advisor and readers as long as they agreed that he could append his original conclusion to the document. With thesis approved, he received his diploma on April 1, 1932.

Judging by his careful cataloguing of incidents fifty years after the event, O'Boyle obviously relished his bouts with teachers at the New York School. Yet what to him clearly represented a successful defense of Catholic principles could also be understood as the overreaction of a largely insulated member of the Catholic subculture to the intellectual bumps and grinds common in the larger, pluralistic society. Granted the not-so-subtle religious prejudices of many academics of the day, O'Boyle's strong response to what might have been merely the insensitive actions of a few professors demonstrated the difficulty experienced by Catholics, long protected in their safe ghetto, as they began to take their place in

17. Ltr., O'Boyle to Msgr. John O'Grady, 18 May 1936, O'Boyle file, National Conference of Catholic Charities [hereafter NCCC] Papers, Archives of The Catholic University of America (hereafter ACUA).

the multicultural mainstream. Like many of his fellow Catholics, O'Boyle was strongly affected by the vicious anti-Catholic prejudices that surfaced during the 1928 presidential campaign and figured in the defeat of their hero, Al Smith. That most recent challenge to their Americanism caused many to retreat even more deeply into a Catholic-only world.[18] O'Boyle was different. Forced by his assignments to deal increasingly with non-Catholic religious and civil leaders and tutored by the example of his bosses, Keegan and McEntegart, he would learn in the 1930s that, to advance the charitable interests of the archdiocese, he must learn to cooperate closely with those of different religious and cultural beliefs.

It was a short step from student to teacher. In 1930 Father McEntegart, who had been teaching a child welfare course at Fordham University's School of Sociology and Social Service, suggested to the dean that O'Boyle be appointed in his place. The school had been organized in 1916 at the urging of then-Bishop Hayes as part of his effort to professionalize Catholic social work and to refute those sometimes overly protective clergymen who held that the harsh and sordid realities of social work were not a proper career for Catholic women. More immediately, Hayes wanted to see more Catholic social workers qualify for the New York civil service examination in social work. In 1922 he offered the school an affiliation with Catholic Charities that opened that office's extensive fieldwork facilities to the student social workers. By the end of the decade Fordham had produced hundreds of professional social workers gainfully employed in scores of private social agencies and public welfare services.[19]

O'Boyle taught his child welfare class for four years (through 1934) in the Jesuit university's downtown Manhattan "campus" in the Woolworth Building. Imitating his teachers at the New York School, he invited student questions and discussion on the cases under investigation. A useful teaching tool, the discussion method also required considerable knowledge and experience on the part of the teacher. O'Boyle recalled a number of embarrassing moments when a student's question exceeded the teacher's depth. Since many of his students had practical experience in the field of childcare, O'Boyle was often able to use one student's natural desire to show off his knowledge to answer another's question. "It got me out of one of the deepest holes I was ever in," he candidly admitted.

18. David J. O'Brien, *American Catholics and Social Reform: The New Deal Years* (New York: Oxford University Press, 1968), pp. 45–46. See also Cohalan, *A Popular History of the Archdiocese of New York,* pp. 247–52.

19. *Fordham University School of Sociology and Social Service Announcement, 1933–1934,* copy in AAW. See also ltr., P. M. Kane, Head of Archives and Special Collections, Fordham University, to author, 14 Apr 1999, AAW, and Brown and McKeown, *The Poor Belong to Us,* p. 76.

Meanwhile Msgr. Keegan had not forgotten his threat to involve his new sub-ordinate in a Catholic experiment in psychiatric social work. Shortly after O'Boyle finished the program at the New York School, Keegan recruited him to help Father McEntegart establish a clinic for children in need of psychiatric care. With McEntegart frequently away, it fell to O'Boyle to organize the new service. He arranged for the facility to be attached to the Foundling Hospital, where two psychiatrists, Drs. James Brochbank and William Doody, directed a staff of psychiatric social workers who treated children from all the local Catholic institutions. As part of an initial survey, O'Boyle arranged for Doody and a psychologist to visit each of these institutions, where they tested thousands of children for their intelligence quotient. O'Boyle took considerable satisfaction from the success of this new agency. Its obvious usefulness reinforced his appreciation of psychiatric social workers, whom he would liberally employ when he assumed direct responsibility for thousands of dependent children later in the decade.

Childcare and the Great Depression

O'Boyle's final years at the New York School coincided with the onset of the Great Depression, a period that would thrust him into the national debate over welfare. The late 1920s had marked the last hurrah for the old city bosses and their massive patronage network, which supported the notion of local charity locally administered.[20] Although these men lacked the reformist spirit of John Mitchell that had so stirred him in his youth, O'Boyle recognized that under new leaders like Charles Murphy and protégés Al Smith and Fiorello LaGuardia, Tammany Hall was now ready to support initiatives concerning workman's compensation, old age pensions, and a state welfare system that would make New York the model of social reform for the whole country.[21] His superiors had likewise come to accept the notion that the state had a major role to play in stimulating recovery and providing welfare. Cardinal Hayes and his subordinates at Catholic Charities strongly supported the state's social welfare initiatives, as in the case of old age pensions and emergency relief.[22]

20. Steven P. Erie, *Rainbow's End: Irish Americans and the Dilemma of Urban Machine Politics, 1940–1985* (Berkeley: University of California Press, 1988), p. 107.

21. Nancy J. Weiss, *Charles Francis Murphy, 1858–1924: Respectability and Responsibility in Tammany Politics* (Northampton, Mass.: Smith College Press, 1968), pp. 32–34 and 94–96, and Charles Garrett, *The LaGuardia Years: Machine and Reform Politics in New York City* (New Brunswick, N.J.: Rutgers University Press, 1961), pp. 14–16.

22. O'Brien, *American Catholics and Social Reform*, pp. 48–51, and Shea, "Patrick Cardinal Hayes and Catholic Charities," p. 252.

During the early months of the Depression private organizations managed to shoulder most of New York City's relief burden, even though for its part the archdiocese was forced to divert most of its current resources to meet the unprecedented demand. Its income exhausted by 1931, Catholic Charities welcomed the city's formation of a Home Relief Bureau, which provided some help for the unemployed with money supplied through emergency state legislation, and readily referred thousands of needy Catholics to that agency.

Msgr. Keegan also insisted that Catholic Charities and agencies of several other denominations play an active role in the Emergency Unemployment Relief Committee (a volunteer organization chaired by Stewart Prosser), which had organized a major relief effort in 1930. Faithful to the so-called "New York System" of dispensing charity, the committee collected the funds to finance an Emergency Work Bureau under which four private organizations, including Catholic Charities, created jobs for heads of households in nonprofit agencies under their control. In the case of Catholic Charities, more than six thousand unemployed men were hired around the diocese. They were paid by local pastors with money received from Catholic Charities, which in turn was reimbursed by the Emergency Bureau. By the winter of 1933 eighty percent of relief in New York City was coming from public sources. Under the leadership of Cardinal Hayes, Catholic Charities had joined "spiritedly and unstintingly" in the joint community planning that decided on the proper distribution of these funds.[23]

These early successes convinced Hayes of the need to cooperate fully with government agencies. The people of his archdiocese, who had strongly supported Governor Franklin D. Roosevelt's social programs, quickly rallied to President Roosevelt's New Deal programs. Church leaders saw a strong similarity between the New Deal and the Church's social teachings as enunciated by the American bishops in the National Catholic Welfare Conference. Appearing with the new president at graduation ceremonies at the Catholic University of America in 1933, Hayes noted that New Deal programs illustrated the Church's philosophy of charity—the principle of the common good based on the commandment to love one's neighbor. In this era of hardship and sacrifice, he reminded Roosevelt, families were holding together remarkably well, thanks in part to the combined efforts of church and state.[24]

23. *Catholic Charities of the Archdiocese of New York Annual Report, 1933,* ACCANY. See also Shea, "Patrick Cardinal Hayes and Catholic Charities," p. 273. The following paragraphs on Hayes and the New Deal are based on this source, pp. 261–74, and on the comprehensive account in Brown and McKeown, *The Poor Belong to Us,* pp. 151–91.

24. Gerald Fogarty, *The Vatican and the American Hierarchy* (Wilmington, Del.: Michael

Hayes and Keegan decided that their social welfare experiences should be brought to the attention of the whole American Church. To do so they offered to host the nineteenth annual meeting of the National Conference of Catholic Charities in October 1933. Keegan was the president of the conference that year (which coincided with the 100th anniversary of the St. Vincent de Paul Society in America), and Hayes invited all the members of the hierarchy to join conference delegates and interested observers at a four-day extravaganza. The Waldorf Astoria ballroom and the cavernous Metropolitan Opera House were obtained to handle the expected crowds. The closing banquet would feature President Roosevelt delivering his first New York address since becoming chief executive. For his part the new president was eager to acknowledge the importance of the Catholic vote to his coalition. He accepted the cardinal's invitation during a meeting with Msgr. Keegan shortly after his inauguration in 1933. Keegan personally secured the president's participation, but it was Father O'Boyle who faced the daunting task of organizing the four-day affair.[25]

He brought it on himself. O'Boyle later admitted that at an initial planning meeting called by Keegan, he had "talked too much" and as a result was stuck with the job of directing all the organizers.[26] The assignment required considerable tact, for Keegan made it clear that the convention was to be a New York affair and under no circumstances should O'Boyle brook interference from Msgr. John O'Grady, the executive secretary of the National Conference of Catholic Charities. O'Boyle expended considerable energy throughout a busy summer of 1933 keeping the Washington-based O'Grady informed, but at arm's length from the action.

The eventual success of the convention helped solidify O'Boyle's reputation as a first-class administrator, but the long planning phase was not without its mini-crises. For example, on the night before the all-important closing banquet at the Waldorf Astoria, where Roosevelt was scheduled to speak, O'Boyle learned that the list of attendees with the seating arrangement had been lost. He conscripted all the priests and stenographers and typists he could find. Divided into groups in rooms around the hotel, they culled lists of names and poured over seating diagrams through the night, with O'Boyle running from floor to

---

Glazier, Inc., 1985), p. 239. Hayes' remarks were reprinted in "The Principle of the Common Good," *Catholic Mind* 30 (22 Jul 1933): 263.

25. Ltrs., Keegan to Msgr. John O'Grady, 10 Nov 1932 and 20 Oct 1933, Keegan file, NCCC collection, ACUA.

26. O'Boyle, Notes, pt. 8, which is also the source of the following account of O'Boyle's personal involvement in the affair.

floor delivering the latest index cards for the VIP seating. About four in the morning, trying to restore drooping spirits, he clapped his hands and exhorted, "Come on, let's get going." One of the workers in that group happened to be his immediate boss, Father McEntegart, who, taking umbrage at his subordinate's remark, shot back with, "What do you think we've been doing? We haven't been riding up and down on the elevator, taking it easy."

During the conference itself Keegan and other charity directors delivered important reports. In turn they listened to experts like Secretary of Labor Frances Perkins, Postmaster General James Farley, and presidential assistant Harry Hopkins expound on the philosophy and aims of the New Deal. Of particular interest was an address by the rector of Catholic University, Bishop James H. Ryan, defending the Roosevelt administration.[27] O'Boyle, always a staunch supporter of the Democratic Party,[28] would have agreed with Ryan and enjoyed listening to the charismatic president, but he reserved his greatest praise for his friend and hero Al Smith. The Happy Warrior spoke to the delegates on the first day of the conference, using as his theme the biblical story of the man who fell among robbers on the road to Jericho. It was one of the finest homilies on that Bible passage he ever heard, O'Boyle recalled many years later.

While the convention served to publicize the American Church's growing cooperation with public agencies in supplying relief for the indigent and its general support for the new president's philosophy of social welfare, it also marked the beginning of a drawn-out battle with the federal government over the role of religious agencies in the distribution of public welfare. Catholic charities around the country had become comfortable with a system in which denominational agencies were allocated public funds for their relief work. Soon after the vast Federal Emergency Relief Administration had been established in the summer of 1933, however, Harry Hopkins, its administrator, announced that federal funds, now the primary source of relief, would be allotted only to public agencies in the states and could be spent only by those agencies.

During succeeding months the actual dispersal of funds varied widely across the country depending on the relative strengths of local public and private relief agencies. Yet despite vigorous lobbying by Msgr. O'Grady and directors of Catholic charities like Msgr. Keegan, federal rules remained unchanged, although under pressure Hopkins agreed that personnel from private (religious) agencies

27. *NYT*, 1 Oct 1933. The *Times* provided full coverage of the convention and used its editorial page to praise the work of the St. Vincent de Paul Society on the occasion of its centennial.
28. On O'Boyle's political affiliation, see Donoghue intv.

could be employed in the distribution of federal relief.[29] Institutions like New York's Catholic Charities were forced to seek other arrangements for obtaining funding. Many members of its staff promptly sought jobs in those public institutions administering federal funds and therefore were able to influence relief operations. Meanwhile Catholic agencies like the Guardian Society continued to direct their pleas for assistance to state agencies not dependent on federal funds.

As director of a major institution supervising the settlement of dependent children, O'Boyle had his work cut out for him. While the emphasis of all early relief had been on the unemployed, mostly heads of households, the Depression was causing a crisis for childcare agencies, in particular those with teenagers approaching the age of discharge. As early as January 1933 O'Boyle had issued a warning about their plight. In the pages of the *Catholic Charities Review,* he reported to colleagues around the country that in New York City alone almost two thousand teenagers between 16 and 18 were being retained in childcare institutions because of the depressed job market. Many of these youths had parents, but they too were unemployed and could not assume responsibility for their children. These cases were properly the responsibility of public relief agencies, he claimed, which should be persuaded to subsidize such families so that their children could return home. He offered his colleagues several suggestions for temporary relief that had helped in New York, but the only lasting solution, he admitted, was jobs for those graduating from dependent care. While that goal remained elusive, he urged his readers to renew their efforts to demand public aid. These young people, he argued, had a legitimate claim on funds being dispersed by municipal and state relief bureaus. Those operating childcare institutions must plead their case, just as others argued the case for unemployed adults.[30]

What particularly incensed him was a recent change in federal regulations that overturned an item in the previous administration's Relief and Construction Act that provided support for the placement of older dependent children in boarding homes. O'Boyle and his colleagues had protested Harry Hopkins' decision to rule out childcare as an activity eligible for federal funds, informing President Roosevelt that his administration was deliberately subordinating the legitimate needs of teenagers to those of adults. Roosevelt referred their protest to the federal Children's Bureau, whose director met with them in December 1933. Msgr. O'Grady served as spokesman at this and subsequent meetings

29. Thomas W. Tifft, "Toward a More Humane Social Policy: The Work and Influence of Msgr. John O'Grady" (PhD dissertation, The Catholic University of America, 1979), p. 83.
30. O'Boyle, "The Dependent Adolescent," *The Catholic Charities Review* 17 (Jan 1933): pp. 6–8. See also O'Boyle, "Fifty Years of Child Care," same source, 33 (Dec 1949): pp. 268–69.

where Hopkins finally agreed to insert a childcare provision in the new relief bill under consideration. Although this left unsolved the problem caused by the ban on direct federal payments to denominational relief agencies, the dependent children in the care of the Guardian Society and others gained substantial help.

O'Boyle made clear that he was not in favor of direct relief payments to teenagers, which he found demoralizing. He wanted jobs. In 1932 he had joined with the directors of the Protestant and Jewish agencies doing similar work in the city in bringing the plight of unemployed youth to the attention of public authorities. They formed a special ten-member Subcommittee for the Working Boy in the Welfare Council of New York City and proceeded to dun the city's Emergency Work Bureau and the state's Temporary Emergency Relief Administration for funds. Their lobbying succeeded. Money was made available for a special project that placed three hundred Catholic, Protestant, and Jewish boys in the Civil Works Service where, after vocational testing, they were placed in positions in the public schools as assistant librarians, messengers, clerks, and the like. The jobs paid enough to make the young men self-supporting for a year while professional employment agencies sought permanent positions for them. Once these boys found permanent work their places in the program were taken by others from one of the after-care agencies.

Emboldened by their success, O'Boyle and his colleagues decided to seek federal funds to enlarge the program to include 1,200 boys. The subcommittee made numerous trips in 1935 to Washington, where its members argued their case before officials of the Works Progress Administration, which had become responsible for all federal relief programs. O'Boyle asked Msgr. O'Grady to use his many government contacts to monitor their request as it worked its way through the Washington bureaucracy. O'Grady promised to do what he could when their petition got to Washington, but he warned O'Boyle that, while the New York group's lobbying might prove effective later on, its petition must first go through regular channels. This meant that before Washington considered the case, the proposal must be first win the approval of the WPA's New York office, which was directed by General Hugh Johnson, a prominent New Dealer.

O'Boyle lost no time in arranging a meeting with Anna Rosenberg, Johnson's assistant, who would later serve in Washington as an assistant secretary of defense during O'Boyle's years in the capital. "So far things look rosy," he reported to O'Grady on July 24th. Following the meeting Johnson reviewed the proposal, and despite existing regulations about the dispensation of federal relief, the WPA agreed to assume responsibility for the project. In 1935 the Guardian Society could report that, in addition to the 725 boys and girls who found jobs through its employment bureau with support from New York relief agencies, an additional 141 youths between the ages of 17 and 21 gained work through the auspices of the WPA.[31]

Fully committed to the idea of a partnership with government in relief programs and child welfare, O'Boyle became closely involved with colleagues from the non-Catholic agencies, actively participating with them in the work of various city and state organizations. During the mid- and late 1930s he served as a member of both the Central Admission and Distribution Center of the Greater New York Fund and the New York City Child Welfare Committee. He sat on the board of directors of the Child Welfare League of America and was an active member of various committees of New York's Welfare Council and the state's Conference on Social Work. He also served as a consultant on child welfare in the state's Department of Social Welfare and was active in the American Association of Social Workers. Not content to be the poster boy for Catholic Charities in these organizations, O'Boyle threw himself into their work, gaining a reputation as a leader in the field of childcare.[32]

National Conference of Catholic Charities

Msgr. Keegan's growing confidence in O'Boyle was reflected in the latter's increasingly important and far-ranging assignments. In particular O'Boyle's association with the work of the National Conference of Catholic Charities in the early 1930s thrust him into the inner sanctum of the American Church's charitable operations. It also tested his ability to work with a second egotistical, impatient, and single-minded champion of charitable work, Msgr. John O'Grady. The NCCC had been organized in 1910 at the Catholic University of America as a largely lay operation under the auspices of the St. Vincent de Paul Society, but in 1920 O'Grady assumed leadership and proceeded to transform the NCCC into a professional organization largely underwritten by the diocesan directors of Catholic Charities.

Foremost among these professionals was Msgr. Keegan, who supported the effort to make the NCCC a united voice in the effort not only to professionalize

---

31. Ltrs., O'Grady to O'Boyle, 19 Jul 1935; O'Boyle to O'Grady, 23 and 24 Jul 1935 (source of quote); and O'Boyle to John J. Butler, 24 Jul 1935. All in O'Boyle file, NCCC Papers, ACUA.

32. *The Catholic Charities Review* 17 (Sep 1943): p. 172. For a summary of the myriad organizations in which O'Boyle served, see ltr., O'Boyle to Msgr. Ready, executive secretary of the NCWC, 13 Aug 1943, NCWC Papers, ACUA.

Catholic charitable operations, but also to represent the Church's interests vis-à-vis the federal government. Although they shared a common vision for Catholic charities, Keegan and O'Grady, as might be expected of two such autocratic leaders, frequently remained at arm's length. More than once O'Boyle was cast in the role of facilitator and conciliator.

O'Boyle's first prolonged association with O'Grady began shortly after the NCCC's 1933 convention in New York. A group of diocesan directors, probably at O'Grady's urging, approached the rector of Catholic University with a proposal for organizing a school of social work. They pointed out the need to prepare a corps of trained clergy and selected laymen for leadership in the field. For decades bishops had become accustomed to sending their priests to Catholic University for advanced study in theology and other subjects. The university, the group argued, was therefore the logical place for a school of social work with the academic and professional standards they sought. Rector Ryan invited the directors to form an advisory committee to assist in preparing plans for such a school. The advisory committee was duly created with Keegan at its head. O'Boyle, although not a member, was drafted to serve as secretary.

The committee met in December 1933 to discuss the group's minimum requirements, which its members presented to the rector. They argued that the enterprise must be organized as a separate school in the university; also, the new school should operate on a quarterly system rather than the university's standard semester system. The directors of Catholic Charities were willing to donate $10,000 annually to the university, which, along with tuition and scholarships supplied by the Knights of Columbus and the Catholic Daughters of America, would cover most of the expense.[33]

To O'Boyle, the recent graduate of the prestigious New York School, fell the task of preparing a detailed plan to be presented to the university's board of trustees. By March 1934 he was ready with an outline of objectives, a curriculum draft that emphasized field instruction, a list of admissions and faculty requirements, and an organizational chart that reflected a comparative analysis of twenty-eight schools across the country. His prospectus emphasized the need for a faculty that combined practical experience in social work with a dedication

---

33. Ltr., O'Grady to O'Boyle, 23 Jan 1934, O'Grady/O'Boyle file, NCCC Papers, ACUA. On O'Boyle's efforts to convene the committee, see ltrs., various dates (c. Nov–Dec 1933), School of Social Work file, same source. See also Dorothy A. Mohler, "The School of Social Work of the Catholic University of America, 1934–1947," a paper presented at the annual meeting of the Council on Social Work Education, 7 Mar 1982, copy in Rector's files, ACUA. Unless otherwise noted the following paragraphs are based on this work.

to pure research. It also stressed the need for both faculty and students to make use of agencies outside Washington in their fieldwork. It called for the training of priests in both casework and administration and proposed admission of students from other disciplines for a minor in social work. O'Boyle even suggested that the majority of priests and sisters attending Catholic University would profit from a social work minor as a means of enlarging their understanding of the many social problems existing in their parishes and schools.[34]

The trio of Keegan, McEntegart, and O'Boyle, representing the advisory committee, presented the prospectus to Bishop Ryan and Dr. Roy J. Deferrari, then dean of the graduate school. Ryan called O'Boyle's work one of the best proposals presented during his time as rector and promised to present it with his endorsement to the trustees. The trustees accepted the proposal in April and appointed Msgr. O'Grady dean. The school opened with forty-five students in September 1934.[35] To O'Boyle's consternation, Msgr. Keegan, confident of his assistant's ability to get the new school operating in "the New York way," proposed to the rector that Father O'Boyle be appointed O'Grady's assistant. Everyone but O'Boyle seemed pleased with the idea. To make matters worse, O'Grady invited O'Boyle to live with him in Washington. That was the last thing O'Boyle could have wanted, but, always the good soldier, he indicated his willingness to take on the job if his superiors considered him capable. He won a last-minute reprieve when Cardinal Hayes refused permission, citing the shortage of experienced priests in Catholic Charities and the delicate negotiations O'Boyle was then conducting with city and state agencies over the distribution of relief funds. O'Boyle, however, was convinced that what really saved him from O'-Grady's grasp was the fact that Ryan had so oversold his abilities that Hayes decided such a paragon should remain in New York.[36]

Although O'Boyle would never serve in the new School of Social Work, he remained intimately connected with its operations, first as secretary and after 1937 as a member of its advisory committee. There he supported O'Grady's plan to open the new school to lay women students. The rector, citing a "gentlemen's agreement" with the board of trustees—all prelates—concerning the enrollment

34. "Program of Proposed Catholic University School of Social Work," 22 Mar 1934, NCCC Papers, ACUA. See also "Report of the Committee of Diocesan Directors of Catholic Charities on the School of Social Work at Catholic University," School of Social Work file (1934), same source.

35. "The National Catholic School of Social Service and the School of Social Work of The Catholic University of America, Pt. 1: The Problem," (c. 1947). Rector's files, ACUA.

36. O'Boyle, Notes, pt. 8. For Hayes' rejection of the proposal, see ltr., Hayes to Ryan, 13 Apr 1934, O'Boyle file, NCCC Papers, ACUA.

of women, was able to defeat the proposal.[37] The ban did not extend to sisters, who at the insistence of the advisory committee had been included as students from the beginning. In fact, Keegan reported that he and his fellow directors had pledged themselves to "exert every effort" to release sisters and priests from diocesan duties to be trained in the new school.[38]

O'Boyle's relationship with O'Grady gradually evolved into a partnership in which O'Boyle, a master of detail, began to offer advice on matters of budget and school programs. Soon he was advising O'Grady on what points he should discuss with the advisory committee. His letters became studded with phrases like "I think you should" and "you might mention." In January 1936, for example, O'Boyle told O'Grady: "I believe two cautions are to be observed in presenting [to the committee] whatever plans you decide to follow." He went on to warn O'Grady not to present his plans in such a rigid fashion that the Catholic Charities directors might consider them already settled, with no room for their input. It would be best, O'Boyle added, to use various members of the committee to explain your plan to some of the directors to win their consideration. If O'Grady would send O'Boyle his notes on his proposals, O'Boyle would fashion them for consideration by both the advisory committee and the directors of Catholic Charities.[39]

By the mid-1930s Keegan and O'Boyle had also developed a strong partnership, even if the younger priest still trod warily, ever mindful of his boss's impetuous responses to both friends and foes. By then, too, O'Boyle had clearly learned how to play the older man, a tactic made easier by the fact that under Keegan's tutelage he had come to agree with him on all the important issues of social reform. Keegan recognized this symbiosis, just as he recognized his subordinate's loyalty and hard work. When he asked O'Boyle to draft his speeches and reports, as he frequently did in this period, he left decisions on what points were to be underscored almost entirely up to the speechwriter.[40]

Shortly after he was elected president of the NCSW in 1935, Keegan was asked to give the keynote address at the Ohio state conference. He was eager to make a good impression, especially because the director of the school of social

37. Ltr., Ryan to Bp. Karl J. Alter, 12 Jul 1935, Rector's files, ACUA.

38. "Report of the Chairman of the Committee of The Catholic University School of Social Work," quoted in *Proceedings of the Twenty-first National Conference of Catholic Charities, 29 Sep–2 Oct 1935.* NCCC Papers, ACUA.

39. Ltr., O'Boyle to O'Grady, 9 Jan 1936, School of Social Work file, NCCC Papers, ACUA.

40. On the closeness of the O'Boyle-Keegan relationship in this period, see Muldoon, Donoghue, and Higgins intvs.

work at Western Reserve University and all her students would be present for the speech. "Make it good," he told O'Boyle without any further instruction. O'Boyle decided the speech should warn social workers against the growing optimism about economic recovery. The conviction that good times were just around the corner and that the recently enacted Social Security legislation would meet all the country's social needs was lulling the public into accepting a sort of cease-fire in the fight for more government involvement in public relief. Employment figures would not soon improve, O'Boyle predicted, because technological advances were making more and more jobs redundant. He had Keegan urge his Ohio audience to publicize the need for fundamental changes in the economic order. If they failed, the public, he predicted, would forget the poor and needy and lapse into a "form of conservatism that is unpardonable."[41]

Keegan readily accepted O'Boyle's draft, but decided that he could enhance it by adding three quotations from Professor David C. Coyle's article in a recent edition of the *Atlantic Monthly.* He explained that Coyle was the brother of the director of the Western Reserve school and citing him would please his audience. An angry O'Boyle vowed that the three quotes from an entirely unrelated article on public works would not be added to his draft. Appealing to Keegan's well-known vanity, he argued, "You are President of the Conference; you don't quote anybody, they quote you." On the night train to Columbus, O'Boyle finally won his point, and the quotations were dropped. A highly favorable reception put Keegan in good humor, which was only reinforced the next morning when O'Boyle brought him a copy of the *New York Times,* which generously quoted from the speech. "Well, you are made," O'Boyle explained. "The headline said 'Keegan Sees Peril to Relief Work.' It doesn't say Keegan of Catholic Charities or offer any identification except the word Keegan. So now you are a national figure." Keegan grabbed the paper, and O'Boyle reported that "needless to say, we had two wonderful weeks afterward; everything went very well."[42]

O'Boyle's most important speech-writing effort for Keegan was the presidential address at the NCSW's national convention in Atlantic City in October 1936. The convention provided the occasion for a major statement by a Catholic official on the status of social reform in America, and at Keegan's insistence O'Boyle went to Washington to discuss the talk with Msgr. O'Grady. O'Grady wanted Keegan to consider the issues philosophically and to place the underlying principles in their historical prospective. To that end he urged O'Boyle to consult

41. Quotes are from a summary of Keegan's address published in *NYT,* 18 Oct 1935.
42. O'Boyle, Notes, pt. 8. The cardinal devoted several pages of his brief notes to this incident.

with Dr. Goetz Briefs, a noted economist and former president of the Reichs-bank. At O'Boyle's request Briefs submitted a twenty-two-page survey of which, O'Boyle confessed, he could understand only the first eleven. Lengthy discussion with these men convinced him that they were not on the same wavelength. "It seems to me," O'Boyle noted, "there is one thing we must avoid, that is, the possibility of becoming quite academic." In the end, after a week of intense labor, he produced an optimistic survey, which Keegan delivered to general acclaim on May 24, 1936.[43]

O'Boyle titled the address "Democracy at the Cross-roads." The crossroads had been created, he explained, by the great concentration of ownership and profit since the Civil War and the simultaneous closing of the American frontier, that symbolic safety valve which had offered to every American a chance at building a career and accumulating wealth. The limitless frontier had in fact tested the idea of individual liberty and freedom of opportunity while protecting the balance between property and non-property that had always mitigated class conflict in America. The Great Depression made clear to everyone that these historic changes—the concentration of wealth and the closing of the frontier—were causing a fundamental shift in America's industrial and agricultural life, a shift that threatened a "feudalization of American wealth" with a permanent leisure class and an unchanging laboring class.

Although it was difficult for a democratic government to avoid falling into the hands of powerful interest groups, O'Boyle was optimistic. He believed that the American government's system of checks and balances would quickly identify any transgression of the constitution. "We need not let phantom fears close our minds to necessary changes in public policy," he wrote, "but we must be alert that such changes conform to the basic pattern of our democracy." He deemed a return to rugged individualism proposed by some "an unprofitable adventure." To those who favored a communist experiment, he argued that Americans had too much faith in spiritual values and human rights "to go the Russian way." For those who believed a vested oligarchy was the answer, he recalled "that from such abuse of power our forefathers came to this country."

The speech offered some specific advice:

Government must encourage individual ownership in every practicable way. By government credit and subsidy, if necessary, we should encourage people

---

43. Ltr., O'Boyle to O'Grady, 19 Nov 1935, O'Boyle file, NCCC Papers, ACUA (source of quote). The same file contains much correspondence on the same subject among O'Grady, Briefs, and O'Boyle between August 1935 and May 1936, in which O'Grady apologizes for his lack of input.

to own their own homes. Government should aid the deserving tenant farmer to own his own land. . . . We cannot forget that this country was built up and stamped mentally and morally by a large group in the middle wealth brackets; it was its pride that it offered to countless immigrants the chance of ownership which they lacked in their native countries. If we deprive the people of this traditional opportunity we shall accentuate the most fundamental of all our difficulties—the appalling lack of a wide distribution of property. What is more appalling we shall be developing a type of citizen, who will be lacking in independence and a sense of responsibility.

Although government intervention in relief was welcome, it must be controlled. Echoing the teachings of recent popes, O'Boyle proposed a rule for a country "living in an atmosphere of emergency and expectancy: a natural order should obtain in the matter of government welfare and relief, an order that is disregarded only with serious consequences. Every social problem must be met at the level at which it arises. Problems, for example, that can be dealt with by local institutions and local government must never be referred to larger units of government. It is only when that economic or social unit cannot cope that a higher government should intervene."[44]

These principles would figure prominently in O'Boyle's direction of a new archdiocese in later years.

44. "Democracy at the Cross-Roads," copies at various stages of preparation located in O'Boyle file, NCCC Papers, ACUA. Generous extractions from the speech appeared in an article and editorial in *NYT*, 25 May 1936.

CHAPTER 4

Other Duties as Assigned

Seasoned bureaucrats are wary of the phrase "other duties as assigned" in their job descriptions. Patrick O'Boyle, who seemed to relish such collateral work, was an exception. During his years at Catholic Charities, where his major task had been supervising and coordinating the work of the archdiocese's many childcare institutions, he readily accepted additional duties that involved him in the day-to-day operation of several of these institutions.

By the close of 1936 New York's Catholic Charities could boast of several successes in the fight for government recognition of the role of religious organizations in relief work. In October the city's Board of Estimates had raised the public contribution for childcare and boarding-out services to $6 per month per child and had pledged nearly a half-million dollars to cover the expenses of these mostly religious institutions. On the national level, O'Boyle had joined those who had lobbied successfully for amendments to the Aid to Dependent Children and the Child Welfare Services sections of the new Social Security Act, which created the first, albeit weak, safety net for the nation's dependent children.[1] Although this left many issues to be addressed in future months, O'Boyle would no longer be among the frontline soldiers. In late 1936 he received a new, all-consuming addition to his other assignments.

Mission of the Immaculate Virgin

In early December 1936 O'Boyle's friend Msgr. Mallick Fitzgerald died. Fitzgerald was the long-time administrator of the Mission of the

1. Brown and McKeown, *The Poor Belong to Us,* p. 177.

Immaculate Virgin for the Protection of Homeless and Destitute Children. At a meeting of the Mission's board of trustees that convened immediately following the funeral, Cardinal Hayes appointed O'Boyle temporary head of the vast orphanage on Staten Island. Hayes wanted O'Boyle to begin by conducting a thorough survey of the institution and its operations, the results of which were to be delivered personally to him within six months. Many changes were in order, but Hayes cautioned O'Boyle to proceed "slowly, prudently, and tactfully." In meetings that same day with the Mission's staff the cardinal called for cooperation with the new boss who, "as to be expected," would have a "different approach to things." Hayes also introduced O'Boyle to the board of trustees, which, at his suggestion, appointed the new administrator treasurer of the Mission and member of the board. What was billed as a temporary appointment would eventually end in a seven-year tour of duty in addition to his other duties. Despite "the difficulties involved," O'Boyle later mused, those years were "among the happiest years of my priesthood."[2]

The Mission was founded in 1881 by the saintly Irish immigrant Father John C. Drumgoole, an extension of his work with New York's abandoned and orphaned children.[3] It was supported by contributions from the St. Joseph's Union, a worldwide charity organized by Drumgoole, and subscriptions to the Mission's annual magazine, *The Homeless Child.* Its enormous building on Lafayette Street sheltered more than four hundred boys; an annex near Ft. Washington sheltered an equal number of girls. All were cared for by the Sisters of St. Francis of Hastings-on-Hudson. About half the children studied either in nearby parochial or public grammar schools or in the Mission's own academic and vocational classes. The rest were employed youths, mostly paper boys, who paid a small portion of their earnings in rent and into a private savings account. Scholarships were available for those able to take advantage of higher education.

In 1883 the energetic Drumgoole obtained a 650-acre tract on Staten Island's Raritan Bay. The site became known as Mt. Loretto, a name chosen by its founder to honor the congregation of sisters who had befriended him in his seminary days. Eventually all the children, including those in a special facility for the

2. O'Boyle Daybook, 7 Dec 1936, Archives of the Mission of the Immaculate Virgin (hereafter AMIV), source of quotes 1–3. [Rare for O'Boyle, he kept a minutely detailed day-by-day account of his activities during the first three months of his tour at Mt. Loretto.] See also O'Boyle, Notes, pt. 9 (last two quotes) through pt. 13. Unless otherwise indicated the personal comments in this section are taken from this source.

3. *To Save the Children* (New York: St. Anthony's Guild, 1981). This brief history of the Mission and its founder was reprinted by the Mission in 1988 under the title *Father John C. Drumgoole, Mount Loretto.*

blind, were transferred to Staten Island. During the next half century Mt. Loretto expanded considerably. By the time O'Boyle arrived in 1936 it housed 1,100 children, ages 5 to 18, cared for by 85 resident sisters and a support staff of 120. Its forty-three buildings included the enormous "cottages"—dormitories that each housed about a hundred children—a grammar school, trade schools, workshops, printing press, a large gothic church, a power plant, and even a special railroad siding. Mt. Loretto's farm with its herd of eighty cows and the rest of the farm animals not only supplied much of the Mission's needs but also provided agricultural training for some of the boys.

The phenomenal growth of orphanages in the nineteenth century had many fathers, not the least of which was the charitable reaction of the public to the Hogarthian conditions in the immigrant slums of the great Eastern cities. There thousands of abandoned or neglected children, many ravaged by hunger and alcohol, struggled to survive in the streets. Charitable organizations, many sponsored by religious groups, responded by establishing orphanages or arranging for foster care, including the controversial practice of exporting children to unsupervised foster homes in Western towns and farms.

The Catholic Church felt a particular responsibility for these children, since many were the offspring of newly arrived Catholic immigrants. Faced with the overwhelming need, Catholic institutions like the one organized by Father Drumgoole responded generously. Despite good intentions, though, and the often selfless labor of the hundreds of sisters, brothers, and priests involved, some institutions were characterized by overly strict regimentation, irregularities in accounting, and other failures in childcare that lent some credibility to the charges of critics.

Leaders of social reform, led by the spokesmen of the Progressive Movement, used the orphanages as the focal point of their drive to abolish the asylum system in favor of public relief for families.[4] The American Church, as represented by the directors of Catholic Charities and the NCCC, supported these aims, especially during the long fight for aid to dependent children. At the same time Cardinal Hayes, stung by the scandalous reports of the Strong Commission, was determined that, while they remained necessary, the orphanages in his archdiocese would be models of institutional childcare. The centralization of this work under his professional staff in Catholic Charities was the result of this resolve.

Mt. Loretto constituted a major challenge to a centralized system. Its greatly

4. Dale Keiger, "The Rise and Demise of the American Orphanage," *Johns Hopkins University Magazine* (April 1996): pp. 34–40.

loved administrator had operated independently for many years, and over time the Mission, once a model for childcare, developed serious problems, especially in a staff grown lax under its aging director. Always at loggerheads with Keegan and the Division of Children staff, old Msgr. Fitzpatrick nevertheless developed a friendship with Father O'Boyle that led him to accept some changes at the orphanage. In 1928, for example, mental health personnel from Catholic Charities began examining the children, and the next year the trade school was reorganized into separate schools for tailoring, electric work, carpentry, and printing, staffed by the city's Department of Education.[5] For the rest, Fitzpatrick continued to go his own way, much to the chagrin of Keegan and his staff. Hayes later admitted privately to O'Boyle that on several occasions he had considered transferring Fitzpatrick, but he could not bring himself to do so "because he was a classmate of mine."[6] Although O'Boyle always assumed that his old classmate, Frank McIntyre, now the chancellor of the archdiocese, was instrumental in all his New York assignments, it seems likely that in this case Msgr. Keegan, who was also close to the cardinal, was responsible. Keegan was anxious to have a loyal, professionally trained administrator in charge of reforming Mt. Loretto. O'Boyle fit the bill. Although he admitted that while his new staff was courteous, they were well aware that he was from Catholic Charities, Msgr. Fitzpatrick's old bugaboo.

This new director never acted like someone filling a temporary assignment. Within a month he had initiated an audit of both the Mission and St. Joseph's Union and ordered a study of the responsibilities and performance of the staff of the Mission and of St. Benedict's, the diocese's home for African-American children in Rye, New York, answerable to Mt. Loretto's board of trustees. To help with the surveys he advertised for an administrative assistant and from the applicants chose the remarkably gifted James Norris. Norris, who would follow O'Boyle to Catholic Relief Services and eventually, as an advocate of world peace, would address the fathers of Vatican Council on that subject, became the mainstay of O'Boyle's administration of Mt. Loretto, involved in every facet of its operations.[7]

5. Minutes of the Board of Trustees, Catholic Charities of the Archdiocese of New York, 3 Dec 1928 and 11 Oct 1929, ACCANY.

6. Hayes' remarks were quoted in O'Boyle's Notes, pt. 13. For an example of Fitzpatrick's assumptions and independent action, see Minutes of the Mission's Board of Trustees, 15 Nov 1936, AMIV.

7. Raymond J. Kupke, "James J. Norris: An American Catholic Life" (PhD dissertation, The Catholic University of America, 1995), pp. 120–24, outlines Norris' career at Mt. Loretto. His duties as conceived by O'Boyle are outlined in O'Boyle's Notes, pt. 14. Summary of O'Boyle's activities in his first weeks at Mt. Loretto is taken from his Daybook, 7 Dec 1936 to 20 Feb 1937, AMIV.

With the help of professional social workers on the staff of Catholic Charities O'Boyle launched a wide-ranging study of the Mission's programs. Even before these studies got under way, he had begun to centralize control of what was in effect a small town. He ordered that all work requests first come to his office, and only then would those approved be directed to the various departments. The seemingly indefatigable administrator was everywhere: out inspecting barns and cows, down among the boilers, up in the damaged cupolas, looking through the books in the old Manhattan office of the St. Joseph's Union, meeting with local school officials, and consulting constantly with the sisters who worked directly with the children.

A canny bureaucrat, O'Boyle checked with Keegan or McEntegart on every issue, obtaining their permission for any major change. In some serious matters, like the audit and changes to the *Homeless Child,* he went directly to the cardinal, whose only recorded caveat was not to make changes in the magazine "too drastic."[8] Members of the board of trustees received a detailed report on all aspects of the Mission's operations prior to their first meeting with the temporary administrator. His frank and detailed discussion of conditions and pressing needs won the board's speedy approval of a budget for 1937 amounting to $200,000.[9]

It is not certain when O'Boyle reported to the cardinal or in what detail, but he made clear in his presentation that at almost eighty years of age, Msgr. Fitzpatrick had increasingly been confined to his office and apartment in Manhattan, victimized by "those in charge" who "gradually took advantage of his absence and failed to fulfill their obligations to the children." O'Boyle made clear that he was not including the sisters, whom he found invariably caring and cooperative, in this condemnation, but he obviously wanted major changes in the support staff. After studying the report for a week, Hayes told O'Boyle that since he was now so intimately acquainted with the situation he should stay to carry out his recommendations.[10]

O'Boyle had warned Father McEntegart that the staff expected more changes, and, if he delayed acting, he would be dismissed as a ten-day wonder, a phrase some of the staff used to denigrate Fitzpatrick's modest attempts at reform.[11]

8. O'Boyle Daybook, 16 Dec 1936, AMIV.

9. Minutes of a Regular Meeting of the Board of Trustees of the Mission of the Immaculate Virgin, Held at the Residence of The President, His Eminence, Cardinal Hayes, 452 Madison Avenue, New York City [hereafter Minutes, Board of Trustees], 18 May and 15 Dec 1937, AMIV.

10. O'Boyle, Notes, pts. 10 (source of quote) and 13. Hayes probably received the report in May 1937.

11. O'Boyle Daybook, 8 Jan 1937, AMIV.

Now armed with a mandate from the cardinal and the pledge of funds from the board, he acted. The head farmer and his assistants were the first to go. O'Boyle considered the replacement, a hard-working farmer from Connecticut, John Dorsey, "one of God's noblemen." Another lucky find was a graduate engineer and former Ford employee to replace the superintendent of buildings and grounds and supervisor of most of the lay staff. O'Boyle created the position of head dietitian, who would also serve as food buyer and manager of the Mission's eight dining rooms. Again he made a good choice in the person of Columbia University graduate Mary Walton. For some reason O'Boyle felt constrained to report to the board that Walton was not a Catholic, a comment that elicited from Cardinal Hayes the remark "Well, the food is not Catholic or non-Catholic, is it."[12] More medical personnel were also hired, and O'Boyle ordered that each child receive a physical examination twice a year. He maintained a convalescent home for the ill and frequently bragged about the excellent health of his charges.[13]

A program was launched to renovate all the existing residences and dining rooms at both Mt. Loretto and St. Benedict's, so that the children's quarters might be more cheerful and comfortable, and less institutional in aspect. With careful planning O'Boyle was able to reduce the number of boys in each of the six three-story "cottages" from ninety-six to a still excessive seventy-two, allowing for the creation of recreation rooms in each building. Further reductions and the closing of two buildings from Father Drumgoole's time, which housed a hundred boys each in dormitories, was delayed for several years until a new archbishop approved the necessary funds. Meanwhile, crowding at St. Elizabeth Hall, the girls' quarters, was alleviated with the erection of Duval cottage, named after its generous donor, for the use of the younger girls.

Improvement in the Mission's education system during the late 1930s included the establishment of St. Aloysius, an academic high school for boys. Arrangements were made to send the lesser number of female students to Holy Rosary High School in Manhattan, although some of the boys and girls would remain at the neighboring public high school in Tottenville. The Mission now boasted two vocational high schools, where boys and girls were instructed by staffs supplied in large part by the local county board of education. Money was even found to establish a separate class for the slightly retarded who, O'Boyle recalled, were

12. Quoted in O'Boyle's Notes, pt. 10.
13. "Annual Letter to His Eminence," 1 Jan 1937, reprinted in *The Homeless Child* 65 (1938–1939), copy in AMIV.

not fooled for a second when the educators decided to name it the "Opportunity Class."

O'Boyle had been concerned about the evidence of poor discipline since his arrival. His idea of dealing with infractions was to withhold privileges. He immediately outlawed corporal punishment when he heard one of the old staff members extol the efficacy of the rubber hose. Most infractions, he concluded, resulted from a lack of adequate recreation. He hired a recreation director and provided each residence with equipped recreation rooms and lounges. Sports teams of every sort were encouraged, and Mt. Loretto joined several of the Catholic sports leagues. The Mission also inaugurated its own movie nights to supplement the usual trips to Tottenville's movie house. The more dubious excursions to Perth Amboy that had become a source of trouble for some of the boys and girls were banned. Boats were found for the youngsters to use on Raritan Bay during the summer season.

Other efforts to improve discipline were begun. The number of counsellors in each residence increased, and these young social workers were encouraged to continue their education by receiving time off for study in Manhattan. In the matter of dress, stress was placed on individual choice. O'Boyle instructed those who purchased the clothes that they be well fitted, and he recalled later that the harried proprietor of Mt. Loretto's shoe store responded to the boys' complaints when their shoes fit poorly. With some pride he reported that the principal of Tottenville High School complained that the Mission children were too well dressed. Much of this improvement was financed by the generous but mostly modest contributions of the many thousands of members of St. Joseph's Union. Their major connection to Mt. Loretto was through the pages of *The Homeless Child,* with its circulation of 300,000. Mindful of its importance to the finances of the Mission, O'Boyle was determined to make it as attractive as possible. Because its production provided valuable training for boys in the vocational school, it continued to be typeset at the Mission, but printing and distribution were turned over to an experienced company. Meanwhile, much of the content was written and designed by O'Boyle and Norris.

O'Boyle grew to love his home on Staten Island and genuinely loved the children. He got a special kick out of the irreverent older boys, who liked to call him Pappy. In his hours of relaxation he took up smoking a pipe and acquired an Irish setter that he had to share with the children. He even learned to drive, practicing on the Mission's empty driveways. (His driving career abruptly ended after a near-collision during his first foray into Manhattan's traffic.)

Vacations during the late 1930s meant, as usual, short visits to Scranton, where he would drop in on his aunt Katie Parks. Often his Muldoon cousins, now young adults with plenty of free time, would visit him on Staten Island. Cousin Tony had a car and was pleased to chauffeur the busy administrator when he needed to get around the city on weekends. It was easy for the well-connected priest to obtain seats at important sports events, and Tony and Steve especially thrilled at the chance to be introduced to the likes of Jack Dempsey and Babe Ruth.[14] O'Boyle also kept in touch with his father's relatives. Closer to home were visits to cousin Bernard O'Boyle and his family at their residence in the Bronx. They too enjoyed expeditions to Mt. Loretto, and Bernard was grateful when O'Boyle arranged to hire one of his in-laws, a recovering tuberculosis patient, to work on the Mission's farm.[15]

A New and Exacting Superior

The death of Cardinal Hayes and appointment of Francis J. Spellman as his successor early in 1939 ushered in a new and dynamic era for the Church in New York. It also marked the beginning of a new chapter in Patrick O'Boyle's career. Once again he was introduced to a hard-working, imperious taskmaster, this one with close Vatican connections thanks to his personal friendship with Pius XII.

Their first meeting was not an unalloyed success. Msgr. Keegan called one day in July to warn that Spellman wanted to make a thorough inspection of the Mission without any fanfare. O'Boyle took him at his word and was working in one of the buildings when the archbishop's party arrived. In fact he had to be fetched to the meeting by his friend Frank McIntyre, now a bishop. Spellman's appointment had been met with apathy by most of the diocese's clergy, and O'Boyle admitted that he had not written the new archbishop a congratulatory note because he did not know the man and did not want to appear presumptuous. Perhaps Spellman was reacting to what he perceived as indifference, or was simply irritated by the delay when he opened the conversation by gruffly commenting on O'Boyle's appearance. "You look sick," he greeted the administrator. "I always look this way," was his equally gruff reply. Spellman pointed to Mt. Loretto's imposing church and asked why had O'Boyle built such a large edifice. O'Boyle explained that the church predated his administration by many years. Aware of O'Boyle's hope to build more residences for the boys, Spellman then pointed to the six large cottages and asked why the need for more. O'Boyle, by

14. Muldoon intv.
15. On O'Boyle's relations with his relatives in the Bronx, see ltr., Kathleen O'Boyle Fay, "Memories of Cardinal O'Boyle," copy in AAW.

then thoroughly exercised, explained that the word "cottage" scarcely described old buildings that even after two years' effort still crammed seventy-two boys into antiquated and unsafe surroundings.[16]

The initial inquisition over, Spellman proceeded on his tour. He was obviously impressed by the efforts to humanize the residences, but he asked why all the effort to paint and otherwise renovate what O'Boyle hoped to replace in the near future. Because, O'Boyle shot back, the same public Department of Welfare that once pilloried Mt. Loretto for its living conditions was scheduled to inspect the Mission within months, and he thought it wise to make the place as presentable as his limited funds would allow. Spellman made no further comment, and as he walked through the place his mood gradually changed. Noticing that the dormitories in the old buildings were divided into separate cubicles with different color schemes for each, he expressed surprise, remarking that many of the pricey New England prep schools were not as attractive as Mt. Loretto.

Spellman then surprised O'Boyle by reopening discussion of what O'Boyle had understood to be a solid agreement. Before he died, Cardinal Hayes had verbally approved the Mission's sale of 100 acres to the local deanery, at $4,500 per acre, for an extension to a nearby cemetery. The money thus realized would be used to build some of the desired boys' residences.[17] Spellman, who obviously did not consider the sale a done deal, told O'Boyle that Msgr. Joseph A. Farrell, the Staten Island dean, had called the Mission's price for the land "exorbitant." Calling that description "most peculiar," O'Boyle explained that it was Farrell himself who had suggested the figure. When Spellman seemed unconvinced, O'Boyle offered to discuss it with Farrell, who was in the inspection party, only to have Spellman brush him off. O'Boyle was not used to having his veracity questioned, and a call he received that night from Msgr. Keegan only added to his irritation. "Well, Pat, I don't know what to tell you about that visit," reported his boss, who would never enjoy with Spellman the intimacy and influence he had had with his predecessor. "After we left Msgr. Farrell at his rectory and started for the ferry," Keegan went on, "the archbishop turned to me and said, 'Who is right about that price, Farrell or O'Boyle?'" Keegan went to bat for his subordinate: "One of the things I know about O'Boyle is this," he told Spellman. "If he tells you something you can be sure it is the truth." Despite this endorsement, Spellman would continue to doubt.

16. O'Boyle, Notes, pt. 13. The Notes, pts. 9–15, contain O'Boyle's recollections (including quoted comments by Spellman and Keegan) of Mt. Loretto. Unless otherwise noted, these are the source for what follows.

17. Minutes, Board of Trustees, 21 Jun 1938.

This opening encounter convinced O'Boyle that the first meeting of the Mission's board of trustees with Spellman in the chair would be an exacting one, and he pressed Jim Norris on the fine points of the financial report. When Norris complained that such details were for the bookkeepers to address, O'Boyle reminded him that neither Norris nor the bookkeepers were the ones about to be grilled. He was right. Although Spellman took little notice of Mission activities, he quickly zeroed in on finances, especially how the St. Joseph's Union operated and the condition of its small investment portfolio. Satisfied with O'Boyle's thorough answers, Spellman hit on the note that among the most generous overseas contributors were people in Ireland. Asking O'Boyle if he had been to Ireland recently, Spellman lectured him on the poverty in that country and added, "I don't think that you should be taking money out of Ireland for the Mission." O'Boyle remained silent, but he noted later that when the Union received a second $10,000 contribution from an obviously wealthy Irish canon, Spellman had nothing more to say about Irish poverty.

At the end of the meeting Spellman seemed anxious to show his appreciation of O'Boyle's thorough preparation by inviting him to dinner. O'Boyle turned him down, citing a prior commitment to meet with Father McEntegart. He was more willing to accept an invitation from fellow board member Judge Alfred J. Talley. When they reached the street Talley turned to O'Boyle and said, "Well, young man, that was one of the longest meetings I've attended in some time. You deserve a good drink; let's go over to the Waldorf bar."

By late 1939 members of the board were increasingly anxious about building the long-planned residences. The war in Europe, they argued, would soon cause a severe price rise and a drop in contributions from overseas. Spellman, however, continued to preach economy. The Mission must, he insisted, find a way to liquidate its debt and pay in full for any new work. The board should scale back construction, limiting itself to two cottages for the present. O'Boyle reported that he could secure a loan at 2 percent that would liquidate all previous obligations and meet current expenditures plus provide help in financing the new buildings. Spellman agreed, but stipulated the Mission must pay off the loan within five years. He accepted O'Boyle's estimate that this was achievable through the sale of land and special grants.[18] When the Martha H. Hall Foundation of New York offered $80,000 for construction, Spellman promised another $60,000 from diocesan funds. O'Boyle lost no time in procuring the services of Andre Foulhioux, the celebrated architect of Radio City Music Hall, to design two cottages

18. Minutes, Board of Trustees, 13 Oct 1939 and 14 Jun 1940.

that would house thirty boys each. In November 1940 the archbishop returned to Staten Island to dedicate the new buildings.[19]

Spellman also offered O'Boyle strong support when the latter proposed closing St. Benedict's. The home for African-American children had opened in 1886 under the sponsorship of St. Benedict the Moor parish in Harlem. From the start the building had proved inadequate, and Father John E. Burke, with help from the Commission for Mission Work Among Negroes and Indians and the sainted Mother Katharine Drexel, purchased a site in Rye, New York, where a building to house 150 children and their caregivers was constructed. In 1897 management of the home was assumed by Mt. Loretto, and the Sisters of St. Francis, the same congregation that worked at the Mission, were installed.[20]

Reflecting later on his frequent visits, O'Boyle's strongest impression was of the warmth and friendliness of St. Benedict's, a feeling he ascribed to the intimate size of the place and the unusual closeness of the children to the loving Sisters of St. Francis. The children received the same educational and spiritual support as their counterparts at Mt. Loretto. O'Boyle had done what he could in the way of repairs and modernization for the old frame building, but an inspection in 1940 concluded that the structure was unsafe and essentially unrepairable. A committee of St. Benedict's trustees agreed, and the decision was reached to close the home.[21]

That left the question of what to do with the children. O'Boyle proposed to the archbishop that they be integrated into the diocese's other childcare homes with Mt. Loretto taking the majority. Spellman immediately agreed, adding that even if he had the money, he would never authorize another home solely for black children. Racial integration of a childcare institution had never been tried before in New York, and no one was sure how the decision would be received. Spellman volunteered to discuss the transfers personally with the superiors of the institutions involved, and he asked the board to avoid any publicity. He agreed with O'Boyle that the transfers should occur over a period of time so as to avoid undue comment.

19. *NYT*, 11 Nov 1940. See also *The Homeless Child* 68 (1941–1942).

20. John M. Ariotta, "Before Harlem: Black Catholics in the Archdiocese of New York and the Church of St. Benedict the Moor," *Dunwoodie Review* 16 (1992–93): 85–93. See also, Sister M. Georgiana Rockwell, S.B.S., "St. Benedict the Moor Mission, New York City: First Negro Catholic Mission North of the Mason and Dixon Line," 3 Mar 1982, Archives of the Sisters of the Blessed Sacrament.

21. Minutes of Regular Meeting of the Board of Trustees of St. Benedict's Home, 13 Oct 1939 and 14 Jun 1940, and Minutes of a Special Meeting of the Board of Trustees, 8 Jul 1940, both in AMIV.

Initiating a method he would adopt with much success later in Washington, O'Boyle conferred first with the sister-superintendents of all the affected institutions. After receiving their pledge of cooperation, he concentrated on Mt. Loretto, where he discussed the change with his own priests and sisters and then followed up with a gathering of the full staff. "All received the message well," he reported. Finally he approached the children in a meeting he considered crucial to the success of his plan. In an emotional talk he explained that the black children were losing their home and had no place to go "except here with us," and that they should be received with open arms.

He was happy to report to the board and to Catholic Charities that all had worked out well. The staff could detect no distinction being made by the children in the classrooms or the recreation halls. In all, ninety-one African Americans transferred to Mt. Loretto; forty more were discharged to their families while another nineteen were accommodated in other diocesan homes.[22] To insure the continued smooth operation of the diocesan integration effort, Catholic Charities ordered the desegregation of all its childcare institutions. It set a quota for the number of black children in every childcare institution so that they would not be concentrated in a few places. Should the demand for care for black children rise, so too would the quotas at each institution.[23] Despite everyone's determined effort to avoid publicity, news spread and for his efforts O'Boyle received a letter of congratulations from the city's Department of Welfare.

By now relations between O'Boyle and his archbishop had warmed considerably. Spellman had come to trust the younger man and depended on his administrative gifts. He showed his gratitude in 1941 when, at his instigation, the Vatican announced that O'Boyle had been elevated to the rank of papal chamberlain. It was the sixteenth year of the new monsignor's priesthood.

O'Boyle would remain at Mt. Loretto until September 1943. By then his demanding job administering an institution with an annual budget approaching half a million dollars had become routine. As usual his duties varied. At any given time he might find himself discussing war regulations with military authorities so as to prepare the Mission for a possible bomb attack after Pearl Harbor, preparing copy advertising a special fund drive by the St. Joseph's Union, phasing out the Mission's school for the blind (operating with just eight pupils in 1941), or working with a reduced wartime staff on upgrading the buildings to

22. Minutes of Regular Meeting of the Board of Trustees of St. Benedict's Home, 17 Jun 1941, AMIV, and O'Boyle, Notes, pt. 10.

23. Minutes, Board of Trustees of Catholic Charities of the Archdiocese of New York, 22 Oct 1940, ACCNY.

meet new fire and safety codes. He worried that the children found him too strict. In fact, he admired their "spunk," as he called their initiative and sense of responsibility. His major goal, he claimed, had been to achieve at Mt. Loretto the highest professional standards commensurate with the best current childcare practices. At the same time he was anxious, he confessed, to make every child in his care recognize the fundamental truth of his or her worth and dignity and to learn to love and respect God, Church, neighbors, and country. "It was the best job I ever had," he claimed.[24]

Institutional Commodity Services

During O'Boyle's years on Staten Island his duties continued to multiply. In 1939, for example, he accepted the post of treasurer and member of the board of Lincoln Hall, a home for boys referred by the courts. A successor to the old New York Catholic Protectory, the Westchester County institution housed two hundred boys in six cottages with a gym, vocational school, and staff facilities. With its population increasing rapidly, O'Boyle was closely involved in the protracted negotiations that led in 1940 to the addition of three new cottages under a grant from the Hayden Foundation. In 1941 he relieved his old boss, Msgr. McEntegart, as assistant secretary and member of Catholic Charities' board of trustees. No mere honorific, this assignment included the time-consuming task of preparing the board's annual report and helping to organize the archbishop's annual charities appeal drive.[25] In 1943 O'Boyle likewise chaired a committee that revised the National Conference of Catholic Charities' Manual on Child-Caring Homes. During these last years at Mt. Loretto he also helped Msgr. O'Grady prepare the NCCC's annual programs. Less arduous but still requiring frequent commutes from Staten Island was his service as a director of the Child Welfare League of America and the city's Child Welfare Committee.

Overshadowing all these additional responsibilities was the part he played in organizing the Institutional Commodity Services, a purchasing cooperative established in the New York archdiocese in December 1941. Commonplace today, the central purchase of goods used by a diocese's institutions was practically unknown at the time. There is evidence that Archbishop Spellman had discussed such a move with his chancellor, Bishop McIntyre, who had been investigating various cost-cutting financial innovations.[26] During one of his early meetings as

24. As quoted in ltr., Msgr. Edmund F. Fogarty to O'Boyle, 9 Oct 1969, AAW.
25. Minutes, Board of Trustees of Catholic Charities of the Archdiocese of New York, 20 Oct 1939, 22 Oct 1940, 25 Apr 1941, and 26 May 1942, ACCNY.
26. Francis J. Weber, *His Eminence of Los Angeles,* vol. 1, p. 37.

chairman of Mt. Loretto's board of trustees, Spellman grilled O'Boyle and the procurator of Dunwoodie about the comparative costs of maintaining orphans and seminarians. The upshot of their discussion was O'Boyle's assignment to plan a central purchasing agency for those and other archdiocesan institutions.[27] His considerable experience at Mt. Loretto in large-scale purchasing aside, O'Boyle's task was formidable. He had to devise a central purchase scheme, line up suppliers, and most important, enlist the cooperation of the archdiocese's many colleges, hospitals, orphanages, old age homes, and the like.

He turned for advice to Harry Patrick Schwarzman, the purchasing agent for the very successful Joint Purchasing Corporation of the New York City Federation of Jewish Charities. From Schwarzman he learned that the key to success was a director who could sell the idea to the various institutions, long accustomed to the free management of their temporalities and suspicious of the increasingly centralized control of the archdiocese instituted by the new archbishop. Fearing a loss of independence, many of the institutional managers wanted the chancery excluded from their business. Moreover, although the chance to save thousands of dollars yearly should have immediate appeal to hard-strapped institutions, buyer loyalty and the comfort of doing things the old way were strong inducements to embrace the status quo. As one college procurator proudly explained to O'Boyle, she had always bought all the school's food from the local A&P. Resistance to change was bolstered by the existing suppliers. Large wholesalers, who regularly ingratiated themselves with small donations of goods or services, remained favored by many institutions. Nor were some Catholic wholesalers above demanding special consideration.

Archbishop Spellman had his own candidate for the sensitive post of director, but to his considerable irritation O'Boyle repeatedly turned the man down, arguing that a retired department store buyer was temperamentally unsuited to the role of selling the plan to the institutions. An exasperated Spellman, tired of the argument, told O'Boyle to find his own purchasing director. A chance encounter introduced O'Boyle to Edward M. Kinney, a graduate of the City College of New York. Kinney was then director of Catholic Charities in Schenectady, where he had succeeded in bringing the Albany diocese's organizations together to present a unified budget for the local Community Chest. Impressed

27. Although, according to O'Boyle's *Notes* (pt. 15), Spellman ordered Father Giblin, the seminary procurator, to participate in this planning, there is no evidence that Giblin played a part in what developed. The following paragraphs are based on this portion of the *Notes* and on a brief fact sheet prepared by Edward Kinney on the Institutional Commodity Services for Cardinal O'Boyle in 1979, AAW.

with the young man, O'Boyle discussed salary, obtained his release from his employer, and with Archbishop Spellman's less than enthusiastic permission, hired him. Thus began an association that would last throughout World War II.

With Schwarzman's guidance, O'Boyle and Kinney developed buying programs for each category of institution and then took to the field to sell their programs. They opened the campaign in December 1941 with a meeting of the heads of all archdiocesan institutions at which Archbishop Spellman urged the directors for their own best interest to enlist in the new service. The O'Boyle-Kinney team then organized a series of regional meetings with institutional superintendents and buyers. They explained the projected savings that could be realized under group purchase and invited all vendors doing business with the institutions to submit counterbids. They even subdivided the larger purchase plans into regional zones so that a maximum number of suppliers could participate. The first item centrally purchased was milk and cream for infant-care agencies. It produced a savings of up to 45 percent for individual agencies, a $72,500 windfall for the diocese. (Central purchases during 1942 generated nearly a half million dollars in savings, the first of many millions over the decades as individual parishes were brought into the program.)

Most directors quickly enlisted in the various programs. Their loyalty was strengthened in the early days of the war when all sorts of scarcities arose. With Kinney at its helm, the Institutional Commodity Service proved a valuable guide through the maze of wartime regulations and rationing. Before O'Boyle severed his ties in 1943, the organization had begun providing advice to the federal Office of Price Administration on the design of guidelines for rationing that recognized the specific needs and problems of charitable institutions, especially hospitals.

O'Boyle as His Colleagues Saw Him

By 1943 Mt. Loretto had been transformed into a financially secure, model childcare institution. That feat, following on the fruitful reorganization of the Guardian Society and the later success of the Institutional Commodity Service, solidified Patrick O'Boyle's reputation. His focused, no-frills approach to problem solving had won the confidence of professional social workers and colleagues in Catholic Charities and the National Catholic Welfare Conference. His stubborn self-assurance, albeit masked by a natural diffidence and considerable personal charm, often led powerful and sometimes irascible superiors to bow to his decisions. His was a mindset nurtured in an archdiocese noted for tough-minded leaders who gave little weight to pious pronouncements, but, rather, looked for speedy action and favorable results. He was part of a clerical culture that placed great emphasis on playing by the rules, a culture endemic to the old Irish-American dioceses where the prelate's word was tantamount to God's.

O'Boyle's method of operation, as described by close colleagues, reflected this milieu.[28] Never a gregarious man, he was uncomfortable in large social gatherings. In small business meetings he usually remained quiet until he had taken the measure of those with whom he was dealing. Nevertheless he was always prepared to stand on principle and when sure of his facts would never back down. Commenting on the meaning of the name O'Boyle, his friend Archbishop John T. McNicholas of Cincinnati once facetiously told him, "It might well mean 'I never seek a fight, but I will never run away from one.'"[29] Still, O'Boyle realized the practical value of remaining on speaking terms with even one's most severe critic. "Never close the door" was his irenic advice to subordinates as they dealt with officials in little sympathy with their causes.

Subordinates might glimpse another side of his character. Their first impression was most often of a formal and authoritarian figure. In fact, O'Boyle's profound respect for the priesthood precluded easy familiarity with the laity, although his stiffness with colleagues invariably thawed as he came to know them and appreciate their work. A man of firm and usually well-thought-out convictions, he was nevertheless willing to listen to counterarguments from subordinates and could be persuaded to change his mind. But they best be prepared. O'Boyle was innately suspicious of high-blown rhetoric or unsupported generalities. He wanted the pertinent facts; he reveled in the fine print and absorbed statistics like a blotter. He had a remarkable memory for the minutiae of things. His letters reflected these inclinations. They were always spare, devoid of florid language, and grounded in facts. He demanded a similar approach in his subordinates' reports and letters. He was a compulsive editor, never hesitating to shorten or simplify the drafts of superiors and subordinates alike. Never one to boast about his many achievements, he was also chary with compliments. The highest accolade one might expect for an outstanding job was his jovial order: "You can cut yourself a piece of cake for that."

To a remarkable extent these techniques and habits could just as well be ascribed to the cardinal-archbishop of Washington thirty years later.

28. The description of O'Boyle's work methods is based on interviews with Wycislo, Quinn, Kinney, and Kelly. See also ltr., Kinney to O'Boyle, n.d. (c. 1971), AAW, and Eileen Egan, *Catholic Relief Services: The Beginning Years* (New York: Catholic Relief Services, 1988), pp. 20–21.
29. Ltr., McNicholas to O'Boyle, 26 Apr 1948, McNicholas file, NCWC Papers, ACUA.

CHAPTER 5

An Organization Man

In early June 1943 Archbishop Spellman, then overseas visiting American troops, ordered Msgr. O'Boyle to understudy Msgr. McEntegart in his role as director of the just-organized War Relief Services. Before McEntegart was even able to recruit a staff or develop programs, his appointment as bishop of Ogdensburg, New York, was announced, casting doubt on his availability to the new national organization. Although decision on a replacement was the prerogative of the American bishops acting in concert, O'Boyle, whose training and administrative experience closely echoed McEntegart's, was obviously Spellman's nominee if and when the post became vacant. While continuing to direct operations at the orphanage and working with Ed Kinney on selling the new buying service, O'Boyle began to participate in the relief service's organizational meetings and to meet with those government officials who would be reviewing WRS's proposals and budget requests.[1]

The idea of a centralized response by Catholics to the needs of war victims and servicemen could be traced to the organization of the National Catholic War Council in 1917.[2] Supported by the American bishops and in conjunction with the Knights of Columbus, the council raised and distributed millions of dollars in relief and recruited volunteers to as-

1. Ltrs., McEntegart to Abp. Edward Mooney, 14 and 24 Jun 1943. Copies of both in Archives of the Archdiocese of Detroit (hereafter AAD). See also Minutes, WRS Organization File, Swanstrom Papers, Archives of Catholic Relief Services.

2. Surprisingly, considering its age and importance, there is no standard history of Catholic Relief Services. The following paragraphs on its origin are based on Egan, *Catholic Relief Services,* pp. 2–18, and a very useful summary in Kupke's "James J. Norris: An American Catholic Life," pp. 145–51.

sist Catholic servicemen and civilian refugees. The council also represented Catholic groups in the United War Work Drive, a joint money-raising effort by American volunteer agencies. The success of this wartime cooperation had an unanticipated result. With encouragement from a Vatican impressed with the American Church's war relief record, the American bishops organized the National Catholic Welfare Council (later renamed National Catholic Welfare Conference) in 1919 "to maintain, for the sake of peace, the spirit of union and coordination of our forces." Thus, a half-century before Vatican II would call for the formation of such groups, American Catholics had an episcopal conference that met annually to discuss and vote on national matters of public policy. The conference's day-to-day operations were left to an administrative board acting in the name of the nation's hierarchy and supported by an expanding secretariat located in Washington.

The NCWC remained largely uninvolved in overseas relief during the interwar years. Finally in 1940 it organized the Bishops' War Emergency and Relief Committee to coordinate and direct American Catholic relief and in 1941 sponsored what would become an annual collection for general overseas needs. The first collection, taken up in every parish in the nation on the fourth Sunday of Lent (Laetare Sunday), netted over $1 million. The bishops' relief committee would be one of more than 200 such agencies registered with the president's War Relief Control Board. To avoid duplication of effort, and fraud, that federal agency, established in July 1942, was empowered to approve budgets and operations of all registered organizations. In response to appeals from the major relief groups, concerned with the many separate collections being conducted by all these registered agencies, the board also created the National War Fund to sponsor a national joint appeal for war relief and distribute the monies thus collected to its member agencies. The president of Chase National Bank, Winthrop Aldrich, served as president of the Fund, which was headquartered in New York. In April 1943 the NCWC applied for enrollment in the National War Fund.

Even in the darkest days of war, the NCWC was contemplating the massive postwar rehabilitation task ahead. Along with other volunteer agencies it feared that the federal government, in the name of operational efficiency, intended to monopolize the task. In fact the State Department had already announced that federal agencies, with the assistance of the quasi-governmental Red Cross, would plan, coordinate, and distribute all aid in liberated areas, unencumbered by the multitude of voluntary agencies. The NCWC joined other organizations in protesting this decree, and in January 1943 the government capitulated. In a joint statement officials of the Office of Federal Relief and Rehabilitation Operations, the Red Cross, and the War Relief Control Board declared that "there are many essential services which can be provided by private agencies that cannot be provided by the government" and announced that volunteer agencies would consequently play a major role in postwar relief.

Following this significant victory, the volunteer agencies decided to organize themselves. They formed the American Council of Voluntary Agencies for Foreign Service. Enlightened leaders such as Archbishops Edward Mooney of Detroit, Samuel Stritch of Chicago, and Spellman in New York understood that the Church's participation in such interdenominational efforts was necessary if it were to have an effective voice in postwar operations. Yet the NCWC faced opposition from those who considered the Bishops' War Emergency and Relief Committee an ecclesiastical body chiefly concerned with sectarian matters. The NCWC's administrative board agreed that while the committee's emergency fund should be retained to provide needed religious aid (e.g., church repair), a new legal organization should be created for general relief. Accordingly, the NCWC incorporated the War Relief Services–National Catholic Welfare Conference on June 7, 1943.[3]

WRS was to be governed by a board of trustees that included twelve bishops from the administrative board of the NCWC, along with Archbishop Spellman in his role as military ordinary, and Bishop John O'Hara, his delegate for military chaplains. Five of the trustees would constitute a governing committee headed by Archbishop Mooney. To further dilute the feeling that WRS was an ecclesiastical body, the board appointed an advisory board of prominent laymen, including Al Smith as treasurer. These organizational matters were considered and approved by the bishops at their meeting on June 29, 1943, at which time they also appointed O'Boyle executive director, effective on the date of McEntegart's resignation.[4]

Even before his official date of service, O'Boyle was fully involved in relief operations. In early July 1943 he joined bishop-elect McEntegart in a meeting with the president of the National War Fund to argue the case for inclusion of the new Catholic organization in the federal program. As a result of this effort the NCWC and the War Fund drew up a memorandum of understanding. Approved by the

3. Ltr.(with appended Depository Resolution), O'Boyle to Msgr. Michael J. Ready (general secretary, NCWC), 20 Jul 1943, copy in AAD.
4. Minutes, Board of Trustees, WRS, 29 Jun 1943, and ltr., Ready to Bp. McIntyre, 16 Jul 1943. Copies of both in AAD.

bishops on July 19, this agreement recognized WRS as a member of the National War Fund entitled to all its privileges, thus guaranteeing financial support for all NCWC projects approved by the federal agency.[5] This agreement also obliged WRS to submit periodic budget requests to the National War Fund and to hold itself accountable for all its expenditures. A relationship between church and state unprecedented in American history, the agreement guaranteed American Catholics a role in the vast postwar rehabilitation effort while providing WRS with millions of dollars for its varied relief activities. Meanwhile, the Bishops' Emergency Fund continued to collect money for purely religious needs in war-torn countries.

McEntegart departed soon after WRS was accepted as a member of the National War Fund. It was up to O'Boyle, not yet officially installed as director and still responsible for the day-to-day operation of Mt. Loretto and the Institutional Commodity Services, to devise a program and obtain approval of an initial budget, hire a staff, and find a home for the new organization. Before he left, McEntegart outlined an approach to war relief that O'Boyle initially followed. McEntegart suggested that WRS limit itself to assisting refugees, prisoners of war, and merchant seamen. To avoid the costly administrative overhead that might delay delivery of aid, he wanted WRS to work closely with Catholic institutions in other countries, using their expertise and manpower to facilitate the transfer of supplies to the needy.

The new director's first challenge was to negotiate with the National War Fund over a budget for the remaining five months of 1943. Following a flurry of consultations that took him to Washington for meetings with State Department officials and the NCWC staff and then to Chicago to brief his superiors on the administrative board, he presented a program to a budget committee of the Fund in late July. He asked for $960,000 to assist refugees (specifying operations in the Middle East, North Africa, Mexico, Malta, and elsewhere), $125,000 for aiding prisoners of war in the United States, and $50,000 to support seamen's clubs in major American ports.[6]

To O'Boyle's surprise, the budget was rejected by the Fund's budget commit-

5. Minutes of Annual Bishops' Meeting, 11 Nov 43, and ltrs., McEntegart to Winthrop Aldrich, 30 Apr 1943 (NCWC application), Ralph Hayes to McEntegart, 1 Jun 1943 (memorandum of understanding), and O'Boyle to Ready, 23 Jul 1943. All in file 250, NCWC Papers, ACUA. See also ltr., Msgr. Howard Carroll (asst. secy., NCWC) to Ready, 16 Jul 43, same file.

6. Ltr., O'Boyle to Mooney, 24 Sep 1943, Archives of the Archdiocese of Baltimore [hereafter AAB]. See also series of O'Boyle's letters and memos concerning his Washington itineraries, Jul–Aug 1943, in file 135, NCWC Papers, ACUA.

tee because one senior official continued to insist that WRS was a sectarian institution, and therefore ineligible. Archbishop Spellman was out of the country at the time, but at Bishop McIntyre's suggestion, O'Boyle hastily assembled a group of prominent Catholic laymen, including the redoubtable Al Smith, to discuss this latest setback. Smith arranged a meeting with Winthrop Aldrich himself at which Aldrich cited O'Boyle as a witness to the memoir of understanding that had recognized WRS membership in the National War Fund. He approved its budget on the spot, noting in passing that his obstinate subordinate was "a good man, only he talks too much."[7]

Later while working out the details of the budget with O'Boyle, the once recalcitrant and still talkative War Fund official reminded the harried new director that any money not spent by the end of the year would revert to the Fund. He asked bluntly: "Can you—it is now nearly the first of August—in the remaining months spend nearly a million dollars on this program?" O'Boyle bravely answered, "Certainly, without any question." Inwardly, he later admitted he was thinking, "How in the name of the good Lord will we be able to do it?" In early August WRS received approval for its first three projects. An NCWC observer reported that with his command of every detail O'Boyle "made a very good impression on the Committee and had no difficulty in obtaining the approval he sought."[8]

Meanwhile, organizing a competent staff took priority. Answering Archbishop Spellman's plea, the bishop of Brooklyn released Father Edward E. Swanstrom to serve as O'Boyle's assistant director. Swanstrom, like O'Boyle a graduate of the New York School of Social Work, had earned a doctorate in political philosophy while ministering to Brooklyn's longshoremen and their families. He would play a major role in the success of WRS, an organization he would lead during its great postwar expansion. Before his departure, Msgr. McEntegart had recommended that O'Boyle try to recruit two other assistants. Thus Eileen Egan left an important position in the New York public schools to work in war relief. A disciple of the saintly pacifist Dorothy Day, Egan became a loyal partner in many of O'Boyle's refugee projects, despite their frequent strong philosophical disagreements.

Also at McEntegart's suggestion O'Boyle had asked Archbishop Stritch to re-

7. O'Boyle, Notes, pt. 17. Unless otherwise noted, the following quotations and personal references to meetings are taken from this source, pts. 17–21.

8. Memo, William Montavon to Ready, 12 Aug 1943, sub: Meeting of Panel of Budget Committee of National War Fund, file 135, NCWC Papers, ACUA.

lease Father Aloysius J. Wycislo, an official in Chicago's Catholic Charities, to work in WRS's yet-to-be organized Polish relief program. O'Boyle, who disliked travel, again endured a wartime trip to the Windy City to recruit Wycislo. Exhibiting a frankness that always seemed to astonish and endear him to his superiors, O'Boyle declined Stritch's invitation to join him in his examination of a group of young clerics for a special degree. "Archbishop," he answered, "I wouldn't know what they were talking about." A fellow guest at Stritch's table, Bishop James A. Griffith, laughingly chimed in, "Well said, monsignor. While the archbishop is conducting his examination we shall take a nap."

With Stritch's permission O'Boyle made his pitch to Wycislo, apparently unaware that the young social worker could not speak Polish. Wycislo eventually agreed to join WRS for a six- to twelve-month tour and visited New York in June to discuss details. When Wycislo finally reported for duty a month later, O'Boyle had taken up temporary residence at the Hotel Roosevelt, where Wycislo would also live until overseas transport could be obtained. He was obviously leery about the new job. When he appeared at the door of O'Boyle's hotel room, baggage in hand and smoldering cigar in the corner of his mouth, his first words to his new boss were a terse, "You stinker." The agreed-upon six-month enlistment would evolve into a sixteen-year tour of duty, including many years of vital service in the postwar period as assistant director.[9]

Other important appointments would be made as the refugee program expanded in Europe, including two lay assistants who proved essential. Edward M. O'Connor became O'Boyle's administrative assistant. A personable man, he did much to promote WRS programs in his many appearances before charity groups around the country. For the all-important task of organizing the purchasing and shipping facilities envisioned for the new organization, O'Boyle turned to Ed Kinney, his partner in the Institutional Commodity Services. Their weekly meetings to review that organization's business had continued even after O'Boyle became the unofficial director of WRS, but their discussion of diocesan programs received increasingly short shrift as the two turned to analyzing the challenges faced by WRS. In the end O'Boyle convinced Spellman to release Kinney to run the acquisition and shipping program that saw millions of tons of food and clothing delivered to all parts of a world at war. O'Boyle also relied on Kinney to negotiate with all the organized labor groups involved in the operation.

9. Wycislo intv. Wycislo would return to Chicago in 1959. He was appointed auxiliary bishop in 1960, and in 1968 bishop of Green Bay, Wis.

McEntegart liked to claim that he had run WRS out of his briefcase. The less fanciful O'Boyle realized that the old orphanage office on Lafayette Street was inadequate, but he rejected Spellman's offer of another building because of the need for costly renovation. He turned once again to his friend Al Smith. The Happy Warrior was then serving as spokesman for the John J. Raskob organization, owners of the Empire State Building. That great New York monument, completed in the darkest days of the Depression, still had many floors unoccupied. Smith arranged for WRS to occupy space on a utility-cost-only basis, with the understanding that should a prospective tenant desire its offices, WRS would move to another floor. The relief organization opened for business in its new suite on the Empire State Building's twelfth floor on August 16, 1943. It gradually moved up the building as occupancy grew, eventually settling on the seventy-ninth floor.[10]

The weeks of living in a large commercial hotel ended later in the fall when arrangements were concluded for O'Boyle to live with his good friend Msgr. James B. O'Reilly, pastor of St. Malachy's Church on West 49th Street. In the heart of New York's theater district, St. Malachy's, with its famed actor's chapel, provided a special apostolate for the denizens of Broadway. In exchange for his small but comfortable quarters on the rectory's fourth floor, O'Boyle insisted on serving on the parish's weekend rota, celebrating Mass, hearing confessions, and answering the night bell. He would remain at St. Malachy's until his transfer to Washington.

O'Boyle's move to West 49th Street followed by a few weeks the announcement of his official appointment as director of War Relief Services. After a series of exchanges, Archbishops Spellman and Mooney set the date at August 19, following which O'Boyle officially severed his ties with the Institutional Commodity Services and resigned his post as secretary of the board of Catholic Charities.[11]

The exchange of letters between Spellman and Mooney over the appointment, friendly and probably sincere, nevertheless adumbrated a peculiar challenge that O'Boyle would face in the next months. In fact there existed a strong suspicion, if not outright hostility, in a bloc of powerful Midwestern prelates on the NCWC administrative board toward what they perceived as a power play by

10. Ltr., O'Boyle to Ready, 13 Aug 1943, NCWC Papers, ACUA. See also undated memo by Edward Kinney (c. 1972, copy in AAW) summarizing his connections with WRS.

11. Ltrs., Spellman to Mooney, 10 Aug 1943, and Mooney to Spellman, 14 Aug 1943, copies in AAD. The appointment was reported in *NYT* on 20 Aug 1943. See also Minutes of the Board of Catholic Charities of the Archdiocese of New York, 16 Nov 43, ACCNY.

the new and well-connected archbishop of New York. These men, lead by Mooney and his close friends Stritch and McNicholas of Cincinnati, suspected that the forceful Spellman was trying to co-opt the new organization.[12] During the first few months of operation, according to one close witness, Spellman "virtually ran WRS" through McEntegart and Bishop McIntyre, Spellman's representative on the administrative board.[13] Although O'Boyle was obviously highly qualified for the job of director, the suspicion lingered that he too would mold WRS to do the will of the archbishop of New York. Mooney and the rest considered WRS an instrument of the administrative board, and they resented what they perceived as Spellman's effort to control it.

O'Boyle was aware of the unspoken division in the hierarchy and the general resentment of the strong New York influence on war relief. He worked hard to convince both sides to back the new organization. A "smart cookie" as well as an "astute Irish politician," according to his close associate Wycislo, he courted Mooney and Stritch, scrupulously reporting to them his every move, soliciting their advice and providing valuable suggestions in turn. At the same time he recognized Spellman's influence with both American and Vatican officials and always reported to him first before moving on his many initiatives. He routinely and openly informed the administrative board on budget matters and appeared before the general body of bishops at their annual November meetings. At the same time he adamantly opposed an effort by NCWC bureaucrats to move his organization's headquarters to Washington. Citing New York's importance as an international distribution center, he declared that the city would remain headquarters for war relief "and that's that."[14] He used his old friend Bishop McIntyre, who proved to be a strong force for getting issues past the administrative board, to win this and other agreements from the bishops. O'Boyle's ability to gain the trust and backing of all factions in the hierarchy ranks among his greatest contributions to war relief.

Relief Operations

The problem of winning approval for its first budget from the War Fund was overshadowed by the operational challenges faced by WRS. On September 24 O'Boyle reported to Archbishop Mooney that the War Fund's budget committee

12. Fogarty, *The Vatican and the American Hierarchy,* pp. 268, 311.
13. Wycislo intv. Wycislo commented extensively on the differences between Spellman and the Midwestern bishops and O'Boyle's success in uniting them behind WRS.
14. Ltr., Heffron to Ready, 30 Aug 1943, file 135, NCWC Papers, ACUA.

had given the final green light to WRS's first specific projects: Catholic services to seamen, aid to prisoners of war, and relief for North African refugees.[15] Yet although Catholic facilities for merchant seamen existed in several American ports, no Catholic agency had ever before attempted to serve the material as well as spiritual welfare of Catholic seamen in major ports throughout the world. Nor had any Catholic agency ever sponsored a program for prisoners of war. In fact the YMCA was the only American agency recognized by the Geneva Convention for this work. Further, although the first wave of war refugees and the countries where they had found haven had been identified, local Catholic agencies to channel American donations to those areas had not. It was apparent to O'Boyle that WRS programs would need to be built from the ground up.[16]

Still shorthanded, but blessed with a healthy bankroll, WRS set out to learn from doing. With over half of his budget to be spent on relief materials for overseas shipment, O'Boyle turned to Ed Kinney to organize purchase and shipping facilities. Kinney procured a processing center on Eleventh Avenue and built up an inventory of supplies from which the growing staff began to make requisitions.

The prisoner-of-war project posed special problems. Unlike the YMCA, the new organization was unable to obtain the right to have its representatives visit the camps. Working through the International Committee of the Red Cross and the Swiss Catholic Mission in Geneva, O'Boyle was at least able to insure that WRS supplies were distributed to American and Allied prisoners in camps in Europe and the Far East and, under reciprocal agreements, to Axis prisoners in America and elsewhere. Packed in kits for ease of distribution, the educational, recreational, and occupational supplies proved effective in combating what O'Boyle called the "barbed wire disease," that is, the boredom and incipient despair inherent in the harsh life of the camps.[17] Beginning in September 1943 WRS shipped some $25,000 worth of material each month to prisoners around the world. The prisoners themselves decided on the specific nature of the supplies. In their letters they requested handicraft kits, carpentry tools, how-to books and pamphlets on technical and nontechnical subjects, and, of course, sports equipment.

Included in the shipments to the camps were religious supplies for men of all

15. Ltr., O'Boyle to Mooney, 24 Sep 1943, AAD.
16. O'Boyle, Notes, pt. 19.
17. As quoted in *NYT,* 17 Apr 1944. See also O'Boyle, Notes, pt. 17, and a brief survey prepared by Edward Kinney, "Twenty Years of American Catholic Overseas Aid," *The Catholic Market* (Jan 1964).

faiths. These goods were purchased with money from the Bishops' War Emergency and Relief Fund. Mindful of critics in the National War Fund and scrupulous in his adherence to the agreement of understanding, O'Boyle kept a careful watch on appeals that might blur the strict line between religious and general humanitarian aid. He bluntly refused requests from the Military Ordinate to reimburse civilian chaplains working in POW camps and to provide for the religious needs of German and Italian priest-soldiers detained in American camps. He insisted that such requests must be sent to the Bishops' Committee, a fact, he told Mooney, he was prepared to discuss with the administrative board. The board respected his decision and throughout the war used their emergency relief fund to respond to such requests as well as to requests from the Holy See for sectarian aid.[18] He also made this distinction very clear to aid recipients. For example, concerning aid distributed in North Africa by the White Fathers in 1943, O'Boyle emphasized that the funds must be used only for health and welfare projects and not for religious purposes. He even instructed the White Fathers in the elaborate financial procedure that must be followed, adding that the work was subject to audit by the National War Fund.[19]

O'Boyle was also concerned about how the large amounts collected for the Bishops' Emergency War and Relief Fund on Laetare Sunday might influence the federal government's decisions concerning his budget. By September 1944, for example, the Bishops' Fund had achieved a balance of more than a million dollars. O'Boyle and others worried that publication of this sum by Archbishop Stritch might jeopardize some of WRS's budget requests, and so they wanted expected grants from the Bishops' Fund expedited to reduce this potentially embarrassing surplus. Stritch agreed and arranged with his friend Archbishop Mooney to speed up approval for requests totaling $615,000 before O'Boyle presented his next budget to the War Fund.[20]

Relief for citizens of the war-torn island of Malta was the first WRS proposal to win specific authorization from the War Fund's budget committee. On August 20, 1943, Archbishop Mooney was able to inform his counterpart in Valletta that help was on the way. This program was quickly followed by aid for orphanages, dispensaries, and clinics in Algeria and Tunisia, using the expertise and facilities of the White Fathers and other Catholic organizations in North Africa. Another

18. Ltr., O'Boyle to Mooney, 23 Sep 1944, AAD. See also *The Catholic Charities Review* (Nov 1943): p. 249.

19. Ltr., O'Boyle to Bp. Joseph M. Birraux (Superior General of the White Fathers), 19 Aug 1943, copy in AAD.

20. Ltr., Stritch to Mooney, 19 Sep 1944, AAD.

budget item provided funds for the Catholic Committee for Refugees, which was finding homes for those fortunate enough to have escaped to the United States.

Refugee relief and the broader program of providing supplementary help for liberated civilian populations consumed the bulk of WRS funds. It was also a ceaseless source of concern and challenge for its director. O'Boyle sent Eileen Egan and Dr. Henri Amiel, who resigned his professorship at Loyola University in New Orleans to join WRS, to Portugal to organize aid for Catholic refugees, mostly Poles, Austrians, and other anti-Nazis stranded in that neutral country. He prevailed upon Bruce Mohler, long associated with Catholic immigration efforts, to survey the situation in Algeria before joining Egan in organizing a refugee office in Lisbon and later one in London. Securing travel arrangements for these WRS agents proved difficult. Only after several trips to Washington to confer with State Department officials did he secure the necessary permissions. All communication with Egan, Amiel, and those who followed would be sent via the State Department pouch after O'Boyle pleaded personally with the secretary of state for this privilege.[21]

The largest program launched by WRS in 1943 was designed to assist Polish civilians and soldiers scattered throughout the Middle East. Bishop Joseph Gawlina, chaplain general of the Polish Army, appealed to WRS for help. Freed from Soviet captivity at the request of the Western allies after the German invasion of Russia in 1941, thousands of desperate Polish war victims were slowly drifting through Iran to places as far away as India and Egypt. Before leaving for Portugal, Eileen Egan had surveyed the proposed refuge for Poles in Leon, Mexico. As a result of her investigation, O'Boyle included $20,000 as part of his 1943 budget proposal to the War Fund for the so-called Colonia Santa Maria. Later in the war Egan and Irene Dalgiewicz, a social welfare administrator from New York's Catholic Charities, worked closely with the 1,500 Poles in Mexico.[22]

Bishop Gawlina's major concern was the thousands of his fellow countrymen in the Middle East. At O'Boyle's suggestion he met with Winthrop Aldrich to describe the plight of the refugees. As a result, O'Boyle found himself in the enviable position of having the War Fund urging his organization to target money for Polish relief. Armed with this endorsement and approvals from the Polish American Council and the president's War Relief Control Board, he faced what ap-

21. The details of providing for the assignment and transport of overseas agents, including mailing privileges, can be found in file 135, NCWC Papers, ACUA.

22. Egan outlined in considerable detail the organization and operation of the hacienda turned over to the Poles by the Mexican government. See her *Catholic Relief Services,* pp. 25–64.

peared to be the final hurdle: pro forma clearance by interested government agencies. Plunging into the bureaucratic maelstrom, O'Boyle pleaded with El-dred Kuppinger, head of the State Department's Special Division, for speedy action because the War Fund required that the allocated money be expended within the calendar year.[23]

One bureaucratic hurdle followed another. With clearances finally secured in early September, O'Boyle then faced the task of getting Father Wycislo to his Cairo headquarters.[24] Frustrated at the long delay, he asked Spellman to pull some strings. Wycislo finally sailed to the British Isles in November. Spellman intervened again to secure his transport from England to Egypt by providing him with a letter of introduction, which opened all doors.[25] Spellman also wisely arranged for Wycislo to be attached to the Chaplain Corps, with the right to wear an Army uniform with a simulated officer's rank.

Thus clad, Wycislo had immediate access to military bases and the use of military facilities including travel on military planes, "without which I would never have been able to operate," he concluded. Wycislo urged O'Boyle to have all WRS agents working overseas attached to the military in some form or other. Without such recognition, he warned, field operations would come to a standstill. Even when WRS gained control of a fleet of supply trucks to transport its relief goods, Wycislo added, they would be useless without access to military gasoline depots, which were closed to civilians. O'Boyle took the point, and WRS relief workers who followed Wycislo were clothed with some kind of military connection so essential to their operations.

Under Wycislo's direction 154 centers for Polish refugees were established in twelve countries throughout the Middle East and Africa. WRS spent some $2 million during the war to maintain and supply these camps. Wycislo kept O'Boyle informed about the difficulty in translating the funds received from New York into the food and clothing needed in the camps. He purchased supplies on the local market, with most coming from the Jewish cities in Palestine. Working through the apostolic delegate in Cairo, he was able to connect with local church authorities, who arranged for the distribution of supplies. Sometimes he simply wrote checks on his WRS bank account so local caregivers could purchase needed food.

23. Ltr., O'Boyle to Kuppinger, 31 Jul 1943, copy in AAD.
24. Ltr., O'Boyle to Mooney, 8 Sep 1943, AAD.
25. Wycislo intv., which is also the source for the information about the Polish program that follows.

Along the way the articulate Wycislo became the WRS poster boy for refugee operations. In succeeding years, when O'Boyle appeared before the War Fund's budget committees or the NCWC's administrative board, he brought Wycislo home to testify in uniform. As usual O'Boyle was crammed with the facts and ready to defend his budget with a myriad of detailed information. The uniformed Wycislo provided the human dimension, explaining to government officials and bishops in turn how he was organizing and supplying the camps.

Father Wycislo's contact with the apostolic delegate in Cairo underscored yet another important contribution Patrick O'Boyle made to war relief. By September 1943 the tide of battle had turned. Allied troops were on the European continent, and the fall of the Italian government was imminent. Now to the thousands of refugees calling for help was added the specter of vast liberated civilian populations in dire need. O'Boyle did not lack the necessary funds to help, but he needed a workable infrastructure to deliver the help in time to avert calamity. Mulling the problem over one evening at St. Malachy's, he was brought up short when his host, Msgr. O'Reilly, who had once directed the Catholic Near East Welfare Association, asked if he had ever considered enlisting the Vatican's network of nuncios and apostolic delegates in the cause. Who were better equipped than these men to analyze local needs, evaluate available distribution facilities, and arrange for the purchase of local supplies? In the office the next morning O'Boyle grabbed his copy of the *Annuario Pontificio,* the Vatican's directory containing the names and addresses of its representatives throughout the world, and fired off cables to all those in the affected areas.

The response was overwhelming. Each replied that he would gladly receive funds, which would be channeled to the refugees in greatest need, while providing WRS with a strict accounting of how the money was used. In many countries the official representatives of the Holy See were WRS's only contact with the refugees until it was able to dispatch its own representatives to work out agreements with the local Catholic welfare agencies. Within days O'Boyle had created a global network connecting WRS to all these hierarchies and welfare agencies. This connection would enable WRS to avoid the costly and time-consuming recruitment of an army of relief workers, thus significantly reducing overhead and channeling most of its money into the actual quick delivery of supplies to the needy.

Just how difficult it would be to establish a WRS presence in countries now falling under Allied control was brought home to O'Boyle when WRS tried to insert its agents into liberated areas of Italy. News of the calamity in war-torn

Sicily and the regions south of the front lines was known early at WRS head-quarters because William O'Dwyer, then an Army Reserve brigadier general and later mayor of New York, visited O'Boyle while on leave from duty in the Mediterranean theater. He urged O'Boyle to get the supplies to the civilians even while the battle was still raging. A similar plea came from Msgr. Walter S. Carroll, a Vatican diplomat who had recently led a team that surveyed the region and who reported to O'Boyle that clothing and food especially were priority needs. Carroll recommended that WRS agents be dispatched even before supplies were shipped, so that they could acquaint themselves with conditions and with the operations of the Pontifical Commission of Assistance for Refugees, the nation-wide relief distribution agency that could provide the expertise apostolic dele-gates were supplying in other countries.[26]

Realizing that funds alone could not produce the desperately needed clothing and food quickly, O'Boyle recommended to the administrative board that WRS conduct a gift-in-kind campaign for the people of Italy. The bishops agreed, with the understanding that the appeal be restricted to those parishes with large Italian-American congregations. Reminiscent of the Catholic Charities drives that occupied so much of his time in earlier years, O'Boyle asked the bishops of the concerned dioceses to appoint campaign directors whom he supplied with organizational kits that gave step-by-step instructions for the publicity, collec-tion, and shipment phases of the drive. Conducted during the summer of 1944, the campaign collected three thousand tons of clothing, bedding, and shoes, along with hundreds of tons of food and medicine. Under Ed Kinney's supervi-sion all this material was baled and stored in three WRS warehouses, ready for shipment.[27]

The great success of this first gifts-in-kind campaign prompted Herbert H. Lehman, the former governor of New York and now director of the newly organ-ized United Nations Relief and Rehabilitation Administration, to launch a simi-lar campaign on a national scale.[28] He invited the Church to participate. Leery that Catholics were being asked so soon to help in a new drive (UNRRA sched-

26. Egan, *Catholic Relief Services,* pp. 107–8.

27. Ltr., O'Boyle to Ready, 15 Sep 1944, copy in AAD. See also O'Boyle's Notes, pt. 19 (a ten-page overview of WRS drafted by Edward Kinney and edited by O'Boyle); and *The Catholic Char-ities Review* 28 (Jun 1944): p. 157. In his "Twenty Years of American Catholic Overseas Aid," Kin-ney reported that the first clothing campaign collected six thousand tons, an error he later corrected in his draft report to O'Boyle in 1973.

28. UNRRA was funded by forty-four nations united to aid liberated populations. Member countries contributed $4 billion (72 percent of which from the United States) to the cause.

uled its collection for the last week of September), O'Boyle nevertheless recommended that the bishops cooperate with UNRRA, which promised to play a major role in postwar relief plans. Eighty-four dioceses responded, at Archbishop Mooney's urging, and WRS again turned to distributing diocesan and parish organization kits. Detailed information on the drive was sent to every pastor in the country through his diocesan campaign manager. After addressing the East Coast directors in New York on September 7, O'Boyle journeyed to Chicago to address the Midwestern contingent while the peripatetic Swanstrom did similar duty in San Francisco. In the end Catholic parishes donated some eighteen million pounds of supplies to the UNRRA campaign in 1944.[29]

Lehman clearly admired the way WRS conducted its operations. He invited O'Boyle and Swanstrom to meet with members of the UNRRA staff at Washington's Mayflower Hotel to talk to them about relief operations. Both O'Boyle and Swanstrom strongly advised against creating a large bureaucracy of social workers to distribute goods, but to rely on local experts already in place. Unfortunately, UNRRA disregarded this advice and spent millions on developing a huge relief infrastructure.

While the gifts-in-kind campaign was in full swing, O'Boyle was embroiled in an increasingly frustrating fight to get the collected supplies and the WRS agents assigned to supervise their distribution to Italy. He later admitted that he should have anticipated the difficulty involved in transporting six civilians (later reduced to four priests) to Italy while the fighting still raged.[30] In May 1944 he had dutifully initiated negotiations with officials in the State and War Departments, forwarding to the Army staff all pertinent information.[31] There the case languished.

The military's intransigence, personified by the attitude of Assistant Secretary of War John J. McCloy, stemmed from its belief that the Army should retain control of all relief programs in the theaters of war. Private relief agencies should restrict their activities to the collection of materiel, which should be turned over to the Army for distribution. O'Boyle would have none of this. On one of his increasingly frequent visits to Washington he outlined the WRS case for Leo T. Crowley, a sympathetic Catholic ally, political advisor to President Roosevelt,

29. Ltr., O'Boyle to Ready, 8 Sep 1944, file 135, NCWC Papers, ACUA.

30. The four priests recruited to supervise the distribution of WRS supplies in Italy, all with a social welfare background and knowledge of Italian, were Fathers Andrew P. Landi of Brooklyn, John P. Boland of Buffalo, Caesar Rinaldi of Newark, and Thomas F. Markham of Boston.

31. Memo, O'Boyle for Leo T. Crowley (Director, Foreign Economic Administration), 29 Aug 1944, copy in AAD.

and, as head of the powerful Foreign Economic Administration, in charge of lend lease.

With O'Boyle's help Crowley drafted a memo for Assistant Secretary McCloy arguing the need for sending the WRS agents to Italy immediately. Crowley followed this up with a phone call, only to find the assistant secretary stonewalling. McCloy claimed that the only civilians in the Mediterranean theater were government employees, a claim that Crowley quickly proved false. McCloy also asserted that the British were opposed to private relief agencies operating in Italy. Finally he promised to ship the WRS goods at some unspecified date, but remained opposed to sending WRS personnel on the grounds that there were sufficient government employees in Italy to distribute relief supplies.[32] This latter assertion was made in the face of the disastrous failure of the Allied Control Commission's relief program.

O'Boyle, undaunted, continued to line up support for WRS. To counter claims of British opposition, his colleagues secured assurances directly from the British embassy that His Majesty's government was standing by awaiting American approval for the WRS operators. O'Boyle himself met with the apostolic delegate Archbishop Amleto Cicognani, who at his urging addressed a personal plea to Secretary of State Cordell Hull. Myron Taylor, the president's personal representative to the pope, joined those calling for speedy action. Meanwhile Crowley discussed the matter with the president, leaving behind a memorandum outlining the whole affair. He also extracted a promise from Roosevelt's secretary, Grace Tully, that the busy chief executive would be reminded of Crowley's memo "at the earliest opportunity."[33]

The president eventually did prod the War Department to act on the transport of the four priests, but his memo was allowed to linger. The matter was finally resolved following a visit by Archbishop Spellman to the White House. Just returned from Rome, Spellman described for Roosevelt and his special assistant Harry Hopkins the suffering of the Italian population under the Allies' disastrous relief policies. Just how effective was Spellman's intervention remains unclear, but in late September Roosevelt sent a stern reminder to the War Department, resulting in the necessary permits being granted.[34] The four priests, including Father Andrew P. Landi, who would continue with Catholic Relief

32. Ltr., O'Boyle to Mooney, 2 Sep 1944, AAD.

33. As quoted in ltr., O'Boyle to Mooney, 2 Sep 1944, AAD. See also O'Boyle's Notes, pt. 24. Unless otherwise indicated, the following section on supplies for Italy, including quotations, are from this source, pts. 19 and 24.

34. Fogarty, *The Vatican and the American Hierarchy*, p. 308.

Services for a record fifty-five years, arrived in Rome, courtesy of the U.S. Army, on October 11. In a surprise move the pope, in a public demonstration of his gratitude for American help, elevated the four priests to the rank of monsignor on the spot.

The effort to transport relief supplies to Italy pushed O'Boyle into another battle with the Washington bureaucracy. He recognized that shipping space was at a premium, but the need was critical and frustration mounted after WRS arranged for a fleet of trucks to be on call in Italy to move the supplies once arrived. In September 1944 O'Boyle appealed again to Leo Crowley, who promised to review the issue with Oscar S. Cox, his assistant at the Foreign Economic Administration, and then with General John H. Hilldring, who as chief of the Army staff's Civil Affairs Division answered directly to the secretary of war. Hilldring strongly defended the principle of military responsibility for civil relief in the initial stages of military operations against those in the War Shipping Administration and elsewhere who pushed for a civilian role. It followed that Hilldring would claim exclusive right to set priorities on the shipment of relief supplies.[35]

O'Boyle refused to be deterred. Back in Crowley's office again, he spoke of the increasing irritation of the thousands of Italian-Americans over the delay in shipping the goods they had donated. Left unsaid was the possible effect of this irritation on Roosevelt's fortunes in the upcoming election in which he was running for an unprecedented fourth term. Crowley took the hint, and in O'Boyle's presence phoned Marguerite "Missy" LeHand, another presidential secretary, and dictated a memo for the president that outlined the problem. He concluded by reminding Roosevelt that this could prove important to his political fortunes, adding, "From here on, I absolve myself completely for any responsibility in this matter."[36] Crowley asked O'Boyle to provide his office with a detailed list of the shipping needs. A grim O'Boyle reminded Crowley that they had been through this before, but finally agreed to draw up a list one more time.

A witness to the colloquy was Bill O'Dwyer, making his round of visits to Washington friends like Crowley. Later that day on the train back to New York, O'Boyle found himself sitting opposite O'Dwyer, who remarked on the monsignor's dour mood. Although he was a Democrat, O'Dwyer pointed out to fellow-Democrat O'Boyle that WRS might want to tell its story to the press. He

35. On the responsibilities and powers of the Civil Affairs Division, see Robert W. Coakley and Richard M. Leighton, *Global Logistics and Strategy, 1943–1945* (Washington, D.C.: Government Printing Office, 1968), pp. 743–44.

36. As quoted in O'Boyle's Notes, pt. 24.

mentioned Robert Bird, a political reporter at the New York *Herald Tribune* as one likely to be interested and offered to put him in touch with O'Boyle. Bird did interview O'Boyle a few days later, but O'Boyle asked him to hold off on the story until he tried Washington one more time.

Back in the capital a few days later, O'Boyle alerted Crowley to the pending *Tribune* story, adding that Roosevelt's advisors were doing him a great disservice by failing to warn him of the feelings of the Italian-American community. He also repeated the warning to Oscar Cox, a rapidly rising star in the Roosevelt administration. Without hesitation Cox put a call through to General Hilldring. After concluding his brief conversation he turned to O'Boyle and repeated Hilldring's about-face: "Those damned clothes and food are going to Italy if I have to carry them on my back." True to his word, Hilldring issued the necessary orders, and sixty-eight railcar loads were readied for transporting the first million pounds of donated goods to the docks at Newport News.[37] Six merchant vessels were involved in the operation, the first supplies from a private charity organization to be delivered to Italy. In some cases bales of donated clothing were used as fillers on ammunition ships. On September 25 O'Boyle received word that the shipments would begin on November 1. WRS objected to the delay, explaining to the Army that the clothing in particular was desperately needed with winter coming on. In the end the first ships sailed on October 10. Summarizing this latest imbroglio together with a long list of other pressing concerns for the general secretary of the NCWC, O'Boyle concluded: "no more gripes for the present—your turn now."[38]

With General Hilldring now reluctantly on board, WRS pressed for transport of goods to England in anticipation of the liberation of France and the Low Countries. Archbishop Spellman, in recently liberated Paris, passed on O'Boyle's request to Cardinal Emmanuel Celestin Suhard, the archbishop of Paris, for permission to enlist the Daughters of Charity in WRS operations. The sisters enjoyed an enviable reputation for their work with the poor and for the heroic stance of their Mother General, who had refused to the point of imprisonment to give the Nazis the names of refugees in hiding. The sisters were ideally situated to help. Their congregation worked out of some eight hundred centers, mostly in city slums throughout France and Belgium. In response to O'Boyle's request, Mother Louise Decq cabled her one-word reply: "Yes."[39]

37. Ltr., O'Boyle to Mooney, 4 Oct 1944, AAD.

38. Ltr., O'Boyle to Ready, 25 Sep 1944. See also ltr., O'Boyle to Mooney, 4 Oct 1944. Copies of both in AAD.

39. As quoted in Egan, *Catholic Relief Services,* p. 67. Unless otherwise noted, the following paragraphs on aid to France are based on Egan's work, pp. 65–104, and O'Boyle's Notes, pts. 19 and 20.

Henri Amiel arrived in Paris in late August and set up WRS headquarters in the congregation's historic motherhouse on Rue du Bac. With the sisters he devised a national network to distribute the materials. Shipments were expected soon at the Normandy ports and at Marseilles, so acquiring means of land transport became the number one priority. Again O'Boyle approached his friend Leo Crowley, who had been a Detroit resident with close ties to the auto industry before the war. He sent O'Boyle and Swanstrom to the main plant of the L. B. Smith Brothers outside Harrisburg, where, despite wartime restrictions, they were allowed to buy a fleet of trucks with extra tires and spare parts. Once the trucks arrived on the Continent they were manned by enlisted soldiers of the Polish army-in-exile. Here the universal brotherhood of non-commissioned officers came into play as the trucks were supplied with fuel thanks to the generosity of the U.S. Army's depots. Thus tons of goods were delivered to those in need.

Worried by reports that the Daughters of Charity, many weakened by malnutrition and overwork, were refusing to use for themselves any of the relief goods coming their way, O'Boyle insisted they feed themselves, pointing out that their good health was vital to the operation. When he heard that many of the sisters were making do with burlap rags for shoes, he asked the chief officers of the Endicott-Johnson Shoe Company in Binghamton, New York, for help. The company's only question was how many sisters were in need. When told seven thousand, they promised on the spot to supply the shoes and ship them at their expense.

Operations in France soon fell into a productive routine. Visiting in France, Winthrop Aldrich, the president of the War Fund, was heard to remark that if he had his way, all the relief in Europe would be put under the Daughters of Charity. O'Boyle was determined to use their well-deserved reputation to WRS's advantage. Passing on a survey of the sisters' work prepared by Dr. Amiel, he told Archbishop Mooney that he planned to send a copy to the War Fund's budget committee. Thinking about upcoming budget battles, he wanted to impress those tough-minded businessmen that the Daughters of Charity got on the job quickly "and did not fool around about personnel such as American Relief For France is doing now."[40]

O'Boyle was referring to one of WRS's secular rivals for National War Fund money. Although the various volunteer agencies were partners in the campaign to assist war victims, they were also rivals for federal money. For example, WRS

40. Ltr., O'Boyle to Mooney, 26 May 1945, AAD.

was just one of forty-five agencies given clearance for relief work in Italy. As a result of Ambassador Myron Taylor's initiative, most of these agencies, with WRS cooperating but not participating, established American Relief for Italy, an umbrella organization that combined their efforts. Taylor asked O'Boyle to suggest a director for the new program, and thus Judge Juvenal Marchisio was selected. O'Boyle did his best to tutor Marchisio in his effort to unite the often warring Italian-American factions and actively supported Marchisio's request for a substantial grant from the National War Fund.[41]

Marchisio proved to be an aggressive spokesman for his organization, and O'Boyle came to realize that he must fend off the judge's repeated attempts to hire away WRS personnel. Worse, Marchisio was inclined to give too much credit to American Relief for Italy, O'Boyle concluded, and would try to create the impression that his organization had collected all the clothing and other goods shipped to Italy, despite the fact that WRS was responsible for over 90 percent of the supplies in 1944. O'Boyle forwarded to the administrative board one of the detailed reports his agents in Italy had compiled describing the extensive distribution network they had created, adding that he was using money from the Bishops' Emergency Fund to counter Marchisio's claims in Italian news sources.[42] O'Boyle wryly commented later that when any relief distribution was made by American Relief for Italy, he made sure that Msgr. Landi or one of his colleagues was present and standing close to the American ambassador when the pictures were taken, so that WRS received full credit for its work.

In contrast, O'Boyle had nothing but praise for the similarly constituted Polish War Relief organization. With the help of Mooney's auxiliary, Bishop Stephen S. Woznicki, WRS guided Polish Relief in devising a program, and the two relief organizations made common cause in selecting Archbishop Adam Sapieha of Cracow to accept and distribute their combined supplies in a Poland now under Soviet control. They agreed to present a united front to the National War Fund in defending their continued support of the Polish refugees scattered in the Middle East and elsewhere. In contrast to aid for refugees, the program devised to support the needy in Poland itself was fraught with diplomatic peril. O'Boyle was involved in lengthy negotiations in the spring of 1945 with Secretary of State Edward R. Stettinius and Herbert Lehman, the director of UNRRA, over obtaining Russian cooperation.[43] In May he drafted a memo to Stettinius,

41. Ltr., O'Boyle to Mooney, 27 Apr 1944, AAD.
42. Ltrs., O'Boyle to Mooney, 28 Nov 1944, and to Ready, 15 Sep 1944. Copies of both in AAD.
43. Ltrs., O'Boyle to Mooney, 4 Oct 1944 and 26 Mar 1945. Both in AAD.

which all the volunteer agencies interested in working in Poland signed, request-
ing government assistance in obtaining admission of their supplies and trained
personnel into the country.[44]

The annual ordeal of winning budget approval consumed much of O'Boyle's
time. Following the arduous task of defining the program for the coming year, the
director presented his budget to the president's War Relief Control Board in
Washington. In this O'Boyle enjoyed an advantage because of his good relations
with the officers of the National War Fund in New York, who advised him on
how to best approach the Washington group. The WRS's budget of $5 million
for 1944 was accepted without much discussion. Similarly, it was with an obvious
sigh of relief that O'Boyle could report to Archbishop Mooney in March 1945
that the final section of the 1945 budget had just been approved. With a special
supplement to provide for the needy in the Netherlands, the War Fund approved
nearly $4.8 million for the last year of the war.[45]

WRS submitted a budget of $5.5 million for fiscal year 1946. Even Archbish-
op Spellman blanched at the amount, asking O'Boyle if that wasn't too large a request so late in the war. O'Boyle defended the amount on the basis of the increased needs WRS faced. By then he had cultivated a wide network of friends
in government agencies, and when a decision on the WRS's budget was delayed
he learned from Elliot Jensen, who dealt with the voluntary agencies for the War
Fund, that some on the budget committee had once again raised an objection to
WRS participation, repeating the old argument that it was a religious agency.[46]

The War Fund appointed an executive committee to review the complaint
made in one of its budget subcommittees in January 1945, but Elliot Jensen recommended that O'Boyle first meet with Winthrop Aldrich and Si Seymour, the
Fund's general manager, before presenting his budget to the entire budget committee.[47] Meeting in Aldrich's office in Chase National Bank, the president of the
Fund reaffirmed the contract between the Fund and WRS, but he explained that
$5.5 million was a difficult request for the Fund to honor that year. O'Boyle im-
mediately offered to reduce the request to $4.8 million, noting that this was "pos-
itively our bottom figure." He knew he was on the right track, he later reported,
when he saw Si Seymour wink at Aldrich and nod affirmatively. Nevertheless,

44. Ltrs., O'Boyle to Mooney, 16 Apr and 18 May 1945. Both in AAD.
45. Ltrs., O'Boyle to Mooney, 15 Mar and 4 Jun 1945. Both in AAD.
46. Memo, O'Boyle for Abp. Mooney, 10 Feb 1945, no subj., AAD. See also O'Boyle, Notes, pt.
21, for this and the quotations in the following paragraph. O'Boyle's memory failed him in his draft
memoirs when he mistakenly put the 1946 budget request at $7.5 million.
47. Ltr., O'Boyle to Mooney, 31 Jan 1945, AAD.

Aldrich asked O'Boyle to go ahead with his presentation to the whole budget committee. Privately, Jensen suggested that O'Boyle "bring some fine men and put on a good show."

Although it appeared his revised $4.8 million budget was safe, O'Boyle was taking no chances. He turned to his board of trustees headed by John Burke, president of B. Altman & Co. Members of the board, which included John Coleman, twice chairman of the New York Stock Exchange, Victor Ziminiski, general manager of Gimbel's, and John O'Shea, chairman of the Democratic National Committee, were in prominent attendance when Burke and O'Boyle defended the WRS contract and its revised 1946 budget. Their presentation lasted twenty-three minutes and elicited no questions from the committee. On the phone later that day Elliot Jensen told O'Boyle: "You put on a good show, and you are going to get the funds you requested." But Jensen had one request. Would O'Boyle please drop his constant reference to the $14 million raised by the Knights of Columbus in World War I? It was a phony claim, the money involved was in a war bond drive, not an outright donation, and O'Boyle knew it. O'Boyle piously promised to drop what he knew was a specious argument, and thus the great battle of the budget ended.

While fighting for his 1946 budget O'Boyle was enmeshed in more campaign drives for food and clothing. The United National Clothing Collection Committee, chaired by Henry J. Kaiser, scheduled a nationwide effort for April 1945, and the Church was fully committed to participate. Members of the hierarchy served prominently on Kaiser's advisory committee. Once again it fell to WRS to coordinate the work of every diocese and parish in the country. Considering this comprehensive appeal, O'Boyle hoped to derail an effort by some Italian parishes and fraternal groups in the States to launch a separate food and clothing drive for Italy.[48] The pastors of largely Italian-American parishes in the New York archdiocese had been advised to deny use of their parish halls to the American Labor Party and other groups organized to drum up interest in such an appeal. But when Judge Marchisio and the Relief for Italy organization entered the picture it became obvious that WRS would lose the propaganda war if it continued to resist.

O'Boyle appealed to the executive director of the president's War Relief Control Board in Washington for permission to conduct a limited campaign for food and clothing in a limited number of Northeastern dioceses. News of the cam-

48. Ltrs., Mooney to Stritch, 13 Feb 1945, and O'Boyle to Mooney, 10 Feb 1945. Copies of both in AAD.

paign spread to predominantly Italian-American parishes throughout the country, and O'Boyle decided to ask Archbishop Mooney to invite all the bishops to participate.[49] Catholics joined in these and other campaigns at the end of the war with results that far exceeded expectations. WRS reported in January 1946 that it was receiving one million cans of food a day in its New York, Chicago, and San Francisco warehouses. O'Boyle emphasized for the press that all this food would be sent overseas as quickly as rail and sea transport could be arranged and would be distributed to all the needy without distinction of race, color, or creed.[50]

Final Challenges

There was no break from the incessant labor of preparing and defending budgets, fighting with federal departments over war relief priorities, negotiating distribution facilities overseas, and smoothing over rivalries both in the hierarchy and among the various volunteer agencies. Although O'Boyle's labors were recognized by his superiors—in June 1944 Pope Pius XII had elevated him to the rank of domestic prelate with the title of Right Reverend Monsignor—O'Boyle was never spared time for even a brief vacation during the war. He later laughingly claimed that working for Archbishop Spellman had given him ulcers, but whether it was ulcers or some other ailment, he did suffer several bouts of illness during the war.[51] In March 1944 he was laid up for three weeks with an unspecified problem, and at least once during the war he traveled to Rochester, Minnesota, for treatment at the Mayo Clinic.[52]

Although admittedly somewhat of a hypochondriac, O'Boyle nevertheless obviously paid a physical price for the unremitting labor. A game of golf with his friends, dubbed "the four O's," was fitted in when possible. Father Wycislo, who saw much of O'Boyle during his visits to New York, gave a hint of how he spent his rare hours of relaxation. The two would enjoy dinner and a long walk on Fifth Avenue. Often these walks would end at the Plaza Hotel where they would linger over a drink and cigar listening to Ruth Welcome entertain the lobby audience with music for the zither.[53]

---

49. Ltr., O'Boyle to Mooney, 31 Jan 1945, AAD.

50. *NYT*, 2 Jan 1946.

51. His remark about ulcers was made at the time of his appointment to Washington. He said: "Yea, in those days working for Spellman I got the ulcers and now I give them." As quoted in Ford intv.

52. Ltr., "Pat" O'Boyle to "Monsignor John" (O'Grady, exec. secy., NCCC), 21 Mar 1944, O'-Grady file, NCCC Papers, ACUA.

53. Wycislo intv.

During his last year as director of war relief, O'Boyle faced two major challenges, one involving personal loss, the other a prolonged battle with the Truman administration. His personal trial began on a rainy Saturday morning in late July 1945. He woke that morning in his room at St. Malachy's to what promised to be an extra-heavy day. Father Swanstrom and two staff members were scheduled to leave for Europe in a few hours on a survey of operations. O'Boyle had prepared a brief the night before and hoped that his secretary could finalize it in time for his final meeting with Swanstrom at eleven o'clock. Then he was due to meet Archbishop Spellman and the Italian ambassador for lunch to discuss the effect of the growing political power of the Italian Communists on postwar relief operations.[54]

After saying the seven o'clock parish Mass and hearing confessions, O'Boyle caught a cab on Broadway. Headed downtown, the fastidious cleric noticed that his pants had been poorly pressed. They would never do for a meeting with his archbishop and the Italian ambassador! He decided that there was time for a quick detour to Rogers Peet, the clothing store on Fifth Avenue, where a suit he had bought earlier in the week was waiting for pickup. He could change in the store and still make it to the Empire State Building in time for his briefing with Swanstrom. His fastidiousness probably saved his life. Sporting the new suit, O'Boyle caught another cab and headed down Sixth Avenue. As they neared 34th Street their way was blocked by a crowd, all peering down the street at the Empire State Building. The driver jumped out to investigate and returned to report that the top of the great skyscraper was on fire. When O'Boyle got out to look he saw at once that the center of the conflagration was the seventy-ninth floor, half of which accommodated the WRS staff. He ran part way down 33rd Street toward Fifth Avenue and with a policeman's help dodged through the lobby of the McAlpin Hotel to 34th Street, where he had a straight shot to the building and pandemonium.

It was only then that O'Boyle learned the cause of the tragedy. An Army twin-engine B-25 bomber en route from its base in New England to Newark airport, with a crew of two and a passenger, a young sailor hitching a ride on home leave,

---

54. O'Boyle's itinerary for 28 Jul 1945 is detailed in Arthur Weingarten's *The Sky is Falling* (New York: Grosset and Dunlap, 1977), pp. 41–42 and 239–40. Weingarten's book provides the most comprehensive account of the disaster, and it and O'Boyle's Notes, pt. 23, are the basis of the following paragraphs. See also Theodore James, Jr., *The Empire State Building* (New York: Harper & Row, 1975), pp. 130–41, and John Tauranac, *The Empire State Building: The Making of a Landmark* (New York: Scribner, 1995), pp. 317–22. *NYT,* 29 Jul 1945, included a lengthy article about War Relief Services in its coverage of the accident that is incorrect in some of its details.

had slammed into the world's tallest building. Flying through dense fog and confused about his location, the pilot had lowered his altitude below the minimum 1,500 feet to get a visual bearing. He found himself in the very middle of Manhattan's skyscraper district. Desperately trying to gain altitude, the plane ripped into the seventy-eighth and seventy-ninth floors of the northern wall of the building. Part of the plane skidded across the seventy-ninth floor to fall out the 33rd Street side. One engine fell into an elevator shaft; it and the car fell into the basement. While most of the wreckage missed the WRS office, a great wall of flame, fed by aviation fuel and exploding oxygen tanks did not. The inferno claimed the lives of eleven staff members instantly. Six others, one fatally wounded, were rescued after spending several terrified hours closeted in Father Swanstrom's corner office.

Most of the staff members on duty that day were in the office when the bomber struck. Father Swanstrom and the two assistants who would be leaving for Europe in a few hours were not present. Preparing for the trip, Swanstrom was taking time out for a haircut at a nearby barbershop. He had asked his two colleagues to join him so that they could continue their planning session. A frantic O'Boyle found himself barred from the few elevators still in operation, so he went instead to a triage station in the sub-basement where he gave absolution to some of the severely wounded. Returning to the lobby he encountered Mayor LaGuardia, who had just arrived. In answer to his plea, LaGuardia shoved O'Boyle and Swanstrom into an elevator and ordered the operator to take the three men to the offices. The car was forced to halt at the sixty-second floor, and they climbed the rest of the way on foot. The scene they encountered was horrific. The fireman had laid the bodies, charred beyond recognition, on the metal desks. To O'Boyle's surprise he found his old classmate, Bishop McIntyre, anointing some of the dead. McIntyre explained that for some unknown reason he had decided to take a morning stroll in the neighborhood and, equipped with the holy oils he had absentmindedly left in his pocket the night before after a sick call, he had followed the firemen up to the WRS office.[55]

A shaken O'Boyle and Swanstrom accompanied the survivors down to the waiting ambulances and angrily fended off requests from radio reporters for an interview. O'Boyle did, however, agree to provide a statement for the district attorney, only to learn when he arrived at the police station that it was all a hoax to get them out of the building. Later joined by McIntyre, O'Boyle and Swanstrom

---

55. Weber detailed McIntyre's role in the accident in his *Catholic California Essays: Some Historical Reflections* (Los Angeles: Archdiocese of Los Angeles Archives, 1992), pp. 94–95.

then went to the city morgue to help identify the victims. Before the dreadful day came to a close O'Boyle visited the survivors in the hospital, and then he and Swanstrom fanned out to visit the families of those who had died.

Archbishop Spellman immediately arranged for a funeral Mass at St. Patrick's Cathedral, but O'Boyle was too broken up to deliver the eulogy. On the day after the tragedy Spellman also broached the subject of future operations, offering temporary office space in the old Cathedral College building at 51st Street and Madison Avenue. O'Boyle decided on the spot that it was best to open for business the following day in temporary quarters. Since Ed Kinney maintained a duplicate set of purchase and payment records at his distribution center, operations could continue without delay. O'Boyle began the challenging task of returning the office to normalcy by addressing the assembled staff. He discussed their shared sorrow and stressed the vital nature of the work they were doing to relieve the suffering of so many. Swanstrom tried to speak, but broke down in the attempt, and soon the whole gathering was in tears. Ironically, War Relief staff members who served in the war zones suffered no harm during the hostilities; those working in the safety of New York made the ultimate sacrifice.

Concerning a permanent home, O'Boyle received a call from General Hugh A. Drum, Al Smith's successor as manager of the Empire State Building. Drum was concerned that the relief office might not return. No doubt worried about his building's public image, Drum emphasized the psychological need for conquering fear by returning. WRS could have any available space. O'Boyle admitted that many on the staff were fearful about returning to a skyscraper, but they were determined to face the challenge. On September 14 the staff found itself ensconced in large offices on the seventy-second floor overlooking Fifth Avenue.[56]

Soon most of the fire's survivors were back at work and making light of the prediction that they would never return to a tall building. But none of the staff, it seemed, escaped severe psychological scarring from the trauma they had undergone. O'Boyle divided them into two categories—those whose breakdown was immediate and recovery swift, and those less fortunate who suffered a delayed reaction. He placed himself in the latter category. Although Father Wycislo, who got through to him from Europe immediately after the fire, detected no change in his mental outlook, O'Boyle later admitted that for many months he suffered nightmares that brought back the horror of that day. He later diagnosed his malady as a nervous breakdown. "I was completely broken by that horrible event, and it was Frank [Bishop McIntyre] who insisted that I take some time off to re-

56. *NYT*, 15 Sep 1945.

cuperate."[57] Always mindful of authority, O'Boyle obediently took himself off for ten days rest at one of his favorite spots, the resort hotel at Hershey in his beloved Pennsylvania.[58]

The Empire State Building tragedy delayed Swanstrom's European tour by weeks. His mission, to coordinate the newly devised displaced persons program, marked the beginning of Catholic relief's major postwar work and O'Boyle's last great battle with the federal bureaucracy. Shortly after the Allies conquered Germany, WRS reached an agreement with the supreme Allied commander, General Dwight D. Eisenhower, to work among the hundreds of thousands of displaced persons, principally Poles, Lithuanians, and other Eastern Europeans, some in special camps, others simply adrift in war-torn Europe. O'Boyle got the National War Fund and the president's War Relief Control Board not only to approve this agreement, but also to agree that WRS funds budgeted for prisoners of war be diverted to this new category of need. Swanstrom met in Paris with Father Wycislo and two other priests working with Polish and Lithuanian refugees to plan the new program. Swanstrom brought with him four laymen who, under the agreement with the American military, would set up operations in the various camps for the displaced in Germany.[59]

Since no WRS agent had yet been allowed into Poland to review relief arrangements in that country, Swanstrom and Wycislo also flew into Warsaw in November 1945, the first American relief workers on the scene. They were on hand to welcome the second shipment of WRS supplies, which were distributed to dioceses throughout Poland by Caritas volunteers in trucks supplied by WRS.[60] As a consequence of this and other agreements Swanstrom reached in Europe, WRS also became the first private agency to begin operations in Austria and Czechoslovakia.

Swanstrom was particularly concerned about the condition of German civilians. Before leaving on the Warsaw trip he had described in an interview their dire plight and severely criticized the American Army and U.S. policy for neglecting the crisis as the helpless, especially the aged and children, faced starvation in the coming winter. While O'Boyle declared Swanstrom "100% right on

---

57. Ltr., Weber to author, 5 Feb 1997, AAW; and Weber intv. of Cardinal O'Boyle, copy in AAW (source of quote). Weber summarized O'Boyle's reaction to the accident in *His Eminence of Los Angeles,* vol. 1, p. 57. See also Arthur and Wycislo intvs. Anthony Muldoon recalled that the accident brought on a nervous breakdown in his cousin that "knocked him for a loop." See Muldoon intv.

58. O'Boyle, handwritten note appended to his ltr. to Mooney, 15 Sep 1945, AAD.

59. Ltr., O'Boyle to Mooney, 5 Jul 1945, AAD.

60. Swanstrom's trip is described in Eileen Egan's *Catholic War Relief,* pp. 158–62.

conditions," he did not want the interview released in its entirety, nor the needs of the Germans broadcast in the publicity for the upcoming foodstuffs campaign. His concern centered on how such a statement might affect his organization's relations with the State Department and the military in future negotiations, and he was determined that such negotiations would take place.[61]

He knew his task would not be easy because of the popular mindset that confused relief for the German destitute with trading with the enemy. In September 1945 he applied to the president's War Relief Control Board for permission to distribute food and clothing in Germany. Predictably, in the weeks that followed he met not only with considerable trepidation on the part of government officials, but also with downright opposition from some of his colleagues in the American Council of Voluntary Agencies. At a meeting of the council's executive committee on October 24, O'Boyle took his stand, making clear his determination to send aid to German civilians, "especially the children, despite hindrance by government regulations and the hesitancy of many volunteer agencies."[62]

The need for an educational campaign was obvious, and O'Boyle welcomed news that a State Department representative had proposed that Bishop Bernard Sheil, one of Archbishop Stritch's auxiliaries, tour Germany with a representative of the Friends (Quaker) Service Committee and report to the American public on conditions among civilians. Methodist Bishop G. Bromley Oxnam and others were also to tour Germany, and, O'Boyle predicted, "You may be sure they will come out with a blast."[63] Still he was adamant that WRS take the lead in such an aid program.

He had his way. In an interview published in the *New York Times* on January 7, 1946, Swanstrom, back from Europe, described the suffering in German cities and demanded that private relief agencies become involved. He denounced the assumption that public opinion would not tolerate private relief for former enemies and concluded: "If Americans could see, as I have, innocent children and the aged literally dying from starvation . . . I'm sure that they would feel as I do, that they, too, come under the mantle of Christian charity." The *Times* noted that this was the first public discussion of the Catholic stand on aid to former enemies.[64]

O'Boyle was also busy working on the bureaucrats. He won Herbert

61. Ltr., O'Boyle to Mooney, 29 Oct 1945, AAD.
62. As quoted in O'Boyle's Notes, pt. 18. See also ltr., O'Boyle to Mooney, 29 Oct 1945, AAD.
63. As quoted in ltr., O'Boyle to Mooney, 29 Oct 1945, AAD.
64. As quoted in *NYT*, 8 Jan 1946.

Lehman's gratitude for the strong endorsement Catholic War Relief gave UNR-RA at its congressional appropriations hearings. His stock with the directors of the National War Fund was already at a new high after he released his assistant, Edward O'Connor, just back from a survey of relief operations, to appear before Community Chest meetings around the nation where he described the effect of American relief on the suffering civilians of Europe.[65] He also made sure that the National War Fund directors received a copy of Archbishop Stritch's letter to his fellow bishops strongly endorsing the work of the Fund and detailing its need for contributions.[66]

On June 10 O'Boyle was able to report that Father James Hoban, then working for WRS in Paris, would go to Berlin to represent WRS on a six-man commission appointed by the State Department and the U.S. Army to arrange a system for the distribution of food and clothing through private agencies. President Harry S Truman approved the commission's decisions, and on March 22 a shipment of WRS food left for Bremerhaven. This first shipment by a private agency and a second that sailed a week later delivered some two million pounds of food and clothing. They, and those that followed every month, were distributed to the needy through Caritas Verband, a federation of German Catholic relief agencies.[67]

Although the war was over, War Relief Services only intensified its operations as one aid crisis followed another. O'Boyle's last great battle began, appropriately perhaps, on St. Patrick's Day, 1946. March 17 marked the opening of UNR-RA's fourth general meeting in Atlantic City. Eileen Egan was there as an observer for WRS. During the opening session she learned from the Associated Press (later confirmed by an AP dispatch on the 21st) that the American military government was about to announce that as of July 1 American authorities would close the displaced persons camps in Germany. Thereafter full responsibility for providing for displaced persons and civilian detainees in the American zone must be assumed by the Germans themselves. Given the prostrate condition of the German economy and the certain starvation of the refugees, such a declaration was tantamount to forcing the refugees, against their will, to return to their Communist-controlled homelands.

By the simple expedient of closing the camps the United States would avoid

65. For a general overview of the postwar refugee crisis, see Michael Marrus, *The Unwanted: European Refugees from the First World War Through the Cold War* (Philadelphia: Temple University Press, 2002), especially pp. 296–324.

66. Ltr., O'Boyle to Mooney, 5 Jan 1946, AAD.

67. *NYT,* 23 Mar 1946, and ltr., O'Boyle to Mooney, 10 Jan 1946, AAD.

the unpopular picture of forcing these unwanted into trains heading east. The Western allies were anxious to solve the problem of displaced persons and had even cooperated in the forced repatriation of many refugees, especially Russian soldiers held in camps in Austria and Germany. Citing the UNRRA charter and provisions of the Yalta agreement, Soviet officials continued to press for the repatriation of civilians as well.[68]

As agreed by the twenty-five nation-signatories in 1943, UNRRA was charged with the reconstruction of devastated countries and repatriation of foreigners located in Germany and Austria. Nothing in the agreement or in the Yalta declaration provided for those displaced to exercise freedom of choice or the right of asylum. As early as February 1945, O'Boyle sounded the alarm. Freedom of choice, valid travel documents, and aid in resettlement, he declared, would be paramount issues for refugees in postwar Europe. Although the crisis applied mostly to the vast number of Catholic refugees from Poland, Austria, Lithuania, and Yugoslavia, it also applied to Jewish refugees. Consequently O'Boyle wanted to make common cause with the American Jewish Joint Distribution Committee on the repatriation issue. He arranged for a strong NCWC statement opposing forced repatriation to be included in a document on the subject issued by the American Council of Voluntary Agencies. Hoping for widespread discussion of the matter, he also sent the Catholic statement to UNRRA and the Intergovernmental Committee on Refugees.[69]

As the war in Europe drew to a close O'Boyle briefed the bishops on the plight of those in DP camps and the principle of freedom of choice. In April 1945 he sent an NCWC position paper on displaced persons to Minnesota's Governor Harold E. Stassen, one of the United States representatives at the forthcoming United Nations Conference in San Francisco. The following month he prepared a strong memorandum outlining the precarious situation facing the many Lithuanian refugees in France through the French ambassador to Foreign Minister George Bidault.[70]

Despite his awareness of the danger, O'Boyle was unprepared for Egan's news when he arrived in Atlantic City in March 1946 after the opening session of the UNRRA meeting. Underscoring the urgency of the crisis, Egan cited the remarks of Sir George Rendel, leader of the British delegation, who noted that

---

68. Egan, *Catholic Relief Services,* pp. 210–14.

69. Ltr., O'Boyle to Mooney, 23 Feb 1945, AAD.

70. Ltrs., O'Boyle to Mooney, 23 Feb, 16 Mar, and 13 Apr 1945. All in AAD. See also ltr., Msgr. Carroll (NCWC) to Abp. Amleto Cicognani (Apostolic Delegate), 23 May 1945, DP file, NCWC Papers, ACUA.

WRS was caught unawares despite the presence of its agents in the DP camps because the American authorities, faced with the task of closing hundreds of such camps, needed to act quickly and in secrecy. There was no use appealing to UNRRA, he added. To overturn this decision WRS must approach its own government.[71]

With Spellman's help, O'Boyle arranged to meet with Secretary of State James F. Byrnes in Washington on March 20. At that meeting he charged that the government was about to make a serious mistake that would sentence many people to death; General Eisenhower had promised these people in the name of the U.S. government that they would remain where they were, taken care of by the United States. Byrnes appeared unmoved by these arguments. Totally misreading the situation, he cited his own experience as a circuit judge in South Carolina, where he would often see men loafing on the courthouse steps. He compared these men to the displaced persons in Germany and asked O'Boyle if he agreed. Seeing his arguments were having no effect, a disgruntled O'Boyle took his leave. Afterward he prepared a memorandum outlining the meeting for the American bishops, and he sent a copy to Byrnes. He also arranged with now-Cardinal Stritch, who had succeeded Mooney as chairman of the bishops' administrative board, to forward a copy to President Truman. Should he not receive a favorable answer from Byrnes by March 31, he wanted Stritch to send copies to three influential senators: Scott W. Lucas from Stritch's Illinois, James A. Mead of New York, and Arthur Vandenberg, Michigan's staunch champion of bipartisan foreign policy.[72]

In a covering letter O'Boyle warned Byrnes that he needed a decision by March 31, "since our organization must determine its future attitude with reference to Displaced Persons." He summarized WRS's position: closing the camps without having a substitute agency ready to care for those who could not be repatriated would be an act of deliberate injustice. Either the Intergovernmental Committee for Refugees should begin work immediately on resettlement or the United Nations meeting in London in April should take "precise and definite steps to care for the non-repatriable" before the camps closed.[73]

A pessimistic NCWC official warned Cardinal Stritch that there seemed little

71. Egan, *Catholic Relief Services,* pp. 212–13.

72. Memo, O'Boyle to Stritch, 20 Mar 1946, no sub, DP file, NCWC Papers, ACUA. O'Boyle described his meeting with Byrnes in his Notes, pt. 18.

73. Ltr., O'Boyle to Byrnes, 20 Mar 1946, copy in DP file, NCWC Papers, ACUA. Archbishops Mooney, Stritch, and Spellman were all elevated to the rank of cardinal at the first postwar consistory in February 1946.

hope of a reversal of the War Department's move unless the president intervened. O'Boyle's March 31 deadline passed without any reaction from the State Department, but in early April came a glimmer of hope. The White House invited representatives of the Catholic Church, the Federal Council of Churches, the AFL, and the CIO to meet with the president. Msgr. Howard Carroll of the NCWC secretariat represented War Relief Services. Carroll's recommendations for the conferees echoed those O'Boyle had offered to Byrnes the previous month: the camps should remain open until the U.N. program on displaced persons was announced, and resettlement plans should be developed and put into operation for those who clearly could not return to their homelands.[74]

On April 28 O'Boyle heard the good news. President Truman informed Cardinal Stritch that, while the Army was correct in its thinking that the camps could not be maintained indefinitely, it would be unwise to close them in August as recommended. He declared that the camps would be maintained until after the United Nations acted on the problem in the fall, when "we can then determine what is best to do with this very difficult problem." Two days later Truman was back giving Stritch an update on the government's latest decisions on the Polish refugee colony in Mexico. The State Department was underwriting some of the costs of the establishment and had arranged for the admission into the United States of the orphans and those adults who could meet immigrant standards established by law.[75] O'Boyle rejoiced in the decision because, as he put it, it initiated an orderly and humane closing of the camps over a period of time.

Although there was much work ahead for Catholic war relief in the frenzied postwar years, the essential outline of O'Boyle's role was now complete. The record of relief is usually expressed in statistics, the number of people helped, the tons of food and clothing shipped, the nations involved. Undergirding this record of achievement, however, was the development of an organization unprecedented in the American Church. As international recognition of his work began to accumulate in the form of medals and awards, O'Boyle insisted on playing down his role in the success of War Relief Services.[76] Yet it was his mastery of

74. Ltrs., Swanstrom to Carroll, 8 Apr 1946, and Carroll to Stritch, 22 Mar 1946. Both in DP file, NCWC Papers, ACUA.

75. Ltrs., Truman to Stritch, 28 and 30 Apr 1946, copies in DP file, NCWC Papers, ACUA.

76. In the coming years O'Boyle would be the recipient of, among others, the French Legion of Honor and Italy's Order of Italian Solidarity, along with other Italian and French decorations and decorations from Luxembourg, Poland, Austria, and China. He was also cited by the president of the United States for "eminent service rendered in the field of humanitarian war relief during World War II." All these awards are summarized in an NCWC news release, 14 Jan 1955. The Vatican

organization that allowed a staff that never numbered more than eighty-five people to supervise the collection and distribution of sixty-nine tons of relief materials valued at $102 million to the overseas needy. It was he who devised the system that recruited a half million volunteer workers in American parishes to conduct ten successful campaigns for food and clothing. It was he who kept the hierarchy united behind him and who fought the federal bureaucracy over the principle that private relief agencies had a primary role to play in war relief.

recognized his war service in 1956, appointing him assistant to the Pontifical Throne and Count of the Episcopal Palace and Court of the Lateran. In 1972 the French government named him Commander of the National Order of the Legion of Honor, the highest honor bestowed on an individual. See *Evening Star,* 4 Feb 1972. [Hereafter *Star;* see list of abbreviations.]

CHAPTER 6

Pomp and Circumstance

On August 31, 1945, Archbishop Mooney received a handwritten communiqué from the director of War Relief Services. O'Boyle's old friend and the chancellor of the archdiocese, Frank McIntyre, had just informed him that Archbishop Spellman was about to name him assistant director of New York's Catholic Charities. With Spellman and Swanstrom both out of the country, O'Boyle confidently predicted that there would be no final steps taken at least until November. Although he admitted he would rather stay to launch the postwar relief program, he logically assumed that Swanstrom would succeed him to carry out their plans. He included a glowing description of Swanstrom's character and ability for the president of the bishops' administrative board.[1]

O'Boyle was in for a surprise. Spellman had no intention of severing his close ties to war relief, insured by the fact that its director was a priest of his archdiocese. Rather, he expected O'Boyle, beginning in September, to work simultaneously in both war relief and Catholic Charities. Aware that Msgr. Keegan's failing health meant the assistant director would bear full responsibility for New York's large charity apparatus, O'Boyle argued that one man should not try to hold down both jobs. Spellman's imperious reply: "That's the way I want it."[2]

Apparently O'Boyle spent little time on Catholic Charities affairs during that winter as he struggled with the thorny problems of relief for German civilians and the threat to the displaced persons camps. In late

1. Ltr., O'Boyle to Mooney, 31 Aug 1945, AAD.
2. As quoted in O'Boyle's Notes, pt. 13. His appointment as assistant director of Catholic Charities in September 1945 was noted in *NYT,* 15 May 1947.

spring he developed severe back and leg pains that sent him for another prolonged stay at the Mayo Clinic. In July Spellman had to appoint Msgr. Charles Giblin, McIntyre's assistant in the chancery, to Catholic Charities while Swanstrom remained in charge at War Relief Services.[3]

The doctors were at odds over the correct diagnosis of O'Boyle's problem. A nonfunctioning right kidney was the chief suspect. The patient underwent lengthy sedimentation tests, and then had to overcome a persistent infection that seemed implicated. The orthopedists and arthritis specialists, on the other hand, suspected a spinal disk problem. O'Boyle reported to Spellman that the pain had eased considerably after physical therapy and after he began wearing a back brace, but some doctors still suspected kidney involvement. A clearly frustrated patient noted that if his kidney proved the cause of the long hospitalization, "I wish they had taken it out." He wanted to come home, but, he told Spellman, his doctor warned him that to return to New York would only mean starting tests all over again.[4]

Spellman agreed that O'Boyle should stay in Rochester for as long as the doctors ordered. Meanwhile, he added, Giblin and Swanstrom "are carrying on well."[5] In fact Swanstrom and Ed Kinney visited the patient in late September, when they helped him prepare preliminary plans for their upcoming fund-raising campaign. O'Boyle obviously considered Spellman's frequent letters beyond what was expected from his boss, and for once his responses revealed a genuine warmth toward "His Eminence," as he would forever after refer to the New York archbishop. Still, he probably received more comfort from Frank McIntyre's practical approach to his confinement. McIntyre's good wishes came with an offer of financial assistance. O'Boyle claimed that he could cover hospital expenses and the specialists at the Mayo Clinic would allow him to pay their fees in installments. He would, he promised, ask for help, if needed. In the end McIntyre did meet some of O'Boyle's expenses and insisted that it was a gift, not to be repaid.[6]

When O'Boyle did return to New York in late October with backache gone but nonfunctioning kidney in place, no further reference was made to his returning to Catholic Charities. To the contrary, O'Boyle plunged back into war relief work. He and his assistants had begun to discuss the enormous problem of resettlement of war-related refugees. This vital work would increasingly occupy his

---

3. *NYT*, 15 Jul 1946. For a summary of all these changes, see Minutes, Board of Trustees, Catholic Charities of the Archdiocese of New York, 12 Mar 1947, ACCANY.

4. Ltrs., O'Boyle to Spellman, 3 Aug and 4 Oct (source of quote) 1946, AANY.

5. Ltr., Spellman to O'Boyle, 5 Aug 1946, copy in AANY.

6. Ltr., O'Boyle to McIntyre, 20 Oct 1946, AANY. See also Weber's intv. with Cardinal O'Boyle.

A New Archbishop. Cardinal Spelman congratulates his director of
Catholic Charities, Monsignor O'Boyle, on O'Boyle's appointment as Archbishop
of Washington.

successor at WRS, but for now O'Boyle concentrated on the equally knotty
problem of financing future resettlement programs and the rest of war relief's
operations.[7] His last major undertaking was to plan and supervise the first direct
appeal to American Catholics for support of WRS. When the National War
Fund dissolved in January 1947, collecting for the multiple needs of war victims
became a major responsibility of private relief agencies. At O'Boyle's urging the

7. On planning postwar projects, see, for example, ltr., O'Boyle to McNicholas, 20 Jan 1947, Mc-
Nicholas file, NCWC Papers, ACUA.

American bishops decided to use their Emergency Fund (now dubbed the Bishops' Relief Campaign for Victims of War) and their annual Laetare Sunday collection to finance the activities of WRS.

The Laetare Sunday collection had realized, on average, $2.5 million during the war years. O'Boyle set a much higher goal. Together with Swanstrom and Kinney he organized the collection down to the parish level.[8] Through the administrative board he asked each ordinary to appoint a diocesan director, and he conducted regional meetings with these appointees, urging them to use the promotional materials prepared by WRS. In this way the needs of the war victims would be brought home to the prospective donors in the pews. These meetings necessitated lengthy swings around the country. Most were by train, but on one memorable trip along the West Coast, O'Boyle, who disliked travel and was especially leery of airplanes, took his first flight.

Using the organizational structure of the Church in such a concentrated effort explained the fabulous success of the first postwar appeal. By the time accounts were totaled in May 1947, the campaign had realized well over $7 million for WRS, almost three times the amount collected in any previous appeal.

Catholic Charities Again

Just as the campaign drew to a close, O'Boyle heard again from Cardinal Spellman. With Msgr. Keegan now totally disabled, Spellman wanted O'Boyle to take over as director of Catholic Charities. Again he insisted, over O'Boyle's protests, that he retain his post at WRS. O'Boyle only learned later that he was Spellman's second choice for director. The cardinal had picked O'Boyle's old friend and golfing buddy, Msgr. John O'Donnell, who pleaded his lack of fitness for the job and pushed O'Boyle's candidacy. O'Boyle was reconciled to returning to Catholic Charities, but he was convinced that the idea of a dual directorship shortchanged WRS and was unfair to Swanstrom, who would end up performing both his and O'Boyle's work. Chancellor, now-Archbishop, McIntyre advised him to ask Spellman straight out to recommend Swanstrom's appointment to Archbishop McNicholas and the administrative board. To O'Boyle's surprise, Spellman merely replied "certainly," and the deed was done.[9] On May 15 O'Boyle succeeded his old boss, Msgr. Keegan, at Catholic Charities, and Father Swanstrom, with Father Wycislo as his deputy, assumed responsibility for war relief. Two months later, in a sign of Spellman's satisfaction with the arrange-

8. Ltr., O'Boyle to Stritch, 11 May 1946, copy in AAD.
9. O'Boyle, Notes, pts. 13 (source of quote) and 25.

ment, O'Boyle was appointed a diocesan consultor, a member of the select body of priests required by Church law to advise and assist the ordinary.[10]

Although O'Boyle had served seventeen years in Catholic Charities, he faced an entirely different situation in postwar New York. Always looming over him in earlier times was the awesome figure of Robert Keegan, who in the days of Cardinal Hayes could enlist anyone he wanted for Catholic Charities and saw his budget demands met without opposition. This influence waned under Spellman, who came to dominate Catholic Charities just as he dominated every aspect of diocesan business. Moreover, Spellman's trusted chancellor, Frank McIntyre, was no particular friend of Catholic Charities. While its new director considered charities a priority issue, McIntyre did not, and during O'Boyle's brief tenure he debated and fought his old friend over personnel and budgets. Meanwhile, as chairman of the Catholic Charities board of directors, Spellman continued to poke and pry into O'Boyle's activities.[11]

As postwar director, O'Boyle found himself responsible for 174 agencies serving 151,443 people with an annual budget of $2.2 million. Msgr. Christopher J. Weldon had stayed on as assistant director and was of considerable help in acclimating O'Boyle to old surroundings. Even before he could settle in, he faced a major crisis. Many of their social workers, Weldon reported, were upset over the wage scale and working conditions. There was even talk of a strike.

O'Boyle's first reaction was to investigate working conditions. To that end he called a meeting of the lay supervisors in the various agency departments. Many of these employees were unaware of O'Boyle's lengthy experience in social work and were probably surprised by his detailed questions about schedules, home visits, and other aspects of social service. Their answers convinced him that changes were in order, but when he learned that these supervisors had engaged a lawyer to negotiate with the CIO to have the Catholic workers unionized, he decided that immediate action was called for.[12]

Talking the matter over with Cardinal Spellman, O'Boyle was told to consult Judge Edward C. Maguire, the mayor's advisor on labor conflicts. To O'Boyle's frustration, repeated meetings with the judge produced only one firm bit of advice: above all else he and his assistants must exercise patience. Convinced he was getting nowhere with the judge, O'Boyle turned to his old friend Msgr. John

10. These appointments were made public by *NYT,* 16 May and 25 Jul 1947.

11. This situation is explained in Donoghue intv. See also Kelly, *Inside My Father's House,* pp. 83–84.

12. O'Boyle, Notes, pt. 25. Unless otherwise noted, the following paragraphs are based on this source.

P. Monaghan, the famed labor priest. For many years Monaghan had taught in the archdiocese's minor seminary, where he instilled in a whole generation of priests respect for the Church's social teachings. He helped organize the Association of Catholic Trade Unionists and served as its New York chaplain. O'Boyle's friendship with the feisty Irish priest began in his early days in Catholic Charities and deepened when in 1939 Monaghan became pastor of a Staten Island parish near Mt. Loretto. The ultraconservative McIntyre considered Monaghan an outright socialist until O'Boyle was finally able to convince him otherwise.[13]

Given Monaghan's strong union sympathies (he would later have a falling out with Spellman over the latter's defeat in 1949 of the striking cemetery workers), his advice to O'Boyle came as a surprise. According to O'Boyle, when apprised of the situation, Monaghan jumped out of his chair and exclaimed, "My God, under no circumstances should they organize a labor union in a charitable organization."[14] Armed with this advice, O'Boyle called a general meeting for all the social workers affiliated with Catholic Charities. They heard him explain that the organization depended on an annual appeal for financing and that the archdiocese could not afford salary increases. They were free to organize and strike, he added, but if they did he would recruit seniors at Mount St. Vincent's and New Rochelle, two local Catholic women's colleges, to work with Catholic Charities clients. His remarks drew no questions. With obvious satisfaction he recalled that the issue of a strike was never again raised during his tenure as director.

It is difficult to reconcile O'Boyle's sincere sympathy for unionism learned in Scranton and reinforced in his years at St. Columba's with his bald threat to use scab labor to break a strike by his employees. Labor expert Msgr. George Higgins, who knew O'Boyle well in later years, observed that O'Boyle was merely exhibiting what was commonplace among Church leaders in those days, a not-in-my-backyard reaction to what they would applaud in a similar challenge to private business. By instinct and training O'Boyle exercised total loyalty to the Church, and he expected no less from the social workers. His sympathy might be wholehearted when it came to the organization of workers in industry, but the Church was not a business, and, according to this reasoning, not a venue for labor organizing.[15]

13. Weber intv. with Cardinal O'Boyle. For an extended analysis of Monaghan's influence, see Lynch, "Above All Things the Truth."
14. As quoted in O'Boyle's Notes, pt. 25.
15. Higgins and Arthur intvs.

Washington

Settling quickly in office, O'Boyle was soon enmeshed in projects such as drafting plans for a new foundling home and reviewing reports prepared for Cardinal Spellman's use at the upcoming conference of Catholic bishops. He was able to spare some time for a visit to Scranton and weekly get-togethers for golf and dinner with the four O's, the old quartet of priest friends that included his host at St. Malachy's. He also enjoyed the company of his friend Msgr. George Guilfoyle, an irrepressible pal who even in later years insisted on calling Cardinal O'Boyle "Uncle Pat." Ranking high among his lay friends in that period was Andrew Maloney, an executive at New York's Bankers Trust. This work and play, however, would abruptly come to an end.

Msgr. Keegan's long invalidism ended on November 3, 1947, and O'Boyle, with his old colleague from Washington, Msgr. O'Grady, attended the funeral on a wet and chilly day. O'Boyle promptly came down with influenza, which confined him to his room at St. Malachy's. His doctor ordered complete bed rest that, after two weeks, left him in a much-weakened state. At that point he got a call from Msgr. Weldon at Catholic Charities, telling him that a letter had arrived for him from the apostolic delegation. Thinking it a request for information about a former associate who was about to receive a papal honor, he asked Weldon to open the letter. Weldon called back to report that the letter contained a sealed document marked "personal," which he sent over unopened. To O'Boyle's surprise, the apostolic delegate was informing him that the pope had appointed him archbishop of Washington. If he agreed to the appointment, O'Boyle was to reply "as soon as possible."[16]

Always a fatalist when it concerned his health, O'Boyle grilled his doctor over his future. The surprised physician assured him that it was just the flu and he would recover, but O'Boyle continued to temporize. Spellman was away at the time, although his puzzled secretary reported that he called frequently to inquire about Msgr. O'Boyle's health. When Spellman did return to New York he immediately visited the patient at St. Malachy's to learn his decision. O'Boyle, reminding Spellman of his several visits to the Mayo Clinic, replied that he believed he should refuse. Spellman brushed aside such concerns, assuring O'Boyle, "I know all about it, and you're in good condition." With that firm push, O'Boyle agreed to inform the apostolic delegate of his acceptance.

Spellman, all business, asked to see the rest of O'Boyle's suite. When in-

16. This and the conversation with Spellman that follows are quoted in O'Boyle, Notes, pt. 26.

formed that the twenty-square-foot room on the top floor was all O'Boyle could claim, Spellman declared the space insufficient for organizing a consecration ceremony and invited O'Boyle to come live in the cardinal's residence, dubbed by one and all "the Powerhouse," on Madison Avenue.

The new bishop-elect agreed to the move, but before any public announcement was made he decided to convalesce for at least a week at Our Lady of Princeton, a retreat house in New Jersey. He asked his friend Father O'Donnell to drive him down to Princeton. Bound to secrecy, he did not break the news, but Jack O'Donnell knew his man, and later back home called St. Malachy's pastor, who himself was recovering from an operation at the Mayo Clinic. He mentioned O'Boyle's unusual quietness on the trip to Princeton and mused about the possibility that "lightening had struck." On December 3, the eve of the scheduled public announcement, O'Boyle heard from Spellman, who warned him to report in at Madison Avenue early in the morning because the press would be expecting interviews. The retreat house provided a ride back to the city, but even at that early hour O'Boyle just escaped visitors approaching the retreat house. He later learned that they were two frustrated reporters who had got wind of the announcement and had driven through the night from Washington to get an exclusive.

As O'Boyle's ordinary, Cardinal Spellman would naturally have known of the pope's decision to appoint O'Boyle to Washington. He had written to both his friend, Pope Pius XII, and the apostolic delegate on June 15 about the vacancies in Baltimore and Washington. What he told them is unknown, but he received word of the Vatican's decision on November 21 and let Father Wycislo in on the secret when they met during Spellman's stopover in Paris.[17]

Given his close friendship with the pope, it would seem likely that Spellman was responsible for O'Boyle's selection, but that has not stopped speculation on this most privileged of Vatican prerogatives. O'Boyle himself claimed that Cardinal Spellman had little to do with his appointment, later declaring, "Oh, no, it was Mooney because, you know, the war."[18] On another occasion he emphatically denied Spellman's involvement—"he had nothing to do with it"—and indicated that the apostolic delegate, Archbishop Cicognani, who had come to know him quite well through war relief, was the instigator. O'Boyle later told his secre-

17. Fogarty, *The Vatican and the American Hierarchy*, p. 314, cites Spellman's diary for this information. See also Wycislo intv.

18. Msgr. James Gillen thus quoted his friend and vacation companion in his interviews both with the author and with Fr. Conley.

tary and probably closest friend, then-Msgr. John Donoghue, "Actually, Cicognani was the one responsible for making me the archbishop of Washington, not Spellman." For confirmation he cited the report of his friend Bishop Joseph McShea of Allentown. McShea was serving as one of Cicognani's secretaries at the time of O'Boyle's elevation. He testified to the central role the delegate played in the selection and explicitly denied any involvement by Spellman.[19] Msgr. E. Robert Arthur, another of O'Boyle's close Washington associates, supported this view. Admitting that the question remained at heart a mystery, he confidently ruled out Spellman and assumed instead that Cicognani played the major role. Finally there is the comment of renowned historian John Tracy Ellis, who recalled that at O'Boyle's installation luncheon the new archbishop turned to the apostolic delegate and said, "I'm here because you wanted me here."[20]

Such opinions tend to reinforce historian Gerald Fogarty's thesis that Spellman's effort to become the unofficial primate of the American Church was effectively blocked by the Midwestern triumvirate of Stritch, Mooney, and McNicholas, who dominated the leadership of the NCWC. These prelates spoke of the Hindenburg Line they had built to restrict Spellman's influence to the East Coast. While Spellman breached that line when he succeeded in obtaining the see of Los Angeles for his chancellor, Francis McIntyre, the appointment of O'Boyle was a different case. Although Spellman had come to trust O'Boyle with increasingly important responsibilities, and O'Boyle had come to respect the boss "who gives me ulcers," there was no love lost between the two. Those who doubted Spellman's role in O'Boyle's promotion could point to the fact the O'Boyle's permanent appointment to Catholic Charities coincided with the death of Archbishop Michael Curley in Baltimore, an event that had opened the Washington position. Would not an astute kingmaker, they pushed the point, leave his candidate in the higher profile war relief assignment? While O'Boyle was learning that he had been Spellman's second choice for Catholic Charities, the trio of Stritch, Mooney, and McNicholas was singing his praises. Their expressions of gratitude for his hard work, acumen, and loyalty during the war were widely aired.[21]

Despite these arguments, the preponderance of opinion points to Spellman as instigator of O'Boyle's elevation. Archbishop Philip M. Hannan, O'Boyle's

19. Donoghue intv.
20. Arthur and Ellis intvs.
21. Ltr., McNicholas to O'Boyle, 11 Jul 1947, copy in AAD. See also Minutes of the Administrative Board, NCWC, Jul 1947, ACUA.

chancellor, noted that O'Boyle would often disagree with Spellman on some is-sue, but would just as frequently add, "You know, he made me the archbishop."[22] Historian Gerald Fogarty, who noted Spellman's communication with both Ci-cognani and the pope on the Washington appointment, conceded that on the East Coast, including Washington, Spellman's influence dominated.[23] Using Spellman's stormy relations with McIntyre as an example, biographer Francis Weber noted that while Spellman was never close to O'Boyle, he recognized tal-ent and loyalty and never let petty arguments cloud his judgment. Weber report-ed O'Boyle's self-deprecating comment on how Spellman offered McIntyre the choice between Washington and Los Angeles, "and I got what was left over."[24] Archbishop Donoghue took Weber's thesis a step farther: "Spellman liked the cardinal [O'Boyle], liked O'Boyle because he realized the cardinal was capa-ble."[25]

Some of these commentators dismissed O'Boyle's bow to Mooney and Ci-cognani as an effort to mask what he knew was Spellman's role. He wanted his new subordinates in Washington to understand that he was his own man and did not necessarily subscribe to Spellman's opinions. Nor, he wanted it understood, was he in any way beholden to or dependent on his former superior. As a new archbishop O'Boyle was never a loyal booster of Spellman's public outcries—the New York cemetery strike, for example—and by his own statements made it ob-vious that he did not intend to be identified with Spellman's viewpoint on many issues.[26]

The identity of his sponsor was probably far from the archbishop-elect's mind in the busy weeks leading up to his consecration on January 14, 1948. The Washington press, especially, reported fully on his remarks following public an-nouncement of the appointment. The *Evening Star* opened its account with a description of the fifty-one-year-old O'Boyle: "About 5 feet 10 inches tall, stocky, with graying hair parted on the left and wearing rimless spectacles. He has a ready and engaging smile." It also took note of a faint Irish brogue. Much was also made of the fact that the appointment marked the first time in the history of the American Church that a monsignor had been elevated directly to the rank of

22. Hannan intv.

23. Gerald Fogarty, *Patterns of Episcopal Leadership* (New York: Macmillan, 1989), p. 230, and *The Vatican and the American Hierarchy*, p. 314. See also Cohalan, *A Popular History of the Arch-diocese of New York*, p. 313.

24. Weber, *His Eminence of Los Angeles*, vol. 1, p. 76. See also his letter to the author, 5 Feb 1997, AAW.

25. Donoghue intv.

26. This point was made by Kelly, Arthur, and Ellis in their intvs.

archbishop. Coverage included the more significant news that the Washington archdiocese would include not just the capital, but also the five southern Maryland counties, including St. Mary's, the site of the landing of the *Ark* and the *Dove* in 1634 and the cradle of American Catholicism.

Speaking from his office at Catholic Charities, O'Boyle offered some biographical details for the reporters, emphasizing his Irish heritage, boyhood jobs in Scranton's mills and nearby farms, and his years at Mt. Loretto. Admitting that he had never lived in Washington, he assured reporters that he had visited the city many times, sometimes twice a week during the war, and had come to know many priests of the new diocese. He also supplied them with a formal statement which singled out Cardinal Spellman and Archbishop Cicognani for special thanks and acknowledged the "grave responsibility" he assumed as new chancellor of Catholic University, "a citadel of Catholic thought."[27]

In later weeks the appointment received major coverage in two important labor journals. *Labor,* a national weekly, underscored O'Boyle's childhood in a trade union family. It noted the new archbishop's pride in his union connections, his "deep sympathy with the labor movement," and his belief that only through organization could workers improve their condition. The paper went on to make a prediction: with Washington rapidly becoming a world capital, O'Boyle would eventually receive a cardinal's red hat. "His simple beginnings thus add to the drama of the occasion."[28] The *United Mine Workers Journal* also informed its readers of O'Boyle's close union connections and quoted from his reply to the union's congratulatory note in which he reported his attendance at the Mitchell rally in Scranton, concluding that "many years have passed since then and the UMW has accomplished great things for the benefit of the men who work so hard."[29]

O'Boyle dutifully responded to congratulations that streamed in from all sides while trying to wind up work at Catholic Charities. He also took time off for a quick trip to Washington at the behest of the apostolic delegate. Archbishop Cicognani advised him on some of the issues he would encounter in the capital and stressed the area's need for Catholic high schools. Cicognani asked him to treat construction as a priority project of his administration. O'Boyle used the trip to discuss pending business with Washington's aging auxiliary, Bishop John M. McNamara. He hoped to keep the visit private, so he asked McNamara to

27. *Star,* 3 Dec 1947 (source of quotes), and O'Boyle vertical file, Washingtoniana Collection, D.C. Public Library. See also *NYT,* 4 Dec 1947.
28. *Labor, A Weekly Newspaper,* 17 Jan 1948.
29. *United Mine Workers Journal,* 1 Feb 1948.

meet at his hotel, the Statler Hilton on Sixteenth Street. As luck would have it, he bumped into the rector of Washington's Sulpician seminary in the hotel corridor. With his secret blown, he decided to include a tour of St. Matthew's Cathedral on nearby Rhode Island Avenue. Msgr. John K. Cartwright, the rector, and his staff greeted O'Boyle on the steps of the cathedral and gave him a guided tour of what would shortly become his principal church.[30]

The day of consecration brought together many of the people who had figured in his life. The first pew on the center aisle of St. Patrick's was reserved for Uncle Stephen's family, Aunt Katie and Uncle Robert Parks, and Aunt Mary, Uncle Patrick Muldoon's widow. Bernie O'Boyle and his family and cousin William Higgins, all from New York, represented the O'Boyle clan. They were among those who received the new archbishop's first pontifical blessing during the *Te Deum* at the conclusion of the consecration Mass. On the altar was O'Boyle's old school friend and recently appointed auxiliary bishop of Scranton, Henry Klonowski, who with Bishop McNamara served as Cardinal Spellman's co-consecrators.

Msgr. Cartwright from Washington served as a deacon of honor along with Msgr. O'Reilly, O'Boyle's friend and landlord at St. Malachy's. Among the scores participating in the sanctuary were a number of Washington's senior priests, including Henry F. Grabenstein, John Tracy Ellis, John J. Coady, and William F. Stricker.[31] Colleagues from war relief, along with now-Archbishop McIntyre assisted, while his golfing buddy, Msgr. Jack O'Donnell, served as deacon and Msgr. Swanstrom as subdeacon. Bishop Bryan McEntegart delivered the homily. Also present watching the new bishop prostrate himself on the altar steps, wearing the vestments Pius XII and Cardinal Spellman wore at their consecrations, were sisters from Scranton's Marywood College. They included his special friend Sister Gemma and Sister Margaret Mary, a seamstress who had made clothes for Mary O'Boyle in the old days.[32]

A contingent of younger Washington priests, including Leo J. Coady, Joseph Teletchea, and Joseph Eckert, also made the trip to snowy New York to see their new bishop consecrated. With no seating reserved for them, they proceeded single file up the main aisle of St. Patrick's and across the sanctuary, hoping to lo-

30. Quinn and Arthur intvs. See also O'Boyle's Notes, pt. 27.

31. The Washington priests who served as chaplains were nominated by Msgr. Cartwright at O'Boyle's request. See, for example, among the many letters on the choices in the St. Matthew's Cathedral Archives, ltrs., Father Bernard Martin to Cartwright, 16, 17, and 24 Dec 1947. On Cartwright's appointment as a deacon of honor, see ltr., Cartwright to O'Boyle, 23 Dec 1947, same source.

32. "Notes by Sister Francis Gabriel, I.H.M., re: Bishop O'Boyle," copy in AAW.

cate the sacristy. Guided through a side passage and down a flight of stairs, they passed through yet another door only to find themselves locked outside on the street! Deciding that they had not come all the way from the capital to stand in the snow, they marched back in and commandeered places on the edge of the sanctuary around the altar. The men were unknown to O'Boyle, who found himself staring at a group of strangers throughout the ceremony. Later Father Coady answered O'Boyle's "What were you doing there?" with the explanation, "Your dang New Yorkers kicked us out."[33]

To O'Boyle's delight, also making the trip from Washington were three officials of the local St. Vincent de Paul conferences, who wanted to join all the other Catholic Charities representatives paying tribute to one of their own. Included in the group was Andrew Gleason, "in his black derby and a nip on his hip."[34] Gleason served as president of the St. Vincent de Paul at St. Aloysius parish where he, along with Msgr. Paul H. Furfey, Mary Margaret Walsh, and workers at the Friendship Houses and volunteers in the Christ Child Society served as the mainstay of Washington's charity network.[35]

Among the three thousand guests at the lengthy ceremony were Myron C. Taylor, representing President Truman, William O'Dwyer, now New York's mayor, former governor Herbert Lehman, and prominent New Dealer James Farley, along with representatives of the Protestant and Jewish relief organizations long associated with O'Boyle. The pontifical procession into the cathedral numbered five hundred participants; fifty bishops and abbots with their chaplain attendants added to the color and splendor of the ancient rite.[36] Of the many gifts and purses received by the new archbishop, probably none was more treasured than the episcopal ring given him by the Immaculate Heart of Mary sisters from Scranton. "We feel that your honor is our honor," the mother general told him, adding that the sisters considered him a member of their family. Another special remembrance: a chalice inscribed with the names of the donors, his old friend Henry Klonowski and three colleagues from war relief, Aloysius Wycislo, Stephen Bernas, and Robert Bates.[37]

33. Coady intv.

34. As quoted in ltr., Kirk to O'Boyle, 19 Jan 1951, St. Vincent de Paul Papers, ACUA.

35. Ltr., Kirk to O'Boyle, 19 Jan 1951, St. Vincent de Paul Papers, ACUA.

36. *NYT,* 15 Jan 1948. For a comprehensive account of the ceremony, see "In Division—Strength," *The Voice* (Feb 1948): pp. 8–9, 24ff. Probably due to Msgr. Cartwright's urging, historian John Tracy Ellis served as one of O'Boyle's chaplains. See ltr., O'Boyle to Ellis, 29 Dec 1947, Ellis Papers, ACUA.

37. Ltr., M.M.M. (Mother Mary Marcella) to O'Boyle, 8 Dec 1947, Archives of the I.H.M. Motherhouse. The chalice remained in O'Boyle's possession until his death and is now on exhibit in AAW. An example of one of the purses sent to O'Boyle was from Lawrence Gorman, S.J., repre-

In what the press dubbed his first public appearance as archbishop, O'Boyle devoted the Sunday after his consecration to a farewell visit to Mt. Loretto. He arrived late Saturday night, delayed by a snowstorm, to find the lights burning brightly in St. Elizabeth Cottage, where the sisters and older girls had stayed up to greet him. He began the next day with Mass in what was always called "the big church on the boys' side." Then with a host of sisters and priests from all over the city in tow, he spent the day with the children, many of whom could recall his living among them. After lunch he was treated to two separate variety shows staged by the boys and girls. Energized by the boys' band playing Irish melodies and the intricate patterns of the baton twirlers, O'Boyle found himself cheering the children while the rest of the audience cheered him.[38]

The new archbishop rode down to Washington on Tuesday, January 20, the eve of his installation. Accompanying him on the train were old friends Frank McIntyre, Bryan McEntegart, and Henry Klonowski. Conversation dwelt on the challenges of organizing a newly independent diocese. McIntyre and Klonowski, both well versed in the arcana of canon law, argued over how and when the new archbishop should formally renew the faculties of his priests. O'Boyle admitted that their discussion was of no interest to him, "because my knowledge of canon law was very, very limited."[39] (Actually his schooling in canon law, if not his experience, left him every bit as equipped in that subject as McIntyre.)

But if O'Boyle paid scant attention to such esoteric matters, he had carefully boned up on the history of his new see. An independent diocese for Washington had been debated for nearly a century. Rome, with an eye on political realities, wanted a prominent representative in the capital. The archbishops of Baltimore, aware that Washington's Catholic population was small and likely to remain so, resisted. Cardinal Gibbons had successfully fended off Vatican pressure, and his successor, Archbishop Curley, vigorously fought the Vatican's intent with the argument that the nation's capital "had occupied in the Archdiocese of Baltimore the place of any small town within the limits of the Premier See." But Rome was not to be denied this time, and "with a gun to his head," as historian John Tracy Ellis put it, Curley reluctantly recommended that the "See of Baltimore be known hereafter as the Archdiocese of Baltimore-Washington."[40]

---

senting some members of the Jesuit Community. See ltr., O'Boyle to Gorman, 23 Dec 1947, Varia Collection, Georgetown University Archives (hereafter GUA).

38. *Staten Island Times* and *NYT*, 19 Jan 1948, and O'Boyle, Notes, pt. 26. See also ltr., O'Boyle to Msgr. Edmund Fogarty (Mission director), 27 May 1981, AMIV.

39. Quoted in O'Boyle, Notes, pt. 26.

40. Ltr., Curley to Cicognani, 6 Mar 1939, Roman Letters, Curley Papers, AAB. Ellis' comment on this letter was made in his intv.

Rome considered such a compromise insufficient, and on July 22, 1939, a date meant to coincide with Washington's 150th anniversary, Pius XII issued a bull announcing the formation of the separate Archdiocese of Washington. With a bow to the loyal Curley, the pope added that "for the time being," the two distinct archdioceses would be united under one ordinary.[41] Although governed by one administration, the two cities would henceforth be canonically discrete entities, and, in an exception to the law that made holding two benefices illicit, Michael Curley was named ordinary of both the oldest and newest archdioceses in the United States. To the consternation of many old Washingtonians and of Archbishop Curley, who considered historic St. Patrick's in the downtown section of the city his pro-cathedral, the papal bull also designated St. Matthew's Church the cathedral seat of the Washington archbishop.

Although no one expected the union of the two jurisdictions to survive Curley's passing, the priests of Washington were left with several questions. Echoing the old Baltimore argument, some wondered how an archdiocese covering only Washington's sixty-four square miles, with thirty-four parishes, only twenty-seven of which were staffed by diocesan clergy, could survive. Speculation centered on the possibility that the new see might be configured to include parts of northern Virginia and nearby regions of Montgomery and Price George's Counties in Maryland. Such a move would correspond to the growing notion of a Washington metropolitan region. Many priests were concerned about their own future. For example, would those native to Baltimore now serving in Washington be allowed to choose where they would be incardinated?

The announcement of O'Boyle's appointment on December 4 answered such jurisdictional questions. With the addition of the five surrounding Maryland counties (Montgomery, Prince George's, Calvert, Charles, and St. Mary's), the new archdiocese now covered 2,104 square miles, with 84 parishes and 89 primary and secondary schools and an estimated Catholic population of 165,000 served by 139 diocesan priests and 55 order priests. All clergy would be incardinated in the archdiocese in which they were assigned as of December 3, 1947.[42]

News of O'Boyle's selection surprised the clergy of the new archdiocese. It also added to the concern of many. In general the clergy recognized the pressing need for a man on the spot. Stories were commonly exchanged about how the Baltimore chancery, clueless about conditions in Washington, nevertheless

41. The full text of the 22 Jul papal letter is found in Roman Letters, 1939, Curley Papers, AAB.
42. Statistics from Msgr. Robert O. McMain (archdiocesan historian), "Archdiocese of Washington is 40 Years Old," Jul 1988, copy in AAW. See also Arthur intv.

blithely decided issues concerning churches in the capital. Archbishop Hannan recalled the time he was assigned to revalidate the boundaries of Washington parishes only to discover that the Baltimore chancery had drawn boundaries through apartment complexes, with the ludicrous result that the living room of one apartment belonged to St. Thomas the Apostle parish while its kitchen was counted elsewhere.[43] Most priests agreed that Auxiliary Bishop McNamara, a forceful orator and tireless celebrant of liturgical functions, lacked essential leadership qualities. At the same time most had never heard of this monsignor from New York. When O'Boyle spoke of his many Washington friends, he could not have been counting local diocesan priests, but, rather, colleagues at the NCWC, the National Conference of Catholic Charities, and those involved in social work at Catholic University. To some his appointment was just another power play by the ambitious New York cardinal. They made much of the popular belief that O'Boyle was a deskman who had never served as a pastor and lacked experience in a parish. They rehashed the false information that "he never heard a confession." In short, Washington's priests had questions about their new boss. His every move would be scrutinized and discussed by a clergy that thirsted for a hands-on leader, but remained fearful that what they may have been given was a latter-day Northern carpetbagger.[44]

None of these misgivings were evident when O'Boyle's train pulled into Union Station on January 20. His party was met by a delegation of clergy led by Bishop McNamara and Msgr. Cartwright and accompanied by a large group of lay people, including cheering school children. After welcoming speeches by McNamara and Cartwright, the party took off for St. Matthew's Cathedral. Following yet another tour they retired to the rectory for dinner. Only then did O'Boyle present his credentials to the half-dozen consultors stationed in Washington, who formally accepted him as the archbishop of Washington.

He spent the night at St. Matthew's for what proved to be the first and last time. In fact O'Boyle was the nation's only ordinary who lacked a place to hang his hat. The cathedral rectory was too cramped to offer lodging, and the Baltimore chancery had made no practical preparations for his arrival in Washington. The rectory at St. Patrick's, which had been built with the idea that it would someday be home for a bishop, was the obvious solution. Like any other pastor eager to retain his independence, Msgr. John J. Russell at St. Patrick's might be forgiven any reluctance to take on so important a boarder. Nevertheless, he

43. Hannan intv.
44. Arthur, Hannan, and Quinn intvs.

Installation in St. Matthew's Cathedral. The new archbishop of Washington receives his staff of office from the apostolic delegate, Archbishop Amleto Cicognani.

bowed to the logic of his assistant, Father E. Robert Arthur. Since it was inevitable that the new archbishop would take advantage of the episcopal accommodations at St. Patrick's until a permanent home could be found, Arthur suggested that the pastor might as well earn credit for having invited him.

The installation ceremony had been carefully choreographed from Catholic Charities headquarters in New York. Msgr. Cartwright handled details in Washington, while O'Boyle provided lists of invitees, including, along with his New York friends and colleagues from Catholic Charities and war relief, many government and labor leaders. He arranged to have an invitation hand-carried to the White House. (President and Mrs. Truman did not attend.) Well into January he was still sending Cartwright additions to the list and suggested seating. (Concerning two Immaculate Heart of Mary sisters, for example: "These are very dear and close friends of mine. I would be pleased if you can arrange to give them good seats.") He also vetted seating arrangements for the head table at the luncheon at the Mayflower Hotel scheduled to follow the ceremony.[45] O'Boyle's old colleague at Catholic Charities, Joe Annin, arranged the public relations aspects of the affair, and Washington specialist Emmett Dougherty dealt with the media in the capital.[46]

These men arranged for the early release of O'Boyle's episcopal coat of arms and motto. As designed by heraldry expert William F. J. Ryan, it featured four quadrants colored in a patriotic red, white, and blue. Two quadrants carried symbols of Ireland, shamrocks borrowed from the coat of arms of Cardinal Spellman and referring to St. Patrick's Cathedral, where O'Boyle was ordained, and an oak tree taken from the traditional coat of arms of the O'Boyle clan in Ireland. Also in the new shield were three stars from the coat of Pius VI, the pope who appointed John Carroll America's first bishop, and three from George Washington's coat of arms. The new coat of arms also carried O'Boyle's motto, drawn from St. Paul's first letter to the Corinthians: *"State in Fide"* (Stand Firm in the Faith). As O'Boyle later reflected, these words were but a spiritual extension of a cardinal rule he had adopted early in life, "When you've got a job to do, do it."[47]

The apostolic delegate installed the new archbishop in his cathedral on January 21. The large church designed by the noted architect Grant LaFarge was

45. A considerable collection of correspondence, including ltr., O'Boyle to Cartwright, 5 Jan 1947 (source of quote), is filed in the Archives of St. Matthew's Cathedral.

46. Ltr., Dougherty to Annin, 8 Jan 1948, Archives of St. Matthew's Cathedral.

47. As quoted in *Star,* 4 Mar 1973.

packed with five hundred clergy, including nineteen bishops, scores of senior government officials and diplomats, and O'Boyle's friends and colleagues from New York. Addresses by Cicognani and McNamara were studded with lengthy references to John Carroll and the development of the American Church as well as to O'Boyle's singular service in war relief. For his part, the new archbishop delivered an inaugural address in which he reminded the local Catholic community of the spiritual dimension of good works while pledging himself to "preserve, promote, and expand all the good works, educational and charitable, with which your generosity and zeal have enriched Catholic life in this community."[48]

At the lunch that followed at the Mayflower Hotel, Archbishop McNicholas spoke on behalf of the American hierarchy. O'Boyle would have a long time to ponder one of McNicholas' asides. Turning to the new archbishop he said, "Archbishop, I do hope that you will have no trouble as Chancellor of the Catholic University."[49] The generous purse presented to the new archbishop to mark the occasion he later used to provide housing for the Newman Club at Howard University. The tiring but momentous day behind him, O'Boyle returned to St. Matthew's to retrieve his baggage and then on to St. Patrick's rectory, which would remain his home for almost a decade.

One ceremonious day followed another. On January 22 O'Boyle was officially introduced to the laity of the archdiocese in a so-called civic reception in Catholic University's gymnasium. Over three thousand invitees, including representatives from every parish and diocesan organization, along with spokesmen for the District of Columbia government and its board of trade, extended their greetings. As O'Boyle walked up the long aisle of the gymnasium, one priest was heard to remark, "I think, from his gait and posture, he's going to make his own decisions."[50]

Sometimes facile prognosticators get it right.

48. Quoted in *Catholic News*, 24 Jan 1948, which provided comprehensive coverage of the ceremony with lengthy quotes from the speakers.
49. Quoted in O'Boyle, Notes, pt. 27.
50. As quoted by Archbishop Hannan in *CS*, 13 Aug 1987.

CHAPTER 7

Learning on the Job

During his second week in Washington, the new archbishop called in a young priest to tell him that he was to be the archdiocese's first vice-chancellor. When Father Leo Coady protested that he did not know that much about canon law, O'Boyle responded, "And I don't know that much about being a bishop either. I've got to learn, and you go up there and learn."[1] In fact on one level O'Boyle's years in New York had superbly equipped him to lead a new ecclesial organization, but his expertise would be severely tested in the months to come. Ultimately, O'Boyle's striking performance at Catholic Charities and in war relief had been in the role of a subordinate. As such, he proposed bold initiatives, but executed decisions made by others. Now he was responsible for all decisions, a responsibility that can produce either inhibiting caution or impetuous activity.

In some other areas, most notably in the essential partnership that must exist between a bishop and the clergy and laity under his care, O'Boyle's experience in New York left something to be desired. His five years of pastoral experience were almost a quarter-century behind him and had occurred in a time and place profoundly different from postwar Washington. Even the episcopal style exemplified by mentors like Francis Spellman and Francis McIntyre would become obsolete in the next decades. As one senior New York cleric admitted, he understood O'Boyle's leadership style because he knew how Spellman and McIntyre operated. "If you talked back to [them] . . . they might wipe up the floor

1. As quoted in Coady intv.

with you, but the next day they could call and say, 'I have rethought. We'll do it your way.'"[2] Not many of O'Boyle's new subordinates, at least initially, were willing to talk back.

While the clergy of Washington would soon come to appreciate their new archbishop's profound respect for the priesthood, many of them would find it difficult to adapt to his quick decisions and his demand for unquestioned obedience. The more astute among them realized that his brusque manner and brook-no-opposition approach to decision making marked the insecurity of a newcomer and, at base, the shyness that the years in sophisticated New York had failed to diminish. Many, however, resented their new bishop's attitude, which proclaimed that the way things were done in New York was the best and only way to proceed in the capital.

Planning for the future of the Church in Washington had been allowed to drift during the war and Archbishop Curley's long illness; many decisions about personnel and property were urgently needed. As he had shown in previous assignments, O'Boyle was quite ready to make these decisions, but his shoot-from-the-hip style would produce some poor results in the early years. Those years were clearly a time of learning, for the clergy and laity of Washington, but most especially for the new archbishop.

Governing from St. Patrick's

Although O'Boyle would admit to learning on the job, that did not mean he had not already put considerable study into his new duties. During his last months in New York he had consulted tribunal officials and canvassed the chancery's department heads. They prepared a notebook that outlined in detail the steps to be taken in organizing a diocese, a tome he carefully studied. He otherwise rarely went outside Washington for advice. He might on occasion consult his friend Archbishop McIntyre on financial matters, deferring to his Wall Street experience. Especially early on, he frequently phoned "the Cardinal" to solicit Spellman's advice on Church affairs. For the most part, though, he relied on his own experiences, what he knew of the governance of the New York archdiocese, and how its principal players operated.[3] He treated his vicar, Bishop McNamara, with respect and kept him informed, but, like Curley before him, recognized Mc-

2. Kelly intv.
3. Quinn intv. Unless otherwise noted, the following information on the organization of the archdiocese is based on this interview and those of Arthur, Donoghue, and Hannan. In what follows they will be cited only when they are directly quoted.

Namara's limitations and rarely sought his counsel. Anxious to appear impartial in his appointments, he turned instead to Baltimore's chancellor, Msgr. Joseph M. Nelligan, for advice.

It was a logical move on O'Boyle's part. During Curley's illness Nelligan had directed personnel affairs, and, furthermore, he was Washington-born. But like many priests in the old archdiocese, Nelligan considered the capital a backwater and was remarkably ill-informed about its parishes and clergy. It was Nelligan who prompted O'Boyle to appoint Father James Cowhig, a young Roman-trained canon lawyer, his chancellor. It would take O'Boyle several years to realize his mistake. The rest of his major appointments were quickly and informally made. During his first evening at St. Patrick's he told Cowhig, who was an assistant at the historic parish, of his appointment and asked Msgr. John Russell, St. Patrick's pastor, to stay on as head of Catholic Charities. The following day he named Father John Spence director of Catholic education and Father E. Robert Arthur vice-officialis of the tribunal. Arthur, like Cowhig Roman-trained and an assistant at St. Patrick's, graduated from the Catholic University with a degree in canon law. He had worked in the Washington branch of the tribunal since 1938, but because of Arthur's youth O'Boyle prevailed upon the nationally respected Msgr. John K. Cartwright, rector of the cathedral, to accept the title of officialis, in this case a sinecure that left Arthur, the trained lawyer, to run the tribunal. Before the end of the first week O'Boyle had selected his ten consultors (four of them holdovers from the previous regime). In addition to McNamara and Cartwright, the board included seven senior pastors and the retired rector of the cathedral, Msgr. Edward L. Buckey. In succeeding weeks he named directors for the various archdiocesan organizations like Catholic Cemeteries and the Catholic Youth Organization.[4] To prevent the development of a curia mentality, and because of the shortage of priests, O'Boyle wisely insisted that all these appointees perform their new duties in addition to regular parish responsibilities.

O'Boyle accepted Msgr. Cartwright's offer of an office for the chancery consisting of two large rooms on the second floor of a townhouse owned by St. Matthew's at 1723 Rhode Island Avenue, N.W. There Cowhig with his reluctant assistant, Father Coady, and Father Arthur set up operations. Meanwhile, Spence opened an education office on nearby N Street, while Catholic Charities continued work at 1441 Rhode Island Avenue. The archbishop appropriated one of St. Patrick's front parlors for an office. A room across the hall was divided into of-

4. All these appointments were mentioned in the city papers. See, for example, *Star,* 12 and 19 Mar 1948. On 12 Mar 1948 *BCR* published extensive biographies of the appointees. Cowhig was initially made acting chancellor and was assigned to the position permanently later in the year.

fices for both his and the parish's secretaries. Cowhig found a typist-receptionist for the archbishop, "a respectful but somewhat breezy" woman, according to O'Boyle, but for many years the chancellor would serve as the archbishop's official secretary. Two of St. Patrick's assistant priests shared duty as chauffeur for a man who had not attempted to drive since prewar New York days and who declared Washington's traffic too dangerous to try again.

O'Boyle later concluded that his nine years at St. Patrick's had been "all in all" a pleasant experience.[5] He seemed to make a genuine effort at first to stay out of parish affairs, quietly saying Mass at a side altar and limiting his public appearances to major feast days and those special events that highlighted St. Patrick's citywide ministry. These included the Pan-American Mass for the hemisphere's diplomats on Thanksgiving Day, the Police and Firemen's Mass on Mother's Day, and the grand celebration of the Irish on St. Patrick's Day. Enlisted as a member of the Hibernians during his first year in Washington, O'Boyle was proud to welcome Eamon De Valera, the great Irish leader, to St. Patrick's.[6] He seemed genuinely uncomfortable with the ceremonial aspects of his new office, and his appearances at the cathedral were only when required. The cathedral staff discovered he needed guidance on how to vest in episcopal attire. His masters of ceremonies—at first young cathedral assistants like Father Louis Quinn, then later his longtime liturgical expert and close companion, the Sulpician Father Walter Schmitz—spent many hours coaching him in the rubrics.

No one, however, could improve his singing. The musical Father Joseph Teletchea tried, so did Father Coady, but even O'Boyle realized the hopelessness of the effort. It was his one failure everyone felt free to kid about. When once he admitted that he "couldn't follow a note," one young priest readily agreed and told him that his efforts at High Mass were "a cruelty" to his audience. One lay friend unexpectedly congratulated him on his singing after a service, only to be told by a clerical wag, "Oh boy, now I know why you're so favored around here." Although even he would joke about his tin ear, O'Boyle could still take umbrage at criticism from fellow bishops. Once while trying to chant during a special Mass at the Shrine of the Immaculate Conception, he noticed a visiting bishop, a liturgical expert, stifling a laugh. After the ceremony an irritated archbishop confided to his cousin, "Did you see that son-of-a-gun laugh? I know I can't sing, but they don't have to insult me."[7] Nor was he an orator in the true sense. Although he

5. O'Boyle, Notes, pt. 27.

6. *BCR,* 29 Jun 1949.

7. Many of O'Boyle's colleagues have commented on his musical limitations. See, in particular, intvs. with Gillen (first quote), McArdle (second quote), and Muldoon (third quote).

would eventually develop into a forceful and effective extemporaneous speaker, his longer sermons and addresses, often written by others and lacking O'Boyle's usual concision and pointed emphasis, failed to engage his audiences.

Despite his new eminence, he never abandoned his taste for simple living. His rooms at St. Patrick's overlooking Tenth Street and a major department store's loading dock were little improvement over accommodations at St. Malachy's.[8] Still, even these modest qualities entailed some sacrifice from those around him. Realizing that O'Boyle was an especially light sleeper, priests on the floor above removed their shoes before entering their rooms at night. His chancellor later recalled that the lights flashing on the multilined telephone could waken the archbishop. Surprisingly in a man from the Broadway district of New York City, he was constantly awakened by the early morning sanitation crews and their noisy trucks.[9] When he finally moved to the calm of the Tenleytown in far-northwest Washington in 1957, one cleric predicted that the boss would soon be complaining about the noise of grass growing. (After his first night in his new home on Warren Street, O'Boyle reportedly told his secretary that he had never realized just how much noise birds made.)

He remained, as always, an early riser. To their considerable discomfort, many Washington priests were apt to receive business calls from their archbishop at 7:00 a.m. At the same time he was remarkably accessible, ready to interrupt office routine for a phone call or even an impromptu meeting. All quickly learned that their calls would not be screened, nor would elaborate appointment procedures prevent almost instant contact. To the delight of many, he placed little emphasis on episcopal dignity. To the overawed domestic who insisted on larding her conversation with "your excellency" this and "your excellency" that, the archbishop suggested, "Eleanor, why not say 'your excellency' when you bring me coffee at breakfast, and just let that once do for the day?"[10]

The rectory staff accustomed itself to his simple habits. Weather permitting, he could be seen every day pacing in the shadowed walkway next to the church as he recited his breviary and daily rosary. Sunday mornings would find him, clad in a plain cassock, chatting with worshippers. His favorite spot was near one

8. The following paragraphs on life at St. Patrick's are taken from the author's *A Parish for the Federal City: St. Patrick's in Washington, 1794–1994* (Washington, D.C.: The Catholic University of America Press, 1994), pp. 323–26.

9. Hannan discussed the noise problem with department store executives. See ltr., Hannan to William Jones (attorney with Hamilton and Hamilton), 24 Jun 1955, Hamilton file, AAW.

10. As quoted in William S. Abell, ed., *Patrick Cardinal O'Boyle As His Friends Knew Him* (Washington, D.C.: Privately published, 1986), p. 47.

of the church's side doors, which he would hold open for departing visitors with a brief greeting or longer conversation. Many parishioners and especially the children from nearby St. Patrick's Academy might fail to associate their amiable doorman with the new archbishop, but he soon became known to the denizens of Washington's old downtown during the thirty-minute constitutional he took around the neighborhood most evenings. Accompanied by one of St. Patrick's young assistants and equipped with a pocketful of quarters to help the neighborhood's down-and-outers, O'Boyle learned firsthand something of the poverty and dislocation that were beginning to grip the core of his adopted city. He knew some of the beggars were professionals (one woman repeatedly received five-dollar bills in response to her pleas for her bogus family). He detested being taken advantage of, but nevertheless continued handouts to one and all. Using this modest charity as a barometer of need, O'Boyle was dismayed to find as the months passed that his cache of quarters was long exhausted before he reached home. One of his close colleagues suggested that this firsthand contact with the victims of poverty and drugs, who were beginning to haunt the old downtown area, provided O'Boyle with experience that would redefine his outlook on the needs of the modern city.[11]

St. Patrick's new resident tried his best to make the rectory a relaxed and amicable place, a difficult challenge at a time when the household was deeply divided over how the parish and the new diocese should function. His sometimes brusque New York style of repartee did not endear him to everyone. The first night in his new home he managed to insult the cook, who took umbrage at his wisecrack about the rich fare at St. Patrick's, overlooking the extra care that had gone into his welcoming dinner. He enjoyed needling and bantering with the "family" and guests, especially at the dinner table, and his more astute companions learned that a snappy comeback was the best response. Yet, as might be expected, no matter how sincerely O'Boyle resolved to remain a non-interfering boarder, no one could remain indifferent to the extended presence of the archbishop in their midst.

It was also inevitable that, despite his good intentions, O'Boyle would begin to insert himself into parish affairs. When, for example, he discovered that the magnificent Oriental rug covering St. Patrick's sanctuary floor also covered a grand shamrock mosaic, he ordered it removed. Although an understandable reaction in a son of proud Irish immigrants, it clearly challenged the prerogatives of the pastor. His reaction to a lengthy pre-Midnight Mass concert by the

11. Hannan intv.

parish's famed choir also demonstrated a curious disregard for the pastor's position. Squirming in his sanctuary seat, he sent someone to the choir loft with the pointed request that they sing "Jingle Bells."

On a far more serious note, O'Boyle listened to Father Cowhig explain that the popular and gregarious Msgr. Russell was unhappy in the old downtown parish and missed the bustle of a close-knit, active congregation with its busy parish organizations. O'Boyle must have been aware of the philosophical differences and increasing tension between Russell and Cowhig, but without bothering to check on Cowhig's story, he appointed Russell pastor of the lively and vibrant Nativity parish when that position became vacant in October 1948. To the consternation of the brash young chancellor's many critics, O'Boyle then appointed Cowhig administrator of St. Patrick's, a premier post in the archdiocese.[12] Father Arthur once asked why Cowhig was appointed simply an administrator. O'Boyle explained that he considered himself St. Patrick's pastor. When the canon lawyer explained that such a move was not permitted under a Church law that forbade anyone's holding two benefices at once, he was ignored. During the rest of O'Boyle's long sojourn in the old parish, Cowhig and his successor served as administrator, never pastor.

Cinderblock O'Boyle

The new ordinary's most immediate challenge was to meet the physical needs of the spectacularly growing Catholic population in the Washington area. This population was destined to almost triple in the next twenty years, and even in 1948 the outlines of this massive growth were discernible. The Baltimore chancery had largely ignored growth predictions. In 1946, for example, one Washington pastor visited the chancery to warn Msgr. Nelligan of the need for a new parish in the rapidly developing Chillum area of Prince George's County, only to be dismissed with the advice that if he thought it desirable, he should purchase land in the area on his own. The pastor considered it a diocesan responsibility and did nothing. Baltimore continued to ignore the situation, and by the time O'Boyle arrived the crisis had extended far beyond the boundaries of Chillum. In another case the Baltimore chancery agreed to buy the last prime piece of land in the Four Corners region of Montgomery County only after the local pastor threatened to buy it himself and sell it back to the archdiocese later at a handsome profit.

12. Dade, Arthur, and Hannan intvs. See especially intv. with Msgr. Joyce Russell, John Russell's brother.

With needs so widespread and funds limited, O'Boyle's first duty was to set priorities. Here his newcomer status only added to the challenge. For example, the first delegation that met with him after his installation represented the Mt. Olivet Cemetery Association. Its president, Msgr. Cartwright, used the occasion to warn O'Boyle that the venerable cemetery was rapidly filling and new cemetery space must be developed immediately. The group pressed their ordinary with the urgency of the matter, but when O'Boyle ordered an inventory he discovered that in fact Mt. Olivet had sufficient capacity left for an indefinite period. Clearly, the association had misread their new man, who reveled in accurate statistics. At the first consultors meeting, on March 9, 1948, he appointed a Commission on Parishes to determine the location of new parishes and set their boundaries. Its members, headed by Bishop McNamara, were expected to hold hearings, conduct on-site inspections, and make recommendations. The consultors would then recommend which properties should be purchased and suggest the order in which the archdiocese would fulfill the many requests for construction in the newly formed parishes as well as for needed improvements and additions to existing buildings.

O'Boyle was heartened by the response of the consultors, who eagerly discussed the need for new churches, schools, and convents. They also asked for immediate consideration of a new Providence Hospital and especially an early beginning to the projected city high school, the one the apostolic delegate had pressed on the archbishop-elect the previous December. This latter subject must have given O'Boyle pause when he learned that only half of the two million dollars needed for the proposed 800-pupil school had been collected. Also cause for concern: at the end of this first meeting the very senior Msgr. Thomas Smyth broke his silence to observe that, while everything discussed that day was worthy, only two were important at the moment, the high school and a home for the bishop, "because if you leave it to these men [gesturing to his fellow consultors] you will be here at St. Patrick's until you are carried out."[13]

The archbishop took the point. He might get plenty of useful advice from these senior pastors, but any action was squarely up to him and his new chancery. He began by tackling finances. Even before his installation he had heard from his old colleague in the National Conference of Catholic Charities, Msgr. O'Grady, about funding sources. Pointing to the numerous legacies left by Washington Catholics to the archbishop of Baltimore, O'Grady argued that most

13. O'Boyle, Notes, pt. 27. The cardinal concluded the notes for his proposed memoirs with a brief summary of the needs of his new archdiocese and his first meeting with the consultors.

were intended by their donors for Catholic agencies and institutions in the capital. He recommended that O'Boyle examine all such legacies over the past quarter-century and use his findings to buttress a demand for a fair share of such moneys as well as the income from any foundations established by Baltimoreans for diocese-wide charities. If it were decided that funds left by Baltimoreans should be used exclusively in Baltimore, then it would follow that funds contributed by Washingtonians over the years should be used exclusively in the new archdiocese.

Since his days in the seminary O'Boyle had showed a willingness to insist on his rights, even at the risk of earning his superiors' disapproval. As O'Grady had implied, Rome had prescribed a fair financial division when it split the two archdioceses in 1948, but, uncharacteristically, O'Boyle made no move to press his fair claim. Nor would Baltimore's new archbishop, Francis P. Keough, offer to redress the imbalance in assets, and, given the need for the postwar expansion of church facilities in both dioceses, could any payment from Baltimore be expected in the near future. (Only in 1961, after years of negotiations, did Baltimore offer and O'Boyle accept what his chancellor later described as a bad deal. As final settlement of the ordered division of assets, Baltimore agreed to pay the debt of St. Augustine's parish. Contracted by Archbishop Curley in 1936, it was the largest single debt in the new diocese.)[14]

O'Grady had also made a pitch for an annual fund drive in Washington similar to the highly successful ones O'Boyle had been so closely associated with in New York. O'Grady denigrated the antiquated parish assessment method of fund raising still favored by some senior pastors. Their argument that membership in the Community Chest precluded an annual drive, he claimed, was untenable, and he urged O'Boyle to adopt the more efficient and effective system of raising funds.[15] Again uncharacteristically, the new archbishop deferred to the pastors, and the annual appeal, which later would bring in millions of dollars for the Church in Washington, was postponed for more than a decade.

Soon after the first consultors meeting, O'Boyle was visited by the vice-president of Washington's leading bank, who offered the archdiocese unlimited financing at three and a half percent. O'Boyle promised to consider the proposal, but his conviction that the bank was not being overly generous was confirmed when, in a conversation with Cardinal Stritch, he learned that the Chicago archdiocese was securing loans at a full percentage point lower. O'Boyle promptly

14. Hannan intv. Hannan was O'Boyle's chancellor at the time of the settlement.
15. Memo, O'Grady to O'Boyle, no subj., 15 Dec 1947, copy in NCWC Papers, ACUA.

called in the banker and asked if he considered the capital in any way inferior to Chicago. After assuring O'Boyle that it was not, the chastened banker promised that the new archdiocese would also get its loans at the lower rate.

Using New York as a model, O'Boyle worked to centralize control of all real estate and construction projects in his chancery. While friends in Congress arranged for passage of a private bill that placed the archdiocese's assets in a corporation sole, all pastors were informed that any expenditure over $1,000 must have his specific approval. As a result the consultors spent long hours balancing the need for heating and organ repair in this parish against the requirement for new lighting, gutters, and desks in that school. This time-consuming scrutiny at least provided a basis for setting priorities within a limited budget.[16]

The pace of construction and rehabilitation was astonishing. During his first forty-six months in town O'Boyle established thirteen new parishes and nineteen new schools. He also completed major property acquisitions and new buildings for twenty-five other parishes and diocesan institutions. All but $788,000 of this nearly $9 million price tag had been paid by December 1951.[17] Some of the new parishes had actually existed before O'Boyle's arrival, in the form of missions of established parishes, and already possessed land and buildings, usually in the form of temporary sanctuaries or, in rare cases like St. Bernadette's in Silver Spring, a large school. Others, however, had necessitated selection and purchase of land and the inauguration of a preliminary building program. The archbishop became an enthusiastic reader of Washington's classified real estate ads—"my other Bible," he called them—and toured the suburban counties, especially those areas scheduled for development, in search of appropriate sites for future parishes.

As time passed his usual guide on these tours was Father Philip M. Hannan. A Washington native and veteran of the famed 82nd Airborne Division in World War II, Hannan was trained in canon law at the Catholic University before being drafted by Cowhig in late 1948 to replace his assistant, Father Coady, who after more schooling had moved on to Catholic Charities. Hannan's family was prominent in the capital's business community, and he was familiar with real estate trends and commercial conditions in the metropolitan region. His first serv-

16. Ltr., Cowhig to Rev. Pastor, 25 May 1948, Chancery file, AAW. For a detailed account of the consultors' work, see, for example, Meeting of Consultors, 19 Mar 1949 through 22 Jan 1950 (see especially meeting of 19 Dec 1949), same file. The bill creating the corporation sole (80th Cong., 2d sess. HR 6203, 12 Apr 1948, approved 29 May 1948) was introduced in the House of Representatives by Joseph P. O'Hara of Minnesota. See *Star*, 13 Apr 1948.

17. "Summary of Archdiocesan Construction Projects to Date," 31 Dec 1951, Progress Report file, AAW.

ice to O'Boyle, a man of considerable organizational skills but no experience in land acquisition and building, was to tutor him in the arcane points of property development.

The archbishop was not a willing student. His conception of parish design was clearly formed by his New York experience and, ignorant of the role of the automobile in the suburbs, was based on the assumption that every Catholic should live no more than a mile-and-a-half from church. Thus parishes should stand three miles apart at the most. Hannan, who familiarized himself with the developers' plans by studying the Suburban Sanitary Commission's projected water and sewer lines, was opposed to any three-mile standard. He argued that the diocese should tie property purchases to the location of projected housing developments. While O'Boyle was extremely cautious about investing in property, Hannan's mantra was "buy, buy." They would drive through the yet empty areas of Montgomery and Prince George's Counties with an eye on the odometer. Hannan discovered that if the parcel he proposed for purchase fell within the three-mile rule, he would earn a grudging "if it's three miles . . . all right." But O'Boyle himself would have clocked the distance, and if the property fell outside his limit, it would require a forceful lecture on the part of his savvy subordinate to win approval.[18]

By far the most costly of these early projects was construction of Archbishop John Carroll High School. O'Boyle had expressed his gratitude to the consultors for their pledge of support for the school project at their first meeting, but old Msgr. Smyth's warning about the lassitude of these gentlemen and the need for a push from the ordinary contained more than a grain of truth. With contributions lagging, O'Boyle decided to impose an assessment on each of the forty-six parishes that would be sending students to the new boys' school. He was reluctant to do so, he told the pastors, but, he reminded them, they had all agreed that assessments spread over a three-year period were preferable to a diocesan fund drive.[19] He tried in vain to recruit James Norris to organize the management of the school, but his old colleague preferred to remain with War Relief Services. He did succeed, however, in recruiting the Augustinian Fathers to provide the teaching staff.[20]

18. Hannan intv.

19. See, for example, ltr., O'Boyle to Very Rev. Arthur A. O'Leary (pastor of Holy Trinity), 1 Mar 1949, Parish file, AAW.

20. Ltrs., O'Boyle to John T. Sheehan, O.S.A. (Augustinian provincial), 5 Jun 1950, and to Joseph M. Dougherty, O.S.A., 10 May 1951, John Carroll High School file, AAW. On O'Boyle's effort to recruit Norris, see Kupke, "James J. Norris," pp. 231–32.

The new school, completed a year ahead of schedule, was dedicated by the apostolic delegate thirty-three months after he pressed the project on O'Boyle. When the first of the now-projected thousand students began classes in September 1951, the total indebtedness on the new $2 million institution was less than $59,000. One fact about this first freshman class merited headlines in Washington's papers: 17 of the 250 students were African Americans, representing a racial breakthrough in the capital.[21]

An unusual aspect of this building program, unheard of in a nonunion town like Washington, was the fact that the son of a Scranton steelworker insisted that, despite the cost, all construction in the archdiocese be performed by union labor. Some pastors objected because, they pointed out, insistence on union labor deprived their own parishioners, mostly nonunion workers, of the chance to bid on parish jobs. O'Boyle was adamant, and for this and his public pronouncements on the rights of working men and women, he earned the high regard of national labor leaders like George Meany and Arthur Goldberg.

Near the end of his life, O'Boyle boasted that every building project in his time employed union labor, but in fact there were exceptions.[22] When union contractors complained to Msgr. Cartwright that the cathedral continued to rely on the services of a nonunion electrical contractor, Cartwright pointed out that the contractor was an African American whose black electricians had performed satisfactorily for some years. O'Boyle, well aware of the poor civil rights record of the unions, backed the nonunion firm's retention. On one occasion, after almost a decade of insisting on union workers, O'Boyle was irritated to learn that some contractors were demanding portal-to-portal pay for a small job on church buildings in Leonardtown, in southern Maryland's St. Mary's County, adding the cost of daily round trips from Washington to the high price of the job. It was a stupid move, and O'Boyle would have none of it. He asked Father George Higgins, the labor expert at the NCWC, to sit in on a meeting he had arranged with a group of union leaders from the building trades. After listening to their arguments for the extra money, he reminded them of his allegiance to the union cause. He was planning an addition to the house he would soon be moving into, he told them. That job was being done by union labor despite the extra cost, "but that's alright *[sic]*, I believe in that." He then asked each of the assembled leaders in turn if their homes had been built by union labor. Such conditions

21. *Star,* 9 Sep 1951, and *WP,* 10 Sep 1951.
22. The retired cardinal reminisced about his building program in the *Catholic Light,* 31 Jul 1986.

were practically unheard of in Washington at that time, and each had to admit that his house was no exception. O'Boyle had made his point. They were dismissed, and the Leonardtown work was given to nonunion contractors. O'Boyle's little drama sought to confirm two trends: his continued commitment to the union cause, as well as his determination not to be hoodwinked by unreasonable union tactics.[23]

This confrontation had a curious aftereffect. Some of the disgruntled union leaders retaliated by arranging for a picket line at Mt. Olivet Cemetery protesting the use of unorganized laborers. O'Boyle was infuriated by suggestions from a Labor Department official that distribution of a few bottles of whiskey among the desultory picketers would solve the problem. He simply ignored the demonstration, and it went away.[24]

While statistically impressive and almost debt free, O'Boyle's early building program proved in the end to be poorly conceived, badly executed, and inadequate to meet its intended goal. Haunted by the specter of debt, he had decided to meet the pressing need for new parishes with functional structures, all-purpose buildings with space for classrooms and a large auditorium doubling as a temporary church. His idea of "get it up and fix it later" proved disastrous, especially when planning and supervision of construction emanated directly from downtown. Critics liked to recall the time a supplier pulled up in his truck at a construction site and announced that he had a load of bricks for somebody named O'Boyle.[25]

Many of the new buildings were found inadequate for the needs of the congregation from the day their doors opened. With the prevailing one-size-fits-all mindset, all plans and construction decisions were centered in the chancery, resulting in costly mistakes and notably poor design. The habit of building first and appointing a pastor later left the archbishop with no one to check if contractors were proceeding correctly and, most important, no one to advise him on the special needs of a particular community and its ability and willingness to finance a building program. One early exception to this sequence in parish development occurred when O'Boyle appointed Father James H. Brooks pastor of a yet-to-be-organized Our Lady Queen of Peace parish in Washington's Southeast section. Brooks moved to the area and spent time exploring the community, surveying its

23. The story is related by Higgins in his intv., which is also the source of the quote.
24. Hannan intv.

25. Donoghue intv. Many witnesses to O'Boyle's years in Washington comment on the failures of his early building program. The word "disaster" was commonly used in their descriptions of the results. See, for example, Arthur, Hannan, Quinn, and O'Brien intvs.

needs, and interviewing the Catholics who would form his new congregation. He even began celebrating Sunday Mass in a theater in the neighborhood and collecting a down payment for a building that met the community's requirements.

The heart of the problem was O'Boyle's imperfect understanding of financing and almost atavistic fear of debt. Taking advantage of an economic downturn in 1953, Father Hannan obtained an offer of a line of credit for the archdiocese at two percent interest, enough to develop a number of new parishes whose congregations could easily handle a two percent debt. But when he approached his boss with the suggestion that he apply for a $20 million line of credit, O'Boyle recoiled in horror. Hannan recorded O'Boyle's reaction: "Wow! That floored him. All he could see was a $20 million debt, while I was only talking to him about a line of credit. I never could get that from him."

O'Boyle wanted no parish saddled with a debt that could not be discharged at a rate of ten to fifteen percent a year. Although many growing postwar congregations could easily afford a large, long-term debt, few could adhere to a strict ten percent annual payoff, especially in their first years. Yet O'Boyle could not bring himself to accept a more optimistic view of the financial future, so loans for construction were sharply limited, and the chance to build adequately and well went by the board. In time he would learn to delegate more responsibility for building to pastors, who, in the case of new parishes, would be installed before building began or even in some cases before the land had been purchased. In time he would even come to take some satisfaction in the nickname "Cinderblock O'Boyle," bragging a little about the $300 million in construction (including the Shrine of the Immaculate Conception) during his administration. It is not all that clear, however, whether the sobriquet "Cinderblock" was meant as a compliment on the quantity of his work, or rather a comment on the quality of those early buildings.

Relations with the Clergy and Laity

Returning from an inspection of future parish sites in late 1948, Msgr. Cartwright posed a question: "Where," he asked O'Boyle, "are you going to get the priests to take care of all these new parishes that we are projecting?"[26] Historically, the capital had not proved to be a fertile source of vocations. Most blamed it on the region's predominantly transient population. If a young man in the city felt called to the priesthood, he would most likely return to his home dio-

---

26. As quoted in O'Boyle, Notes, pt. 28.

cese. Over the years, therefore, Washington had come to depend on Baltimore for most of its clergy. These priests automatically became part of the new archdiocese after the split. With the Baltimore source now dried up, the need to develop a diocesan clergy was an urgent priority despite the part-time help of religious priests studying at Catholic University. It appeared that O'Boyle had netted his first recruit during his installation ceremony. As the new archbishop received the pledge of fidelity from each of his priests, he was surprised to find one of his old New York colleagues kneeling before him. When asked why he was pledging obedience, the visitor explained that he had joined the wrong line during the procession and could not find a way out!

Alas, the archbishop was unable to keep the New Yorker in Washington, but shortly after Msgr. Cartwright raised the issue of the shortage of priests O'Boyle launched a systematic effort to recruit personnel. He could depend on old friends in New York to encourage young men to study for Washington. Thus Msgr. Monaghan, the labor priest, directed Joseph O'Brien to the new archdiocese, while another colleague was instrumental in pointing stock trader James Gillen away from Wall Street to the priesthood and to Washington. Some of his fellow bishops proved very generous. In those early years O'Boyle received four candidates from the Diocese of Newark alone. When he asked Scranton's Bishop William J. Hafey to direct some of his surplus candidates to Washington, O'Boyle's new director of vocations, Father Hannan, was invited to recruit among Hafey's seminarians. Within a few months he had three of them signed up. Hannan also made numerous trips to Ireland where, with the permission of various bishops, seminary rectors provided him with lists of suitable candidates to approach. These young seminarians would agree to serve in Washington for three to six years, after which they could return home or apply for incardination. Washington would pay half their education fees and all travel expenses. In later years these agreements became less formal, and during O'Boyle's tenure in office, Ireland supplied Washington with scores of priests.[27]

Ex-paratrooper Hannan proved a good choice for vocation director. A regular guest in religion classes at Georgetown and Catholic Universities, he also talked frequently with seniors in the area's high schools about the priesthood. These talks proved a major source for local candidates, but as late as October 1951, while O'Boyle could point to 101 seminarians preparing for service in the archdiocese, the thirty-two students entering the first-year class included only

27. Hannan, O'Brien, and Gillen intvs. See also O'Boyle, Notes, pt. 28.

four Washingtonians. He used this disturbing statistic to highlight the transient nature of the Church in the capital and to issue a challenge: "That is a problem that really is a problem—to get people to think about the diocese as a diocese—to get some solidarity in it." Once this mindset was achieved, he reasoned, a native clergy would follow.[28]

Under pressure to build churches and schools, the archbishop made no move to establish a seminary. After inspecting Detroit's new seminary in 1950, he told Cardinal Mooney that while he would welcome a similar establishment in Washington, it would probably be left to his fourth successor to do the job.[29] During his years in Washington he enrolled men in many seminaries around the country, especially St. Mary's in Baltimore and Theological College at Catholic University. Although he always retained a jaundiced view of the products of the North American College in Rome, Washington was represented in each year's class. He left selection of candidates for the prestigious Roman education up to his chancellor in consultation with the professors at St. Mary's, but he did maintain a lively interest in the students. In keeping with his usual aversion to any hint of elitism, he needled the Roman-trained priests and kidded them about their supposed European ways.[30] The archbishop would in time found a minor seminary. Before then he encouraged boys with an interest in the priesthood to attend St. Charles College in Catonsville, Maryland. Signaling his encouragement of such schooling, he participated in the school's centennial celebration in November 1948 and enthusiastically asked that, as one trained by some noted Sulpicians, he be considered an honorary Sulpician.[31]

In the case of young priests especially, O'Boyle readily assumed the role of spiritual father. A man of simple faith and piety, he made a point of meeting with candidates on the eve of their ordination to encourage them to retain the ardor they felt that night throughout their priestly lives. Should they encounter any difficulties they were urged to give him a call. He placed special importance on their spiritual exercises; the annual clergy retreat always was a highlight of his year. He even revived the priests' choir and appointed the talented Father Elmer T. Fisher to lead its performances at the retreats and other clergy functions such as the funerals of priests.[32] The tough exterior so esteemed in the New York

28. As quoted in *CS*, 2 Nov 1951.
29. Ltr., O'Boyle to Mooney, 3 Jul 1950, AAD. He was off by one. Cardinal McCarrick, his third successor, established a diocesan seminary in 2002.
30. Duffy intv. Duffy was in the third postwar class at the North American College.
31. "Joy Begins at Home," *Alumni Bulletin of St. Charles College* (Mar 1949).
32. Ltr., Chancellor Cowhig to Rev. Elmer T. Fisher, 9 Apr 1949, Chancery file, AAW.

archdiocese demanded that priests avoid any show of kindness or humility. Such virtues were considered private and personal. Thus O'Boyle used a brusque exterior to mask a caring leader, solicitous of the feelings of others.[33] Some could attest to receiving a reprimand from the archbishop, only to be greeted the next morning with a phoned apology. Few, however, subjected to his chilly, businesslike interviews, would ever know how much he agonized over the placement of his young priests. He personally pored over and altered assignment rosters designed by the chancery, worrying whether each new assistant would be happy and productive in his duties.

Only his closest associates would ever know how often he was guilty of private acts of kindness. Once, for example, he learned that one of the Holy Cross deacons who helped out at St. Patrick's was about to be ordained and, because of differences in his non-Catholic family, would celebrate his first Mass privately without fuss in his congregation's house of studies. Instead, O'Boyle arranged for a first Mass with all the splendor St. Patrick's could provide followed by a bang-up reception for the young man's friends.[34] When he learned that young Father Gillen was practically commuting to New York to care for his aged mother, O'Boyle quietly pulled strings for her transfer to the Carmelite Sisters' care in Georgetown. (Later during a pastoral visit to the institution, O'Boyle told the elderly and somewhat confused resident that he had recently promoted her "Jimmy," whereupon she shot back, to O'Boyle's delight, "Did you give him a raise?") In later years close associates witnessed the doughty old warrior worrying about the situation of those leaving their priestly duties during the birth control controversy. He wanted to make sure that they were provided for and retained their medical insurance.

According to O'Boyle's code of conduct, kindnesses were never to be broadcast, and he made sure that all such evidences of a softhearted, caring executive were rigidly suppressed. Unaware of this facet of their new archbishop's character, most priests were left with the impression of a rigid, rule-bound boss, cursed like so many Irish-Americans who considered "what will the neighbors think" a major criterion for conduct. From the earliest days they endured his badgering about a proper dress code for priests, exemplified by his campaign to make them wear hats in public and cassocks in the rectory. A man who enjoyed an extremely

---

33. Donoghue, Arthur, and O'Brien intvs. These three witnesses all agreed that O'Boyle tried to mask his deep regard for the priests with his brusque manners.

34. As related by Bp. Lyons in Sister Virginia Hughes, *Through His Eyes: A Memoir of Bishop Thomas Lyons* (Washington, D.C.: Abbeyfeale Press, 1992), pp. 35–36.

simple life style, he railed against any sign of ostentatious living. He urged boat lovers among the clergy to abandon their "cruiser cabins," his risibly mistaken reference to the craft some priests used on their days off to ply the area's water-ways.[35]

Nor was disconnect between bishop and clergy limited to the lower ranks. Like their assistants, senior pastors tended to resent O'Boyle's frequently used expression "my boys."[36] What he meant in a spirit of paternal care they under-stood as a patronizing attitude. While even the Baltimoreans among them recog-nized the need for a local ordinary and especially for one with executive experi-ence, some questioned the theological competence of a man who bragged that he had learned all the theology he needed to know at his mother's knee. Chancellor Cowhig was openly critical of O'Boyle's competence in matters of canon law, and even the cathedral rector, the erudite Msgr. Cartwright, differed frequently with the newcomer. A nationally known preacher with close connections to Church leaders throughout the country (he was a classmate of Archbishop Spellman's), Cartwright found it difficult to work with the Scranton steelwork-er's son. Exasperated over some difference, he once resigned his post, only to have second thoughts and return a few days later saying he had reconsidered and asking O'Boyle to reinstate him. Aware of the extreme embarrassment Cart-wright was enduring, O'Boyle immediately agreed, telling him that he was doing a fine job. In fact, O'Boyle respected Cartwright for his work at the cathedral and as an intellectual and cultural ornament in the diocese.

Another intellectual star in the local Catholic firmament, Father John Tracy Ellis, also had strong disagreements with O'Boyle. Although the archbishop showed the eminent professor of church history many courtesies—e.g., a per-sonal invitation to his consecration in New York and appointment as the arch-diocese's censor of books—he was not above pricking the academic's high self-regard. O'Boyle once quizzed Ellis about progress on his monumental biography of Cardinal Gibbons. Ellis offered a summary and was chagrined to hear O'Boyle's offhand response, "Well, it's a nice hobby." Early on O'Boyle, chancellor of Catholic University and the ecclesial authority whose imprimatur would be sought for the biography, expressed his strong conviction that it should contain no reference to bishops arguing among themselves. Of course the book recounted many such arguments, and although O'Boyle, whom Ellis de-scribed as "a very fretful man," did grant the imprimatur, he pointedly ignored

35. Gillen and Arthur intvs.
36. As referred to in Abell intv.

the book's existence until he heard the apostolic delegate praise it in public. Ellis later noted the irony: only after the critically acclaimed work received praise from an Italian churchman did O'Boyle, so worried about washing the American Church's dirty linen in public, begin to give copies to his friends in the hierarchy.[37]

In contrast to his austere relations with the clergy, which masked a warm and caring concern, O'Boyle was outwardly friendly with the laity but never enjoyed the warmth and closeness that had developed between Cardinal Gibbons (and even to some extent Archbishop Curley) and Washingtonians. His arrival was greeted with much good will by area Catholics pleased to have an ordinary of their own. Nevertheless, whether through a punctilious regard for episcopal protocol or merely further evidence of his underlying shyness, O'Boyle remained somewhat aloof from the public. The "good people," as he referred to Washington's laity, were embraced in the abstract. His lay friends and colleagues would always remain limited in number, consisting mostly of business associates and a few personal friends like publisher Walter McArdle, Speaker of the House of Representatives John McCormack, and, later, attorney William Abell. It was only with this very exclusive few that he might relax, remove his clerical collar, and enjoy a scotch and a cigar.

On the official and ceremonial level, O'Boyle conscientiously played his assigned role. Countless hours were spent blessing new buildings, laying cornerstones, and encouraging lay organizations with his presence at their affairs. One of his first official appearances was at the joint meeting of the area's Knights of Columbus councils in February 1948, when he was invested as a fourth degree knight.[38] Shortly thereafter he presided at a Mass for the dead sponsored by the Knights at Arlington National Cemetery. By his presence at their functions he energized the Catholic Youth Organization, Legion of Mary, Ladies of Charity, and the Sodality of Our Lady. During his first fall in Washington he led ten thousand marchers in the Holy Name parade down Constitution Avenue.[39]

The new archbishop seemed especially attracted to these mammoth demonstrations of faith, as typified by his role in the Family Rosary Crusade in October 1951. Organized by a lay group headed by Leo A. Rover and featuring a talk by the popular orator Father Patrick Peyton, the rally on the Washington Monument grounds attracted a prayerful audience of seventy thousand. Although he

---

37. Ellis intv. See also Kelly intv.
38. *BCR*, 12 Mar 1948.
39. *BCR*, 5 Nov 1948.

willingly presided over such impressive ceremonies, the self-effacing prelate made sure that others occupied the spotlight. One outdoor Mass at the Monument's Sylvan Theater featured a sermon by the well-known orator Bishop Fulton J. Sheen. After the ceremony, the crowds pressed upon Sheen, pleading for autographs. Finally one young girl approached O'Boyle and asked him to sign her program. After signing with great care, he jokingly told her, "God bless you, little girl, for saving my reputation."[40]

Of particular note during his early years in Washington was O'Boyle's sponsorship of two new lay organizations. Calling it the most important work started in the local Church since his arrival, he extolled the new Nocturnal Adoration Society, which, beginning in 1951, enlisted Catholic men by the hundreds to spend a holy hour in specially designated churches at appointed times throughout the night of each First Friday. He also expressed satisfaction with the reaction of the city's Catholic professionals and businessmen to the invitation to enroll in the John Carroll Society, which he sponsored at the urging of prominent laymen. Also begun in 1951 was the society's sponsorship of the annual Red Mass, an imposing ceremony calling God's blessing on the nation's lawmakers and attended by many government leaders. The society also provided a forum at its breakfast meetings for prominent leaders in government, education, and the Church to address topics of the day. O'Boyle himself frequently used talks at society meetings to promulgate his opinion on pressing social and moral concerns.[41] But above all, he saw the existence of such organizations, along with the quiet work of the St. Vincent de Paul Society, as signs of the spiritual vitality of the laity, without which "the Church is dead, no matter how beautiful a building it might have."[42]

Although he clearly would have preferred to play down the ceremonial aspects of his new position, O'Boyle willingly submitted to a perpetual round of appearances because, he realized, that was what the priests and people expected of him. In November 1948 a packed congregation at St. Matthew's watched as the apostolic delegate conferred the pallium (the wool collar symbolizing the of-

40. The O'Boyle file, AAW, contains numerous memos, news clippings, and reports detailing the archbishop's participation in these lay organizations. In addition to the weekly editions of *BCR* in 1948–49, see also *Star*, 24 Feb, 28 Mar, 29 Oct 1948, 29 Oct 1949, 29 Oct 1951, and 12 May 1952. See also "Memories," by Archbishop Hannan in *CS*, 13 Aug 1987, and Abell, *Patrick Cardinal O'Boyle*, p. 44 (source of quote).

41. O'Boyle's estimate of the Nocturnal Adoration Society was reported in *Star*, 4 Jun 1951. For his role in the genesis of the John Carroll Society, see the author's *The John Carroll Society, 1951–2001* (Washington, D.C., 2001).

42. As quoted in *CS*, 13 Nov 1953.

fice of archbishop) on O'Boyle. That Thanksgiving he presided at his first Pan-American Mass, and in January 1949, to the delight of local Catholics, he pronounced the benediction at the inauguration of President Harry S Truman (a task he would repeat four years later for President Eisenhower).[43]

Those who assumed, given his New York education and experience, that the new archbishop would immerse himself in the day-to-day affairs of diocesan charities were mistaken. In 1949 he made that clear to Father Coady, now ensconced in Catholic Charities after a brief classroom stint at Catholic University "to learn the jargon," as O'Boyle put it.[44] Attention to the desperately needed new parishes, he explained, must take preference over new charity projects. For the present he was content to let Msgr. Russell, the nominal director, and Coady work with their especially strong lay advisory board without interference from him. His long-term aim was to imitate the New York system, in which Catholic Charities acted as an umbrella organization, overseeing everything in the social service field. He looked to the day when Washington's Catholic Charities would sponsor a comprehensive funding program that not only underwrote the diocese's social agencies, but also provided local support for national projects like the recently redesignated Catholic Relief Services. Such an ambitious plan would have to wait. For the present O'Boyle looked to a rejuvenated St. Vincent de Paul Society to shoulder much of the charity burden and to donations from the Community Chest, which he praised in a radio address as an "efficient charitable and social welfare program."[45] In appointing Coady to Catholic Charities he remarked, "You go up there, you're on your own, you run the place, don't bother me unless you need me. I'm as close as the telephone."

It didn't quite work out that way. As Coady noted, he never called the archbishop as often as he received calls from the archbishop. O'Boyle would learn from the morning paper of some family about to be evicted, or some alien about to be deported, or some young boy in trouble with school authorities. He wanted Catholic Charities to do something about it immediately and to report back to him as soon as possible. To remind him, an experienced social worker, about established procedures and ordered business methods would win a reply like

43. These and the rest of the religious and secular events received generous coverage in both the local papers and *BCR.* See, for example, *Star,* 21 Jun, 27 Sep, and 10 Nov 1948; *NYT,* 11 Nov 1948; and *BCR,* 15 Oct 1948. The prayer O'Boyle delivered at the Truman inauguration was reprinted in *NYT,* 21 Jan 1949.

44. Coady and Arthur intvs. Coady began his long career in Catholic Charities in 1949, succeeding Russell as director when the latter left to become bishop of Richmond in March 1950.

45. As quoted in *Star,* 27 Nov 1948.

John F. Kennedy addresses the John Carroll Society. Archbishop O'Boyle, who sponsored this prestigious organization of Catholic professionals, listens with officials of the society to the presidential aspirant in 1959.

"Sure, sure, I know that," and with a wink and a grin, "but you'll take care of the poor soul."[46]

Meanwhile, O'Boyle kept close tabs on the St. Vincent de Paul Society. Working with Harry J. Kirk, president of Washington's particular council, the diocesan body charged with coordinating the activities of the individual parish conferences, he scheduled frequent appearances at society meetings and pushed recruitment in parishes that had yet to establish a conference. He received Kirk's confidential and sometimes critical reports of parish conferences. Once noting the wide variation in the amount of money collected and spent in the various parishes, he suggested to Kirk that "it would be a source of edification" if the fig-

46. As quoted by Bishop Thomas Lyons, in his eulogy.

A Christmas Party. Archbishop O'Boyle with the children of St. Ann's Infant Home during one of his annual visitations.

ures for each conference were published in the *Baltimore Catholic Review.*[47] He was always ready to provide publicity for the society's projects as well as the work of other social services under his jurisdiction. Beginning in 1949, for example, he was the honored guest at the annual Christmas party at St. Ann's Infant Home, providing the press with a seasonal photo op featuring a smiling arch-

47. The St. Vincent de Paul Papers in AAW contain considerable correspondence on these subjects. See, for example, ltrs., Kirk to O'Boyle, 21 Apr 1950, O'Boyle to Kirk, 14 Jan 1948, 15 Jan 1950 (source of quote), and 7 Oct 1950. See also *Star,* 16 Feb and 6 Dec 1948.

bishop, often with the apostolic delegate in tow, enjoying himself with the toddlers and their caregivers in their home on California Street.[48]

A glimpse of O'Boyle's early and sometimes problematic management technique was evident when Catholic Charities came to plan the archdiocese's new home for the aged. For almost a century the Little Sisters of the Poor had cared for Washington's needy old folks. The only other Church-affiliated elder care facility in the area opened shortly before World War II on P Street in Georgetown. Sponsored by St. Matthew's rector, Msgr. Buckey, the home, consisting of two connected houses, was operated by a committee of Georgetown matrons. After Buckey's death in 1948 the directors fell on financially hard times and asked the archdiocese to assume control. O'Boyle agreed on condition that the institution be placed under the professional management of the Carmelite Sisters for the Aged. The sisters, in turn, agreed, provided O'Boyle promise to build a modern facility in the near future. Although the architect's plans for Carroll Manor would not take final form until 1954, O'Boyle was from the outset deeply involved in the process.

In this and other Catholic Charities projects Father Coady learned to accommodate to the archbishop's management style. He learned that the archbishop was a great one for reports, since frequently a phone call from O'Boyle would begin with the question, "When is that report coming in?" Coady's submissions seemed to satisfy him. Coady would first state the problem and then develop three possible solutions with reasons for each. O'Boyle, he concluded, liked answers in threes—probably, Coady reasoned, because in providing three options you had pretty much covered the thought process needed for making a decision. O'Boyle might accept one or reject all the options, but he appreciated the saving in time when a subordinate summarized the options.[49]

Sound management practices tended to break down from time to time. In reviewing plans for Carroll Manor with the architect, Philip Shrier, and Sister Bernadette, the diminutive Irish Carmelite who represented the sisters, O'Boyle would often find himself outfoxed. When the sister would demurely ask if some little extra might be added, O'Boyle would turn to the architect, asking, "Can we do it, Phil? How much would it cost?" When Shrier assured him that the requested addition would cost about $20,000, O'Boyle would say, "Oh, that's peanuts, put it in." Sister Bernadette would then propose another little improve-

---

48. See, for example, *Star,* 29 Dec 1950.

49. Coady intv. is the source of this and the following paragraph. The quotations are as reported by Coady.

"Cinderblock O'Boyle." The archbishop lays the cornerstone of Carroll Manor home for the aged, part of his $300 million building program.

ment, and again, after getting a modest price estimate from his architect, O'Boyle would order it added. After several such sessions with Sister Bernadette, the cost of Carroll Manor had increased a quarter of a million dollars. O'Boyle seemed flabbergasted that these piddling little additions had added up to real money. Still, he may well have had the last laugh. When it opened later in the decade, Carroll Manor was recognized as the state of the art in what was still a new field in social service.

Some Lessons Learned

Patrick O'Boyle was a man of ordered habits. He did not, his colleagues agreed, take work home from the office, but that observation overlooked the countless appearances he made at evening gatherings of Catholic organizations. In fact the establishment of an independent archdiocese, along with the many hours spent addressing the thorny issue of race relations in the capital and carrying out his growing responsibilities at the NCWC, precluded any true respite from work. Sometime during those first years in Washington he resumed his highly imperfect golf game, playing with colleagues like Father George Higgins of the NCWC at the Burning Tree Country Club in Montgomery County. His desk calendar likewise noted a brief hiatus in each of those first summers, probably marking his annual return to Pennsylvania, but nearly all out-of-town trips were for charity conferences or religious events. The most prolonged of these events, one that included his first visit to Rome and put him in daily contact with two hundred Washington priests and laity, was the archdiocese's Holy Year pilgrimage in April–May 1950.

O'Boyle's decision to join the pilgrimage might seem puzzling. He was never a happy traveler, and even though his time on the tour was abbreviated, it did include a whirlwind dash through France and Italy with five days in Rome, all sandwiched between lengthy (nine-day) Atlantic crossings. Still, the chance to visit the tomb of St. Vincent de Paul, celebrate Mass at Lourdes, and attend the canonization of St. Anthony Claret made it a "glorious trip" in his judgment.[50] His stopover in Paris also included receptions by the archbishop and the mayor of the city, both anxious to honor him for his efforts during the war to feed and cloth the French people. In Rome he had his first private audience with Pope Pius XII, who also alluded to America's aid to the stricken peoples of Europe and Asia. In a further sign of his gratitude, the pope left his seat at the conclusion of the lengthy canonization ceremony and walked over to the archbishop of Washington seated among his fellow bishops from around the world to give him a public embrace.[51]

Only two incidents caused unease during the trip. O'Boyle had invited Father Ellis to join the pilgrimage and to brief the Washington group on the places they would be visiting. Ellis saved his comments about Ireland for last, concluding that visitors would find there much unemployment and "more dirt than there ought to be." Although O'Boyle's shortened itinerary precluded his visiting Ireland himself, he was furious at what he considered a slur on his parents' birthplace. Summoning Ellis to his stateroom he told him in a loud voice, "You have slighted Ireland!" Ellis afterward concluded that all his troubles with O'Boyle

---

50. Postcard, O'Boyle to Kirk, 9 May 1950, St. Vincent de Paul Papers, AAW. The trip itinerary was reported in *Star,* 3 May 1950, and "Holy Year 1950 Washington Archdiocesan Pilgrimage to Rome," copy in AAW.

51. O'Boyle honored the pope's request to pass his sentiments on to the American public in an address in St. Matthew's on May 21, the day after his return. See *Star,* 21 May 1950 (source of quote).

began that day.[52] An incident on the long train ride to Rome had a less enduring but more anxiety-provoking effect. A minor rail accident tossed luggage around, causing O'Boyle's bottle of after-shave lotion to break, spewing its contents over the vestments he was to wear the next day at the canonization. An anxious Father Schmitz, with the damaged vestments on appropriated hangers in hand, paced the train's open passageways in an attempt to rid the watered silk of the odor of bay rum.[53]

Shortly after his return from Europe, Archbishop O'Boyle scheduled a two-week vacation with his old New York pals at Tupper Lake in the Adirondacks.[54] There he no doubt caught up on all the news about life under Cardinal Spellman, but in fact by 1950 there were indications that New York was exerting less of a pull on his thinking as he began to adjust to the realities facing the Church in the capital. Members of his staff took heart from his occasional remarks to the effect that "we don't always need to look elsewhere for help; we've got guys right here who know how to handle things."[55] Discovering that local talent could produce satisfactory results coincided with a noticeable relaxation in some regulations considered sacrosanct in his old world.

Regulations governing so-called mixed marriages were a case in point. In New York and elsewhere such unions were strictly forbidden in the church proper, restricted instead to the sacristy or more commonly to rectory parlors. At first O'Boyle enforced a similar rule in Washington. In a commodious church like St. Matthew's Cathedral, the sacristy was often a large room that could be adapted to some extent for the occasion. In most Washington churches, however, sacristies were no more than crowded workspaces and the rectory parlor a cramped room in a modest house. At the urging of some pastors O'Boyle finally agreed to cancel the old strictures, although he insisted on strict conditions and regulations that must be followed. Henceforth in Washington, where Catholics composed only a small portion of a relatively transient population and where mixed marriages were commonplace, the ceremony would take place at the altar rail.[56] This meant that such wedding parties enjoyed all the trappings of a traditional church celebration.

A similar change of heart could be detected in O'Boyle's relaxation of the

52. Ellis intv.

53. Gerrity intv. Ms. Gerrity was one of the pilgrims who enjoyed the opportunity to socialize with the archbishop on the lengthy journey.

54. Plans for the trip were outlined in ltr., O'Boyle to Mooney, 29 Jul 1950, Mooney Papers, AAD.

55. As quoted in Arthur intv.

56. O'Boyle, "Conditions *'Sine Qua Non'* for Mixed Marriages in Church," 19 May 1948, AAW.

rules governing burials. He came from a jurisdiction that required Catholics to be interred in Catholic cemeteries, and subordinates in Washington soon came to understand that their new archbishop looked upon burials in non-Catholic or secular cemeteries as "absolutely immoral."[57] His opposition was underscored soon after his arrival when he refused permission for a prominent state department official to bury his wife in a Protestant cemetery. In Washington, where many families with mixed religious heritages owned plots in some of the city's historic, nondenominational cemeteries, such a rule created real hardship. The demand also affected Catholics in southern Maryland, who were long accustomed to burying their dead with their neighbors. Also to be considered were the many burials in the local military cemeteries. Although O'Boyle may never have given up his old certainty that Catholics should be interred communally in blessed ground, he nevertheless came to realize that it was a belief impossible to enforce. By 1951 the rule was quietly relaxed.

Given O'Boyle's lifelong dedication to personal loyalty, it must have surprised some when he abruptly dismissed his chancellor in 1951. He had been aware for some time that now-Msgr. Cowhig (among the first group of Washington priests to be so honored through O'Boyle's intercession) had a low opinion of the archbishop's grasp of canon law, openly denigrated his leadership style, and told one and all that he should never have been raised to the episcopacy. Apparently unfazed, O'Boyle would even josh about remarks of Cowhig's that somehow filtered back to him. He obviously appreciated the hard-working chancellor's abilities, and in fact Cowhig's considerable organizational and managerial skills were partly responsible for the extraordinary development program of those early years. A brusque man himself, O'Boyle also appeared to ignore Cowhig's callous treatment of his fellow priests.

By 1951 the chancellor's swashbuckling style had antagonized many priests in the diocese. Aware of Msgr. Cartwright's willingness to take a forthright stand on issues that engaged him, some priests asked him to intervene. Cartwright recognized Cowhig as a man of talent and consequence, but one, he believed, wrongly assigned. He decided that he could not stand idly by and so pointed out to O'Boyle his mistake in appointing Cowhig. He described the growing split between chancery and clergy and mentioned Cowhig's effort to recruit a like-minded priest for his staff. "You don't need men like that representing you," Cartwright concluded.[58] O'Boyle agreed, and Cowhig was transferred to St.

57. As quoted in Arthur intv.
58. As quoted in Arthur intv.

Jerome's in Hyattsville, Maryland, where he served for some time as administrator before O'Boyle relented and appointed him pastor. Affirming Cartwright's conclusion, Cowhig thrived in his new post, where he won the loyalty and support of his congregation as he transformed St. Jerome's into a model modern parish.

Philip Hannan succeeded Cowhig as chancellor, a post he would hold for fourteen years. A man of many interests with a notable capacity for work, Hannan offered a looser management style, but his pragmatic approach to the job appealed to O'Boyle. "Your canon lawyer shouldn't spend time telling you what as ordinary you can't do," Hannan explained. "Tell me what you want done, and I'll find the way to do it." That O'Boyle would welcome such a philosophy in 1951 suggested a shift in attitude. Fresh from New York he could be expected to find such advice unnerving. Under Hannan's guidance it became far less so.

Archbishop O'Boyle's maturing in his new post also produced a change of view on the question of a Catholic newspaper. Shortly after his arrival he had agreed to share the cost of the *Baltimore Catholic Review,* which in turn agreed to provide full coverage of the Washington Church. The *Review* had many Washington readers, and initially it remained true to its pledge. O'Boyle's first years in office received generous coverage, as did Washington's parishes and schools. In late 1948 he and Archbishop Keough concluded that the format and content of the paper should change. O'Boyle created a committee under Msgr. Cartwright to advise him on what the reformatted paper should cover.[59] Whatever the committee recommended, the *Review*'s coverage of news in the capital gradually diminished over the next two years, until news of the Washington archdiocese was frequently restricted to a one-page summary. O'Boyle once joked that he would need to jump off the Washington Monument to gain notice in the *Review.* He was exaggerating, but seemed open to Father Hannan's argument that despite the price, it was important for an ordinary to have a news organ of his own to keep his diocese informed about the things that concerned him. In 1951 O'Boyle severed his ties with the Baltimore publication in favor of his own *Catholic Standard.* Ignoring advisors, he appointed the busy Hannan the paper's first editor.

Other examples might be cited to demonstrate how early experiences in Washington moderated O'Boyle's New York mindset. In fact, in his approach to local racial practices and later in his progressive stance on social justice issues, he set a pace that far exceeded changes in policies and practices in his old archdio-

59. Ltr., O'Boyle to Ellis, 8 Oct 1948, Ellis Papers, ACUA.

cese. At the same time his respect for authority and his demand for loyalty, inculcated in him by his seminary experience and years of service under hard taskmasters, never wavered. Historian Florence Cohalan's description of Cardinal Spellman could, with only slight modification, also be applied to O'Boyle in 1951 Washington:

> Only a very superficial observer could miss his intense awareness of his own authority and his determination that it be recognized and accepted by his subordinates on every level. He could be, as a number of them learned, very demanding and even inconsiderate of them as he often was of himself. At the same time, few could miss his sense of duty, his capacity for work, his grasp of affairs, his willingness to settle things promptly, his quite exceptional confidence in his own judgment. . . .[60]

The question remained just how far the radical changes coming to the postwar Church and American society would alter these realities.

---

60. Cohalan, *A Popular History of the Archdiocese of New York*, p. 276.

CHAPTER 8

‑‑𝕸

Fighting Jim Crow

Washington may have shed its sleepy, small-town image after the war, but many of the city's old, insular habits, including its laws and customs governing race relations, remained. The capital never experienced the overwhelming influx of immigrants that transformed the great cities of the East during the last century, and its social attitudes continued to reflect the outlook of a leadership comfortable with its Southern traditions. Many of those who arrived during and after World War II, including many African Americans from the rural South seeking a better life in the District, quietly accommodated to the city's unremarkable but very real segregation.

The capital's Jim Crow rules were reinforced by Congress, which was constitutionally mandated to govern the District of Columbia, and were jealously guarded by the congressional committees appointed to prepare legislation and run the city through a board of commissioners. The chairmen of these committees, usually senior members from the South, were dedicated to maintaining the racial status quo. In theory the court-sanctioned separate but equal doctrine ruled race relations in Washington. In practice segregated housing, churches, hospitals, restaurants, and most other establishments catering to the public proved anything but equal. Only on the city's buses and streetcars and in the tiers of Griffith Stadium, where Washington cheered on its hapless Senators, did black and white citizens receive similar treatment.

The Church in Washington readily accommodated itself to these racial practices. Blessed with one of the largest concentrations of black Catholics, the Archdiocese of Baltimore and Washington theoretically welcomed African Americans in all its churches. In fact it maintained a separate grid of black parishes and rigidly segregated those African Americans who attended the so-called white churches. With the exception of two grade schools and a small high school in southern Maryland and the four black parish schools in the city, all Catholic educational institutions excluded African Americans. (Catholic University, which reopened its doors to black students on a restricted basis in 1936, was a notable exception.) Martin Luther King, who once famously observed that Sunday morning was the most segregated time in America, might well have been referring to Washington's Catholic churches. Only St. Augustine's, the mother church of the city's black Catholics, was truly integrated. Hundreds of white Catholics, drawn to the imposing old structure on Fifteenth Street by its convenient Mass schedule and the beauty of its choir, joined African-American parishioners in praising God as equals.

The local Church's racial policies would present Patrick O'Boyle with his first moral challenge as ordinary. Little in his career had prepared him for the event. His experience with race matters was limited to his years of social work in an archdiocese with a limited black Catholic population and in particular to the integration of the orphans at Mt. Loretto. The racial rivalries that racked blue-collar populations in many of America's industrial cities were absent from the nearly all-white Scranton of his boyhood. Nevertheless, in a sensitive youth like O'Boyle, his immigrant background and social conditions in his hometown led him to identify with the underdog and stimulated an abiding sympathy for the underprivileged whatever their color.

For O'Boyle the goal of workable race relations boiled down to a question of elementary justice as prescribed by the Church's social teachings. To him the issue was crystallized in his oft-repeated comment: "I just don't see any reason why a little black boy or girl doesn't have the same right to a Catholic education as a little white boy or girl."[1] The only acceptable response to this statement was incompatible with the practices in his new archdiocese, and O'Boyle made no secret of his determination to change things. But how to effect change both in the city and especially in the southern Maryland counties with its three-hundred-year tradition regarding race without stimulating a backlash? A pell-mell approach might not only prove counterproductive but also, as in the later cases of some Southern dioceses, rend the Catholic community for years to come. Without any rules or prior experience to guide him, O'Boyle opened the campaign against Jim Crow during his first days in Washington.

1. O'Boyle claimed that he was quoting St. Louis Archbishop Joseph Ritter, an ardent champion of racial justice, when he made this observation. The statement has been reported many times, the latest in *WP*, 7 Jun 1999.

As It Was

At the time of O'Boyle's arrival, nine Washington parishes were reserved for black Catholics, their boundaries dividing the city in a separate pattern superimposed on the boundaries marking the city's white parishes. The creation of these parishes had been actively sought and gratefully accepted by most black Catholics before World War II.[2] Weary of being merely tolerated in their neighborhood parish, they envied the status of congregations at St. Augustine's and St. Cyprian's, churches established in the nineteenth century for African Americans. The archbishops of Baltimore accepted the idea of black parishes with the truthful claim that African Americans wanted separate churches and the dubious assertion that all churches welcomed all Catholics. In fact, the dual system of parishes had strengthened the notion that black Catholics should be limited to attendance at black parishes. Catholics thought in terms of "your" church and "our" church, and that made it easier for racist congregations and their racist or complacent pastors to "refer" any African American entering "their" church to the nearest "black" church with a clear conscience.

Racial division in parishes was made easier by the continued racial separation of the city's neighborhoods. Even in the days of slavery and well into the post–Civil War decades, Washingtonians had lived peacefully in integrated neighborhoods. By the end of the nineteenth century, however, Jim Crow's triumphant conquest of the city had produced an urban scene rigidly divided by race, with a carefully defined black community arching across the inner wards of the capital from the Anacostia River in the south and east through the area to the north around Florida Avenue and U Street before ending in Foggy Bottom in the west. Unknown and largely ignored by the white establishment, this area, marked by large pockets of poverty and noisome slums with alley dwellings, was aptly dubbed the Secret City by historian Constance Green.[3]

The lines demarking the two cities remained relatively stable until World War II, when the new wave of black migration and a concomitant movement of white Washingtonians to the rapidly developing suburbs ushered in a time of speedy

---

2. The following paragraphs are taken from the author's *The Emergence of a Black Catholic Community: St. Augustine's in Washington* (Washington, D.C.: The Catholic University of America Press, 1999). See especially pp. 233–36.

3. Constance McLaughlin Green, *The Secret City: A History of Race Relations in the Nation's Capital* (Princeton, N.J.: Princeton University Press, 1967). Green's comprehensive survey of Washington's race history provides a detailed look at the legal and social elements of the fight for racial justice in Washington. See especially chapters 11 and 12.

transformation. The change produced much racial tension exacerbated by racially designated covenants that sought to exclude blacks from white neighborhoods and by "block busting," a technique used by unscrupulous realtors to encourage white flight. Even as black neighborhoods expanded into the far reaches of the city and despite signs of progress in the fight for racial justice on the national level, Washington's political and business leaders, supported by their congressional allies, tried to reinforce the capital's strict segregation practices. When St. Patrick's Academy accepted a black pupil during the war in a rare case of racial fairness, its principal faced questioning by city officials for violating the District's racial code.[4] As late as 1948 the city's schools and most of its restaurants and theaters (but not its parks, which were controlled by the federal government) remained strictly segregated.

Historian Father Rory Conley has identified eleven parishes affected by the city's racial demography. Six of these were white parishes in what were largely black neighborhoods; the other five were located in those transition areas that were rapidly becoming black. Conley concluded that "the proximity of nearby black churches and the racial sensitivities of individual pastors" partially explain how the latter parishes evolved into bastions of segregation.[5]

It was the egregious prejudice emanating from these parishes that fueled demands from the slowly emerging crusaders for racial justice. For example, the pastor of St. Martin's on North Capitol Street was cited for purchasing several nearby properties in a vain effort to preserve his white-only neighborhood. When a priest at St. Mary's on Fifth Street, N.W., in keeping with that parish's policy, directed a black worshipper to find a "colored church," the possibility of an international incident ensued. Unfortunately for the hapless cleric, the worshipper proved to be a Panamanian diplomat. His expulsion was the one specific incident of prejudice in a Washington church cited in the 1948 report issued by the prestigious National Committee on Segregation in the Nation's Capital.[6]

---

4. Arthur intv. Ignoring the city's investigation at first, Father Arthur ended the matter by reporting to the Board of Education that accepting the student, a graduate of St. Patrick's grade school, was a matter of Church policy.

5. Rory T. Conley, "'All One in Christ': Patrick Cardinal O'Boyle, The Church of Washington and the Struggle for Racial Justice, 1948–73" (MA thesis, The Catholic University of America, 1992), p. 85.

6. National Committee on Segregation in the National's Capital, *Segregation in the Nation's Capital*, p. 7. On the establishment and work of the committee, see Green, *Secret City*, pp. 286–88. Unless otherwise noted, the following information on segregated parishes is based on Albert S. Foley, "The Catholic Church and the Washington Negro" (PhD dissertation, University of North Carolina, 1950), pp. 158ff. See also the author's *Emergence of a Black Catholic Community*, pp. 268–301.

The rigid segregation of the congregation at Immaculate Conception on N Street, N.W., near Howard University and the historic black neighborhood of Le Droit Park, found its cramped black section overflowing at most masses while the few white parishioners rattled around in the rest of the church. Adding to the stress was the fact that the black worshippers, labeled "troublemakers" by the pastor, included distinguished teachers and idealistic young students from Howard and Catholic Universities. Catholic chaplains at Howard estimated that dozens of these black students drifted away from the Church out of frustration over their treatment at Immaculate Conception. Until shortly before O'Boyle's arrival, St. Matthew's Cathedral had maintained segregated seating, its clergy responding to requests for assistance from black Catholics with a formal statement issued in the pastor's name: "We do not serve colored."[7] The standard explanation for such treatment was that black Catholics should attend St. Augustine's because its pastor "needed their support."

In the face of such systematic discrimination, a reform movement began to attract progressive clergy and laity to the cause of integration. Efforts by students from the area's Catholic colleges and Howard University's Newman Club along with newcomers flocking to wartime Washington had stimulated the city's nascent Catholic settlement house movement. Inspired by the work of Dorothy Day and the Baroness Dorothy DeHueck, Catholic University's Father Paul H. Furfey and Dr. Mary Elizabeth Walsh organized a group in the mid-1930s to serve the poor, mostly black, residents of the inner city. By the time of O'Boyle's arrival a network of organizations that depended on the labor of an interracial staff of university students and part-time volunteers was offering support and bearing witness to many of Washington's most desperate residents. In 1940 Walsh opened Fides House in the eastern Shaw neighborhood, where the needs of black youth were emphasized. Later the Blessed Martin de Porres Hospice, a Catholic Worker House of Hospitality operated by the saintly Llewellyn Scott in the Swampoodle section, opened its doors to homeless men.[8] Both served as models of racial equality in a segregated city and Church.

Signs of change were also evident in Catholic organizations like the Third Order of St. Francis, the lay auxiliary of the Franciscans, which routinely en-

7. Hannan intv. Hannan asserts that Msgr. Buckey's habit of relegating black Catholics to the back pews of St. Matthew's and referring African Americans to St. Augustine's was continued by his successor, Msgr. Cartwright, until O'Boyle put a stop to it in 1948. The fact of segregated seating at the cathedral in 1948 was noted in *Star,* 4 Mar 1973, at the time of O'Boyle's retirement.

8. For a useful summary of this work, see Jenell Williams Paris, "*Fides* Means Faith," *Washington History* 11 (Fall/Winter 1999–2000): pp. 25–45.

rolled black Catholics, the Archdiocesan Council of Catholic Nurses, and the Catholic Evidence Guild, an organization dedicated to street evangelism. But the quiet dedication to Christian principle exhibited by these groups remained a rare exception to the general policy of the many spiritual and social organizations that continued to exclude African Americans. The most noted organization bearing witness to the ideal of an integrated Church, and one that would have close contact with the new archbishop, was the Washington chapter of the Catholic Interracial Council. The local council, organized in 1944 by a distinguished group of black and white Catholics, many of them educators and senior civil servants, was affiliated with the organization founded by the Jesuit John LaFarge in New York. LaFarge believed that black and white activists should merge in a common effort to change attitudes and influence Catholic institutions through education, dialogue, and witness.[9]

Especially pertinent for O'Boyle's education on conditions in Washington, the council's steering committee decided to document the Church's racial practices. In early 1947 it conducted a series of surveys in which on a given Sunday biracial teams entered churches across the city before the principal Mass, walked down the main aisle, and seated themselves in the center section. Although the council concluded that Washington's Catholics were "ready to accept blacks equally," in fact only half the churches surveyed allowed the biracial teams to remain undisturbed. This dolorous news was confirmed by a second survey a few weeks later.[10]

The council also gathered data on other Catholic institutions, including such parish-related organizations as the Holy Name Society, the Sodality, and various fraternal groups. It found these organizations closed to black Catholics in all "white" parishes, even at churches where significant numbers of African Americans attended without discrimination, such as St. Patrick's in old downtown.[11]

Despite prevailing practices, progressive forces like the Interracial Council enjoyed some powerful allies in the city. St. Patrick's pastor, Msgr. Lawrence J.

9. On the formation of the Washington council, see *Catholic Interracial Review* (hereafter *CIR*) (Jun 1947): p. 86. The activities described in the following paragraph were detailed in the "Washington Reporter," articles written for this journal by John J. O'Connor. For an account of the often harsh reception afforded members of the council, see Foley, "The Catholic Church and the Washington Negro," pp. 156–58 and 224–25.

10. The survey was described in *CIR* (Mar 1947): p. 44 (source of quote), and in a brief history of the council published on its fiftieth anniversary in December 1994, copy in AAW. See also Pauline Jones intv. Ms. Jones was a team member in the follow-up survey.

11. William and Mary Buckner, Paul P. Cooke, and Father George V. Joyce intvs. All were members of the council and participated in its surveys.

Shehan, who as head of Catholic Charities had thoroughly integrated the staff and operations of that organization, also served as host for council meetings. Both Shehan and his successor, Msgr. John Russell, were strong supporters of the council's efforts and faithfully attended its sessions in St. Patrick's hall. The apostolic delegate also showed his support for the council's work. Archbishop Cicognani celebrated Mass for its members at the Vatican delegation, located among the embassies on Massachusetts Avenue, and on occasion hosted their social receptions.

After years of neglect from Church officials in Baltimore, the Washington council had several reasons to greet the arrival of the new archbishop with optimism. The founder of their movement, Father LaFarge, who had firsthand knowledge of the plight of black Catholics in the region from his many years of service in St. Mary's County, had sent a congratulatory letter to the archbishop-elect in December 1947 in which he broached the subject of race relations in the new archdiocese. In reply, O'Boyle confessed that, although "somewhat aware" of the racial climate in the region, he was "not at all well posted on the situation." He promised to read LaFarge's booklet on Catholicism in southern Maryland, and arranged to meet LaFarge before his installation to discuss the matter. La-Farge later reported that the two discovered themselves of a mind on the goal of integration and the techniques that should be employed to achieve that goal. The Washington Catholic Interracial Council, in turn, received a reply to its welcoming wishes in which O'Boyle expressed the desire to meet with them to learn more of their work.[12]

True to his word, O'Boyle met with officers of the council, including its president, former Assistant Secretary of State G. Howard Shaw, and its chaplain, Jesuit Father Wilfred Parsons, at St. Patrick's on February 17, 1948.[13] The council members, presuming from previous exchanges a sympathetic audience, launched into a general discussion of the treatment of African Americans in the city, specifically in Catholic churches and schools. Actually, the officers had planned to concentrate on the school situation, especially the lack of high schools for black Catholics. The eagerly awaited new boys' high school was a case in point. If it

12. Ltrs., O'Boyle to LaFarge, 15 Dec 1947 (source of quote) and 9 Jan 1948, and LaFarge to O'Boyle, 12 Dec 1947, 15 Nov 1948, and 7 Nov 1949. All in LaFarge Papers, AGU. See also *CIR* (Feb 1948): pp. 28–29.

13. The meeting was reported in *CIR* (May 1948): p. 45, and O'Boyle's Notes, pt. 29, which are the source for the following paragraph. Father Parsons, a member of the CUA faculty, was LaFarge's predecessor as editor of *America*. Contrary to O'Boyle's recollection, their meeting did not occur during his first week in Washington, although it might well have been, as he claimed, the second group to meet him at St. Patrick's.

were to bar black students, they charged, the cause of racial justice in the capital would be set back a quarter-century.

Ever cautious, O'Boyle was not about to be railroaded into action. He reminded the group that he was new to the city and promised to study the situation prior to making a decision. A frustrated Father Parsons interjected, "When does the decision come? We have had so many studies, and nothing has really been done." The group had to be satisfied with O'Boyle's promise to take action after "in all fairness" he had verified what they had told him.

Integration of Washington's Parishes and Schools

O'Boyle revealed his thinking on the volatile subject soon enough. At the first meeting of the Commission on Parishes on March 12, he spoke to his consultors about the status of black parishes. The time would come, he announced, "when parishes would not be designated as colored parishes and that parishes would be established without such designation."[14] O'Boyle later noted that the consultors were "most cooperative," but he could not have missed the undercurrent of opposition, especially when his vicar, the usually diffident Bishop McNamara, bluntly asked if the new policy had been recommended by the apostolic delegate. To its credit the Vatican had been pressing the American bishops to address the subject of race relations for decades, so McNamara and those unsympathetic to integration might naturally suspect that the pope's representative had pushed the proposed change. O'Boyle forcefully denied the implication and insisted that integration was his idea; in fact it represented his "strong personal convictions," he told them. Underscoring his intentions, he declared that he meant to break down racial barriers "whatever the price to be paid." He expected them to come up with a workable plan to accomplish that goal.[15]

O'Boyle's comments not only succinctly expressed his determination to integrate, but also hinted at the tactic he planned to adopt. Change would be gradual and carefully orchestrated without any public announcement. If his determination disconcerted the racial traditionalists, his rejection of any public notice was bound to disappoint some racial progressives who longed for a Jovian thunderbolt to smite the miscreants and integrate the Church's institutions instantly. O'Boyle, however, saw wisdom in quiet gradualism. As he would later tell members of the New York Interracial Council, he believed that he should declare the

14. As quoted in O'Boyle, Notes, pt. 28.

15. O'Boyle, Notes, pt. 28 (first quote), and Abell, *Patrick Cardinal O'Boyle,* p. 9 (second and third quotes). It is not clear if Abell is quoting the archbishop's exact words.

Church's "norms of practice clearly and without any hesitation while at the same time working quietly and prudently for their fulfillment." While Father LaFarge expressed enthusiasm for this strategy, calling it "pretty much the key to handling the situation in the more explosive areas," the Washington chapter of his organization might well have felt excluded from the process.[16] O'Boyle's attendance at its reception held in his honor clearly signaled his sympathy with its aims, but there would be no follow-up meetings about the future role of the council nor answers to its specific questions about integrating the Church's institutions. Instead, members had to content themselves with the archbishop's celebrating their anniversary Mass, during which he stated that charity could not be legislated.[17]

In the weeks that followed his meeting with the Commission on Parishes on March 12, the archbishop settled on a procedure. His first objective was to dismantle the system of segregation in Washington's churches and schools. Only later, after the city and neighboring counties had complied, would he order change in southern Maryland, where feelings were bound to run high. Meanwhile, he would seek to improve the archdiocese's outreach to the urban, mostly black, poor. Concerning a timetable for the schools, O'Boyle planned to be flexible. Parishes could admit eligible black children to their schools on a gradual schedule devised by his consultors, but they must make a start. None of his directives concerning integration were published; indeed none were ever written down. Any discussions or negotiations occurred during private meetings with individual pastors. O'Boyle probably discussed the general outline of the new policy at a conference of the archdiocesan clergy in late March 1948.[18]

To avoid public controversy and backlash, O'Boyle insisted on step-by-step, low-key change. Later scenes of ugly resistance to published decrees in other dioceses attested to the wisdom of his decision. In the case of school desegregation he resorted to a tactic impossible in later decades. Using Father Hannan as his agent, he successfully persuaded local newspaper publishers to impose a blackout on the desegregation story. The glare of publicity, he argued, could hinder progress. Appealing to their better natures, he had Hannan point out to the publishers that a court decision affecting Washington's public schools was ex-

16. Ltr., LaFarge to O'Boyle, 7 Nov 1949 (both quotes), LaFarge Papers, AGU.

17. *CIR* (Nov 1948): p. 174. On the lack of response to council questions, see Cooke intv. (Dr. Cooke was an official of the council at the time.) On the O'Boyle reception, see Buckner intv. and *CIR* (May 1948): pp. 77–79. On the anniversary Mass, see same publication (Nov 1948): p. 174.

18. Conley points to a clergy conference on March 31 as a possible occasion when the desegregation plan was aired. See "'All One in Christ,'" p. 83.

pected before long, and the successful integration of a large school system such as that of the Washington archdiocese would help allay the fears of officials faced with integrating the public schools.[19] To questions from traditionalists and activists alike O'Boyle offered the same simple and disarming response: "Anyone who comes to Church to pray will be welcome. Anyone who comes to cause trouble will be asked to behave or leave."

Clearly, while the gradual approach addressed long-term goals, it also caused some immediate problems. Most commentators reported that integration of Washington's churches was uneventful, but in fact the intransigence of several pastors and administrators seemed at times to be strengthening the status quo and caused O'Boyle and the archdiocese public criticism.[20] On the very day the archbishop announced that the era of separate black parishes was passing, a committee of his consultors visited Holy Name parish and the site of the proposed St. Benedict the Moor parish, eleven blocks apart in the central section of northeast Washington. Learning that more than 700 African Americans now attended the still-segregated Holy Name, the committee discussed a proposal that "Holy Name be turned over to the colored and that Holy Name School be used for a new parish."[21]

Further underscoring the impression that nothing was about to change, the chancery published new boundary decrees during the course of the following year. These notices retained the separate grid of black and white parishes across the center city. For example, the decree defining the boundaries of Holy Redeemer, the black parish on New York Avenue near North Capitol Street, covered a gerrymandered swath of the city that included parts of nine white parishes.[22] Vice-Chancellor Hannan, who wrote many of these decrees, later explained that they were meant to protect the integrity of the historic black parishes, which, if restricted to their immediate neighborhoods, could not remain viable. Furthermore, their parishioners, who willingly traveled from across the city to enjoy the fellowship of their black friends and to play leadership roles in a parish, would be denied these pleasures. Valid explanations, but the publication of the boundary decrees (they would not be amended until a decade later) prom-

---

19. Ltr., Bp. Thomas Lyons to O'Boyle, 9 Feb 1970, O'Boyle Papers, AAW.

20. William Abell, for one, argued that the integration of Washington's churches was trouble-free. See *Patrick Cardinal O'Boyle*, p. 9.

21. Report of the Parish Committee (Holy Name Parish, 12 Mar 1948), AAW

22. Archdiocese of Washington Chancery Office, Decrees, Holy Redeemer Boundaries, 3 Oct 1949, AAW. See also same source, decree for St. Cyprian's Parish in ltr., Father Francis Carney (pastor of St. Cyprian's) to Hannan, 13 Sep 48.

ised a measure of comfort to those pastors who looked for a continuation of the old system.

A number of these unreconstructed pastors received personal warnings from their new archbishop in the months after his arrival. The racial barriers in their parishes must come down, he told them. No exceptions, no islands of privilege, would be tolerated. The choice was simple: abolish discrimination or face "official action."[23] These confrontations took place in various private meetings in the spring of 1948. Citing entries in the archbishop's desk calendar, historian Conley has identified a number of probable occasions, including back-to-back sessions in March with the pastors of St. Mary's and Immaculate Conception, two of the most notorious discriminators.[24] In some cases these behind-closed-doors exhortations had little immediate effect, and the usually exacting administrator took no action against the recalcitrants. His low-key approach to converting the practices, if not the hearts and minds, of his subordinates endured even under severe provocation. Public correction would no doubt appeal to the increasingly vocal progressive critics, but it would also add obstacles to his long-term aim. Unlike the thundering leader of later decades, O'Boyle chose a low profile, shouldering a share of adverse national publicity in the bargain.

Father LaFarge warned his friend in November 1948 that the National Committee on Segregation in the Nation's Capital would be holding its final meeting before publishing its long-awaited report. The committee's investigation of conditions in Washington predated O'Boyle's arrival, LaFarge explained, and some last-minute corrections in its very critical report were still possible. He wanted the archdiocese to send a representative to explain the reforms being put in place. The archbishop, uncharacteristically, dithered. Not responding initially, he finally answered LaFarge's second reminder, because "I was taking up the matter of the policy we might pursue." He agreed with LaFarge's decision to send the Catholic Interracial Council's G. Howard Shaw to the meeting, adding that he would discuss with Shaw points he wanted brought before the group. The intervention proved useless. In the end the committee's report, which gained national headlines, featured the incident at St. Mary's involving the ejection of the Panamanian diplomat. O'Boyle's forthright but tempered response would characterize all his public comments on the subject during the next several years:

23. Foley, "The Catholic Church and the Washington Negro," p. 139 (source of quote). See also Donoghue intv.
24. Conley, "'All One in Christ,'" p. 87.

I never heard of any such incident. If such a thing happened and I heard of it I would have acted immediately to correct the situation and prevent it from ever happening again.

An incident of this kind is contrary to the teachings of the Catholic Church. The doors of every Catholic Church in Washington are wide open to all who wish to come in to pray and to worship Almighty God.

The report of the committee is of real social value. I am sorry that this part of the report jumped to a general indictment based on one incident.

The *New York Times* called O'Boyle's statement "reassuring," adding that race relations was an area in which the public should look to the churches for leadership.[25]

This public notice was followed shortly by an account of race relations in 1949 Washington in *Ebony*, the national African-American magazine. *Ebony* cited incidents in which black Catholics were curtly barred from a church and told that there was a church in Northwest "for your people." The article also contained photos of the segregated seating at St. Paul's where, as late as 1949, African Americans were restricted to the last eight pews. Although its notoriously bigoted pastor had died in 1947, St. Paul's parish, situated in the heart of Washington's embassy district, prided itself on its distinguished international congregation, and its new pastor had allowed the old racial practices to continue. In a later issue the magazine published a lengthy letter by Father Hannan in which he called the *Ebony* article "very misleading" and the charge that St. Paul's excluded blacks a "falsity." *Ebony* had made no such charge, and Hannan's apologia provided the national journal the opportunity to cite further specific evidence of Jim Crow's continued strength fifteen months after O'Boyle said segregation would end.[26]

Even as the inner-city parishes slowly began to adjust to the realities of neighborhood change, the pace of conformity at Immaculate Conception must have tried O'Boyle's patience to the limit. In 1950 he called on Father George L. Gingras to prepare a plan for reorganizing the parish. Gingras, who had been serving as administrator of St. Augustine's since the legendary Msgr. Olds' retirement in 1949, had shed the traditional attitudes of a native Washingtonian to become the archbishop's principal advisor on racial matters. (His conversion to a racial pro-

25. O'Boyle was quoted in *NYT*, 11 Dec 1948. He was mentioned in the editorial on 12 Dec. See also ltrs., LaFarge to O'Boyle, 15 and 24 Nov 48, and O'Boyle to LaFarge, 29 Nov 1948. All in LaFarge Papers, AGU.

26. *Ebony* (May 1949): pp. 13–18. Pictures of the segregated seating at St. Paul's appear on p. 15. See *Ebony* (Sep 1949) for Hannan's letter and editor's response.

gressive once prompted conservative Chancellor Cowhig to label him a "turn-coat" and to ask who had gotten to him.)[27] Gingras based his recommendations for Immaculate Conception on the proposition that racially separate parishes were being phased out. First, he urged a change in pastors. The incumbent's views were well known, Gingras added, and a new face "would give a big boost to the whole plan." While boundary adjustments could be delayed, he discussed agreements that must be reached with neighboring parishes and proposed a checklist for the new pastor: conduct a census to identify all black and white Catholics in the area; issue envelopes to all and publish lists of contributors so all might feel they belong; begin a convert class, with a particular welcome to African Americans; admit all children to the schools; immediately integrate the choir, ushers, altar boys, and all parish organizations; and finally, establish a strong St. Vincent de Paul Society to tend to the many poor in the neighborhood.[28]

O'Boyle would later adopt a variation of this proposal at Immaculate Conception and, with further modification, when he combined St. Paul's and St. Augustine's parishes and then Capitol Hill's Holy Comforter and St. Cyprian's in the next decade. But there was no immediate change at Immaculate Conception, because, despite his threat of "official action," O'Boyle was not yet ready to go to the extreme of firing a pastor. Not surprisingly, the complaints continued until, a full year after Gingras proposed the change, O'Boyle finally lost all patience. His move came shortly after he received a protest from the visiting chancellor of the vicariate apostolic of Jamaica, Msgr. Gladstone Wilson. Following proper procedure, Wilson had sought to offer a memorial Mass at Immaculate Conception for a deceased member of a Jamaican family living in the parish, only to be told by the pastor that the "sensitive" request was "if not impossible, at least extremely difficult" and that the black monsignor should go to St. Augustine's instead. A furious archbishop once again called the pastor on the carpet. That reverend father said illness had prevented him from making the necessary arrangements. O'Boyle refused to accept this transparent excuse and apologized to the visitor. He pledged that there would be no repetition of an incident of this kind.[29] Three months later Immaculate Conception had a new pastor and integration of the parish began along the lines suggested by Gingras.

27. Hannan intv. For an account of Gingras' transformation into a racial progressive, see the author's *The Emergence of a Black Catholic Community*, pp. 296–97.

28. Ltr., Gingras to O'Boyle, 20 Dec 1951, copy in AAW. Gingras' proposal is discussed in detail in the author's *The Emergence of a Black Catholic Community*, pp. 307–9.

29. Ltrs., Wilson to O'Boyle, 13 Aug 1952, and O'Boyle to Wilson, 18 Aug 1952, copies of both in SAA.

Like these problem city churches, the integration of the schools also got off to a slow start. Surprisingly, the private high schools and colleges led the way. O'Boyle, concerned that these institutions might use their rigorous entrance requirements to maintain racial barriers, scheduled meetings with their administrators at which he and Father Spence emphasized that to work, integration could not be restricted to parochial schools and that every Catholic school in the archdiocese would eventually be expected to participate.[30] All cooperated. Dunbarton College, which had admitted its first black student shortly before O'Boyle's arrival, was joined by Trinity College in 1948. That same fall Georgetown University matriculated five African Americans in its law school. Mackin High School, a small school operated by the Holy Cross Sisters, enrolled a black student in 1949. At the prestigious Gonzaga High School, the Jesuit administrators ignored protests by some parents, alumni, and faculty and accepted two out of seven black applicants into the freshman class. For the most part these very modest changes in these schools were accepted matter-of-factly.[31] In contrast, only one black child was accepted in a parochial grade school in 1949. Employing one ruse or another, at least seven Catholic grade schools were able to turn aside black applicants. After the mother of a ten-year-old black child personally asked Vice-Chancellor Hannan to intervene, the pastor of St. Aloysius agreed to admit her son into his elementary school.[32]

The slow pace of change distressed the activists. Where most diocesan officials tended to view Catholic schools as a means of preserving the faith, black parents saw them as a means of advancement for their children. Reflecting this belief, the Interracial Council had made the need for Catholic education its first priority when its representatives met with the new archbishop. It also continued to publish critical examples of resistance to the archbishop's intent. In 1949 the council charged that, instead of admitting black children to unfilled white schools, some parishes were going to extraordinary lengths to find white pupils, even busing in children from outlying neighborhoods. It pointed to Sacred Heart parish, where qualified African-American children were denied admittance to the school. Commenting on the fact that the white parents and students of Sacred Heart provided a Thanksgiving dinner for 300 children from Holy Re-

30. Donoghue intv.

31. Foley, "The Catholic Church and the Washington Negro," p. 214. For a useful account of Gonzaga's integration, see *WP*, 7 Jun 1999.

32. Ltr., Bp. Thomas Lyons to O'Boyle, 9 Feb 1979, O'Boyle Papers, AAW. See also Hannan intv. Conley's "'All One in Christ,'" pp. 92–93, recounts the various reasons the schools cited in rejecting black applicants.

deemer, a black parish without a school, a council spokesman noted, "Charity is a good and noble thing, but Catholic Negroes in this area would like to see charity preceded by, accompanied by, and followed by justice."[33]

O'Boyle might ignore demands for speedy change, but he had to be disappointed with the proposals submitted by his consultors in January 1950. Referring to what they called the "defects and evils of the present situation," the consultors cited some doleful statistics. Five black children now attended Catholic high schools while at least 1,425 others who had made a retreat in a Catholic parish that year were forced to attend segregated public schools. The four black parish schools were overcrowded and geographically remote from many black Catholic homes. For hundreds of these children, the only recourse to religious training was in packed Sunday school classes. The consultors noted the "contradiction of Catholic principles inherent in these statistics," but went on to list a host of "dangers to be avoided," including violation of the rights of white people, yielding to pressure groups, and hasty efforts to let down the barriers of segregation. Their recommendations tested the limits of gradualism. O'Boyle should "try to secure the consent of all high schools" and "try to secure the consent of all pastors" to admit a few black students each year. They even recommended that he convert a high school (Immaculate Conception was a possibility) "not designated as a colored school" to serve the bulk of black high school students.[34]

The consultors still had much to learn about their new archbishop if they thought "try to secure the consent of the pastors" would fly. Their idea of some kind of quota, on the other hand, appeared more useful, and during the next few months the archbishop, ignoring the consultors, worked out a plan with Fathers Spence and Hannan. He called in the pastors particularly affected and ordered them to accept at least two black children in their kindergarten and grades one through three in 1950, continuing in succeeding years as those first pupils advanced into higher grades. At a later meeting the city's Catholic principals learned about the open enrollment policy adopted for the new diocesan high school scheduled to open in 1951. Meanwhile, Father Hannan met with the principals of the city's Catholic high schools, who agreed to begin accepting black students on a regular basis.[35]

Clearly, O'Boyle intended to bypass the consultors. Integration of the schools, including the later changes in southern Maryland, would henceforth be

33. *CIR* (Dec 1949): p. 188.
34. "Colored Question," att. to Minutes of the Meeting of the Board of Consultors, 24 Jan 1950, AAW.
35. Ltr., Lyons to O'Boyle, 9 Feb 1979, O'Boyle Papers, AAW.

directed by himself in concert with his sympathetic aides. At the same time events were occurring that strengthened O'Boyle's determination to go slowly. Archbishop Ritter's blanket integration order in 1947 concerning schools in St. Louis, and, closer to home, the effort by progressives to integrate Washington's public swimming pools in 1949 had precipitated the strong opposition and civil disorder that he was determined to avoid.

Other archdiocesan institutions seemed to consider themselves immune from the new directives, as the Catholic Interracial Council, by now a self-appointed watchdog, was quick to point out. The city's major Catholic cemetery, it reported, continued to maintain a separate and decidedly inferior section for the African-American dead. "Even in death segregation pursues colored Catholics," the council concluded. Local Catholic hospitals continued to segregate patients by race. Reports circulated that the sisters at Providence Hospital hastily integrated some semi-private rooms when anticipating an episcopal visit, but, if true, O'Boyle was not deceived by any such Potemkin-like efforts. He was determined to break through their color barrier, but it would take some years before, plagued by continuing complaints from black doctors, he acted. Threatening to "take the cross off the top" of the hospital he built, O'Boyle visited Providence and ordered the sisters to integrate.[36]

The Interracial Council was particularly concerned about the treatment of black children in the Catholic Youth Organization. When Father Thomas B. Dade organized Washington's CYO in 1946 with the help of a board of prominent Catholic business and professional men, he established a separate league for the city's black parishes. Only two white parishes would agree to play them, and consequently, the black teams, lacking adequate facilities and forced to beg practice and play time from black public schools, were left to play each other. A group representing black parishes led by Father George V. Joyce from St. Augustine's discussed the problem with Dade in 1948. Aware of the new archbishop's racial policy and the stated aims of the national CYO, Joyce abruptly demanded that Dade integrate his organization immediately. A flustered Dade dismissed the notion, explaining that his board had threatened to resign if the organization sponsored integrated games.

The next day Joyce received a call to report personally to the archbishop. O'Boyle preceded to bawl him out, not because he disagreed with the priest's in-

36. Ltr., Dr. Mitchell W. Spellman to Father Gingras, 2 Jul 1957, SAA. See also Baroni intv. (second quote). On segregated cemeteries, see *CIR* (Dec 1949): p. 188 (first quote). For more on segregation in the hospitals, see the author's *The Emergence of a Black Catholic Community*, pp. 302–3.

tentions, but, the archbishop explained, because the timing of the demand threatened to cause a backlash in the city that might derail his long-range plan for peaceful integration.[37]

O'Boyle's subsequent actions achieved the goal, albeit in a less contentious way. Two weeks after his confrontation with the archbishop, Joyce learned that the CYO would sponsor a championship game between its black and white leagues. The *Interracial Review* claimed that the game between St. Augustine's and St. Dominic's marked the first time the color line in sports had been breeched in Washington. Under orders, Dade followed up this game by inviting the black league to renew its request for integrated games "at a later date." Instead the black parishes quietly withdrew from the CYO in 1949. The Catholic Interracial Council was not so quiet. Local newspapers published a letter from its spokesman protesting the current $25,000 fund drive for the CYO and charging that its segregation made it impossible for many Catholics to support the organization.[38]

Undeterred by the hoopla, O'Boyle continued the quiet pressure at his own pace. In 1951 he personally appointed three prominent black Catholics to the CYO's board of directors and let it be known that he expected the board to produce an integrated sports program. Eventually the major black parishes accepted a renewed invitation to organize CYO teams, which in the next few years began playing the white teams on a regular basis as a matter of course.

In retrospect the racial changes achieved by the new archbishop in those early years seem slight, but contemporaries knew better. Among Washington's churches, the Catholic archdiocese was practically alone in declaring a policy of integration. Adopting reforms that would directly impact thousands of citizens, one of the area's major institutions was defying the status quo. Although great changes were on the horizon, segregation had yet to loosen its grip in 1950. Almost without exception, businesses continued to resist calls for equal access. National Theatre, Washington's sole professional stage, had dimmed its lights rather than allow mixed audiences. The city's major drugstore chain and department stores closed their lunch counters when black customers demanded service. Restaurants in the city continued to refuse African Americans service, despite pending suits in the federal courts. Violent confrontations frequently accompanied efforts by black residents to use city parks and pools. In the midst

37. Joyce and Dade intvs. The account in these paragraphs is more fully developed in the author's *The Emergence of a Black Catholic Community*, pp. 289–91.

38. *WP* and *Star*, 15 Feb 1950.

of this resistance, the actions of the new archbishop attained special prominence. Exulting in President Truman's call for civil rights legislation in his 1949 inaugural address, the *Interracial Review* noted that the archbishop was the leader in the fight for racial justice in the capital.

In fact, the council readily gave notice to what it considered the archbishop's often-overlooked victories. Citing O'Boyle's "high competence" as an administrator who was content to let his actions speak for him, Dr. John J. O'Connor, the council's Washington reporter, listed some achievements that had gone unnoticed even by many Catholics. In addition to the peaceful integration of the churches and the enrollment of black students in the new archdiocesan high school, O'Boyle's had lent vital support to organizations dedicated to social action.[39]

While Catholic Charities remained the archdiocese's principal source of aid for Catholic needy, O'Boyle's open purse proved an important subsidy for the lay apostolates dedicated to Catholic action and social service, especially those working with inner-city residents. Catherine de Hueck Dougherty herself cited O'Boyle's support of the Friendship House movement as a sign that some in the hierarchy were conscious of the need for such work and understood its implication for the Church and for American society.[40] In January 1949 O'Boyle celebrated the opening of a new Friendship House, the St. Peter Claver Center, at 1513 U Street, N.W., and appointed Father Joyce its spiritual moderator and Mary Houston, a veteran of the New York Friendship House, director. He also provided financial support for a permanent three-person staff.[41] His actions, predictably, upset some of Washington's old guard. On the new Friendship House specifically, one Washington matron expressed her horror at the archbishop's sponsoring a place where young white girls were encouraged to associate with black people in such a neighborhood. This activity will lead to intermarriage, she predicted, adding, "Washington is a southern city. You are from the north and will expose yourself to a lot of criticism by such actions." Even those supporting an end to segregation, she concluded, draw the line at social mingling.[42]

Criticism only seemed to spur O'Boyle on. When the Friendship House's lease expired in 1950 he suggested that it resettle in the city's Southwest section and purchased a building for it on Seventh Street. Citing the Friendship House constitution, which emphasized lay control, Mary Houston asked O'Boyle to

39. *CIR* (Oct 1951): pp. 158–59 (source of quote).
40. Ltr., Dougherty to Father Furfey, 10 Jun 1948, Furfey Papers, ACUA.
41. *Star*, 14 Jan 1949.
42. Ltr., Ms. Ross to O'Boyle, 3 Feb 1949, O'Boyle Papers, AAW.

At Camp Florence, a summer program for inner-city kids and a favorite charity of the archbishop who willingly posed for publicity photographs.

consider his purchase an interest-free loan which the center would repay on a regular basis. Although he had intended the purchase as a gift, O'Boyle agreed to the proposal to underscore the fact that the center was a lay enterprise. In the following years the center forwarded its monthly payment of $100 when it could. In turn, the archbishop sent the center $500, usually on a monthly basis, to help cover operations. O'Boyle also took to dropping in on the lively group. After one such surprise visit left him cooling his heels at the door of an empty building because the staff was on retreat, he began to announce his coming down to the minute.[43]

Fides House also received O'Boyle's strong support. Soon after his arrival in Washington he visited the tiny house on New Jersey Avenue and congratulated its live-in staff. The city's papers recorded his observation that since its members had become part of the neighborhood, they had become true neighbors of the poor and were living a vital part of their religion. "You are pointing the way," he added.[44] Important for the staff, O'Boyle added Fides House to the list of organizations receiving subsidies from Catholic Charities.[45] In 1949 he purchased larger quarters for the organization on I Street in Washington's Swampoodle area, and there hundreds of local children received medical care and special after-school education.

Concern for needy children, fostered by his experiences in New York, made O'Boyle a pushover when the St. Vincent DePaul Society asked for help with its summer camp program. This unheralded charity, which provided vacations for some five hundred inner-city, mostly black, children became one of the archbishop's favorite projects. Father Gingras' appointment in 1950 as director of Camp St. Florence in southern Maryland came with a detailed set of instructions from O'Boyle on just how the operation should be run and how funds should be solicited. Periodic visits and generous bank drafts from the archbishop followed on a regular basis. In 1952 O'Boyle promised to get an "offering" from Catholic Charities to help with the cost of camp operations.[46]

Despite its modest beginnings, integration of the city's Catholic parishes and schools attracted praise from civil rights leaders. The Washington branch of the NAACP included O'Boyle in its list of honorees in 1949. Citing his continuing efforts to achieve "a more truly Christian social order," the venerable civil rights organization noted that, despite the many problems he faced in his new post, O'Boyle had constantly sought "to foster the best interests of all his flock."[47]

43. The relations between O'Boyle and the center are fully documented in the St. Peter Claver Center file, AAW. See especially ltrs., Houston to O'Boyle, 5 Nov 1950 and 23 Jun 1952. On the interest-free loan, see O'Boyle, Memo for the Record, 18 Jun 1951.

44. The visit and the archbishop's comments were widely quoted in the city's press. See, for example, *Star* (source of quote), *WP*, and *Washington Times Herald*, 8 May 1948. See also *BCR*, 14 May 1948.

45. Ltrs., Russell to Furfey, 15 Mar 1949, Furfey to Coady, 5 Aug 1953, and Coady to Furfey, 22 Jan 1956. All in Furfey Papers, ACUA.

46. Ltrs., O'Boyle to Gingras, 7 Oct 1950 and 2 Apr 1952. The modest program generated a large file of reports, financial statements, and O'Boyle observations. See Chancery file, AAW.

47. The NAACP award was granted in January 1949. See *CIR* (Feb 1949): p. 61, and (Apr 1949): p. 61.

Recognition also came from fellow Catholics. In October 1949 the Catholic Interracial Council asked him to preside at its prestigious Hoey Award ceremony in New York City, where leaders of the Church's fight for racial justice were recognized.[48] At that ceremony O'Boyle chose to speak on the United Nations Declaration on Human Rights.

He reserved his first major public statement on race relations for a sermon in his own cathedral in March 1950, when he elaborated on the pope's recent statement on the Church's mission to African Americans. He reminded Catholics that the brotherhood of man derived directly from the Church's doctrine of the fatherhood of God and the truth that all are one in the Body of Christ. This doctrine demanded justice for all, and white Catholics, under God their father, must welcome African Americans and resist manmade racial divisions. His frequently quoted conclusion summarized his reasoning on race relations:

> Unless the resources of the Church are placed at the disposal of every single member of the Church and made available to every man, there is no Catholicism worthy of the name. Our Sacraments and our societies, our Mass and mysteries of the Faith are a common possession, just as God is OUR Father. What is Catholic is ours—it is of *all* of us united as one, just as God is OUR Father and not the special Father of any one of us.[49]

The integrationists were jubilant. An Interracial Council spokesman claimed that O'Boyle's strong attack on the "racist heresy" had created a moral climate for peaceful change. The archbishop's "clear and definite instruction" could leave no one ignorant about the Church's teachings on race. Integration, he added hopefully, was now the official policy of the archdiocese.[50] In fact O'Boyle's constancy seemed to convince all but the most obdurate that their new archbishop was serious about changing racial patterns. Two prominent critics of his racial policy made conciliatory moves. A few weeks after the archbishop's headline-making sermon, Msgr. Cartwright invited members of the Interracial Council to a special Mass and breakfast at the cathedral, where they heard the NCWC's Father George Higgins discuss the American Church's evolving racial stance. The Cartwright gesture closely followed an invitation to the same group from Bishop McNamara to attend an interracial gathering at St. Gabriel's, his parish in North-

48. *NYT*, 31 Oct 1949.

49. O'Boyle, "The Apostolate of Justice to All Men," 12 Mar 1950, copy in AAW. The Interracial Council published an extract of the sermon, ten thousand copies of which were distributed throughout the city's parishes. See also lengthy quotes from the sermon in *Star*, 13 Mar 1950.

50. *CIR* (May 1959): p. 61.

west Washington. In fact by 1950 black Catholics were quietly attending churches throughout the city without incident.

By the early 1950s also several of the parochial schools in transitional neighborhoods were exceeding the quotas for the admission of black students. St. Martin's, for example, began its 1950 academic year with ten black children in attendance, while Holy Name counted twenty African Americans in its student body. By 1954 approximately one-third of the pupils at St. Martin's and Holy Name were African American. With most parishes exceeding the goals set for them, recruiting quotas were abandoned. In a laudatory report, the *Evening Star* estimated that some 1,600 black students were attending Catholic elementary schools, 10 percent of the total enrollment.[51]

These statistics masked the true pace of reform and the difficulty in achieving an integrated diocese, since the great majority of those 1,600 students attended four schools in the traditionally black parishes. More revealing were the statistics on the high schools, which attracted students from across the city. Here the number of black students remained low. By 1954 both Mackin and St. Dominic's, small co-ed schools under archdiocesan control, were ten percent black; the new Archbishop Carroll High School six percent black. African Americans were enrolled at all the other high schools, but in statistically insignificant numbers. Putting the best light on it, Msgr. Spence expressed pleasure with the trouble-free transition, predicting that the public schools could expect a similar result when they integrated in the wake of the Supreme Court's historic *Brown v. Board of Education* decision in May 1954.[52]

The Struggle in Southern Maryland

Actually, Spence was not far off the mark. The integration of the city's Catholic churches, schools, and organizations, if somewhat halting, was approaching its goal, and without the development of any kind of organized opposition. The success of O'Boyle's low-key gradualism did not go unnoticed. As guest of honor, Chief Justice of the Supreme Court Earl Warren sat next to the archbishop at the luncheon following the Pan-American Mass on Thanksgiving Day, 1954. The court had recently reached its historic decision that rejected the separate but equal principle and outlawed segregation in the nation's schools and, by extension, in most areas of American life. Turning to O'Boyle, Warren confessed that

51. *Star*, 23 May 1954. See also John Daley, Draft Article Prepared for *CS* (c. May 1954), copy in AAW.

52. *Star*, 23 May 1954.

*O'Boyle with Chief Justice Earl Warren and Speaker of the House
John W. McCormack at the Pan American Mass, 1963. Warren sought
the archbishop's advice on racial integration.*

he was worried about the process of achieving an integrated society, and he
wanted to discuss the archbishop's experiences in Washington.[53] O'Boyle's response went unrecorded, and there were no follow-up meetings between the
two. Both were left to witness in the months to come the riots and bloodshed in
places like Little Rock and at the University of Alabama when the government attempted to enforce the court's decision.

O'Boyle's resolve would be tested in the months to come as he tackled segregation in the parishes of southern Maryland. Although he tried to use the same
technique that had proved successful in Washington, he soon learned that the
time for a low-key, nonconfrontational approach had passed. "No matter what
you do," one angry Maryland resident told the archbishop at the height of the
crisis, "you're not going to cause me to lose my faith." "I'm glad," O'Boyle shot
back, "because I'm going to integrate the schools."[54]

Events would prove he should not have spoken so surely. Nothing in

53. Archbishop Hannan offered the most complete account of the exchange in *CS*, 13 Aug 1987.
54. As quoted in Donoghue intv.

O'Boyle's background, including his years of service in New York's Catholic Charities, would prepare him for his encounter with the widespread, visceral opposition to change among many of the Catholics in Charles, Calvert, and especially St. Mary's Counties. The region was served by twenty-six parishes and four missions, all under the care of the Jesuit fathers. Although the most distant of these churches, St. Michael's in Ridge, was less than eighty miles from the capital, their largely rural congregations more closely resembled those in the deepest South in social outlook. Relations between the races had changed little since Civil War times, a condition faithfully mirrored in the local Catholic Church. With the exception of the all-black congregations at St. Peter Claver near Ridge and St. Dominic's in Aquasco, the churches included black and white congregants, although in rigidly segregated areas, and, following ancient custom, also placed African Americans last during all phases of the liturgy. For the most part black Catholics were excluded from parish organizations. The region boasted two black parochial schools. The pastor of St. Peter Claver also directed the nearby Cardinal Gibbons Institute, a vocational institution specializing in agricultural subjects, and the region's only Catholic high school for African Americans.

The new archbishop's determination to learn about what must have seemed an exotic region was apparent in his discussions with Father LaFarge before his arrival in Washington. In 1949 he had asked Msgr. O'Grady, his old friend from the National Council of Catholic Charities, to tutor him in the economic and social problems of the southern counties. While O'Grady's lengthy report on Charles and St. Mary's Counties no doubt familiarized O'Boyle with economic conditions and existing social services in the region, it did not address the realities of race relations.[55] As a result it seems that O'Boyle was genuinely surprised by the vicious reaction to the hesitant efforts of some of the more progressive Jesuit pastors in 1951 to discuss the idea of integration with their congregations.

Anxious for the success of his ongoing integration program in Washington, O'Boyle was reluctant to countenance any precipitate action in St. Mary's County. In this he had the support of Father William F. Maloney, the local Jesuit Provincial, a cautious leader. Neither was willing to sanction the actions of progressive Jesuits like the saintly Horace McKenna, pastor of St. Peter Claver; his housemate, the provocative Richard T. McSorley, pastor of St. James (a forerun-

55. Ltrs., O'Boyle to O'Grady, 8 Apr and 2 May 1949. See also O'Grady's report, "An Outsider Looks at St. Mary's and Charles Counties, April 11–14, 1949." All in O'Boyle file, NCCC Papers, ACUA.

ner of St. Cecelia's in St. Mary's City); and Michael Kavanagh, pastor of St. Joseph's in Morganza. McKenna had already threatened to close St. Peter's school, calling the effort to continue the poorly staffed and subsidized institution a misguided effort "to put a bandage on the Mystical Body of Christ."[56]

On April 18, 1951, these pastors conducted a Novena of Grace at their parishes during which each delivered a sermon on racial justice. Two days later, Father McKenna, facing a shortage of priests that morning, decided to combine the student bodies of St. Michael's (white) school and St. Peter Claver's for the weekly student Mass. His action set off a firestorm of protest. Children at St. Michael's were yanked out of class while parents and troublemakers kept the party-line phones busy. Feelings were running so high that the Jesuit superior, fearing for the safety of Father McSorley, who was considered an agent provocateur by local Catholics, rushed him out of town. McSorley later attempted to analyze the situation for the archbishop. He claimed that the opposition sensed that the Jim Crow era was passing and, fearing the "tide of Negro life engulfing them irresistibly," they were determined to resist. McSorley welcomed such protests because, he believed, they confirmed the small minority in their determination to integrate and gave their opponents much to think about.[57]

O'Boyle didn't see it that way. Following the contretemps at St. Michael's, the chancery was flooded with complaints and petitions from segregationists. After reviewing the testimony of these witnesses, O'Boyle decided that "all the petitioners proved was that they knew how to sign their names."[58] He also succeeded in countermanding the Jesuit provincial's decision to transfer the three priests because it would seem he was caving in to pressure from the segregationists. Nevertheless, he was still convinced that a quiet approach had the greatest chance of success, and during the next year he agreed to the transfer of the three men.

O'Boyle did not specifically address the racial situation in the counties until the early fall of 1952 when his chancery distributed a "Suggested Program for Meeting Interracial Situation in Southern Maryland" to the priests of the region. Based on what they had learned from their efforts in Washington, O'Boyle's assistants, none with experience in or special knowledge of southern Maryland, sought to provide a formula for ending "compulsory segregation of any kind in the churches." They specifically exempted the schools, calling their integration a

---

56. As quoted in John Monagan, *Horace: Priest of the Poor* (Washington, D.C.: Georgetown University Press, 1985), p. 88. Monagan's book, pp. 87–93, provides a useful account of the 1951 protest in Ridge.

57. Ltr., McSorley to O'Boyle, 2 Jul 1951, AAW.

58. As quoted in Monagan, *Horace*, p. 96.

far more complicated question over which Church authorities lacked complete control. The question of integrating the classrooms, they concluded, should be postponed until success in the churches could be evaluated. Predicated on the belief that the laity as a group would follow, even if reluctantly, the lead of the pastor, the program called on priests to present a united stand on integration and prudently and tactfully discuss the race question with their congregations.[59] Declaring a united front and a common effort essential to success, the authors predicted that if applied "prudently, perseveringly and sympathetically, say for a couple of years," the program should produce some marked improvement in race relations.

The authors went on to suggest a long list of measures that might lead to better race relations, but in an awkward attempt at evenhandedness tended to blame the victim for the crime. Noting that the "aloofness" of whites from their black brethren was not based solely on race, they went on to discuss the lack of refinement, social graces, good manners, and personal hygiene of many local black Catholics. In addition to a self-improvement program for African Americans, they called on pastors to encourage their black parishioners to work with them on solving the segregation problem. Finally, the authors warned that the desire for progress should not blind pastors to the need for extreme caution lest their actions lead to "incidents." If incidents should occur, the chancery expected the archdiocese's role in the matter to be kept to a minimum. Opposition should be addressed locally, and pastors should "work out their solution locally."

Although Spence was probably the author of this optimistic directive, it could not have been issued without the archbishop's knowledge and approval. It is difficult to see how even with his limited understanding of the region O'Boyle could have envisaged such a plan workable. It was unrealistic to ask the priests of southern Maryland, some of them natives of the region and many allied to a provincial generally satisfied with the racial status quo, to unite solidly in an effort to change centuries-old customs. It was also unrealistic to expect pastors to confront opposition alone. Finally, it was unrealistic to expect pastors to act when their colleagues who had tried to fight Jim Crow were being transferred out of the region.

Nothing came of the vague program for converting the hearts and minds of Catholics dedicated to preserving their way of life. In May 1954 Father LaFarge reported to O'Boyle that, setting aside the question of schools for a time "and as

59. "Suggested Program for Meeting Interracial Situation in Southern Maryland," issued by the Chancery between 25 Aug and 17 Sep 1952, AAW.

I see it, it can *only* be for a time," nothing had changed in the parishes of southern Maryland. According to LaFarge, his fellow Jesuits in St. Mary's County were awaiting direction from their archbishop. Was it not time, he probed, for O'Boyle to act? While nothing might be expected from the older clergy, LaFarge admitted, the new men might show some initiative and "under favorable auspices" might take the lead. Even if only slight improvement was achieved, "some initiative is better than passive resignation." O'Boyle's answer must have given scant comfort. He and Msgr. Spence had recently surveyed the situation with three of the senior clergy of the region, O'Boyle noted, and he was scheduled to visit southern Maryland in the next weeks to obtain firsthand information from pastors on the ground.[60]

O'Boyle seemed anxious to follow the spirit of LaFarge's suggestions, even if he began by going to the very men most likely to oppose his wishes. As promised, he met with the pastors, using his so-called fact-finding mission as a vehicle for getting the word out: he intended to begin the integration of the churches in southern Maryland. He would be flexible. There would be no fixed timetable, but he expected to see a start made everywhere. As in Washington, no provocative announcements would be issued and unnecessary skirmishes with the diehards would be avoided.

His intervention produced no obvious changes in the rigid segregation in most parishes. Lacking an organized lay group to push for change or pastors willing to take the lead, reform was severely limited. Representatives from Washington's Interracial Council tried to integrate seating at St. Peter's in Waldorf later that year by commandeering a pew at the principal Sunday Mass. The incident and an inept attempt by the pastor to explain the confrontation to the press threatened to produce a noisy standoff the following week. Chancellor Hannan was sent to defuse the situation by speaking at all the Masses, while the parish launched a plan to abolish the practice of renting reserved pews to white parishioners. In fact, the only noticeable integration in the mid-1950s occurred in the two parishes near the Patuxent River Naval Base in St. Mary's County. Black Catholics stationed at the base, accustomed to integration, ignored local custom and without incident were accepted among the white congregants at the recently established Immaculate Heart of Mary Church in Lexington Park. Curiously, some of the white employees at the base, living in the neighborhood of the all-black St. Peter Claver, attended, though not without objection from some in the

---

60. Ltrs., LaFarge to O'Boyle, 27 May 1954 (source of quotes), and O'Boyle to LaFarge, 1 Jun 1956. Both in LaFarge Papers, AGU.

congregation, what they assumed was their local parish, thereby integrating a formerly all-black church.[61]

Despite the unsatisfactory response to his directive on church attendance, O'Boyle decided to begin integrating the schools in the region. He kicked off the campaign by asking all the pastors in southern Maryland to deliver, beginning in September 1955, a series of seven monthly sermons on racial justice. Following every sermon he or a member of his staff would interview the pastors about changes in attitude in their parishes. By the third sermon, most reported, their congregations were coming to understand where all this talk was leading, but none reported any marked change in attitude.[62] The archbishop himself delivered a widely publicized speech on the subject before the John Carroll Society in February 1956. Expounding on his theme that racial tolerance was grounded theologically in the concept of the Mystical Body, he called on Christians to reject discrimination and promote the cause of equal opportunity for all citizens. Until these goals were reached, he warned, America could not assume the mantle of leadership in the cold war struggle for the allegiance of the third world. To the high achievers of the John Carroll Society he added a telling footnote. It was not so long ago, the steelworker's son reminded them, that their Irish, Italian, and Polish forbears, refugees from Old World slums, came to prosper in America because their white skins eventually afforded them an equal opportunity. Discrimination based on color was neither morally nor legally defensible.[63]

Convinced that the inevitable protest would be muted if integration began unannounced, the archbishop wanted the pastors to begin accepting a limited number of black children in their schools in September 1956 after giving only a two-week notice to their congregations. The pastors, however, feeling isolated and exposed, tried to convince him that an official proclamation was needed. For his part Chancellor Hannan argued that Catholics in southern Maryland sprang from a tradition that demanded an open airing of controversy. An official announcement sometime in the spring would provide time for them to vent their opposition and in the long run serve to soften protest. Accordingly, on May 20, Pentecost Sunday, O'Boyle ordered a statement read at all Masses announcing that the ten parochial schools in the region would register black students, begin-

61. These incidents are discussed in the Hannan intv. Unless otherwise noted this interview, which provides the most comprehensive, first-hand account of the fight to integrate the schools of southern Maryland, is the source of the following paragraphs.

62. Donoghue intv. See also Conley, "'All One in Christ,'" p. 106.

63. O'Boyle, "The Christian Impact," 28 Feb 1956, *The John Carroll Society Quarterly* (Fifth Anniversary Issue, 1956), p. 6ff.

ning with grades one and two, in the fall. Speaking to the press, Hannan noted that the order was "a normal development which brings the schools into line with the rest of the archdiocese" and was unrelated to the pending court cases stemming from the *Brown* decision.[64]

Hannan and Spence, serving as O'Boyle's representatives, attended the many parish meetings that ensued. To all the condemnations and demands for retraction the official response was the same. Their concerns would be addressed by the archbishop, who promised to be flexible. If, for instance, a parish determined that only a small number of black students could be accommodated at the start, O'Boyle would accept this judgment so long as a beginning was made. In return, the congregations must agree to respect the compromise reached. In some cases O'Boyle himself traveled to St. Mary's County to meet with select committees, mainly with the intent of encouraging the priests to persevere. Some of these men found themselves under extreme pressure to break ranks with him. For example, Father James Wilkinson, pastor of Holy Face and a native of the region, learned that plans were afoot to boycott his brother's hardware store because of the priest's support of O'Boyle's order. O'Boyle called Wilkinson a "tower of strength" in those troubled times. He was also relieved to learn that the pastors in southern Maryland were calling on their archbishop to "stand your ground."[65]

Numerous groups insisted on presenting their arguments to the archbishop personally, and O'Boyle readily agreed to such meetings. The most noted of these occurred in August 1956, when a large delegation representing the major parishes of St. Mary's County came to St. Patrick's for a discussion that lasted seven hours. Far from the raucous crowd that had confronted Father McKenna in 1951, this group included some of the most distinguished and thoughtful Catholics from the region. O'Boyle patiently answered their questions and debated their opinions. Recognizing the sincerity of their views and the depth of their feelings, he even arranged an impromptu lunch for the group. In the end they pleaded that he postpone any changes in their schools until the state ordered integration in the public schools. To those who claimed that the area would not be ready for integration for at least a decade, O'Boyle replied, "Well,

64. *Star* (source of quote) and *WP*, 26 May 1956. The press was citing an announcement from the archdiocese on 25 May. No mention was made in their coverage of the announcement read at Mass the previous Sunday.

65. Ltr., O'Boyle to Very Rev. William F. Maloney, S.J., provincial, Maryland Province, 20 Jun 1956, Jesuit Appt. File, AAW (first quote), and Ellis intv. (second quote). On the Wilkinson boycott, see Donoghue intv.

gentleman, we're going to do it tomorrow."[66] The delegation took its leave knowing it had failed. Yet up to the last minute O'Boyle was not at all sure of how the vast majority of Catholics in the region would react. On September 5, just days before schools were scheduled to open, he privately warned his priests that "because of certain circumstances in Southern Maryland," the archdiocese might well need to support many of the schools in the area.[67]

Opening day of school was filled with alarms and excursions. Threats to shoot any black child attempting to enroll prompted the state police to escort the black students entering the Catholic school at Great Mills. The anxious pastor of St. Aloysius in Leonardtown called Hannan to tell him that, fearing an outbreak of violence from an angry group pledged to blocking the schoolhouse door, he was calling in the police. Hannan overruled him. Rather than relying on the police, he argued, it was incumbent on all Catholics to order themselves and respect the archbishop's decision. In the end the demonstrators made their noise, but the black children entered peacefully. Some parents removed their children from the school, but, ironically, their spaces were promptly filled by non-Catholics seeking a superior education.

The token successes of opening day seemed to break the spirit of the opposition. Although progress during the next nine years would be slow, an increasing number of black children enrolled in some of the region's parochial schools and at St. Mary's and Ryken High Schools without undue notice or commotion. Finally in 1965, with closure of St. Peter Claver's school and with state-ordered integration on the horizon, the significant integration of the region's Catholic institutions began.[68] Chided by black critics for the slow pace of reform, O'Boyle offered them a metaphor: "Gentlemen, I will take the dishes of segregation off the table one at a time. If I pulled the table cloth off, I would break many of the dishes."[69] Yet at times even the patient champion of gradualism could sound discouraged. When Dr. Paul Cooke of the Interracial Council reported in 1963 that, on a visit to St. Michael's at Baden, he and his colleagues were treated politely but found the parish's CCD children still strictly segregated by both race and sex, O'Boyle replied, "You know, there is only so much I can do down there."[70]

Still, as his later exploits would demonstrate, setbacks like this were not about to end the fight for racial justice that, for O'Boyle, represented a basic moral and

66. As quoted in Higgins intv.
67. Ltr., O'Boyle to Dear Father, 5 Sep 1956, AAW.
68. Ltr., Lyons to O'Boyle, 9 Feb 1979, AAW.
69. This oft-quoted remark was published in Abell, *Patrick Cardinal O'Boyle,* p. 11.
70. Quoted in Cooke intv.

social issue. Few of his brother bishops in those early civil rights times saw the need to challenge traditional race relations, but to O'Boyle the issue of racial justice was not just theological. Msgr. Ellis, that most rigorous of Church historians, offered an unhistorical, but convincing explanation for O'Boyle's stance. The archbishop was a fretful man, Ellis noted, who usually stewed over a policy before acting. But in this case the decision was a private one, from the heart, and immediately arrived at. Often critical of O'Boyle's policies, Ellis concluded that this potentially fractious decision came directly from the abundance of the heart—"ex abundantia cordis"—of a steelworker's son.[71] Looking back on his career, an elderly O'Boyle offered some support for Ellis' conclusion. His years of social work in New York had confirmed what he was rapidly learning about race relations in Washington: African Americans had been treated most unfairly, both by the Church and civil society, and both the Church and the nation were going to pay a price for those injustices.[72]

Although his understanding of Christian principles was certainly at the heart of his deep-rooted conviction that change must come, class and economic issues were clearly an added incentive. His easy identification with the economic have-nots, a legacy of his Scranton childhood, also informed his decision to act, as underscored in his address to the John Carroll Society in 1956. As Archbishop Hannan, a leader in the integration of the archdiocese, later observed of O'Boyle:

> He had very deep-seated convictions, and they went back to the days in Scranton even. By the time he got to New York he had formed his mind about this. And there was no doubt in my mind that he was going to prevail, no matter what difficulties.[73]

O'Boyle's patience with the opposition was based on a genuine sympathy for people who he realized found it difficult to bridge the social, cultural, and economic gulf that separated them from their black brothers and sisters. He was preaching what the old seminary professors used to call one of the "hard sayings" of Christianity, and he was content to give his hearers time to absorb it. At the same time, if his sympathy was obvious, so too was his determination. To a surprising degree his effort to avoid drawing a line in the sand produced a solution that comforted both sides of the issue without inciting confrontation. Time was his ally. Catholics in the archdiocese were not immune to the liberalizing effects of World War II that were beginning to change America's racial attitudes.

71. Ellis intv.
72. He later expressed this view to his secretary and close associate. See Donoghue intv.
73. Hannan intv.

Signs of such a liberalizing trend were not apparent in the capital in 1948. Yet from his first days in Washington it was obvious to all who knew him that O'Boyle was determined to integrate his archdiocese. The difficulty of the task he set for himself must have appeared daunting. With few exceptions, segregation in Catholic institutions had been unquestioned since the time of slavery. Separation of the races was a given. It went unquestioned. It was never an issue.

Until the new archbishop made it one.

~iho

A Capital Pulpit

Americans of a certain age tend to wax nostalgic about the 1950s. Overlooking the onset of the cold war and the battle for Korea, they remember most clearly a time of sleepy innocence filled with weighty matters like the direction of popular music and the size of tailfins on the family car. In a certain sense this selective recall is understandable because, weary of a world at war and its austerities, the public was reluctant to address signs of yet other revolutions threatening their way of life. The postwar reconstruction of Europe and Asia was already forcing the United States into a cold war against communism. Demands by African Americans, supported by the federal courts, were about to generate a mighty movement that would transform the country's awareness of civil rights. Weakened family ties, soon to be exacerbated by development of "the pill," threatened to alter much of the nation's traditional moral value system. Nor to be overlooked, inequities in the national economy were strengthening working-class demands for a greater share of the postwar prosperity.

The Catholic Church had a legitimate interest in all these issues, and its bishops were called on to provide guidance on all sorts of new moral and social questions. At the same time the American Church itself was entering a period of self-examination. Its unique and fruitful relationship with the state was coming under increased assault from conservative forces in Rome. The need to defend America's freedom of religion, along with questions of liturgical reform and Church authority, was being hotly debated, adding to a ferment that would explode on the world stage at the Vatican Council.

As a new archbishop faced with building a new diocese, Patrick O'Boyle might be excused if, like so many Americans, he avoided the swirling turmoil. Instead, he became one of the Church's leading spokesmen on issues of the day. His place in the spotlight was due in part to his unique relationship with his brother bishops, in part also to the fact of his geographical proximity to the seat of government and the secretariat of the bishops' conference, which made him a logical point of reference for those seeking a Catholic response to a moral question. But most of all, many of the issues of the day directly related to the expertise O'Boyle had developed in his years in social work and international relief. His interests in these subjects seemed to compel his speaking out. His response to questions, quotable and candid, revealed a leader stern and unrelenting in defense of the Church's teachings on faith and morals while innovative and farsighted on social and economic issues. This dichotomy allowed him to form comfortable partnerships with both the traditionalist and progressive leaders of the American Church. An O'Boyle trademark, it manifested itself especially in the postwar decade.

On Becoming an Advocate

Ten months after becoming archbishop of Washington O'Boyle was elected by his fellow bishops to the National Catholic Welfare Conference's administrative board. He would serve in this executive body, in effect the Conference's board of trustees, for seventeen years, five as chairman, and later as a member of the executive committee of the NCWC's successor organizations, the National Conference of Catholic Bishops and the United States Catholic Conference.[1] The Conference's bylaws limited election to its board to five successive one-year terms (cardinals served as *ex officio* members). O'Boyle, therefore, was elected by his colleagues in every year he was eligible. He also served for nine years as episcopal chairman of the NCWC's Social Action Department, eighteen years on the Conference's Committee to Complete the National Shrine of the Immaculate Conception, and fifteen years on its Community Services Committee, which addressed the religious needs of the armed forces and the defense industry. The man typically played down this singular demonstration of respect from his colleagues. "If the bishops had their way," he remarked to an assistant, "I'd always

1. These elections were the subject of interest in the secular press. See, for example, *Star,* 18 Nov 1948 and 21 Nov 1955, and *NYT,* 19 Nov 1956 and 10 Apr 1959. Details of these elections, including appointments given to board members, are included in Minutes of the Administrative Board, NCWC Papers, ACUA.

be on the executive committee and be their representative in Washington. They figure I'm on the scene so why not put me on there [the board] and let's use him in town."[2]

Actually, while O'Boyle's observation contained a grain of truth, relations with his colleagues were more complicated than that. True, members of the board naturally welcomed the fact that one of their own was on hand in Washington to treat with any pressing matter rising between their periodic meetings. But if this selfish motive prompted O'Boyle's recurring assignments, it does not explain his repeated election by all the bishops at their annual meetings. Here his close relationship with the various factions of the hierarchy was the critical point. Since the mid-1930s the NCWC had been led by a group of Midwestern bishops coalescing around Cardinals Mooney and Stritch and Archbishop Mc-Nicholas. Their interest focused mainly on developments within the American Church, in contrast to the group counted among the allies of Cardinal Spellman, whose considerable political gifts and personal friendship with both government leaders and the pope prompted him to concentrate on the Church's international role, especially the U.S. government's relations with the Vatican and the communist threat to Western society.[3]

O'Boyle was closely allied to both factions. He maintained a respectful allegiance to his old boss, Cardinal Spellman. Even after he had joined Spellman in the college of cardinals, his correspondence was always respectful, ever deferential. ("May I express formally my deep appreciation and heartfelt gratitude for your genuine kindness," he wrote Spellman after the latter spoke in Washington. "Without any flattery, your appearance here and your address really made the conference.")[4] After O'Boyle moved into his own home, he insisted that Spellman stay with him when in Washington. He willingly paraded with the rest of "Spelly's boys," as the cardinal's protégés were called, at the mass celebration of his twenty-fifth episcopal anniversary in Yankee Stadium in 1957. At the same time O'Boyle was well aware of Spellman's reputation for ruthlessness and avoided any involvement in the contentious cardinal's many public controversies. A case in point was Spellman's tendency to link labor unrest with international communism, an association that O'Boyle would deny.[5] But he kept his

2. As quoted in Arthur intv.
3. These divisions in the NCWC are fully explored in Fogarty *The Vatican and the American Hierarchy*, pp. 311ff.
4. Ltr., O'Boyle to Spellman, 8 Nov 1950, O'Boyle file, AAW.
5. Higgins intv.

peace. Prelates like Cardinal Mooney might joke about Spellman's highly publicized use of seminarians as scab gravediggers, but O'Boyle never commented on the matter in public.[6]

Similarly, O'Boyle never expressed himself publicly on the subject of Joseph R. McCarthy and his notorious hunt for communists in American institutions. O'Boyle had some awareness of the Wisconsin senator's agenda through their mutual friends Msgr. Cartwright and Father William Awalt, the latter of whom had received McCarthy's wife into the Church. He even shared McCarthy's suspicion that there were some instances of communist infiltration that needed to be addressed. But unlike Cardinal Spellman, who embraced the controversial Wisconsin senator, awareness of his own ignorance in the matter and distaste for McCarthy's methods made O'Boyle refrain from any public comment.[7]

At the same time O'Boyle enjoyed close relations with Spellman's opponents. The Midwestern leaders had come to admire the hard-working administrator of their war relief program, and, in turn, O'Boyle showed a genuine affection for Cardinal Mooney and Archbishop McNicholas and his successor, Karl Alter. Early in their acquaintance, the younger man discovered Mooney's interest in golf and thereafter challenged him to a game at every opportunity. Many of his letters to Mooney, no matter how serious the subject, contained some reference to their game.[8] For duffer O'Boyle there was no need to shave his strokes to insure a Mooney win. Nor was the warmth of his relations with the influential archbishop of Cincinnati in the least exaggerated. Their friendship stemmed from their business association after McNicholas succeeded Mooney as chairman of the administrative board, but it quickly exceeded that expected of episcopal colleagues. Shortly after O'Boyle arrived in Washington, McNicholas addressed him in typical fashion: "May I, as an older brother, urge you never to worry, because worry solves no problems; and secondly, not to work so fast that your health may be impaired."[9]

O'Boyle enjoyed genuine friendships with a number of his fellow bishops. He was particularly close to old New York friends like Spellman's auxiliaries John McGuire and George H. Guilfoyle. He was also fond of Richard Cushing, easily

---

6. O'Boyle's position is recounted in Higgins intv. On O'Boyle's relations with Spellman, see also Donoghue intv. On the Yankee Stadium event, see John Cooney, *The American Pope: The Life and Times of Francis Cardinal Spellman* (New York: Times Books, 1984), pp. 248–49.

7. Hannan and Awalt intvs.

8. See, for example, ltrs., O'Boyle to Mooney, 29 Jul and 4 Oct 1950 and 1 Jun 1953, Mooney Papers, AAD.

9. Ltr., McNicholas to O'Boyle, 27 Feb 1948, McNicholas file, ACUA.

relating to the Boston archbishop's blunt, simple style of expression. O'Boyle took great pleasure in Cushing's stories about his famous friends, and frequently entertained him as a houseguest. Busy in Washington, he nevertheless frequently traveled considerable distances to help colleagues celebrate important occasions. He was on hand when his "dear old friend" Karl Alter was installed as archbishop of Cincinnati in 1950.[10] He was always ready to return to Scranton for any ceremony involving his boyhood friends, now both bishops, Henry Klonowski and Martin O'Connor. Klonowski remained a close personal friend even though O'Boyle disapproved of his blunt, autocratic treatment of his parishioners. He also enjoyed telling stories about his efforts to teach Klonowski to play golf. Klonowski's habit of moving his ball to a better lie naturally irritated other members of the foursome O'Boyle had recruited to play.

Philosophical differences or personal foibles were never allowed to interfere with friendship. For example, O'Boyle maintained warm relations with Philadelphia's Cardinal John Krol despite their frequent clashes over issues.[11] O'Boyle also understood that many people had legitimate complaints about some of Archbishop McIntyre's decisions and imperial style, but he never allowed this to color relations with his old classmate, even though his patience seemed sometimes tried by the often-fretful McIntyre. At one meeting of the Catholic University board of trustees, the impulsive McIntyre, rushing ahead of the agenda, was demanding a vote on an issue, forcing O'Boyle to interject: "For God's sake, Frank, wait until the motion has been made."[12]

Relations with Washington's other archbishop, Apostolic Delegate Cicognani, were more complicated. Although always properly respectful and businesslike, O'Boyle nevertheless resented the Italian diplomat's forays into the affairs of his archdiocese. Sometimes acting like the paterfamilias of a parish in the old country, Cicognani would bypass O'Boyle and personally involve himself in the workings of Holy Rosary, the Italian-American parish in downtown Washington, and Villa Rosa, a retirement home spearheaded by Holy Rosary's feisty, independent-minded pastor, Father Nicholas de Carlo. Because O'Boyle recognized the usefulness of his relationship with Cicognani, which had developed from their work during the war, he held his tongue and relations remained proper, if cool. He believed the delegate's interference only encouraged de Carlo's

10. O'Boyle, Notes, pt. 28.
11. Gillen intv. Msgr. Gillen was frequently associated with Cardinal Krol on the latter's trips to Washington.
12. As quoted in Ellis intv. For an extended discussion of O'Boyle's episcopal friendships, see Higgins, Donoghue, Gillen, Arthur, and O'Brien intvs.

shenanigans and once exclaimed, "There is only one archbishop of Washington." Yet he prudently kept his silence.[13]

O'Boyle's colleagues in the NCWC were attracted by his cheerful personality, sense of humor, and especially his straight talk.[14] O'Boyle firmly believed that the Conference was the place where bishops should air their opinions and openly debate their views. He harbored strong opinions on many subjects and over the years never hesitated to speak out. At the same time he was usually careful to avoid alienating a colleague, and, moreover, made clear his genuine respect for each bishop's autonomy. He was never tempted to become a king maker, and adamantly refused to play clerical politics, a stand his colleagues readily recognized and appreciated. They felt safe with his straightforward, no-nonsense way of doing business.

Like many American institutions, the NCWC was changed by its wartime experiences. As historian Gerald Fogarty has pointed out, where before the Conference was merely tolerated by Rome, the war had led to its recognition by the Vatican as an official voice of the American hierarchy. Rome had also come to accept that, despite ethnic diversity, Catholics in the United States now constituted an organic unity, an American Church. This important step on the way to a more sophisticated concept of episcopal collegiality was prompted in part by the American Church's work to succor the victims of war, a program in which O'Boyle, Mooney, and McNicholas were intimately involved. The war also provided American Catholics the means to demonstrate their wholehearted patriotism. While bigotry was by no means eradicated, the war led most citizens for the first time to genuinely accept Catholics as equals. The Midwestern coalition of bishops hoped to build on this war-induced shift in opinion to win from the Vatican acceptance of America's church-state relations while winning from Washington a Catholic voice in the reshaping of postwar society. O'Boyle, as evidenced in his public statements, was an eager partner in this plan.

The bishops turned to their Social Action Department for a greater understanding of many of the country's postwar concerns. O'Boyle's department, as its mandate outlined, was designed to assist Catholic institutions apply the Church's social teachings, especially to the fields of industrial relations, social legislation, health care, and family and rural welfare. These lofty responsibilities

13. As quoted in Arthur intv. For an extended discussion of de Carlo's relations with O'Boyle and with Cicognani, see Hannan intv. Hannan was often called in to establish a truce among the men.

14. Baum intv. Cardinal William Baum, who would succeed O'Boyle in Washington, worked with O'Boyle as a member of the NCWC staff in earlier years.

were performed by a small permanent staff, including Fathers George Higgins (general labor problems), John Cronin (race issues), and Raymond A. McGowen (social action planning and operations). The staff drew up position papers on subjects such as international peace and race relations, reported on pending legislation, and testified for the bishops before congressional committees.

Truth be told, the episcopal chairman had little to do with the day-to-day work of his department. He did, however, press several pet subjects in his annual statements to the administrative board. In 1951 he warned that the St. Vincent de Paul Society had lost its prewar robustness. Less than one-third of the nation's parishes supported a conference, and he wanted permission to address a letter to all the bishops urging them to organize more confraternities in their dioceses. The following year he made a special plea for Labor Day Masses, which he wanted celebrated in every diocese. Meanwhile he outlined how his department had organized conferences and labor schools around the country to demonstrate how relations between labor and management would improve with the formation of labor councils in the various industries.[15]

Nowhere was O'Boyle's elevation to the see of Washington more celebrated than among his old friends and colleagues in the National Conference of Catholic Charities and the St. Vincent de Paul Society. "It is our hope," the *Catholic Charities Review,* the joint publication of the two organizations, editorialized, "that his [O'Boyle's] continued guidance and influence may be felt in the movement to which he has already contributed so much." When the apostolic delegate announced O'Boyle's appointment as spiritual director of the national St. Vincent de Paul Society later in 1948, the *Review* predicted that he would give new impetus to the development of a lay apostolate in Catholic charity and institute closer ties between the society's laymen and the clerical directors of diocesan Catholic Charities. Rounding out his credentials in the charity field, O'Boyle also accepted in 1948 the post of president-councilor of the newly founded Inter-American Catholic Social Action Confederation, an organization created by Catholic Charities representatives from twenty-three nations in the Western Hemisphere.[16]

O'Boyle's old colleague and general secretary of the NCCC, Msgr. John O'-Grady, was especially jubilant when it became clear that a Catholic Charities stal-

15. Minutes of the Administrative Board, 1951, 1952. NCWC Papers, ACUA. For details on the Social Action Department's work see *Catholic Action* (various years).

16. *The Catholic Charities Review* 32 (Jan 1948): p. 1 (first quotation), 32 (Oct 48): pp. 34–35 (second quote), and 33 (Jan 1949): p. 44. See also *NYT,* 10 Oct 1948.

wart would be a prominent member of the NCWC. "It looks more and more like a new day all around," the hard-charging O'Grady predicted.[17] Although O'Boyle had always kept a certain distance from the politically canny but impatient Irish-born activist, he clearly had absorbed many of O'Grady's theories about the role of the Church in social service. As archbishop he would continue to support federal programs while claiming for the Church its legitimate role. He also agreed with O'Grady's thinking on the operations of a now-reduced St. Vincent de Paul.[18]

Never shy, O'Grady in effect anointed the new archbishop as national spokesman for Catholic Charities and the St. Vincent de Paul Society and proceeded to bombard him with suggestions. He repeatedly offered drafts of speeches he wanted O'Boyle to deliver. He also sought O'Boyle's support for a reorganization of the St. Vincent de Paul superior (national) council, which, he charged, was "at a complete standstill." He was especially critical of the national leaders for failing to adopt new programs and urged O'Boyle to push the presidential candidacy of George J. Gillespie.[19] Although O'Boyle would pass O'Grady's suggestions on to the secretary of the NCWC, he did not, as a rule, press matters. He did, however, use some of O'Grady's ideas in his speeches and collaborated in his effort to revitalize the St. Vincent de Paul Society. Correspondence between the two clearly indicated that they carefully orchestrated the annual meetings of the NCCC and the St. Vincent de Paul Society. The 1950 national conference, for example, was clearly an O'Boyle-O'Grady affair, carefully programmed to include an appropriate audience for the guest speakers. The sessions were held at Catholic University, and O'Boyle addressed personal notices to some of the professors, urging attendance. Concerning the session featuring an appearance by Cardinal Spellman he told Father Ellis, "Our people would be edified to see a goodly number of our priests at this largest meeting of the conference. Come if you can."[20] He also arranged for a special papal message to be delivered at the closing session.

Whether Spellman's address stimulated as much delight in this captive audience as O'Boyle diplomatically noted was open to question, but there is no

17. Ltr., O'Grady to O'Boyle, 19 Nov 1948, NCCC Papers, ACUA.
18. Higgins intv. The noted labor priest discusses O'Grady's philosophy and provides examples of his public advocacy of Catholic Charities causes.
19. Ltrs., O'Grady to O'Boyle, 11 Sep 1948; 15 Mar (source of quote), 19 Sep, and 20 Oct 1949; 4 Nov 1950; and 31 Mar 1953. All in NCCC Papers, ACUA.
20. Ltr., O'Boyle to Ellis, 27 Oct 1950, Ellis Papers, ACUA.

doubt that the selection of speakers was carefully thought out. Early on O'Grady, an old Washington hand, had warned O'Boyle against inviting prominent members of the Truman administration. They were displeased by Catholic Charities' stand on health insurance and social security, he said, and they had done all they could to divide Catholic opinion. They would use their appearance to reiterate their position in hopes of converting some Catholics. At the least they would feed the impression that positions taken by the NCCC were not fully representative of the Catholic point of view.[21] O'Boyle took the point, and no government official spoke at the 1950 conference.

By 1953 O'Boyle was asking O'Grady for his recommendations for episcopal advisors in his Social Action Department to oversee organizations like the Family Life Bureau and Catholic Charities. O'Grady canvassed his colleagues to provide O'Boyle with comments on potential candidates.[22] He also continued to provide O'Boyle with material for his increasingly busy speaking schedule. He never seemed abashed when his client rejected his approach.

The gift of eloquence, like the gift of song, was notably absent from the blessings bestowed on Patrick O'Boyle by his Irish forebears. Over the years he would develop a style of delivering extemporaneous remarks that could both charm an audience with their warmth and directness and convince them with their concise logic, but he never mastered the ability to read well from a prepared text.[23] A busy man, O'Boyle's formal addresses were often prepared for him. O'Grady was only one colleague providing materials. Associates in the Social Action Department, especially Higgins and Cronin, prepared most of his talks on labor, peace, and race. John Tracy Ellis worked on parts of his sermons that involved historical topics; even Msgrs. Cartwright and Hannan were called on to contribute drafts. O'Boyle, who had spent years writing material for his old boss, Msgr. Keegan, seemed decidedly uncomfortable using the work of others. Thanking Ellis for ghosting a foreword for a book, he called it "a pity that another signs it." The book was "all Greek and Hebrew to me," he admitted, and Ellis' stylish foreword, he claimed, would set him up for potshots from friends.[24] As in his own experience with Keegan, O'Boyle rarely told his collaborators what he wanted to say. So in tune with his views were Higgins and Cronin, they could

21. Ltr., O'Grady to O'Boyle, 3 Oct 1949, NCCC Papers, ACUA.

22. See, for example, ltrs., O'Boyle to O'Grady, 21 Sep 1953, and O'Grady to O'Boyle, 24 Sep 1953 and 16 Nov 1954. All in NCCC Papers, ACUA.

23. Quinn intv. Msgr. Quinn was a first-hand witness to O'Boyle the speaker, and offers a careful analysis of the cardinal's speaking style.

24. Ltrs., O'Boyle to Ellis, 3 Mar (second quote) and 4 Apr (first quote) 1949. Both in Ellis Papers, ACUA.

grind out an address without particular direction. In any case, a review of the scores of speeches and sermons O'Boyle delivered in his Washington years reveals, in addition to parochial matters, a man deeply concerned with the cold war and the role of private charity in the midst of growing governmental involvement in public assistance.

The Issues: Communism

Tutored by his years in war relief, Patrick O'Boyle came early to an understanding of the menace of postwar communism. Again and again during the 1950s he delivered impassioned condemnations of the Soviet system. Imitating his old hero Al Smith, he frequently called on his listeners to "look at the facts."[25] In all sorts of forums he examined the dangerous rivalry between the superpowers and appealed to Americans to use the principles their nation was founded upon as moral weapons in the cold war. For example, his reaction to the imprisonment of Cardinal Josef Mindszenty in 1948 was quoted in the *New York Times.* "Governments, which owe their existence, in large measure at least, to the lives and valor and labor of American soldiers and American citizens," he posited, "should be bluntly apprised of the fact that they may not with impunity defy the very principles which our blood and sacrifice purchased for them."[26]

Usually O'Boyle's exhortations on communism carried a positive theme, some practical step he wanted his country and his Church to take to counter the multifaceted assault on the West. At the same time he could fulminate with the best of the cold war warriors. For a prestigious New York audience in 1949 he contrasted the Soviet Union, "which stands against the rest of the world as a symbol of immoral brute force cloaked in the iron robes of war," with the United States, whose laws were "fashioned by men with reverent fear of God and generous love of man."[27] The *New York Times* reported on his charge that communism's war on religion was "unparalleled in history." Speaking on Reparation Day in November 1952, a date set aside annually by the American bishops to pray for oppressed peoples, O'Boyle recalled that Christians were commanded to forgive their enemies. "With God's grace we can do that, but I do not think that we can say of the new enemies of Christ that they know not what they do."[28]

25. Extemporaneous remarks at Anti-Communist Meeting sponsored by the Knights of Columbus, 1 Nov 1948, quoted in the *Star,* 2 Nov 1948. See also O'Boyle's speech before the Catholic Press Association, as quoted in *The Commonweal* (17 Jun 1960): p. 303.

26. *NYT* and *Star,* 3 Jan 1949. The complete quote is taken from an article in *CS,* 7 Jan 1949.

27. Address at New York Red Mass, Sep 1949, as reported in *Star,* 14 Sep 1949 (source of quotes).

28. As quoted in *NYT,* 29 Dec 1952, and *Star,* same date.

As acting president of the NCWC's administrative board in 1953, and reacting to the arrest of Cardinal Stefan Wyszynski, he charged that the Polish communist regime "struck one more infamous blow against a heroic and helpless people." Wyszynski, he claimed, had stood firm against the "ruthless efforts by men devoid of decency or conscience to deprive his beloved people of rights, which because they derive from God, are more precious to them than life itself."[29]

In 1956 O'Boyle called for an "agonizing reappraisal" of America's cold war tactics. The communists, he charged, "utter their lies bluntly and fearlessly," monopolizing slogans of justice, peace, and equality "while we have the truth muted and gagged." His reflections, later inserted in the *Congressional Record* by Congressman John W. McCormack, went on to elaborate on his point that the free world found itself "outmaneuvered and outgunned in the very area where our strength should be greatest."[30]

He reiterated this charge in 1959 in another speech reprinted in the *Congressional Record*. The communist world had youth and vigor, he warned; "if we weaken and falter . . . they will fill the vacuum." The West, he insisted, must make the communists understand that it would not compromise with evil.[31] In reaction to a visit by Soviet Deputy Premier Anastas Mikoyan, O'Boyle reminded his follow citizens of the communist achievement: persecution "total, unceasing, and systematic." "In sober truth," he added, "this is the worst persecution in the 2000 years of Christianity. The enemy would cover this horror with a mantle of silence . . . the victims of this tyranny are numbered in the hundreds of millions."[32]

Fiery rhetoric aside, both in public statements and behind-the-scenes negotiations O'Boyle worked for practical approaches to cold war problems. For example, he played an active role in the bishops' efforts to alleviate the suffering of persons displaced by the cold war. As bishop-elect he became a member of the Episcopal Committee for Displaced Persons, and one of his first acts in Washington was to appoint a diocesan delegate to the National Catholic Resettlement Council.[33] Support of displaced persons was also the subject of his first pastoral letter to the Catholics of Washington.

29. Encl to ltr., O'Boyle to Mooney, 7 Oct 1953, Mooney Papers, AAD.

30. O'Boyle, "The Struggle Against Communism," Sep 1956. Extracts quoted in *Catholic Mind* (Sep 1956): pp. 484ff.

31. "The American Stand," reprinted in *JCS Quarterly* (Summer 1959): pp. 15–18.

32. "The Oppressed Peoples," 28 Dec 1958, reprinted in *JCS Quarterly* (Spring 1959): 9–13.

33. Ltrs., McNicholas to O'Boyle, 19 Dec 1947, and to Mooney, 1 Jan 1948; O'Boyle to McNicholas, 10 Jan 1948, and 6 Mar 1948. All in McNicholas Papers, ACUA.

O'Boyle found himself elevated to the position of public spokesman for the bishops on the subject of displaced persons after his disagreement with the Daughters of the American Revolution on the subject gained national attention. The DAR had passed a resolution attacking the refugee legislation pending in Congress. He expressed regret that "this grand group of estimable women should adopt a resolution so at variance with the sacred tradition of our country to be a friend and a charitable neighbor to the needy, the oppressed and the afflicted." Pending legislation, he pointed out, was not intended to change immigration law, but to provide emergency and temporary assistance to victims of communism.[34]

Yet O'Boyle too was critical of the Displaced Persons Resettlement Act as it finally emerged from Congress. He clearly sympathized with President Truman who, while signing the bill on June 25, 1948, dubbed the legislation a mockery. By limiting displaced persons to those so declared in August 1945 (the end of World War II), the legislators had eliminated from consideration refugees from communist Eastern Europe who had been displaced since the war. Truman reluctantly signed the bill, which would admit 205,000 refugees over a two-year period, because to veto the imperfect legislation would deny refuge to everyone in the near future. The new law created the National Resettlement Conference, which accredited volunteer agencies (including the NCWC) for participation in the program and for federal funds.

Serving as spokesman for the NCWC on the issue, O'Boyle participated in the effort by volunteer agencies to ameliorate the discrimination inherent in the 1948 law. Their effort bore fruit in 1950 when Congress authorized admittance of an additional 415,000 refugees, a category now redefined to include those who had escaped from behind the Iron Curtain in the postwar years, along with Italian refugees from prewar fascism. A further group of 215,000 refugees was welcomed under a law signed by President Eisenhower on August 7, 1953.

The displaced persons legislation was separate from the country's immigration law. Congress had reviewed its immigration policy in 1952 and enacted new and stricter legislation, the so-called McCarran-Walter Act, over President Truman's veto. This law established a quota system that frankly discriminated against Asian and Eastern European immigrants.[35] O'Boyle strongly criticized the legislation. "There is something very unchristian and un-American about

34. *NYT* and *Star*, 26 Apr 1948. Both papers provided lengthy excerpts from O'Boyle's remarks (and are the source of the quote).
35. *NYT*, 26 Jun 1952.

our immigration policy," he told the distinguished Committee on Italian Migration in a widely quoted speech.[36] He wanted the restrictive quotas changed, but his political instincts told him that was a fight for another day. He concentrated instead on further liberalizing the country's refugee quotas. In 1955 he called for further liberalization of the displaced persons legislation to admit 200,000 persons a year for an indefinite period. He would continue to push for such legislation throughout the decade.[37]

Long experience in New York social work and war relief had taught O'Boyle that effective operations often depended on the Church's full cooperation with secular organizations and other religious denominations. In April 1950 he urged the administrative board to support a proposal by an Australian archbishop for a Pan-Pacific Conference on Communism. The bishops turned him down, citing the expense of such an enterprise, but they approved his proposal to participate in an All-American Conference on Communism sponsored by the American Legion.[38] Similarly in 1953, O'Boyle called on America's religious leaders to join together in demanding a United Nations investigation of communism's war on religion. His call for an interreligious "crusade of prayer and protest" won headlines in the national press.[39]

His idea of united action involving close cooperation with other faiths was best illustrated by his crucial support of the Foundation for Religious Action, a group organized by Charles Lowry, an Episcopal priest, and Edward Elson, pastor of Washington's National Presbyterian Church.[40] O'Boyle's request for an NCWC representative to the foundation prompted much discussion among the bishops that revealed old fears about interfaith activity. O'Boyle, who had consulted the apostolic delegate and several key colleagues like Archbishop Cushing and Bishop John J. Wright, argued the practical advantage of concerted action. The administrative board finally agreed that he should proceed with the project, provided that the foundation would agree to soften the interdenominational implications of its title by adding "Against Communism." O'Boyle got the title changed and, more importantly, helped the foundation get started with desperately needed financial support, even dunning some of his fellow bishops for contributions.[41]

36. *NYT,* 6 Dec 1955, and O'Boyle, "Speech to American Committee on Italian Migration," NCCC Papers, ACUA (source of quote).
37. NCWC News Service, Bio 210, 14 Jan 1955.
38. Minutes, Administrative Board, 18 Apr 1950, NCWC Papers, ACUA.
39. *NYT* and *Star,* 28 Dec 1953.
40. Ltr., Rev. John Cronin to Hannan, 8 Apr 1954, Foundation file, AAW.
41. Minutes of the Administrative Board, 27 Apr 1954, and Minutes of the Bishops' Annual

Similarly, O'Boyle remained a staunch supporter of the United Nations, re-peatedly referring to the American bishops' 1945 statement endorsing the country's participation in that body. He frequently reminded audiences of the bishops' conclusion that "a sound world organization is not a Utopian dream." To those Catholic critics of what they liked to call "internationalism" who were campaigning "to get the U.S. out of the U.N. and the U.N. out of the U.S.," he pointed out, "To yield to the fear that this thing [international cooperation] cannot be done is defeatism." Addressing the Catholic Association for International Peace in 1952, he recalled the urging of recent popes to join in the effort to achieve "worldmindedness." Despite its imperfections and Soviet obstructionism, the U.N., he claimed, "is, humanly speaking, the last best hope of international peace."[42]

O'Boyle had just appointed a diocesan representative to the local affiliate of the American Association for the United Nations.[43] He followed this up by composing a prayer asking God's guidance for the U.N., which he ordered offered at Masses throughout the archdiocese. In 1956, in the wake of the Soviet invasion of Hungary, the bishops issued a special statement prepared by O'Boyle's Social Action Department. It declared that the U.N. "offered the world the only present promise for sustained peace," before going on to praise the Eisenhower administration for its effort to solve world problems through the world organization.[44]

In 1953 O'Boyle was given the job of integrating the overseas work of the NCWC's various departments and agencies.[45] In short order he presented an agenda which in effect devised a new organization that placed all relief activities and refugee assistance under one episcopal committee and elevated the office dealing with immigration legislation to equal status with the other departments. These and a series of new directives also proposed by O'Boyle to govern the conduct of various agencies affiliated with the NCWC in their dealings with the Vatican, the federal government in Washington, and the Church in other countries were approved by the administrative board in April 1953.[46]

Meeting, Nov 1956. Both in NCWC Papers, ACUA. See also ltr., O'Boyle to Bp. Michael J. Ready, 23 Aug 1954, O'Boyle Papers, AAW.

42. Address to the Catholic Association for International Peace, 14 Nov 1953, as quoted in *America* (28 Nov 1953) and includes O'Boyle's quote from the 1945 bishops' statement. The speech was given prominent coverage in *Star,* 15 Nov 1953, and *CS,* 20 Nov 1953.

43. Memo, Hannan to O'Boyle, 7 Jul 1953, O'Boyle Papers, AAW.

44. Ltr., O'Boyle to Theodore Smith, Exec. Dir., U.S. Committee for the United Nations, 26 Nov 1956, O'Boyle Papers, AAW. See also *NYT,* 18 Nov 1956 (source of quotes).

45. Rpt. of Treasurer, Bishops' War Relief Committee, Minutes of Bishops' Annual Meeting, Nov 1948, NCWC Papers, ACUA.

46. Minutes of Meeting of Survey Committee, 22 Jan 1953, and of the Administrative Board, 14

Throughout his years in Washington, the archbishop would remain intimately associated with overseas relief. Father Swanstrom, director of what was now called Catholic Relief Services, turned to him repeatedly to press special appeals on the administrative board, and O'Boyle secured an appointment for his old associate Aloysius Wycislo to the board of Catholic Relief Services. He remained involved in the annual fund-raising operation and helped stimulate closer cooperation between Catholic Relief Services and the Catholic Charities international organization. But he was under no illusion that private charity could shoulder the burden alone. As he had in the early postwar months, he continued to call on the U.N., especially its relief and rehabilitation agency, as well as the international offices of the American government, for assistance. As early as 1951 he was blasting Western governments for their "abysmal failure to observe the precepts of Christian charity" by withholding surplus goods from those in need. Citing the plight of the starving millions reported by the Indian bishops, he admitted that the need was too great for voluntary agencies to handle and called on the government to ship surplus food. "Catholics can not sanction that difference of opinion between nations should cause our charity to grow cold."[47] He encouraged men like Msgr. O'Grady to keep the public informed about the practical benefits accruing from international aid to places like Italy, where American relief was helping keep the country from going communist.[48]

Social Action Issues

Speaking to the Catholic Press Association in 1960, Archbishop O'Boyle admitted that the Church appeared solely preoccupied with communism, birth control, indecency, and other readily identified evils, and he urged Catholics to broaden their concept of moral law. He wanted more attention paid to the country's social and economic failings, especially in the areas of labor relations, civic corruption, racial discrimination, urban development, and health and welfare for the poor. These were complex issues, he agreed, and when moral principles were applied to complex issues it was not unusual for men of good will to differ on solutions. But he expected Catholics to cooperate with all Americans of good will to form a truly Christian social order.[49]

Apr 1953, NCWC Papers, ACUA. O'Boyle proposed all the recommendations approved by his survey team.

47. Address to the Washington Retreat League, 15 Apr 1951, copy in O'Boyle Papers, AAW.

48. Ltr., O'Boyle to O'Grady, 17 Jan 1956, NCCC Papers, ACUA. See also O'Grady, Letter to the Editor, *WP*, 14 Jan 1956.

49. O'Boyle outlined this thesis in two addresses: "Truth, Charity and the Press," a sermon

The archbishop's primary social concern was with the future of the Church's charity projects in a period of increased governmental involvement in welfare. The increasing secularization of welfare, he had warned in an address to the National Conference of Catholic Charities in 1948, would eventually cause a "lowering of human values and cheapening of human life." Attempts to divorce religion from welfare, the inevitable consequence of what he called the "cold professionalism" of government social work, would in the end crowd out the work of individuals and groups of volunteers bonding together to help the needy.[50]

The government had an important role, he frequently admitted, but charity was the personal responsibility of every Christian. The national press reported his 1950 speech applauding efforts to ensure greater participation of the laity in the work of charitable institutions. The abundant signs of increased interest in such work, especially among Catholic youth were, he claimed, "the most hopeful sign of our times." His vision of this work was perhaps most touchingly summed up in an extemporaneous remark made at the dedication of new buildings at his old Staten Island orphanage in 1952. "The litany of charity is endless," he told his Mt. Loretto audience, "endless as the vital need of men to be rightly regarded, to be protected, and to be loved. Charity is a debt never fully discharged. . . . There are everywhere the poor to be succored, the sick to be visited and comforted, the homeless to be sheltered, mouths to be fed, and bodies to be warmed."[51]

Such sentiments were particularly true in the field of child welfare, an area in which O'Boyle had special knowledge. As early as 1949 he had detected efforts to repeal the requirements written into most state laws that protected the religious welfare of children cared for in public institutions. He had collaborated with Msgr. O'Grady in warning the bishops on public welfare legislation working its way through Congress in 1949. Particularly troubling in the bill was provision for the government to exert direct control over orphaned and dependent children receiving federal aid. O'Boyle viewed that as an effort by bureaucrats in

preached at the golden jubilee of the Catholic Press Association in May 1960 [text reprinted in *The Commonweal* (17 Jun 1960): pp. 303–4]; and "Social Responsibility," a talk before the Loyola Retreat League, Mar 1961 [summary printed in *JCS Quarterly* (Summer 1961): pp. 11–12].

50. O'Boyle, "The Apostolate of Catholic Charity," 12 Oct 1948, reprinted in *The Catholic Mind* (Mar 1949): pp. 153ff. (source of first quote). See also NCCC speech, 7 Nov 1954, excerpts reprinted in *NYT*, 8 Nov 1954, and *CS* news release, Nov 1954 (second quote).

51. O'Boyle, welcoming remarks to delegates to NCCC Convention, 3 Nov 1950, as quoted in *NYT*, 4 Nov 1950 (first quote), and speech delivered at Mt. Loretto, 28 Jun 1952, excerpts reprinted in *CS*, 4 July 1951 (second quote). See also *Staten Island Advance*, 28 Jun 1952.

the Federal Security Agency (predecessor to the Department of Health, Education, and Welfare) to reduce the influence of volunteer childcare agencies and to divorce religion from every aspect of welfare. Especially troubling to the directors of Catholic Charities was the effort by some leaders of the Community Chest to pressure Catholic organizations to turn an even greater number of children over to government agencies for care.[52]

Not content with rhetorical warnings, O'Boyle was ready with practical advice. The 1950 White House Conference on Children and Youth had passed, among its many resolutions, several judged inimical to the Catholic childcare philosophy.[53] O'Boyle pointed out to the president of the administrative board that most of the conference's recommendations relating to religion were nevertheless, in his opinion, better and more pointed than any before proposed by a government group. The Church could readily support the majority of these resolutions about future federal programs, and he wanted the bishops to appoint representatives to the conference's follow-up committees. These representatives could air their objections to individual proposals while influencing the future course of federal welfare programs.[54] In the end he got his way. Msgr. John McClafferty and other Catholic representatives served on the White House committees.

O'Boyle's frequent appeals for a close and equitable partnership between public and volunteer agencies received national attention. The partnership must be balanced, he cautioned audiences in the mid-1950s. While the state possessed its own proper sphere of influence in promoting the common welfare, it must never exceed its authority and intrude upon the domain of voluntary religious efforts. Rather, each must supplement the work of the other. "Statism is a great evil," he went on with a warning that earned headlines, and the government should never be allowed a monopoly in charity work. Efforts by the government to expand its role would not only smother the work of Christian charity, but also be a "catastrophic event blasting America's foundation of freedom," and therefore must be resisted.[55]

His solution: Christians must follow "Christ's most revolutionary teaching," his social gospel. That meant they must become actively involved in charitable

---

52. Ltrs., O'Grady to O'Boyle, 12, 17, and 19 Mar 1949. All in O'Boyle file, NCCC Papers, ACUA.

53. Ltr., O'Grady to Msgr. Howard Carroll, NCWC General Secretary, 4 Nov 1949, NCCC Papers, ACUA.

54. Ltr., O'Boyle to Keough, 21 Dec 1950, copy in NCCC Papers, ACUA.

55. O'Boyle's observations were made in addresses to successive NCCC conventions in November 1954 and 1955. See excerpts in *NYT,* 8 Nov 1954 (first quote) and 7 Nov 1955 (second quote).

work. Mass involvement was the way to assert the rights of religions and other volunteer organizations and preserve the American tradition of private charity. Catholic Charities must demand that living standards be raised and emphasize in its own programs the preservation of family unity by strengthening its family services. Likewise, volunteer religious organizations must collaborate with the state in the war for better housing. Catholic Charities must "be in the forefront, shaping public opinion, and guiding the way" toward wholesome family life in decent neighborhoods.[56]

Especially for the St. Vincent DePaul Society, an organization that historically emphasized a person-to-person approach to charity, O'Boyle's emphasis on modern social services required a change in direction. The rapid development of suburban communities at the expense of city centers, which were left with largely transient or economically depressed populations, posed severe problems for many American dioceses. O'Boyle wanted the society to expand its horizons, as he put it, to broaden its social vision beyond mere almsgiving into every phase of modern social action. A tall task, he admitted, and he urged society members to become leaders in the fight to alleviate the complex social woes that engulfed those left in the city core, while at the same time providing a spiritual foundation for the new social class emerging in the suburbs.[57]

Improvement of labor-management relations was also a continuing goal of the NCWC and a specific project for its Social Action Department, to which O'Boyle brought an instinct for the old labor traditions of the Pennsylvania mills and minefields. National labor leaders appreciated how important Washington's archbishop was to their cause. They highly esteemed O'Boyle, not only for his very vocal defense of their position, but also because of his practical support in a non-union city. O'Boyle's insistence on a union work force for his large building program gave the unions a strong bargaining tool to use in other capital building projects.[58] His support, however, was not unconditional. He demanded that labor leaders live up to their own standards when it came to offering opportunities to black workers. He was harsh on the unions and their poor racial record, even threatening to stop employing unions who discriminated.

Subordinates like Father Higgins came to appreciate the archbishop's willingness to fight for greater economic equity in American society. Behind the

56. "Five Decades of Service in Charity," 25 Sep 1960, reprinted in *The Catholic Charities Review* 44 (Oct 1960): pp. 8–11.

57. "Widening Vincentian Horizons," speech delivered at the NCCC convention, 21 Sep 1958, text in *The Catholic Charities Review* 42 (Nov 1958): pp. 17–20. O'Boyle's talk was fully covered in *NYT,* 22 Sep 1958.

58. Higgins intv.

scenes he worked with his subordinates to fight the so-called "right-to-work" laws that posed a threat to unionism.[59] Soon after O'Boyle became its chairman, the Social Action Department prepared, over his signature, a thirty-year retrospective of the bishops' 1919 "Program of Social Reconstruction." Typical of so many statements associated with Washington's archbishop, the 1949 retrospective contained a careful prescription for action. It called on citizens to make further adjustments in the economic order to better pattern their society on the natural law and the Gospels. New legislation was necessary, but new laws could not root out the causes of economic disorder and social injustice. In harmony with Catholic thought developed in the wake of the great social encyclicals, the statement rejected the idea of class warfare in favor of reciprocal obligations between owners and workers. Above all, labor and management needed to form cooperatives in their own ranks so that an organized management and an organized labor could come together and decide on practical programs, which, in cooperation with the government, would lead to a more just and stable society.[60]

To school Catholic leaders in the goals of such cooperation, O'Boyle published a manual containing pertinent sections of the Church's recent social documents. He wanted seminarians in particular to make a serious study of the papal encyclicals. He also believed his manual could serve as a handy primer for bishops and teachers when called on to answer questions about the Church's position on labor issues.[61] In 1950 he appointed a committee of lay and clerical experts to study the application of *Quadragesimo Anno* to current labor conditions, and the following year he issued a public plea for Catholic schools to do all they could to revive interest in the social encyclicals. Three years later he was back again, urging a national celebration of the labor encyclicals to remind Catholics of this "powerful source of guidance" for better labor-management relations.[62]

In a modest way O'Boyle's Social Action Department sought ways to structure labor-management relations in unionized industries. It worked with management and labor groups in a search for new areas of cooperation. In 1953 it sponsored industry conferences in Boston and Portland, Oregon, under the aus-

59. Ltr., Higgins to O'Boyle, 3 Jan 1956, NCWC Papers, ACUA.

60. Ltrs., O'Boyle to McNicholas (circa 29 Jan 1949), and McNicholas to O'Boyle, 16 Feb 1949. Both in McNicholas file, NCWC Papers, ACUA.

61. Ltr., O'Boyle to McNicholas, 4 May 1949, McNicholas file, NCWC Papers, ACUA.

62. O'Boyle, "May 15th Anniversary of the Social Encyclicals," reprinted in *Catholic Action* (April 1951): p. 3. See also Report of the Social Action Department, Minutes of Administrative Board, 18 Apr 1950, NCWC Papers, ACUA, and ltr., O'Boyle to Mooney, 7 Feb 1956, Mooney Papers, AAD (source of quote).

A Friend of Organized Labor. O'Boyle *congratulates AFL-CIO leader George Meany on his receiving the University of Notre Dame's Laetare Medal, 1955.*

pices of the local bishops. During succeeding years similar conferences were organized in regions where closer cooperation seemed possible. In Washington the department maintained close liaison with national labor and employer organizations like the AFL and the U.S. Chamber of Commerce.[63]

O'Boyle willingly identified himself with labor leaders. In 1953 he presided over a convocation at Catholic University at which George Meany, president of the AFL, discussed the social encyclicals. Just days later he delivered the invocation at the convention of the AFL's Maryland–District of Columbia regional organization. In his prayer at the dedication of the headquarters for the International Union of Electric, Radio and Machine Workers in 1955, O'Boyle noted that the history of American labor "had often been one of struggle, a fight for justice and the dignity of man." Pleading that in the future these goals could be achieved more peacefully, he called for greater labor-management cooperation.

63. Reports of these efforts over the years were made to the bishops at their annual meetings, for which see minutes of the Administrative Board and the annual meetings of the NCWC.

"It is good that men are willing to fight for the right, but it is even better when all parties can unite in a spirit of brotherly love in the quest for the common good."[64] At the presentation of the University of Notre Dame's Laetare Medal to George Meany in 1955, O'Boyle issued an endorsement of the American labor movement:

> The Church in America has always had explicit confidence in the aims of organized labor and has urged her members to take an active part in labor activities. The Church believes that unions are necessary for developing sound social order as well as for protecting workers' rights.[65]

Such support was not unconditional, as O'Boyle reminded a Washington audience some weeks later. The Church was pro-labor, he declared, but not in the "sense of rationalizing or condoning or winking at labor's defects nor . . . in the sense of being anti-management or anti-anything else." That needed to be stated, he claimed, to clear away the confusion that too often surrounded discussion of the Church and labor. Basically, O'Boyle concluded, labor and management were "partners in production; they prosper and decline together." Rather than each continually rehashing the historic faults of the other, did it not make better sense, he asked, for each to devote its energy to putting the Christian idea of society into practice, making the social Gospel an effective force in American economic life?[66]

Racial Justice

While the bishops' position on labor-management issues was well known through their many statements over the years, their views on America's miserable record on race relations was never articulated as clearly. Any statement on the subject had been issued at the insistence of the Vatican and discussed the Church's teachings only in the broadest of terms. A few individual bishops had won a national audience for their forthright condemnation of discrimination, and in Washington the new archbishop had quickly made known his intention to integrate the diocese. From his cathedral pulpit in March 1950 he condemned segregation ("nothing could be more hostile to this divine religion") and demanded full access for African Americans to all the resources of the Church (without which "there is no Catholicism worthy of the name").

64. As quoted in *CS*, 17 Jun 1955.
65. As quoted in *Catholic Mind* (Feb 1956): pp. 81–86.
66. O'Boyle, "The Christian Impact," 28 Feb 1956, reprinted in *JCS Quarterly* (Summer 1956): pp. 6–15.

Race matters were in the purview of O'Boyle's Social Action Department, and soon after his appointment he was involved in obtaining the services of the dean of the Catholic University's National Catholic School of Social Service to testify before a congressional committee in favor of making the Fair Employment Practices Committee a permanent agency of the government. O'Boyle personally approved Msgr. John McClafferty's statement, which spelled out the need for retaining the nondiscrimination clause in all federal contracts, but "keeping in mind the Southern attitude," as he alluded to the lingering anti-Catholicism in some areas of the country, and to relieve the concern of Catholic University's rector, he arranged for the articulate McClafferty to identify himself to the congressmen as a representative of the Washington Catholic Interracial Council.[67]

Reflecting the challenge he was facing in southern Maryland, O'Boyle returned to the subject of race relations in a widely quoted speech to the John Carroll Society in 1956. Inviting his distinguished listeners to examine their consciences in regard to the discrimination suffered by African Americans, he seemed also to be asking his brother bishops to, as he put it, "make an honest audit of the race problem that is currently so much discussed in the United States." He reminded his audience of Catholic lay leaders how "our ancestors" had been regarded by their fellow Americans not so many years before. Their position in society had not been so different from the poor undereducated African Americans struggling in the inner city. Only the accident of color provided them the equality of opportunity denied to so many black Americans.[68] While he treated his audience to a clear and concise condemnation of prejudice, his appeal to their sense of fairness and better natures was more winning and likely more effective.

In the wake of the race riots that impelled President Eisenhower to dispatch federal troops to Little Rock High School in 1957, the Social Action Department's Father Cronin prepared a statement on race that echoed O'Boyle's appeal to conscience the year before. It called on reflective citizens of all faiths "to act now and act decisively" to end discrimination. Declaring that "the heart of the race question is religious and moral," the document specifically criticized those who in the name of prudence opposed any attack on segregation as well as those who were demanding radical solutions to the country's racial problems. Although sympathetic to these sentiments, Cardinal Mooney, the ranking Ameri-

67. Ltr., O'Boyle to McNicholas, 18 May 1949, McNicholas file, NCWC Papers, ACUA. The bill to make the FEPC a permanent agency was defeated in 1950 and again in 1952.

68. O'Boyle, "The Christian Impact," reproduced in *JCS Quarterly* (Summer 1956): pp. 6–15, and later widely distributed in a special reprint.

can prelate, feared that to call for a vote on the statement might divide the NCWC. He refused to consider Cronin's proposal in 1957, pleading that it was too late to act. His intention was made clear the next year when he again rejected an appeal to bring the statement before the administrative board for a vote.

Matters appeared to change in October 1958, however, when the Vatican intervened. The apostolic delegate received a cable from Pope Pius XII ordering the American bishops to issue the statement at once. Only a few bishops had had the opportunity to review the text, and when the pope suddenly died, the apostolic delegate convened an emergency meeting of the cardinals before they left for Rome. They decided to suppress the pope's order, calling it unofficial since it had been sent in irregular form and lacked the papal seal. Described as "furious," O'Boyle ordered Cronin to write Mooney, now in Rome, asking him to present the draft statement to the bishops ahead of their forthcoming annual meeting. Again Mooney, in concert with now-Cardinal McIntyre, refused.

Again death intervened. On the eve of the conclave (after declaring to his colleagues that he intended to vote for Francis Spellman for pope on the morrow), Mooney died. Following election of the new pope, O'Boyle cabled McIntyre and Spellman, the two remaining American cardinals, asking them to meet him in Washington before the bishops' meeting. There Spellman and O'Boyle either outvoted McIntyre or otherwise changed his mind, and the statement was submitted to the administrative board, which approved it unanimously. O'Boyle argued that the statement would be more effective if it were issued by the entire hierarchy. The board agreed, and the archbishop personally appealed to his brethren for approval. With only four dissenting votes, the statement was approved and immediately released to the press, which afforded it national headlines.[69]

Closer to home, O'Boyle tried to publicize the often pernicious connection between poverty and racial discrimination when he discovered that welfare authorities in Fauquier County, Virginia, were referring poor and mostly black women to a voluntary sterilization program. In a nationally reported sermon he especially excoriated the government program as an "obvious and crudely selfish materialistic" attempt to reduce the local tax rate by cutting relief payments. Not only Catholics, he claimed, but all who believe in the dignity and inalienable rights of humans should agree on the immorality of sterilization. To adopt this immoral act as government policy, he charged, betrayed a lack of confidence in

69. Cronin, "Religion and Race," *America* (30 Jun 1954): p. 472, and Minutes of the Administrative Board and of the Bishops' Conference, 1958, NCWC Papers, ACUA. See also Conley, "'All One in Christ,'" pp. 113–14, and Higgins intv.

the nation's ability to solve its economic and social problems. Here poor people, especially disadvantaged African Americans, were being treated as second-class citizens, being told that because of their poverty they were not in fact equal to their neighbors. Treated like irresponsible children, these poor women were being denied the dignity owed them.[70] O'Boyle would later mark the Virginia case as the first step in his campaign to connect birth control with misguided economic policy.

Federal Aid to Education

Although Catholic education did not fall within the purview of the Social Action Department, O'Boyle's interest in the subject was well documented by his frantic building program in the early 1950s. The cost of the enterprise in his archdiocese, particularly the expense of building high schools in the rapidly expanding suburbs, focused his attention on the thorny subject of federal aid. He was thoroughly familiar with the arguments about public subsidies for religious institutions since his days in New York Catholic Charities, but by the end of the 1950s he had decided that, rather than rehash the old constitutional arguments about direct federal aid, the bishops should develop a practical program to secure long-term federal loans for their education projects. On the advice of friends in Congress, he recommended in March 1961 that the bishops seek federal loans for parochial schools. He wanted a prominent Catholic layman recruited to approach President John Kennedy and seek his support and to secure the services of a leading constitutional lawyer to argue their case at congressional hearings. The politically astute O'Boyle also recommended that the bishops find an articulate mother of Catholic schoolchildren to testify to the need for federal help. He wanted the NCWC to start an educational program on federal loans and to get the laity involved in the campaign.[71]

In 1962 the bishops learned that their effort to secure this new kind of help was doomed. The threat that the Church would seek special privileges from the government, most recently aired by Paul Blanchard in his popular anti-Catholic treatise, *American Freedom and Catholic Power,* helped the opposition. But O'Boyle never gave up the fight. In subsequent public discussions he left unspoken the appeal for direct aid and concentrated instead on selling the usefulness of Catholic schools to the commonwealth. He recalled the value of the old Protestant-dominated public schools of earlier times, contrasting their teaching

70. O'Boyle, sermon delivered at St. Matthews Cathedral, 9 Sep 1962, copy in Sterilization file, AAW. For reaction to the sermon, see, for example, letters to the editor, *WP,* 15 Sep 1962.

71. Minutes of Administrative Board, Mar 1961, NCWC Papers, ACUA.

about the reality of God and the importance of his commandments with the "vague secular humanism" of today's public schools, which ignored the "deeper inner need of so many of our young people for basic roots." The answer, he proposed, was the modern parochial school, which combined a good secular and religious education without causing divisiveness in a pluralistic society.[72]

Building the Shrine

The 1950s also saw "Cinderblock O'Boyle" operating on the national stage when he led the effort to complete the Shrine of the Immaculate Conception, the church, one of the world's largest, that dominates the capital's northeast skyline aside Catholic University. O'Boyle's somewhat stuffy observation that, as ordinary of Washington, he was expected "to husband the effort to a successful conclusion" was neatly balanced by Bishop Wycislo's breezy comment: "the Shrine was O'Boyle's baby." In fact, the bishops underscored Wycislo when in 2001 they installed near the entrance of the building a plaque bearing O'Boyle's likeness and proclaiming his leadership in the project.[73] As the local bishop and chancellor of Catholic University, O'Boyle might have expected appointment to the bishops' committee that oversaw the Shrine in November 1948, but a place on the committee not explain his assuming direction of the arduous project. Close associates point to his extraordinary dedication to the Blessed Mother as the center of his devotional life and as the impetus for his role in constructing the Shrine in her honor.[74] Practically every nation in the world had a great shrine to Mary, he claimed, and he was in the habit of urging his Catholic countrymen "to show that we yield to no people in our loyal devotion and affection." He was convinced that a Marian shrine in the capital would become a major place of pilgrimage. Where others blanched at the projected cost, he insisted that the American laity would be quick to support "anything done for the Blessed Mother."[75]

The Shrine, begun by the bishops in the early 1920s, saw only the completion of a crypt church before work was halted by the Depression and the war, and, probably most significantly, by the death of Bishop Thomas Shahan, the undisputed leader of the Shrine program. Money continued to be collected in the ear-

72. Quotations from O'Boyle, "Address to the Rotarians and Kiwanians of Washington," 26 Nov 1969, copy in AAW. On O'Boyle's continuing efforts to secure federal aid, see ltrs., O'Boyle to McIntyre, 21 Aug 1962, and to Spellman, 5 Sep 1962 and 8 Jun 1964. All in NCWC Papers, ACUA.
73. O'Boyle's Notes, pt. 30 (first quote); Wycislo intv. (second quote).
74. Both Archbishop Hannan, as quoted in *CS*, 4 Jan 2001, and Bishop Lyons in his eulogy, copy in AAW, noted that O'Boyle's singular effort to complete the Shrine was a result of his personal devotion to the Blessed Mother.
75. Pastoral ltr., Nov 1953, as quoted in *Star*, 5 Dec 1953.

ly postwar period, an effort spearheaded by Bishop John F. Noll of Fort Wayne, longtime publisher of *Our Sunday Visitor* and chairman of the bishops' Shrine committee. Despite several national campaigns, total contributions by 1950 still fell far short of the estimated $7 million needed to complete the project.[76] In fact most recognized that the long-touted $7 million estimate was increasingly unrelated to the reality of postwar prices, and Noll was not even able to muster a quorum for his committee's annual meeting in 1951. With little new money coming in, the Shrine stood, an aging, deteriorating eyesore on the edge of the university campus. Noll repeated the architects' warning: the deteriorating foundation, built at the cost of $2 million twenty-five years earlier, would be unable to bear the weight of the superstructure if building was postponed much longer.[77]

O'Boyle was skeptical of the desultory, piecemeal approach. His successes in the national collections for war relief convinced him that a similar, highly publicized national effort would provide for the Shrine. Working with an ailing Noll, he prudently discussed his ideas first with the four American cardinals and won their support. The next step was to develop some firm figures. In October 1952 he and Bishop Bryan McEntegart, now the university rector, met with the architects and members of the bishops' budget committee to prepare an up-to-date estimate for completing the building.[78] Three options were developed, ranging from $19 million for a completely furnished Shrine to $12 million for a stripped-down structure that omitted temporarily the campanile and other expensive features. The university trustees, who exercised a special oversight, agreed on the least expensive plan and proposed that the NCWC make the necessary commitments. They agreed with O'Boyle that no money would be borrowed to build the Shrine and that building would begin only after the bishops guaranteed the funds.

All this was aired for the bishops at their November 1952 meeting. Challenging his colleagues to "either build the thing or fill in the hole," O'Boyle added, "It's been an embarrassment to the Church in Washington long enough."[79] He warned that, with only $4 million on hand, the bishops must commit themselves to an extensive fund-raising campaign before any contracts were signed. Carefully marshaling his supporters, he arranged for Cardinal Stritch to propose an $8

76. Shrine Committee Rpt., Minutes of the Annual Bishops' Meeting, Nov 1950, NCWC Papers, ACUA.

77. Shrine Committee Rpt., Minutes of the Annual Bishops' Meeting, Nov 1951, NCWC Papers, ACUA.

78. Eugene Kennedy (Maginnis and Walsh Architects, Boston), "Report of Architectural and Engineering Work," n.d. (ca. Oct 1952), Mooney Papers, AAD.

79. As quoted in Arthur intv.

million campaign centered on a national collection on December 6, 1953. He also left to Cardinal Spellman the task of pointing out that the campaign would impose a quota on each diocese (approximately thirty-six times a diocese's annual payment to the bishops' conference). The bishops agreed, and Archbishop Cushing, a new member of the Shrine committee, announced to the press that building would begin in 1954 following a national appeal for funds.[80]

Using the approach he had pioneered during the war, O'Boyle gathered his old team under Ed Kinney to prepare brochures, parish promotion kits, and the inevitable collection envelopes for diocesan officials. Elaborate timetables were established for publicity, with radio and television spots planned and posters distributed. In June 1953 the bishops received notice of the exact amount each was expected to donate.[81] To oversee the management of the funds collected, O'Boyle drafted Father John B. Roeder, from his own chancery. Roeder endeared himself to his colleagues in chanceries around the country when he carefully credited to their accounts money received from individual donors from their dioceses who had contributed directly to the Shrine office in Washington.[82]

Meanwhile, O'Boyle personally went after the big givers. In 1953 the Catholic Daughters of America presented him with a $300,000 donation, and three years later, after negotiating with its supreme council, he received a million dollars from the Knights of Columbus (one dollar for each member of the fraternal order) to underwrite the cost of the Shrine's campanile. The timing of the gift enabled the architecturally important tower to be completed on schedule with the rest of the superstructure.

The results of the collection were gratifying. O'Boyle reported that over $6.3 million had been collected in the 126 dioceses, 39 of which exceeded their quotas. This left the bishops $4 million short of their goal, but they agreed to conduct collections in succeeding years, allowing O'Boyle to sign a contract with builder John McShain and architect Eugene F. Kennedy from the Boston firm of Maginnis and Walsh to commence building in November 1954. Weeks later, threading his way through the maze of scaffolding that now covered the crypt, the archbishop of Washington blessed the mighty enterprise. Commencement of

80. Minutes of the Annual Bishops' Meeting, Nov 1952, NCWC Papers, ACUA. See also *NYT*, 1 Dec 1952.

81. Shrine Committee, "Nationwide Appeal for the Completion of the National Shrine of the Immaculate Conception," Agenda, 27 May 1953, and ltr., O'Boyle to Mooney, 1 Jun 1953. Both in AAD. See also O'Boyle's Notes, pt. 30.

82. Ltrs., Roeder to Msgr. John Donovan, 14 Dec 1953, and Donovan to Roeder, 16 Dec 53, both in AAD.

building seemed to spur donations. The following year, with forty-six dioceses yet to reach their quota, the committee had on hand $12.3 million.[83]

Always sensitive to the enduring differences between the Midwestern bishops and the Spellman camp, O'Boyle sought a Midwesterner for the post of Shrine director. He hoped in this important appointment, he told the NCWC's Father Higgins, to avoid the impression that the Shrine was strictly an East Coast show. Higgins may have helped, but it was Chicago's Cardinal Strich who recommended one of his priests, Msgr. Thomas J. Grady, for the job. O'Boyle met Grady in 1956 during a subsequent visit to Montreal studying food services at large institutions. He was impressed with Grady's grasp of the logistics of feeding the expected hordes of Shrine visitors and decided on the spot to nominate him for the job.[84] He later quietly appointed a Washington priest, John Murphy, as assistant director.

Another political foray was less successful. O'Boyle was concerned about parking and other space needs for the giant edifice. He approached his friend Congressman John McCormack concerning the possible purchase of forty-nine acres controlled by the university's neighbor, the U.S. Soldiers' and Airmen's Home. Negotiations between O'Boyle and General Wade Haislip, governor of the home, had bogged down. McCormack recommended that several of the American cardinals ask President Eisenhower to talk with his old classmate Haislip about the Church's pressing need. In the end the bishops were allowed to purchase a small parcel for a parking lot, dashing O'Boyle's hope for using the undeveloped acres for a school for the retarded.[85]

As the date of the dedication of the completed structure neared, O'Boyle typically busied himself in the details. Weeks before he had arranged with Luke E. Hart, the Supreme Knight, for a 300-man contingent from the Knights of Columbus to form an honor guard for the ceremony. He wanted the honor guard to include some seventy men from the Knights of St. John, an African-American fraternal organization. It would be a great mistake, he told Hart, if the dedication of the Shrine did not include representatives of the black Catholic community.[86] Preparation for the dedication, which took place on November 20, 1959, found O'Boyle closely involved in the invitation list and seating arrangements for the entire American hierarchy, scores of government officials, and a host of lay digni-

---

83. Shrine Committee Rpts., Annual Bishops' Meetings, Nov 1954–56, NCWC Papers, ACUA.
84. Higgins intv. See also *WP*, 24 Apr 2002.
85. O'Boyle, "Memorandum on Soldiers Home Property," n.d. (c. 1956), O'Boyle Papers, AAW.
86. Ltr., O'Boyle to Hart, 24 Sep 1959, Knights of Columbus file, AAW.

taries. He approved a carefully timed schedule for the procession and stressed to his masters of ceremony the importance of that schedule. "I'm telling you, I want it on time. You're responsible. I don't care who is missing. I don't care who says anything to the contrary. I want it starting on time."[87]

O'Boyle was not mentioned in the many news accounts of the ceremony. But if his role went largely unknown to the public, it was fully recognized by his brother bishops, who appointed him an Apostle of the National Shrine for his years of service. In fact O'Boyle continued working on the project long after the dedication ceremony. Much of the money used to furnish the gigantic church was collected through his efforts. Looking back on his career in his late years, he admitted that the Shrine was one of its major landmarks.[88]

Coda

If a common thread could be said to run through all of O'Boyle's public discourses and activities in the bishops' conference it would concern the Scranton native's simple understanding of religion. Many turn to religion, he once observed, as some sort of benign sedative "to soothe their nerves and to settle their minds." While commenting that he did not wish to sound cynical about a person's search for faith, he went on to outline his own belief:

> Religion is not a thing of mere sentiment or personal escape from fears and dissatisfactions. . . . It means the voluntary subjection of one's self to God. It is the complete acceptance of the will of God as our way of life, loyalty to Him in His suffering as in His hour of glory.[89]

For him the great tragedy of modern times was mankind's loss of its sense of social sin. The relevance of religious and moral principles to all spheres of human life and conduct were now largely ignored, he warned. It was a mistake, he argued, to believe that people could be clubbed into decency and respect for their neighbor through the constraints of public law, just as it is a mistake to seek laws to remedy what are essentially moral problems. As for the latter, O'Boyle believed the obvious needed to be underscored: civil statutes cannot make an action right when the action, by its nature, is morally wrong.[90] Stern words from the new Jeremiah on the Potomac.

87. As quoted in Quinn intv. Quinn served as the master of ceremonies for the event. See also *NYT*, 21 Nov 1959, for details of the ceremony.

88. *Star*, 4 Mar 1973. See also *CS*, 28 May 1970.

89. As quoted in *McCall's Magazine*, ca. 1955, extract preserved in AAW.

90. O'Boyle, sermon at Mass for Catholic Hospital Association, Sep 1951, as quoted in *CIR* (Jun 1951): p. 95.

CHAPTER 10

The Measure of the Man

If the Second Vatican Council is seen as beginning a new chapter in the history of the Church, then the years immediately preceding its opening in 1962 represent some kind of ending. In fact an autumnal feeling was evident during those years in the American Church. Although its unprecedented postwar development, evident in its crowded schools and newly constructed sanctuaries, its thousands of charitable institutions, and its busy seminaries and convents, had transformed the Church into a powerful presence in American society, it was also an institution ripe for change. Even while old ways lingered, an increasingly educated laity was showing restlessness within the confines of its old womb-to-tomb ghetto society, and both clergy and laity were beginning to question the autocratic style of their bishops. It was a time too when American theologians were beginning to rethink some of the old expressions of faith. Some of these scholars were also quietly preparing a defense against Vatican critics of America's unique church-state relationship.

The gift of hindsight allows historians to detect widening fissures in the communion of believers during what would later be considered the last days of the old Church, but leaders in those times like Patrick O'Boyle were not so privileged. His duties, as he perceived them, were not unlike those of his predecessors in past generations: protect and defend the Faith, firmly guide those in his charge, and develop institutions that met their spiritual and physical needs. A timeless assignment perhaps, but in the eyes of most bishops then, one that demanded unquestioned obedience from a faithful clergy and from the "good people"— O'Boyle's favored term—placed in their care. If the archbishop of Washington showed singular foresight about race and labor issues, in general he shared the outlook of most of his colleagues—unquestioning in matters theological and liturgical, defensive in the face of secular society, and autocratic.

O'Boyle derided "the ignorant and the quack intellectuals" who criticized the Church as authoritarian, intransigent, and undemocratic. A thing was not bad because it was not democratic, he reasonably pointed out, before going on less reasonably: "The Church is constitutionally what Christ instituted, and that is all that needs to be said on that." As for intransigence, he argued that all truth, like the laws of nature and mathematics, is intransigent. Regarding authoritarianism, he denied that it was an ignoble or menacing trait. The Church was authoritarian, he admitted, but in so acting it was merely echoing its Founder, who was supremely authoritarian.[1] Issues would arise in the next decade to question such reasoning, but for the archbishop of Washington the years before Vatican II were a period of business almost as usual, a time of relative peace and quiet in which clergy and laity would get to know their shepherd well. It was a time when authority expected ready compliance. In that, the period truly marked the end of an era.

Business Almost As Usual

Throughout the 1950s Archbishop O'Boyle continued to focus on the physical development of his see. The frequent meetings with his consultors resembled nothing so much as the town planning meetings going on all over the rapidly growing Washington suburbs. Here he and his consultors discussed new programs, considered requests from pastors for permission to enlarge or remodel, and endlessly reviewed diocesan finances.

Although most observers agreed that he possessed a comprehensive grasp of the financial aspects of large organizations, they also recognized his consuming interest in the minutiae of business. Facts and figures fascinated him. It seemed that he memorized the financial statements of all his parishes, since he would quote with ease just what amounts pastors held in various funds. With his quick grasp of things financial, O'Boyle knew the right questions to ask. Woe to those unprepared with detailed answers! Those who came prepared and could argue their case with facts and figures would get a hearing. On rare occasions O'Boyle would even be won over to their point of view, but usually his decision stood. He would cut off further rebuttal with "But I'm the archbishop." Occasionally a

1. O'Boyle, "Our Heritage—The Apostolate of Charity," Feb 1952, reprinted in *The Catholic Charities Review* (May 1952): pp. 119–23.

hapless soul would dare to oppose his plans. One monsignor who jealously guarded a large building fund at his wealthy parish and refused to loan the archdiocese money found himself quietly transferred to another parish, one far removed from the building fund, which the archbishop then tapped for one of his projects.[2]

Meeting with his consultors satisfied ecclesiastical propriety, but his decisions were in fact reached with little consultation from those experienced men. O'Boyle sought advice on an informal, ad hoc basis from those he considered expert in different fields, like Msgr. Hannan on property purchases, Msgr. Spence on schools, and eminent Washington bankers, lawyers, professional fundraisers, and business leaders on other issues. By nature a decisive man, he often made snap decisions that could later prove difficult to rescind. This was especially true when it came to real estate. He frequently quoted the saintly Cardinal Hayes of New York to a frustrated Hannan: "The Church is not in the real estate business," overlooking the fact that the timely purchase or sale of Church property represented a prudent management of its patrimony. Some found his management style especially irritating. To the consternation of those charged with performing a task, he would constantly involve himself in the smallest details. "Remember I'm only a telephone call away" became as much a threat as a comfort to project managers.

In February 1954 O'Boyle called a temporary halt to new building programs. The archdiocese owed more than $6.5 million, he reported to the consultors, and twenty-nine of its parishes carried a substantial debt. With one major project underway, the new Providence Hospital, the other proposed projects, including four regional high schools, a home for the aged, and numerous parish buildings, must wait until at least 75 percent of the funds needed for their construction was in hand. He went on to predict that it would take at least seven years to amass the necessary funds. The archdiocese was realizing an annual income of $6 million and was reducing its debt by 10 percent a year, but, ignoring pleas from Hannan and others that further indebtedness was both prudent and practicable, he was reluctant to assess parishes for many of the new capital projects.[3]

Yet, while he was obviously determined to avoid further indebtedness, in fact there were signs even then that he was willing to ignore his own ukase. Within weeks of his announced moratorium on further building, the first appeals for an

---

2. Conway intv. Unless otherwise noted, this summary of O'Boyle's management techniques is based on intvs with Quinn, Donoghue, McArdle, and Duffy.

3. "Statement Made by Archbishop O'Boyle at Consultors Meeting—February 12, 1954," Consultors file, AAW.

old-age home were published, and affected parishes were informed about future assessments for the new high schools. In July 1955 O'Boyle set off on an extended trip to inspect ongoing construction projects in several Midwestern dioceses.[4] Back home he was busy raising funds for Providence Hospital. The issue of replacing the venerable Civil War structure on Capitol Hill was raised at the first consultors meeting. Fifteen acres in northeast Washington were later purchased from Catholic University for that purpose, although the estimated $7 million price tag for a 350-bed modern facility seemed to preclude action indefinitely. The picture changed suddenly in July 1951 when Congressman John McCormack shepherded through Congress an amendment to the 1946 Hospital Center Act that authorized federal funds for construction of additional private hospital facilities in the capital. With a pledge of $3.5 million from the federal government and $2.5 million from the Sisters of Charity, who had built the old Providence and operated it since 1861, the archbishop launched a million-dollar building campaign in early 1952.[5]

He focused the fund drive on major donors. He would invite a group of pastors of prosperous parishes to dinner and then over cigars begin by pressing one, "Joe, could you come up with $5,000 to help us?" After one pastor reluctantly agreed, he would canvass the table, usually netting a goodly sum for the fund.[6] With help from Msgr. O'Grady and Morris Cafritz, a prominent Washington real estate magnate, he hosted a dinner meeting for wealthy capital businessmen who also donated large sums. O'Grady played a major role in rounding up donors, including such diverse organizations as the St. Vincent de Paul Society, B'nai B'rith, and the *Washington Post* and *Evening Star.* O'Boyle was appreciative. "Your letter on the hospital drive," he told the well-connected Catholic Charities leader, "is a real tonic. It has the real snap and vigor that is needed for the campaign."[7]

Msgr. George Higgins organized a campaign kickoff dinner hosted by the archbishop, while Chancellor Hannan formed a labor committee to solicit funds from the various unions represented in town. To a dinner audience that included the secretary of labor and the nation's union leaders O'Boyle spoke of the largely

4. *Star,* 13 Jul 1955, discussed the application of what O'Boyle learned on this trip to future building in Washington and its suburbs.

5. Ltr., O'Boyle to Mooney, 31 Aug 1951, Mooney Papers, AAD. See also commentary by Dr. Phillip Caufield in *WP,* 15 Jul 1951. The building fund and the projected costs were discussed in *CS,* 11 Jan 1952.

6. Gillen intv. Msgr. Gillen was one of the witnesses to O'Boyle's fund-raising technique.

7. Ltrs., O'Grady to O'Boyle, 12 Jun and 8 Sep 1952; O'Boyle to O'Grady, 25 Jun 1952 (source of quote). All in O'Boyle file, NCCC Papers, ACUA.

unsung contribution American labor had made to public and private charities. The dinner, he added, was not just to inaugurate his labor committee's drive, but for him to become better acquainted with the national leaders. Although he had already earned the respect of local unions by his insistence on their participation in his building projects, he took the occasion to make a promise: "Encouragement and support [of the labor movement] shall not be wanting in the Archdiocese of Washington."[8] The first to respond were the bricklayers, whose Local 4 pledged $3,000. Other unions kicked in, and labor spokesman and O'Boyle friend Arthur Goldberg arranged for the Phillip Murray Memorial Foundation to donate $150,000. In less than two years the hospital fund netted more that $900,000, enough for construction to begin. On March 25, 1956, the debt-free building was dedicated, as O'Boyle described it, truly a community effort.

Construction of a home for the aged necessarily took a back seat to the hospital project. Thanks to O'Boyle's enthusiastic response to additions suggested by the sisters, the estimated price tag for a 200-bed home stood at $2 million. The archdiocese was ready in 1951 to provide the land, but not the money, as O'Boyle reported to his old friend from New York days Mother Angeline Teresa, whose Carmelite sisters had been promised a new facility. In the end Msgr. O'Grady, working with John McShane, the builder, found support for the project through the Federal Housing Authority.[9] A federal subsidy plus an assessment on parishes secured the funds, and Carroll Manor opened for business in November 1957.

O'Boyle never left any doubt about his dedication to Catholic education, and despite periodic moratoriums on incurring new debt, construction or enlargement of elementary and regional high schools continued apace well into the 1960s. On his arrival in 1948 the archbishop could count 22,000 students in parochial and private Catholic schools; by 1965 the diocese was educating 59,600 students. Yet by the early 1960s, he had come to realize that the Church would never reach its goal of educating every Catholic child. The first accurate census of the archdiocese, the so-called Survey of Souls conducted by the Council of Catholic Men in 1957, revealed that some 20,000 Catholic students, approximately a third of all Catholic school-age children, attended public schools. (A follow-up census six years later found the proportion rising to 47 percent.)

Addressing the needs of those in public schools, the archbishop inaugurated a Confraternity of Christian Doctrine program throughout the archdiocese.

8. Remarks as quoted in *CS*, 4 Apr 1951. See also *The Catholic Charities Review* (Jun 1952): p. 141.
9. Ltrs., O'Boyle to Sister Angeline Teresa, 19 Jun 1951, and O'Grady to O'Boyle, 30 Oct 1951. Both in O'Boyle file, NCCC Papers, ACUA.

Where once Sunday school was an unorganized catechism class usually conducted by the parish's teaching sisters, the archdiocese, one of the first in the country so fully committed to the concept, established a new apostolate involving hundreds of carefully trained lay men and women that sought to educate thousands of public-school children in their faith. In 1958 O'Boyle assigned his secretary, Father D. Joseph Corbett, to organize the program and procured the services of four Mission Helpers of the Sacred Heart as full-time coordinators who soon had teacher training sessions operating in all the area's Catholic colleges. Classes began in several city, suburban, and rural parishes that were expected to serve as models for the rest. The archbishop added to the visibility of the program by attending graduation ceremonies and bestowing annual awards for superior performance in each parish. Wanting to be kept informed, he demanded from Father James Gillen, who succeeded Corbett as director in 1960, a detail report on what was discussed at each directors meeting and how the directors voted. He wanted Gillen to investigate personally any complaints. The hard work paid off. Within two years of opening its first classes, the CCD program had enrolled almost 20,000 students.

Two other school projects won O'Boyle's special attention. When the Kennedy family offered to underwrite a Lt. Joseph P. Kennedy Institute for the developmentally disabled, he negotiated purchase of six acres from Catholic University's Sisters College and arranged for Notre Dame de Namur sisters to run the operation. With the Kennedy family donating $500,000, the rest of the cost was covered by private donations solicited by the archbishop.[10] The project was his first association with the Catholic president, who in April 1961 donated his auto (a 1959 Pontiac) to a benefit raffle for the institute. The White House asked that there be no public notice of the donation, but O'Boyle saw advantage in making the donation a news event, calling the president's gesture "an inspiration to those working to support, spiritually and financially, the Institute." He agreed, however, to honor the While House request. In this exchange, O'Boyle was correct, to the point, and uneffusive, although in the case of the Kennedy Institute Charity Ball he did depart from his customary policy and agreed to serve as honorary chairman along with Jacqueline Kennedy and Robert F. Kennedy.[11]

Lacking both the manpower and candidates to operate a diocesan seminary, the archbishop settled on a first-rate prep school for boys interested in religious

10. Minutes, Consultors meeting, 29 Oct 1958, AAW.

11. Ltr., Joseph Coyne to Hannan, 31 Oct 1961, Hannan to John F. Kennedy, 5 May 1961, and O'Boyle to Kennedy, 5 May 1961 (source of quote); Memo, Hannan to Roeder, 26 Nov 1957, and Hannan, Memo for Record, 25 Apr 1961. All in Chancery file, AAW.

life. When St. Ann's orphanage vacated its spacious but dilapidated home in Washington's fashionable Kalorama area, he decided to remodel the building and establish Cathedral Latin School, initially detailing six of his priests to serve as faculty.[12] By 1962 the school was ensconced in its new quarters. Despite the severe drain on his personnel resources, O'Boyle took considerable pride in the institution. He supported the costly project for a decade. Among the hundreds of young students who received a strong Catholic education, some fifteen went on to become priests.[13]

Like most prelates of his day, O'Boyle went out of his way to emphasize the importance of Catholic education. The opening Mass for teachers was a liturgical highlight of his Washington year. There he would underscore what he believed was the link between good citizenship and Catholic schools: "You are doing more to teach patriotism and the virtues that really count than any other group I know of," he told 1,200 teachers in 1963, the great majority at that time still brothers and sisters.[14] The year before he had organized an archdiocesan school board to advise him on policies and procedures for the 123 schools under his control.[15] School construction dominated the eighteen major parish projects in 1960–61, as it had throughout the previous decade. Yet as the decade wore on he began placing more and more emphasis on the CCD classes and Father William Awalt's reenergized CYO social program. Schools were no longer necessarily the first order of business for new parishes. When Father Michael Farina was sent out in 1966 to found Holy Spirit parish in Forestville, Maryland, O'Boyle told him to postpone any thought of a school and concentrate on building a church with enough classroom space for a good CCD program. Father Thomas Duffy received similar instructions when he was sent to establish St. Raphael's in Montgomery County: "Don't start talking about a school. I don't know whether we have any staff for [it]."[16]

An archdiocesan financial statement, compiled in February 1960, shows outstanding loans totaling $7.3 million, a modest increase over the $6 million in 1954, and indicates that the moratorium as well as the continuing willingness of parishioners to meet parish debt obligations had had a retarding effect on debt. But the projects approved for the next two years would double the archdiocese's

12. At a cost of $388,000. The sisters donated the building in return for the archdiocese's underwriting the new St. Ann's. See Minutes, Consultors meetings, 29 Oct 1958 and 1 Feb 1961, AAW.

13. D. Joseph Corbett, "Cathedral Latin School (1961–1969)," AAW. Father Corbett, who was O'Boyle's first secretary, was also first principal of the school.

14. O'Boyle sermon at annual teachers' Mass, 4 Sep 1963, as quoted in *Star,* 4 Sep 1963.

15. For a list of members, see *Star,* 5 Oct 1962.

16. Farina and Duffy intvs.

indebtedness. It was as if Bishop Hannan's advice to take advantage of low interest rates had finally sunk in. The largest item on the list of new spending was St. Ann's Infant Home. At first O'Boyle proposed covering the $2 million price tag through a general, house-to-house collection, but in the end he listened to the suburban pastors, whose congregations were already heavily burdened by their pledges to pay for ongoing parish building projects. Instead he secured a commercial loan for the home, relying on help from wealthy donors who formed an advanced gifts committee to make up the rest.[17] St. Ann's was only the most expensive in a host of new approved building; by 1962, the archdiocese's debt was $14 million. Clearly there had been a significant change in O'Boyle's attitude toward borrowing.

Too much could be made of these changes. The archbishop continued building churches and schools at a furious pace well into the 1960s. He did not experience an epiphany when it came to investment acumen. With his usual explanation that the Church was not in the real estate business, he dismissed his chancellor's plan to lease St. Patrick's deteriorating downtown property for a lucrative office/department store complex. Not every missed opportunity, however, was his fault. When he saw the advantage in selling Church property to the General Accounting Office, then building on G Street, he left negotiations up to an inept pastor who botched the job.

Still, a discernible retreat from centralization could be seen by the mid-1960s. The decade before found O'Boyle happily bogged down in the minutiae of parish finance. For example, he personally authorized the outlay of $5,000 at Holy Trinity for a new organ, but only after lecturing the pastor on the need for a contract for both repair of the old organ and purchase of the new. In 1955 his approval was needed before $1,133 could be expended on exterminating termites at St. Peter's on Capitol Hill.[18] A decade later he was sending young Father Duffy to the wilds of Falls Road in Montgomery County with instructions simply "to build a church." When Duffy came in with a proposal that exceeded diocesan guidelines by $100,000, O'Boyle blustered, but Duffy went ahead, plans for his $400,000 church unquestioned and undisturbed.[19]

The early 1960s also presented O'Boyle with his first personnel crisis. In the early, heady days of bursting seminaries, the archbishop had had little trouble

17. On O'Boyle's approach to donors, see ltr., O'Boyle to Gingras, 11 Jun 1959, Archives of St. Augustine Church.
18. Ltr., O'Boyle to Emory Ross, S.J., 14 Feb 1954, and Agenda of Consultors Meeting, 9 Feb 1955. Both in AAW.
19. Duffy intv.

finding priests to man new parishes. In fact when in 1957 the Propagation of the Faith, which sponsored advanced study for its missionaries at Catholic University, offered the services of these priests for weekend duty in the archdiocese, the chancery was hard-pressed to find uses for all of them.[20] A sudden proposal by the Jesuit fathers in 1961 transformed this surplus into a deficit. Citing their expanding education program and its need for priest-teachers, the Jesuits asked to turn over immediately to the archdiocese the thirty-some parishes in southern Maryland, many dating to colonial times, still under their care. The archbishop, while anxious to establish his direct control over this significant segment of the new archdiocese, lacked the manpower. He offered instead to take several of the poorest parishes immediately, with additional transfers in succeeding years. He insisted that the Jesuits retain St. Ignatius at Chapel Point, for centuries the headquarters of their operations in the region. Under a very satisfactory arrangement, Holy Face at Great Mills and St. George's at Valley Lee were placed under diocesan clergy in 1961. O'Boyle understood the need for diplomacy. He advised the priests assigned to the two parishes to refrain from any changes that might be considered controversial by parishioners.[21]

The stress on personnel resources caused by these acquisitions was not long in appearing. When Cardinal Spellman asked O'Boyle in 1962 to add to the ten Washington priests already serving as military chaplains, O'Boyle was forced to say no. Pleas in succeeding years were similarly rejected until, in 1966, despite signs that the stream of new diocesan clergy was dwindling, he arranged for three men to join the armed forces.[22]

Continuing his earlier habit of understating his appreciation for a job well done, O'Boyle was apt to offer a hard-working subordinate a simple word of thanks rather than a tangible reward. Still, at the end of his first year in office he had requested Vatican honors for five Washington clergy, including Cowhig in the chancery and Spence in the education department. In 1952 Rome complied with his request for seven more papal chamberlains, including Fathers Hannan (the new chancellor) and Arthur (in the tribunal). A notable shift in attitude occurred four years later, thanks in part to the apostolic delegate. After attending a ceremony at the cathedral, Archbishop Cicognani commented on the "lack of color" in the sanctuary and urged O'Boyle to petition Rome for more honors. O'Boyle took the hint and in the next two years obtained Vatican recognition for fifty-nine priests and laymen living in the diocese, including a significant number

20. Hannan, Memo for Record, Sep 1957, Chancery file, AAW.
21. Donoghue and Arthur intvs. See also *Star*, 18 Aug 1961.
22. Ltrs., O'Boyle to Spellman, 7 Sep 1962 and 10 Oct 1966, Chancery file, AAW.

of senior educators at Catholic University. He declared a temporary halt to the promotions in 1958, explaining that after that year's crop "we just can't go back to the Pope for more."[23]

The most important of the new appointments occurred in August 1956, when Phillip Hannan was consecrated Washington's second auxiliary bishop. O'Boyle recognized that his hard-working chancellor had not only created a bureaucracy responsive to his demands, but could be trusted for advice. In fact, by the late 1950s, letters to O'Boyle on all sorts of subjects were forwarded to Hannan especially, but also at times to Spence and to the new Msgr. Gingras, with a "What do you think? O'B" or "Any recommendations? POB" scrawled across the top. Moreover, the archbishop frequently endorsed their recommendations. Paradoxically, the man who came to town determined to control every aspect of the Church's operations was now, secure in his authority, finally willing to share control with others.

In the case of some of the honorees, the touch of purple hardly compensated for the stress of trying to satisfy an impatient archbishop. With the possible exception of Msgr. John "Jake" Roeder, Hannan's successor as chancellor, O'Boyle was not personally close to any of his administrators, all of whom felt his bark on many occasions. Always demanding of himself, he was equally demanding of them and was quick to criticize any of their perceived errors. A no-nonsense straight shooter, he considered phoniness in any form a capital sin. "Faker" was his strongest epithet. In a playful moment of self-deprecation he once announced that his long-awaited memoirs would be titled "Fakers I Have Known, Including Myself."[24] If O'Boyle's candor made clear exactly where one stood, it also created some awkward moments. Here the diplomatic Hannan served well as an ameliorator, smoothing over the rough edges of his boss's quick judgments. His was the face and voice most often representing the archdiocese at government and social functions, substituting for a superior who found such occasions particularly onerous. The sensible Hannan saved the archbishop many a heartbreak, but the men were never especially friendly. After years of burning the midnight oil to keep up with the business of a growing archdiocese, Hannan finally asked to be relieved of some duties. "You don't have to do them all at once, do you?" was the equally hard-working archbishop's quick retort.[25]

The contrast between the no-frills archbishop and his director of education,

23. Ltr., O'Boyle to Rev. John O'Connor, 22 Jun 1959, copy in AAW. A list of the new papal chamberlains and domestic prelates was carried in *WP,* 23 Dec 1958.

24. McArdle intv. See also Donoghue and Arthur intvs.

25. As quoted in the Hannan intv.

Msgr. John Spence, could hardly have been greater. Naturally pompous, Spence frankly delighted in the trappings of episcopal rank. When he was named an auxiliary bishop in 1964, he promptly made a courtesy call on O'Boyle. When O'Boyle greeted him at the door with a handshake, the disappointed Spence asked, "Aren't you going to give me the *abbraccio?*"[26] The ancient tradition of a new bishop's receiving a ceremonial embrace from his fellow bishop might be deemed important to Spence, but was clearly beyond O'Boyle's understanding. O'Boyle endured these innocent vanities because Spence was effective in educational matters. He had a quick grasp of what was feasible in the school system and was particularly successful in attracting teaching orders to serve in Washington. Spence also served as a healthy influence on diocesan policy-making. Where his colleagues often desisted from questioning a decision to avoid the archbishop's growl, the guileless Spence would speak his heart. His questions might earn him a blistering retort, but they sometimes caused O'Boyle to rethink a hasty decision.

Over time the archbishop would develop close ties to several priests, principally his secretary, Father Joseph Corbett; his master of ceremonies, Father Walter Schmitz; his frequent vacation companion, Father James Gillen; and his great friend of later years, his secretary and chancellor, John Donoghue. Probably none was any closer in the early years than Father Roeder. Perhaps O'Boyle saw some of himself in the hard working, down-to-earth chancellor. No intellectual, Roeder was a practical man of uncommon good sense who spent high energy and long hours at his job. He was particularly adept at finances, and his sudden death in 1966 was a severe blow to O'Boyle.

A Simple Life

In June 1957 Archbishop O'Boyle moved into his own home on Warren Street just off Wisconsin Avenue in Washington's Tenleytown. He had realized it was time to move, he joked, when a visitor at St. Patrick's announced that she had come to see the bishop. When asked which bishop, she replied, "The younger one." For some time he had been resisting efforts to find him a proper home. "They're trying to get me out of town," he complained to a fellow tenant at St. Patrick's when talk arose about an available historic mansion in the suburbs.[27] But, in truth, despite his undemanding ways, nine years in a busy parish

26. As quoted in Donoghue intv.
27. Abell, Patrick *Cardinal O'Boyle*, p. 47 (first quote), and Telechea intv. (2d quote). The following paragraphs on O'Boyle's lifestyle are based in these sources and intvs. with Donoghue, Wolfe, Gillen, and O'Brien.

rectory, especially for a tenant whose family and close friends were all from out of town, had to be trying. Some time before, he had switched his office to the chancery, and when businessman John Maloney, one of O'Boyle's generous advisors, offered to sell him a solid but unpretentious house for $60,000, he decided to move. After a minimum of remodeling, principally to accommodate a small chapel, the house was ready for the archbishop and his secretary, with a guest room and quarters for Lotti and Patrick Lastowski, a Scranton couple who would run the household for more than a decade.[28]

Another resident was added when the archbishop acquired a dog. Back in Scranton the family always had room for a dog, and Father O'Boyle himself owned a series of pets when he lived at Mt. Loretto. Once again finding himself in his own quarters, he thought of a pet. When visiting St. Aloysius parish in Leonardtown one Sunday, he was introduced to the pastor's dog, which had recently produced a litter of puppies. "Why don't you give me one?" he impetuously asked, and the next morning Lotti was upset to find the new addition ensconced in her basement. Over her protests, the archbishop predicted that she would soon grow fond of the animal. He was right. When Lotti returned to Scranton in 1970 the dog went with her. Thereafter O'Boyle contented himself with the company of the Muldoons' Irish setter on his frequent trips to Scranton.

Now in a home of his own, the archbishop felt freer to entertain visitors. Old friend Henry Klonowski as well as dignitaries like Cardinals Spellman, McIntyre, and Cushing enjoyed his hospitality. When his Muldoon cousins visited, the women would stay at the house while the men were put up at the University Club on Sixteenth Street. O'Boyle was a longtime member of the club, where he would occasionally dine, knowing that his privacy would be respected. He avoided restaurants because people would constantly interrupt his meal in their desire to greet him. From time to time he hosted small dinners at home. His doctor, Thomas Collins, Walter McArdle, and Congressman McCormack and their wives were typical guests at these simple affairs. Thanksgiving and Christmas also found him hosting dinners, this time for the so-called orphans, a group of priests whose families lived at great distances and who therefore were alone at the holidays. Aided by his gregarious vacation companion, Father Gillen (who as a pastor in later decades would carry on the tradition), O'Boyle found himself carving the turkey for an increasing number of "orphans," including the apostolic delegate. Once he entertained a large group of bishops with a buffet served in the

28. Patrick died in 1969, and Lotti retired to Scranton a year later.

recreation room, but such occasions were probably too much for the house, and when it came his turn to host his Dunwoodie class's annual reunion, he had Father Gillen arrange the affair at the Mayflower Hotel. A man of simple tastes, the archbishop much preferred a plain meal with a few friends, preceded by a "holy hour" in which he moderately imbibed his favorite, a scotch and water.

Actually Patrick O'Boyle was universally admired for his simple, almost austere lifestyle. Both friends and critics were quick to point to his total lack of pomp. No collection of episcopal finery for him. The modest gold pectoral cross and ring given him in 1948 would remain the same throughout his years in Washington. No spacious living quarters either. A two-room suite, smaller than his rooms at St. Patrick's and Mt. Loretto, served his needs. The old Harris and Ewing portrait made in 1948 remained his official picture for decades. Later a lucky photographer caught him at a rare outing, ensconced in the full cardinal's regalia of the day, the broad-brimmed red hat on his head and a slightly bemused expression on his face.

Washington's chief pastor also avoided limousines and chauffeurs. In fact he did not own a car, but relied instead on his secretary or master of ceremonies to drive him everywhere. One of his secretaries was eventually forced to sell his Chevrolet Supersport. He had been using the car to drive the archbishop until a group of priests spotted O'Boyle alighting from the high-powered machine and began to josh him about his racy transportation. After that only the sedate diocesan sedan would do.[29] Once a close lay advisor inveigled him into taking a spin in his jazzy red sports car. The mercifully brief trip found O'Boyle's chunky form squeezed into the low-slung seat and his hat threatening to sail away while, all episcopal dignity forgotten, he held on for dear life. Thus ended his forays into the high performance world.

The habit of shining his own shoes and caring for his clothes had endured from his Scranton days. But if he was notably self-sufficient when it came to personal appearance, he was at sea when faced with the simplest problem of home maintenance. He was so unmechanical, his secretary reported, that he found sharpening a pencil a challenge.

In keeping with his simplicity was a carefully structured workday. His routine called for a 5:30 rising and early arrival at the office after Mass and breakfast. He would lunch with the chancery crowd, take a brief walk, then return to work until five o'clock when, unless some meeting or ceremony intervened, it was back to

29. Donoghue intv.

Warren Street for dinner, television or reading, and then bed at ten o'clock. His secretaries reported little variation in this routine over the years. He was not the kind of executive who brought work home. "Forget about it," he told a chancellor about some pending business, "it'll be there tomorrow when you get back to the office."

The *New York Times* once reported that his favorite television show was *McHale's Navy,* for which, when schedules permitted, he reserved Thursday evenings. Otherwise his television viewing was limited mostly to news and ball games or golf tournaments. Although the New York Giants remained his football team and coach Don Shula his hero, he religiously followed the Washington Redskins and occasionally took in a game with his visiting cousins Steve and Tony Muldoon. The tickets were gifts from team owner and O'Boyle friend Edward Bennett Williams. But O'Boyle always insisted on grandstand seats. Somehow the idea of a box seat did not feel appropriate. He once entertained the idea that professional football might serve as a resource for Catholic Charities when Vince Lombardi came to town to lead the Redskins. While in Green Bay Lombardi had arranged for the proceeds of the last preseason game to go to Bishop Wycislo's diocesan charities. O'Boyle was disappointed when the famous coach turned him down for a similar deal in the capital.

The archbishop had brought his golf clubs to Washington and occasionally got up a foursome to play at Burning Tree Country Club. But his free time was limited, and the posh surroundings of the club made him uneasy. This, plus the fact that most of Washington's courses imposed racial restrictions, made him abandon the game. By the mid-1960s the clubs were stored away and his exercise regime reduced to brisk noontime and evening walks.

Moderation in all things no doubt contributed to a healthy constitution, which served him tolerably well until the last months of a long life. O'Boyle was uncharacteristically docile when it came to obeying his physician. When Dr. Collins told him in the mid-1960s that cigars were not contributing to his well-being, he immediately set aside a forty-year habit. When Collins remarked on extra weight, O'Boyle immediately and without complaint cut back on food. On one of his trips to Rome in the late 1960s he experienced abdominal pain. Unlike the wise students at the North American College who when ill in those times went to the airport rather than a Roman hospital, O'Boyle consulted a local doctor who diagnosed diverticulitis. When he got home Dr. Collins immediately put him in Providence, where Dr. Louis Goffredi, the chief surgeon, removed his inflamed appendix. Recovering from the emergency, O'Boyle received a surprise visit from the District's assistant coroner, Dr. Linwood Rayford. Never at a loss, the groggy archbishop told the man whom he had suggested for his position, "I thought you coroners waited till the body was cold."[30]

The archbishop would endure one other hospital stay in the 1960s, this time at the Mayo Clinic. Before the last session of the Vatican Council opened he flew to Minnesota to check on a chronic disk ailment. The doctors discovered a diseased prostate. He underwent successful surgery on September 20, 1965, and was back in Washington a week later. Although the doctors stressed the need for a longer recuperation, O'Boyle predicted, accurately as it turned out, that he would be joining his brother bishops in Rome before the end of October.[31]

The archbishop's vacations were in keeping with his simple lifestyle and his aversion to travel. Where many brother bishops found excuses for frequent trips to Rome, O'Boyle went only when he considered it absolutely necessary. Before the sessions of the Vatican Council opened in 1962 he had visited the Eternal City just four times, as a pilgrim during the 1950 Holy Year, for the required ad limina visits in 1954 and 1959, and for the beatification of Mother Seton. Trips around the United States were more frequent, but only because he thought attendance at the installations of colleagues and at charity meetings was something he ought to do. Personal invitations were another matter. Cardinal McIntyre tried in vain to get him to Los Angeles. McIntyre even asked Father Ellis to relay the news that modern jets made the trip in less than five hours, making a quick weekend visit feasible.[32]

In later years O'Boyle would fly to California several times to visit his aging friend, but while in office vacations were brief and close to home. There were occasional forays to the Adirondacks with old New York colleagues and to Hershey, Pennsylvania, a resort he found particularly restful, but almost always his two-week break centered on Scranton. Cousin Tony would be recruited to drive him around the area to spend time with his "good friends," like his old high school teacher, Sister Brendan, and Mother Beata, superior general of the Immaculate Heart of Mary sisters and an old advisor.[33]

For years O'Boyle would return to the Muldoons' cottage at Moosic Lake in the mountains east of Scranton. The Muldoon brothers even added a small chapel for their cousin and his priest guests. The Muldoon sisters would buy

30. As quoted in Goffredi and Rayford intv. The exact date of the operation cannot be pinned down because, to avoid publicity, O'Boyle always insisted on using an alias when hospitalized.

31. Ltr., O'Boyle to Kirk, 11 Oct 1965, St. Vincent de Paul Collection, ACUA. See also *Star,* 23 Sep 1965.

32. Ltr., Ellis to O'Boyle, 2 Aug 1960, copy in Ellis Papers, ACUA.

33. Ltr., O'Boyle to Mother Beata, 27 Mar 1962, Marywood Archives. See also *Scranton Times,* 28 Jul 1965.

and deliver supplies once a week. Father Gillen, who could cook, was a perennial fixture in a party that often included Henry Klonowski, Fathers Schmitz and Roeder, and in later years, Father Donoghue. On some evenings priests from the area would join them for dinner. The archbishop followed his usual careful routine. After Mass, Bishop Klonowski and others would enjoy a swim, but O'Boyle would content himself with two daily walks around the lake, rosary beads in hand and the Muldoons latest Irish setter at his side. Father Gillen, swearing that he had memorized every cobblestone along the way, was usually recruited for the quotidian journey and prayer session. The archbishop would while away the rest of the day on the shaded patio with its statue of the Blessed Mother, saying his breviary, playing with the dog, and napping. He unbent to the extent of wearing a short-sleeve shirt opened at the throat. After a brief period for libations, dinner was served exactly at six o'clock or Father Gillen would hear about it. The archbishop insisted on sharing the chores. He brewed the morning coffee and put out the garbage.

The image of O'Boyle walking around the lake, rosary in hand, might well serve as a metaphor for the man's simple and conventional spirituality. While daily Mass and praying the breviary formed his spiritual center, he remained faithful to the traditional devotions common to pious Irish immigrant families, especially those honoring the Blessed Virgin. He recited the Angelus three times a day, and his rosary beads were always at hand. Usually faithful to the rules, he ignored the admonishments of the liturgists who considered recitation of the rosary and other private devotions inappropriate during Mass. Once while presiding at a solemn Mass, he was caught by his chaplain saying his beads. In response to the chaplain's quizzical look, he whispered, "Nobody can see me, can they?"[34] Ireland's great saint, and O'Boyle's personal patron, also received faithful attention. A statue of St. Patrick occupied a prominent place in the hallway of his home and received an affectionate pat from the archbishop whenever he used the staircase. A very priestly and prayerful man, O'Boyle also found inspiration in religious texts. His reading, however, did not include the theologically advanced books of the times, but rather the pious literature popular in his youth.

O'Boyle came from a generation that considered open discussion of spirituality unmanly and was, therefore, intensely private about his own devotions. Nevertheless he was convinced of the efficacy of organized community spirituality for his priests and people. He made the annual priests retreat an obligation, and he checked on attendance. As in other things he kept a careful record of who at-

34. As quoted in Farina intv.

tended what sessions, decided on the retreat master, and even set the dates. Not content with annual retreats, he pressed the priests to attend days of recollection as well. Calling his 1952 announcement of these exercises "the most important in many respects I have made since coming to Washington," he spoke of the need for times of prayerful reflection when priests could periodically concentrate on their personal salvation and consider how they were living out their calling. He claimed that these events, for which he selected speakers, differed from the annual retreats in that they were completely voluntary. Nevertheless a count was kept of attendees, and the archbishop carefully reviewed the figures. He was heartened to learn, contrary to his early assumption, that many of the younger priests were attending.[35] Even though the days of recollection never attracted a full complement of busy priests, he remained optimistic. "I hope next year we shall do better," he told Msgr. Gingras after reviewing the statistics for the 1959 sessions.[36]

O'Boyle also considered annual retreats essential for the spiritual life of the laity, so he urged them to attend those sponsored by the Laymen's Retreat League and the Lay Women's Association. He was particularly pleased with the large turnout for nocturnal adoration devotions sponsored by the Confraternity of the Blessed Sacrament. Still, many Catholics were "unwilling to give God more than the minimum Sunday worship, if that," he told his priests. In 1953 he called for the active participation of all schools and parishes in the League of the Sacred Heart. Similarly, he urged Catholics in the area to join in the work of the Family Life Bureau in its effort to strengthen the spiritual life of the Catholic family. He himself accompanied Washington delegates to Family Life conferences and presided at ceremonies where Catholic couples renewed their marriage vows. He believed the archdiocese should be busy in the work of evangelization and backed the work of the Catholic Television Guild. He was especially supportive of the innovative "TV Mass," a weekly service, sponsored by the John Carroll Society, that was begun in 1952.

The archbishop never lost his love for massive outdoor devotions, which he considered grand public demonstrations of faith. Msgr. Cartwright finally talked him into abandoning the Holy Name parades down Constitution Avenue, arguing that in a city with elite military units often on display, the ragged marchers in the parish contingents were an embarrassment. Even so, the mass rallies continued. In October 1958 O'Boyle presided over a celebration of the centennial of

---

35. Ltrs., O'Boyle to Ellis, 5 Nov 1952, Ellis Papers, ACUA, and O'Boyle to Gingras, 13 May 1957, ASA.

36. Ltr., O'Boyle to Gingras, 11 Jun 1959, ASA.

the apparitions at Lourdes with 125,000 Catholics gathered on the Washington Monument grounds. A choir of 2,500 schoolchildren accompanied by the Metropolitan Police Band performed as some 300 prelates and lesser clergy moved to their seats on the platform under the raised swords of Knights of Columbus in full regalia. In October 1961 O'Boyle assembled a similar crowd for the climax of the Crusade of Prayer for World Peace. He was joined by the apostolic delegate and Cardinal Spellman, who urged the crowd to pray for the new Kennedy administration's efforts in face of the intensifying cold war. Until his last days O'Boyle would recall his thrill at the spectacle of such massed devotions.[37]

A final aspect of O'Boyle's essential simplicity was his unabashed pride in his immigrant family. He frequently referred to the struggles of the newcomers in the Scranton of his youth. Nor was he loathe to extol the glories of Ireland and the bravery of her emigrating sons and daughters. He considered it a special honor when the Hibernians asked him to serve as their national chaplain in 1956.[38] He was always ready to take umbrage at any perceived slight to the Irish. Once after hearing diplomats at a Pan-American Mass wax enthusiastic about the greatness of the Hispanic world, O'Boyle responded, "All true. All true, but of course, as you know, the Irish are a pretty good group, too."[39] Like many first-generation Americans whose knowledge of the old country was largely limited to the stories of immigrant parents, O'Boyle was apt to romanticize Irish history and the lifestyle of the modern Irish. In his sermon delivered on St. Patrick's Day, 1956, for example, he defined the mission of the Irish as the conquest of "our sad and sullen world" by a charity founded on the faith that would lead man back to the "joy of the Father's house." Surpassing the excesses of rhetoric tolerated on a national feast day, his analysis of the Irish character stretched credulity:

> Charity is the supreme law of Irish life, the reason for Irish laughter and gaiety. A happy people who could never take too seriously the treasures of this life because they are so certain of the infinite superiority of the next; a people so confident of their destiny that they can mix laughter with their tears even at a wake; a people so conscious of their God-given dignity that they can enjoy jokes about their foibles; a people that deserves its national emblem, the harp, an instrument that can conquer only by its appeal.[40]

37. *WP*, 30 Oct 1961. For O'Boyle's reaction to these affairs, see McArdle intv. McArdle served as chairman for some of these events.
38. *CS*, 14 Sep 1956.
39. As quoted in Abell, *Patrick Cardinal O'Boyle*, p. 45.
40. O'Boyle, "Mission of the Irish," sermon delivered on 17 Mar 1956, copy in AAW.

Despite his assertion, O'Boyle himself showed little tolerance for those joking about Irish foibles. When the irrepressible Msgr. George Higgins decided to needle the Irish during a St. Patrick's Day sermon, an indignant archbishop rose to tell the Irish ambassador and "all you who would like to be Irish," that the preacher they had just heard "is only half Irish."[41] One prejudice O'Boyle would carry to the end. As archbishop he always received but never accepted invitations to the queen's birthday party at the British Embassy. When Msgr. Gillen, who accompanied O'Boyle's successor to the event in 1974, next met O'Boyle, he found himself only half-jokingly denounced as a traitor for going.

As His Priests and People Knew Him

In 1986 William Abell, a friend and advisor, published *Patrick Cardinal O'Boyle As His Friends Knew Him.* This brief, anecdotal portrait was meant to reverse the impression of a man who, thanks to the controversies that raged during his last years in office, was perceived by many as the personification of the unbending autocrat more concerned with Church rules than with the genuine struggles of his priests and people. Abell's engaging work countered that perception and provided documentation for the complimentary obituary in the *Washington Post,* which provided the following portrait in 1987:

> . . . Cardinal O'Boyle often came across as a conventional Irish priest. He had a twinkle in his eyes and what colleagues described as a genuine warmth and affection for his flock, and he was an engaging conversationalist during an evening of drinks and cigars.[42]

Neither Abell's work, based as it was on the reflections of O'Boyle's inner circle of friends and colleagues, nor the *Post* obituary was inaccurate in its description, but a more nuanced and believable picture emerges when the memories of O'Boyle's subordinates are taken into account.[43]

To a remarkable extent these men agreed on the archbishop's strengths and weaknesses. Many, for example, conceded the appealing image of the twinkle-eyed Irishman, but they also recalled the forbidding mien often focused on them. Like many administrators, O'Boyle's anxieties and tensions could lead him to fly off the handle with subordinates. Almost all commented on his gruffness, the harsh talk and rough treatment they received at his hands. Most attributed such

41. As quoted in Higgins intv.
42. *WP,* 11 Aug 1987.
43. The following paragraphs are based on the many interviews of priests in the archdiocese contained in the O'Boyle collection, AAW. See, in particular, the interviews with Donoghue, Quinn, Herrmann, O'Brien, McMain, Higgins, and Arthur.

246 The Measure of the Man

performances to his essential shyness and an insecurity that lay deeply suppressed under a pose of determination and long-suffering. One of the amateur psychologists among his subordinates posited that the archbishop's shyness could be traced to his roots in a poor immigrant household. While his rise from humble circumstances was a source of pride, it also filled him with insecurity. He never seemed to forget the jokes his more sophisticated New York classmates told about Scranton, and throughout his career in letters and interviews he would express wonder at how "Little Patrick," his habitual term of self-belittlement, ever ended up under a bishop's miter. Whatever the cause, those consulted for this study agreed that Patrick O'Boyle was a shy man who frequently masked his shyness with a grim and irascible exterior that belied a caring but lonely leader. The more astute understood that the harsh treatment did not affect their relationship as long as they performed their jobs well. His overbearing attitude was just something they learned to tolerate. Some sensitive souls, however, found the man frightening, even forbidding.

Subordinates were somewhat ambivalent about the archbishop's vaunted reputation as an administrator. Most conceded that his frequently impetuous decisions, those famous quick judgments that many referred to as "shooting from the hip," betrayed a sure grasp of the big picture and proved correct in the long run. But several noted his inability to recognize blank spots in his understanding, a failure that was matched by a stubborn streak that resisted change. As one subordinate observed, once he put his teeth down on something "*state in fide—* bang, that was it."[44] But not always. There were times when one would earn a quick no for a suggestion only to be surprised by a note the next day reversing the episcopal denial. On the other hand, what he wanted done, he wanted done immediately, and he was not above checking back again and again to see that a task was being accomplished. Impetuosity sometimes caused him to bawl out a subordinate by mistake. Abashed by his error, O'Boyle would typically call the wronged man and apologize. One of his endearing traits was the habit of saying he was sorry.

In fact O'Boyle's criticisms were often mildly, even gently put (e.g., "you should have done. . ."), and they were usually fair. One observer called the sometimes harsh words "affirmative candor." When one unfortunate pastor published an advertisement in the *Evening Star* for a parish musical that pictured a dancer doing her high kicks, O'Boyle's subsequent tongue-lashing convinced the poor man that he was about to be dismissed from the archdiocese. With some time to

44. Coady intv. See also Farina intv.

cool off and after an intercession by Walter McArdle, O'Boyle assured the hapless pastor that such was not the case. He just wanted to be sure, he explained, that such a scene would not be in the show. Couldn't the girls, he suggested, "do something like what they used to do in New York, dancing, you know, timid steps?"[45]

O'Boyle's blunt criticism was ruefully accepted by many priests because it actually proved his openness. He would talk plainly about things. Unlike some of his colleagues, who were known for talking out of both sides of their mouth, O'Boyle let one know exactly where one stood with him. Nor, as in some other dioceses, did subordinates find layers of bureaucracy imposed between them and their ordinary. Micromanagement was endurable where one enjoyed access to the final authority. One administrative weakness, more risible than fearful, was O'Boyle's inability, more noticeable in later years, to discriminate among important projects. A feature of the annual priests meeting was an address by the archbishop, a sort of state of the diocese report. Before each of the items on his interminable list, O'Boyle would invariably add, "now Fathers, this is a really important point that you must concentrate on." With every item considered "really important," none seemed especially important, leaving an audience either frustrated or bemused. An efficient deskman, O'Boyle tended to grade subordinates on their administrative tidiness. Upon the death of one elderly pastor he was visibly upset by evidence of unanswered correspondence and unpaid bills that had accumulated during the man's long illness. Why hadn't the assistant priests taken care of these things, he wanted to know.

Underpinning the archbishop's administrative philosophy was the belief that everything done must be easily understood and therefore accepted by even the least sophisticated of the laity. To highlight this tenet, he referred to "Mrs. McGoosla," a mythical character meant to personify the loyal but undereducated and easily scandalized person he might well have met in any parish. Frequently his advisors would find themselves forced to defend their proposals by answering the question, "What's Mrs. McGoosla going to think about that?" Actually the often-blustering archbishop was a complex man. His usually traditionalist, uncompromising approach to church affairs was occasionally interrupted by a striking innovation. Yet because of Mrs. McGoosla's possible reaction, the man who fearlessly ordered the integration of the diocese's churches and schools years ahead of secular institutions also battled to make priests wear hats in the streets and cassocks in the rectory.

45. As quoted in McArdle intv.

His dress rule was a manifestation of his belief that priests should everywhere and in all circumstances project a priestly image. In his mind that image corresponded to the customs and costumes of prewar New York. Once he complained to Msgr. Higgins because his otherwise correct hat sported a blue hatband. "What difference does it make?" asked the straight-talking Higgins. "It makes a lot of difference," came the retort. "You're supposed to be a priest, not a layman." Higgins dismissed the correction as a not-uncommon attitude among older clergy trained in a clerical culture that invested great importance in rules of dress and behavior that were supposed to distinguish those in religious life from the laity. In fact it was Higgins who finally convinced O'Boyle that his annoying insistence on hats for the clergy was a mistake. "Everybody loves a fighter, someone who stands up for what he thinks is right, but nobody really admires somebody who's fighting a losing battle," he told O'Boyle. "You've lost this one. It's a dead issue. I don't wear a hat, and most priests don't wear a hat. I don't know why you're wasting your time." Although he responded with a "that's what you think," O'Boyle begrudgingly surrendered. The following week at the annual priests meeting he added a final item to his usual long list: "One other thing. I was going to give you a talk about wearing a hat, but Higgins, down there at the [National Catholic Welfare] Conference—they know everything down there—he tells me I've lost this one. All right, to hell with it."[46]

If hats were an idiosyncrasy, simple living and avoiding scandal were unbending rules of life. O'Boyle believed that priests should live the Gospel values. Thus the admonition against what he called "cruiser cabins" and fancy cars. He would sometimes needle those serving in wealthy parishes. When Father Duffy was assigned to a church in the affluent Northwest area of the city, he received the warning: "Be careful of some of those lifestyles out there."[47] Convinced that Roman-trained priests often considered their education superior, he never tired of needling alumni of the North American College. He worried about theological experimentation and wanted to protect his seminarians. To the four men setting off for training in Rome in 1954 he said, "When you're there for four years I want you to be the best prayers in the house. Many people have degrees in theology, and their personal lives are scandalous. I want you to be great prayers. I want you to get the degrees, too."[48]

It was well understood that the archbishop was not a party man. He seemed

46. As quoted in Higgins intv. Abell's *Patrick Cardinal O'Boyle,* pp. 26–27, offers a slightly different version of this story.
47. As quoted in Duffy intv.
48. As quoted in O'Brien intv.

socially at ease only in his small inner circle, where he never dominated, but remained always informal, unpretentious, and warm. Even in receptions for fellow priests he was decidedly awkward with party chitchat. One subordinate suggested that, unlike the patrician Msgr. Cartwright, the archbishop was largely untutored in subjects that men tend to discuss at parties, like the latest sports news, and was genuinely at a loss for words in an informal situation. Still, there were those who claimed he enjoyed informal gatherings. At one St. Patrick's Day party he spotted Father Edward Herrmann without a drink, only to learn that the young priest had some time to go in fulfilling the no-alcohol pledge demanded of new priests by Archbishop Curley. In a notable exception to his usual attitude toward law and discipline, O'Boyle bluntly ordered Herrmann to have a drink. He knew that such pledges were a thing of the past, and he did not want one of his priests, even one of German descent, to miss celebrating the great saint's feast day in the proper Irish manner.

O'Boyle enjoyed humorous stories in the Irish vein and had a good repertoire of his own. He would use funny stories to ease a difficult situation. Some subordinates, emboldened by the archbishop's friendly needling, might try to kid back. Sometimes O'Boyle enjoyed the sally, but sometimes the priest quickly learned his mistake. He was more tolerant when others were the target. Once, news reached him that one of his Roman-trained priests frequently performed a notoriously accurate takeoff of the pompous rector of the North American College and O'Boyle's old Scranton friend, Archbishop Martin O'Connor. He called the culprit on the carpet, but his only comment was to tell the chastened mimic, "Now don't say I didn't talk to you about this."[49] In fact O'Boyle was never above poking fun at himself. Hearing that Msgr. Ellis had scheduled a retreat at a Trappist monastery, he kidded, "If you decide to sign up with the Trappists, let me know." As for himself, he added, "I think it would be an altogether good thing for me to keep silence for a long period."[50]

No one could fault the archbishop's work ethic. He was demanding of subordinates, but equally demanding of himself. He admired hard workers and shrewdly surrounded himself with the likes of Father Corbett and Bishop Hannan. Some of his exhortations had their humorous aspects. Once, concerned that there be a large audience for a ceremony, he called the priest in charge and warned him, "If that church isn't full up tomorrow, you're out of a job." After a brief silence from his end of the phone, he suddenly added, "Wait a minute, you

---

49. As quoted in Higgins intv.
50. Ltr., O'Boyle to Ellis, 13 Feb 1953, Ellis Papers, ACUA.

don't get out of a job that easy."[51] O'Boyle displayed a good sales technique when he set out to enlist somebody's help. "You're doing a great job, and now I've got a bigger one for you," was one approach. Another sure-fire formula: he would temper an undue demand by adding ruefully, "Maybe I'm asking too much." Most often the subordinate would fall into the trap by assuring him that indeed he was not.[52]

Even O'Boyle's critics lauded a charitable nature he earnestly tried to hide. Stories circulated about his thoughtful treatment of elderly, declining priests when the time came for them to be relieved of their parishes or their automobiles. His handling of priests with alcohol problems, those with special family burdens, the blind pastor who needed special reassurances, new priests who lacked adequate housing in old parishes, even the dissenters under penalty who needed medical care and living expenses revealed kindnesses that he hoped would go unnoticed. Courtesy was a major concern, and he spoke often of how those in his spiritual care should treat one another, especially how they should remain friends with their colleagues who dissented from his orders.

He deeply respected the priesthood and felt a great obligation to priests, especially those under his supervision. Except for a few close friends, he never appeared at ease with the laity. Despite a lifetime of working closely with lay men and women, he never seemed comfortable in their company, and while always polite never treated them with the warmth he reserved for the ordained. The O'Boyle the laity most often heard in the days before the Vatican Council was the strict moral teacher who, in addition to his frequent exhortations about communism and the rise of secularism, issued repeated warnings about the decline in public morality. Several stern letters were addressed to those who increasingly used Sunday for shopping. Suggesting that both the retailers and their Sunday customers might well be "contributing to the ultimate destruction of our beloved country," he reminded the laity that honoring the Sabbath was a solemn commandment, and the Church demanded that all form a right conscience on the proper observance of the day.[53]

The laity also heard from him about Hollywood's assault on sexual morality. In 1953 he appealed to them to avoid *The Moon is Blue,* condemning the movie as an occasion of sin and calling for a boycott of theaters that showed it. Even before Cardinal Spellman launched his well-publicized attack on *Baby Doll,* O'Boyle

51. As quoted by Bp. Lyons in *Through His Eyes,* p. 19.
52. As quoted in Donoghue intv. (first quote) and McArdle intv. (second quote).
53. Episcopal letters published in *CS,* 21 Jun 1957 (source of quote) and 21 Feb 1958.

had singled out the film as "gravely offensive."[54] Criticized by playwright Tennessee Williams and others for condemning their work before seeing it, O'Boyle replied that he trusted the Legion of Decency's assessment. In fact, he concluded that this movie further demonstrated the urgent need for the Legion, and he made certain that the Legion's pledge was administered annually in every parish in his own archdiocese.[55] In 1961 he addressed a letter to the laity concerning the "terrifying" amount of pornography circulating in the country. He warned against those who confused liberty with license. While Americans cherished liberty, he argued, they must not condone indecent literature anymore than they would condemn the sale of drugs.

He derided those who claimed that obscenity laws were unworkable because of the lack of agreement on what was obscene, comparing it to those arguing that traffic laws were impractical because of a lack of agreement on what constituted safe speed. "One of the rights and duties of the authorities," he concluded, "is undoubtedly to protect people against moral contagion."[56] Later he spoke out against what he called the cultural disease that was engulfing America, a disease typified by scandalous fashions and entertainment full of sex and violence. With rare foresight he focused on violence "that teases, a violence that pleases some latent fascination all of us have for cruelty, for the nastiness that becomes a stimulus of our vindictive feelings."[57]

It was unfortunate that, in the nature of things, the stern voice of the moralizer was all that most Catholics knew of their archbishop. They would no doubt have enjoyed many of his pet peeves. He had little time for the rich and famous, and like most in the community, he liked to poke fun at their often-phony ways. "He's a 24-caret phony" was a favorite putdown. Acquainted with Washington political and social elite, he never sought their company. He was said to hold the speed record for getting in and out of the many receptions he was forced by his position to attend. In addition to his antipathy to Washington's so-called cliff dwellers and the diplomatic crowd, he simply wanted to avoid the fuss and bother of the capital's social scene. He might become a prince of the Church, but a picture of his hero Al Smith still graced his office wall.

O'Boyle was ready to take laymen who considered themselves among an elite down a peg. To the twenty-six doctors, lawyers, and other prominent Washing-

54. Cooney, *The American Pope*, pp. 202–3.
55. *Star*, 11 Jul 1953 and 7 Dec 1956 (source of quote).
56. As quoted in *Star*, 20 Nov 1961.
57. O'Boyle, "The Christian in Today's World," address to the John Carroll Society, 20 Oct 1968, reprint in AAW.

tonians being invested as papal knights he said, "Well, you've all been made big shots, Knights, now." Instead of speaking flowery compliments, he reminded them that the honor merely meant that they now had an even greater responsibility to serve the Church.[58] In a similar vein he wanted the John Carroll Society, which prided itself in those days on its exclusive membership of professional and business leaders, to become more democratic by broadening recruiting. He especially warned its founders to avoid at all cost the impression that they were established as some kind of elite power group trying to influence national policy.

Keenly aware that he was the archbishop of the political capital of the nation, he nevertheless stayed at arm's length from the politicians. Unlike Cardinal Spellman, he was determined not to become a political bishop. A lifelong Democrat, he avoided political discussion, even with intimates. Although ready to be the gracious host, as when he welcomed President Eisenhower to Catholic University to receive an honorary degree in 1953 and to Georgetown University in 1958, he shunned the political limelight. Bishop Hannan concluded that his boss somehow thought federal officials were "nine feet tall." Hannan, a Washington native, had no such illusion and willingly substituted for O'Boyle at many official functions. The number of O'Boyle's visits to the White House during his twenty-five years as archbishop could be counted on two hands. He was Eisenhower's guest at a 1953 stag dinner and was brought along by Cardinal Cushing to visit John Kennedy in 1962. He later accepted an invitation from President Lyndon Johnson to a state dinner for the Italian president. Quizzed later about his seatmate at the affair, he replied, "Oh, some nice young man named John Matthews." His conversation that evening with American singing idol Johnny Mathis must have been somewhat puzzling to both parties. Pressed by President Johnson to head a committee on poverty, he was abashed to find himself delivering his final report to a roomful of reporters at the White House from behind a podium bearing the presidential seal. He never wanted to be perceived as trading on his office and was at all times sensitive to the issue of church-state separation.

His New York experiences taught him that some Church projects would require government intervention. On matters concerning wished-for federal legislation, O'Boyle relied on his friendship with Congressman McCormack or Senator Mike Mansfield, but he avoided discussing national legislation with these leaders. On rare occasion he would speak to a federal official on behalf of one of his colleagues, as he did in 1957 when at Cardinal McIntyre's request he ap-

58. As quoted in McArdle intv. McArdle was one of those laymen being invested as a papal knight.

At the Presidential Rostrum. As head of a presidential commission on poverty, a decidedly uncomfortable archbishop delivers the final report to President Lyndon Johnson from behind the White House seal.

proached Senator William Knowland to explain why his assistance was needed to counter bigotry in a California school tax fight.[59] But these encounters were rare. He preferred that they be handled by the appropriate official at the NCWC. He respected and worked well with Washington's popularly elected mayor, Walter Washington, as well as with Maryland officials. In 1952, for example, he publicly congratulated Maryland's leaders for their aid in the construction of a hospital for the Christ Child Society's farm for sick children, specifically praising them for not raising the church-state issue in providing their important help.[60] In contrast to his general habit, O'Boyle always seemed willing to pose with Scranton pols for their hometown newspaper, as he did with that city's postmaster when they both appeared at the National Postal Forum in 1968.[61]

In view of the controversy that swirled around the election of the nation's first

59. Weber, *His Eminence of Los Angeles,* vol. 1, p. 138.
60. *Star,* 11 May 1952.
61. *Scranton Tribune,* 25 Jul 1968.

Catholic president, the White House was particularly anxious to avoid much public fraternization with Church officials. When President Kennedy attended the Red Mass in January 1961, just days after his inauguration, the John Carroll Society was careful to have him met on the steps of the cathedral by its president, Dr. Charles A. Hufnagel, without benefit of clergy. That particular occasion found O'Boyle greatly incensed. At the conclusion of the Mass, he had retired to the sacristy to divest, meaning to return in street clothes to accompany the distinguished guest to the door. Instead, he returned to find that the president had slipped out without waiting to greet him. Interpreting the action as a direct snub, O'Boyle blew up: "He can go to hell!" he told a startled Msgr. Ellis.[62]

Nor was O'Boyle inclined to associate with the president surreptitiously. In September 1962 he reported to Cardinal Spellman that Kennedy had told the pastor of the Catholic church near his weekend retreat in Middleburg, Virginia, that, while he had some contact with a few of the younger bishops, he had had none with members of the senior hierarchy. He wanted to talk to them about current problems, especially the thorny issue of federal aid to education. Through the Middleburg pastor he expressed the wish that Archbishop O'Boyle visit him in the Virginia countryside some Sunday afternoon. O'Boyle told Spellman he was not at all keen on the idea and would only do it if Spellman and the rest of the NCWC's administrative board approved. Arriving at the heart of the matter, he told Spellman:

> As a matter of fact, and not putting on a "high hat," I do happen to be his [Kennedy's] bishop here in Washington, and I don't see why I couldn't go to the White House and have a session with him if such a thing is really in the cards at all.[63]

Actually O'Boyle, like so many Americans, greatly admired the dashing young president and was in the sorrowing throng among many world figures who attended his funeral at St. Matthew's. He did not, however, deliver the eulogy as requested. When he discovered that the family wanted him to use the occasion to read excerpts from Kennedy's speeches he demurred. If he were going to speak as archbishop of Washington, he reasoned, he was not interested in reading from someone else's speeches. Bishop Hannan, who had been serving as an unofficial liaison between the administration and the Catholic Church, volunteered. O'Boyle offered no objection, but he wanted no part of a gesture that smacked of an assault on the sacred church-state separation.[64]

62. As quoted in Ellis intv.
63. Ltr., O'Boyle to Spellman, 7 Sep 1962, copy in Vatican II Preparation Committee file, AAW.
64. This incident is fully explored in the Arthur and Hannan intvs.

President Kennedy's death in November 1963 coincided with the onset of fundamental change in both the nation and the American Church. American presence in Southeast Asia was about to escalate into a war that would generate profound social unrest and lead many citizens to question the concept of authority in every aspect of their lives.[65] Also that fall, the American bishops returned for the second session of an ecumenical council that, following a rebuff of the guardians of the status quo the year before, promised to reexamine the nature of authority in the Church, the Church's mission to the world, and its interpretation of liturgy and codes of conduct.

Patrick O'Boyle was once described as a man of simple tastes and complex humanity. In his first fifteen years as pastor of the Church of Washington he clearly demonstrated both these traits. He had been the perfect man for what is often called "the old Church," comfortable with its established relationships, steadfast in his loyalty to Church authority, and famously successful in building his archdiocese. It remained to be seen how this complex figure would react to the challenges of the turbulent era that was about to begin.

65. For examples of how other bishops reacted to the challenge, see Thomas T. McAvoy, *Father O'Hara of Notre Dame: The Cardinal-Archbishop of Philadelphia* (Notre Dame, Ind.: University of Notre Dame Press, 1967), and Steven M. Avella, *This Confident Church: Catholic Leadership and Life in Chicago, 1940–1965* (Notre Dame, Ind.: University of Notre Dame Press, 1992).

CHAPTER 11

Vatican II

Pope John's call to the world's bishops on January 25, 1959, to participate in an ecumenical council did not meet with universal approval. Some conservatives, to use the title universally applied, considered the elderly pontiff's initiative a dangerous gesture that threatened the time-honored order of Church doctrine and discipline. These men, chiefly curial officials and their allies in some dioceses, Vatican embassies, and schools of theology, feared that the pope's often-quoted intention of *aggiornamento,* of updating the Church and opening its windows to the modern world, would openly encourage the growing demand not only for changes in the liturgy and increased unity with Orthodox and Protestant groups but also for new ideas about religious freedom, redefinition of the role of bishops, priests, and laity, and delegation of some governing powers to the bishops in their national conferences. Ironically, their blatant effort to ward off what they considered a new threat from the old evil of Modernism actually served to awaken in a majority of the 2,860 bishops who attended a determination to update the Church's discipline and its formulation of doctrine.

Although in the minority, the conservatives enjoyed distinct advantages. It was they who set the agenda through the Central Preparatory Commission, which ordered the schedule and content of debate. They also chaired most of those commissions that would produce the schema, or draft constitutions. These papers were supposed to organize the views of the world's bishops as reflected in their suggestions *(vota)* submitted prior to the council, but they were drafted under the curia's supervision with help from experts initially chosen for their traditionalist views.

The number of American bishops was second only to that of the Italian cohort, but the Americans were not considered an especially influential group by the council's progressives, chiefly prelates from northern Europe and the third world. Some American bishops, along with American theologians and biblical scholars, had kept abreast of the growing demand for updating Church discipline and formulation of doctrine. Most, however, preoccupied with developments in a Church that was just emerging from its ghetto past in a predominantly non-Catholic country, were largely uninformed about issues beginning to embroil their colleagues. Msgr. Higgins, who attended all four sessions of the council, once observed that Rome during those heady months served as "one big Adult Education Institute" for the bishops and their advisors.[1] Indeed, the council, in particular its first session, provided many of the Americans with a quick education. Men like Patrick O'Boyle, who had witnessed firsthand the hardball tactics of the old Tammany Hall denizens, quickly came to understand the dynamics, if not all the implications, of the contest playing out under the dome of St. Peter's.

To help them better comprehend the meaning of the various schema and the undercurrents of the debate, the Americans agreed to meet weekly at the North American College, where committees of bishops and *periti* (experts brought to Rome by individual bishops as advisors) would report to the body on subjects being debated in council sessions. Since the council coincided with Archbishop O'Boyle's tenure as chairman of the National Catholic Welfare Conference's administrative board, it fell to him to obtain permission for such meetings shortly after his arrival in Rome. Permission was needed because the Vatican remained opposed to anything that suggested a formal organization of a region's bishops with juridical powers. Days after his arrival in Rome, O'Boyle, accompanied by Bishop Hannan, approached Cardinal Cicognani, an old friend of the Americans after his long residence among them and now the pope's secretary of state. Cicognani approved the American request for meetings, but stressed that there must be no publicity lest other bishops, misinterpreting the purpose of the American arrangement, demand formation of their own national bodies. O'Boyle so promised, but surely Cicognani was aware, if the archbishop of Washington was not, that few secrets last long in Rome.[2] Soon other national bodies of bishops were meeting to discuss their mutual interests.

The Americans had other concerns. All council business was conducted in Latin, and perhaps more so than most of their international colleagues the Amer-

1. As quoted in Gerald Costello, *Without Fear or Favor: George Higgins on the Record* (Mystic, Conn.: Twenty-Third Publications, 1984), p. 125.
2. Ltr., O'Boyle to Spellman, 10 Oct 1962, Vatican II Papers, AANY.

icans lacked facility in a language that, despite the pleas of many for simultane-

ous translation, the conservatives insisted on retaining, in yet another effort to

control the proceedings. For his *peritus* Archbishop O'Boyle drafted a theolo-

gian, but one best known for his expertise in Latin, the dean of Catholic Univer-

Through their control of the Vatican news sources and the press blackout of

the daily sessions, the conservatives were able to suppress information about the

council. Yet from the beginning, the American bishops provided background in-

formation for the host of English-speaking reporters and commentators, and in

the wake of Pope Paul's order in 1963 that council sessions be fully reported,

they established their own press bureau. At midday an official, usually Holy

Cross Father Edward L. Heston, would provide a summary of events at that

morning's general congregation, while later in the afternoon a panel of experts

The information thus gleaned by widely read correspondents, along with

council decisions that first began to appear in 1963 with the pope's promulgation

of the Constitution on the Liturgy, strengthened the demands of a growing num-

ber of American progressives for immediate change. But change, the council fa-

thers had agreed, was to be regulated by the bishops acting in concert with Vati-

can authorities. Long after the excitement of the council sessions faded, the

impulses it unleashed and the efforts to channel these impulses would preoccu-

py the bishops. Washington was no exception. If Patrick O'Boyle was only a mi-

nor contributor to deliberations in Rome, he would be a major player in the

The First Sessions

Archbishop O'Boyle spelled out his own hopes and expectations for the

council in August 1959, more than three years before the opening ceremonies,

when he submitted his suggestions *(vota)* for subjects to be considered. With ad-

vice from his subordinates but drafted by himself, his list addressed five topics

pertaining to interpretation of matters of faith and four referring to Christian

morals. New to the ways of the curia and clearly putting his best foot forward, he

carefully prefaced his proposals with assurances that he was conversant with

what the magisterium had already pronounced on these issues. His list was inter-

larded with references to specific papal encyclicals and the decrees of the sacred

His submission contained some surprises for anyone familiar with the man's traditional outlook on theological topics and his strong social conscience. Referring to the disputes over the historicity of sacred Scripture among modern biblical scholars, he wanted the council to give more specific direction in these matters and determine norms of scholarly inquiry. Although he recognized the doctrine that "outside the Church there is no salvation," he nevertheless believed that the Church's belief needed further explanation, especially in view of the excommunication of Father Leonard Feeney, the radical defender of the doctrine. Moreover, he believed further clarification of the pontifical declaration on Mary as mediatrix of all grace would be worthwhile. The same applied to the Church's teachings on human evolution, as defined by Pius XII in *Humani Generis*. On a very current topic, O'Boyle referred to the possible existence of extraterrestrial rational life. He himself believed that the Incarnation and Redemption could not apply to creatures "on other planets," and he believed that a council declaration on the subject would offer the light of the Church's doctrine for the guidance of modern scientists.

The archbishop saved his most eloquent pleas for several social issues current in the United States. Reminding the council officials of the existence of strong racial hatred and racial inequality, especially in his own country, he called for the council to solemnly declare the essential equality of all men. Similarly in America and elsewhere there existed much dissension between management and labor. He called on the council to provide a further exposition of the economic justice issues enunciated in the great social encyclicals of Leo XIII and Pius XI. Also, referring to arguments of the times, he called for a declaration on the conditions required for a just war. This, he claimed, would foster world peace. Finally, O'Boyle recommended that the council confirm the Church's teaching that the primary purpose of marriage was procreation. Such information, he concluded, would shine new light on the holy state of matrimony.[3] Indeed, he concluded, on all the matters he had just enumerated the council might shed more light.

O'Boyle's optimistic, but limited, expectations for the council were spelled out in a document prepared under his direction and with his direct input for publication by the NCWC on the eve of the first session. While Pope John had made clear that world conditions lent special timeliness to the council, O'Boyle postulated that the immediate objective of the gathering would be the internal renewal of the Church in doctrine and discipline. All reforms and external changes, if they were to come, would flow from the "renewal of the spirit of the

3. Ltr., O'Boyle to *Eminentissime Domine*, 26 Aug 1959, printed in *Acta et Documenta Concilio Vaticano II Apparando*, Series I (*Ante Oecumenico praeparatoria*), vol. II (*Consilia et Vota Episcoporum ac Praelatorum Septemtrinalivet Centralia*), pt. 6 (*America*) [Vatican City, 1960], pp. 463–64.

Gospels." The American bishops would go, not as representatives of the Church in the United States, but as individual successors to the apostles. Even so, they would be expected to bring with them the wisdom and experiences gained in America. Significantly, in enumerating the elements of this experience, O'Boyle concentrated on the Church's growth from its immigrant beginnings, including its blossoming fellowship with people of other religious beliefs. No specific allusion was made to the demonstrable blessings of religious freedom and the separation of church and state that had so promoted the advancement of the Church in his native land.[4]

A month before leaving for Rome, O'Boyle learned that Secretary of State Dean Rusk wished to meet with the American bishops before the council began. Rusk was anxious to exchange views with them "on any and all matters pertaining to U.S. foreign relations." Since some had already left for Rome, a general meeting was impossible, but O'Boyle suggested that a smaller group could be assembled.[5] The meeting apparently never took place, but the Rusk-O'Boyle exchange was interesting in that it demonstrated that the American government certainly looked on the American bishops as the influential representatives of the nation's Catholics. Moreover, despite his earlier protestations to the contrary, O'Boyle revealed that the idea of a national organization of the bishops was not alien to his own thinking.

With Msgr. Cartwright left in charge, the archbishop, along with Bishop Hannan and Father McCormick, jetted to Rome on October 7, 1962, where, as a guest of the Trinitarian fathers at their comfortable Roman college, his basic costs were covered. The Trinitarians had invited the ordinaries of all those American and Caribbean dioceses in which their congregation served. That allowed O'Boyle to relax during leisure time with colleagues and friends like Archbishop James Davis of Santa Fe. Although these men enjoyed the convivial atmosphere, the Trinitarian house never became a setting for debates about council politics, as did Villanova, the Jesuit-operated residence where some of the most progressive prelates and experts like George Higgins and John Courtney Murray resided. Villanova quickly gained a reputation as the vibrant American meeting place in Rome. Actually, one observer noted, the heated strategy sessions at Villanova were the exception.

4. "Statement on the Ecumenical Council," July 1962, Vatican II file, AAW. See also ltr., Bp. James H. Griffiths to O'Boyle, 9 Aug 1962, copy in George A. Hoehmann's "'My Eminent Friend of New York,' Francis Cardinal Spellman and the Second Vatican Council" (MA thesis, St. Joseph's Seminary, 1992), appendix. Griffith had been asked to comment on the draft and made suggestions for additions.

5. Ltr., O'Boyle to Spellman, 7 Sep 1962, Vatican II file, AAW.

Unlike some of his colleagues, O'Boyle could not have thought of those months as a Roman holiday. During an organizational session on October 22, the world's bishops gave him a singular honor when they elected him to the permanent Commission on Seminaries, Studies, and Catholic Schools with the greatest number of votes cast for anyone on any commission. This recognition by 2,059 of his colleagues no doubt reflected the international reputation he acquired at the helm of the American Church's war relief effort.[6] His commission was charged with revising the schema issued by its preparatory commission in light of the comments of the council's presidents, a select group of senior cardinals responsible for the day-to-day running of Vatican II.

The commission's work was delayed during the first session. It was just as well. In addition to attending all council meetings in St. Peter's, the archbishop was kept busy with his duties on the NCWC administrative board. On October 21 the American bishops convened their annual meeting at the North American College (as they would during subsequent sessions of the council). As chairman, O'Boyle also presided at the session where the bishops organized their weekly meetings for which he had obtained Cardinal Cicognani's permission. The bishops decided to elect a committee consisting of seven bishops and their advisors for each of the twenty (later reduced to thirteen) schemata produced by the council commissions. These committees would review the schemata and present an analysis that sought to enhance the bishops' understanding of the nuances of the ongoing debates, familiarize them with the issues to be voted upon, and, especially in the later sessions, help them strategize over what would become American positions.[7]

Despite the exotic setting and the focus on the council, the administrative board meetings, also held at the North American College, continued routine discussion of the usual topics that concerned operations of the Church in the United States. In 1962, for example, a major subject was financing for the Vatican exhibit planned for the upcoming New York World's Fair. A far more delicate issue was discussed by chairman O'Boyle and the five American cardinals when they decided on a response to the Cuban missile crisis. The dangerous confrontation between the Soviet government and the Kennedy administration over the American blockade of Russian vessels carrying ballistic missiles to Cuba had prompt-

6. Guiseppi Albergo, ed., and Joseph A. Komonchak, ed. of English edition, *History of Vatican II* (Maryknoll, N.Y.: Orbis, 1995).

7. Costello, *Without Fear or Favor,* p. 126, and Hoehmann, "'My Eminent Friend of New York,'" pp. 54–55. Here and elsewhere Hoehmann offers a useful description of the bishops' weekly meetings. Msgr. Higgins recalled that the meetings began during the second session, but, as Hoehmann demonstrated, they were organized in October 1962.

ed the pope to call for negotiations. The pope's impassioned exhortation was favorably headlined in the Soviet press and was featured in the *New York Times,* but generally went unnoticed in the United States. For their part O'Boyle as chairman and the cardinals issued a joint statement calling on American Catholics to observe the upcoming feast of Christ the King as a day of prayer asking God's blessing on the president and the U.S. government. Leaving little doubt about their sentiments, they concluded by praying that God "grant that peace with freedom be preserved."[8]

Shortly after returning home on December 9, O'Boyle provided Washingtonians with an upbeat assessment of the council's first session. Nowhere was there a hint of the great changes about to take place. He defended the first session's lack of production, citing the time-consuming task of organizing the council and predicting that important decisions would issue from the next session, which was scheduled to begin the following September. The lengthy interval, he explained, was meant to give the commissions time to complete their work. He noted that a recommendation on the use of the vernacular in the liturgy "might well emerge during the next session." Such changes, he warned, if they came, would be limited to the first part of the Mass. "The Canon would not be affected." Perhaps in a backhand notice of the tensions that had arisen, O'Boyle claimed that the session was one of the most democratic meetings he had ever attended.[9]

Work on the seminaries and schools commission found O'Boyle airborne much more than he liked. He was back in Rome in February and again in March 1963, when the group met to revise its preparatory schemata in light of the criticisms of the council fathers. The commission tried to meet much of this criticism in its revised text, but O'Boyle and the American *periti* who served on the school subcommission objected, for example, to the section that condemned coeducation. Back home at a special meeting of the American bishops in August, he called for the schema to give greater attention to the education of those not in Catholic schools, with special recognition of the Confraternity of Christian Doctrine and the Newman apostolate. He rejected the effort to extend Vatican control beyond a general supervision of universities and theological faculties to the courses of study themselves. Most important, he wanted the schema to clarify the role of the state in education. A distinction must be made, he asserted, between society and the state, which is the political arm of society. Until this was done, the Church's demand for equal treatment for all parents and pupils could not be

8. As quoted in *NYT,* 26 Oct 1962.
9. As quoted in *Star,* 12 Dec 1962, and *CS,* 14 Dec 62.

presented "in a coherent synthesis." Catholic schools were dedicated to the service of society, not simply for the sole good of the Church, a fact that he wanted recognized in a council document. He asked his colleagues to support his demand for further change.[10]

The death of Pope John in June 1963 cast a cloud over the future of the council until Pope Paul VI endorsed his predecessor's program and promised concrete steps to expedite the work. The opening ceremonies of the second session confirmed the new pontiff's determination to simplify the proceedings, and his subsequent subtle interventions proved his openness to change. Archbishop O'Boyle, who arrived in Rome on September 18, found himself busy juggling his duties on the schools subcommission and his NCWC responsibilities between council meetings. With the new pope's relaxation of the previously strict rules on news coverage, the Americans produced a "Council Digest" daily for the hungry reporters. As chairman of the administrative board, O'Boyle authorized spending $10,000 for the project.[11] He also worked with Msgr. Swanstrom on preparing requests for supplemental funds for Catholic Relief Services that he would present to the board at its semiannual meeting at the North American College.[12] He found time to welcome James Norris to Rome. His old protégé had been appointed a lay auditor and would eventually address the council fathers, the first layman to do so. Norris, anxious to serve but reluctant to ask for O'Boyle's intervention, had turned instead to Msgr. Landi, still directing relief operations in Italy, to help secure the appointment.[13] Norris was on hand when O'Boyle, Spellman, and a host of luminaries joined in celebrating the tenth anniversary of Catholic Relief Services at a grand party in its Roman headquarters.

Also pleasing to O'Boyle was the appearance in Rome of the battle-scarred Father John Courtney Murray, S.J., whom Cardinal Spellman appointed as his private *peritus* when he discovered that Archbishop Vagnozzi, in cooperation with some of the conservative leaders, had tried to block Murray's participation.[14] Murray would rapidly assume direction of the American bishops' efforts to produce a strong council statement on religious liberty. When the Americans discovered early in the second session that discussion of the subject had been dropped from the agenda, they decided to protest. Murray, the theological expert on the subject, drafted a memorandum for the bishops demanding that dis-

10. Vincent A. Yzermans, *American Participation in the Second Vatican Council* (New York: Sheed & Ward, 1967), pp. 562–63.

11. Shelley, *Paul J. Hallinan,* p. 165.

12. Ltrs., Swanstrom to O'Boyle, 31 Jan 63 and 5 Sep 63, Archives of Catholic Relief Services.

13. Kupke, "James J. Norris," pp. 275–76.

14. Fogarty, *Patterns of Episcopal Leadership,* p. 233.

cussion of religious liberty be restored. He also proposed in outline form what the Americans believed the statement should include. The bishops agreed unanimously to a letter that Cardinal Spellman would sign in their name and present both to the council officials and to the pope personally. Paul VI subsequently ruled that the subject of religious liberty would be included in the schema being drafted on ecumenism. Murray later contended that without this united action, the council might well have ignored this subject all-important to the Americans.[15] O'Boyle publicly predicted that, after lengthy "discussion," the council would produce a statement on religious liberty. Such a statement on the individual's right to religious freedom, he concluded, would abrogate the necessity of any lengthy discussion of church-state relations.[16]

The pope's promulgation of the Constitution on the Sacred Liturgy on December 4, 1963, prompted O'Boyle to explain its implication for Washington's Catholics. To curb experimentation, he stated that the new constitution called for change, but only after the bishops had decided on a series of recommendations in these matters for the Church in the United States. He spoke of the use of the vernacular "in parts of the Mass pertaining to the people" and also in the administration of the sacraments, but in America, as elsewhere, only after "approval of regional or territorial episcopal conferences." As chairman of the board of the American conference, he would be appointing two of his colleagues, Archbishop Paul Hallinan of Atlanta, a noted spokesman for liturgical reform, and Bishop James Griffith of New York, to serve on a ten-member commission of bishops from the English-speaking world. With the help of experts in the field, this commission would draw up plans for a common English text for the Mass and sacraments. Hallinan and his colleagues were scheduled to report to the American bishops in early 1964. After approval by the bishops, the English text would then be sent to Rome for final approval and only then put into use. O'Boyle expressed confidence that the changes would be welcomed by most Catholics.[17]

The O'Boyle Interventions

In an effort to speed up proceedings, council officials simplified the submission of several schemata. Thus the schema on Christian education was eventually reduced to a series of propositions, which the council's coordinating commis-

15. Hoehmann, "'My Eminent Friend of New York,'" pp. 118–20. See also Fogarty, *The Vatican and the American Hierarchy,* p. 393, and *Patterns of Episcopal Leadership,* p. 233.

16. "Interview with the Archbishop," *CS,* 13 Dec 1963.

17. *CS,* 18 Oct (source of quotes) and 13 Dec 1963.

sion proposed to offer to the council fathers for a vote without debate. Unhappy with the proposed text, Archbishop O'Boyle submitted what he termed five irreducible points. Reflecting his discussion with his American colleagues the previous August, he wanted the text to acknowledge the importance of Catholic schools in the mission of the Church. The council should also recognize that these schools contribute to the common good and serve society in general. The text should clarify the concepts of "society" and "state." He called for public support of Catholic schools in the name of justice. Finally, he wanted the council to encourage the laity in its role in Christian education, both in and outside Catholic schools. He was the first to intervene when the education commission met in September 1964. Criticizing the proposed text as "utterly inadequate and scarcely defensible," he called for a full debate on education by the council fathers.

The commission subsequently abandoned its original draft and substituted a brief text that, after further debate in the commission and finally in the council itself during its last session, was approved. The promulgated declaration, journalist Vincent Yzermans concluded, generally sustained the views of the Americans. Although it did not address all of O'Boyle's points, it offered a series of general principles that were expected to be amplified at a later date by a papal commission. Meanwhile, the national councils of bishops were invited to interpret these principles for themselves and put them into practice in their countries.[18]

Early September 1964 found the archbishop back in Washington, trying to clear up business by working overtime. "Yes, I know this is Labor Day," he kidded one of his priests, "but somebody's got to work in this diocese!"[19] He also told subordinates to relay their questions and requests for action to the chancellor, who would discuss them with Msgr. Cartwright, the vicar general. He explained that during the first two sessions "everyone and his brother" had written him for decisions. "I needed eight hands, keeping in mind that I had to reply in longhand."[20] Such admonitions apparently failed to reach the vicar general, who continued to bombard the busy archbishop with all sorts of questions and chatty observations.[21]

The council's third session began on September 14, 1964. Cardinal McIntyre suffered a fainting spell during the opening ceremony, some wag insisting that

18. Yzermans, *American Participation*, pp. 563–65, outlines O'Boyle's intervention and its aftermath as quoted above.

19. Ltr., O'Boyle to Father Louis Quinn, 7 Sep 1964, St. Matthew's Cathedral Archives.

20. O'Boyle, Memorandum for Msgr. Gingras, 7 Sep 1964, ASA.

21. See, for example, ltr., Cartwright to O'Boyle, 10 Nov 1964, St. Matthew's Cathedral Archives.

the ultra-conservative prelate was overcome at the sight of a concelebrated Mass.[22] This third session would find O'Boyle at his most active. He would make three interventions, including two speeches in Latin from the rostrum before more than two thousand of his fellow bishops. According to Archbishop Hannan, O'Boyle himself drafted all his papers and speeches. Msgr. Higgins later spoke with admiration of O'Boyle's courage in undertaking what must have been a daunting task. But he considered it his duty, and in his Scranton-Oxford-accented Latin he spoke to the council fathers about Jewish sensibilities and race relations. Probably by then he had lost some of his awe of the Roman princes of the Church. After all, he had "fed those guys during the war," he told Msgr. Arthur. Referring to the never-disguised condescension of Archbishop Pericle Felici, the general secretary of the council, toward the Americans, he told a friend, "I would like to send some shoe leather in the right direction."[23]

O'Boyle was also growing impatient with Archbishop Egidio Vagnozzi, the apostolic delegate in Washington and a close friend of Cardinal Alfredo Ottaviani, leader of the conservative forces at the council. Historian Fogarty noted that Vagnozzi, lacking his predecessor's deftness in dealing with the Americans, impeded their preparations for the council. As O'Boyle put it, "I can't get anything done with that fellow breathing down my neck."[24] Ironically, Vagnozzi proved a valuable ally for the Americans: his constant interference goaded the powerful Cardinal Spellman into making several uncharacteristically progressive moves, to the delight of many of his colleagues. Cardinal Spellman led the American bishops in their opposition to the declaration concerning Jews and non-Christians. The schema had originated in Cardinal Augustin Bea's Secretariat for Promoting Christian Unity. The widely admired ecumenical leader was frustrated by the changes inflicted on his group's proposed text. When it emerged from the council's coordinating commission, the sentence stating that Jews were not guilty of deicide in the death of Christ had been omitted. Cardinal Bea looked to the Americans for help.

Msgr. Higgins estimated that 90 to 100 percent of the Americans supported Bea.[25] At their special meeting on September 16 they pledged a united effort to strengthen the statement on the Jews. Six of them, including O'Boyle, agreed to

22. Shelley, *Paul J. Hallinan,* p. 214.

23. Ltr., Bp. Robert Tracy to Abp. Paul J. Hallinan, 16 Sep 1964, as quoted in Shelley, *Paul J. Hallinan,* p. 214. See also Arthur intv.

24. As quoted in Arthur intv. See also Fogarty, *The Vatican and the American Hierarchy,* p. 383.

25. Costello, *Without Fear or Favor,* pp. 149–50. Costello outlines Higgins' important role in the development of this declaration.

speak. Cardinal Cushing and Bishop Stephen Levin of San Antonio spoke first, concentrating on the deicide issue.[26] On September 29 O'Boyle addressed the council on the emotional topic. He declared that even in the improved version now under consideration, the schema differed from the Council of Trent and the *Summa Theologiae*, both of which clearly stated that none of the Jews at the time of Christ was formally or subjectively guilty of deicide.

O'Boyle explained, as a man from a country with a large Jewish population and as a personal friend of many Jews, why he found the section of the schema on conversion not only objectionable but incorrect. To express hope for conversion, he argued, not only offended Jewish sensibilities with the memory of past persecutions so vivid, it also "oversteps the precise boundaries of Catholic teaching." It would be better, he continued, to accept "the limitation of our knowledge and the unknown ways of Divine Providence." In eloquent sentences he called on the fathers to declare that "the mysteries of salvation depend not on us, but on the action of God." He proposed an insertion that would be perceived by Jews as respecting their sincerity:

> It is well to remember that the union of the Jewish people and of our own people is part of our Christian hope. This union, which the Church ardently hopes for with undaunted faith, will be accomplished by God in His own time and in a manner known to Him alone.[27]

As promulgated on October 28, 1965, the Declaration on Non-Christian Religions did reject the charge of deicide (but the word itself was omitted) and strongly condemned anti-Semitism. Significantly for O'Boyle, any mention of conversion was omitted, and in words that sounded much like his intervention instead declared: ". . . the Church awaits that day, known to God alone, on which all peoples will address the Lord in a single voice and 'serve him shoulder to shoulder.'"[28]

O'Boyle rose a second time on October 28 to speak "in the name of all the bishops of the United States" on the proposed Constitution on the Church in the Modern World. He praised the draft statement, but then went on to propose the addition of a separate section on racial discrimination and other forms of

26. Arthur Gilbert, *The Vatican Council and the Jews* (Cleveland: The World Publishing Co., 1968), pp. 149–50.

27. "Declaration on the Relationship of the Church to Non-Christian Religions," *Acta Synodalia Sacrosanti Concilii Oecumenici Vaticani II* (hereafter *Acta*), vol. III, pt. 3 (Vatican City, 1975), pp. 39–41.

28. Xavier Rynne, *The Fourth Session* (New York: Farrar, Straus and Giroux, 1965), pp. 161–67 and 335 (source of quote).

racial injustice. Reflecting his long dedication to the principle of racial justice, he pointed out that discrimination "in various forms and in varying degrees" could be found throughout the world. He urged the council to condemn racism unequivocally and to outline the theological basis for its condemnation. The council, he continued, should stress the obligation of all Catholics to work to eliminate the scourge of racial injustice and "to advance the cause of interracial brotherhood under the fatherhood of God." The American experience, he added, suggested that such an obligation calls for close cooperation with those of other faiths. The American bishops considered racism one of the most serious moral and religious problems of the age, and, O'Boyle warned, if the council failed to treat it adequately that neglect would suggest that the Church was either unaware of the evil, or worse, insensitive to the plight of millions throughout the world. He concluded by quoting Pius XII on brotherhood, adding, "Unless I am mistaken, the whole world is looking to us to reaffirm this simple but very profound truth in a solemn conciliar statement and to do so unequivocally and with all clarity, precision and forcefulness at our command." [29]

October 28 proved a red-letter day for Washington's archbishop. Shortly after completing his intervention in St. Peter's, he was received in private audience by Pope Paul. Three weeks later he again met with the pope, this time with the rest of the American hierarchy. The discussion focused on the charitable work of the Americans as manifested in the efforts of Catholic Relief Services. Further recognition of O'Boyle occurred on November 21, when he and twenty-three other bishops from around the world, concelebrated Mass with the pope.

Before the third session ended, O'Boyle submitted a written intervention, which under the revised council rules was considered the equivalent of an oral presentation. This time he turned to some practical reforms he believed were needed in seminaries. Here could be seen reflected many of the lessons he had learned since his own seminary training. He wanted the curricula amended to include social studies, with special emphasis on the Church's great social encyclicals and the "many ideas derived from modern science." Theology students should be encouraged to study in the various social disciplines at summer schools. Scholastics should be allowed to read newspapers and encouraged to read secular magazines and journals.

Turning to the so-called preparatory seminaries, O'Boyle argued that they should be limited to day students. He questioned whether it was good to sepa-

---

29. *Acta*, vol. III, pt. 5, pp. 726–28. See also translation in Yzermans, *American Participation*, pp. 239–41 (source of quotes). Yzermans discusses the significance of the document on pp. 198, 200–201.

rate adolescents from their families if they were to develop emotionally. "Will he be able to establish rapport with families in his parish later on?" he asked. Further, if young men never experienced honest labor during their summers, would they ever be able to understand the economic and social problems confronting today's families? Concerning both the seminarians and the young aspirants, O'Boyle urged the council to consider the danger arising from "excessive shielding and sheltering of such students."[30]

Near the close of the third session Pope Paul promulgated *Lumen Gentium,* the council's Dogmatic Constitution on the Church. In the weeks following, the NCWC's administrative board decided to reorganize the conference along the lines outlined in that document. As O'Boyle put it, "The conference had grown like Topsy, and now is a good time to reorganize." For his pains he was named chairman of the reorganization committee, a job that would take many months to complete.[31]

The Final Session

The council's fourth session opened on September 14, 1965. Archbishop O'Boyle, recovering from prostate surgery, missed the first month of meetings and a number of important debates and votes. The Declaration on Religious Liberty provided the most drama during those weeks. This widely celebrated document is considered the American bishops' great contribution to the council. As conceived by Father John Courtney Murray, the declaration replaced the old Church formula that "error has no rights" with the general perception that the state cannot coerce conscience. Never should any person be forced to endorse Christianity or the Church.[32]

To the end the conservative minority sought to defeat the declaration. It saw the American effort as an expedient means of answering their neighbors' criticisms in a nation where Catholicism was in the minority. The opponents continued to hammer away on the theme that "heresy has no rights" and that governments were obliged to establish the Catholic religion as the exclusive religion of the state. The Church, the conservatives claimed, deserved special favor and privilege in governing society. Only when Catholics were in the minority could religious liberty be tolerated.[33] As early as January 1964, after the council's sec-

30. *Acta,* vol. III, pt. 7, pp. 878–80.

31. Minutes of the Administrative Board, Nov 1964, NCWC Papers, ACUA.

32. Costello, *Without Fear or Favor,* pp. 135ff, provides a useful survey of the arguments as seen from the perspective of Msgr. Higgins.

33. Murray's view of the contest as quoted in Hoehmann, "'My Eminent Friend of New York,'" pp. 151–52. See also p. 129.

ond session, Cardinal Joseph Ritter of St. Louis had warned his fellow American bishops that the opponents had enlisted many bishops to question various paragraphs in the schema on ecumenism. He wanted the Americans to counter this "death by many small cuts" with interventions of their own. Father Murray was also concerned about the effect of interventions engineered by the opposition, so at the beginning of the third session he orchestrated a series of interventions by American bishops, each addressing a different aspect of the subject, to strengthen the document and secure a yes vote.[34]

Archbishop O'Boyle was a strong proponent of the declaration and believed that the Americans should be heard on the subject. He volunteered to participate in Murray's plan. As prepared by Murray, O'Boyle's speech focused on the acceptable limits of government intervention in the free exercise of religion. Specifically, the declaration should claim religion's immunity from government control except in cases where the religious practice caused a serious breach of the peace or violated standards of morality or health.[35]

When the council fathers voted to end debate at the end of the third session, they left it to the Secretariat for Christian Unity to revise the text in light of the mainly American interventions. The task fell to a group that included Father Murray. Once again the opponents tried to scuttle the issue by wresting control of the revision process. An appeal to the pope blocked this effort, and a new text (now separate from the schema on ecumenism) was distributed to the council fathers. Murray considered the final version weaker than its predecessor, but still satisfactory. The opponents, however, had not given up. On the last day of the session, the council presidents announced that the revised text was essentially a new document, and therefore the bishops must be given time to examine it and submit their views in the coming months. Left to their own devices, the opponents could then simply let the declaration die. The declaration supporters, who understood the threat, dubbed the day of the announcement "Black Thursday." They immediately counterattacked by circulating a petition that garnered about a thousand votes, and Cardinal Meyer of Chicago personally appealed to the pope. In response Pope Paul promised that the declaration would be the first order of business in the next session. For his part, Cardinal Ritter called on the Americans to express support for the proposed text and send any suggestions for improvement in the brief time period permitted.[36]

34. Donald E. Pelotte, *John Courtney Murray: Theologian in Conflict* (New York: Paulist Press, 1976), pp. 92–99, provides a useful discussion of the fight for the declaration and is the basis of the following paragraphs.

35. *Acta,* vol. III, pt. 2, pp. 718–20.

36. Hoehmann, "'My Eminent Friend of New York,'" pp. 182–83.

Addressing the John Carroll Society on December 15, 1964, O'Boyle offered an optimistic assessment of the situation as it stood after the third session. He predicted that the council would approve the declaration by a large majority. "Even those of a more conservative way of thinking were calling for its passage, as long as it's based on solid grounds and avoids all traces of indifferentism." Although "it is true that anyone who honestly and sincerely follows his conscience is pleasing to God and can be saved," he added, "the Church must avoid the idea that all religions are equally good." At the same time, he echoed Murray's logic, accepting the Church's claims did not mean that government, even in an overwhelmingly Catholic country, should limit religious activity. All religions should be granted freedom.[37]

The archbishop's forced stay at the Mayo Clinic prevented attendance during the debate on religious liberty that marked the opening weeks of the fourth session. On September 20, the day of O'Boyle's prostate operation, the council fathers heard his name announced as one of the scheduled speakers in the upcoming religious liberty debate.[38] His remarks, which included a five-point list of proposed minor changes to the text, were submitted as a written intervention instead. He offered the bishops an optimistic assessment of the declaration and called for their vote of approval.[39]

Back in Rome in late November, O'Boyle would end his participation in the council on a less positive note. During the final days of discussion about *Gaudium et Spes* (The Church in the Modern World), Archbishop Hannan, recently installed as the ordinary of New Orleans, took exception to its condemnation of the possession and use of nuclear arms. He succeeded in obtaining the signatures of nine other bishops, including Spellman, O'Boyle, and Shehan, on a letter that called for correction of these "errors." Hannan argued that the possession of nuclear arms had "preserved freedom in a large part of the world," that recent popes had never condemned total war, and, moreover, no consensus had been reached on the subject among competent theologians.[40]

The objection was doomed to fail. Archbishop Shehan repudiated his own endorsement, and the pope let it be known that he was in full accord with the schema as it stood. Msgr. Higgins was quoted in the *New York Times* as calling

---

37. O'Boyle, Address to the John Carroll Society, 15 Dec 1964. See also quotes in *Star*, 16 Dec 1964.

38. *Acta*, vol. IV, pt. 1, p. 335.

39. *Acta*, vol. IV, pt. 2, pp. 232–35.

40. *Acta*, vol. American interventions, pt. 3, p. 859. See discussion in Yzermans, *American Participation*, pp. 220–21, and Hoehmann, "'My Eminent Friend of New York,'" pp. 204–6. See also *NYT*, 5 Dec 1965 (source of quote).

the petition "inopportune" because it left the impression in the council that it represented the views of all the Americans, which it did not. Cardinal Spellman also let it be known that he too had retracted his support. For his part, O'Boyle later said that he had signed the letter out of loyalty to his old auxiliary, who had sought his backing.

Compared to most of his senior American colleagues, Archbishop O'Boyle was not a particularly visible participant in the council. He was unfamiliar with Roman ways, and, as Msgr. Higgins observed, he was no big-picture man. O'Boyle was never an avid student of theology and hence did not think in broad theological terms. He was pleased that his special interests—racial justice, social welfare, and Catholic-Jewish relations—received council endorsement. He was obviously pleased with the success of the declaration on religious liberty. O'Boyle fully supported Murray's work and, like his colleagues, believed that the Roman curia did not understand the American mentality nor the American concept of democracy. To celebrate passage of the declaration, he hosted a gala party for the ailing Murray, who was clearly the darling of the Americans.[41]

His council experience plainly illustrated the dichotomy in O'Boyle's outlook—progressive, even innovative, on social issues; traditional, ever fearful of experimentation, on issues of liturgy, theology, and church governance. Not that he eschewed change. On the contrary, anything the Church ordered, he was ready to accept, however reluctantly, but seldom a step ahead of the Vatican's wishes. His formula was to be sorely tested in his remaining years in Washington, as demand for change and experimentation, stimulated by the council's work, flowered.

41. Higgins and Donoghue intvs.

CHAPTER 12

A Fretful Shepherd

Many American bishops returned from Rome in December 1965 pleased with what they had accomplished at the council and ready to work with the clergy and laity on beginning the renewal mapped out at their historic gathering. They would have agreed with Patriarch Maximus Cardinal Singh's conclusion that the council had put the Church "into a permanent state of dialogue." Henceforth, he predicted, dialogue within the Church over continuous renewal, with other Christians over ecumenical initiatives, and with the modern world, "those men of good will in all their diversity," on subjects of mutual concern would be the order of the day. As one observer put it, "After the council the three evangelical vows will be those of poverty, chastity, and dialogue."[1] Nevertheless, the road to liturgical and structural change within the Church, the first objectives of this ongoing dialogue, promised to be a rocky one for those American bishops who looked to carefully paced, orderly transformation firmly guided by Rome and their national conference.

Archbishop O'Boyle was squarely in this camp. He was clearly pleased with the council's accomplishments, especially its stand on social issues, but by temperament and training he was cautious and conservative in matters of liturgy and governance. He accepted the need for change, but expected it to be slow and always under the direction of proper authority. "Change can be useful in sweeping away the accumulated cobwebs of outmoded thinking," he told a Washington audience, "but change must have order, or it quickly becomes chaos." He recognized the right of Catholics to dissent, but added, "someone has to call

1. As quoted in Costello, *Without Fear or Favor*, pp. 190–91.

the shots . . . otherwise we would have a half-billion Catholics each claiming the right to follow his own doctrine and his own liturgy."[2] The art of dialogue was not among O'Boyle's more prominent gifts, and for certain the idea of experimentation was anathema to him.

Yet dialogue and experimentation were exactly what a large and articulate segment of the American clergy and laity, inspired by the council debate and its final declarations, wanted and expected. The Washington archdiocese had its share of those looking for speedy change. Even before the council closed some were openly experimenting with the liturgy and publicly offering the archbishop suggestions concerning diocesan affairs. This latter effort did not, one pastor wryly noted, "sit very well, as you can imagine." Accompanying the demand for dialogue and experimentation was a new attitude toward authority. The same pastor sadly noted that "the spirit of contempt for authority (perhaps I put it too strongly) is quickly filtering down, and it is becoming more and more difficult on the level at which I act."[3]

O'Boyle was especially concerned with the effect of experimentation and questioning on the less sophisticated. He was determined to protect the "Mrs. McGooslas" in his care from the worry and confusion of rapid, often conflicting, and certainly unauthorized change. He wanted time to prepare them for renewal with a carefully orchestrated education program, and he expected his priests to be the prime agents in the venture. To that end he offered the clergy a theological seminar at which "the most competent scholars in their respective fields" would lecture on the council's intentions. He also arranged for continuing education classes at Catholic University. (Although 175 priests signed up for the initial classes, lack of interest had reduced the number to 17 by 1968, when for this and other reasons O'Boyle withdrew his support.)[4]

Overlooking O'Boyle's willingness to foster authorized change, critics have unfairly linked him to those like Cardinal McIntyre who seemed determined to scuttle much of the council's work. O'Boyle actually recognized the need for renewal and promptly set about achieving it in his diocese. That he could not control the pace of change intensely irritated him. He labeled those subordinates who tried to innovate disloyal, a major sin in his lexicon. He became chronically

2. As quoted in *Star*, 7 Oct 1967.

3. Ltrs., Rev. Joseph Coyne to Msgr. John Tracy Ellis, 23 Jan 1966 (first quote) and 10 Nov 1965 (second quote), Ellis Papers, ACUA. For a contemporary discussion of this tension, see, for example, "Authority Under Fire," *Time*, 19 Mar 1965.

4. Ltr., Hannan to Reverend and Dear Father, 10 Feb 1965, AAW (source of quote), and *WP*, 4 Oct 1968. See also Donoghue intv.

fretful, Msgr. Ellis observed. Even his master of ceremonies and close friend, Father Walter Schmitz, admitted in January 1966 that the boss had been in a foul mood for some time.[5] Yet his often irascible reaction to events in the late 1960s aside, O'Boyle dutifully led the Church in Washington on its pilgrimage of renewal.

The Fight for Liturgical Change

Of those subjects that preoccupied the post-conciliar Church in America, none was more pressing than liturgical reform. Updating the way Catholics carried out the central rites of their religion went to the very heart of Church renewal, as those on all sides of conciliar debate understood. It followed that any significant change would lead to controversy, as progressive liturgists, typified by leaders of the National Liturgical Conference, sought to push the envelope with demands for experimentation and innovation in the face of episcopal efforts to control and limit change.[6]

It was during this time of controversy that the archbishop of Washington developed a reputation as a conservative, if not reactionary, leader, a reputation that would dog him for the rest of his career. An old-fashioned prelate who "favored a heavy-handed assertion of episcopal authority" was historian Thomas Shelley's later summation of what would become an almost universal judgment.[7] Clearly apprehensive, O'Boyle fretted publicly over unauthorized change and threatened to punish violators. Fearing confusion among an uninformed laity, he privately criticized some of his colleagues, like Archbishop Paul J. Hallinan of Atlanta, for their support of experimentation. Ironically, under O'Boyle's willing leadership the Church in Washington embraced all the innovations recommended by the bishops and approved by Vatican authorities in a timely and orderly fashion and with few of the problems that plagued many other dioceses.

He began shortly after the council's Constitution on the Sacred Liturgy was promulgated. Early in 1964 he set up a series of diocesan commissions—liturgical, sacred art, and building (a sacred music commission would be added later)—to ensure that all new construction or renovation of churches, chapels, and

---

5. Ltr., Coyne to Ellis, 23 Jan 1966, Ellis Papers, ACUA (source of quote). See also Ellis intv. Archbishop Donoghue discussed at length O'Boyle's embrace of change in the post-conciliar period. See intv. See also Herrmann and Arthur intvs.

6. Xavier Rynne, *Vatican Council II* (New York: Farrar, Straus and Giroux, 1968), p. 39. For background on the pre–Vatican II liturgical changes, see Keith F. Pecklers, *The Unread Vision: The Liturgical Movement in the United States of America, 1926–1955* (Collegeville, Minn.: Liturgical Press, 1998).

7. Shelley, *Paul J. Hallinan*, p. 257.

church auditoriums conformed to the requirements of the Sacred Liturgy Commission in Rome and with the directives of the bishops' conference. Under the general supervision of Bishop Spence, who chaired the building commission, and with the assistance of Msgrs. Arthur (liturgy) and Cartwright (sacred arts), these bodies were expected to become conversant with the latest revisions of liturgical rules and pass judgment on the spiritual and artistic aspects of any proposed work in the archdiocese. The commissions in turn were charged with advising the archbishop on the merits of all proposed projects, since O'Boyle made it clear that he intended to have the final say on all changes.

The building commission was the channel through which he operated. It issued strict guidelines for the pastors, explaining how their proposals must be submitted for review by the three commissions. Only after the details (including the architect's drawings) were approved by the liturgical and sacred arts bodies would the building commission decide if the project could proceed. It would then closely supervise construction in a series of specific reviews. [8]

As in most bureaucracies there were bottlenecks. In this case an early impediment proved to be Msgr. Cartwright. The rector of the cathedral was rightly celebrated for his knowledge of sacred art and for the beauty of the liturgy at St. Matthew's. Unfortunately he found it extremely difficult to adapt to change and used his position to frustrate the efforts of pastors to provide effective settings according to the new liturgical directives. One pastor, for example, submitted plans for a renovated sanctuary in strict compliance with the latest comments of the Vatican's Liturgy Commission, only to have Cartwright reject them, tartly adding that the proposed arrangement would look like a Methodist meeting house. Cartwright had already informed the archbishop of his disapproval, which, he told the pastor, was based on what was artistically admirable. The more flexible archbishop reviewed the proposal and merely told the pastor that he "wished" the plans could be modified. But if his decision in this case betrayed sympathy for the beleaguered pastor, he nevertheless continued to support his awkward commission system and the close control over change that it symbolized. Even as he complied with O'Boyle's compromise solution, the pastor in question, Father Joseph Coyne, noted that Cartwright and others seemed determined to hold back the tide of change, and as a result many of the young pastors and an even greater number of young priests were completely frustrated. [9]

8. Bp. Spence, "Procedural Guide Lines To Be Followed By All Pastors with Building Programs," n.d. (c. 1964), Building Commission file, AAW. See also series of undated, untitled memos defining the work of the three commissions, same file.

9. Ltr., Coyne to Ellis, 12 May 1965, Ellis Papers, ACUA.

The archbishop made a significant change in February 1965 when he approved celebration of Mass facing the people. No doubt with the "Mrs. Mc-Gooslas" in mind, he assured the laity that what might seem a radical move had always been an option in the Roman rite. Nevertheless, he set down strict rules. The new position could be taken at two Sunday Masses and one on weekdays provided that there was at least one other scheduled Mass celebrated every day "in the usual manner." The directive included comprehensive instructions on the proper furnishing of the temporary altar, which must immediately be moved aside after Mass to allow an unobstructed view of the main altar.[10]

To prepare for this change O'Boyle sent Father Louis Quinn to demonstrate the new configuration to a major gathering of diocesan priests. Saying Mass facing the congregation as well as reciting the prayers in English was disconcerting to many priests. When Quinn confessed his uneasiness, O'Boyle admitted to his own discomfort with the new ways, but added, "This is the way it's to be, it's to be done." From this Quinn came to realize that no matter what it cost O'Boyle personally, loyalty to the Church and the pope compelled him to act.[11]

The first important changes in the Latin Mass, authorized by the bishops with Vatican approval, were scheduled to go into effect on March 7, 1965. A full five months before this date O'Boyle began an education program to familiarize the laity with the alterations. He outlined a series of sixteen sermons that were to be preached by all parish priests in the archdiocese. To enhance their oratorical skills for such an important assignment, he offered each the opportunity to make a practice recording, using the facilities at Cathedral Latin School. He wanted the priests to follow his outline, but to write their own sermons. He also wanted each parish to develop a "strong program to 'sell' the liturgical changes to the people." Meanwhile men like Father Walter Schmitz, the archbishop's master of ceremonies, offered a series of workshops on the coming changes, and the clergy were invited to listen to a recording of the so-called participated Mass recently celebrated at the National Liturgical Conference.[12]

O'Boyle would employ similar techniques during the next two years as liturgical changes multiplied, especially the introduction of English (in what was later titled the liturgy of the Word) and publication of the new Vatican Instruction

---

10. Ltr., Hannan to Reverend and Dear Father, 10 Feb 1965, copy in Higgins Papers, ACUA. See also *CS*, 1 Nov 1963.

11. As quoted in Quinn intv.

12. Ltr., Msgr. Arthur to Reverend and Dear Father, 22 Sep 1964, copy in Higgins Papers, ACUA. See also Donoghue intv. For the many announcements concerning liturgical changes, see Chancery file, AAW.

on Church Music. This latter directive authorized a more flexible approach to
the selection of music and instruments in the liturgy. It might well be true, as
Msgr. Ellis observed, that O'Boyle had hoped for only minimal change in the
liturgy, but he did appreciate the usefulness of parts of the Mass in English and,
out of loyalty perhaps, overcame his aversion to the use of the guitar, at least to
the extent approved by his own sacred music commission.[13]

The deliberate pace of change in Washington only seemed to embolden some
of the priests and people to gather for Masses outside the regular parish system,
where they experimented with the liturgy according to their interpretation of the
council's declaration. With emphasis on lay participation, their Mass featured
sermons that included observations from the congregation, petitions expressed
by the congregation at the offertory, and contemporary music accompanied by
guitars and drums. These groups coalesced into a loose entity called The People
and began to attract a significant number of enthusiastic, well-educated members
to their so-called Action Mass. Divorced from any parish affiliation, they recruited priests for the most part from local universities and held their celebrations at
any available college chapel or school auditorium. The archbishop was particularly upset by the extra-parochial aspect of the movement, as well as by reports of
notable deviations from the authorized Mass. For their part, The People invited
the archbishop to witness their celebration and hoped to gain his permission to
establish an experimental, nongeographical parish like those found in some other
dioceses. O'Boyle would have none of it.

While beleaguered by demands for innovative and unorthodox liturgies, the
archbishop had to deal with an aggressive apostolic delegate. Archbishop
Vagnozzi, in collaboration with the more conservative element in Rome, was anxious to expose any minute deviation from the letter of the law as interpreted by
officials generally opposed to change. As chairman of the bishops' administrative
board and archbishop of Washington, O'Boyle frequently heard from Vagnozzi
with complaints about innovations great and small. For example, in January 1965
Vagnozzi reported on a series of "abuses," including the celebration of community Masses at a number of seminaries. "This must be forbidden," he told O'Boyle.
He also reported that the pope was worried about the de-emphasis on Latin in
seminary training. "In this delicate period of transition and arrangement that we
are experiencing," he pontificated, "it is requested that there be an alert vigilance
to avoid conflicts and difficulties." Again claiming papal concern, this time about
the "excesses in some of the ecumenical services in the United States," Vagnozzi

13. Ellis intv.

warned that until the new norms were set by Rome, participation in such ceremonies should be avoided.[14]

The reform spotlight turned toward the bishops' conference in November 1966, as it began to consider major initiatives proposed by its liturgical commission. Archbishop O'Boyle was just completing his term as chairman after successfully managing the post-conciliar reorganization of the NCWC. To reflect the post-Vatican II realities, the bishops formed the National Conference of Catholic Bishops, a canonical body through which they could exercise their joint supervision of the American Church. (They also established a separate civil corporation, the United States Catholic Conference, to conduct the Church's multifaceted religious and social works.) His work done, O'Boyle stepped down as chairman, and the archbishop of Detroit, John Dearden, was installed as the first president of the NCCB.

Archbishop Hallinan, the new head of the bishops' liturgical commission, lost no time in presenting the bishops with a long list of proposals. Two prompted the most discussion: use of English in the canon of the Mass and establishment of centers in "controlled communities" for experimenting with the structure of the Mass with the approval of the local ordinary.[15] Such Church-sponsored experimentation, Hallinan contended, would help neutralize the efforts of those, like The People, who were freely exploring new forms without guidance. The bishops agreed to seek Rome's permission, although whether O'Boyle voted with the majority is unclear. He did, however, brand The People's Action Mass a "sorry travesty" and pointed to specific "flagrant violations" of the service.[16]

Months of negotiation and petitions to reluctant Roman authorities followed on the subject of an English canon, until August 1967 when Hallinan and Dearden announced a stunning victory. The Holy See had approved the use of the English text prepared by the International Commission on English in the Liturgy and recently endorsed by the American bishops, provided the American bishops agreed. At the September meeting of the NCCB's administrative committee, Hallinan proposed that the text be formally approved and put into effect in churches throughout the country beginning in October. He added that the Canadian bishops, who had also received approval, had already instituted the change. A speedy vote of approval from the Americans seemed likely, until the

---

14. Ltrs., Vagnozzi to O'Boyle, 18 Jan 1965 (first quote), to Hannan, n.d. (c. Jan 1966) (second quote), and to O'Boyle, 16 Jan 1965 (third quote). All in Chancery file, AAW.

15. Shelley, *Paul J. Hallinan*, p. 243. Unless otherwise indicated, the following paragraphs are based on this source, pp. 239–58.

16. As quoted in *Star*, 9 Oct 1967.

archbishop of Washington took the floor. He opposed the move, he told his colleagues, because he opposed the words of consecration being spoken in English. His stand should have come as no surprise. Earlier that year he had voted against accepting the text proposed by the English language commission for the same reason. The use of the vernacular, he feared, "would open the way to innumerable abuses," in particular "the introduction of numerous and perhaps invalid versions of the sacramental form." He called on his colleagues to retain Latin for the words of consecration.[17]

Chairman Dearden told O'Boyle that he was out of order in proposing change in a text that had already received the approval of the bishops at their last general meeting and more recently from the Holy See, which had specified that the text be employed exactly as proposed. Nevertheless O'Boyle remained unmoved, and Cardinal McIntyre rose to second his objection. Oakland's Bishop Floyd L. Begin joined them, questioning the administrative committee's competence to decide the matter. He proposed that a decision be postponed until the general meeting of the bishops in November. At that, powerful voices like those of Dearden and Cardinal John Krol of Philadelphia were raised in defense of Hallinan's proposal. Finally, in an effort to compromise, Chicago's Cardinal John Cody suggested that all members of the conference be polled. A ballot was sent out in September and five days later Dearden reported the results: an overwhelming vote for the proposed text, which would be used in all Masses beginning October 15.[18] Undeterred, O'Boyle again raised the question of retaining Latin in the consecration at the general meeting of the bishops in November. He was aware that a vote on the subject had already been taken, he added, and he did not plan to push the matter further. Nevertheless, he wanted his colleagues to remember, "Latin is unchangeable while English is not." His question was tabled with no action taken.[19]

This rearguard attempt to retain some Latin in the Mass is difficult to explain. Msgr. Higgins dismissed the incident as "a little friendly gesture to McIntyre," adding that O'Boyle's "hang-up" on a Latin consecration was something he most likely got from his old friend. Certainly defense of Latin was never the con-

17. The quote is from a summary of O'Boyle's remarks in the Minutes of the NCCB Administrative Committee Meeting, September 1967, p. 31, NCCB Papers, ACUA. With the establishment of the NCCB, the old administrative board was renamed administrative committee.

18. Later changed to October 25. Minutes of the NCCB Administrative Committee Meeting, Sep 1967, p. 31, NCCB Papers, ACUA. Shelley's *Paul J. Hallinan,* pp. 250–51, provides interesting details concerning this meeting.

19. Minutes of the NCCB Meeting, November 1967, NCCB Papers, ACUA.

cern for O'Boyle that it had become to some of his more traditionalist colleagues.[20] Whatever his motive, the incident underscored one of his most endearing traits. No matter how uneasy he may have felt about the speedy and wholesale change that was going on around him, he had no problem in obeying the decisions of the Holy See and the American bishops even to moves that he personally opposed. The English canon was included in all Masses in the Archdiocese of Washington beginning on October 25.

He even endured joshing about his quixotic stand. After presiding at a Latin Mass on the following St. Patrick's Day, O'Boyle found himself sitting near the irrepressible Higgins, who deftly applied the needle. Why, he asked, a Latin Mass on St. Patrick's Day, since "the Irish don't know any Latin"? (Higgins sarcastically claimed that O'Boyle knew no more Latin than Higgins knew Chinese.) As Higgins reported the rest of the colloquy:

O'Boyle [loud and angry]: What do you mean? Can't I have a Latin Mass when I want to?

Higgins: You can have it in any language you want as far as I'm concerned, but I just wondered why you had it in Latin.

O'Boyle: I suppose you are one of those fellows who would like guitar Masses.

Higgins: Well, I don't mind them. I don't know how to play the guitar, but I noticed that you had an organ Mass, and you know the organ was forbidden for almost a thousand years in the Catholic Church.

O'Boyle [still loud]: Who told you that?

Higgins: Look it up. Organ music was forbidden for many years in the Church.

O'Boyle: Yeah? Will you just get off that damn Latin Mass?

O'Boyle was unambiguous in his opposition to liturgical experimentation. "It is difficult to stop experimentation once it starts," O'Boyle warned his fellow bishops.[21] He had in mind those in his own archdiocese who were pressing ahead with unauthorized alterations to the liturgy. Many bishops were experiencing similar revolutions led by some of their articulate priests and laymen. But where Hallinan and his liturgical commission sought to counteract the radical reformers by co-opting experimentation under control of the bishops, O'Boyle believed that such a move would only encourage the more radical element.

The focal point of this radicalism was the National Liturgical Conference. A

20. Higgins intv.
21. As quoted in Minutes of the NCCB Meeting, Nov 1967, NCCB Papers, ACUA. See also Shelley, *Paul J. Hallinan*, p. 252.

private organization unaffiliated with any Church authority, the conference was founded in pre-conciliar days as a forum for serious-minded liturgists. Their annual Liturgical Week, celebrated in various cities throughout the country, provided members the opportunity to discuss their aspirations for a renewed liturgy. The council's declarations and the Church's new legislation not only opened new horizons for the conference, but also marked the emergence of new leaders, both priests and laity, whose agendas far exceeded the more modest aims of most of the bishops, who opposed the eccentric changes proposed by the increasingly radical group as well as the liberties they were taking in their liturgical celebrations.[22]

Roman officials were also concerned. Fed reports by the apostolic delegate, they directed the bishops to exert control over the liturgists. Hallinan, in trying to explain to the Holy See that the bishops could do no such thing to a private group, sought to use this fear of radicalism to argue for officially sanctioned experimentation. Undiscouraged by Rome's rejection of the NCCB's earlier proposal on the subject, he pressed his fellow bishops to recommend a broader program of experimental liturgy centers at several Catholic universities as well as authorization for bishops to open experimental centers in their own dioceses. At the November 1967 meeting of the NCCB, O'Boyle tried to modify Hallinan's proposal by suggesting that in the section on centers at universities the word "control" be added before the phrase "by the Conference in conjunction with the local Ordinary." Hallinan considered the word "control" too restrictive, but accepted the addition of the less restrictive "supervision" suggested by Chairman Dearden as a compromise.[23]

Hallinan won approval for his proposal from a large majority of the bishops, who accepted his thesis that controlled experimentation would dampen the efforts of the radical reformers. O'Boyle, who by that time had become identified as a major opponent of experimentation, opposed. He had banned the freewheeling liturgy of The People the previous year. Predictably, this only gained more public notice for the Action Mass. The eleven-member executive committee of the informally organized Vatican II Study Group, representing some ninety of O'Boyle's own priests, expressed their concern over the ban and declared that the Church must appeal to modern man in his language. They urged the archbishop to authorize Masses for small groups in private homes. As if this were

22. Baum intv. Baum, then a monsignor, served on the board of the National Liturgical Conference until its increased radicalism prompted him to resign in 1967.
23. Minutes of the NCCB Meeting, November 1967, NCCB Papers, ACUA.

not enough, O'Boyle was also concerned about reports of clandestine groups celebrating the liturgy not only in private homes, but even hotels.[24] In response O'Boyle issued a stern pastoral letter warning, "No one is to proceed faster than Church authorities." Pleased with his work, he sent a copy of his letter to every ordinary in the country.

O'Boyle also reacted sternly when the new president of the National Liturgical Conference, Father Joseph Connelly of Baltimore, came to tell him that his group had selected Washington as the venue for its 1968 Liturgical Week. The increasingly radical tone of the speeches at recent Liturgical Weeks had succeeded in driving out a number of the conference's moderates, leaving the extremists a free hand. O'Boyle told Connelly that the conference was under suspicion and that he forbade its meeting in his archdiocese. Connelly, who dearly loved confrontation, tartly reminded O'Boyle that he lacked authority to bar a private group from the capital. Both parties stood their ground even after Hallinan, the liturgical conference's most prominent member, urged Connelly to hold the meeting elsewhere and threatened to resign if he did not do so. In the end it was the archbishop of Washington who relented. To the great disappointment of Hallinan and those other bishops pushing for authorized experimentation, the Roman Consilium, the curial body charged with supervising the liturgy, rejected the NCCB's proposal for experimentation. O'Boyle used the decision to push his idea of liturgical reform. In a volte face, he welcomed members of the liturgical conference to Washington, but he provided its officers with a long list of dos and don'ts. In so informing Connelly of his permission, he noted that he had changed his mind, in part because several lay advisors had strongly urged him to do so. His refusal had been prompted by the fact that some priests were introducing on their own authority changes in the Church's rites. They must conform to Church rules, he told Connelly, and he wanted all the conference's members so informed.[25] This Connelly failed to do. "I'm not at all happy about this meeting," O'Boyle told a friend. "I may have more to say on this subject later."[26]

Confrontations over the liturgy would fade as authorized changes continued to be issued piecemeal. As each change was announced, it was promptly put into effect in Washington. O'Boyle made it a practice never to be one step ahead or

24. O'Boyle used his friend William Abell to learn what went on at some of these gatherings. See Abell intv. The editor of the *Catholic Standard,* Father William O'Donnell, also reported on one such Mass. See ltr., O'Donnell to O'Boyle, 5 Jun 1970, AAW. For articles on the Action Mass see, for example, *WP,* 11, 25, and 26 Sep 1967, and *Star,* 25 Sep 1967.

25. Ltr., O'Boyle to Connelly, 1 Dec 1967, Chancery file, AAW.

26. Ltr., O'Boyle to Philip Frohman, 13 Jan 1968, Chancery file, AAW.

behind the magisterium. He even came to enjoy the innovations. On the eve of his third concelebrated Mass with Pope Paul he told reporters that new changes in the liturgy would be introduced during the celebration, adding, "I think that adds even more to the ceremony, at least for me." In subsequent years he readily joined in such Masses, especially on Holy Thursday, which the Congregation on Divine Worship marked as a time when such a concelebrated liturgy was particularly appropriate.[27]

Church Governance

As he had in the disputes over the new liturgy, Archbishop O'Boyle consistently emphasized an ordered and controlled approach to the other changes flowing out of Vatican II. It was not always easy to maintain this stand when Church intellectuals like John Tracy Ellis were publicly calling for a more democratic method of selecting bishops, and groups like the National Federation of Priests Councils were winning headlines with their demands for a larger role for priests in governing the Church. Nor were Catholics in the Washington archdiocese immune from the turmoil when they heard influential figures like Ellis argue that the present system of selecting bishops produced conservative-minded financiers, not pastors of souls.[28] Pastors like Father Joseph Coyne were disturbed by "the defection and rebellion of so many of our priests." Addressing his worry to his friend Msgr. Ellis, of all people, he added that "for the sake of the faith and the good of souls" priests should close ranks behind the archbishop. If they have honest differences of opinion, he concluded, let them take them to O'Boyle. "There are channels for this kind of dissent," he pointed out, but they did not include the pages of the inflammatory *National Catholic Reporter* or the secular press.[29]

Beginning in 1966 O'Boyle had set about creating just such channels of communication between himself and the clergy and laity, as encouraged by the council's declarations. First on his agenda was the Clergy Advisory Council. Familiarly called the priests' senate, this group was elected by all the diocesan clergy, who voted for three men in each of six groups that classified priests by years ordained. By October 1966 the votes had been counted and the eighteen members installed, along with four others appointed by O'Boyle to represent the Jesuit

27. Ltr., Herrmann to Fr. Horace McKenna, 12 Mar 1971, McKenna Papers, AGU. The quote is from *Star,* 28 Jun 1967.

28. See Ellis on the selection of bishops in *Commonweal,* 10 Mar 1967, pp. 643–49.

29. Ltr., Coyne to Ellis, 16 Oct 1967, Ellis Papers, ACUA. The Ellis charge was the subject of an article in *WP,* 8 Mar 67.

and Josephite communities (both operating parishes in the archdiocese) and a man to represent the priests in St. Mary's and Calvert Counties. At the organizational meeting O'Boyle directed that the group draft a constitution, which he would review and approve. To assist them in the task, he read them the conciliar documents that set out the objectives of such groups as well as reports from three dioceses that had already organized priests' senates. He asked the clergy to submit suggestions for discussion by the senate, calling this a right that must be included in the constitution.[30] Here O'Boyle's acceptance, even if guarded, of advice from his priests contrasted sharply with the resistance of several of his fellow bishops—Cardinal Cody's well-publicized confrontations with the Association of Chicago Priests, for example—produced a generally irenic condition in the Washington archdiocese.[31]

In April 1967 the senate received its constitution from the archbishop (with only minimal changes, he assured them); elected its first president, Msgr. George Gingras; and created two committees. The clergy affairs committee was to advise the archbishop on such topics as salaries, appropriate lengths of assignment, and criteria for appointments and retirement. A personnel board was established to assist those priests seeking counsel for institutional and attitudinal problems. Consideration of a third committee, "to counsel" the archbishop on personnel assignments, was tabled. Counseling on assignments might well exceed the senate's charter as a strictly advisory body, the majority agreed. They decided to postpone action until clear guidelines were developed.[32]

Actually O'Boyle was decidedly ill at ease with the idea of advisory committees, but a good soldier, he followed the Church's guidelines on the matter in a strict and timely fashion. Like it or not, Washington was going to have its advisory bodies.[33] A few members of the senate, though, wanted to go further. During the organizational phase, Father Joseph O'Donoghue, one of the younger members, suggested that, given the council's call for representative direction of the Church's life, the senate should consider developing methods leading to an active role for the priests in decision making.[34] Gingras ignored the proposal.

---

30. Minutes of Meeting of Priests' Senate, 10 Oct 1966. See also memo, Gingras to All Priests, 28 Feb 1967, sub: Priests' Senate. Both in SOP roll c-46, AAW. (Unless otherwise indicated, sources cited in the following paragraphs are located in this microfilm collection.) Apparently the titles Clergy Advisory Council and Priests' Senate were synonymous. In time the latter was most often used.

31. See, for example, Charles W. Dahm, *Power and Authority in the Catholic Church: Cardinal Cody in Chicago* (Notre Dame, Ind.: University of Notre Dame Press, 1981).

32. Minutes of Senate Meeting, 4 Apr 1967, SOP file, AAW.

33. Duffy intv. Msgr. Duffy was a member of the priests' senate during its early days.

34. Ltr., Joseph O'Donoghue to Gingras, 11 Oct 1966, SOP file, AAW.

The senate got involved in priest assignments in February 1968. The archbishop agreed that the renamed priests' personnel committee would, in addition
to counseling priests with personal or work-related problems, serve as an inter-
mediary between the archbishop and troubled subordinates and advise him on
assignments. O'Boyle, very much a hands-on executive when it came to the
placement of priests, had until then shared this responsibility only with his closest associates. During these post-conciliar years he still continued to meet periodically with Bishop Spence, his chancellor, Bishop Herrmann, and his vice-
chancellor, Father Donoghue, to review candidates. He would then personally
interview those considered for pastorates, leaving the assistants to the others. He
described this duty as his toughest job. As an experienced bureaucrat, he instinctively considered advisory committees impractical and made clear that he
intended to retain much control in the assignment process. He produced a set of
guidelines for the personnel committee that laid out the very limited duties of its
members. Msgr. Thomas Dade, the chairman of the new committee, hastened to
reassure the archbishop that the group fully understood its advisory role and
would operate strictly at his direction.[35]

Despite such assurance, Dade was back just two months later recommending
that his committee review the latest slate of appointments drawn up by the archbishop and his assistants. Such a review might help "avoid further problems"
arising from bad choices, Dade explained, and would certainly enhance the committee's prestige among the clergy. Although the committee realized that its mandate was limited, many priests assumed such reviews were part of the committee's function, as it was in some other dioceses. Through an assistant O'Boyle
informed Dade that the appointments were already made and that he was in the
process of interviewing the priests scheduled for change.[36] If in later years
O'Boyle allowed the personnel committee certain leeway in recommending alterations to his assignment decisions, he nevertheless always retained firm control of the process.

Over time the archbishop enacted a number of proposals advanced by the
senate. For example, he accepted its recommendation for a new salary scale for
the clergy. He also took the senate's point and called on all priests to complete a
questionnaire, a kind of curriculum vitae. He was at pains to reassure the clergy,
whom he called to a special meeting on the subject, that the questionnaire was

35. Ltrs., O'Boyle to Reverend Fathers, 27 Feb 1968, and Dade to O'Boyle, 6 and 22 Mar 1968.
Both in SOP file, AAW.
36. Ltr., Dade to O'Boyle, 13 May 1968, and memo, Donoghue to Committee, 15 May 1968. Both
in SOP file, AAW.

not some kind of scrutiny, but rather an effort to learn about their priestly work in parishes and elsewhere as an aid in the assignment process.[37] He was also ready to listen to members of the personnel committee when they made recommendations concerning priests in conflict with their pastors or perhaps otherwise enduring problems that an ordinary should know about. In some cases the archbishop acted swiftly on these recommendations, but only after he had made his own investigation.[38]

Even as he came to accept advice from the elected representatives of the clergy, O'Boyle was clearly not convinced of the practicality or even usefulness of large advisory bodies. When he thought priests were trying to take on too much authority, he was quick to tell them so.[39] A discussion arose about representatives of diocesan agencies forming a cabinet-style organization under the archbishop, and the priests' senate agreed that its president should be represented in such a body. O'Boyle immediately made the point that the senate existed only to advise the ordinary, who could take its advice when he saw fit. It was not empowered to make recommendations to anyone else. When the senate voted in April 1968 to affiliate with the National Federation of Priests Councils, O'Boyle rejected the proposal, merely noting that affiliation "would not be opportune."[40] In October that same year the senate unanimously approved Father Raymond Cahill's proposal that it recommend to O'Boyle that "as many policy decisions as possible be referred to the Senate for prior consultation."[41] O'Boyle, who obviously saw a clear distinction between advice and consultation, never even bothered to respond.

The archdiocesan lay organization that grew out of Vatican II declarations proved easier for him to live with. As an architect of the new United States Catholic Conference, which included many lay men and women as voting members of its committees, O'Boyle was familiar with the concept of lay advisors even if he would reject Archbishop Dearden's vision of "a collaborative body of shared responsibility."[42] The archdiocese's pastoral commission, its members chosen by O'Boyle, was organized in February 1967. The forty-nine members included fifteen priests and thirty-one lay men and women representing every segment of

37. Ltr., O'Boyle to all Priests, 29 Sep 1967, copy in McKenna Papers, AGU.
38. O'Donnell intv. Msgr. O'Donnell was a charter member of the personnel committee who intervened on behalf of several priests.
39. Duffy intv.
40. Ltr., Gingras to Fathers, 16 May 1968. See also Minutes of Meeting of Priests' Senate, 28 Apr 1968. Both in SOP files, AAW.
41. Minutes of Meeting of Priests' Senate, 8 Oct 1968, SOP files, AAW.
42. Dearden's ideas were explored in *National Catholic Reporter*, 4 Oct 2002.

288 A Fretful Shepherd

the Catholic population. Especially noticeable was the number of black Catholics and others from inner-city parishes.

At the organizational meeting O'Boyle explained the origin of the commission, one of the first to be formed in the United States. The council's decree on the pastoral office of bishops called for such bodies "to investigate and weigh matters which bore on pastoral activity and to formulate practical conclusions regarding them."[43] As then vice-chancellor Donoghue later noted, despite its title and the weighty words from the council, the Washington group was strictly an advisory body that met (infrequently) at the call of the archbishop, who introduced subjects for discussion. Primary among them was the "role of the Church in a changing metropolis." He asked for their ideas on how the differing needs of the inner city and suburban parishes and the problems generated by a mobile population were affecting the mission of the Church. At their organizational meeting the commission added several more topics and appointed members to subcommittees on vocations, formation of parish councils, and religious education.[44] The unwieldy size of the commission and lack of strong leadership and regularly scheduled meetings, severely limited its influence. From time to time the archbishop sought the views of individual members, usually his close business friends, but for the most part he seemed content to follow the letter, if not the spirit, of the Church's call for commissions to formulate practical conclusions regarding matters bearing on pastoral activity. Even so, Washington was recognized as a pioneer in the field, and the chancery was kept busy answering questions from dioceses considering the formation of similar groups.

O'Boyle himself responded to a survey from the NCCB regarding the establishment of national norms for pastoral commissions. He agreed that every diocese should have one, but despite the obviously unwieldy operations of his own commission he suggested that fifty members was the optimum number for such groups. Without mentioning the limited interests of his group, he reported that only ten areas of diocesan business were excluded from its purview, chiefly fiscal matters, construction, and schools. He agreed that there could be some kind of relationship between these commissions and the priests' senates provided that it was of an informal nature, keeping in mind that both are advisory bodies. Concerning the advisability of forming a national commission or national norms that would confer more responsibilities on such bodies, O'Boyle recommended wait-

43. As quoted in unsigned memo, 11 Feb 1967, sub: Pastoral Commission Holds First Meeting, CS file, AAW.
44. Ltr., Donoghue to George Castoria, Diocese of Santa Fe, 16 Mar 1967, Chancery file, AAW.

ing several years so that bishops might benefit from the experience of those already in operation.[45]

The archbishop was more enthusiastic about the idea of lay participation at the parish level. He attended a meeting of the priests' senate at which the subject of parish councils was introduced. One senior, unreconstructed pastor complained, "Why should they [the laity] tell us how to run our parish?" To which O'Boyle shot back, "Because it's their parish," thus ending any opposition in that body.[46] In October 1967 he summoned all pastors to a workshop to discuss the operation of parish councils. Again there were objections. Msgr. Henry Grabenstein worried that such groups would not be content for long to remain strictly advisory. He pointed to the troubles the Episcopal Church was having with its vestries and the problems the pastor of Little Flower parish was having with his advisory school board.[47] The archbishop was undeterred. He had asked Father Quinn to submit material on councils, including his own experiences at Holy Cross parish. In 1961 Quinn had called on some of his talented parishioners for advice when he launched a major building program. Out of this useful collaboration emerged the Holy Cross Parish Advisory Board, which operated to the satisfaction of both pastor and congregation. Armed with this experience, Quinn, with the archbishop's backing, had become a strong advocate of parish councils.[48]

O'Boyle set no deadlines for the formation of parish councils, allowing pastors to decide when such an organization was appropriate for their parishes. As a result formation of such groups was far from uniform throughout the archdiocese. Some parishes would wait some years before forming one. Some councils were appointed by the pastor; others were elected by the congregation as its representatives. Most parish councils adhered to their mandate as a strictly advisory group. A few, like the lively council at SS. Paul and Augustine, quickly exceeded that restriction and, with compliant pastors, became active participants in parish operations. Surprisingly, given his emphasis on the advisory nature of all lay and clerical boards, O'Boyle voiced no objections to these advances.

45. Questions submitted by Bishop James Malone, 30 Dec 1968, with O'Boyle's handwritten comments attached. Copy in Chancery file, AAW.

46. As quoted in Quinn intv.

47. Ltrs., O'Boyle to All Pastors, 27 Oct 1967, and Grabenstein to O'Boyle, 25 Oct 1967. Both in Chancery file, AAW.

48. Quinn intv. See also ltr., Quinn to O'Boyle, 27 Oct 1967, Chancery file, AAW.

Ecumenism

Long experience in working with people of other faiths in New York charities and war relief colored Archbishop O'Boyle's approach to ecumenical affairs. Even in the more restricted days before the council, his relations with Jews and other Christians were uncomplicated, straightforward, and friendly.[49] At the same time indifferentism, the idea that one religion is as good as another, was alien to him. Always a sponsor of the Church's Unity Octave observances, he left no doubt that its familiar prayer "that all may be one" meant for him union under the Roman pontiff. Nevertheless, from his early days in Washington he promoted interdenominational activities, always within the guidelines set by Rome. O'Boyle was personally involved in the local Confraternity of Christians and Jews. He enlisted priests to participate in interfaith meetings of a nonliturgical nature in Protestant churches, to join in honoring non-Catholic clergy at citywide celebrations, and to sponsor joint activities with other clergymen at area universities.[50]

All such actions were carefully circumscribed. Every event endured scrutiny by chancery officials to ensure that it fell within current Vatican rules.[51] O'Boyle, for example, decided that the guidelines forbade the attendance of priests at the consecration ceremony for the incoming Episcopal bishop, Paul Moore, and ordered one of Moore's priest friends to skip the ceremony. He "regretted" that he could not attend, O'Boyle told Moore, assuring him that he was looking forward to meeting him. He sent a layman to represent the archdiocese at the consecration.[52] To Methodist Bishop John Wesley Lord he promised to enlist members of the Council of Catholic Men to join in the anti-gambling campaign in southern Maryland. Lord sought Catholic priests to participate, but O'Boyle insisted that it was a job best done by laymen.[53]

Vatican II stimulated O'Boyle's interest in ecumenism. Assured that the Church wanted its bishops to take an active interest in the subject, he spearheaded creation of the Bishops' Commission on Ecumenical Affairs during his term

49. Hannan intv.

50. See, for example, ltrs., O'Boyle to Cartwright, 9 Aug 1951, and Cartwright to O'Boyle, 11 Aug 1951, copies in St. Matthew's Archives; ltr., Pastor, Grace Episcopal Church, to O'Boyle, 16 Feb 1962, and O'Boyle to Pastor, 17 Feb 1962, Chancery file, AAW.

51. Scores of these investigations are retained in chancery files, 1951–65, AAW.

52. Ltrs., Hannan to Father Bernard Strange, 15 Jan 1964, and O'Boyle to Moore, 27 Jan 1964. Both in Chancery file, AAW.

53. Ltrs., O'Boyle to Lord, 24 and 28 Jan 1961, Chancery file, AAW.

as chairman of the administrative board. He asked the new commission's chairman, Cardinal Lawrence Shehan, to add Bishop Spence (a convert to Catholicism) to his group.[54] He faithfully applied the commission's interim guidelines to ecumenical events in his archdiocese and organized an ecumenical commission. With ten members, including a sister, brother, and layman, the commission prepared guidelines for ecumenical activities, served as a clearinghouse for all inquiries on the subject from both Catholics and non-Catholics, and acted as a watchdog for the archbishop.

One of the commission's major projects was eliminating the Church Unity Octave services at the Shrine of the Immaculate Conception in favor of similar services at many individual parishes. Over the years, with the general relaxation of Church rules, O'Boyle approved the participation of Protestant ministers in these services where they led prayers, read Scripture, and eventually preached. Catholic priests were encouraged to reciprocate in Protestant sanctuaries.[55] Changes in the Church's guidelines allowed Protestant and Jewish leaders, clothed in their robes of office, to process with Catholic bishops into St. Matthew's Cathedral at Bishop Edward Herrmann's consecration as auxiliary bishop in 1966. Later, O'Boyle, in the scarlet robes of a cardinal, participated in a thanksgiving service at St. Mary's Armenian Church welcoming the Armenian Patriarch, Vasken I, to Washington.

The Tangled Groves of Academe

Nowhere were the meaning and implications of conciliar decrees more fiercely debated than in the country's Catholic colleges, most notably among the theologians at Catholic University. Although the archbishop of Washington had little direct involvement in these arguments, as university chancellor he nevertheless played a significant if largely symbolic role in a gathering crisis that would earn him unwelcome and largely unfair press.

Patrick O'Boyle would readily admit that he was not one of the hierarchy's intellectual stars. Throughout his years in Washington he demonstrated a deep respect for intellectuals like John Courtney Murray, George Higgins, John Tracy Ellis, and the host of philosophers and theologians who were contributing mightily to the Church's growing reputation as a promoter of academic distinc-

54. Ltr., Shehan to O'Boyle, 21 Jun 1965, Chancery file, AAW.

55. Memo, Spence for O'Boyle, 5 Nov 1965, sub: Candidates for Ecumenical Commission. See also Commission's "Statement of Purpose and Objectives," Jan 1966, and "Report From Archdiocesan Commission on Ecumenism," n.d. (ca. 1968). For an example of the commission's policing activities, see ltr., Spence to Dear Superior, 26 Aug 1966. All in Ecumenical file, AAW.

tion. Although largely untutored in theological debate, he was a bright executive who frankly harbored strong reservations about the practicality of some opinions expressed by professors. Indeed he concluded that many theologians did not know what they were talking about, even as he respected their right to dissent from Church teachings that were not deemed infallible.[56] He supported serious theological discussion. At the same time he wanted to see carefully researched contributions discussed in appropriate academic circles or published in learned journals and not aired in the popular press. As always he was concerned lest their debates fall in the hands of the unsophisticated, who might conclude that theologians were questioning the faith rather then seeking its clarification. For example, when he appointed Msgr. Arthur to serve as censor of the *Catholic Biblical Quarterly,* he explained that such journals were the proper venue for theological discussion and speculation. He was not interested in debating an author or checking on his scholarship. Colleagues would do that. Rather, he wanted to ensure that in their debates the theologians were courteous and uncontentious.[57]

Like many bishops of his generation, O'Boyle was particularly concerned that scholars not wash the Church's dirty linen in public. When Msgr. Ellis' monumental biography of Cardinal Gibbons was finished in 1952, he had told the abashed author that he "hoped there were no evidences in the book of bishops quarreling with each other." Again, Ellis' 1955 essay on the American Church's intellectual history worried O'Boyle. "You better let it alone for a while," was his stern admonition. At about the same time Ellis was invited to give a paper on church-state relations at the International Congress of Historical Sciences in Rome. O'Boyle was concerned about introducing the controversial subject, especially in Rome, where the concept of religious liberty had many powerful enemies. Curiously, he was also concerned about the possible reaction of critics at Catholic University like Msgr. Joseph C. Fenton and his conservative colleagues at the *American Ecclesiastical Review.* O'Boyle was sympathetic to the historian's take on the subject, but after consulting his friend Bishop Bryan McEntegart, at that time the university rector, he decided Ellis should not speak.[58]

Cordial relations between the two survived this rejection, even as earlier they had survived O'Boyle's detailed criticism of the biography of John Carroll pre-

56. O'Boyle's attitude toward academics is discussed in detail in the Donoghue, Arthur, and Kelley intvs.

57. Arthur intv.

58. Ltr., Ellis to Father Walter Burghardt, 15 Oct 1968, copy in John Courtney Murray Papers, AGU. See also Ellis intv. (source of quotes).

pared by Annabelle Melville, one of Ellis' star pupils. Again O'Boyle was concerned, not with the author's scholarship, but with the fact that the work "will most likely be read by people who will not have the proper appreciation of the frailties of bishops and clergy and when it is not necessary to emphasize these to make a point, I would prefer that they would be omitted."[59] In fact O'Boyle's relations with Ellis and many of the luminaries at Catholic University remained cordial and even warm. The archives are full of examples of his thoughtfulness and generosity to academics. Msgr. Paul Furfey's sentiment in a letter to O'Boyle, "I am proud to be a priest of your archdiocese and I continue to cherish a warm regard for you," was not an isolated example of the often-expressed gratitude of these men and their fruitful collaboration with the archbishop in the days before controversy finally surfaced.[60]

Roman authorities had decided in 1948 to designate the Washington archbishop chancellor of Catholic University. O'Boyle had not sought the job. From early times he recognized the potential for friction, especially with the theology faculty, considering Rome's particular control over what was America's only pontifical university. He also knew that he lacked any real control, which was exercised in the main by the rector and the academic senate answering to a board of trustees composed of the American archbishops and selected laymen.

O'Boyle was proud of the university's achievements, and he served as its spokesman in the bishops' conference. As chancellor he readily participated in all the school's ceremonies. At the 1965 graduation convocation, for example, he bestowed an honorary degree on President Lyndon B. Johnson. He never appeared overawed on such occasions. At the conclusion of Johnson's speech, many on the dais rushed to shake the president's hand. Amid the ranks was a youthful Msgr. Theodore McCarrick, who remembered earning a look of surprise from the president and disapproval from school officials when he tripped on the crowded platform, unseating several distinguished faculty members in the process. An embarrassed McCarrick was gratified to see that O'Boyle merely shook his head and laughed heartily at the consternation of the dignified academics.[61]

A member of the board of trustees, O'Boyle worked assiduously at raising money for the university. His effort to attract major donors and secure grants resulted in a significant improvement in the school's material development. He

59. Ltr., O'Boyle to Ellis, 7 Nov 1951, Ellis Papers, ACUA.
60. Ltr., Furfey to O'Boyle, 21 Aug 1966, Furfey Papers, ACUA.
61. McCarrick, "A Graduation Memory," *CS*, 17 May 2001. Cardinal McCarrick judged his predecessor a "great chancellor."

rarely intervened in the university's internal affairs. Early on he did join those around Dr. Vincent Burke, chairman of the biology department, in an unsuccessful campaign to establish a university medical school, but this was a rare exception.[62] He usually remained safely above academic infighting.

There was ample controversy, and by 1963 the heated debates between the traditionalists associated with the *Ecclesiastical Review* and the progressives centered round the *Catholic Biblical Quarterly* were earning headlines. That year the rector barred four distinguished theologians, John Courtney Murray, Hans Küng, Gustav Weigel, and Godfrey Diekmann, from speaking at the university. Msgr. William J. McDonald argued that sponsoring appearances by these noted liberal scholars would make it appear that the university was endorsing one faction in the ongoing debate at the Vatican Council. In fact, McDonald, who was appointed rector in 1957 without any input from O'Boyle, was a close ally of the apostolic delegate and other fervent supporters of Cardinal Ottaviani, leader of the traditional forces at the council.[63] When Msgr. Ellis charged that barring the four speakers was merely the latest in a censorship policy that had gone on for a decade, the incident became a rallying point in progressive Catholic circles and was picked up in the national press, where the always lively issue of academic freedom was raised.[64]

Although several members of the hierarchy, including Cardinal Ritter, strenuously objected to McDonald's actions, the university's board of trustees listened to Cardinal McIntyre defend the rector. McIntyre even called for a censure of the university's academic senate for its criticism of the rector, adding that complaints should have been directed to the board of trustees and not the press. An angry Bishop Bryan McEntegart, McDonald's predecessor, demanded without success that the trustees censure Ellis for his charge.[65] O'Boyle, who was purportedly furious at Ellis' remarks, refrained from commenting on the affair, and his auxiliary, Bishop Hannan, arranged over the apostolic delegate's objections for Father Küng to speak at Georgetown University.[66] O'Boyle's undisguised support for

62. On the effort to establish a medical school, see Gofreddi intv.

63. Higgins and Ellis intvs. See also C. Joseph Nuesse, *The Catholic University of America: A Centennial History* (Washington, D.C.: The Catholic University of America Press, 1990), pp. 395–96.

64. Ellis, *Catholic Bishops: A Memoir* (Wilmington, Del.: Michael Glazer, 1984), pp. 37–39. See also "Crisis at Catholic U," *Time,* 29 Mar 1963.

65. Minutes of the Board of Trustees, 24 Apr 1963, book 5, ACUA. Ltr., McIntyre to McDonald, 17 Apr 1963, as quoted in Weber, *His Eminence of Los Angeles,* vol. 1, pp. 275–76. See also Ellis, "The Catholic University of America, A Personal Memoir," *Social Thought* (Spring 1979): p. 53.

66. Ltrs., Vagnozzi to Hannan, 5 Jun 1963, and Hannan to Vagnozzi, 10 Jun 1963. Both in Chancery file, AAW.

John Courtney Murray and sympathy for that theologian's thesis on religious freedom and church-state relations also put him at odds with the apostolic delegate, who strongly opposed Murray.

O'Boyle also refrained from involvement in two faculty disputes in 1966. When some forty members of the arts and science faculty, claiming that the dean had refused to consult them on important business, walked out of a meeting, the incident was front-page news. Just days later the faculty of the School of Sacred Theology protested the merger of its school with the department of religious education. The Academic Senate, the theologians claimed, was a rubberstamp for the administration, again a charge aired in the press. Regarding the ensuing brouhaha, Msgr. Higgins asked his old friend Msgr. Ellis, "Aren't you glad you live in SF [San Francisco]?"[67] Actually, Higgins had decided that Father Schmitz, recently appointed dean, had done a "remarkable job" in revitalizing the university's School of Sacred Theology. He had hired new faculty, including Father Charles E. Curran, a popular teacher, lecturer, and author. Higgins predicted that, absent interference from the apostolic delegate, the school would soon become best in the country.[68]

By early 1967 many at the university had become demoralized by the state of affairs under the hapless rector whose second five-year term was nearing completion. A large group of senior faculty formed an Assembly of Professors with the intent of presenting a united appeal to the board of trustees in the matter of selecting a new rector. The assembly rehearsed the reasons for having a layman in the job and proposed a list of suitable candidates. Its chairman alerted O'Boyle to "a serious crisis in confidence within the faculty," a condition, he argued, that would be allayed by a qualified lay rector selected by the trustees in accordance with the procedures established by the national associations of higher education. O'Boyle's response has not survived, but as one commentator put it, Chancellor O'Boyle "generally pursues a hands off policy, but dislikes controversy or boat-rocking."[69] Whether he liked it or not, the archbishop of Washington was about to become a principal player in the university's greatest controversy.

Trouble erupted over the tenure of Father Curran in the theology school. His

67. Ltr., Higgins to Ellis, 16 Feb 1966, Ellis Papers, ACUA. With O'Boyle's permission, Ellis had taken a position at the University of San Francisco in 1963.
68. Ltr., Higgins to Ellis, 18 Jul 1966, Ellis Papers, ACUA.
69. Ltr., Professor Malcolm Henderson to O'Boyle, 10 Mar 1967, Curran file, AAW (first quote), and Norma K. Herzfeld, "The Problem of Catholic University," *Commonweal* (31 Mar 1967): p. 40 (second quote).

work, which explored new directions in moral theology and questioned certain reserved truths in light of the Second Vatican Council, made him an extremely controversial figure whose detractors included the apostolic delegate and his confidant, the university rector.[70] At McDonald's request in October 1966, Curran was questioned about press accounts of his recent lectures. During a subsequent meeting with the rector, Curran argued that he should be judged by his writings, not press accounts. The hostile questioning prompted the theology faculty to pass unanimously a resolution in support of their colleague and expressing "our full confidence in his teaching." There was no reason for making Curran defend his orthodoxy, the teachers asserted. They also objected to the unspecified charges and the consequent harassment he was forced to endure.[71]

Father Curran's views were discussed at the trustees' November 1966 meeting. It might be assumed, given Curran's views on sexual morality and their widespread publication outside the scholarly community of theologians, that O'Boyle was among those who supported formation of a committee to investigate the matter. The committee, consisting of Archbishops Krol and Hannan, and the rector, now Bishop McDonald, informally decided to judge Curran's work on his latest book, copies of which they provided to interested trustees as well as to the chairman of the bishops' committee on doctrine.[72]

Archbishop Krol was not inclined to wait for a report from the bishops' committee, and he and his colleagues agreed to recommend that Curran be dismissed. In view of the priest's general popularity, McDonald predicted that to offer no reasons for the decision would "cause trouble," but Krol argued that Curran should merely be informed that his contract would not be renewed, a proper course of action covered by the trustees' bylaws. Hannan wanted the task of informing Curran given to the rector, who, he hoped, would act with tact and circumspection. At the time Krol and Hannan were unaware of the intense feelings in the theology faculty over a similar case in which one of their number had recently been dismissed without a hearing. The committee reported to the trustees in early April. Krol pointed out that while Curran's orthodoxy was not being questioned, "his views on certain key matters were unclear and were sub-

70. Nuesse, *The Catholic University of America,* pp. 399–401.

71. Minutes of faculty meeting of the School of Sacred Theology, 19 Oct 1966 (source of quote). See also ltr., Curran to McDonald, 21 Oct 1966, and a useful chronology of the Curran affair, "Summary of the Rev. Charles E. Curran Controversy," encl. to ltr., Walter Schmidt to O'Boyle, 18 Apr 1967. Copies of all in Curran file, AAW.

72. Ltr., Hannan to O'Boyle, 5 May 1967, Curran file, AAW. See also E. Michael Jones, *John Cardinal Krol and the Cultural Revolution* (South Bend, Ind.: Fidelity Press, 1995), on Krol's role in the Curran affair.

Campus Protest. Catholic University erupted over the trustees' decision not to reappoint Father Charles Curran to the theology faculty, April 1967.

ject to serious concern." The board agreed with the committee's recommendation; only Archbishop Paul Hallinan, warning that the trustees should not act without giving specific reasons, dissented.[73] On April 17 the rector informed Curran that his appointment would not be renewed. Curran responded by declaring the trustees' action arbitrary and unfair, adding that the press would be so informed. The theology faculty threatened to resign en masse. Archbishop Hannan, belatedly realizing the mistake of not holding hearings, offered to return to Washington immediately to discuss the matter with Curran. In the end Curran rejected the offer of a meeting.[74]

By Wednesday, April 19, a boycott of all classes threatened by the general student population and supported by most of the faculty began. The press was treated to photographs of clergy, including Father Schmitz, dean of the theology school and O'Boyle's master of ceremonies, along with sisters and lay students

73. "Summary of the Rev. Charles E. Curran Controversy" (source of quote), Curran file, AAW.
74. Ltr., Hannan (signed Phil) to O'Boyle, 5 May 1967, Curran file, AAW.

298 *A Fretful Shepherd*

forming picket lines before the university's main buildings. That Friday Father Curran addressed the students in front of Mullen Library, part of a mass demonstration in support of him. In the absence of any explanation from the trustees for their action, the press and many in the faculty and student body rightly assumed that Curran's dismissal resulted from his "liberal views on moral theology and his liberal attitude toward birth control."[75]

The trustees were inundated with letters, most in support of Curran. Critics like Ellis and Higgins blamed the bishops for the crisis. They noted that Baltimore's Cardinal Shehan, who had voted with his colleagues, was now calling for Curran's reinstatement. Cardinal Cushing, an ex officio member of the board who absented himself as a protest against the lack of academic qualifications of most trustees, joined the fray. He was "absolutely opposed to the methods the trustees pursued in regard to the curriculum and professors," he was quoted in the press, adding, "I would not condemn this man. He must teach all sides. That's scholarship."[76] As for O'Boyle, Krol, and the others, Ellis predicted, "One has grown accustomed to expect nothing from those quarters." He blamed O'Boyle especially for appointing members of the Krol committee, none with an academic background.[77]

Despite the desertions, some bishops wanted to tough it out. The apostolic delegate urged the trustees to stand firm, even if it required closing the school for the rest of the semester. He appealed to the chairman of the trustees, Cardinal Spellman, who begged off the fight. "I'm too old," he told Vagnozzi, let us do "whatever Archbishop O'Boyle says we have to do."[78] Archbishop Krol was adamant. He considered the central point of the controversy not Curran's views on moral theology, but the trustee's right to dismiss untenured teachers.[79] Many of his fellow bishops were less interested in asserting such arbitrary power. Trustees like Archbishop Dearden, Cardinal Shehan, and Bishop Fulton J. Sheen, for example, saw the boycott, which its leaders vowed to continue indefinitely, underscoring the profound shift in attitude toward episcopal power and presenting a tremendous threat to the Church's reputation and to the academic standing of its many colleges and universities.[80]

75. As quoted in "Summary of the Rev. Charles E. Curran Controversy," Curran file, AAW.
76. As quoted in *Boston Pilot* and distributed to other papers by the Catholic News Service, 21 Apr 1967. The quote was carried in *NYT*, 22 Apr 1967.
77. Ltr., Ellis to Higgins, 21 Apr 1967, Ellis Papers, ACUA.
78. As quoted in Kelly intv.
79. Ltr., Hannan (signed Phil) to O'Boyle, 5 May 1967, Curran file, AAW.
80. Kelly intv. Although Kelly might be considered an opponent of this point of view, he also provided an insider's report on the change of mood in the hierarchy.

Dean Schmitz reiterated this warning on April 18. The trustees' failure to explain their action was damaging to Curran's reputation and contrary to the spirit of Vatican directives, he told O'Boyle. The theology faculty, therefore, urged the board to rescind its decision.[81] The next day the theologians upped the stakes, transmitting to the individual members of the board their resolution to boycott classes until Father Curran was reinstated. The chairman of what was dubbed the April 20th Assembly of the Entire Faculty of Catholic University cited the "unusual exercise of administrative power" in dismissing a teacher recommended by his school and the academic senate for promotion to associate professor. The entire university faculty, Professor Malcolm C. Henderson reported to O'Boyle, would not resume work unless and until Curran was reinstated.[82]

Paramount in O'Boyle's view of the matter was the fact that Curran had not been given a hearing. That, he concluded, had placed the board of trustees in an untenable position.[83] He polled the board for authority to negotiate with the faculty of the school of theology. His conversations with Dean Schmitz and others had convinced him that nothing less than abrogation of the trustees' action would accomplish the university's return to normalcy. He wanted the board's approval to negotiate the point with Curran and representatives of the theology faculty.[84] He asked that the poll be kept confidential, but by April 22 the *New York Times* was discussing its implications and predicting an early end to the boycott, now entering its fifth day.[85] The trustees approved O'Boyle's request, although one, his friend Cardinal McIntyre, suggested that he "sell the damn place." O'Boyle later reflected that McIntyre's was probably the best advice he ever received, but, he joked, "I couldn't find the deed."[86]

With the students still staging protest marches and all classes suspended, O'Boyle met several times with Dean Schmitz, Archbishop Hannan, and Rector McDonald. Before he made any public announcement he also called Archbishops Krol and Dearden and Bishop John Wright of Pittsburgh. As O'Boyle later put it, "They agreed, like ourselves reluctantly, that it was the only thing to do under the circumstances." At the same time and despite Curran's soon-to-be-

81. Telegram, Schmitz to O'Boyle, 18 Apr 1967, Curran file, AAW.
82. Telegram, Henderson to O'Boyle, 22 Apr 1967, Curran file, AAW. The School of Education was an early holdout in the boycott, but it too joined the other schools in shutting down classes.
83. Ltr., O'Boyle to Bp. Lambert Hoch, 26 Apr 1967, copy in Curran file, AAW.
84. Night ltr., O'Boyle to Board Members, 20 Apr 1967, Curran file, AAW.
85. *NYT*, 22 Apr 1967.
86. As quoted in Weber's intv. with O'Boyle.

confirmed reinstatement, O'Boyle still wanted the bishops' commission on doctrine to examine the theologian's writings and render a final decision.[87]

Standing on the steps of the university library before a cheering crowd of some 2,500, the archbishop announced the trustees' concession. He noted that the reinstatement in no way affected the theological issues raised in press speculation; in particular, "it in no way derogates from the teachings of the Church and statements by popes and bishops on birth control." As with any appointment in Catholic schools, he continued, statements concerning doctrine were subject to the teaching authority of the Church.[88] Curran agreed, declaring that the boycott was not a revolt against authority, but a protest against arbitrary action, specifically the failure to renew a contract without charges or a hearing.

O'Boyle was anxious to put it all behind him. Along with Father Schmitz, whose break with the archbishop had yet to occur, he was a guest that night at a dinner preceding confirmation ceremonies at SS. Paul and Augustine Church. He seemed happy to ignore the subject, but of course Msgr. Higgins brought it up. For once Higgins took pity on the man. He congratulated O'Boyle for the way he handled the situation. O'Boyle replied that he did not know whether he should be congratulated or not. Another guest reassured him that the general reception of his concession speech was favorable because of the way he handled himself. He had sown no animosity and was willing to talk to members of the faculty. It seemed to some witnesses that O'Boyle was pleased by these compliments even though he obviously did not want to get into the pros and cons of the issue.[89]

On a personal level, the crisis led O'Boyle to sever one of his closest friendships. He asked Dean Schmitz how it looked that his master of ceremonies publicly supported Father Curran. He asked Schmitz to "see if you can see your way clear on this thing."[90] But they never reconciled and went their separate ways until many years later when the cardinal visited Schmitz in Georgetown University Hospital where his old friend lay seriously ill.

Looking back later, Msgr. Ellis concluded that the faculty made academic history when the boycott forced the trustees to rescind their decision.[91] But, O'Boyle's statement made clear, the bishops had not been won over to the prin-

87. Ltr., O'Boyle to Hoch, 26 Apr 67 (source of quote), copy in Curran file, AAW.
88. As quoted in *WP*, 26 Apr 1967.
89. Ltr., Msgr. Francis T. Hurley, United States Catholic Conference, to Ellis, 29 Apr 1967, Ellis Papers, ACUA.
90. As quoted in Abell intv.
91. Ellis, "CUA, 1927–1979, A Personal Memoir," p. 53.

Chancellor O'Boyle Announces Curran's Reinstatement. From left: Curran; Bishop William McDonald, university rector; O'Boyle; and Father Walter Schmitz, dean of the theology school.

ciple of academic freedom envisioned by American educators. As O'Boyle saw it, Catholic freedom had its limits: it must accept dogmatic definitions made by the Church in the fields of faith and morals; and it must always exercise prudence. Although every teacher had the right to speculate on matters not clearly defined by the Church, prudence and justice demanded that these personal opinions not scandalize the faithful.[92]

Major reforms in the university followed fast on the Curran controversy. Msgr. Higgins' prediction that "Bill McDonald's days are definitely numbered" was proved correct, and with the Vatican's approval, Father John P. Whalen was appointed acting rector.[93] O'Boyle, citing his responsibility under canon law for

92. O'Boyle, "As a Man Believes," sermon at Catholic University's celebration of the Year of Faith, 15 Oct 1967, *Catholic Educational Review* (Dec 1967): pp. 577–79.

93. Ltr., Higgins to Ellis, 9 Feb 1967, Ellis Papers, ACUA (source of quote). See also ltr., O'Boyle to Spellman, 13 Jul 1967, copy in AAW.

teaching the faith throughout his archdiocese, successfully argued against a proposal made at the bishops' conference that the president of the NCCB, not the archbishop of Washington, should be the chancellor of the university. The Vatican agreed with O'Boyle.[94] The archbishop of Washington would remain chancellor, but in the aftermath of the Curran fight the university's board of trustees voted for a major reorganization, reducing its membership from forty-three to thirty members, with laymen accounting for half the total. In July 1968 the trustees elected their first lay chairman. The selection of Carroll Hockwalt, a retired vice-president of Monsanto Chemical, was widely interpreted as "a step in the dramatic process of the hierarchy loosening its control over the university."[95]

Just how far the bishops would go in loosening their control was debated in the following months as the trustees considered the issue of a lay president. (The title of rector, considered too European-sounding, was dropped.) Some in the hierarchy, including Chancellor O'Boyle, were openly opposed to the idea. Archbishop Hannan attributed O'Boyle's stand to his general uneasiness in dealing with a layman in such a sensitive position. In particular he was concerned with how the relationship of chancellor to lay president might be defined. At the very least he insisted that the schools of theology and canon law, and department of religious education, retain clerical directors. A search committee began in the fall of 1968 the difficult task of locating suitable lay candidates. O'Boyle interviewed the four finalists, and after a vote by the board and with the approval of the Vatican's Congregation for Catholic Education, Chairman Hockwalt announced that Clarence C. Walton, a Columbia University dean, would assume office as the first president of Catholic University, beginning in September 1969. With a bow to O'Boyle's concerns, the trustees also announced that a priest would be appointed to oversee ecclesiastical studies and a committee formed to review all the university's schools. A separate committee of bishops would review the religious schools.

O'Boyle publicly expressed his pleasure with the appointment and described his own role in university affairs. The chancellor, he explained, was responsible "for enforcing orthodoxy of doctrine." As for possible changes in the chancellor's role, he added that university statutes were then in the process of a revision, due to be completed in April. "We won't know until then what his [the chancel-

---

94. Shehan, *A Blessing of Years: The Memoirs of Lawrence Cardinal Shehan* (Notre Dame, Ind.: University of Notre Dame Press, 1982), pp. 261–62. Cardinal Shehan was the chairman of the subcommittee investigating the NCCB's proposed change.

95. *WP*, 28 Jul 1968 (source of quote).

lor's] new role is. I was going to put in 'if any,' but I'll leave that out."[96] The revised bylaws, approved by the American bishops and the Vatican and announced on February 5, 1970, did in many ways reduce Rome's control of the university and in President Walton's words brought its governance "in line with that of other American universities." The new rules, however, left the role of chancellor intentionally vague, merely stating that his rights and duties with respect to the schools of theology, philosophy, and canon law would be in accord "with the norms and regulations established by the Holy See."[97]

O'Boyle's solution to a controversy he did not create was purely pragmatic. Given the unanimity of the faculty and student body in their support for Father Curran, the trustees had no choice but to capitulate. No matter the embarrassment to the Church and to him personally, it had to be done. The alternative pushed by the apostolic delegate and Archbishop Krol, O'Boyle realized, would only lead to more turmoil and further damage the Church's reputation. He was prepared to alter the way the bishops dealt with the academic community, and he went along with the majority of his colleagues in granting a larger measure of freedom to lay educators. To be expected, this progressive attitude did not extend to abrogating any aspect of the teaching authority of the Church. The thorny problem of academic freedom in Catholic schools was yet to be squarely addressed. In a way the Curran crisis could be seen as a foreshadowing of an all-consuming controversy about to erupt in the Archdiocese of Washington.

96. *NYT*, 31 Jan 1969. The *Times* ran not only a lengthy news article but also a profile of the new president.

97. All quotes from *NYT*, 31 Jan 1969.

A Civil Rights Crusader

In response to congratulations from well-wishers at the time of his elevation to the college of cardinals in 1967, Patrick O'Boyle stated that the
honor was not meant especially for him. Rather, he insisted, it was an expression of the pope's gratitude, not only to Washington's Catholics, but
also to "the many clergy and laymen of other faiths who have labored beside us in attacking the problems of racial and social injustice which are
of common concern."[1] A generous remark that understated O'Boyle's
considerable importance as a leader in the American Church, it nevertheless underscored what was probably his principal preoccupation
since coming to Washington.

No national movement evolved more rapidly than the fight for civil
rights during the turbulent 1960s. Much had changed since the day in
1955 when a tired Rosa Parks refused to relinquish her seat to a white
passenger on a Montgomery, Alabama, bus. Her gesture signaled the onset of a revolution that treated the nation to the spectacle of peaceful
demonstrations and sit-ins in the face of attacks by police dogs and sher-
iffs' batons. It also hastened formation of alliances among like-minded
activists of both races. For the most part these alliances were religion-
based and led by clergymen who fought for integration on the local level
while providing leverage for federal legislation that redefined the nation's
concept of civil rights.

Almost twenty years had passed since Archbishop O'Boyle launched
his integration campaign. By 1967 this notable achievement only evoked

1. His remark was widely quoted. See various versions in *Star,* 26 Jun 1967, and *NYT,*
23 Sep 1968.

a sense of nostalgia in reformers faced with ardent demands for equal treatment and opportunity as well as the need for complex and costly solutions to discrimination. That many Catholics shared the negative attitude of their fellow citizens toward civil rights only complicated the archbishop's continuing efforts. No social philosopher, he clung to the belief that a gradualist approach to reform would achieve better results because it would avoid a violently divided laity. Pell-mell action, on the other hand, might well galvanize a united opposition to the Church's teachings. Yet his old aim of clearing the table one dish at a time was no longer practical in the face of increasingly strident demands from progressive reformers of both races in the swirling turmoil of the 1960s. The question remained: could a man of good will, but one committed to gradual change, transform himself into the civil rights crusader demanded by a more aggressive generation?

A Red Hat

Speculation about a red hat for the archbishop of Washington had circulated since the early 1960s, especially after O'Boyle's years as chairman of the bishops' administrative board and election by his fellow bishops to represent them at several synods called by the pope in the wake of Vatican II. The rumor also reflected the obvious importance of America's capital in international affairs and the elevation of the archdiocese to the status of an ecclesiastical province (including the Diocese of the Virgin Islands).[2] Despite the rumors, O'Boyle reported that he was totally surprised when Apostolic Delegate Vagnozzi woke him at midnight on May 29, 1967. For once Father Donoghue had not heard the phone, and so a pajama-clad archbishop, standing sleepily at his bedside, learned that Pope Paul intended to enlist him in the sacred college of cardinals.[3]

The archbishop, accompanied by Fathers Donoghue and Henry Yannone, the latter fluent in Italian, arrived in Rome on June 21. O'Boyle was back at the airport three days later to welcome a contingent of relatives, friends, and associates, including, on his initiative, representatives of Washington's Protestant and Jewish communities. All 160 of them stayed at one of Rome's deluxe hotels, where they enjoyed a round of parties and get-togethers. The lucky ones also found good seats for the ceremonies of that week. Meanwhile Father Donoghue stayed with the archbishop in the more somber surroundings of the North American College.

2. See, for example, early speculation on O'Boyle's future in *Star*, 12 Dec 1963.
3. Donoghue intv. See also *Star*, 29 May 1967.

The Red Hat. Cardinal O'Boyle receives the symbol of his new office from Pope Paul VI, June 1967.

O'Boyle was particularly concerned about his aunt Margaret Muldoon. Now in her eighties, she had insisted on the trip against her children's wishes. O'Boyle assigned responsibility for her welfare to Father Gillen, who was well acquainted with the family from his many vacations at Moosic Lake. Far from needing help, Aunt Margaret exhausted Gillen with her participation in every activity, using their spare time for long shopping sprees throughout the city.[4] As for O'Boyle, for once he was able to smother his antipathy to pomp and ceremony as his friends made a great fuss. One can only imagine the look on his face when as guest of honor one evening he was escorted to the head table by a phalanx of acolytes bearing massive, lighted candles in keeping with an ancient Roman tradition.

The consistory itself was a three-phased affair. On June 26 O'Boyle and the

4. Gillen intv. The image of the vigorous senior appealed to many. See, for example, Donoghue, McArdle, and Muldoon intvs.

rest of the nominees waited on the stage of a Vatican audience hall before a throng of friends. There they were to receive official notice of their acceptance by the college of cardinals, which was meeting in secret session with the pope. Two days later the new cardinals in their scarlet robes knelt before the pope, swore their loyalty, and vowed to labor for the peace and tranquility of the Church "even to shedding blood." The pope then bestowed on each a red hat as a sign of his new office and his vow.[5] In keeping with tradition, the pope also assigned each new member a titular church in the Eternal City. The last phase of the consistory occurred on the 29th, when the new cardinals concelebrated Mass with the pope in St. Peter's Square before 100,000 worshippers and each received from him a ring signifying his new office.

Congratulations continued to pour in from President Lyndon Johnson and other high government officials, and there were many festive meals and receptions to attend before all could return home. Through it all the new cardinal maintained his usual self-deprecating mien, repeating his claim that his elevation was meant as an honor for the clergy and all the people of Washington. Before leaving Rome O'Boyle, along with most of his new colleagues, received his appointment to a Vatican office. The pope assigned him to the Congregation of Rites, an appropriate choice given his notably strict adherence to every letter of the Vatican's decrees on liturgical reform. O'Boyle also took formal possession of his titular church, St. Nicholas in Prison.[6] The 800-year-old basilica was in urgent need of repair, and on the spot he pledged $15,000 for emergency restorations.

Back in Washington, O'Boyle faced another round of festivities, including a dinner on July 9 for the city's leading clergymen. Labor notable and former Supreme Court justice Arthur Goldberg also hosted a dinner to honor his old friend. Over the next several months O'Boyle's promotion would be celebrated by various organizations, which emphasized his dedication to social justice. In September his alma mater, now reorganized as the University of Scranton, made him a doctor of laws. His acceptance speech was a variation on his constant plea for racial justice. Reminding his audience that the Scranton region had been the birthplace of the American labor movement, he added: "What a proud boast if

5. Actually, the headgear was scarlet and not a hat, but a biretta. The great red tasseled hats, which were never worn, were hung inside a cardinal's cathedral after his death.

6. St. Nicholas of Myra was the prototype of the modern Santa Claus. The "in prison" had nothing to do with the saint, but with the fact that the church was located next to an old Roman prison. Father Henry Yannone would represent O'Boyle in his future dealings with the rector of the church. Yannone, the archdiocesan archivist, translated a history of that church.

the anthracite region could today again gain a reputation as one of the nation's principal sources of dedicated champions of social and economic justice."[7] Weeks later the American Jewish Committee presented him with its first Isaiah Award for human relations. This honor represented a singular gesture in those early days of interfaith dialogue. He also managed to squeeze in an overnight visit to Mt. Loretto, on Staten Island, where the children noisily celebrated his new honor.

The cardinal may have been grateful for the receptions, but he was also anxious to get away from all the fuss. To his usual announcement that "little Patrick is going away for two weeks," he now admitted to colleagues, "It's a great year for getting away."[8] Summer's end found him traipsing the shores of Moosic Lake, where "Father O'Boyle," as his family addressed him, was finally allowed a little peace and quiet.

An End to Gradualism

Most often Cardinal O'Boyle responded to the many well-wishers by asking them to work harder for social justice in the capital. On one occasion, however, he turned the spotlight on himself, confessing that he had missed opportunities to serve better and asking forgiveness for failing to lead the way. Such a statement from some clergymen might have sounded self-serving, but coming from this tough and blunt New Yorker it rang true. O'Boyle was justifiably pleased with the results of his integration campaign and his support of unionism. He frequently recited gains made in integrating the archdiocese's churches, schools, charitable institutions, even its hospitals and youth organizations during his first decade in Washington. He also liked to emphasize the fact that no Catholic church had closed or sold its property because of the changes in the racial composition of a neighborhood. This latter claim, while technically true, neglected to take into account the loss of two parishes, and eventually their property, when he merged two white parishes with two neighboring black parishes. His statements also tended to overlook the continuing problem in the Catholic hospitals, which were slow to integrate their staffs, especially in allowing full status to black doctors.[9]

7. As quoted in *CS,* 28 Sep 1967.
8. Ltr., O'Boyle to Higgins, 9 Aug 1966 (first quote); note to staff, 31 Jul 1967 (second quote). Copies of both in AAW.
9. For example of O'Boyle's listing these accomplishments, see his "Brotherhood, Belief and Practice," reprinted in *CS,* 24 Feb 1961. On the hospitals, see ltrs., Joseph Nuesse (leader of the Catholic Interracial Council) to William Buckner, 5 Nov 1962, to Dr. Paul Jaquet, president of the

Yet even as he exulted in the archdiocese's progress, he was coming to realize that achieving racial justice was a complex challenge that demanded far more aggressive leadership. Influenced by the rapidly unfolding civil rights movement and the militant ideas of some of his subordinates, he blossomed into a civil rights activist. The transformation did not occur overnight or without fits and starts. One chancery officer observed that the archbishop "was liberal in the morning, conservative in the afternoon, and reactionary at night."[10]

O'Boyle's concern about the effect of urban renewal on the displaced poor and about fair housing was a case in point. Soon after arriving in Washington he began collecting information on the city's plans for urban renewal. He used his old colleague Msgr. John O'Grady to study the problem and report on the work of the Redevelopment Land Agency, which was charged with planning the redevelopment of much of the inner city.[11] He also made sure that a Catholic was appointed to the city's Urban Renewal Council—"most important that we are represented," he told his chancellor. Likewise, he arranged for a representative to serve on an interfaith committee organized to deal with the Redevelopment Land Agency. Yet when it came to a more visible role for himself, O'Boyle seemed less positive. For example, when invited by the D.C. commissioners to present his views on urban renewal and a freeway project that would demolish most of old Southwest Washington, he demurred, sending Msgr. Hannan instead. Hannan later remarked that the archbishop should have voiced his opposition in person, but O'Boyle still shunned the limelight. He once confessed his error in avoiding a more active role. In an address to the Council of Catholic Men about the relocation of poor Southwest residents and their inadequate housing, he added, "Gentlemen, I accuse myself for not knowing about it and speaking forthrightly about it."[12]

In the wake of the resettlement fiasco involving citizens from Southwest, O'Boyle determined to involve the archdiocese more closely in city affairs. He organized an Office of Urban Renewal and in June 1960 appointed Msgr. George

St. Luke's Guild, 25 Mar 1963, and to O'Boyle, same date. All in Nuesse Papers, ACUA. Conley's "'All One in Christ,'" provides a detailed account of O'Boyle's racial efforts in this period.

10. Floyd Agostinelli as quoted in Lawrence M. O'Rourke, *Geno: The Life and Mission of Geno Baroni* (New York: Paulist Press, 1991), p. 45.

11. See, for example, ltrs., O'Grady to O'Boyle, 1 Nov 1949, 23 Aug 1953, and numerous reports on urban renewal and block busting, various dates. All in NCCC Papers, ACUA.

12. O'Boyle, "Concluding Remarks at Fourth Annual Convention of Washington Archdiocese's Council of Catholic Men," 12 Feb 1962, copy in CCM file, AAW. See also Note to Msgr. Hannan attached to ltr., D.C. Commissioners to O'Boyle, 5 Nov 1958, and memo, Harry Buswell to O'Boyle, 20 Mar 1961, both in Chancery file, AAW. See also Hannan intv.

Gingras, pastor of SS. Paul and Augustine, director. Gingras promptly secured a seat on the city's Human Relations Commission, and although his time in office proved short, he continued to be a regular witness before city and federal groups concerned with city planning. One of his first moves was to hire Floyd H. Agostinelli as secretary of the new organization, the first layman in a position of influence in the chancery. Agostinelli, a self-described "constant thorn in O'Boyle's side," developed a network of contacts among the civil rights activists in the archdiocese and the city's non-Catholic clergy.[13] With O'Boyle's approval, Gingras and his staff worked to keep inner-city parishes abreast of developments in housing and employment opportunities. They also promoted the formation of credit unions in city parishes. As Father Geno Baroni pointed out, modern man didn't live on bread alone, but on credit, and in fact the effort of inner-city residents to improve their neighborhoods was tied directly to home improvement loans.

The new organization came just in time to counter the growing perception that the archdiocese was largely resting on its laurels. As the leader of the local Catholic Interracial Council pointed out to O'Boyle in 1961, once again the Church had lost the initiative, this time when Agnes Meyer, wife of the owner of the *Washington Post*, formed an Urban Youth Corps to work in the slums. "We missed the boat again," John O'Connor claimed. Anything the archbishop did now, he continued, would look like "me too." The archdiocese was great on enunciating fine principles, O'Connor continued, but when it came to action it was Mrs. Meyer, not the archdiocese, who produced results. O'Connor expressed sympathy for O'Boyle because, as he put it, "if it had been humanly possible to get a social action program started, you would have."[14]

Coming from an old battle-scarred warrior like O'Connor, these remarks were not meant to comfort the archbishop, but to spur him to action. As O'Connor was aware, O'Boyle had made his position on racial justice abundantly clear. In a series of public statements in 1960–61 he had campaigned to convince Catholics that social justice was a moral issue. This was the position of America's bishops and the theme of their 1958 statement on race that O'Boyle had pushed through the bishops' conference.[15] Now two years later he explored the causes of discrimination, which he traced to a denial of the Christian message,

13. As quoted in O'Rourke's *Geno*, p. 45. See also ltr., Gingras to O'Boyle, 24 Sep 1960, Chancery file, AAW.
14. Ltr., O'Connor to O'Boyle, 19 Apr 1961, Chancery file, AAW.
15. "Discrimination and Christian Conscience," 14 Nov 1958, Hugh Nolan, ed., *The Pastoral Letters of the U.S. Bishops*, vol. 2 (Washington, D.C.: NCCB-USCC, 1983), pp. 201–6.

and later in a series of sermons and public appearances he exhorted Catholics to work for fairness, especially in the volatile area of housing, which was embroiling the Washington region. Specifically he referred to the ongoing dispute over block busting, white flight, and the resulting creation of a largely segregated black inner city surrounded by all-white suburbs. His job, he believed at that time, was not to devise specific programs, but to remind Catholics of their obligation to seek racial justice.

Some weeks before he received O'Connor's letter, O'Boyle had outlined the connection between the Christian's obligation and discrimination. Before a large New York audience he praised community efforts to erase racial barriers, but he went on to note that the real test was in personal encounters between individuals. He called on Catholics to ascertain the true state of race relations in their community and to cooperate with those of other faiths in seeking justice.[16] In February 1961 he had also urged the *Catholic Standard*'s fifty thousand subscribers to commit themselves to the fight against discrimination. He specifically endorsed the upcoming interdenominationally sponsored Brotherhood Week, during which local church leaders would ask their congregations to sign pledges expressing their opposition to discrimination in housing. He went on to argue that the root cause of discrimination in housing transcended prejudice and that those who would correct this evil must also look to the economic and social problems that contributed to current conditions.[17] Beyond outlining these problems, however, he had yet to suggest any concrete course of action.

In March 1963 he endorsed a joint statement by local religious leaders that publicized the gross inadequacies in the city's public welfare apparatus and called on the federal government to increase its support. At the same time he began to explore possible programs the archdiocese might undertake to improve race relations. In April he established the Archbishop's Committee on Human Relations, with subcommittees devoted to concerns like housing, education, and welfare.[18] While its twenty-one members worked to fulfill their mandate, some

16. Both Conley's "'All One in Christ,'" pp. 119–20, and *NYT*, 14 Feb 1960, quote extensively from this sermon, delivered in St. Patrick's Cathedral on the occasion of Father LaFarge's eightieth birthday.

17. O'Boyle, "Brotherhood: Belief and Practice," *CS*, 24 Feb 1961. Conley's "'All One in Christ'" provides a useful summary of O'Boyle's activities in race relations during the early 1960s and is the basis for the paragraphs that follow.

18. The work of the committee and its membership are detailed in Minutes of Meeting of Archbishop's Committee on Human Relations, 26 Apr 1963, AAW, and Minutes of Board of Directors, Catholic Interracial Council, 6 May 1963, Nuesse Papers, ACUA. Floyd Agostinelli served as secretary of this committee, and at his suggestion J. Francis Polhaus, legal council at the NAACP, became a member.

also joined their non-Catholic neighbors in demanding that local governments enact ordinances barring housing discrimination. O'Boyle began an address to Washington's Urban League by quoting the bishops' assertion that "the heart of the race question is moral and religious." He went on to recommend four specific areas where men of good will could take action to improve conditions. He called on all employers to adopt the merit principle in hiring and training workers. He demanded that local jurisdictions make public housing available to low-income families and establish youth programs to combat delinquency. Finally, he called on religious leaders to destroy what he termed "the ghetto of ignorance and indifference that poisoned race relations."[19]

To translate these proposals into action O'Boyle helped organize the Interreligious Committee on Race Relations in June 1963 and agreed to chair the group during its early years. Its forty-two members pledged to adopt the goals outlined in the archbishop's four-point program, using their economic and political muscle to move the city toward equal employment opportunity and fair housing. Overcoming his reluctance to appear in political gatherings, O'Boyle spoke at the invitation of President John Kennedy on behalf of the administration's civil rights bill at a White House meeting of religious leaders. He also was the lead witness, testifying before Washington's Board of Commissioners in favor of a ban on housing discrimination. Specifically, he proposed that the pending city ordinance bar discrimination in sales, rentals, and financing of housing and the enforcement of fair employment practices in city contracts.[20] Again, he led the fight to halt extension of the city's freeway system, at least until adequate housing could be provided for people displaced by the project. (In the end, the Interreligious Committee, in collaboration with other activist groups, succeeded in halting the freeway project before it invaded most of Northeast Washington.) O'Boyle's stint as chairman provided a bonus. Just as the subject of ecumenism was being discussed at the Vatican Council, he was entering into close contact with numerous clerical and lay leaders of other faiths, some of whom became personal friends and close collaborators in the ongoing equal rights campaign.

In a pastoral letter read at all Masses in July 1963 he again stressed the point that the heart of the race question was moral and religious. "No Catholic with a

19. O'Boyle, "Address of Archbishop O'Boyle to Washington Urban League," May 6, 1963, copy in AAW. The speech received wide coverage in the press. See, for example, *Star*, 7 May 1963, and *NYT*, same date.

20. Documents covering all aspects of O'Boyle's testimony are located in Fair Employment Practices file, Nuesse Papers, ACUA. The testimony itself has been preserved in the Chancery file, AAW.

Crusader for Social Justice. O'Boyle testifies, with Bishop Smallwood Williams of the Bible Way Church, on behalf of a measure to ban housing discrimination in the District of Columbia.

good Christian conscience can fail to give the Negro people the legitimate opportunity to secure proper housing, equal opportunity for a job, proper and adequate welfare needs, and full participation in our public and private educational facilities."[21] In effect he was staking the Church's claim to a leadership role in the civil rights fight.

He soon found himself in the national spotlight when in August 1963 he agreed to give the invocation at the March on Washington for Jobs and Freedom. The demonstration was organized by such activists as A. Philip Randolph, Bayard Rustin, Roy Wilkins, and a young Georgia clergyman, Martin Luther King, Jr. They had enlisted the support of many civil rights leaders in the white community, including Walter Reuther representing the labor movement and Eugene

21. As quoted in *CS,* 7 Jul 1963. See also *Star,* 1 Jul 1963.

Carson Blake of the National Council of Churches. Federal authorities were of two minds about the event. The Kennedy administration hoped to use the mass demonstration to support its civil rights bill, then fighting its way through Congress. At the same time it feared that the presence of tens of thousands of marchers would create the impression that it was being pressured into new legislation or, even worse, criticized for doing "too little, too late." The administration was also concerned that the demonstration could turn violent. Attorney General Robert Kennedy and his assistant, Burke Marshall, welcomed the involvement of O'Boyle and other respected allies of the movement as insurance that the event would remain peaceful. Even before accepting the invitation, O'Boyle had Bishop Hannan, who was close to the Kennedy family, inquire about his participation and received assurances that his presence would be welcomed.[22]

Bishop Hannan was not so much concerned about the administration's reputation or the possibility of violence as he was of the appearance that the Church was endorsing a pressure group whose goals were excessive and critical of the gradualist approach adopted by the archdiocese in the past. It was wrong, he argued, to promote the notion that employment could be obtained through political pressure instead of personal effort and achievement. He advised O'Boyle to permit local Catholics and groups from around the country organized by the Catholic Interracial Council to participate, but to withhold any personal endorsement of the affair, which could lead, he predicted, "to many difficulties."[23]

O'Boyle's participation in the Interreligious Committee on Race Relations had convinced him of the need for government action on civil rights. Ignoring Hannan's advice, he accepted the invitation to participate and endorsed the goals of the march leaders. In informing the region's pastors and religious superiors of his approval, he quoted from his recent statement as chairman of the Interreligious Committee in which he urged citizens to consider the purpose of the upcoming demonstration "as a legitimate expression of the support for the moral

22. See Coady, Hannan, and Donoghue intvs. There exists considerable secondary literature on O'Boyle's participation in the march. See especially Taylor Branch, *Parting the Waters: America in the King Years, 1954–63* (New York: Simon & Schuster, 1988); Thomas Gentile, *The March on Washington, August 23, 1963* (Washington, D.C.: New Day Publications, 1983); and the useful surveys by Rory Conley in "Cardinal O'Boyle and the 1963 March on Washington," *The Catholic Historical Society of Washington Newsletter* (Nov 1993): pp. 1–2, 8, and his dissertation "'All One in Christ,'" pp. 134–40. For a critical account, see John Lewis, *Walking With the Wind: A Memoir of the Movement* (New York: Simon & Schuster, 1998), pp. 219–27. Unless otherwise noted the following paragraphs are based on these sources.

23. Memo, Hannan for O'Boyle, n.d. (ca. 10 Aug 1963), Chancery file, AAW.

The March on Washington, 1963. O'Boyle offers a prayer as Whitney Young and Walter Reuther flank Dr. Martin Luther King, Jr., just before the latter delivered his "I Have a Dream" address.

right of the American Negro to equal opportunity. It [the situation] leaves it to each citizen to make a considered judgment on his participation in the demonstration." Use of the word "his" was not accidental. With an eye to the remote possibility of violence, he explicitly barred participation by women religious. They, he advised, could best serve the cause by spending the day in their convents, praying for the success of the march.[24]

Leaving the organization of Catholic participation to the Interracial Council and the hospitality of many city parishes and Georgetown University, O'Boyle greeted the six American bishops, including his neighbor, Baltimore's Archbishop Shehan, who came to Washington for the event. O'Boyle felt constrained to curb the enthusiasm of the organizers who announced that the archbishop had "urged" participation by local Catholics and pleaded for contributions to cover expenses. (The Knights of Columbus already had contributed $25,000 toward the cost of accommodations for those coming from far away.) O'Boyle had his chancellor state that the Interracial Council's announcement, which actually was

24. Ltr., O'Boyle to All Pastors and Superiors of Religious Orders of Men and Women, 19 Aug 1963, Chancery file, AAW.

written in his own chancery, had not been authorized and that under no circumstances were funds to be solicited.[25] Through its national chapters, the Interracial Council was advising visiting clergy and religious to obtain permission to march from their local bishop. Some complied, but many simply came to town. Large numbers of women religious from around the country ignored O'Boyle's well-meant but patronizing directive and joined the massive throng.[26]

The archbishop's endorsement of the march gained him favorable notice in church circles, but it was his reaction to the draft of one of the speeches that won him national attention. If the march is principally remembered as the setting for Martin Luther King's stirring "I Have a Dream" speech, numerous other leaders also spoke that day to the crowd from the steps of the Lincoln Memorial. One was John Lewis, the youthful activist and spokesman for the Student Non-Violent Coordinating Committee (and in later years a U.S. congressman from Georgia).[27]

SNCC had been in the front lines of the civil rights struggle, most notably in its "Freedom Rides," which earned beatings and jailing for many of its nonviolent student members. SNCC was particularly critical of the administration's civil rights bill, and Lewis was prepared to say so with flaming rhetoric. Floyd Agostinelli obtained an advance copy of Lewis' speech and passed it on to the archbishop. O'Boyle could overlook criticism of the Kennedys, but Lewis' draft also included lines like "We will march through the South, through the Heart of Dixie, the way Sherman did. We shall pursue our own 'scorched earth' policy and burn Jim Crow to the ground—non-violently."[28] Phrases that called for "revolution" by the "masses" convinced O'Boyle that the speech was seriously out of line with the true meaning of the day. Lewis' contempt for any call for patience also rankled O'Boyle and others who believed the gradualist approach to reform had proved successful. After consultation with his brother bishops, he informed both the Kennedy administration and the march leaders that he would not give the invocation unless Lewis' address was altered.

25. Ltr., Roeder to All Pastors and Superiors of Religious Orders of Men and Women, 22 Aug 1963, and memo, Catholic Interracial Council of Washington (Joseph Nichols) to All Religious of the Archdiocese of Washington, n.d. (ca. 20 Aug 1963). Both in Chancery file, AAW.

26. See, for example, ltrs., Rev. Anthony Robinson to Chancellor, 23 Aug 1963, Chancery file, AAW, and O'Boyle to President, Georgetown University, 30 Aug 1963, Varia file, GUA. See also Pauline J. Jones intv. for details of one parish's participation.

27. Lewis devoted considerable critical attention to O'Boyle's intervention in his *Walking With the Wind*.

28. As quoted by Godfrey Hodgson in his "The March on Washington: 20 Years After the Dream," *Potomac Magazine (Washington Post)*, 1 Jul 1983, p. 13.

Early on the day before the march Robert Kennedy personally called O'Boyle and pleaded with him to remain on the program. Kennedy was under the illusion that O'Boyle's objection to the Lewis draft was its criticism of the administration's bill, when in fact O'Boyle was concerned about what he perceived as a threat of violence. He stood his ground: he would not appear unless Lewis toned down his rhetoric. Lewis and his group were equally adamant that no changes would be made. The more conservative march leaders feared what O'Boyle's defection might mean to the general support they sought from the government.[29] They pressured Lewis, the battle-scarred Randolph pleading with SNCC members to save the march he had planned for so long. As the ceremony was about to begin, Bayard Rustin, whom the archbishop respected as a moderate and effective leader, was able to assure O'Boyle that the speech would be changed, so O'Boyle went out and addressed the throng. Meanwhile a reluctant Lewis and his colleagues in SNCC redrafted his speech, accepting the changes dictated by Rustin and Randolph.

The invocation, hastily prepared by O'Boyle with Archbishop Shehan's help, explicitly called for Americans to shun violence while asking for a special blessing for the leaders of the struggle for justice and harmony among the races. "As Moses of old," O'Boyle added, "they have gone before their people to the land of promise. Let that promise become a reality so that the ideals of freedom, blessed alike by our religious faith and our heritage of democracy, will prevail in our land."[30]

O'Boyle's demand that Lewis moderate his speech was not without its critics among the civil rights activists who interpreted his stand as demonstrating a less than full commitment to racial justice. To counter this impression, a group of Washington clergymen, including the Episcopal and Methodist bishops, wrote in the *New York Times* that critics were mistaken to brand O'Boyle's "quiet determination, desire to be thorough, and concern to commit himself only to what can be carried out" as less than total dedication to the cause. These were men who had worked with the archbishop on the Interreligious Committee, and, they reminded the critics, his demand that the Lewis speech be changed meant that the march would be remembered for Dr. King's stirring rhetoric rather than a diatribe against John Kennedy and Congress.[31]

O'Boyle's forthright endorsement of the march, as well as his participation,

29. Hodgson, "The March On Washington," p. 13.
30. As quoted in *CS*, 13 Aug 1987.
31. *NYT*, 14 Nov 1964. See also same source, 23 Sep 1968.

influenced many of his fellow bishops and American Catholics. Thousands of religious and laity, marching under banners that proclaimed their parish affiliation, provided a visual affirmation of the Church's commitment to racial justice. As for O'Boyle's personal reaction to the main event of the day, he told a friend that Martin Luther King "really knows what he's talking about."[32] In the brief interval before King's talk, Ralph Bunche, the distinguished United Nations official, leaned over to O'Boyle and said, "Now you're going to feel just a little like you are in a black Southern Baptist church."[33] It was a moment of high purpose and exciting theater to savor, especially for the doughty prelate, who had fought long and hard for racial justice in Washington.

A New Civil Rights Activist

In 1964 the *New York Times* quoted one observer's description of Patrick O'Boyle as a bishop who had always understood the evil of segregation, but had been restrained "by prudence and bureaucracy from his big move," only to be transformed in his late years "against formidable odds of personal temperament and ecclesiastical tradition" into a very public leader in the fight for civil rights.[34] Although this analysis tended to discount O'Boyle's persistent efforts to make Catholics see racial justice as a moral imperative, it did underscore the noticeable transition, beginning in 1964, from teacher to social activist. This change not only resulted from a newfound conviction that a more active stance was called for, but also reflected the influence of several persuasive subordinates dedicated to involving the resources of the Church more completely in the fight.

Actually, a multifaceted social program was already operating in the archdiocese, led by Geno Baroni, a newcomer to Washington informally serving under Msgr. Gingras at SS. Paul and Augustine. O'Boyle might have been taken aback by some of Baroni's high-flying activities, but in fact the archbishop was always a firm supporter of the dynamic priest's ideas. They had much in common. Like O'Boyle, Baroni had grown up in an immigrant family in a Pennsylvania mining town where his father, a miner, and mother, a domestic, eked out a living. Baroni himself earned school money working in an amusement park and in a factory, where he was eventually dismissed for trying to organize the workers.[35] Baroni

32. Quoted in McArdle intv.
33. Quoted in Hannan intv.
34. As quoted in *NYT*, 29 Oct 1964.
35. Baroni's career was the subject of countless articles and news reports. See, for example, Arthur McNally, "Green Pastures in a Black Ghetto," *Sign* 43 (Jan 1966): pp. 18–27, and Gerald R. McMurray, "Remembering Geno Baroni," *America* 156 (22 Sep 1984): 145–48. For a comprehensive account, see O'Rourke's *Geno.*

arrived at Sts. Paul and Augustine in 1960, when the inner-city neighborhood around 14th and V Streets, N.W., was at its nadir. Poverty and crime were rampant, and a sense of hopelessness pervaded a community that rarely heard from the government agencies created to help it. Baroni's instinct was to organize the people. He enlisted like-minded clergy of other faiths to help convince the community of the need for a united effort. The opportunity arose when the old, rambling convent at 1419 V Street became available. He persuaded Msgr. Gingras—who, along with assistants like Carl Dianda and later Raymond Kemp, Ralph Dwan, and Andre Bouchard, had been influenced by Baroni—to see the possibilities for neighborhood improvement. Gingras approached O'Boyle with the idea of using the building as a center, not only for parish activities, but also for ecumenical organizations trying to unite the community in its dealings with school, welfare, and housing agencies. O'Boyle bought the idea and from the start proved an enthusiastic sponsor of the center, including providing timely financial help.[36]

With respected insider Gingras dealing with the archbishop and the often suspicious chancery, Baroni was free to develop many programs that used the V Street Center, as it was dubbed, as their headquarters.[37] A cadre of social workers and community organizers under the center's director, Mary Houston, and in time people like Barbara Mikulski and other local civil rights activists, offered a list of programs that addressed all manner of parish and community concerns. Here neighborhood groups, aided by talented young people from around the region, became a political and social force in the face of an often-indifferent city bureaucracy.

It was also during this period that Baroni began to ponder the mutual interests of the country's ethnic minorities and their need for alliances. He had a genius for building coalitions, and he urged the African-American groups working out of the center to engage with their Hispanic neighbors. He looked to the time when neighborhood groups, alliances of ethnic minorities, might negotiate with city officials on local needs. Such alliances were bound to attract the support of the son of an immigrant blue-collar worker. O'Boyle frequently alluded to the struggle of past generations of Catholic newcomers and translated their struggle to current conditions. The energetic Baroni allied with friends in the Protestant clergy like William Wendt, James Reeb, and Philip Newell, along with the popu-

36. See, for example, ltr., O'Boyle to Gingras, 26 Mar 1963, SAA. On Baroni's influence among the priests of the parish, see Kemp intv.

37. For details on the many programs emanating from the V Street center, see the author's *The Emergence of a Black Catholic Community*, pp. 332–37.

lar black preacher Walter Fauntroy, to support many civil rights issues of concern not only to African Americans, but also to the other minorities arriving in Washington.

At first O'Boyle was taken aback by some of the activities at the center. After Baroni and his friends were photographed demonstrating their opposition to local welfare regulations, for example, O'Boyle responded promptly: "The next time somebody suggests that you deposit a coffin on the Capitol steps, say that's something that Protestants do, but not Catholics." But O'Boyle would come around to Baroni's way of thinking. Soon after the Capitol incident, the irrepressible Baroni participated with his Protestant friends in picketing the White House, an event pictured in the *Washington Post*. Baroni, who feared this would be the end of his priestly career in Washington, was ordered to report to O'Boyle's office, where the stern-visaged prelate sat at his desk with the *Post* opened to the picture. O'Boyle asked what the demonstration was about. When he learned that Baroni had participated as a sign of support for Rev. Fauntroy and for Martin Luther King's efforts, O'Boyle simply responded, "All right, Father. By the way, I was pleased to see in this picture you had your hat on. That's the way I like my priests to appear in public. You can go now."[38] For once the sartorially indifferent Baroni had met the always-correct O'Boyle's standard for clerical attire. On a more serious level, the conversation convinced Baroni that his method of bearing witness in the fight for civil rights had his boss's backing. It also taught him a lesson: do not seek permission; act as though you had it and, if need be, apologize afterward.

As chairman of the Interreligious Committee, O'Boyle used Baroni's expertise to inform him on inner-city housing issues, and in 1963 he had the young priest craft the committee's statement on the subject.[39] In the wake of the march on Washington and no doubt prodded by Baroni, the archbishop began to assume a more visible and active role as chairman. At his urging, the city's religious leaders pledged their congregations to favor contractors who identified themselves as equal opportunity employers. To foster personal communication between the races, which he believed essential to achieving racial justice, O'Boyle convinced the committee to sponsor Washington's participation in National Home Visit Day. After a slow start the annual visits of blacks and whites to each other's homes grew in popularity and, O'Boyle was convinced, produced closer understanding in the community. The Interreligious Committee's most signifi-

38. Both as quoted in O'Rourke, *Geno,* pp. 36–37.
39. Baroni intv.

cant activity during O'Boyle's tenure as chairman was its strong support for the Kennedy-Johnson civil rights bill. The archbishop presided over a convocation at Georgetown University in April 1964. One planner concluded that, to be effective, they would need a huge crowd. A record-shattering seven thousand attended, many recruited by O'Boyle from the city's seminaries and convents. The next day the archbishop led a delegation of 150 religious leaders to the White House, where he pledged to President Johnson the group's support for the bill.[40] He later arranged for seminarians to join their non-Catholic counterparts in a twenty-four-hour prayer vigil on the day the bill was debated in the U.S. Senate.

Probably nothing drew O'Boyle to the attention of the nation's Catholic civil rights advocates more than his widely advertised support of Martin Luther King's march in Selma, Alabama. On March 7, 1965, TV programs were interrupted to show the brutal treatment meted out by the Alabama state police and sheriff's deputies to a group of civil rights marchers setting out on a trek to the state capital to protest Alabama's racial restrictions. Seventy of the brutalized marchers, some struck down after seeking refuge in a church, required hospitalization. Dr. King responded by announcing plans for a repeat march, this time by religious leaders from around the country. Given the American bishops' general aversion to priests and religious demonstrating, King included few Catholics in his invitation.

Father Baroni immediately grasped King's implication that Catholics were somehow less than fully committed to the cause. He convinced his pastor of the need for a Catholic presence in the march and got Floyd Agostinelli, their ally in the chancery, to ask O'Boyle for permission for their participation. Agostinelli explained to the archbishop why the participation of laymen alone would not do in this case. O'Boyle agreed that four priests, properly attired in black hat and Roman collar, could go to Selma. He added the altogether proper caveat that they first must obtain permission from the local ordinary, in this case the bishop of Mobile, Thomas J. Toolen.

Broadly interpreting O'Boyle's consent, the Catholic Interracial Council sprang into action. Using its national network of contacts it not only invited Catholics from around the country to participate in a Walk For Freedom and all-night vigil at the White House, but also informed its allies that a "large delegation of priests was being sent to Selma by His Excellency, Most Reverend Patrick A. O'Boyle, D.D."[41] Of course the archbishop had done no such thing, but that

40. *NYT*, 29 and 30 Apr 1964.
41. Catholic Interracial Council Newsletter (vol. 5, no. 1), March 1965.

did not stop priests and religious around the country from heading to Alabama. Conveniently assuming that O'Boyle's direction applied to all, many did not bother to seek approval from their own ordinaries.

Back in Washington Gingras and Baroni faced another obstacle to participation, namely Bishop Toolen, who, they correctly assumed, was opposed to demonstrations by Catholic clergy in his diocese. They resorted to subterfuge. Learning that Toolen was not in Mobile, Agostinelli directed their request to that city, repeatedly informing O'Boyle's office that they had not yet reached Toolen, but continued to try. Borrowing a page from Baroni's manual, they decided to act first and apologize later. They accepted an invitation to join the other religious delegations at National Airport for a chartered flight to Selma. Meanwhile Bishop Spence and the watchdogs in the chancery learned of the ruse and frantically sought to contact them to cancel the trip. A madcap chase ensued, with Gingras and the other priests anxiously waiting for the plane to take off from National Airport while the Methodist bishop stood on the tarmac expounding on coming events for reporters.

Agostinelli prudently put himself out of reach of the archbishop's office, but his allies in the chancery led Spence to assume the plane was taking off from Dulles Airport, where he repeatedly and unsuccessfully had Gingras and Baroni paged. A nervous Agostinelli, who had been dodging repeated efforts by chancery officials to locate him, stood by to see if the plane would take off before Spence was able to locate the Catholic delegation. The marchers finally took to the skies, but not before Baroni identified himself to reporters as a representative of the archbishop of Washington, who, he claimed, fully supported those demonstrating for civil rights in Selma.

The effort to locate Agostinelli and the priests going to Selma during that hectic day has been used by some as proof that the archbishop had changed his mind and had rescinded his permission for the trip. This assumption presumed a naïve archbishop comically outwitted by wily subordinates. On the contrary, the evidence suggests that O'Boyle allowed the drama to unfold as it did for his own purposes. As Agostinelli reported, when first approached on the matter "the old boy had an uncanny sense of what was going on. I felt he could almost read what I was about to say before I said it."[42] Moreover, as an important member of the bishops' conference O'Boyle certainly was aware of Bishop Toolen's presence in Washington for a meeting of the hierarchy. He could easily have

---

42. As quoted in O'Rourke's *Geno,* p. 46. O'Rourke's book, pp. 43–53, provides a comprehensive account of the Selma trip. See also Baroni and Agostinelli intvs.

called Agostinelli's bluff when he repeatedly reported on the continuing failure to locate Toolen.

Actually, the way the little drama played out allowed O'Boyle to avoid any difficulty with Bishop Toolen and the apostolic delegate, both of whom were opposed to having Catholic clergy participate in demonstrations. In response to a complaint from Delegate Vagnozzi, O'Boyle agreed that sisters should be excluded from all demonstrations except those sponsored by the Church, but that priests and male religious should be allowed to participate if the local ordinary and their religious superiors approved. (Interestingly, the usually much stricter Cardinal Spellman, answering a similar complaint from Vagnozzi, defended the presence of both priests and sisters in Selma.)[43] After providing the apostolic delegate with a brief assessment of the major civil rights organizations and the radicalism of some as demonstrated by John Lewis' speech during the march on Washington, O'Boyle offered a general observation. Usually only the laity, he believed, should participate in demonstrations; priests and religious "only when unjustice [*sic*] to the Negro demands a positive religious image."[44] When Vagnozzi later pressed the bishops' conference to consider the subject at its November meeting, the conference's administrative board agreed with O'Boyle that a decision on participation in demonstrations was best left to individual bishops.[45]

Left to men like Bishop Toolen, priests would never have marched at Selma.[46] Finally reached, not by Gingras or Baroni but by Bishop Spence, Toolen expressed his opposition and asked that O'Boyle be informed and the priests stopped. However sincere Spence's effort to stop the demonstrators, the subsequent cops and robbers chase served to demonstrate that O'Boyle, following protocol, had tried to comply with the decision of a fellow bishop. Yet it seemed likely that Washington's civil rights champion was playing a double game. When Agostinelli finally reappeared at the chancery, he later recalled, "O'Boyle gave me hell for being gone from the office for so long without telling anybody where I was going. But I had the feeling he didn't mean it." In fact Agostinelli felt bold enough to remind O'Boyle that a Methodist bishop was demonstrating in Selma and asked, "Wouldn't it be great if Bishop Hannan would go?" Knowing Han-

43. Ltr., Spellman to Vagnozzi, 29 Jun 1965, cited in Fogarty, *Patterns of Episcopal Leadership,* p. 234.

44. Ltr., O'Boyle to Vagnozzi, 3 Jul 1965, Apostolic Delegate file, AAW.

45. Minutes of the Administrative Board, 13 Nov 1965, NCWC Papers, ACUA.

46. Toolen justified his stand in a candid letter to Agnes M. Cline, 6 Mar 1965, copy in SAA.

nan's aversion to demonstrations and knowing that Agostinelli also knew, O'Boyle merely growled.[47]

O'Boyle's position on Selma, which he shared with Archbishop Ritter of St. Louis and a few others in the hierarchy, marked a turning point in the American Church's role in the civil rights struggle. Following on the Selma experience, priests and male and female religious in ever-increasing numbers participated in civil rights events that followed in those tumultuous times, a fact that provided a formerly skeptical audience convincing evidence of the Church's wholehearted commitment to the cause of racial justice and equal opportunity. O'Boyle never decried the fact that his name had been invoked by civil rights activists around the country. Nor did he show any irritation with his subordinates. His relations with Gingras remained warm. In fact Gingras was made one of his official consultors. As for Baroni, O'Boyle called him in because of a complaint from a senior member of the hierarchy. As Baroni described the scene:

> The cardinal told me that I had been in all the papers with King marching arm and arm without a hat on, that this kind of action was not priestly, and that he could not tolerate this any longer. I asked what he was going to do, and he said, "Geno, next time wear a hat."[48]

Baroni interpreted such scenes as tacit approval of his methods, and indeed during remarks at a conference of archdiocesan clergy a few weeks after Selma, O'Boyle pointed Baroni out to his fellow priests, saying, "Here's a man who has been fighting in the front lines for a long time. I think we ought to give him a hand." When the applause died down the archbishop announced that he was appointing Baroni executive secretary of his new Committee on Community Relations, the archdiocese's version of the war on poverty. In effect he was telling Baroni to continue on an archdiocesan level the work he had started at the V Street Center.[49]

Reflecting on the accelerated civil rights activities, O'Boyle worried that he might "oversell" the cause. To a concerned layman he explained, "We can alienate more people by giving them an overdose than by ignoring the subject altogether." The immediate task was to consolidate the gains realized "by turning words into deeds, particularly in the fields of housing and job opportunity."[50]

---

47. As quoted in O'Rourke, *Geno*, p. 49.

48. As quoted in *America* (22 Sep 1984): p. 146.

49. Ltr., O'Boyle to Gingras, 1 Sep 1965, SAA. The quote is as reported in *Sign* (Jan 1966): p. 27.

50. Ltr., O'Boyle to William Carolan, 4 Sep 1965, Chancery file, AAW.

But if the archbishop spoke out less frequently in the next two years, he actually increased his activities behind the scenes. In early 1966 he sponsored a series of seminars for all priests on open housing. He also assigned a group of progressive pastors to parishes recently acquired from the Jesuits in southern Maryland, where earlier racial gains had been allowed to atrophy.[51] Vowing that he would not close one inner-city school "as long as we can get a dime to support them," he arranged for suburban parishes to subsidize these institutions. (At the time of his retirement he boasted that not one school had closed.)[52] Meanwhile, he ordered that an effort be made to pool the resources and programs of the poorer parishes, thus making them eligible for grants available through the Economic Opportunity Act.[53]

Time and again O'Boyle returned to the subject of fair housing, the premier source of racial tension in the capital area. In May 1966 he reminded priests of the archdiocese that block busting and similar tactics designed to perpetuate segregated housing were "immoral and unworthy of Christians." All have the moral right, he declared, to acquire and occupy any house that their means allowed. At the same time he issued a statement coinciding with the Fair Housing Sunday effort in which he bluntly stated that to deny African Americans the right to buy a house and enjoy equal education and job opportunity "is in effect denying that right to Christ Himself."[54] In his first official statement as a cardinal, O'Boyle called on the Montgomery County Council to adopt an open housing ordinance. "What is morally right and just is likewise sound public policy," he posited. To those who claimed such an ordinance would deflate property values, he declared that the right to private property "was not absolute and unconditional and could not be exercised to the detriment of the common good."[55]

Activism in the Archdiocese

The Selma march, demonstrating a unity among the nation's clergy, had proved peaceful. Gingras and Baroni, who at the advice of march organizers had placed their breviaries inside their hats to ward off the anticipated blows of police batons, returned home unscathed. But violence, this time initiated by African Americans in the inner cities, was not long in coming. In August 1965 the

51. Ltrs., Coyne to Ellis, 23 Jan and 6 Apr 1966, Ellis Papers, ACUA.

52. *America* (24 Mar 1973): p. 254.

53. For details on school programs and subsidies, see ltr., Hannan to O'Boyle, 19 Apr 1965, and O'Boyle to Msgr. Thomas Lyons, 14 Dec 1967. Both in Chancery file, AAW. The quote is as recorded in *Star*, 10 Apr 1967. See also *CS*, 9 Jun 1966, and *WP*, 19 Apr 1967.

54. As quoted in *NYT*, 23 May 1966.

55. As quoted in *WP*, 7 Jul 1967.

Watts section of Los Angeles exploded in a deadly riot. Two years later Newark and Houston were in flames. Although Washington had been spared, it seemed to some only a matter of time. President Johnson declared Sunday, August 5, 1967, a national day of prayer for civil and racial harmony.

During the previous week Cardinal O'Boyle had hosted a dinner for Cardinal Krol and others. When the conversation turned to the riots, Msgr. George Higgins offered the bishops a challenge: "Instead of talking cheap, do something about the race question." When O'Boyle pointed out that the bishops had issued a statement on the subject the year before, Higgins replied, "Yeah, that was last year." The challenge nettled O'Boyle. The next morning he called on Higgins and Baroni to prepare a pastoral letter for him on the riots. He approved their work and ordered that it be read at all Masses a week after Johnson's national day of prayer. Higgins and Baroni objected, explaining that if the statement was not read on August 5, Johnson's designated date for prayer, its impact would be nil, and "we just wasted our time if you wait for a week." O'Boyle grumbled about the logistics involved in getting it to the pastors in one day and asked sarcastically if they planned to run the diocese. Higgins replied that they were happy to leave the diocese to its bishop, but pointed out that Western Union would get the statement to the pastors in time. O'Boyle finally agreed. His mood brightened considerably when he received a personal call from President Johnson, who praised the statement for its "great contribution" to the cause.[56]

The pastoral letter, which was reprinted in the *Congressional Record*, analyzed the cause of the riots:

> We must come to realize that riots, however senseless they may be, are the frenzied cry of alienated people who are trying to tell us, out of a sense of despair and utter hopelessness, that they want to be heard. . . . We must be willing to acknowledge our responsibility for perpetuating a system which sooner or later was inevitably bound to erupt in violence.

The nation must provide an antidote to this sense of despair, he stated, by inaugurating a dramatic and far-reaching escalation in its war on poverty. He branded past efforts to eliminate segregated housing "feeble" and the welfare system "paternalistic" and "demeaning." Specifically on the local level, he called on Congress to allocate more money for Washington's schools and low-income housing projects.[57]

56. As quoted in Higgins intv.
57. The pastoral letter was printed in *CS*, 3 Aug 1967, in *Social Justice* (Oct 1967), pp. 204–6, and the *Congressional Record*, Senate, 90th Congress, 1st Sess, S11322, 10 Aug 1967.

Cardinal O'Boyle's instincts, honed by fifty years' experience with the results of urban poverty and neglect and the arguments of Father Baroni, led him to accept the proposition that housing for the poor was a moral issue and therefore the Church should be directly involved in revitalizing urban neighborhoods. His earlier reluctance to commit the archdiocese to specific housing projects was overcome by his exposure on the Interreligious Committee on Race Relations, where he had come to see that ecumenical cooperation might achieve remarkable results. He was clearly impressed, as he put it, with those clergy of different faiths "all working together with true religious dedication" to speed the day when the racial issue would no longer exist in America.[58] In October 1967 he called for an urban coalition for the District of Columbia. With the support of Mayor Washington, George Meany, head of the AFL-CIO, and the National Council of Churches, he outlined a united effort to meet the racial crisis that included a $2 million revolving fund for housing development. He introduced the idea during a press conference at Fides House, where he exhorted the city's leaders: "The time has come, indeed has long past, to act rather than to debate. Our goals are clear enough; what remains is to put ourselves on the line, in the forum and in the market place."[59] He was optimistic about the usefulness of a union of the area's business, labor, religious, civil rights, and government agencies along with education and social service institutions in a concerted attack on poverty and discrimination. (Mayor Washington accepted the challenge and the new Urban Coalition began operations in February 1968 under its first chairman, Walter McArdle.)[60] O'Boyle also endorsed the idea of a development fund organized by a coalition of local Protestant clergymen that would supplement government efforts by providing loans to nonprofit sponsors of federally financed housing. He pledged $10,000 to the fund's kick-off drive. It was important, he explained to his fellow bishops, that where such organizations existed, the Church be represented.[61]

The cardinal used the same press conference to announce the archdiocese's own private war against urban poverty. He was expanding his Committee on Community Relations, he declared, renaming it the Archdiocesan Office of Urban Affairs and appointing Father Baroni executive director. This office would oversee the archdiocese's own Urban Rehabilitation Corporation to promote

58. Ltr., O'Boyle to Mr. and Mrs. A. L. Neves, 7 Apr 1965, Spence Papers, AAW.
59. *Star,* 27 Oct 1967.
60. The purpose of the coalition and McArdle's plans were outlined in *CS,* 14 Mar 1968.
61. Minutes of the USCC Meeting, Nov 1967, ACUA. See also ltr., Isaac Frank to O'Boyle, 8 Feb 1968, and reports of coalition meetings. All in Chancery file, AAW.

nonprofit housing projects in the District of Columbia. Although the corporation would apply for federal grants to support construction, O'Boyle promised an initial $400,000 contribution. Just five months before he had thrown cold water on a Baroni-inspired proposal to launch a nonprofit housing project. The archdiocese did not possess any suitable site in the inner city for such a project, he explained, and he rejected out of hand any imitation of Sursum Corda, the large-scale Jesuit-initiated new housing project then in the final stages of planning. He did, however, overrule his financial advisors and agree to support Baroni's seemingly modest proposal for the rehabilitation of seven houses. Baroni confidently predicted (but not to his boss) that this small beginning would bring in enough money to finance a constant increase in the number of dwellings—he was thinking in terms of hundreds—that the archdiocese would rehabilitate.[62]

By the time of his press conference in late October, the cardinal had reversed himself. In addition to rehabilitating the seven homes in Washington's Northwest 1 urban renewal area as a demonstration project, he pledged the archdiocese to join five Protestant churches and three synagogues in rehabilitating ten houses on Capitol Hill. Further aligning himself with ecumenical action, he announced that in cooperation with Washington's Presbyterian churches the archdiocese was establishing an ecumenical center at 1419 V Street. With financial support from both denominations the center would offer an expanded list of outreach programs beyond what Baroni and his associates had begun in the fields of job training, legal aid, and community organizing. In conjunction with the local Episcopal diocese, the cardinal was opening an Ecumenical Training Center, where newly ordained Catholic and Episcopal priests would be schooled in current racial issues. He also listed a number of additions to the archdiocese's neighborhood social service centers, including a center for Latino immigrants, as well as a list of projects to be manned by lay volunteers.

Casting aside his earlier reservations, the cardinal went on to announce that the archdiocese, with the approval of the board of trustees of St. Vincent Home and School and the City Regional Planning Program at Catholic University, would develop 1,100 units of nonprofit housing for low- and moderate-income families as well as senior citizens on the orphanage's property on Fourth Street, Northeast. (St. Vincent residents were being transferred to group homes, then considered more effective in meeting the children's needs.)[63] With this agree-

62. Ltr., O'Boyle to Wilberding, 21 May 1967, Chancery file, AAW. O'Boyle met previously with Baroni and his associates to discuss their housing proposal on 19 Sep 1967. For details, see same file. See also O'Rourke, *Geno*, p. 66.

63. Details of the archdiocesan anti-poverty agenda were announced in *CS*, 2 Nov 1967. See also

*Recognition for a Community Activist. President Johnson presents the annual
brotherhood award of the National Conference of Christians and Jews to Cardinal O'Boyle,
February 1968.*

ment the archdiocese found itself in the forefront of the fight against urban poverty. For O'Boyle personally it represented the end of an evolution from the moral teacher who denounced the evils of racial discrimination and neglect of the inner-city needy to social critic suggesting specific programs for government action, and finally into a willing sponsor of urban renewal projects.

The cardinal's newfound activism did not go unnoticed. In February 1968 the National Conference of Christians and Jews gave him its annual brotherhood award. In the presence of Chief Justice Warren and other dignitaries of church and state, President Johnson (the previous year's recipient) bestowed the honor on a decidedly uncomfortable O'Boyle. Yet he was comfortable enough to preach a little homily to the crowd. He derided the term brotherhood as a "fatuous, not to say cynical slogan" if it did not include a personal commitment to break down barriers. Minorities must be "wanted, welcome, and accepted," he concluded, challenging his fellow citizens to a vigorous effort to influence organizations like labor unions, educational institutions, and neighborhoods.[64] The National Association for the Advancement of Colored Peoples added its plaudits. Echoing what it called liberty-loving Americans on the Washington scene, it awarded O'Boyle a special citation for his recent efforts to achieve "full democracy for all."[65]

Riot

In keeping with his own cherished belief in nonviolence, Cardinal O'Boyle found himself in sympathy not only with Martin Luther King's goals (although not the civil rights leader's strong opposition to the Vietnam War) but also with his methods of protest. In March 1968 King announced plans for yet another demonstration in Washington; this time a contingent of needy people would petition government officials for help. While in the city they would camp near the Lincoln Memorial in what was dubbed Resurrection City. The archdiocesan priests' senate endorsed what it called the mobilization of the poor and recommended that O'Boyle order the chancery to use its resources to support King. Not only did O'Boyle agree, but he also arranged for a group of priests to visit Resurrection City periodically and for Catholic Charities to contribute bedding and other supplies to the protestors.[66]

Star, 26, 27, and 30 Oct 1967, and 4 Mar 1973. See also ltr., O'Boyle to Dear Friends in Christ, 18 Apr 1968, AAW.

64. *America* (2 Mar 1968): p. 283 (source of quotes). See also *NYT*, 16 Feb 1968.

65. As quoted in *CIR* (vol. 33): pp. 128 and 264.

66. Minutes of the Priests' Senate, 27 Mar 1968, SOP file, AAW. See also Arthur intv.

The spirit of nonviolence suffered a major defeat when "the apostle of nonviolence," as O'Boyle called King, was assassinated in Memphis on April 4. When word reached Washington late that afternoon, groups of angry black residents, especially those in the upper Fourteenth Street corridor near SS. Paul and Augustine Church and within sight of the V Street Center, took to the streets. Only later that night did overextended police managed to gain control, but not before scores of businesses and residences were burned and looted. Father Baroni could smell the tear gas in his rooms. When he and Msgr. Gingras, both well known to the people of the area, ventured out to view the damage in their parish, they were warned by friendly neighbors to return to the safety of the rectory. Following a night of relative calm the violence escalated. President Johnson called in federal and National Guard forces as a shocked nation watched veteran Army units with rifles and bayonets at the ready patrolling the streets of the capital.[67]

Mayor Washington invited Cardinal O'Boyle and several other church leaders to join him at the government's command center. Using back streets Father Baroni chauffeured the cardinal downtown, using the time to brief him on what the mayor was going to propose. As Baroni had learned through his civil rights network, Washington was going to urge the religious leaders to issue a televised plea for calm and order. The street-savvy priest was skeptical of such a plan. "The rioters aren't watching TV," he told O'Boyle, "they're stealing TVs."[68] More important, the mayor hoped to get O'Boyle and the others to side with him in opposing the many business executives who were demanding that the president order the troops to shoot to kill. Not only would such a tactic lead to many innocent deaths, O'Boyle and Baroni agreed, but it would also extend the riot, which was already showing signs of petering out in the face of the strong military presence. O'Boyle followed this line of reasoning in speaking to those in the command center. He argued forcibly against a shoot-to-kill order, and subsequent to the meeting federal and city authorities rejected the businessmen's request.[69]

At the same time the cardinal was aware of the need to impose order on the marauders. At that same meeting he told the mayor, "Walter, take hold of the city." Yet even as he urged officials to go on the initiative, he showed sympathy for those roaming the burned-out streets. "If you and I had to live like that," he

67. The most comprehensive description and analysis of the Washington riots is found in Paul J. Scheips, *The Role of Federal Military Forces in Domestic Disturbances, 1945-1992* (Washington: GPO, 2005), chapter 10.

68. As quoted in Dianda intv.

69. O'Rourke, *Geno*, pp. 57-58.

told Baroni, "we'd have burned the town long ago."[70] Although it was unlikely to reach his intended audience, the cardinal nevertheless issued a call for calm, arguing that the way to honor Dr. King's memory was by striving constantly to use his methods to achieve the goals for which he gave his life.[71] The cardinal expressed much the same ideas in a pastoral letter read at Palm Sunday's Masses on April 7. Viewing the riots in Washington and the disturbances that week in 125 other American cities, he concluded that the greatest danger came from extremists who could never defeat King in life and were now trying to convince people that violence worked. Palm Sunday found the cardinal at the Shrine leading a congregation of four thousand in a memorial service for the slain civil rights leader. With the return of relative calm on Monday, he spent the day with Father Baroni visiting the Catholic service centers around the city, where hundreds of volunteers were busy with the task of feeding and clothing great numbers of citizens who lacked access to stores and homes in their burned-out neighborhoods. The next day he and Mayor Washington flew on Vice-President Hubert Humphrey's plane to Atlanta, where they attended King's funeral.

The riot appeared to spur O'Boyle to greater involvement. On April 18 he announced a temporary moratorium on all new ecclesiastical building with the exception of emergency projects. Anticipating objections, he added a postscript: the moratorium covered those funds parishes received from the archdiocese; it would not assess parish funds, which had been amassed by congregations for specific building and renovation projects. O'Boyle explained that the moratorium, the first imposed in any diocese, was needed because of the increased outlay for social services in the wake of the riot. Noting that many considered decent and safe housing one of the highest forms of Christian charity, he asked for generous support for a planned special collection even while acknowledging the burden that the accelerated programs of the Urban Coalition and his own Urban Rehabilitation Corporation would impose on local Catholics.[72]

Undeterred by critics, O'Boyle continued his personal anti-poverty campaign, never deviating essentially from the course he laid out before the riot. In May 1968 he notified Archbishop Dearden, president of the NCCB's administrative board, about efforts of the National Medical Association Foundation to develop an approved health care system for the urban poor. "I'm on board," he

---

70. Herrmann intv. (first quote) and Baroni intv. (second quote).

71. *WP*, 5 Apr 1968.

72. Ltr., O'Boyle to Dear Fathers, 11 Apr 1968, copy in McKenna Papers, GUA. See also *Star* and *NYT*, 18 Apr 1968.

Resurrection City. Led by Father Geno Baroni, Cardinal O'Boyle and his secretary, Father John Donoghue, visit the headquarters of the civil rights protesters, March 1968.

told Dearden, who quickly added his endorsement. O'Boyle also allocated more funds for the growing number of service centers financed by Catholic Charities.[73] In a decidedly unusual reaction to unsolicited suggestions from subordinates, he listened to a group of priests who had boldly suggested that some black Catholics be added to the chancery staff. He promised to give their suggestion serious consideration.[74] In subsequent months several African Americans were added.

Six months after the riot the cardinal was on hand to dedicate the seven remodeled houses on K Street at North Capitol. He surprised Baroni by granting permission for the purchase of three hundred more properties and urged the

73. Ltrs., O'Boyle to Dearden, 14 May 1968 (source of quote), and Dearden to O'Boyle, 31 May 1968. For extra funds for service centers, see, for example, ltr., O'Boyle to Rev. Ralph Dwan, 10 May 1968. All in Chancery file, AAW.

74. Ltr., O'Boyle to Dwan, 13 May 1968, copy in McKenna Papers, GUA.

334 Civil Rights Crusader

head of his Urban Rehabilitation Corporation to apply for federal funds for the project before the just-elected Richard Nixon scuttled the program.[75] In the end O'Boyle gave the corporation $135,000 to re-do fifty-one houses, which were then sold to low-income families who borrowed the necessary money from the federal government's so-called 221H program. Nor did O'Boyle give up on Richard Nixon. Reacting to rumors that the president wanted to tour the K Street homes and meet their new owners, he extended an invitation through H. R. Haldeman, Nixon's chief of staff, asking him to make an appointment with Father Baroni.[76]

The federal government's war on poverty, which O'Boyle strongly endorsed, underwent dramatic change in the months following the riot. Many African Americans, reflecting growing black self-awareness and self-reliance, turned away from programs associated with their white allies in the civil rights movement. Many white volunteers resented their exclusion from prominent places in the movement and turned instead to other pressing issues, principally the anti–Vietnam War movement. Even Cardinal O'Boyle, who after September 1968 was deeply involved in a debate with a significant number of priests over birth control, was diverted from his previous concentration on the subject. Nevertheless he never abandoned his personal war on poverty. As he declared to a gathering of the John Carroll Society in October 1968:

> Today there are poor people—too many people—who are really poor, miserably poor. . . . Right here in Washington there is a terrible contrast between the poverty of many of our people living in the inner city and the affluence that is evident when you walk along Connecticut Avenue or drive across the park to the northwest—where I live. . . . This contrast between poverty and luxury is no mere fact of nature like the difference between winter and summer. To a great extent poverty resulted from injustice in the past and it continues to exist because of injustices we have not yet taken the trouble to end. . . . More important than money are the lives salvaged, the homes and families preserved, the young given a chance, the aged sheltered and cared for.[77]

A warrior pronouncing his creed in the fight against poverty, O'Boyle would cherish these sentiments throughout his remaining years as the shepherd of Catholic Washington.

75. Baroni intv. See also *Star*, 10 Nov 1968.
76. Ltr., O'Boyle to Erlichman, 19 Mar 1969, copy in Chancery file, AAW.
77. O'Boyle, "The Christian in Today's World," speech given before the John Carroll Society, 20 Oct 1968, copy in JCS Files, ACUA.

CHAPTER 14

'State in Fide'

The Archdiocese of Washington found itself at the center of the controversy over artificial birth control that erupted in 1968. Pope John XXIII had exempted the subject from the deliberations of the Vatican Council and instead appointed a commission of experts to examine the matter. Bypassing the recommendations of the reconstituted commission's majority, his successor, Paul VI, reiterated in July 1968 the Church's traditional condemnation of contraception in his encyclical *Humanae Vitae.* Among those who sought a different approach to this moral problem was a loosely formed group of priests in Washington. Encouraged by the judgment of some American theologians, principally faculty members of Catholic University, they issued a Statement of Conscience that denied the dogmatic nature of the encyclical and insisted that couples should consult their own consciences in deciding if in their particular case birth control was licit.

Such an approach was entirely alien to Cardinal O'Boyle. His unwavering fidelity to the pope and his own responsibility as a bishop, his moral sensibilities formed in the pre–Vatican II Church, and his determination that theological debate should not be allowed to confuse the faithful prompted him to demand that the dissenting priests renounce their position and in their preaching and counseling as well as in the confessional adhere strictly to the explicit teaching of the encyclical. To counsel souls contrary to the express directions of the papal decree, he was convinced, was clearly wrong, and actions contrary to those teachings were immoral.

A significant number of those who had signed the Statement of Conscience, including members of religious orders in the area, spurned his demand. Thus the battle lines were drawn in a conflict that would be played out in the glare of national publicity and would result in the loss of many talented priests before the issue was finally adjudicated in Rome.

Early Skirmishes

No one doubted the cardinal's opposition to artificial birth control. Some of his critics attributed his stand to a lack of pastoral experience. He never assumed confessional duties in Washington—his secretary was convinced that he had even forgotten the form for absolution. Yet while his experience was not recent, his many hours "in the box" as a curate and during his years of residence in various New York parishes must have provided him with some understanding of the issue.[1] And if it were true, as one of his closest colleagues observed, that O'Boyle's life experiences had denied him any real appreciation of the sexual aspects of marriage and even the mechanics of contraception, his many years of association with the Family Life Movement familiarized him with the sociological and economic consequences of a large family and the sacrifices it demanded of a Catholic couple.[2] Actually, such speculation was beside the point. Throughout his life Patrick O'Boyle looked to Rome and the pope for the ultimate judgment on all moral matters. The Church had always considered artificial birth control illicit, a position reaffirmed by Pope Paul. So be it.

In August 1965 the cardinal delivered a sermon on the subject of contraception in St. Matthew's Cathedral. He was particularly concerned that the continued silence of the bishops was encouraging federal officials in their eagerness to offer information on birth control, thereby intruding into the moral lives of citizens. Moreover, he criticized those so-called Catholic experts who, he said, by predicting imminent change in the Church's traditional teachings were causing moral confusion in the unsettled period during which the pope and his commission continued studying the matter.

Adopting a new approach, the archbishop used constitutional rather than theological arguments to press his opposition. Proposed legislation dealing with contraception, especially the dissemination of birth control information through the Johnson administration's antipoverty program, he declared, was "a clear invasion of the sacred right of privacy which the Supreme Court holds to be invio-

1. Many of those interviewed, including Archbishops Hannan and Donoghue and Father Higgins, underscored O'Boyle's lack of pastoral experience, which they saw as one of the factors in what followed.

2. Donoghue and Gillen intvs.

late." While the government might properly research the subject, he conceded, the minute it presumed to give advice on contraception "it opens the door to influencing the free decision of its citizens." Pointing to those who were already calling for "motivating" citizens to limit the size of their families, he warned that only a thin line now existed between availability and coercion, especially among poor African Americans.[3]

The sermon earned not only national headlines but editorial criticism. O'Boyle had timed his talk to coincide with Senate hearings on increasing the government's role in family planning. The subcommittee chairman invited him to testify, but with the last session of Vatican II pending, he declined. Instead William Ball, a lawyer who often worked with the bishops' administrative board, delivered a statement before the committee that also stressed the privacy issue. At its November meeting in Rome, the administrative board authorized Ball to prepare a brief for Sargeant Shriver, head of the Office of Economic Opportunity, in opposition to the claim that the Economic Opportunity Act of 1964 authorized funds for birth control programs.[4]

O'Boyle pressed his fellow bishops to publish a declaration defending the Church's traditional position and its opposition to government initiatives. He won the administrative board's agreement to draft a statement for Vatican review. With Rome's approval and following lengthy discussion by the board, a statement reflecting O'Boyle's criticism of public policy on birth control was issued on November 14, 1966, more than a year after his strenuous condemnation in St. Matthew's.[5]

If the 1965 sermon signaled O'Boyle's firm stand against contraception, the publication of the "Guidelines for the Teaching of Religion" in 1968 solidified his reputation as a leader of those opposing change. In light of the confused and sometimes contradictory instruction offered by the nation's teachers of Christian doctrine following Vatican II, Cardinal Shehan of Baltimore and O'Boyle, along with the bishops of Richmond and Wilmington, sponsored an authorized guide to teaching. The guidelines contained a statement that adumbrated the firm line

3. The sermon was widely quoted. See, for example, *NYT* and *Star*, 29 Aug 1965. The archdiocese published it under the title "Birth Control and Public Policy," copy in AAW. *Sign* (Nov 1965): pp. 37–38, offered an extensive analysis. For the many letters and comments on the sermon, see Chancery file, AAW.

4. Minutes of the Administrative Board, 13 Nov 1965, NCWC Papers, ACUA. See also ltr., Francis Hurley (assistant general secretary, NCWC) to Ellis, 13 Sep 1965, Ellis Papers, ACUA.

5. Minutes of the Administrative Board, 19 Apr and 5 Oct 1966, NCWC Papers, ACUA. For text, see "A Statement on the Government and Birth Control," in Nolan, ed., *Pastoral Letters of the U.S. Catholic Bishops*, vol. 3, pp. 65–73.

on birth control soon to be endorsed by the pope. O'Boyle wholeheartedly agreed with the sentence warning every teacher of religion in the region: "He may not permit or condone contraception practices." Ironically, Shehan, who was responsible for the wording of this document, had, as a member of the pope's birth control commission, supported the majority call for modification of the Church's traditional stand.

Publication of the guidelines aroused public protest by a number of priests and educators, most notably by the newly created Association of Washington Priests.[6] The association, which at its height claimed a third of the diocesan clergy as members, originated in a series of informal meetings of priests interested in fellowship and study, jokingly referred to as the "scotch and Scripture crowd." Later reorganized as the Vatican II Study Group, the still largely informal organization sponsored lectures and held discussions about theological and pastoral implications of the recently concluded council.[7] Several activist members sought to have the group express an opinion on the archdiocese's implementation of various changes in the liturgy, but they despaired of finding a consensus among their colleagues and decided instead to create a more formal organization.[8] Under the leadership of Father T. Joseph O'Donoghue, a dynamic, intellectually engaging young assistant pastor at St. Francis de Sales, they invited all the clergy in the archdiocese to join an Association of Washington Priests, the first group of its kind in the nation. They promised members the opportunity to discuss mutual concerns and get to know one another in a relaxed atmosphere where they could speak their minds. They also planned to invite experts to lead discussions of current topics. An executive committee was soon busy drawing up guidelines for study panels and preparing a definition of the organization's "ultimate aim," which was "to stimulate action when, where, and how this is warranted."[9]

No doubt unaware of this aim, Cardinal O'Boyle never objected to the formation of the association, nor did he discourage priests from joining. He was probably disconcerted by the group's continuing support for liturgical experimenta-

6. The guidelines were reprinted in *Social Justice* (Jul–Aug 1968): pp. 125ff. See also George A. Kelly, *The Battle for the American Church* (New York: Doubleday & Co., 1979), p. 167.

7. On the evolution of the Vatican II Study Group, see various memos and statements collected in the Chancery file, AAW.

8. Ltr., Rev. T. Joseph O'Donoghue to Ellis, 16 Apr 1967, Ellis Papers, ACUA.

9. "Suggested Guidelines for Study Groups of the Association of Washington Priests," n.d., copy in Chancery file, AAW. In his study "Dissent: The *Humanae Vitae* Controversy in Washington, D.C." (MA thesis, University of Maryland, 1987), Christopher M. Meagher offers a sympathetic account of the AWP. See especially pp. 74–101. See also Duffy intv. Father Duffy was one of the original members of the organization's executive committee.

tion and its defense of "the People." Nevertheless, he agreed to meet with its members to discuss reform. The meeting—a dialogue, O'Boyle called it—found the association and the cardinal in agreement on all the points discussed. O'Boyle promised to promote further liturgical reform; in turn the association called the meeting fruitful and a genuine addition to renewal.[10]

That October 1967 meeting proved to be the end of comity. While it is unfair to blame O'Donoghue for the rising animosity in the following months, his some-times strident confrontations with those directing reform in the archdiocese, probably a necessary element in his impatient effort to reshape the role of the Church in the lives of the people, was radicalizing the association by driving out some of its moderate members. These colleagues had become convinced that a few members of the association were using their position for their own purposes. Chancellor John Roeder went even further. During one of their daily post-lunch walks, he warned the cardinal that the archdiocese harbored about fifteen priests who were looking for trouble and just waiting for an issue "to hang their hat on." These priests were readily identifiable at the periodic clergy conferences, for they were the ones who poked fun at all sorts of earnest but sometimes ineffectual sug-gestions made by chancery officials. Pushed too far by such tactics at one meet-ing, O'Boyle invited the offenders to take their complaints to the apostolic dele-gate and offered to give them his address on Massachusetts Avenue.[11]

A second chance for better relations occurred in May 1968 when Father John (Jack) Corrigan, a popular assistant at St. Gabriel's with a large following throughout the city, informed the cardinal before it was publicly announced that he had been elected the association's new chairman. Further demonstrating his characteristic courtesy and tact, Corrigan added that the association firmly sup-ported the cardinal's 1968 charity appeal and looked for it to exceed his goal. Yet courtesy and tact did not prevent Corrigan, like his predecessor, from pushing the association's agenda. When O'Boyle vetoed a proposal that the priests' senate join the National Federation of Priests Councils, Corrigan supported O'-Donoghue's successful effort to secure their association's membership in the fed-eration. The national federation existed to speak out on issues of the day, and true to its word provided vital support for the Washington group when trouble erupted.[12]

10. Ltr., O'Boyle to Father Joseph Byron, 28 Sep 1967; Association Press Release, 17 Oct 1967. Both in Chancery file, AAW. On O'Boyle's view of the association before the *Humanae Vitae* crisis, see Donoghue and Duffy intvs.

11. As quoted in Coady intv.

12. Ltr., O'Donoghue to Dear Members, 22 May 1968, Chancery file, AAW. See also ltr., O'-Donoghue to Ellis, 21 Apr 1968, Ellis Papers, ACUA.

Crisis in the Capital

On June 24, 1968, Father Joseph Coyne, a pastor usually sympathetic to the cardinal's efforts to carry out council reforms, confessed that his hopes for the archdiocese were not high. In many areas it was business as usual, he explained. Duly constituted bodies like the priests' senate and the personnel committee were for all practical purposes ignored. A number of priests, convinced that the chancery was growing resistant to change and, doubtful that a more forward-looking attitude would ever emerge, were drifting off on their own. In place of unity in the archdiocese, Coyne saw only an increasing fracture that served mainly to scandalize the people.[13]

Publication of the "Guidelines for the Teaching of Religion" in July 1968 provided a further example of the conditions lamented by Coyne. The cardinal had failed to consult the priests' senate or the archdiocese's Advisory Board for Religious Education before approving the document. At this point the Association of Washington Priests waded in. Claiming to reflect the view of 142 local clergy, its spokesman asked, "What would these groups ever be consulted about if not such a document?" In an open letter to the cardinal on July 27, the association declared that many diocesan priests could not follow the directive on contraception because "it gives no room for either probable opinion regarding the practice of contraception or the right of conscience so clearly enunciated in the documents of Vatican II." Citing the judgment of several European bishops who respected the consciences of those practicing responsible family planning, the association told the cardinal that for him to brand such actions sinful was "a judgment the association regarded as excessive."[14] O'Boyle, no doubt aware of the imminent publication of the encyclical that would confirm the guidelines, but anxious to keep it secret, rejected the association's request to discuss the matter.

Considering the prominence the secular press gave to the association's statement, reaction to *Humanae Vitae,* issued on July 29, seemed almost anticlimactic. A group of fourteen theologians on Catholic University's faculty, with Father Curran in the lead, issued a statement on July 30 that offered detailed arguments against the infallibility of the document. Citing the "common teaching of the Church" that Catholics might dissent from non-infallible declarations of the magisterium "when sufficient reasons for so doing exist," they concluded that

13. Ltr., Coyne to Ellis, 24 Jun 1968, Ellis Papers, ACUA.
14. As quoted in *NYT,* 28 Jul 1968.

spouses could decide in conscience that artificial birth control was "permissible and indeed necessary" to preserve and foster the value and sacredness of marriage.[15] The fourteen original signers were soon joined by seventy colleagues phoning in from around the country. Eventually scores of other theologians lined up with their Catholic University friends.

Emboldened by the theologians, who would provide expert support in the coming conflict, the leaders of the Washington priest-dissenters issued their Statement of Conscience the same day. Hastily prepared, the public dissent from the pope's encyclical was verbally agreed to by sixty or more diocesan priests, many of whom had not yet read the encyclical or the statement prepared by their chairman, Father Corrigan.[16] The Statement of Conscience quoted the conclusions of the theologians on the primacy of conscience, adding that this position was "perfectly compatible" with loyalty to Christ and the Church. Pastoral ministry, they declared, must take into account not only papal decrees and theological judgments, but also "the practical day-to-day lives of those who are striving to live in the grace of Christ." The signers concluded with the hope that they could enter into dialogue with the cardinal and the whole community "to explore the dimensions of this most complex issue."[17]

Some critics later concluded that O'Boyle reacted impetuously to these statements and, once so committed, found himself unable to dismantle the confrontation he created. This thesis is not supported by the facts. The cardinal learned of the two statements while in Hershey, Pennsylvania, a favorite stopover on the way to his annual vacation in Scranton. Believing as he did that as bishop he had no choice but to give his full support to the pope, he called in a brief statement to his secretary in Washington for release to the priests of the archdiocese.[18] He began by citing Vatican II's Dogmatic Constitution on the Church, which declared that the pope's teaching authority extended beyond *ex cathedra* declarations and must be adhered to "according to his mind and will." While not precluded from

15. "Statement of Catholic Theologians," 30 Jul 1968, copy in Higgins Papers, ACUA.

16. The number of dissenters at any time during the crisis is open to debate. Meagher (in "Dissent") lists sixty-one association members who verbally agreed to the document. Later he discusses the fifty-two members who actually signed. Father O'Donoghue claimed that 71 out of 101 members signed. *Star* (5 Aug 1968) printed the names of fifty-one signers, a number of whom were nonmembers. *WP* (5 Aug 1958) counted fifty-two priests issuing the statement, again including nonmembers.

17. "Statement of Conscience," 30 Jul 1968, issued by John E. Corrigan, copy in Higgins Papers, ACUA.

18. Donoghue intv. Archbishop Donoghue accompanied the cardinal during that Pennsylvania trip.

theological discussion, *Humanae Vitae,* he declared, was nevertheless the authentic teaching of the Church, binding in conscience and exempt from public questioning. He concluded by instructing his priests to follow this authentic teaching in their preaching, instructing, and hearing of confessions. He added optimistically that he knew all would present the pope's decision to the faithful.[19]

With the threat of a canonical process looming, O'Boyle turned to his lawyer, Msgr. E. Robert Arthur, for advice. But if he listened to Arthur about procedure, he consulted Father John Ford, the Jesuit theologian who had helped develop the birth control statement in the recently issued guidelines for teachers, on the substance of the dissent. Ford agreed to help and recommended that O'Boyle also seek the advice of Georgetown professor Germaine Grisez, an expert on the theological implications of the dissenters' position. Actually, Grisez had provided O'Boyle with advice the year before during the Catholic University crisis. Although his suggestions had been rejected by O'Boyle at that time, he was willing to join Ford in helping the cardinal develop his arguments. At the time the cardinal was convinced that he could demonstrate to the signers of the Statement of Conscience that their reading of the encyclical was in error and thus secure a hasty retraction. It was inconceivable to him during these first weeks that he could not make them see the light and recant.[20]

Grisez and Ford worked for several days drafting a pastoral letter for O'Boyle, which they went over with him in detail on August 2, 1968. Redrafted at the cardinal's direction, it was read at all Masses the following Sunday. The document was deeply pastoral, uncharacteristically personal, even confessional in spirit, yet allowed for no compromise from obedience to the pope's teaching. In the letter O'Boyle even admitted that he could never really appreciate how difficult it was for Catholic couples to follow the Church's rules, but asked all to obey "as we are in conscience bound to do," and to accept "the cross Christ was asking us to bear."

At the same time he claimed that America's bishops were solidly behind the pope, who had simply reiterated what the Church had always taught. "Even the most expert theologian," he declared, "must accept the teaching authority of the Church—that authority which resides in the Bishops, and especially in the successor of Peter." He went on to develop his argument. The bishops, with the

19. Ltr., O'Boyle to Reverend and Dear Father, 1 Aug 1968, copy in Higgins Papers, ACUA.
20. Donoghue intv. Again the number of dissenters is open to question. The cardinal's letter, signed on August 2, was sent out to sixty-four priests.

pope at their head, were the successors of the apostles. It followed that those who dissent from the pope's teachings actually are refusing to listen to Christ. The point at issue, he concluded, was not only the Church's moral teaching authority, "but her very unity which is centered in the Vicar of Christ."[21] He confessed how difficult it was to be a bishop in the face of opposition from priests and theologians, but he remained optimistic that the dissenters would soon come to accept the encyclical. In fact, he reported, some had already changed their minds. In the trying months of strife ahead Cardinal O'Boyle would never issue a more personal, simple confession of his faith in the Church and his uncomplicated loyalty to its teachings than in this hastily prepared pastoral letter.

While dining with Grisez and Ford on August 2, the cardinal asked the young professor to work for him for a year on the issue. Grisez's role would increase in importance during that time. Their collaboration informed their very similar reading of the crisis. Two of O'Boyle's closest associates concluded that Grisez was his most influential advisor, at least in the first, critical months of dissent. Of particular importance was O'Boyle's wholehearted acceptance of Grisez's blunt "my way or no way" approach to the demands of the dissenters.[22]

Only as the crisis deepened in late September 1968 would the cardinal begin to widen his pool of advisors. In truth, he was losing the argument in the press, which the dissenters skillfully exploited to their advantage. It was obvious that the often unvarnished and provocative expression of his views led to the inaccurate impression of an impatient and petulant leader dealing unfairly with dedicated subordinates. He belatedly realized that his being cast as an inflexible tyrant dealing with a group of sincere defenders of the primacy of conscience was generating sympathy for the dissenters and, his major concern, causing some loyal Catholics in the pews to waver in their support of traditional Church teaching. The cardinal admired Grisez's forthright and inflexible approach to a subject they agreed upon, but as Grisez would warn O'Boyle on a later occasion, sometimes a response should be "brief and soft, and I'm not the one to know how to write that way!"[23]

To help counter the generally received impression, O'Boyle enlisted the advice of some of his close lay supporters, principally Walter McArdle, William Abell, and Ray Dufour. All prominent Washington figures with considerable knowledge of the local scene, these men would meet informally with O'Boyle to

21. Ltr., O'Boyle to Dear Friends in Christ, 2 Aug 1968, copy in Higgins Papers, ACUA.
22. Arthur and Donoghue (source of quote) intvs.
23. Ltr., Grisez to O'Boyle, 24 Dec 1971, *Humanae Vitae* file, AAW.

discuss the best way to present his position. McArdle confessed that at times they seemed to have convinced the cardinal to adopt a course of action only to learn that he reversed himself after consulting with Grisez. O'Boyle once admitted that McArdle and the others had recommended that he not address the crisis too often, "either in person or by issuing letters," but he would listen to Grisez and published yet another pastoral letter on the subject in late September, an especially hard-line statement which he read from St. Matthew's pulpit.[24] Such decisions bothered McArdle, perhaps O'Boyle's closest personal friend in the city. He considered Grisez a hard-liner whose lack of "resiliency" precluded any debate on a course of action. Msgr. Arthur noted that Grisez served as a "burr under the saddle" of the others. For his part the cardinal appeared to ignore the tension and took what advice he wanted from either side.[25]

Leaving Grisez and Ford to draft a detailed response to the dissenters during that hectic August, O'Boyle joined Cardinals McIntyre, Cody, and Krol (Cardinal Shehan was notably absent from the group) in a hasty trip to Rome. When discovered by the press, they explained their unexpected presence as an attempt to get the pope to stop over in the United States during his forthcoming visit to South America. The ruse fooled no one, and it became common knowledge that they were at the Vatican to be reassured about the pope's intentions in his encyclical.[26] The Washington chancery denied reports that the cardinals never even secured an audience, explaining that "the one who spoke Italian best" represented the four in a meeting with the pope. The Holy Father assured them that he meant exactly what he wrote in *Humanae Vitae* and he expected the world's bishops to enforce it.[27] The highly unusual picture of three princes of the Church cooling their heels while their colleague consulted with the pope may well be accurate, since growing Vatican concern about the critical reception of the encyclical precluded any hint of a formal meeting with hard-line supporters.

Back from Rome, O'Boyle reviewed the draft statement prepared by Grisez and Ford that outlined at length his views and those of the dissenters as he understood them, along with a disquisition on freedom of conscience and his formula for a speedy resolution of the crisis. It was sent in the form of a ten-page letter to each of the sixty-one priests still associated with the Statement of Conscience. If the tone of the document was nonconfrontational and low-key, its

24. Ltr., O'Boyle to George H. Hern, 23 Oct 1968, copy in *Humanae Vitae* file, AAW.
25. McArdle, Abell, and Arthur intvs.
26. Donoghue intv.
27. As quoted in *NYT Magazine*, 24 Nov 1968. See also *NYT*, 11 and 17 Aug 1968.

conclusion was forthright and presented the position from which O'Boyle would never deviate in the long months ahead. I am your bishop, he reminded the priests; I commissioned you to teach and preach Catholic doctrine in strict accordance with the Church's teachings. To present this teaching as only one alternative is not in accordance with that doctrine. "I cannot allow you to diverge from this *[Humanae Vitae]* teaching, because I can only authorize you to do what I am authorized to do myself." He begged the priests to reject the spirit of dissent "which could tear [the Church] apart, could rip the body of Christ limb from limb."

Regarding the multiple requests for some sort of arbitration, O'Boyle stated that a bishop could not carry on a public disputation with his priests when they refuse to accept a teaching clearly articulated by the pope. That kind of debate, he declared, "would burn the Church down, not build it up." In the letter's final page his steely resolve revealed itself most clearly. "My conscience as a Bishop and your public statements . . . are forcing me into a position where I will have to do what I do not want to do. Will you help me find a happier way of resolving my dilemma?" Finally, he requested individual responses outlining each dissenter's reaction to his letter wherein each would state what he planned to do. He would be overjoyed, he concluded with a muster of hope, "if you are able to tell me you have changed your mind."[28]

Responding on August 21 for most of the dissenters, Father Corrigan rejected the idea of individual answers. Since theirs was a corporate statement, only a corporate response was appropriate, he claimed. He went on to lament the cardinal's implication that the Statement of Conscience was not in accord with authentic teaching, especially in light of those bishops around the world who had issued similar statements. Despite O'Boyle's obvious determination to avoid debate, Corrigan appended a list of questions, largely a rehash of issues the cardinal had already addressed.[29]

Nine dissenters responded individually to the cardinal's letter and were eventually reconciled. Included in this group was Msgr. Paul F. Furfey, Catholic University's preeminent social scientist, who had worked with O'Boyle on many inner-city projects. Furfey's response was significant because his conclusions not only foreshadowed the Vatican's ruling three long years ahead, but also

28. Ltr., O'Boyle to Fathers. There is some confusion about the date of this letter. Some were marked 10 August, others 14 August 1968. Apparently they were mailed in two batches. For a copy of the letter see Furfey Papers, ACUA.

29. Ltr., Corrigan to O'Boyle, 21 Aug 1968, copy in Furfey Papers, ACUA.

demonstrated that, despite his words, the cardinal was willing to compromise to a degree. Furfey gently posited that encyclicals were not infallible. Some, in fact, had been reversed. He recalled for the cardinal the example of the Church's teaching on money lending. *Humanae Vitae,* he believed, should be treated in the same manner as the great social encyclicals, likewise vital Church teachings. They were never considered infallible, and many thoughtful Catholics differed from the pope on numerous social issues. Like those encyclicals, *Humanae Vitae* should be considered an authoritative statement on contraception. Since many competent theologians disagreed on the encyclical's infallibility, Furfey admitted that he would not refuse absolution to a person who, in good faith, dissented.

Furfey slightly amended his position a few days later. He had come to believe, he reported again to O'Boyle, it was necessary to consent internally to the doctrine set out in *Humanae Vitae,* that is, in the abstract, contraception was evil. But, he added, circumstances sometimes change the nature of an act to such an extent that it ceased to be evil, and he could find nothing in the encyclical that declared contraception evil "under all conceivable circumstances," a belief, he claimed, that would guide him in the confessional. At the same time he admitted he was no theologian and promised to keep his beliefs to himself.[30]

Writing to Corrigan at about the same time, Furfey confessed that he could not understand precisely what the pope and the hierarchy wanted the dissenters to admit.

> The only point about which I feel strongly is my belief that it is not certain that birth control is under all circumstances a mortal sin. Well, strangely enough, no one seems to contradict me on that. The Encyclical didn't. The Cardinal didn't. No one has told me that I must give up my belief on that particular point. So what is all the fuss about?[31]

Confrontation

Furfey heard no more from O'Boyle on the subject, and he remained a priest in good standing in the archdiocese. But he would learn what all the fuss was about when the cardinal began meting out punishments. Actually, O'Boyle had not lost hope that at least the majority would respond to his plea and be reconciled. Ignoring the flood of negative publicity, he tried to contain the issue. His dealings with the men during mid-August were patient, even fatherly, and always

---

30. Ltr., Furfey to O'Boyle, 16 Aug 1968, and an undated addendum (ca. 20 Aug 1968). Copy of both in Furfey Papers, ACUA.
31. Ltr. Furfey to Corrigan, 20 Aug 1968, copy in Furfey Papers, ACUA.

respectful. His approach proved productive, as demonstrated by those few who once supported the Statement of Conscience only later to disassociate themselves from public dissent. Still, there was a limit to his patience. If priests would not comply with the Church's teaching, he believed, then as bishop he had to act. It was not a matter of choice or opinion. Like the dissenters and unlike the great majority of bishops, the cardinal found himself painted in a corner with no room for compromise. Toward the end of August he had come to believe that he must adopt a new, altogether hard-line approach. His decision to do so, which he sincerely believed was forced upon him, only served to unite the opposition and dash his hope for a speedy and favorable outcome to the crisis.

And so in his role as chancellor of the university, he called a meeting of the Catholic University theology faculty for August 20. The cardinal faced a critical audience, which listened to his views and demands and in turn argued for the right to dissent. O'Boyle also read a statement on freedom of conscience. In it he addressed the criticism that he was out of step with many other bishops around the world. He stood with the pope, he added, and any disagreement between him and his brother bishops was matter for the pope to judge.[32] At the end of the meeting the cardinal announced that he would probably refer the matter to the university's board of trustees. Particularly ominous for teachers so lately involved in issues of academic freedom, O'Boyle added that disciplining the faculty would involve "complex legal problems and due process" not only in law but also in academic procedure.[33]

As he proved in the university controversy the year before, Father Curran clearly knew how to play the media. O'Boyle was never so skilled, and the whole affair degenerated into a highly publicized Irish dogfight. O'Boyle was clearly irritated when Father Curran and others reported that the meeting had showed that both sides were essentially in agreement. In a statement released to the press, an angry O'Boyle accused the theologians of "spreading propaganda," of "purposefully causing confusion among the faithful," and of being "unfair" to him personally by deliberately misrepresenting his views. Listening patiently to them, he added, in no way implied agreement.

The meeting with the theology faculty was followed on August 30 by a similar session with thirty-five of the dissenting priests (O'Boyle would meet with the

32. "Freedom of Conscience," a statement by Cardinal O'Boyle read to priests at the Theological College, encl., Vice-Chancellor Donoghue to Reverend and Dear Father, 11 Sep 1968, copy in Higgins Papers, ACUA.

33. As quoted in *WP*, 22 Aug 1968. See also *CS*, 22 Aug; *Star*, 18 and 22 Aug; and *NYT*, 24 Aug 1968.

rest the following week). The cardinal ordered them to retract their statement, and he set a deadline: by September 14 they must accept his pastoral instruction to "teach, preach, and hear confessions in accordance with the encyclical" or face "canonical penalties."[34] Adopting an authoritative tone, O'Boyle directed that each priest at the meeting rise and identify himself. One young dissenter, to gales of laughter, identified himself not by his own name but by the name of one of the archdiocese's notorious milquetoasts. O'Boyle probably caught the implied criticism, but wisely ignored an act which so obviously amused his audience.[35] He did not, however, overlook the abrupt departure of Father O'-Donoghue from the meeting before receiving the cardinal's admonition. Actually, unknown to O'Boyle, O'Donoghue had pressing parish business that afternoon. O'Boyle, on the other hand, only saw one of the ringleaders walking out while he was speaking.[36]

The cardinal's order left the dissenters little room for maneuver. With no avenue of appeal except to a decidedly unsympathetic Roman curia, they seemed left with a stark choice. But on the day following his meeting with the dissenters, the cardinal handed them a whole new issue to exploit. Throughout his long career as an administrator, O'Boyle had always been noted for his prudent response to all sorts of provocations, but that weekend he lost his temper and for once acted impetuously. On Saturday evening, August 31, he phoned Father O'-Donoghue and told him to present himself at the chancery to receive the pastoral admonition he had missed because of his early departure from the meeting the day before. O'Donoghue refused unless he was allowed to bring counsel. With that the cardinal had his secretary drive him to the St. Francis de Sales rectory, where he confronted a surprised O'Donoghue, suspended his faculties to teach, preach, or offer Mass publicly, and ordered him to vacate the premises within four days.

Actually O'Donoghue had been a thorn in O'Boyle's side for some time. Clearly impatient with the pace of reform in the archdiocese, he would use the Association of Washington Priests to provoke action in a whole variety of areas, contraception and the role of conscience in interpreting Church law among them. When the cardinal ordered his first pastoral letter on contraception to be

34. As quoted in Pastoral Instruction to the Priests of the Archdiocese of Washington, encl. to ltr., O'Boyle to Reverend and Dear Father, 2 Sep 1968, *Humanae Vitae* file, AAW. See also page one reports in *Star* and *WP*, 3 Sep 1968. See also *WP*, 4 Sep, and *NYT*, 3 and 4 Sep 1968.
35. Dignan intv. Father Dignan was one of those in the audience called on to identify himself.
36. Meagher, "Dissent," pp. 46–49, provides a detailed account of the incident based on his interview with Father Corrigan. See also *NYT Magazine,* 24 Nov 1968, and Donoghue intv.

read without comment at every Mass on August 4, O'Donoghue had read the letter and then, without stating his own views, read the statements of several European bishops and American theologians, which appeared identical to the association's Statement of Conscience and contrary to O'Boyle's letter. During the tense meeting at St. Francis de Sales, O'Boyle told O'Donoghue that he had received calls and visits from several unidentified parishioners who were concerned and confused by O'Donoghue's readings during Mass on August 4.

O'Boyle's action, the Federation of Priests' Councils later claimed, penalized O'Donoghue without benefit of counsel, without the chance to confront his accusers or even know their identity, and without learning the specific charges being leveled against him. There were no provisions in canon law to adjudicate such issues, but every American grasped instinctively that the priest's rights were being violated. O'Donoghue would take full advantage of this basic understanding of justice and overnight became a sympathetic victim, giving his colleagues a new issue that revived their flagging hopes. Reaction was immediate and earned the cardinal front-page headlines and critical editorials in the press as well as lengthy notice in *Time* and *Newsweek*.[37] To attend the annual Labor Day Mass on September 2, he was forced to walk through a noisy picket line of The People carrying placards that read "Boil O'Boyle in Oil." Meanwhile the National Federation of Priests' Councils, while conceding that assistant priests had no due process rights under canon law, insisted that such priests should enjoy some basic rights. It called on O'Boyle to reconsider his action and appoint an impartial investigator. It also announced its intention to appeal to the administrative committee of the bishops' conference, not only to work toward a resolution of the O'Donoghue case, but also to study what it saw as the underlying problem, the lack of due process in the Church.

To make his position clear to the faithful, the cardinal took the unusual step of holding a press conference on September 3, during which he publicized the deadline he had imposed on the dissenting priests and warned that his duty as bishop required him to remove any priest who rejected the teachings of the pope. For its part the Association of Washington Priests immediately countered with a news conference of its own. Standing on the steps of the cathedral, Father Corrigan, among others, used the occasion to demonstrate what they saw as O'Boyle's arbitrary behavior, asking why O'Donoghue was singled out when the parish's other assistant, Father James C. Kennelly, had read the same statements at his Masses. Corrigan also announced that the dissenters were appealing to

37. See, for example, *Star* and *WP*, 6 Sep 1968. See also *Time*, 13 Sep 1968.

Archbishop Dearden, president of the bishops' conference, to establish a special board to mediate the dispute. *Commonweal,* the prestigious magazine run by laymen, waded into the fray. Predicting that O'Boyle's tactics would drive conscientious priests out of ministry, it warned that "the course the ultramontane followers like O'Boyle are following" could only lead to disaster.[38] Finally, in a slap at the cardinal, the newly formed parish council at St. Francis de Sales invited O'Donoghue to stay in the parish.

The O'Donoghue case gave the dissenters a new issue, but they still faced the cardinal's deadline for a response to his pastoral instruction. In the weeks before that date, both O'Boyle and his allies made last-ditch efforts to avert a showdown. One grew out of discussions among a group of moderate members of the Association of Washington Priests with Father Louis Quinn (president of the priests' senate) and Bishop Spence during the Labor Day-week clergy retreat. Fathers Quinn, Thomas Duffy, and Joseph Byron, the latter a stalwart of the dissenters and one of the few pastors involved, cobbled together a statement that would have pledged its signers to accept the Church's teaching on contraception as well as its traditional teaching on conscience. The authors proposed that every priest in the archdiocese be asked to sign this broad statement. Those who did would be automatically considered in good standing. An optimistic Bishop Spence took the draft to the cardinal, who was also attending the retreat, only to have it rejected: only a formal rejection of the Statement of Conscience by the individual dissenters would effect reconciliation.[39]

Still seeking an end to the crisis on his terms, O'Boyle relaxed his expressed resolve to treat each priest individually and met for one more round with several groups of dissenters before and during the clergy retreat. Thinking that perhaps straight talk from committed laymen might help, he enlisted his advisors McArdle and Dufour to meet with fifteen of the dissenters at the Mayflower Hotel. He also asked Father Gillen, head of the Family Life Bureau and a strong supporter of *Humanae Vitae,* to debate some of the dissenters on local radio shows. Beset on all sides with questions about the strength of O'Boyle's commitment, Gillen boldly asked if he was in the fight for the long haul. O'Boyle's firm response: "This is it; this is what we have to do." Thus reassured, Gillen engaged in a series of appearances during which he defended the magisterium.[40]

---

38. *Commonweal,* 4 Oct 1968. The *NYT* provided a detailed account of these events on 5 Sep 1968.

39. Duffy, Quinn, and Donoghue intvs.

40. As quoted in Gillen intv.

To make his position crystal clear O'Boyle arranged for all the priests of the archdiocese to receive a copy of his own statement of conscience, the one he had addressed to the theologians at Catholic University in August, in which he deemed statements contrary to the Church's official teaching "erroneous, scandalous, and offensive to faithful Catholics." Referring to statements by European bishops, which the dissenters were using to support their position, he observed that if those bishops were teaching doctrine expressed by the pope and the council, "I shall have no disagreement with them." If their teaching "amounts to, implies, or supports" the position of the dissenters, "to that precise extent I shall be compelled to disagree with them." He concluded by offering his personal creed: "I intend to teach in unison with the Catholic teaching of Vatican II and Paul VI, and I must reject whatever is incompatible with this teaching."[41]

Nothing came of all the various efforts at reconciliation, and on September 14 the dissenters, who now numbered forty-four, issued their corporate response to the cardinal's instruction. It stressed not only their respect for the papal encyclical, but also respect for "the intelligently and responsibly formed conscience of the people we serve."[42] Some of the priests appended their personal comments on the issue as the cardinal had requested.

The cardinal's personal interviews with the forty-four priests were scheduled to begin on September 18. On the day before he confirmed in a lengthy news conference that the appeal of the dissenters to the bishops' conference to intervene had been rejected. Their hope that Cardinal Shehan, who had quietly and without any threat of penalty dealt with dissenters in his archdiocese and who was chairman of the bishops' mediation board, would take their case was dashed. Speaking for the bishops, Shehan had pointed out that the dispute was "not one of authority and obedience in the sense in which that might usually be understood," but rather was doctrinal in nature and, hence, not subject to mediation. O'Boyle went on to outline for the press the nature of the penalties he was contemplating. The "degree of exclusion" faced by those who remained in dissent would be determined by the specific nature of the individual's dissent as revealed in the interviews about to begin and an evaluation by the cardinal and his advisors of their written responses.[43]

The impetuousness evident in his treatment of Father O'Donoghue and in

41. Ltr., Donoghue to Reverend and Dear Father, 11 Sep 1968, with encl., copy in Higgins Papers, ACUA.
42. As quoted in *NYT*, 15 Sep 1968.
43. As quoted in *Star*, 18 Sep 1968. See also *WP*, same date. Both papers provided full coverage of the news conference.

some of his less than careful responses to reporters was under strict control when O'Boyle conducted the individual interviews with forty-four dissenters over a three-day period beginning on September 18. Flanked by Msgr. Arthur, his canon lawyer, and John Donoghue, his secretary/vice chancellor, and in the presence of Father Louis Quinn, who as president of the priests' senate served as a witness to the proceedings, he began each interview by proposing that they start with a prayer. After briefly kneeling together, the cardinal asked the priest being interviewed to explain his position as expressed in his personal letter and his understanding of the Statement of Conscience. He then asked if the priest could promise not to teach, preach, or council anyone contrary to the strictures of *Humanae Vitae* and could promise to resume his parish duties without further discussion of the encyclical. For the most part the meetings were cordial, and over the three days five of the priests were reconciled.[44]

Most interviewed on the first day stood their ground, however, and penalties were meted out to eleven of them on the spot; the rest were told they would be notified at a later date. The penalties, meant to reflect the individual declarations of the dissenters, varied. Hardest hit the first day was Father John Fenlon, who was suspended from all public ministry. The rest had their faculties to hear confession suspended while a few, including spokesman Corrigan, were also barred from preaching and counseling. Far from cowed by these events, the dissenters and their lay allies met at a nearby hotel to debrief the priests who had been interviewed and present reporters with a summary of the day's doings. Their comments underscored what they regarded as anomalies in the penalties.[45] To staunch the speculation, O'Boyle announced that all further penalties would be made public simultaneously later in the month. He also invited all the dissenters to meet with him again at any time, but none took advantage of the offer.

Without denigrating the sincere position of any of the dissenters or the painful choice each made during his meeting with the cardinal, the case of the universally admired and saintly social activist Father Horace McKenna stands out for special notice. No one respected the elderly McKenna more than O'Boyle, who had supported the Jesuit's fight for racial justice in southern Maryland and later his work in the inner city. He was especially exasperated and saddened by McKenna's stand. Even before the interview McKenna had pub-

44. The years have dimmed the memory of some of the participants consulted. The following intvs. generally agreed on the course of the proceedings: Arthur, Dignan, Donoghue, Kemp, and Quinn.

45. On the reports, see, for example, lengthy articles in *WP* and *NYT*, 19 Sep 1968.

licly clashed with the cardinal at one of the meetings with all the dissenters. At that time McKenna justified himself by explaining:

> I'm not a prince of the Church like his Eminence and I'm not a learned theologian like Father [Ford], but I'm a simple parish priest who for all my priestly service has been associated with the poor, and I think there comes a time in the life of every devoted priest when he must stand up and represent the faith of his people. . . . I am here to represent the faith of my people. I know for certain that there are good people, who are totally loyal to the church, who believe that in conscience that they can use contraceptives in marriage. And that's all I have to say.

O'Boyle asked his old friend by what authority did he differ from the Church, only to receive McKenna's celebrated response: "Forty years in the confessional."[46]

McKenna's explanation best summarized the position of those arguing for the primacy of conscience. At his meeting with O'Boyle he explained that when he first came to Washington he carefully upheld the strict doctrine on birth control, but he soon found that loyal Catholics were being hopelessly burdened. He came to believe that such people should be free to do what they thought right and best. His simple, pastoral approach to the debate was easily grasped and provided a powerful antidote to O'Boyle's rigid orthodoxy. He was the young dissenters' hero.

Not being permitted to hear confessions was especially painful for McKenna, but his determined stand seemed to bring out a gruffness in O'Boyle usually reserved for younger priests. On another occasion McKenna playfully, but obviously sincerely, asked O'Boyle for his blessing. A frustrated O'Boyle responded, "I'd like to give you a crack on the jaw." Nevertheless, McKenna got the blessing. McKenna publicly summarized the crisis for the cardinal by painting it as "a matter of conflict between authority and supposed experience." The "supposed" was his humble way of describing his forty years as a confessor. Privately, he offered a more pungent explanation. His dispute with O'Boyle, he noted, was "what you get for trying to argue sex with an Irishman."[47]

For McKenna at least there was the comfort of living with a group of sympathetic Jesuits. For some of the Washington dissenters it was a different story. For example, Father George Pavloff, an assistant at St. Patrick's, found serving under

46. As quoted in Monagan, *Horace*, p. 143. Monagan offers a detailed account of McKenna's role in the *Humanae Vitae* crisis.
47. All quotes from Monagan, *Horace*, pp. 145–54.

a conservative, decidedly hostile pastor only added to his difficulties in a time of inner turmoil.[48]

The crisis intensified when the executive board of the National Federation of Priests' Councils met in emergency session on September 25 and decided to seek an interview with the cardinal, but only after telling the press that O'Boyle had refused to use the structures devised by the American bishops for arbitration. Their spokesman was finally received by O'Boyle's secretary, who dismissed the offer of mediation as "interfering and intruding in the affairs of the archdiocese."[49]

Meanwhile O'Boyle began an ill-starred effort to wean lay support from the dissenters. By now it was obvious that appeals to the media by both sides were feeding the controversy and magnifying the tension. It was also obvious that O'Boyle was at a loss on how best to counter the dissenters' ability to enlist widespread lay support. Instead of scholarly debates and quiet appeals to authority that were the norm in the Church he grew up in, public debate on issues was now being aired by dissenters and laity, most of whom were of a younger generation using techniques they had learned during the turbulent demonstrations against racial injustice and the Vietnam War. "You can't be half Catholic," he declared at a press conference on September 21. "No one is compelled to be a Catholic, but if he is he should follow the teachings of the Catholic Church." Public dissent, he concluded, was neither permitted nor condoned.[50]

If O'Boyle regretted the strength of lay support for the dissenters and their skillful use of the press, he never deviated from his resolve. Against the advice of Walter McArdle and William Abell, he published a pastoral letter that he ordered read at all Masses on September 22. Strongly influenced by Germaine Grisez, O'Boyle spoke about "false prophets" who claimed that contraception was a matter for individual consciences. He included in their number "even a few of my fellow bishops in other lands." He asked the laity to help him persuade those priests who disputed the pope's order to renounce their stand. He also had a warning for those who accepted the dissenters' view of conscience by quoting an awful curse from Deuteronomy, chapter 29: "The Lord will blot out his name from under Heaven." He could not stand by, O'Boyle told his listeners, "and let you be misled by an idea of freedom of conscience that could bring down on you so horrible a curse."

48. Pavloff intv.
49. As quoted in *Star*, 26 Sep 1968. See also same source, 23 Sep 1968.
50. As quoted in *Star*, 21 Sep 1968.

This passage, so uncharacteristic of O'Boyle's style, embarrassed many of his supporters. Some priests simply skipped over it when reading the letter,[51] but not so the press, which highlighted the curse in their reports. With advance warning of the letter and of O'Boyle's decision to read it personally during the principal Masses at the cathedral, an alliance of the dissenters' lay supporters, the so-called Committee for Freedom in the Church and the Washington Lay Association, called for a public protest. As the cardinal mounted the pulpit to read his letter, more than two hundred people rose and walked out. (Similar walkouts occurred in a number of parishes throughout the archdiocese.) Fore-warned, the press was on hand to record the event for their readers. In fairness, most of the media also reported on the standing ovation afforded the cardinal by the more than eight hundred remaining members of the congregation.[52] The cardinal's secretary noted that both the walkout and the ovation were unprecedented acts in the history of the American Church.

After the demonstration in St. Matthew's, *Time* magazine and other journals publicized the statements of the various episcopal conferences around the world. While all these statements were careful to stress the authority of the papal encyclical, they also emphasized the importance of individual conscience. It followed, therefore, that the pope's teaching was being presented in many countries "more as an ideal to strive for than an absolute norm to be followed," a point constantly stressed by the cardinal's critics.[53]

Penalties for thirty-nine dissenters were officially announced on October 1. The most severe sanctions were meted out to five priests, including Fathers O'-Donoghue and Corrigan, who were suspended from all public ministry and evicted from their rectories. The cardinal also warned Corrigan that any further public dissent would be considered an act of defiance, "and further action on my part will be contemplated." To which Corrigan replied via the press, "What more can he do, burn me at the stake?"[54] In the weeks that followed, several of those barred from public ministry took up quarters in a house on Kenyon Street in Northwest Washington donated by a group of supporters spearheaded by Mrs. Philip A. Hart, wife of the Michigan senator, along with Minnesota's Sen-

51. Quinn intv. At the time Father Quinn was president of the priests' senate.
52. Accounts differ on the number who left. *Newsweek* (7 Oct 68) reported 150 who walked out at the 12:30 Mass; *WP*, 23 Sep 68, counted 200 leaving, as did *Life* (28 Oct 68); *Star* (23 Sep 68) estimated 400 at various Masses around the archdiocese, including 300 during O'Boyle's principal Mass; while *Time* (4 Oct 68) reported one-third of the cathedral congregations, roughly 400.
53. *Time* (4 Oct 1968), p. 57.
54. As quoted in *NYT*, 2 Oct 1968.

Defending 'Humanae Vitae.' O'Boyle inveighs against the dissenters from the pulpit at St. Matthew's Cathedral in September 1968.

ator Eugene McCarthy.[55] Dubbed the Center for Christian Renewal, the old three-story building became the unofficial headquarters for the dissenters, who hired a group of canon and civil lawyers to consider their options and pursue a legal solution.

Support also came from another quarter. Fifteen Jesuits at Georgetown University issued a statement declaring that the position of the dissenters "seems

55. Contributions for the upkeep of the house came from all over the country. See, for example, ltr., Msgr. Ellis to Corrigan, 4 Oct 1968, Ellis Papers, ACUA. See also *Time*, 13 Oct 1968.

firmly grounded in the teaching of Vatican II and the tradition of theologians."
Nine Jesuits stationed at Washington's Gonzaga High School, including its
headmaster, also informed the cardinal that they wanted to be associated with
the dissenters' Statement of Conscience.[56] At the same time growing numbers of
lay Catholics were showing their support for individual dissenters who had received lesser penalties by attending their Masses in droves. The dissenters did
not give up hope. They hammered away at the issue of primacy of individual
conscience and looked forward to the chance of winning support at the upcoming meeting of the American bishops. Even so, some began to drift away. Early in
October three priests obtained employment in local government and private industry, two of them after receiving a leave of absence from the cardinal.[57]

In the weeks leading up to the bishops' November meeting Cardinal O'Boyle
sought to counter the conscience issue and the belief that somehow a distinction
was being made between *Humanae Vitae* and the great social encyclicals of the
recent past. Heeding the advice of friends, he adopted more diplomatic language,
offering in a statement accompanying the official announcement of the penalties a
temperate defense of *Humanae Vitae,* not necessarily as an infallible expression
but one nevertheless binding on the conscience of every Catholic. Before an invited audience of lay leaders, he also argued that the basic prohibition in the social encyclicals—that one may never deprive workers of a fair wage or that discrimination on the basis of race is morally reprehensible—had a power equal to
the prohibitions against artificial contraception as expressed in *Humanae Vitae.*[58] In response the dissenters quoted the Belgian Jesuit theologian Louis
Dupre: "The right, or better the duty, to follow one's conscience is so sacred and
has been so universally accepted by the Church in recent decades that Cardinal
O'Boyle's voice seems to be coming from another century."[59] In a way the two
sides were arguing apples and oranges. The cardinal saw the issue in terms of objective morality while the dissenters looked to personal accountability.

If resolution of the crisis in their favor was appearing increasingly remote to
the dissenters, the cardinal was also experiencing setbacks in his effort to restore
orthodoxy in his archdiocese. He considered those theologians at Catholic Uni-

56. As quoted in *NYT*, 7 Oct 1968. See also *WP* and *Star,* same date.

57. *Star,* 13 Oct 1968. Fathers Meyer, Spellman, and Fenlon were the first dissenters to leave the
active ministry for outside employment.

58. O'Boyle, Statement on Penalties, issued 1 Oct 1968, and "The Christian in Today's World,"
an address delivered to members of the John Carroll Society and others, 20 Oct 1968. Copies of
both in AAW. See also *NYT*, 21 Oct 1968, and Abell intv.

59. As quoted in *Star,* 26 Sep 1968.

versity who were aiding and abetting dissent a key ingredient in the crisis, and when they rejected his admonitions he had threatened to take action. The trouble was that, although he was chancellor of the pontifical university responsible for orthodoxy, he was also but one on a reformed and diverse board of trustees increasingly sensitive to the issue of academic freedom. Aware of the practical limits of his position, he asked the board, not his fellow bishops, to discipline the theologians. Meeting in early September, the board voted to ask the university's rector to investigate with "academic due process" whether the theologians had violated their responsibilities to the school "under its existing statutes."[60] At the same time the theologians involved were suspended from teaching, pending outcome of the inquiry.

The academics proved remarkably adept at avoiding speedy decision. Only in June 1969, after considerable discussion, including an angry rejection of their decision by Cardinal McIntyre, a board member, did the trustees accept a report from the school's committee of inquiry, approved by the academic senate. The university endorsed the academic propriety of the theologians' actions without passing judgment on the theological issues involved. Calling the decision a sign of the university's dedication to academic freedom, the academic senate, with the approval of the board of trustees, reinstated the theologians whom Cardinal O'Boyle had hoped to see disciplined.[61]

A frustrated O'Boyle clearly anticipated the conclusion of the lengthy investigation and began disassociating his priests from the school as early as October 1968. Declaring "the worst mistake I ever made was to send you fellows to that university," he withdrew his considerable financial support for the university's continuing education program for parish priests in the theology school.[62] Instead, he created his own program under the auspices of the Josephite Pastoral Center. The new program was meant to emphasize modern social problems. Explaining the shift O'Boyle declared, "This time I am confident of the genuine benefit that all who attend this course will derive from this thoroughly orthodox yet updated series of lectures."[63]

60. As quoted in Minutes of General Meeting, NCCB, Sep 1968. See also Minutes of Meeting, CUA Board of Trustees, 15–16 Jun 1969. Both in ACUA. See also James P. Shannon, *Reluctant Dissenter* (New York: Crossroads Publications, 1998), pp. 148–50. There was much reporting and speculation in the press on this issue. See, for example, *NYT*, 8 Sep 1968, *WP*, 5 Sep 1968, and *Star*, 1 Sep 1968.
61. Minutes of Meeting, CUA Board of Trustees, 15–16 Jun 1969, ACUA, provides a detailed account of the debate.
62. As quoted in *NYT Magazine*, 24 Nov 1968. See also *NYT*, 10 Oct 1968.
63. As quoted in *Star*, 24 Oct 1968.

Meeting the Press. O'Boyle ponders a question about the birth control crisis at one of his numerous meetings with reporters in 1968.

Although the cardinal's interpretation of *Humanae Vitae* and his defense of Church authority were shared by the large majority of his fellow bishops, support for his confrontational approach was by no means unanimous among them. This distinction had surfaced during the meeting of the NCCB's administrative committee on September 18. Following O'Boyle's report on the Washington crisis, Cardinal Krol recommended that the committee endorse the actions taken by Washington's archbishop in dealing with his priests. No doubt aware that Krol's proposal would not receive unanimous approval, O'Boyle replied that a pledge of solidarity might be more properly addressed to the pope. Cardinal Shehan, citing his experience in Baltimore, pointed out that the crisis might be handled in a different fashion. The committee's president, Archbishop Dearden, cautioned that a statement of support for the cardinal appeared to exceed the mandate of the administrative committee, which was at the service of the bishops' conference, which might object to an action taken by the committee touching on the affairs of an individual diocese.

Cardinal O'Boyle later spoke of his irritation over Cardinal Shehan's remarks. His Baltimore confrere had promised to stand beside him, only later to change direction and refuse support. In fact, since their work together on the guidelines for teaching religion, relations between the two were strained. O'Boyle was particularly amazed that Shehan had voted with the pro-contraception members of the papal commission.[64] Nevertheless O'Boyle sidestepped the issue by proposing that instead of a statement of support for him the committee reaffirm its strong support of *Humanae Vitae*. With unanimous approval, the committee subsequently published a new appeal to the nation's Catholics for support of the encyclical, adding that the American bishops joined with the pope in calling on the priests and people to "form their consciences" in light of the encyclical.[65]

At the same meeting O'Boyle proposed that the bishops establish a foundation that would sponsor research aimed at making the Church's teachings on sex in marriage "more livable for contemporary believers." He specifically mentioned research into the rhythm method of birth control and pledged $25,000 to the enterprise. The committee agreed and appointed O'Boyle to chair an ad hoc group to make specific proposals. O'Boyle would win agreement at the bishops'

64. Ltr., Msgr. Weber to the author, 5 Feb 1997. Weber spent days interviewing O'Boyle in preparation for his biography of Cardinal McIntyre and is here quoting O'Boyle. See also Arthur intv.

65. Minutes of the Administrative Committee, 18 Sep 1968, NCCB Papers, ACUA (source of quote). See also *NYT*, 19 Sep 1968.

general meeting in November for a Human Life and Natural Family Planning Foundation. Supported by assessments on individual dioceses, the new foundation began its work in February 1969 with a $600,000 grant and a prestigious board of directors. Its first executive director was O'Boyle's old friend and supporter Lawrence Kane.[66]

Reconciliation

The apostolic delegate, most likely at the direction of the Vatican, made a last attempt to defuse the crisis before the meeting of the American bishops in November 1968 by bringing in an unofficial arbiter. The press reported and the dissenters believed that Cardinal O'Boyle had invited Bishop Joseph Bernardin, then general secretary of the NCCB, to mediate the dispute. O'Boyle never bothered to correct that impression, going as far as telling the press that he had asked Bernardin "to approach those priests on my behalf."[67] The claim made no sense given O'Boyle's repeated insistence that the crisis was doctrinal and therefore excluded from mediation by outside groups. Also to be considered was the cardinal's generally poor regard for young Bishop Bernardin.[68] Although O'Boyle may have suspected intervention by the apostolic delegate in the matter, he may also have concluded that Bernardin was acting on behalf of some of his fellow bishops. At any rate he went on with the charade.[69]

Bernardin's effort was doomed from the start. Never allowed to reveal the source of his mandate, indeed not even aware of its exact nature, he was expected to bring about a miraculous reconciliation. His initial interviews with the cardinal and the individual dissenters convinced him of the impossibility of any compromise in positions. For their part the dissenters, who generally admired Bernardin, concluded that his mission was not a sincere attempt at mediation, but a ploy to keep the matter off the bishops' agenda. They also concluded that it was impossible for one man to succeed.[70] They were right. The Bernardin mission quietly faded away, though not before Bernardin prepared a report that eventually found its way to Rome.

66. The Human Life Foundation file, AAW, contains numerous documents demonstrating O'Boyle's continuing support for this work and his selection of Kane to direct it.
67. As quoted in *Star*, 6 Nov 1968. See *NYT*, same date.
68. Arthur and Donoghue intvs. In an aside, Msgr. Arthur added: "I know that Cardinal Bernardin did not rank among the top bishops in Cardinal O'Boyle's estimation. I don't think he saw him as any great person."
69. For an extended discussion of the Bernardin mission, see Higgins intv. Msgr. Higgins lived with Bernardin at the time and gained some insight into what still is a mysterious mission.
70. As reported by Father Corrigan in *WP*, 7 Nov 1968.

The bishops might well have decided to ignore the Washington crisis during their meeting that began on November 11, but if so it would not have been the fault of the dissenters and their lay supporters. A coalition of lay groups, including the Washington Lay Association, had succeeded in contacting 100,000 prominent Catholics around the country to enlist them in a national demand for action by the hierarchy. On the eve of the meeting some five thousand cheering Catholics gathered at the Mayflower Hotel in a display of unity with the penalized priests. They listened to several well-known lay people, including Senator Eugene McCarthy reading one of his celebrated poems. Spokesmen for the crowd called on the bishops to intervene and to argue for the development of a more democratic process to resolve such confrontations by immediately establishing a due-process proceeding. On opening day some 399 priests from sixty-two dioceses, including more than forty representatives of priests' senates, also called on the bishops to intervene. Some of them staged a sit-in in the lobby of the Hilton Hotel where the meeting was taking place. They confronted Archbishop Dearden, who promised to give their demands "careful consideration," but added that the bishops had no competence to intervene in an individual diocese.[71] Several smaller groups that supported the cardinal's position also staged meetings and prepared resolutions. All this was part of the larger era of protest and counter-protest that characterized the 1960s, but it was new to the bishops. As Professor Grisez noted, "The bishops had a bellyful of the priests in the week they spent in Washington."[72]

As the bishops gathered, their spokesman, Bishop James P. Shannon, announced that the draft of a pastoral letter on artificial contraception as well as social issues including war aims and arms control would be debated and published by the 270 bishops during their meeting. He went on to predict that the letter would take a position on *Humanae Vitae* "similar" to that of "other hierarchies."[73] Since many of the hierarchies had emphasized the role of individual conscience in deciding the morality of birth control, Shannon's remarks stimulated much speculation. O'Boyle's old friend Bishop Wycislo noted that many of the cardinal's fellow bishops had adopted a stand-off, noncommittal position on the question that was embroiling the Church in Washington. Almost all had experienced some degree of dissent in their own dioceses, but many, unfamiliar with O'Boyle's leadership style, were surprised by his truculent reac-

71. As quoted in *NYT*, 12 Nov 1968. In this country's so-called paper of record, the dissenters received exhaustive coverage. See, for example, articles on 20 Oct and 10, 11, 13 Nov 1968.

72. As quoted in *NYT Magazine*, 24 Nov 1968.

73. As quoted in *NYT*, 12 Nov 1968.

tion.[74] O'Boyle enjoyed strong support from powerful colleagues like Cardinals McIntyre and Krol and others of the more traditional outlook, but he never asked his colleagues to endorse his action. Despite the obvious hesitation among some bishops, he never considered himself abandoned. They were all in the crisis together, he told an associate. If others had no problem in their dioceses— good for them.[75] Nor did he press for their support, in part because he respected their individual circumstances, but also, his intimates suggested, because he knew such support would not be unanimous and therefore would weaken the American Church's strong endorsement for the encyclical.

Respect for differing interpretations did not mean that Cardinal O'Boyle was indifferent to what he saw as error. The prestigious Catholic news organ in Great Britain, *The Tablet,* published an insider's report by its special correspondent. In an article reminiscent of Xavier Rynne's work at Vatican II, the author described O'Boyle's reaction to the constant references by bishops to the decidedly different conclusions of other national hierarchies. Grabbing the microphone, he reportedly branded the Canadian bishops "liars" and the French "kooks." He also reportedly dismissed Detroit's auxiliary Bishop Thomas Gumbleton's attempt to speak in favor of due process for priests.[76]

The bishops' long-awaited statement, "Human Life in Our Day," was released on November 14, 1968. A key section of the lengthy document explicitly supported *Humanae Vitae,* but added an ambiguous phrase that would prove important in events that followed in Washington and Rome. The statement read in part:

> We feel bound to remind Catholic married couples, when they are subjected to the pressures which prompt the Holy Father's concern *that however circumstances may reduce moral guilt,* no one following the teaching of the church can deny the objective evil of artificial contraception itself. With pastoral solicitude we urge those who have resorted to artificial contraception never to lose heart but to continue to take full advantage of the strength which comes from the sacrament of penance and the grace, healing and peace in the Eucharist.[77]

74. Wycislo intv. Bishop Wycislo attended the sessions of the meeting and offered his reflections on the cardinal's role.

75. Arthur intv. O'Boyle's opinion, reported by Bishop Wycislo, Arthur, and Archbishop Donoghue, three of his close associates, is discussed in their interviews. See also Kelly, *The Battle for the American Church,* p. 14.

76. "American Self-Scrutiny," *The Tablet,* 18 Jan 1969, pp. 55–56. The story earned page one treatment in *WP,* 17 Feb 1969. O'Boyle refused comment. At the same time he did not deny the *Tablet* report.

77. "Human Life in Our Day." Hugh J. Nolan, ed., *Pastoral Letters of the United States Catholic Bishops,* vol. 3 (Washington, D.C.: United States Catholic Conference, 1983), pp. 164–99. Emphasis added.

The bishops went on to devote considerable attention to the obligation to form a correct conscience according to the Church's moral dictates. They restated the traditional Church teaching that conscience "though inviolable is not a law unto itself."[78] Commenting on the letter, Cardinal O'Boyle asserted that it contained no compromises about artificial birth control and urged Catholics to read the whole document. He also warned against the distorted interpretation given by the media.[79]

Those who saw the document as more in line with the European hierarchies pointed to the phrase "however circumstances may reduce moral guilt" and the fact that nowhere did the authors attempt to define such circumstances. No matter how adamantly the O'Boyles and Wrights claimed that the letter presented a clear-cut defense of *Humanae Vitae* as advanced in Washington, it must be conceded that in their effort to provide a careful exposition of the moral imperatives involved, the bishops did create some ambiguity. The dissenters claimed to see vindication for their position in the pastoral letter.[80] In fact the bishops offered no support for the dissenters specifically, but rather underscored O'Boyle's long-held position that disagreement with the pope's encyclical was acceptable only when expressed prudently by competent theologians and "such as not to give scandal."

In the next months almost half of the penalized priests left the active ministry. Some immediately took up secular positions; some married and began families. By February 1969 nineteen had left; fewer than thirty remained, under various degrees of restriction. Six months later only eighteen were still living in rectories or working in archdiocesan offices.

In the wake of the bishops' meeting Cardinal O'Boyle received an indication that the Vatican supported his actions. While attending a consistory in early May 1969 he had a private audience with Pope Paul. Shortly after his return to Washington he received a letter from the pope in which he praised the cardinal not only for his acceptance of the encyclical, but also for his zealous effort to secure a similar acceptance from the priests and laity of Washington. The pope concluded with the wish that the dissenters reconsider their position and reestablish full communion with their bishop.[81] Armed with this endorsement, the cardinal, with Bishop Bernardin in tow, met with twenty-five of the dissenters, some no longer active in the ministry, to present what he called his revised conditions for

78. Ibid., para. 37.
79. The cardinal's comments were carried in *CS,* 21 Nov 1968. See also *Star,* 17 Nov 1968.
80. As reported in *NYT,* 16 Nov 1968.
81. Ltr., Pope Paul to O'Boyle, 15 May 1969, copy in AAW.

reconciliation. His conditions represented only slightly altered demands most recently expressed to Bernardin during that prelate's abortive effort at mediation. As one condition the dissenters must admit in a public statement that *Humanae Vitae* represented the authentic teaching of the Church and they must so present it in the pulpit and confessional. They must also retract their position as outlined in their Statement of Conscience, which, O'Boyle charged, was misleading and in apparent contradiction to the bishops' pastoral letter. In a bow to Bernardin's efforts, the cardinal added that the dissenters should express in a positive way what they now accepted and need not apologize for their previous stand.[82] Predictably, the priests rejected O'Boyle's offer, charging that he had misrepresented their position: they had never attacked the moral judgments expressed in the encyclical, but contended that it also allowed for the judgment of the individual.

Convinced that he had taken the correct course ("the only thing that's right," he told advisor Walter McArdle), O'Boyle bore his critics with studied indifference. But perhaps he was not altogether indifferent. He had received "much abuse for the position I took," he told a sympathizer, but "I have also received much support and consolation from many priests and members of the laity throughout the country and the world."[83] Subordinates marveled at his ability to compartmentalize. Discussion of the crisis was limited to his few closest advisors. Even his secretary and housemate recalled that the subject was never discussed outside working hours.

Many years later, in describing the cardinal's visit to Scranton during the 1969 Easter season, his cousins noted that in contrast to the usually humorous and sarcastic "Father 'Boyle," they were host to a "torn, torn" tearful man who spent much of his time in his room in prayer. He was a distraught father who brooded over "his boys." He worried about the priests he was losing, adding "I just can't forget those guys."[84]

As the number of dissenters who had left the ministry increased, the cardinal urged the rest of the priests to maintain friendships and treat those leaving charitably. Meanwhile he stood by to provide practical assistance. He quietly an-

82. Apparently no transcript of the cardinal's remarks was preserved. The Association of Washington Priests issued a press release on 28 Jun 1969 outlining his remarks. See also "Conditions for the restoration of faculties to the priests from whom they have been withdrawn in virtue of their dissent from *Humanae Vitae*" (The cardinal's version, 10 Dec 1969, and Bishop Bernardin's revised version, 20 Dec 1969). All in AAW. See also *NYT*, 29 Jun 1969.

83. Ltr., O'Boyle to Msgr. P. C. Conway, 21 Jun 1970, copy in *Humanae Vitae* file, AAW.

84. As quoted in the Muldoon intv.

nounced that some of those relieved of their duties would continue to receive salaries and any other needed financial help. For Father Joseph Haslinger, who was living on Kenyon Street but already under treatment for what would prove a fatal illness, O'Boyle cut off laicization proceedings to preserve his medical insurance. The cardinal always showed a preference for priests who dared to disagree, to stand up to his gruff manner. Now he was losing some of the brightest and most articulate. He especially hated taking away faculties to hear confession, which he considered the crux of a priestly vocation. Although he retained the support of the great majority of priests in the archdiocese, a significant number of them were critical of his handling of the dissenters and were sympathetic to letting them have their say. At other times the cardinal might well have endorsed such sentiment, but in this case he was convinced not only of the dissenters' basic errors, but that their actions were confusing the people in the pews.

As the months passed the cardinal proved agreeable to taking advantage of the ambiguities in the bishops' statement. In August 1969 four of the dissenters—Fathers Raymond Kemp, Andre Bouchard, John Cunico, and Shane McCarthy, all serving inner-city parishes—sought an agreement with O'Boyle that would allow them to resume their full responsibilities. As Kemp later explained, his parishioners had pointed out that birth control was not their issue, that they liked and respected the cardinal for his stand on racial justice, and they wanted Kemp to settle his differences and get back to full-time work. Kemp and the others also wanted to be part of the archdiocese's new initiatives in the inner city.[85]

O'Boyle was ready to talk. Calling the dissent "water over the dam," he agreed to abandon his insistence on a public apology if they agreed to teach in accordance with *Humanae Vitae* as spelled out in the bishops' "Human Life in Our Day" pastoral. No mention was made of a public renunciation of the dissenters' Statement of Conscience. Father McCarthy, one of the four, rejected O'Boyle's offer. Father Byron, speaking for the remaining dissenters, explained that "no matter what the words say they still come out sounding like a retraction."[86] Byron would have reason to remember his words two years later after Rome intervened. The three priests who accepted O'Boyle's terms were promptly restored. The trio saw no difficulty in agreeing that *Humanae Vitae* was correct in declaring artificial contraception wrong. The dissenters had accepted that proposition (as had so many other national hierarchies), but in agree-

85. Kemp intv. See also *NYT*, 6 Aug 1969.
86. As quoted in *NYT*, 6 Aug 1969.

ing to the bishops' pastoral they could take refuge in its statements about moral imputability and the role of individual conscience.

Few avenues were left open to dissenters remaining in the ministry. With legal assistance from a volunteer Committee of Concerned Canon Lawyers under-written by the National Federation of Priests' Councils, nineteen of them under the leadership of Father Joseph Byron submitted their case to the archdiocese's tribunal court in September 1969. They were at pains to emphasize that they did not designate Cardinal O'Boyle the defendant in the case, but the court decided otherwise and declared itself incompetent to judge a cardinal. The court of appeals (in the case of Washington, the Archdiocese of Cleveland served as the appellate court) concurred.[87] The nineteen decided to appeal directly to the pope. Citing the lack of correct judicial process, the National Federation of Priests Councils urged the NCCB to support the appeal, but the bishops agreed not to intervene, in keeping with their administrative committee's decision in September 1968.[88]

The appeal to the pope evoked a response from the papal secretary of state, Cardinal Jean Villot, who advised the nineteen to reopen conversation with their archbishop. Explaining his position to Villot, O'Boyle characterized the dissenters' Statement of Conscience as a "public, pastoral dissent." He had, therefore, refused to agree to arbitration, which he understood to imply a decision by a third party, because that would mean "arbitrating Church teaching itself." In seeking reconciliation with the priests, he concluded, he had followed proper procedures outlined in canon law. For their part the dissenters contended that their statement echoed those issued by other hierarchies and that O'Boyle demanded a statement from each of them that "would represent a clear retraction of our statement of conscience."[89]

The stalemate was unexpectedly broken by Cardinal Villot's surprise announcement that the case of the nineteen would be turned over to the Sacred Congregation for the Clergy for examination and decision. Thus the dissenters achieved one of their key demands: a hearing before a neutral third party. The prefect of the congregation, Cardinal John Wright, skillfully devised a three-

87. Joseph Byron, "The Case of the Washington Nineteen: A Search for Justice," in *Judgment in the Church*, ed. William Bassett and Peter Hurzing (New York: Seabury Press, 1977), pp. 104–12. Byron presents a useful summary of the judicial cases through conclusion of the crisis in Rome. Unless otherwise indicated, the following paragraphs are based on this summary.

88. Minutes of Meeting, NCCB, Apr 1970. See also Minutes of Administrative Committee, NCCB, 18 Sep 1968, pp. 25–29, NCCB Papers, ACUA.

89. Memo, O'Boyle to Villot, 26 May 1970, and Statement by spokesman for the disciplined priests. Both quoted in *CS*, 18 Feb 1971.

phased approach that employed proxies to represent the principals, thus avoiding a confrontation between O'Boyle and the priests. O'Boyle selected Msgrs. Arthur and Donoghue as proxies; the dissenters Father Raymond Goedert and Donald Heintschel from the Committee of Concerned Canon Lawyers.

In April 1971, after weeks of studying documents and discussions with the proxies, the congregation issued its findings and recommendations. It agreed with the proxies of both parties that Cardinal O'Boyle had observed all requirements of existing canon law in his treatment of the priests, and, as a result, all parties agreed to collaborate in seeking a pastoral solution to the issue. Proxies for the priests agreed to substitute a more considered statement of their views for the controversial Statement of Conscience. Finally, the congregation prepared a statement of theological principles that each dissenter was expected to endorse. These findings declared "without ambiguity, doubt or hesitation the objective evil of contraception is an authentic expression of this magisterium" and all who receive priestly faculties should communicate this teaching. The congregation went on to discuss conscience and, quoting the American bishops, added "particular circumstances surrounding an objectively evil act, while they cannot make it objectively virtuous, can make it inculpable, diminished in guilt or subjectively defensible." It also quoted the bishops where they had summarized the Church's teaching that conscience was invaluable and no one could be forced to act in a manner contrary to conscience.[90]

Although Cardinal Wright may very well have agreed with the point long advanced by Cardinal O'Boyle, that those who dissent in public should be made to recant in public, he later admitted that the decision was taken out of his hands.[91] Thus Pope Paul ended the crisis by ruling, as conveyed by the congregation, "that without further delay, formality or necessity for written or oral explanations, each priest who accepts the 'findings' set forth above present himself individually, at his earliest convenience, to his Ordinary and declare his desire to enjoy the full faculties of the Archdiocese." The congregation went on to declare with "confidence" that Cardinal O'Boyle would respond promptly and gladly to each request so made. In fact, the dissenters subscribed to the findings and so indicated to the cardinal, who promptly restored their faculties.[92]

90. *Sacra Congregatio Pro Clericis*, "Official Communication," 26 Apr 1971, copy in AAW.
91. Arthur intv. Arthur and Wright were friends from student days, and Wright frequently consulted Arthur informally during the proceedings.
92. One exception: Father O'Donoghue, by then a professor in New York, was questioned further on his statements, the chancery arguing that he was not one of the nineteen to whom the Vatican's directive was addressed. See also Arthur intv. Msgr. Arthur was involved in restoring faculties to Father Byron and the others.

Stand Fast in the Faith

Cardinal O'Boyle never publicly referred to the crisis after Rome spoke. Nor did he reveal the contents of the three-page, handwritten private letter he received from Pope Paul at the time of his fiftieth anniversary as a priest. Asked why he never published this personal expression of papal gratitude unprecedented in modern times, O'Boyle explained, "It would only have further compromised the Holy Father."[93] Pope Paul was not so diffident. A public letter from the pope was read during the anniversary Mass. No doubt aware of his loyal subordinate's disappointment at the outcome of the Vatican deliberations, Pope Paul publicly hailed O'Boyle as "a father, teacher and leader" and as a "guardian and defender of the faith, undiminished and unblemished." The pope also thanked the cardinal for his bulldog-like loyalty—"Yes, for us and to us." Somewhat later the pope made yet another public display of his gratitude. During the 1976 consistory, at which Cardinal Baum, O'Boyle's successor in Washington, received his red hat, the pope interrupted the ceremonies to embrace O'Boyle, thanking him for his support.[94]

At first O'Boyle had resisted the idea of an anniversary Mass. The priests' senate, citing the need for healing, finally persuaded him to participate by making it a celebration not only for him but for three other diocesan priests also ordained in 1921. In fact the day was really all about O'Boyle. He entered to a thundering ovation, unusual in that it was led by the younger clergy, an act widely interpreted as a sign of their admiration for the old warrior's long fight. O'Boyle had strictly charged the arrangers that in a ceremony honoring the four men his name was not to be mentioned. Bishop Spence, true to the letter of the ruling, never mentioned the cardinal's name in his homily. Instead in a lengthy tribute he repeatedly praised the individual achievements of the "cardinal archbishop of Washington." During the Mass the apostolic delegate read the pope's letter. Ever after, O'Boyle would refer to the occasion as one of the highlights of his career.[95]

Ceremony and demonstrations of loyalty could not mask the impact of the decision made in Rome. Some of the dissenters interpreted the Vatican's find-

93. The text of this letter appears to be lost. During his interview with Msgr. Francis Weber, O'Boyle showed him the letter and answered Weber's question, which produced the O'Boyle response (quote). See ltr., Weber to author, 5 Feb 1997, AAW.

94. Baum intv. The pope's public letter, read at the anniversary Mass, is quoted in *CS*, 27 May 1971.

95. Quinn and Arthur intvs. See also the *WP*, 22 May 1971, and *Star*, 27 May 1971.

ings as a vindication of their position. The cardinal remained silent, but his close associates and advisors were aware of his deep disappointment. (His old friend from New York, Msgr. George Kelly, reported that O'Boyle was "furious" at the settlement, which "left him out to dry.")[96] The cardinal was especially disappointed with the leadership of his old ally Cardinal Wright, but it soon became known that the resolution recommended by Wright's congregation was actually the work of the pope himself. While O'Boyle thought in terms of absolutes, which some of his subordinates believed should have been fought for harder, the pope and his congregation—displaying an "Italian mentality," as Msgr. Gillen, a long-time Roman resident, put it—offered an ambiguous solution that would end the crisis.[97] O'Boyle may have been disappointed, but the congregation's findings went little beyond what he had demanded of Father Kemp and the others he had reconciled in 1969. Actually, the cardinal should have been disappointed with his fellow bishops, whose 1968 "Human Life in Our Day" was quoted verbatim by Wright's congregation in its findings.

There has been no end of analysis of the crisis by O'Boyle's subordinates. Several criticized the one-sided advice the cardinal received, especially in the initial months of the crisis. If only Hannan had still been in Washington, several posited, he would have moderated the response to the dissenters and avoided stalemate; he had frequently succeeded in changing or modifying his superior's position. "You don't need to go down that road" was one of his frequent remarks to his boss.

Another supposition: if only moderate Father Byron had led the dissenters from the crucial beginning weeks, the emotionally charged clash between the cardinal and men like Fathers O'Donoghue and Corrigan, which fueled the fight and led to such draconian penalties, might have been avoided. Yet another supposition: if so many of the dissenters had not studied and maintained close ties to their teachers at Catholic University, the influence of those theologians, the intellectual architects of the dissent, would have been lessened. It was also argued that if Bishop Bernardin had been given a clear mandate by the Vatican, O'Boyle's resistance to mediation would have been modified. Finally, the suggestion was frequently advanced that the cardinal's lack of pastoral experience was a factor in all his decisions during the crisis. This was especially important when he was forced to confront problems of a pastoral nature. Cardinal O'Boyle tend-

96. On O'Boyle's disappointment, see Donoghue, Arthur, Abell, and Gillen intvs. See also Kelly, *The Battle for the American Church*, pp. 13–16 (source of quote).

97. Gillen intv. See also Donoghue intv. and Kelly's *The Battle for the American Church*.

ed to respond to issues, not ideas. As one of his fellow bishops commented: "His mind is like that of a big-city mayor."[98]

However intriguing these suppositions might be, they were also beside the point. To suggest that O'Boyle would have acted substantially differently is to deny the nature of his beliefs, which he consistently evoked throughout the crisis.

> I cannot give back faculties, which are official authorizations to exercise the priestly ministry, to priests who have asserted that they will use these faculties contrary to the Church's teaching, which must be the principle of her pastoral practice. . . . It would not be charitable—it would in fact be dishonest and irresponsible—if I were to give my blessing to such an abuse.[99]

The cardinal took his motto, "Stand Fast in the Faith," seriously. Father Byron, later reminded of his confident prediction on the eve of the interviews ("He [O'Boyle] can't suspend fifty-two priests"), ruefully admitted that he proved to be a poor prophet who clearly had not understood the cardinal's resolve.[100] It is probably true that if the crisis had been less public and O'Boyle had not reluctantly become embroiled in a media war, he would not have felt compelled to impose such stern penalties. But no one and nothing was going to relax his deep unity with and loyalty to the pope, as expressed in his defense of the encyclical. The constant invocation of the judgments of other national bishops' conferences left him unmoved.

Although the doctrinal issue in the conflict could not be discounted, it was also obvious that by training and experience O'Boyle believed that ecclesial authority existed to be obeyed. He concluded that the widespread distrust of authority that had begun to pervade society in the 1960s was also beginning to erode Church discipline as well. Thus, while he might overlook the fine distinctions in doctrine advanced by priests like Msgr. Furfey, he could not give way to what he considered the flagrant disobedience of men like O'Donoghue and Corrigan.

In its effort to end the crisis over birth control, the Vatican tried to meld authority and conscience, an effort readily subscribed to by the dissenters. Since then conservative commentators like George Weigel and Msgr. George Kelly

98. As quoted in *NYT,* 10 Nov 1968. The suppositions referred to in these paragraphs were discussed by Donoghue, Hannan, Higgins, Arthur, O'Brien, and Duffy.

99. Ltr., O'Boyle to John M. McAlinden, 22 May 1970, copy in *Humanae Vitae* file, AAW.

100. As quoted in Duffy intv. Byron was also off in his count of the remaining dissenters, who actually numbered forty-four.

have claimed that removing the sanctions sent a message to the laity that resulted in its widespread rejection of *Humanae Vitae*. The ultimate result of the Washington crisis, they argued, was a culture of dissent that reached critical mass in the Church in recent decades.[101] Offering an overview of the crisis, Cardinal William Baum concluded:

> He [O'Boyle] acted with consistency, defending the integrity of Catholic doctrine. . . . I think he was a hero for doing so. And subsequent events have proved him right. The rejection of *Humanae Vitae* has had grave consequences. Pope Paul foresaw it in the encyclical. . . . He said [that] denying the Church's doctrine on one point leads to others. And Cardinal O'Boyle saw all that. He was very clear. People didn't consider him a theologian, but he was a sound bishop, a *magister fide* in the way a bishop should be.[102]

The *Humanae Vitae* crisis reinforced the public's perception of Cardinal O'Boyle as a conservative and tough-minded Irishman, the standard bearer for the cause of papal authority in the American Church. This perception has endured beyond his death. However true, it overlooks O'Boyle's humanity. For the rest of his life Cardinal O'Boyle would suffer over the loss of so many talented priests. He bore no grudge against those who were reinstated. They were treated fairly with all the usual preferments opened to them. He once defined the ultimate victory in the crisis as reconciliation with all the dissenters. He failed to achieve that goal, and thus the crisis ultimately became a tragic chapter in the life of a loyal churchman.

101. George Weigel, *The Courage to be a Catholic: Crisis, Reform, and the Future of the Church* (New York: Basic Books, 2002), pp. 68–70, and Kelly, *The Battle for the American Church*, pp. 167–87.

102. Baum intv.

CHAPTER 15

"What'll They Think of Next?"

Cardinal O'Boyle retired in April 1973, five years after the Washington riot and just twenty-four months after adjudication of the *Humanae Vitae* crisis. A brief time, it was nevertheless long enough to demonstrate again those different elements in his philosophy of stewardship. On one hand, his genuine sympathy for labor and the poor, particularly those suffering because of racial discrimination, continued to be manifested in numerous social programs that placed him in the forefront of the progressive bishops in the post–Vatican II era. At the same time his narrower theological vision, along with an abiding reluctance to meet the demands of a clergy and laity anxious to share responsibility for operations of the Church in Washington, also ordered his actions. His increasingly public clashes over diocesan policy earned him the opprobrium of many in the Church who criticized him for what they considered reactionary ways.

Cardinal O'Boyle was a man firmly grounded in the pre–Vatican II Church, where power was centered in Rome and the local ordinary. Like many of his colleagues he believed the bishop's power in his see absolute and his responsibilities all-encompassing. While he usually found it easy to support the council's decisions, he found it difficult to accept the evolving relationship between a bishop and his people encouraged by the council fathers. His repeated question about the latest actions of subordinates—"What'll they think of next?"—was less a criticism of their proposals than an effort to understand a new age.

The Dissenters and Their Issues

New dissenters, both lay and clerical, had many issues to raise with Cardinal O'Boyle. Frustrated by the pace of reform as ordered by the

American bishops, they sought a more active role in the direction of diocesan affairs. If they met opposition, so be it. They were prepared to stand firm, as one put it, in hopes of eventually being reconciled to "an authority that is credible to me."[1] In Cardinal O'Boyle they met a man who neither age nor recent battles had worn down. He stood the strain of controversy well, as a close associate observed: "His adrenaline was always up for a battle."[2]

One of his most vocal critics during his last years in office was the Washington Lay Association. Organized in October 1967, it enrolled hundreds of Catholics from all the professions anxious to participate in Church activities, particularly its social programs, and to have a say in its finances and administration. The association's first priority was housing for the poor. On this subject there was much on which both sides could agree, so initial relations between the cardinal and the new group were cordial. Association representatives congratulated O'Boyle on his plan to involve the archdiocese in a comprehensive housing program; in turn the cardinal thanked the association for its interest in social action and welcomed its members' request for a meeting.[3]

O'Boyle met with the association's leadership in January 1968, at which time James P. Gibbons, soon to become president of the organization, outlined a plan that would involve the archdiocese with the association in a multimillion-dollar housing project. Stunned by the grandiose proposal, O'Boyle turned them down, explaining that his Urban Rehabilitation Corporation was already fully committed to a housing project as part of the archdiocese's long-term commitment of $14 million to social programs. Gibbons' reaction to the meeting foreshadowed the association's future relations with the archdiocese. He called the cardinal's advisors "a group of old men," and vowed that with or without O'Boyle's approval his group would seek money from individual parishes for its project. He figured his group had O'Boyle boxed in. There were ways to obtain parish lists, he noted, and, if needed, the association could go to the press.[4] Without diocesan help the association was forced to scale back its plans, but not before explaining to the press that the cardinal had rejected its proposal and refused to supply it with parish lists.[5]

1. Quotation from *The Voice*, Feb 1969.
2. Gillen intv.
3. Telegram, Joseph W. Lowell et al. to O'Boyle, 27 Oct 1967, and ltr., O'Boyle to Lowell, 2 Nov 1967. Both in WLA file, AAW. See also *WP*, 14 Oct 1967.
4. As quoted in memo, Bp. Herrmann for O'Boyle, 12 Jan 1968, sub: Meeting of the Washington Lay Association, WLA file, AAW.
5. *WP*, 27 Jan 1968.

Undeterred, the association announced its program, dubbed Project Share, and enlisted Robert F. Kennedy as honorary chairman. The project sought $259,000 to purchase and rehabilitate three hundred homes, which would then be rented for $100 a month. It planned to kick off its fund drive on May 4, when some thousand canvassers would call on members of 60,000 Catholic households identified in the area. The cardinal in turn announced that the Project Share canvassers were not authorized by the archdiocese and that the Catholic Charities collection scheduled for May would be used to support his ongoing housing project.[6]

Gibbons used O'Boyle's announcement of a moratorium on church construction to renew the association's request for help in obtaining contributions from Catholics now relieved of the expense of new parish buildings. O'Boyle again turned Gibbons down. For him to sponsor the association's "laudatory effort" while pressing the archdiocesan project would, he argued, "impose an undue moral obligation on our people." This was the last cordial exchange between the two. Shortly after, Gibbons publicly branded the cardinal a fraud on racial matters, while O'Boyle concluded, "These people are out to destroy me."[7]

Meanwhile the association pursued its agenda on several fronts. In February 1968 it called on O'Boyle to begin publishing archdiocesan budgets. Justifying the request, the board of directors quoted the statement accompanying Archbishop Hallinan's published financial report as reflecting "an openness, a 'sharing of authority' between the laity and hierarchy." O'Boyle promised to consider the proposal and even suggested to Archbishop Dearden that the matter be discussed at the next bishops' meeting. He personally considered it a good idea, he added, but the opinion of all the bishops needed to be considered.[8]

After receiving legal advice on his obligations as a corporation sole, O'Boyle considered telling the association that he would await a decision from the bishops. Instead, convinced (as he told Cardinal McIntyre) that the association was "really an anti-clerical group," he merely informed Gibbons that the proposal was being given "proper consideration." Although that ended discussion of the subject, in fact in the months to come increasing numbers of bishops, including O'Boyle, began publishing financial statements.[9]

6. *WP*, 12 Apr 1968, and *Star*, 3 May 1968.

7. As quoted in *Potomac* (*WP* Sunday magazine), 1 Jun 1969. For Gibbons' charge, see *NYT*, 24 Nov 1968.

8. Ltrs., Board of Directors, WLA, to O'Boyle, 17 Feb 1968 (source of quote); O'Boyle to Gibbons, 21 Feb 1968; O'Boyle to Cardinal Cody, 21 Feb 1968. All in WLA file, AAW. The discussion became public knowledge. See *WP*, 24 Feb 1968.

9. Ltrs., O'Boyle to McIntyre, 1 Mar 1968 (first quote), and to Gibbons, 19 Mar 1968 (second

In August 1968 the WLA, in union with the Washington Association of Priests and others, attacked the widespread exceptions to the cardinal's building moratorium. It asked O'Boyle specifically about the expensive projects under active consideration in three parishes.[10] Here the cardinal was vulnerable to adverse publicity because of his loosely defined exemptions mentioned in the moratorium announcement. By February 1969 nine parishes had been granted exemptions for building projects, reflecting an ongoing struggle between the traditional Catholics who wanted most of their contributions used in their own parishes and the social activists. In defense of the exemptions the vice-chancellor explained that almost a half-million dollars from the recent bishop's appeal had been applied to social projects, as had $300,000 from the archdiocesan development fund.

Despite Father Baroni's successful efforts to convince suburban parishes to meet with black Catholics to discuss inner-city concerns and the archdiocese's outlay for two hundred more houses, it was difficult to explain such large building projects like the new church at St. Camillus and the school at St. Ann's. The chancery confirmed that the moratorium was still in effect, but that did not stop the *Washington Post* from concluding that the $3.5 million in construction projects launched in four parishes since the moratorium demonstrated that "like so many brave statements of the Cardinal's it was followed up by no action, and today the building programs of the archdiocese are in full swing."[11]

Cardinal O'Boyle vigorously defended the archdiocese's record. In a rare appearance before a civic group, he told the businessmen in the Reciprocity Club that he was trying to translate the Church's social teachings into action. Without mentioning his critics by name, he defended the exceptions to the moratorium and ticked off the projects sponsored by the Urban Rehabilitation Corporation and other archdiocesan offices. He also stressed the need for greater government involvement because of the limits to the churches' efforts to cure social ills. "What they can do—all of them—is only a drop in the bucket."[12]

By this time the protesters had significantly escalated their charges. Firmly allied with the Association of Washington Priests, the Center for Christian Renewal, and the Committee for Freedom in the Church in the *Humanae Vitae* contro-

---

quote). In his ltr. to O'Boyle (27 Feb 1968), McIntyre had outlined the legal rights under corporation sole, an analysis confirmed by O'Boyle's lawyer (ltr., George Hamilton to O'Boyle, 28 Mar 1968). See also proposed reply to the Washington Lay Association, 19 Mar 1968. All in WLA file, AAW.

10. Ltr., Frank W. Reilly to O'Boyle, 12 Aug 1968, WLA file, AAW.
11. *WP*, 1 Jun 1969.
12. As quoted in *Star*, 29 Mar 1969.

versy, the WLA issued a blanket statement condemning what they saw as racism in the Church. Dubbing the archdiocese's social programs paternalistic and self-serving, they attacked the cardinal's financial, personnel, and education policies. Judging the archdiocese's social actions "ineffective," they called for a series of sweeping changes in financial and personnel policies.[13]

The protesters sought to explain their position in a series of "teach-ins" at the cathedral and various parishes with building programs. During or immediately following Sunday's principal Masses, representatives of the Center for Christian Renewal and the WLA would attempt to recite their charges against the archdiocese and their proposals for sharing authority with the bishop. These efforts and the resistance to them produced a circus-like atmosphere that ended with the spectacle of organists loudly drowning out Gibbons and the others and groups of opponents screaming an impromptu recitation of the rosary. During a melee on Good Friday at the cathedral, one parishioner knocked Gibbons down with a punch to the jaw. Gibbons filed charges, but later dropped them. Not so the cathedral pastor who, during a later teach-in, summoned the police and had a protester arrested for unlawful entry and disturbing a church service (by throwing what appeared to be blood on the altar). Cardinal O'Boyle stated his regret for the arrests, but this was the ninth such disturbance, he explained. Despite offers to provide the protesters facilities for their teach-ins outside the church proper, they had insisted on pursuing their program of interrupting Mass.[14]

The city's corporation counsel dismissed charges against those arrested, but not so the charges against several protesters who attempted to pass out literature during Mass at Blessed Sacrament Church on August 10. The police were called in to arrest the intruders, and subsequently Cardinal O'Boyle was served with a subpoena to appear at a hearing. The subpoena was later vacated, and the protesters found guilty and fined. The parish council had made available to them an area outside the church building, but the offer was refused. The pastor, Father Louis Quinn, expressed the sentiments of the chancery when he explained to the assistant corporation counsel that a church congregation made a "ready captive audience for any group if there is no protection against disorder and disruption."[15]

13. "A Statement on Racism in the Church," 10 Jun 1969, copy in Center for Christian Renewal file, AAW. The allies' charges were spelled out in detail by the Catholic News Service, 23 Jun 1969, copy in Chancery file, AAW.

14. Ltr., O'Boyle to Reverend and Dear Fathers, 22 Jul 1969, copy in St. Matthew's Cathedral Archives with enclosed statements by the cardinal and cathedral rector.

15. Ltr., Quinn to Louis D. Harrington, 2 Jan 1970, AAW. See also *CS*, 1 Jan 1970, *The Voice*, Sep 1969, and NC News Service Release, 21 Aug 1969.

Once again the cardinal was losing a press war. As distressed as he must have been over the disruptions, however, he dismissed them as irrelevant. Churches were never meant to be a public forum for discussion, he argued, and such activities always carried with them the potential for violence. He expressed himself open to a free discussion of social justice issues elsewhere, but, he added, such discussions could be fruitful only when animated by Christian generosity and charity.[16] Up close O'Boyle had a disarming way with the protesters. Spying a group of angry dissenters as he emerged from the Shrine of the Sacred Heart after the annual Labor Day Mass, he immediately walked over to them and began shaking hands. A friendly chat ensued, completely diverting the group from its original purpose.[17] Unfortunately the overarching debate over Church authority and the correct role of the laity could not so easily be resolved.

By 1970 the cardinal found himself under assault from yet another group of protesters, this time representatives of the local black Catholic community. The archdiocese counted some 60,000 African-American parishioners, a figure rapidly growing, with adult converts averaging a thousand a year. Many of these Catholics, frustrated by lingering discrimination and lack of progress toward racial justice, had come to believe that real progress was impossible as long as all authority was held by white men. The quest for black leadership in local community affairs was behind their demands in the early 1970s. According to Father Baroni, it represented "a valid kind of separation," not unlike efforts by Irish newcomers in earlier times to preserve their religion and culture.[18]

As the author of many racial reforms in past decades, O'Boyle was disappointed with demands for autonomy, even while recognizing the need for greater self-expression in the African-American community. Showing a peculiar myopia to the realities facing black citizens, he also expressed disappointment over the ever-escalating demand for further reform. Typical of his reaction to pressure groups, he refused to be pushed beyond what he considered proper. When the Black United Front demanded reparations for historic wrongs done to their ancestors, the cardinal refused to endorse the call. He would struggle in behalf of the "legitimate" aspirations of the black race, he said, but further than that he would not go. Called a racist by some for his stand, he confided to a friend, "That's what you get for adopting a fair attitude and staying with it."[19]

16. As quoted in *Star*, 9 Jun 1969.
17. As described in Coady intv. Msgr. Coady had accompanied O'Boyle to the Mass and watched the interchange from the Shrine's steps.
18. Buckner intv. See also *WP*, 1 Jun 1969.
19. As quoted in Archdiocese of Washington Biographical Release (ca. 1983), AAW (first quote), and McArdle intv. (second quote).

Cardinal O'Boyle supported the bishops' decision to create a National Office for Black Catholics devoted to the "liberation of black Catholics" by providing them with an official voice in Church affairs.[20] The office was organized in July 1970 under the direction of Brother James Davis, S.M., who pressed the bishops for an annual operating budget of $650,000 to help black parishes and support efforts of African Americans to gain control over institutions in their community. Plans to achieve these goals were devised by representatives of the Black Catholic Clergy and Sisters Caucuses and the Black Catholic Lay Caucus.

The archdiocese had its own Black Lay Caucus, which sponsored a national convention at Catholic University in August. Cardinal O'Boyle supported the group, calling on the clergy to cooperate in informing their congregations about the event. He also agreed to speak at the opening Mass. In his remarks on that occasion he referred to what he called a new hope based on the fact that black Catholics were taking the initiative in working toward self-determination in the African-American community.[21]

Despite these sentiments, O'Boyle was ill-prepared for the proposals that emerged from the convention. Brother James, labeling the Church a white man's institution, concluded: "If the Church is to be our home, it needs us in its jobs and leadership." The shortage of black priests, he charged, was not because of a lack of vocations, but because of the opposition of many bishops. Declaring "we are blacks first and Catholics second," the delegates sent a petition to the apostolic delegate demanding the ordination of four black bishops to head regional dioceses to which all black Catholics would belong.[22]

Close to home, O'Boyle faced the demands of the Black Catholic Clergy and Religious of Washington, a group organized in 1970. Its leaders announced their intent to survey Washington's black Catholic community and stress to the archbishop the urgency of the actions they would propose.[23] The new group's first objective was to reverse the decision of the superintendent of Catholic schools to close the Academy of Our Lady, a high school for girls in the inner city. The decision was made without consulting the school board or anyone in the black community, the group charged. It branded the promise to place all the girls in

20. As quoted in NC News Service Release, 2 Jul 1970.
21. Remarks by Cardinal O'Boyle, 21 Aug 1970, at National Convention of Black Catholics. See also ltrs., Sister Martin de Porres, S.C., to Fellow Catholics, 15 May 1970, and Gingras to Reverend and Dear Father, 24 Jul 1970. All in Black Lay Caucus file, AAW.
22. *WP*, 23 Aug 1970 (first quote), and NC News Service Release, 25 Aug 1970 (second quote).
23. Memo, Black Catholic Clergy and Religious Executive Board to Cardinal O'Boyle, 13 May 1970, sub: Organization of the Black Catholic Clergy and Religious of Washington, Black Catholic Clergy file, AAW.

other schools "bribery," and O'Boyle's promise that no urban schools would be closed "perfidious." Vowing not to allow "this death dealing paternalism to survive," they demanded greater black membership on the school board and reversal of the decision on the school closure.[24] Overlooking the fiery rhetoric, the cardinal acceded to the group's demand and reversed the decision of his school superintendent to close the school. He went on to settle a debate over the naming of a principal for the school.

No sooner had the school crisis ended than the group demanded more. In July 1971 Brother James complained about the lack of black leadership in an archdiocese with the fourth largest number of black Catholics and the largest number of black priests in the nation. There were no black pastors, he noted, and despite O'Boyle's declaration that the development of black leadership was a slow and laborious process, no effort had been made to hire African Americans in chancery positions beyond secretaries and custodians.[25]

There was no reply to this latest demand as the cardinal worked on social justice issues at his own pace. He continued to support the Black Catholic Lay Caucus, sending its leader $250 to help with its second convention while ignoring demands for creation of a black ombudsman to report, among other things, on the conduct of his education office.[26] He also tried to adjudicate lingering racial problems in the southern Maryland parishes.[27] Yet while vigorously working on projects he believed would advance the cause of racial justice, O'Boyle refused to be pushed along lines he considered inappropriate. For this stand he, who had been lauded in earlier decades as a crusader for racial justice, now earned the opprobrium of black Catholics pushing for a greater say in the operations of the Church.

At times the canny old reformer had the last say. A group of activists, seeking a greater voice in the Church's distribution of welfare, demanded that Fides House be given a full-time, paid black director. Actually Fides House depended on diocesan funds for all its work and its staff consisted of the unpaid members of the Missionary Servants and volunteer lay men and women. By the early 1970s when the demand was made, enrollment in the Fides programs had declined sig-

24. Memo, Black Catholic Clergy and Religious to His Eminence, 17 Apr 1971, no sub, Black Lay Caucus (hereafter BLC) file, AAW.

25. Brother James Davis, "Remarks at Black Leadership and Christ's Kingdom Society Dinner," 27 Jun 1971, copy in BLC file, AAW.

26. Ltrs., O'Boyle to Joseph Dulin, 10 Jun 1971, and Robert Robinson to O'Boyle, 3 May 1972. Both in BLC file, AAW.

27. Minutes of Meeting in Chancery Office attended by Cardinal O'Boyle and others, 22 Jun 1971, BLC file, AAW. See also McKenna intv.

nificantly. Far from considering demands for a paid director, the cardinal was about to withdraw support from what had become a fading institution. Commenting on their timing, O'Boyle told the activists, "You blew it."[28]

The spirit of protest, albeit in a more subdued form, was also affecting Washington's priests. Although the great majority had stood with Cardinal O'Boyle during the controversy over *Humanae Vitae,* many in that majority agreed with the Association of Washington Priests that the clergy should play a greater part in the administration of the archdiocese. The elected priests' senate was the usual avenue for communicating their recommendations, but O'Boyle was not deceived by that body's often-sugarcoated suggestions. He clearly understood that many of his priests wanted to share his responsibilities and just as clearly rejected the proposition. He was simply unable to shake off a lifetime's experience with a regimented Church structure. Nor could he dismiss his conviction that committee decisions were an inefficient way of doing business. His distrust of corporate decisions showed when he was visited at this time by a group of sisters. When he asked which of them was the superior, the women explained that there was no superior, that they shared the responsibility. His one-word retort: "Nonsense."

In March 1969 Father Joseph Byron, a member of the senate, had recommended that the regular deanery meetings throughout the archdiocese be used to discuss topics of concern suggested by a committee formed for that purpose in each deanery. The senate unanimously approved the recommendation, but the cardinal insisted on a change. While topics could be chosen by the deaneries, they must receive approval from the chancery prior to any discussion.[29] When the following month he asked the senate's personnel committee for a few suggestions on assignments, he felt it necessary to remind its members that their recommendations were "always advisory."[30] The committee submitted a few suggestions along with the offer to help him, in the wake of the crises over *Humanae Vitae,* establish closer rapport with his priests. If O'Boyle had any points he would like to discuss, the committee was ready to meet with him. O'Boyle obviously had no intention of turning to the committee for substantive work. There was a great deal of consultation, he commented wryly, "sometimes, I think, too much."[31]

28. Quoted in Coady intv. See also Paris, *"Fides* Means Faith," p. 44.

29. Minutes of Priests' Senate Meeting, 5 Mar 1969, SOP file, AAW.

30. As quoted by Msgr. Thomas Dade, see Minutes of Priests' Senate Meeting, 29 Apr 1969, SOP file, AAW.

31. As quoted in Duffy intv. See also Memo, Father Montgomery (for personnel committee) for O'Boyle, 9 Jul 1969, sub: Personnel Committee, SOP file, AAW.

O'Boyle's chancellor was concerned about yet another personnel committee suggestion. The group wanted the archdiocese's priests surveyed to ascertain their interests and qualifications for future assignments. Bishop Edward J. Herrmann saw no problem with a survey as long as it was voluntary, but he was skeptical of the committee's claim that the priests had little confidence in the senate's effectiveness, especially since it was so rarely consulted on assignments. One member of the senate, reflecting on the fact that a hundred priests in the diocese had failed to cast a vote in the last senate election, reported that many were upset because they viewed the senate as an impotent organization unworthy of their notice. Father Michael J. Arrowsmith, a member of the priests' senate, admitted that the cardinal could and did often ignore the senate's advice, but suggested that for the future of the body O'Boyle should at least explain why in any given instance he refused its recommendations.[32]

The cardinal made some effort to respond to the criticism. Putting on a happy face, he told the members of the senate that he appreciated their work and believed that he enjoyed a good relationship with them. But the cordiality stopped there. It would do well, he added, if the senate limited its work to advising the ordinary "and not expand itself into a body that would offer advice to all the Ordinaries." In effect he was warning the group to stay away from general pronouncements on the state of the Church, like its discussion of shared ministry and priestly celibacy. He was ready to submit a draft of his proposed assignments to the personnel committee for its advice, but only if he and the committee chairman polled all its members for their views. He also planned a change in the committee's makeup. In addition to the six elected members, he would appoint two auditors whose job would be to explain to the committee why some personnel suggestions were being rejected. Finally, the cardinal reversed himself on the subject of an arbitration board. When the senate first recommended such a body in the early stages of the *Humanae Vitae* crisis, he dismissed it out of hand, explaining, "You can't administer with all that." His thoughts had evolved by late 1971. He announced that he planned to create a board of arbitration and conciliation for the archdiocese, which would include two members chosen by the senate.[33] On minor matters, the cardinal proved to be considerably more flexible. For example, in 1972 he promptly approved a whole set of senate proposals on

32. Memo, Herrmann for O'Boyle, 7 Aug 1969, sub: Personnel Committee. See also Minutes of Priests' Senate Meeting, 8 Dec 1970. Both in SOP file, AAW.

33. Minutes of Priests' Senate Meeting, 21 Sep 1971, SOP file, AAW (first quote). See also Duffy intv. (second quote).

the quotidian concerns that any group of employees might have about personal expenses, continued education, and vacations.[34]

The cardinal continued to believe that the assignment and discipline of priests were basic responsibilities of the bishop and could not be shared. Nor did he consult any committee when he wanted to discipline a priest. When Father Raymond Kemp announced plans to run for a seat on the District of Columbia's school board, O'Boyle opposed it. Although he admitted that things might have been different if the elections were held in Scranton, he was convinced that in Washington the largely non-Catholic and black electorate "will kill you, they'll kill me, and they'll destroy the Church." Kemp ignored the cardinal, reasoning that if O'Boyle was adamant he could end the candidacy by transferring him. (Kemp won the election, and as predicted by O'Boyle, suffered through a short and turbulent term on the school board, constantly under fire from black extremists.)[35] Nor did the cardinal seek consultation or offer any explanation when he summarily dismissed an assistant from his post at St. Aloysius Church in Leonardtown, Maryland. Minus official explanations, the *Washington Post* speculated that the priest's long hair, "mod" clothing, and peace symbols had upset some of the parishioners.[36]

The cardinal's dedication to defending traditional Church teachings continued in the face of the impulse, even among his fellow bishops, to revise their position on some issues. At the 1972 bishops' meeting, for example, a gruff and unconverted O'Boyle insisted, over the objections of its authors, that the resolution "The Imperative of Peace" be amended to include a reassertion of the right of self-defense. It was clear that anything that might be interpreted as a retreat from traditional Church teaching only strengthened his determination to defend the old ways.[37]

During these last years in office O'Boyle also faced dissent in the academic community. Once again the underlying thread was divergent views on academic freedom at a Catholic university. In July 1971 Father Robert J. Henle, S.J., president of Georgetown University, published a letter in *Georgetown Today* explaining why his school took no stand on controversial subjects like Vietnam and *Humanae Vitae*. Faculty and students were expressing all shades of opinion on these subjects, he pointed out, and his duty was to protect openness and free-

34. Ltr., O'Boyle to Reverend and Dear Fathers, 17 Jul 1972, SOP file, AAW.

35. As quoted in Kemp intv. See also *The Advocate* (Newark, N.J.), 25 Sep 1971.

36. *WP*, 4 Dec 1971.

37. Thomas J. Reese, S.J., *A Flock of Shepherds: The National Conference of Catholic Bishops* (Kansas City, Mo.: Sheed & Ward, 1992), p. 159.

dom of expression on the campus. The conservative Jesuit theologian and O'Boyle friend Father John Ford openly debated Henle on this issue and kept O'Boyle informed. The cardinal was clearly pleased that someone was taking a stand against this kind of thinking. He congratulated his old comrade in the *Humanae Vitae* fight, telling Ford that he looked forward to Henle's reaction to the criticism.[38]

The cardinal, who had been keeping tabs on the university's reported liturgical innovations, again found himself in the midst of a very public dispute with Georgetown's president in 1972. Once again the issue was academic freedom, centering on the university's distribution of a sex manual. The booklet had been prepared by a group of medical students for their fellow students. Along with a frank discussion of all aspects of human sexuality, the forty-six-page work contained a nonjudgmental discussion of artificial birth control, abortion, and homosexuality. It also included an introduction by the authors' academic adviser, Father Robert C. Baumiller, S.J., describing the work's aims and offering the following disclaimer: "Moral questions, so important in this area, were not able to be handled because of lack of time and expertise and because the strict informational quality of this endeavor would be overwhelmed."[39]

The first reaction from official Church sources appeared in a lengthy editorial in the *Catholic Standard* on November 9, calling the manual "not only ill-advised; it is dangerous . . . a shabby project for any Catholic school." When a member of Catholic University's campus ministry attempted to refute the editorial in a letter to the editor, O'Boyle ordered the letter quashed. "I know this party so forget it," he added.[40] The cardinal entered the fray a week later. In a lengthy letter to Father Henle, he outlined the moral objections to the manual and demanded its withdrawal. "I feel I have no alternative," he added, "but to state that in view of this latest number of serious deviations from the teachings and discipline of the Church . . . there is serious doubt in my mind that Georgetown University can any longer consider itself a Catholic University." The cardinal was especially rankled by Father Baumiller's disclaimer. He asked Henle whether as president he approved the work and if not, what course of action he was prepared to take.[41]

38. *Georgetown Today,* Jul 1971, and ltrs., Ford to O'Boyle, 14 Jul 1971, and O'Boyle to Ford, 20 Jul 1971. Both in *Humanae Vitae* file, AAW.

39. *Human Sexual Response-Ability* (1972), copy in GU file, AAW.

40. Handwritten note signed PAO, attached to ltr., Brother Richard J. Albert, S.A., to Editor, *CS,* 10 Nov 1972, GU file, AAW.

41. Ltr., O'Boyle to Henle, 14 Nov 1972, GU file, AAW.

After talking with Henle he agreed to withhold publication of his denuncia-tion for a week and so informed the apostolic delegate.[42] When Henle's response finally arrived, it disclaimed responsibility for the publication and made no offer to withdraw it from circulation. True to his word, O'Boyle had his hard-hitting letter published in the *Catholic Standard,* and soon the secular press was all over the story. The debate took the expected turn when on November 24 a university spokesman, Father Edmond G. Ryan, S.J., defended the publication because "the rights of students to publish material without censorship by the university is key to the issue of academic freedom. . . . Students have the right to express themselves without fear of reprisal from the university." As for O'Boyle's threat to strip the university of its Church affiliation, Henle replied, "If you do, I'll sue you."[43]

Once again Cardinal O'Boyle found himself on the uncomfortable side of a debate over academic freedom. Msgr. Donoghue, now chancellor of the archdio-cese, issued a statement challenging Father Ryan's premise. The concept of aca-demic freedom in Catholic schools, he argued, did not apply when exercise of such freedom conflicted with the Church's moral teachings. What had hap-pened, Donoghue asked, to the concept that the Catholic college served *in loco parentis* for students entrusted to the faculty for a true philosophical and theo-logical education?[44] Donoghue's statement proved to be the parting shot in the affair. The manual, which had already been circulated throughout the campus, was not withdrawn, and threats to sue the archdiocese over the issue of academ-ic freedom faded away, as did O'Boyle's threat to take away the university's Church affiliation.

Behind the Times

Even as the various protest groups advanced their right to share in the Church's fiscal and operational decisions, none saw cause to criticize the cardi-nal for his long stewardship of the archdiocese. By 1969 local Catholics, number-ing more than 395,000, worshiped in 126 parishes, 47 of them established since 1949.[45] O'Boyle had supervised construction of scores of churches and schools

42. Memo, O'Boyle for Abp. Raimondi, 15 Nov 1972, GU file, AAW.

43. Ryan's explanation as quoted in *Star,* 25 Nov 1972. Henle's remark as quoted in Donoghue intv.

44. *CS,* 30 Nov 1972. See also Donoghue intv.

45. Accurate statistics for this period are hard to come by. Those used here come from a chancery study prepared for the NCCB in late 1968 and the December 1968 report for the Vatican's "Annuario Pontifico." See ltr., Vice-chancellor to Abp. Raimondi, 16 Feb 1969, AAW.

needed to accommodate this growth as well as the many charitable institutions which had opened during the past twenty years. He also had served as principal fund-raiser for an archdiocese with few of the financial resources needed to undertake such a vast building program. The cardinal cheerfully accepted the popular sobriquet "Cinderblock O'Boyle." He was a prime example of those brick-and-mortar bishops who had fostered the amazing growth of the American Church for more than a century.

Although now in his mid-seventies, O'Boyle continued to work a full day in the office, supervising every aspect of operations. Yet signs had appeared that cast doubt on the methods of administration that had served him so well since back in his New York days. His administrative style, which featured a very close control over every aspect of diocesan life, was proving inadequate in meeting the sudden acceleration of social programs and all the other complexities associated with a post–Vatican II diocese. He seemed to sense the problem. In a rare moment of reflection he complained in December 1970 that so many issues were referred directly to him, he was unable to give each the time and attention it deserved. Equally worrying, the present system frustrated his desire to follow through on each issue to its solution. Yet he seemed loath to change his ways. He had no intention of isolating himself from the work of the diocese, he told his immediate subordinates, but "given the temperament that I have, I always want to know what's going on, and I admit that I have injected myself into situations which have been assigned . . . [to others]." Seeking some sort of compromise, he asked all those in the chancery to list their current assignments and to note to whom they reported.[46] The investigation did little good. At the end of his career a poll revealed that no fewer than twenty-nine officials still reported directly to him.

Looking on the positive side, O'Boyle's direct involvement in the minutiae of the archdiocese and the people involved obviated any need for sophisticated organization. Yet as the archdiocese grew in size and its government in complexity, incidents began to occur demonstrating the busy executive's failure to follow through on important issues. In 1969 the priests' senate recommended that the archdiocese associate itself with Philadelphia's Institutional Procurement Service. Why such a proposal needed to be brought to the attention of the man who had organized New York's precedent-setting system years before is unclear. In his defense, the cardinal may have ignored the subject in previous decades, thinking that the Church in Washington was then too small to make central pur-

---

46. Memo, O'Boyle to Bp. Spence et al., 2 Dec 1970, Chancery file, AAW (source of quote).

chasing practical. Certainly he lacked a subordinate with Ed Kinney's genius for organization to start such a system. For whatever reason, it was indicative of the archdiocese's organizational weakness in 1969 that although the cardinal, calling the recommendation "a good idea," asked a subordinate to investigate the possibility of a Philadelphia connection, nothing came of it. Years would pass before the archdiocese established central purchasing under O'Boyle's successors.[47]

Another expensive mishap occurred when the archdiocese refused to purchase the campus of the recently closed Dunbarton College in the upper Connecticut Avenue region. The Holy Cross sisters offered the campus to O'Boyle for a song, but the man who always reminded those around him that "the Church isn't in the real estate business" turned them down. That left the valuable property to others and meant that the archdiocese lost a useful source of revenue for its many social programs. Archbishop Hannan later commented that, while he had made mistakes as chancellor of Washington, none was that big. When he heard of the proposed sale, he called O'Boyle from New Orleans urging him to get the contract rescinded. O'Boyle, who, Hannan realized, had never learned a thing about the real estate business in all his years in the capital, merely fretted, and the sale went through.[48]

Actually, the failure of the hard-pressed administrator to retain close supervision of all construction projects sometimes worked to the benefit of the archdiocese. Father Farina, for example, suggested building a new and very different style rectory at Holy Family parish in the Maryland suburbs in keeping with post–Vatican II concepts of priestly living. Without the usual searching questions, the cardinal ordered Farina to "go ahead and see what happens." His reaction prompted many pastors to seek permission to plan and construct buildings in keeping with their needs without enduring the old and often inhibiting scrutiny from above.

Also puzzling, given his New York experience, was O'Boyle's delay in applying modern fund-raising techniques to the archdiocese's charities. For twenty years his major effort was the annual appeal for Catholic Charities. Parishioners were constantly dunned to contribute to second collections for the many agencies not directly affiliated with Catholic Charities. Often these collections failed to meet the needs of the many social programs, which then had to devote time and personnel to fund-raising. Finally in 1969 Msgr. Coady, the director of Catholic Charities, got the cardinal to organize an annual appeal that combined giv-

47. Minutes of Priests' Senate Meetings, 5 Mar (source of quote) and 26 Jun 1969, AAW.
48. Hannan intv.

ing for most of these agencies.[49] A committee of chancery officials was formed to allocate the funds collected, while an executive gifts committee solicited large contributions from wealthy donors. The cardinal himself proved to be the most effective fund-raiser. One subordinate learned his technique when he overheard a telephone conversation during which, after an affable exchange, O'Boyle bluntly asked the donor what he planned to pledge that year. He then reminded his hapless listener how good God had been to him and successfully negotiated a substantial increase. Most often such soft pressure tactics proved profitable for the campaign. Commenting on the distasteful job, O'Boyle remarked, "I'm never embarrassed or ashamed to beg for God's poor."[50]

The first Cardinal's Appeal, conducted in May 1969, realized over $527,000, more than doubling the Catholic Charities appeal of the previous year. The 1970 campaign showed further increase. Father James F. Montgomery, the appeals director, finally persuaded O'Boyle that the diocese's major charities, still independently collecting money, should be included in the 1971 campaign. For some reason, Msgr. Coady noted, O'Boyle believed that $600,000 represented the most that the traffic would bear in Washington. His advisors finally convinced him to set the goal for the 1971 appeal at $725,000. The area Catholics responded by pledging over $800,000. The appeal and Cardinal O'Boyle's personal comments on the needs of the archdiocese received general coverage in the press.[51]

A Last Hurrah

Throughout his career O'Boyle tended to regard the press as an adversary. Only in his last years in office did he learn to use trusted laymen to deal directly with the fourth estate. In 1970, for example, he sent a group to discuss with the *Post*'s executive editor, Benjamin Bradlee, some recent Oliphant cartoons that, he believed, ridiculed the Church. The group's spokesman, Walter McArdle, told O'Boyle that they made significant progress and were generally satisfied with the outcome of the lengthy talk about the *Post*'s coverage of the Church. In response, the cardinal, always pushing for further concessions, asked an exasperated McArdle why he had not complained to Bradlee about the paper's religion reporter.[52] The success of the delegation in their meeting with Bradlee con-

49. Coady intv.

50. Bishop Thomas Lyons, "Eulogy Delivered at the Funeral of Cardinal O'Boyle," copy in AAW.

51. A history of the collection was prepared by the Appeals Office in 1979. For press coverage, see, for example, *Star*, 28 Mar 1970, and *WP*, 3 Apr 1971 and 26 Jan 1973.

52. Memo, Walter McArdle to O'Boyle, 1 Apr 1971, sub: Memo of meeting regarding cartoon in *Washington Post*, Chancery file, AAW. See also McArdle intv.

Pro-Life Champion. O'Boyle, armed with the pink carnation that symbolized the movement, greets a child at a pro-life Mass.

vinced O'Boyle that such rebuttals were best left to laymen. He encouraged friends like McArdle and other prominent Catholic Washingtonians to respond to critics, using the letters to the editor columns and personal contacts to advance the Church's position. What he really wanted, he said, was a Catholic equivalent of the Anti-Defamation League, which successfully countered anti-Semitism. He never succeeded in that, a failure he always regretted.[53]

Even though he lost the media war on several important occasions, Cardinal O'Boyle was actually quite skilled at winning publicity for his causes. Thanks to the press, the shepherd of Washington's Catholics had become a latter-day Jeremiah, preaching morality to every subscriber of the city's great newspapers. "American Culture Is Polluted," screamed the *Post* headline in June 1971 over its summary of the cardinal's analysis of what he called "the new morality," which sanctioned sexual license and abortion, contrary to all Christian teaching.[54] The statement would not have surprised any diligent *Post* reader, since that newspaper, like its competitors in Washington and New York, had been reporting the cardinal's no-holds-barred condemnation of the practices. In December 1969 the *New York Times* had reported O'Boyle's denunciation of the District government for practicing "extermination medicine" in its ruling that D.C. General Hospital could perform abortions upon request. Those who claimed that publicly financed abortions were meant to help the poor, he asserted, were in reality hoping to eliminate poverty by eliminating the poor.[55]

Passage of a population control bill in the U.S. Senate in September 1970 found the cardinal ready for battle. Once again he expounded the thesis that such legislation "exposes the proposition that the simplest way to get rid of poverty is to get rid of poor people." Though the legislation would only have provided contraceptives to those who needed them, O'Boyle said nothing in it precluded the use of abortion as a method of birth control. Should the bill become law, he reasoned, "the country would take a giant step toward espousing the anti-life philosophy . . . as a public policy."[56] The bill did become law, but to make sure Catholics understood his arguments, he called on all priests in the archdiocese to attend a right-to-life seminar so that they might become better informed on a subject he expected all of them to preach in the coming months.[57]

O'Boyle continued to write and preach against abortion, especially on the an-

53. McArdle and Abell intvs.
54. *WP*, 20 Jun 1971.
55. *NYT*, 10 Dec 1969.
56. As quoted in *Star*, 24 Sep 1970.
57. The order was reported in the *CS*, 4 Mar 1971.

In Retirement. Well into his ninth decade O'Boyle kept busy traveling and attending conferences, Here, in October 1984, at age 88, he was a speaker at the Catholic Charities Awards Dinner.

nual Right to Life Sunday, but he saved his mightiest salvo for an attack on the District's mayor and city council for adopting regulations governing abortion clinics. He accused local officials of "giving an aspect of legitimacy to a procedure that kills." Alluding to the Nazi-ordered abortions on Jews and the fact that seventy-one percent of the city's population and most of its poor were African American, he told a cathedral congregation, "No one can ignore the implication of genocide."[58] The press reacted instantly to what one editorial called "extrava-

58. Quoted in both *Star* and *WP*, 7 Aug 1972.

gant rhetoric." Using the "electric" word *genocide,* the cardinal had shattered the city's tranquility, it claimed, "by his wild assertion."[59] In January 1973, when the Supreme Court decided in the case of *Roe v. Wade* that a woman had the right to an abortion in the first trimester of pregnancy, he branded the decision "a catastrophe for America . . . a hideous and heinous crime" and likened it to the Dred Scott decision, which once protected the institution of slavery. He made it clear to his flock that the Supreme Court could never rule abortions morally permissible. He concluded: "No court can do that." He wanted all the homilies at Sunday Masses to be devoted to reminding Catholics that abortion was morally evil and that the laws of the Church must be obeyed.[60] Because of such unambiguous and outspoken condemnations, he earned the mantle of leader in the Church's reaction to government's growing intrusion into the debate.

Other issues engaged Cardinal O'Boyle during his later years. He continued to defend the legitimacy and usefulness of parochial schools. To an audience of Rotarians and Kiwanians he ignored the Church's historical position and defended the moral impact of public schools in earlier times. In those days, influenced by the Protestant ethic, students learned of the reality of God, the importance of the Commandments, and the efficacy of prayer. Unfortunately, he charged, that ethic had given way in modern times to a secular humanism that failed to meet the needs of young people. In contrast, he described the parochial school's combination of secular and religious education as a kind of natural successor to the public schools of earlier days. People of many faiths had come to realize this, he claimed, as well as the fact that parochial schools in no way caused divisiveness in a pluralistic society.[61] In a headline-generating statement he branded the concept of "religious neutrality" a myth and stated that public schools were beginning to show increasing favoritism to one or another religion. He was referring to what he called the humanistic and secular concept at the heart of public education, which he said was itself a religion. He agreed with the recent Supreme Court decision that Catholic schoolteachers were unlikely to maintain neutrality in regard to religion, but neither, he argued, would schoolteachers of every kind of religious view, including atheism, remain neutral.[62]

Public aid for parochial schools was one argument he would never win. He met with more success in his call for social justice for agriculture workers. The

59. *Star,* 10 Aug 1972.

60. As quoted in *WP,* 25 Jan 1973.

61. O'Boyle, "On Educational Values," 26 Nov 1969, copy in AAW.

62. O'Boyle, "On Public School Teaching Religion," 3 Oct 1969, copy in AAW. See also *NYT,* 4 Oct 1971.

bishops had avoided a public statement in 1969 when Cesar Chavez led the United Farm Workers in a strike against California's grape growers. Instead they organized a commission, which under Bishop Joseph Donnelly and Msgr. Higgins was instrumental in bringing about a useful agreement.[63] When Chavez sought to organize the lettuce harvesters in 1972, a call again went out for a boycott. This time the bishops' Social Development Committee urged Catholics to observe the boycott.[64] Although the NCCB itself remained noncommittal, O'Boyle took his cue from the Higgins group. In a statement read at the 1972 Labor Day Mass he called on the public to support the migrant farmworkers. In standing with the laborers he referred to his Scranton boyhood and the plight of the immigrants in that era. Living conditions for the California farmworkers, he charged, were similar to the deprivation families he knew in his hometown were forced to endure. Although his statement was addressed to Catholics in his archdiocese, it received wide and favorable notice. The AFL-CIO cited him for his leadership in the fight for social justice.[65]

In October 1972 the cardinal made one of his rare references to the Vietnam conflict, a war that had enveloped the nation in a debate that was producing violent demonstrations around the country. Back in 1966, after being assured that his action could not be interpreted as a criticism of the Johnson administration or an attempt to dictate its foreign policy, he called on priests, "without editorializing in any manner," to lead their congregations in prayer for American troops.[66] Later he began to condemn the cost of the war, but without change in his intention to remain neutral. In a sermon on the worth and dignity of human life in 1972, he remarked that the nation's domestic problems were another victim of the war. American society, he added:

> has yet to find a way to disentangle itself from one of the longest and most tragic wars in the nation's history—a war which has seriously divided our people and has crippled our efforts to solve our most pressing social and economic problems here at home.

Although the statement no doubt reflected his focus on the cost of the war, he approved the 1972 resolution by the American bishops, "Imperative of Peace."

63. Interview with Bishop Joseph F. Donnelly, chairman of U.S. Bishops' Ad Hoc Committee on Farm Labor, NC News Service, copy in John Carroll Society files.
64. *NYT*, 12 Jul 1972.
65. Text of Statement by Cardinal O'Boyle, reprinted in *CS*, 7 Sep 1972. See also *Star*, 4 Sep 1972, and *Catholic Mind* (Dec 1972): 7–10.
66. Memo, Spence to O'Boyle, 20 Dec 1966, sub: Regarding Prayers for our Military in Vietnam, and ltr., Roeder to Rev. Fathers, 23 Dec 1966. Both in Chancery file, AAW.

His approval, however, had been contingent on the inclusion of his amendment asserting the right of self-defense.[67] It might be assumed that the cardinal did not condemn American involvement in the war because he did not want to see the Vietnamese people, especially the Catholics, abandoned and handed over to Communist domination. Unlike Cardinal Spellman in his oft-quoted defense of national policy ("My country right or wrong . . ."), O'Boyle offered commentary rather than condemnation. He remained neutral on the issue. Clearly the old lion in the winter of his career was ready to roar out against abortion and all matters of social injustice, but was reluctant to make a clear judgment on the morality of a war that was preoccupying citizens above all else.

67. Reese, *Flock of Shepherds*, p. 159. For text of the resolution, see Nolan, *Pastoral Letters of the U.S. Bishops*, vol. 3, pp. 229–40.

CHAPTER 16

Finale

Responding to a papal directive to the world's bishops on the age of retirement for senior clergy, Cardinal O'Boyle submitted his resignation in July 1971, days before his seventy-fifth birthday. By all accounts the letter was a pro forma gesture. In good health, with a number of new social programs under way, and with the *Humanae Vitae* controversy just winding down, he was pleased that the pope did not respond immediately to his offer. While bishops, and especially cardinals, were often retained in office long after their seventy-fifth birthdays, O'Boyle was retired just twenty-one months later. (He would remain another two months as apostolic administrator of the archdiocese until his successor was installed.)[1]

Although the pope had on several occasions expressed his deep gratitude for O'Boyle's stalwart defense of *Humanae Vitae*, some in the Vatican were less appreciative of the cardinal's unsubtle approach to the controversy over the encyclical, which had revealed deep divisions in the Church. Immediate acceptance of his resignation was unthinkable. Coming just months after the Vatican's response in the case of the Washington dissidents, it would be widely perceived as a defeat for the cardinal. It was only after celebration of his twenty-fifth anniversary as archbishop of Washington, during which the pope again praised him for his "vigorous defense" of the faith, that the change was announced.

Soon after the cardinal's letter of resignation was published, the Black Catholic Lay Caucus pressed him to recommend an African American as his successor. In October 1971 its representatives arrived in Rome with

---

1. On O'Boyle's thoughts on retirement, see Donoghue intv. See also *NYT*, 16 Jul 1971.

the hope of personally petitioning the pope on the matter.[2] Nothing came of these efforts, and in April 1973 William Wakefield Baum, the youthful bishop of the Diocese of Springfield–Cape Girardeau, Missouri, was named to head the Church in Washington. On May 9, after the apostolic letter of appointment was read, Cardinal O'Boyle led his successor to the bishop's throne and handed him his staff, the symbol of his new office. Baum readily agreed that O'Boyle should continue to live in his Warren Street home, where Msgr. Donoghue would remain his house companion. Baum, who had known O'Boyle for years through his work on the NCCB staff, disagreed with those who pointed out the potential trouble in having a retired but still active predecessor residing in the city. Baum understood the cardinal's deep respect for the proprieties and knew he would never interfere.[3] When quizzed by a group of reporters on the subject, O'Boyle admitted that he did not relish idleness, "but that's up to my successor." A new man was in charge, he added, and it was O'Boyle's duty to help him in any way possible.[4]

True to his word, O'Boyle attended all the public ceremonies to which he was invited during the next few years. He officiated at confirmations, St. Patrick Day Masses, even the blessing of the fleet at St. Clement's Island, until the phlebitis in his leg became too painful. He rarely appeared in the cathedral and with few exceptions did not again offer Mass in public. Sometimes he was forced into the limelight. When Washington's clergy welcomed Pope John Paul II in 1979 at a ceremony at St. Matthew's Cathedral, O'Boyle, feeling under the weather, decided only at the last minute to attend, and then quietly, in a back seat. He was mortified by what happened, he recalled: "Wouldn't you know, the Holy Father spotted little Patrick and insisted that I walk with him up the aisle. How I ever made it was miraculous. It seemed like a ten mile trek."[5]

One ceremony he was determined to attend occurred in September 1973, when he and Archbishop Baum dedicated the monastery for the Carmelite nuns at Great Mills in southern Maryland. For many years a dedicated group known as the Restorers had worked for the acquisition and renovation of the 200-year-old Carmelite monastery at Port Tobacco, the first convent in English-speaking America. The site became the venue for popular pilgrimages, one of which the cardinal joined. The Restorers' hope had always centered on the return of the

2. *NYT,* 23 Jul and 2 Oct 1971.
3. Baum and Abell intvs. See also Higgins intv. Msgr. Higgins was one of those questioning the wisdom of having a predecessor so nearby.
4. As quoted in *Star,* 4 Mar 1973.
5. As quoted in Weber's intv. with O'Boyle.

Carmelites to their historic home, and O'Boyle's interest encouraged them.[6] His interest had first been sparked by Mother Teresa of the Cross, at one time his secretary before entering the Carmel. Soon after his appointment to Washington, she approached him for help in returning the nuns to their historic home. O'Boyle was torn. He wanted the Carmelites back in the diocese and was impressed with the fervor of the pilgrims and the Restorers, but he considered Port Tobacco too remote from Catholic population centers. In the end he rejected the idea of restoring Port Tobacco as a working monastery, but supported efforts to build a pilgrim hall and acquire more of the monastery's original property.

Mother Teresa was undaunted. She continued to broach the subject until he finally agreed to petition the Father General of the Carmelites to bring the nuns back to the archdiocese. The formal dedication of the Holy Face Carmelite monastery at Great Mills in 1973 was an interim step. Three years later found the nuns restored to their historic home. Although retired, the cardinal kept a careful eye on the new monastery. One of the nuns recalled that during particularly cold snaps in the winter he would suddenly call to ask if they were warm enough. He once accused Father Farina of being "cheap" at the nuns' expense for constructing poorly insulated hermitages. Farina had to explain that the huts were built according to the nuns' specification. All he did was supply the funds.[7]

Another ceremony O'Boyle continued to enjoy was the feast day of his namesake. Three weeks after his retirement he officiated at St. Patrick's Church, reminding the congregation of the 700 years of oppression suffered by the Irish and the need for America's Irish to keep the faith as their ancestors had.[8] The following year found him in Scranton addressing the Friendly Sons of St. Patrick. But there was a limit to his extolling all things Irish. In 1978 he ended his usual practice of sponsoring the annual St. Patrick's Day parade because the Irish Northern Aid Committee was scheduled to march. The group was widely believed to be a secret supporter of the outlawed Irish Republican Army.[9]

Like many new retirees, Cardinal O'Boyle was uneasy about the future. He seemed to miss all the bustle and fuss of the last decades as well as the give and take with his critics.[10] He began his new life with a flurry of activity. He traveled.

6. Nuns of the Port Tobacco Carmel, *Who Remembers Long: A History of the Port Tobacco Carmel* (Washington, D.C.: privately published, 1984), pp. 28–39.

7. Sister Mary Ann, O.Carm, and Msgr. Farina intvs. Sister Mary Ann was one of the nuns who accompanied Mother Teresa when the restored convent was opened.

8. *WP*, 18 Mar 1973.

9. *Staten Island Advance*, 8 Mar 1978.

10. Abell intv. Abell provided a carefully nuanced portrait of O'Boyle in retirement.

Several times he flew to Los Angeles to visit Cardinal McIntyre, and in 1979 to help bury him. He traveled to Ireland, one time with his friend Archbishop Thomas J. Donoghue of Louisville, later for a comprehensive tour with Msgr. John Donoghue that found them visiting the O'Boyle family in Mayo. His last trip was arranged by his Muldoon cousins, but he spent the time in a Dublin hotel with Msgr. Joseph Corbett while the rest of the party toured the country in miserable weather. Closer to home he made several sentimental trips to Mt. Loretto. In 1973 he spent Thanksgiving day with his Staten Island friends, and in 1976 he participated in the dedication of its rebuilt church, now considerably smaller than the grand structure criticized by Cardinal Spellman forty years before.[11]

In August 1976, the eighty-year-old cardinal attended the Eucharistic Congress in Philadelphia, where he spoke before 12,000 seniors on the aging process and the reaction of modern society to its aged members. A civilization was truly developed and blest by God, he contended, when it respected and cared for both its very old and very young.[12] He also felt well enough that year to travel to Rome to celebrate his successor's installation as a cardinal. When an anxious travel mate asked the old gentleman why he was leaving his seat, O'Boyle remarked, "I'll let you know—even a cardinal has to go once in a while."[13]

During the early years of retirement the cardinal faithfully attended the annual bishops' meetings. Turning eighty in 1976 meant that he who for so many years had had a significant role in the bishops' conference was now barred from voting with his fellow bishops. He resented the ban and quit attending meetings. Observers like Msgr. Ellis noted that during these years the cardinal had become less aggressive, had in fact mellowed into a warm person. Yet there were still times when the old Irish temper blew hot. O'Boyle had little respect for Archbishop Bernardin since the latter's intervention in the *Humanae Vitae* controversy. He abruptly left the opening meeting of the bishops' conference in 1974, proclaiming audibly, "The only reason I came was to vote against him."[14]

11. Ltrs., O'Boyle to Msgr. Edmund Fogarty (director of Mt. Loretto), 7 Feb 1973, and Fogarty to O'Boyle, 22 Oct 1976. Copies of both in Mt. Loretto Archives. O'Boyle was a faithful benefactor of the institution, at one time contributing $1,000 to the chapel fund.

12. Address to the Senior Citizens at the 41st Eucharist Congress, 3 Aug 1976, copy in AAW. According to Archbishop Donoghue the speech was drafted by O'Boyle's director of Catholic Charities, Msgr. Leo Coady.

13. As quoted by Joseph Vaghi, Sr., in his intv.

14. As quoted both in Eugene Kennedy, *The Now and Future Church: The Psychology of Being an American Catholic* (Garden City, N.Y.: Doubleday & Co., 1982), pp. 23–24, and Reese, *A Flock of Shepherds,* p. 49.

Until near the end of his long retirement, the cardinal exhibited the same self-discipline that had ordered his life since boyhood. Except for periods of travel, his routine never varied. He rose at six, offered Mass, fixed his own breakfast, and, weather permitting, took a walk in the Warren Street neighborhood. He was then ready to greet his secretary, Ann Wolfe, who came to help with the large volume of correspondence. In time the stream of letters would slow to a trickle, and with little to occupy him, he finally succumbed to the pleas of old friends to write his memoirs. But his heart wasn't in the project, and after dictating a series of brief vignettes on events, mostly those that occurred before he came to Washington, he gave up the task. Wolfe continued to come in, if only to share tea and donuts with the cardinal and administer his eye drops. Concerned for her safety, he insisted on walking out with her when she left the house and standing on the curb to signal when it was safe for her to drive off.

After lunch he usually puttered a bit in the yard and always took a nap. Isabel Marin, his long-time housekeeper, was on hand to prepare dinners that he shared with Msgr. Donoghue or guests like the McArdles, Benjamin Rome, and old colleagues like Bishop Wycislo. Occasionally there were longer visits. His Muldoon relatives regularly arrived for brief stays. In 1982 Msgr. Francis J. Weber, Cardinal McIntyre's biographer, spent a week discussing O'Boyle's old friend with him. Weber was taken aback, as he put it, by how he, a simple priest, was received by a prince of the Church. O'Boyle met him personally at the airport, prepared his lunches, and even brought him his towels.[15] Periodically O'Boyle would dine with friends, but only at the McArdles did he seem to relax enough to remove his clerical collar and enjoy a pre-dinner scotch on their patio.

In 1984 the pope selected Msgr. Donoghue to be the bishop of Charlotte, North Carolina. His departure was a mighty blow to O'Boyle, who had come to think of the younger man as a son. A distraught Donoghue even considered refusing the appointment, but O'Boyle insisted that he obey. The cardinal, now eighty-eight, never bounced back after the separation. Donoghue was replaced by the director of communications, the ebullient Father Maurice T. Fox, and in the final months by a youthful Father Kevin T. Hart. For a time Father Thomas M. Duffy, the chaplain of the city's police and firemen, joined the household. By then many of the cardinal's old friends and colleagues had died. In addition to Frank McIntyre and Jim Norris, his assistant at Mt. Loretto and at War Relief, he lost younger subordinates like Joseph Corbett and Geno Baroni. Most wrenching was the loss of his long-time friend and physician Tom Collins. By then, also,

15. Weber, *California Essays*, no. 16.

the cardinal, who had enjoyed relatively good health all his long life, was beginning to show the debilities of extreme old age. It became difficult for him to
sleep. Most nights found him dozing in his chair, only to wake at 3:00 a.m. About
this time a young Seventh-Day Adventist physician from India, studying at
Georgetown for his U.S. board certification, was employed to give O'Boyle his
medicine and otherwise ease his infirmities.

The cardinal rarely talked about death. He liked to repeat the story his old
New York pastor told about the thought of a friend who was watching Cardinal
Hayes being installed at St. Patrick's Cathedral. He had to smile, the friend reported, thinking that, as Hayes was being seated with great pomp on his throne
directly above the cathedral's crypt, the all-powerful prelate was actually "sitting
on his own grave." Although saddened by the death of old friends, he was un-
afraid. "We're all born to die," he reminded Donoghue.[16]

On some days he failed to recognize visitors. Father Gillen and Walter McArdle had to remind him who they were. When Father Hart first appeared at the
Warren Street house he was faced with a grouchy cardinal who demanded,
"Who the hell are you?" Hart explained that he had been sent to live there by
Archbishop Hickey, to which O'Boyle replied, "Well, who the hell is he?" When
reminded that Hickey was his successor, he immediately changed his tone and
invited Hart into his home. Even in the haze of old age he remembered that duly
authorized orders must be obeyed. He also remembered the tough road faced by
the Irish immigrants of his youth. By now he used a cane to help get around.
Each time he passed the fireplace he gave the iron coalscuttle a good whack with
the cane, announcing, "That's for Scranton."[17]

On the eve of a visit by the Muldoons in July 1987, the cardinal fell in the
shower, breaking his hip. He underwent surgery at Georgetown Hospital to insert a rod that would enable him to walk again. He soon recovered enough to
stay with the Little Sisters of the Poor, where he received physical therapy. Before
much progress was made, he suffered a series of strokes that led to pneumonia
and kidney failure. He was taken to Providence Hospital to await the inevitable.
The morning of August 10 found him in a mostly unconscious state. Until then
he had continued to fight, but he seemed to understand Father Hart's consoling
words that it was all right to let go. He squeezed the priest's hand and, as the old
Irish saying put it, went home to God.

16. O'Boyle, Notes, pt. 3 (first quote), and Donoghue intv. (second quote).
17. As quoted in Hart intv.

In Retrospect

The cardinal's obsequies continued over several days, culminating in the funeral Mass on Friday, August 14, attended by 7 of the 8 American cardinals, 40 bishops, 225 priests, and some 1,100 lay men and women. During the funeral and the ceremonies preceding it, the archdiocese heard a host of speakers eulogize their departed leader. Former mayor Walter Washington reminded his audience of the cardinal's stand on social reform, especially his work for racial justice. President Ronald Reagan's tribute, read at the service, referred to O'Boyle as the son of immigrants who epitomized the finest qualities of a loving father in a turbulent era in the nation's history. William Bennett spoke on behalf of the federal government. The most moving moments occurred just before the cardinal's body was interred in the special crypt prepared in the cathedral, when Bishop Lyons spoke about his old friend. In summarizing the cardinal's life, he concluded that the greatest tribute that could be paid to his memory would be the "recommitment of our lives, whatever our station or calling may be, to stand fast in the faith." He concluded by referring to O'Boyle as "a complex man, but a man of simple, direct, and strong faith. A man fully committed to the fulfillment of the responsibilities of the life to which he was called."[18]

Even before his death, the picture of a complex Patrick O'Boyle, liberal on social issues and conservative on matters of theology and Church authority, had become a cliché. Scranton in the time of his youth made an indelible impression on the cardinal. Just as he continued throughout life to return repeatedly to the city and friends of his boyhood, he constantly referred to the conditions endured there by the immigrants of those days and related it to the problems faced by Washington's poor. The experience of his family in Scranton's mills and mines, reinforced by his respect for the Church's social encyclicals, made him a strong proponent of the American labor movement. O'Boyle's support of unionism was especially important in Washington, where most workers were not organized.

It might seem difficult to trace a line between his childhood experiences in Scranton and his later championship of racial justice, but the cardinal frequently made the connection. In his many exhortations against discrimination, he would remind his audience of the desperation of Scranton's immigrant and largely Catholic population and relate their plight to the black experience. He was one of Washington's earliest civil rights champions, instrumental in shaping the city's

18. As quoted in *CS,* 20 Aug 1987. This paragraph is based on the *Standard's* full coverage of the cardinal's funeral.

response to discrimination. Walter Fauntroy, the District of Columbia delegate in the U.S. House of Representatives, said his friend played a pivotal role in the resolution of civil rights problems in the region. "He was a gentle giant of a man on questions of civil and human rights."[19]

If experiences in his Scranton youth nurtured his belief in the God-given dignity of humans of every race and creed, it was his assignments in New York that formed his attitude toward authority and discipline. Following exactly the rules and procedures set by the Church guided his years in Washington. Assignments in the New York archdiocese instilled in him a great respect for the office of bishop. He was also aware that his consecration as archbishop invested him with great authority. Although he frequently asked advice from his old New York colleagues, he demonstrated complete assurance in his new powers from his first days in town.

His parish experience, though brief, instilled in him a conservative, but never austere, approach to the laity. In the decades before Vatican II the American Church had developed a womb-to-tomb Catholicism that priests like O'Boyle respected and nurtured. It followed that nothing must subvert the laity's respect for priests. Thus came his eccentric insistence on cassocks in the rectory and hats in public because "people expect it." His abiding concern was that by their dress or behavior priests must never scandalize the simple Catholics in the pews. The increasing sophistication of Washington's laity never seemed to quiet his fears.

Thanks to his New York training and experiences O'Boyle became in the literal sense one of the country's first social-worker priests. His training at the New York School exposed him to the latest understanding of childcare institutions. His increasing responsibilities in New York's vast social welfare system provided him with administrative skills. Experience in dealing with Church and secular authorities at every level taught him the usefulness of mixing tact with stratagem. The experience of his long years in Catholic Charities, reinforced by his innovative direction of Catholic War Relief, made him a perfect choice for the new archdiocese of Washington.

In the wake of Vatican II, the Washington archdiocese experienced a series of crises that altered the way many Catholics regarded their spiritual leader. O'Boyle had openly welcomed some of the changes ordained by the council fathers. Some, he believed, like the declarations on race, the Jews, and religious freedom, should have been enacted years before. In other matters, however, he

19. As quoted in *CS*, 13 Apr 1987.

would have preferred a slower approach. Age seemed to have strengthened his natural conservatism, especially in regard to the liturgy. While he faithfully enacted those modifications approved by the Vatican, he summarily rejected efforts by an element of the clergy and laity to experiment with new forms of worship. He appeared deaf to their insistence that they too must share responsibility for the renewed direction of the Church. Some bishops understood the need to work with these often sincere and loyal Catholics in fashioning a new model of Church authority and discipline, but Cardinal O'Boyle never came to appreciate the subtleties and complexities of this new way of perceiving the Church.

Debate over liturgy and the accelerated social action programs in the late 1960s paled in comparison to the crisis over *Humanae Vitae*. At times Cardinal O'Boyle seemed to stand alone. Even the Holy See appeared to distance itself from him in the end. A good pastor, he was usually sensitive to the viewpoint of others, even when it differed from his own, but in this matter he could see no compromise on what he believed was an assault on authentic Church authority. This standoff caused the archdiocese to lose some of its most effective priests. It cost O'Boyle personally a heartache that remained with him for the rest of his life.

Patrick O'Boyle was an attractive human being, modest and humble. He was honestly amazed that the son of a poor steelworker had become a cardinal. To those who knew him well he was a warm gentleman free of any kind of cant. He had little regard for the many honors bestowed on him, but rather took immense satisfaction in carrying out his duties well. His approachability was an attractive feature known to all his colleagues. He never stood on protocol. He had all the dignity he needed to project the Church's authority, but he never lost sight of his own humanity. His foibles were obvious. Often blind to important suggestions from subordinates, he was notorious for making hasty and sometimes ill-conceived decisions. Subordinates need not worry about offending him, but his gruff and sarcastic style, commonplace in New York, tended to upset young Washington priests. Many never came to understand that beneath the harsh exterior lurked a heart full of respect for their priesthood.

Famed Church historian John Tracy Ellis, who knew the cardinal well, concluded that any account of his life would need to present his career in a balance that was weighted toward the positive. Msgr. George Kelly, O'Boyle's ally in the *Humanae Vitae* fight, offered a different judgment. "The O'Boyle type did a hell of a lot for the Church and not much harm." The cardinal himself would have been wary of such judgments. In his later days he never rued the past, never looked back. He believed that many of the changes in his archdiocese during his years in charge were good, especially the increased regard for the needs of the poor and for racial justice. As for others, changes initiated by the council fathers, he would have preferred a slower approach. No one summarized his thought process better than himself. At the time of his retirement he told a reporter, "There have been difficulties, sure, but I can go to bed at night and say I tried my hardest."

Indomitable, loyal, steadfast in the faith, he did his best.

Bibliography

Abbreviations

AAB	Archives of the Archdiocese of Baltimore
AAD	Archives of the Archdiocese of Detroit
AANY	Archives of the Archdiocese of New York
AAW	Archives of the Archdiocese of Washington
ACCANY	Archives of Catholic Charities, Archdiocese of New York
ACUA	Archives of The Catholic University of America
AGU	Archives of Georgetown University
AMIV	Archives of the Mission of the Immaculate Virgin (Mt. Loretto)
AUS	Archives of the University of Scranton
BCR	*Baltimore Catholic Review*
CIR	*Catholic Interracial Review*
CS	*Catholic Standard*
NCWC	National Catholic Welfare Conference
NCCB	National Conference of Catholic Bishops
NCCC	National Council of Catholic Charities
NYT	*New York Times*
Star	*The Washington Star* newspapers (including the *Evening Star* and the *Sunday Star*)
WLA	Washington Lay Association
WP	*Washington Post*
WRS	War Relief Services

Manuscripts and Archival Material

As might be expected, the archives of the Archdiocese of Washington contain the largest concentration of useful documents for an O'Boyle biography. Although there exists only a small collection of personal papers, the records of the various offices and institutions in the archdiocese are rich in letters and notes from a man who was not overly fond of the telephone. Especially important are the files of O'Boyle's chancery. Their usefulness made the laborious task of plowing through a largely unorganized microfilm collection well worthwhile.

The archives of The Catholic University of America are another important source. Among other collections mentioned in the footnotes, the records of the NCWC, including summaries and transcripts of its meetings, as well as the meetings of its administrative board, are especially important for an O'Boyle study. Likewise, the university's collection of the records of the NCCC are important for documenting O'Boyle's role in Catholic Charities, both in New York and during his Washington years. Mention must also be made of the very informative papers of John Tracy Ellis and Paul Furfey in these archives.

O'Boyle's long association with Cardinal Edward Mooney resulted in much correspondence, especially concerning war relief. All this material has been preserved in the Mooney papers in the archives of the Archdiocese of Detroit. Curiously, the well-organized archive of Catholic Relief Services contains little of its World War II history.

The Georgetown University archives are useful for its collection of the papers of Horace McKenna and John Courtney Murray. Its university file also contains correspondence between O'Boyle and various university officials. The District of Columbia Public Library's Washingtoniana Collection also contains useful O'Boyle information. Finally, the Library of Congress and the Family History Center operated by the Church of Jesus Christ of Latter Day Saints contain much important information on O'Boyle's Irish connections and conditions in nineteenth-century Mayo and Sligo.

Interviews

To a great extent this biography depends on interviews. Fortunately, many of the cardinal's close collaborators with vivid memories of their dealings with the man were available for questioning. Many of these interviews were conducted by Father Rory Conley, the Washington archdiocesan historian. His work is especially important, because some of the key figures he questioned were no longer alive when this book was in preparation. Some of those interviewed by Conley submitted to a second and even a third questioning by the author. To a remarkable extent, those interviewed by both historians, a decade apart, offered exactly the same answers and often quoted the cardinal in exactly the same words. Six of the interviews were conducted by others. Msgr. Geno Baroni was questioned by the staff of the archdiocese's Office of Black Catholics. Marilyn Nichols interviewed Father Horace McKenna and William and Mary Buckner. Researchers John O'Brien and Timothy Cleary interviewed Ignatius Henry. Two O'Boyle interviews exist, one (only partially intact) by a group of seminarians from Mount St. Mary's College, in Emmitsburg, Maryland, the other by Msgr. Francis Weber. All the interviews, most in the form of verbatim transcripts but some only summaries of the conversation, are now on file in the archdiocesan archives.

William S. Abell
Personal friend and consultant

Floyd Agostinelli
Chancery official; secretary of the diocesan racial office

Msgr. E. Robert Arthur
Tribunal official, pastor

Msgr. William Awalt
Director, Catholic Youth Organization, pastor

Msgr. Geno Baroni
Civil rights activist, advisor to the cardinal on social justice matters

William Cardinal Baum
NCCB official, later archbishop of Washington

William and Mary C. Buckner
Civil rights activists, members of the Catholic Interracial Council

Msgr. Leo J. Coady
Director of Catholic Charities of the
Archdiocese of Washington

Rev. David J. Conway
Pastor

Dr. Paul Cooke
Educator, civil rights activist

Msgr. Thomas B. Dade
President, Priests' Senate, pastor

Rev. Carl F. Dianda
'Humanae Vitae' dissenter, pastor

Rev. Eamon Dignan
'Humanae Vitae' dissenter, pastor

Archbishop John F. Donoghue
Secretary to the archbishop, chancellor, the
cardinal's housemate on Warren Street

Msgr. Thomas M. Duffy
Pastor

Msgr. John Tracey Ellis
University professor, archdiocesan censor of
books

Msgr. Michael D. Farina
Pastor

Rev. John C. Ford, S.J.
Theologian, advisor to Cardinal O'Boyle

Elizabeth Gerrity
Holy Year (1950) pilgrim

Msgr. James G. Gillen
Director of the Family Life Bureau, pastor

Dr. Louis Gofreddi
The archbishop's surgeon

Archbishop Philip M. Hannan
Chancellor, vicar general, editor of the
'Catholic Standard,' participant in
Vatican Council II

Msgr. Kevin T. Hart
O'Boyle's housemate during his last days on
Warren Street

Ignatius Henry
Principal, Rockford Normal School, County
Sligo, Ireland

Bishop Edward J. Herrmann
Chancellor, auxiliary bishop

Msgr. George Higgins
NCWC official, social justice activist

Pauline J. Jones
Member of the Catholic Interracial Council,
civil rights activist

Rev. George V. Joyce
Chaplain, Friendship House, social justice
activist

Msgr. George Kelly
Author, Archdiocese of New York official

Rev. Raymond B. Kemp
Social justice activist, 'Humanae Vitae'
dissenter, pastor

Walter McArdle
Publisher, friend and consultant to Cardinal
O'Boyle

Rev. Horace McKenna, S.J.
Social justice activist, 'Humanae Vitae'
dissenter, pastor

Anthony, Stephen, and Margaret Muldoon
Cousins of Cardinal O'Boyle

Patrick Cardinal O'Boyle
Archbishop of Washington

Rev. Joseph A. O'Brien
Chaplain, St. Elizabeth's Hospital

Msgr. William F. O'Donnell
Editor, 'Catholic Standard'

George Pavloff
'Humanae Vitae' dissenter

Msgr. W. Louis Quinn
Assistant at St. Matthew's Cathedral, pastor

Linwood Rayford, M.D.
Assistant coroner, District of Columbia

Sister Mary Ann Roe, O.Carm.
Member of the Port Tobacco Carmel

Msgr. Joyce Russell
Pastor

Msgr. Joseph L. Telechea
Assistant pastor, St. Patrick's Church

Joseph Vaghi, Sr.
Architect, advisor to the archbishop

Sister Miriam Andre Williams, C.S.C.
Principal, St. Patrick's Academy

Anne Wolfe
Secretary to Cardinal O'Boyle

Bishop Aloysius Wycislo
War Relief Services official, bishop of Green Bay, Wis.

Newspapers

The author systematically screened the columns of the *New York Times, Washington Star* (including the *Evening Star* and the *Sunday Star*), *Catholic Standard,* and selected years of the *Washington Post* and *Baltimore Catholic Review* for their many articles about and quotations from Cardinal O'Boyle. Useful articles were also found in the *Scranton Times, United Mine Workers Journal,* and *Labor.*

Secondary Materials

Abell, William S., ed. *Patrick Cardinal O'Boyle As His Friends Knew Him.* Washington, D.C.: Privately published, 1986.

Acta et Documenta Concilio Oecumenici Vaticani II. Vatican City, 1960.

Acta Synodalia Sacrosanti Concilii Oecumenici Vaticani II. Vatican City, 1975.

Albergo, Guiseppi, ed., and Joseph A. Komonchak, ed. of English edition. *History of Vatican II.* Maryknoll, N.Y.: Orbis, 1995.

Arlotta, Jack M. "Black Catholics in the Archdiocese of New York and the Church of St. Benedict the Moor." *The Dunwoodie Review* 16 (1992–93): 69–108.

Avella, Steven M. *This Confident Church: Catholic Leadership and Life in Chicago, 1940–1965.* Notre Dame, Ind.: University of Notre Dame Press, 1992.

Beck, John. *Never Before in History: The Story of Scranton.* Northridge, Calif.: Windsor Publications, 1980.

Bernstein, Saul, et al. *The New York School of Social Work, 1898–1941.* New York: Institute of Welfare Research, Community Service Society of New York, 1942.

Branch, Taylor. *Parting the Waters: America in the King Years, 1954–63.* New York: Simon & Schuster, 1988.

Brody, David. *Steelworkers in America: The Nonunion Era.* Cambridge, Mass.: Harvard University Press, 1960.

Brown, Dorothy M., and Elizabeth McKeown. *The Poor Belong to Us: Catholic Charities and American Welfare.* Cambridge, Mass.: Harvard University Press, 1997.

Casey, Marion R. "'From the East Side to the Seaside': Irish Americans on the Move in New York City." In *The New York Irish,* edited by Ronald Bayor and Timothy J. Meagher. Baltimore: Johns Hopkins University Press, 1996.

Coakley, Robert W., and Richard M. Leighton. *Global Logistics and Strategy, 1943–1945.* Washington, D.C.: Government Printing Office, 1968.

4

Cohalan, Florence D. *A Popular History of the Archdiocese of New York.* Yonkers, N.Y.: United States Catholic Historical Society, 1983.

Conley, Rory T. "'All One in Christ': Patrick Cardinal O'Boyle, The Church of Washington and the Struggle for Racial Justice, 1948–73." MA thesis. The Catholic University of America, 1992.

———. "Cardinal O'Boyle and the 1963 March on Washington." *The Catholic Historical Society of Washington Newsletter* (Nov 1993).

Cooney, John. *The American Pope: The Life and Times of Francis Cardinal Spellman.* New York: Times Books, 1984.

Costello, Gerald M. *Without Fear or Favor: George Higgins on the Record.* Mystic, Conn.: Twenty-Third Publications, 1984.

Dahm, Charles W. *Power and Authority in the Catholic Church: Cardinal Cody in Chicago.* Notre Dame, Ind.: University of Notre Dame Press, 1981.

Daniels, Roger. *Coming to America: A History of Immigration and Ethnicity in American Life.* New York: Harper Perennial, 1990.

Diner, Hasia R. *Erin's Daughters in America: Irish Immigrant Women in Nineteenth Century America.* Baltimore: Johns Hopkins University Press, 1983.

Dolan, Jay P. *The Immigrant Church: New York's Irish and German Catholics, 1815–1865.* Notre Dame, Ind.: University of Notre Dame Press, 1983.

Dubofsky, Melvyn. "Organized Labor and the Immigrant in New York City, 1900–1918." *Labor History* 2 (1961): 182–201.

Earley, James B. *Envisioning Faith: The Pictorial History of the Diocese of Scranton.* Devon, Pa.: William T. Cooke Publishing, 1993.

Egan, Eileen. *Catholic Relief Services: The Beginning Years.* New York: Catholic Relief Services, 1988.

Ellis, John T. *Catholic Bishops: A Memoir.* Wilmington, Del.: Michael Glazier, Inc., 1984.

———. "The Catholic University of America, 1927–1979, A Personal Memoir." *Social Thought* 5 (Spring 1979), pp. 35–62.

Erie, Steven P. *Rainbow's End: Irish Americans and the Dilemmas of Urban Machine Politics, 1940–1985.* Berkeley: University of California Press, 1988.

Fitch, John A. *The Steelworkers.* New York: Charities Publication Committee, 1910. Reprinted by University of Pittsburgh Press, 1989.

Fogarty, Gerald. *Patterns of Episcopal Leadership.* New York: Macmillan, 1989.

———. *The Vatican and the American Hierarchy.* Stuttgart, Germany: Anton Heissmann, 1982. Reprinted by Michael Glazier, Inc., 1985.

Foley, Albert S. "The Catholic Church and the Washington Negro." PhD dissertation. University of North Carolina, 1950.

Fordham University School of Sociology and Social Work. *Service Announcement, 1933–34.*

Gallagher, John P. *A Century of History: The Diocese of Scranton: 1868–1968.* Scranton, 1968.

Gannon, Michael V. "Before and After Modernism: The Intellectual Isolation of the American Priest." In *The Catholic Priest in the United States: Historical Investigations.* Collegeville, Minn.: St. John's University Press, 1971.

Garrett, Charles. *The LaGuardia Years: Machine and Reform Politics in New York City.* New Brunswick, N.J.: Rutgers University Press, 1961.

Gentile, Thomas. *The March on Washington, August 23, 1963.* Washington, D.C.: New Day Publications, 1983.

Gilbert, Arthur. *The Vatican Council and the Jews.* Cleveland: The World Publishing Co., 1968.

Green, Constance M. *The Secret City: A History of Race Relations in the Nation's Capital.* Princeton, N.J.: Princeton University Press, 1967.

Grossman, Jonathan. "The Coal Strike of 1902—Turning Point in U.S. Policy." *Monthly Labor Review* (Oct 1975): 21–28.

Hodgson, Godfrey. "The March on Washington: 20 Years After the Dream." *Potomac Magazine, Washington Post,* 1 Jul 1983, 6–14.

Hoehmann, George A. " 'My Eminent Friend of New York,' Francis Cardinal Spellman and the Second Vatican Council." MA thesis. St. Joseph's Seminary, 1992.

Hogan, Peter E. "Archbishop Curley and the Blacks." *The Catholic Historical Society of Washington Newsletter* 4 (Jan–Mar 1990).

Hughes, Sister Virginia. *Through His Eyes: A Memoir of Bishop Thomas Lyons.* Washington, D.C.: Abbeyfeale Press, 1992.

Hunton, George K. *All of Which I Saw; Part of Which I Was: The Autobiography of George K. Hunton.* Garden City, N.Y.: Doubleday & Co., 1967.

James, Theodore, Jr. *The Empire State Building.* New York: Harper & Row, 1975.

Joy, Agnes. "John Mitchell and Religious Leaders of the Period 1900–1910." MA thesis. The Catholic University of America, 1954.

Keiger, Dale. "The Rise and Demise of the American Orphanage." *Johns Hopkins University Magazine,* Apr 1996, 34–40.

Kelly, George A. *The Battle for the American Church.* New York: Doubleday & Co., 1979.

———. *Inside My Father's House.* New York: Doubleday & Co., 1989.

Kelly, Neil A. " 'Orphans and Pigs Fed From the Same Bowl': Catholics and the New York Charities Controversy of 1916." MA thesis. St. Joseph's Seminary, 1991.

Kennedy, Eugene. *The Now and Future Church: The Psychology of Being an American Catholic.* Garden City, N.Y.: Doubleday & Co., 1984.

Kisseloff, Jeff. *You Must Remember This: An Oral History of Manhattan from the 1890s to World War II.* New York: Schocken Books, 1989.

Kupke, Raymond J. "James J. Norris: An American Catholic life." PhD dissertation. The Catholic University of America, 1995.

LaFarge, John. *The Manner is Ordinary.* New York: Harcourt, Brace, 1954.

Lewis, John. *Walking With the Wind: A Memoir of the Movement.* New York: Simon & Schuster, 1998.

Lynch, Thomas. "Above All Things the Truth: John P. Monaghan and the Church of New York." *Dunwoodie Review* 16 (1992–93): 109–65.

MacGregor, Morris J. *The Emergence of a Black Catholic Community: St. Augustine's in Washington.* Washington, D.C.: The Catholic University of America Press, 1999.

———. *A Parish for the Federal City: St. Patrick's in Washington, 1794–1994.* Washington, D.C.: The Catholic University of America Press, 1994.

McAvoy, Thomas T. *Father O'Hara of Notre Dame: The Cardinal-Archbishop of Philadelphia.* Notre Dame, Ind.: University of Notre Dame Press, 1967.

McColgan, Daniel T. *A Century of Charity: The First One Hundred Years of St. Vincent de Paul in the United States.* 2 vols. Milwaukee: Bruce Publications, 1951.

McConnon, Tom. *Angels in Hell's Kitchen.* Garden City, N.Y.: Doubleday & Co., 1959.

McLoughlin, Anne Marie. "The Catholic Guardian Society of the Archdiocese of New York: Its Origin and Development (1902–1945)." MA dissertation. Fordham University, 1947.

McMurray, Gerald R. "Remembering Geno Baroni." *America,* 22 Sep 1984, 145–48.

McNally, Arthur. "Green Pastures in a Black Ghetto." *Sign* 43 (Jan 1966): 18–27.

Meagher, Christopher M. "Dissent: The *Humanae Vitae* Controversy in Washington, D.C." MA thesis. University of Maryland, 1987.

Meier, Elizabeth G. *A History of the New York School of Social Work.* New York: Columbia University Press, 1954.

Monagan, John S. *Horace: Priest of the Poor.* Washington, D.C.: Georgetown University Press, 1985.

Nuesse, C. Joseph. *The Catholic University of America: A Centennial History.* Washington, D.C.: The Catholic University of America Press, 1990.

Nuns of the Port Tobacco Carmel. *Who Remembers Long: A History of the Port Tobacco Carmel.* Washington, D.C.: privately published, 1984.

O'Boyle, Patrick A. "The Dependent Child." *The Catholic Charities Review* 17 (Jan 1933).

———. "Fifty Years of Child Care." *The Catholic Charities Review* 33 (Dec 1949).

———. "Five Decades of Service in Charity." *The Catholic Charities Review* 44 (Oct 1960).

O'Brien, David J. *American Catholics and Social Reform: The New Deal Years.* New York: Oxford University Press, 1968.

Ochs, Stephen J. *Desegregating the Altar: The Josephites and the Struggle for Black Priests, 1871–1960.* Baton Rouge: Louisiana State University Press, 1990.

O'Grady, John. *Catholic Charities in the United States: History and Problems.* Washington, D.C.: National Conference of Catholic Charities, 1930.

O'Rourke, Lawrence M. *Geno: The Life and Mission of Geno Baroni.* New York: Paulist Press, 1991.

Paris, Jenell W. "*Fides* Means Faith: A Catholic Neighborhood House in Lower Northwest Washington, D.C." *Washington History* 11 (Fall/Winter 1999–2000): 24–45.

Pecklers, Keith F. *The Unread Vision: The Liturgical Movement in the United States of America, 1926–1955.* Collegeville, Minn.: Liturgical Press, 1998.

Pelotte, Donald E. *John Courtney Murray: Theologian in Conflict.* New York: Paulist Press, 1976.

Phelan, Craig. *Divided Loyalties: The Public and Private Life of Labor Leader John Mitchell.* Albany: State University of New York Press, 1994.

Reese. Thomas J. *A Flock of Shepherds: The National Conference of Catholic Bishops.* Kansas City, Mo.: Sheed & Ward, 1992.

"Resources and Future of Scranton." *Scranton Board of Trade Journal,* Oct 1915, 14–23.

Rynne, Xavier. *The Fourth Session.* New York: Farrar, Straus and Giroux, 1965.

———. *Letters From Vatican City, Vatican Council II, First Session, Backgrounds and Debates.* New York: Farrar, Straus and Giroux, 1963.

———. *Vatican Council II.* New York: Farrar, Straus and Giroux, 1968.

St. Paul's Church Centennial Jubilee Book. Scranton, 1989.

Scanlan, Arthur J. *St. Joseph's Seminary Dunwoodie, New York, 1896–1921.* New York: The United States Catholic Historical Society, 1922.

Scheips, Paul J. *The Role of Federal Military Forces in Domestic Disturbances, 1945–1992* (Washington: GPO, 2005).

"Scranton Bolt and Nut Company." *Scranton Board of Trade Journal.* Nov 1914.

Shannon, James P. *Reluctant Dissenter.* New York: Crossroads Publications, 1998.

Shea, Sister Mary Margretta. "Patrick Cardinal Hayes and the Catholic Charities in New York City." PhD dissertation. New York University, 1966.

Shehan, Lawrence J. *A Blessing of Years: The Memoirs of Lawrence Cardinal Shehan.* Notre Dame, Ind.: University of Notre Dame Press, 1982.

Shelley, Thomas J. *Dunwoodie: The History of St. Joseph's Seminary Yonkers, New York.* Westminster, Md.: Christian Classics, 1993.

———. *Paul J. Hallinan: First Archbishop of Atlanta.* Wilmington, Del.: Michael Glazier, Inc. 1989.

———. "Slouching Toward the Center: Cardinal Francis Spellman, Archbishop Paul J. Hallinan, and American Catholicism in the 1960s." *Catholic Historian* (Fall 1999).

Spalding, Thomas J. *The Premier See: A History of the Archdiocese of Baltimore, 1789–1989.* Baltimore: Johns Hopkins University Press, 1989.

Stephenoff, Bonnie. "'Papa On Parade': Pennsylvania Coal Miners' Daughters and the Silk Worker Strike of 1913." *Labor's Heritage* (Winter 1996): 4–21.

Tauranac, John. *The Empire State Building: The Making of a Landmark.* New York: Scribner, 1995.

Tentler, Leslie W. *Seasons of Grace: A History of the Catholic Archdiocese of Detroit.* Detroit: Wayne State University Press, 1990.

Tifft, Thomas W. "Toward a More Humane Social Policy: The Work and Influence of Msgr. John O'Grady." PhD dissertation. The Catholic University of America, 1979.

WPA Guide to New York City. New York: Random House, 1932. Reprinted by New Press, 1992.

Weber, Francis J. *Catholic California Essays: Some Historical Reflections.* Los Angeles: Archdiocese of Los Angeles Archives, 1992.

———. *His Eminence of Los Angeles: James Francis Cardinal McIntyre.* 2 vols. Mission Hills, Calif.: St. Francis Historical Society, 1997.

Weingarten, Arthur. *The Sky Is Falling.* New York: Grosset and Dunlap, 1977.

Weiss, Nancy J. *Charles Francis Murphy, 1855–1924: Respectability and Responsibility in Tammany Politics.* Northampton, Mass.: Smith College Press, 1968.

Wilson, Susan. "President Theodore Roosevelt's Role in the Anthracite Coal Strike of 1902." *Labor's Heritage* (Jan 1991): 4–23.

Yarina, Margaret. *Marywood College, the First Seventy-Five Years: A Retrospective.* Scranton, 1990.

Yzermans, Vincent A. *American Participation in the Second Vatican Council.* New York: Sheed & Ward, 1967.

Index

abandoned children, 69–70
Abell, William, 154, 245; birth control controversy and, 343–44, 354
abortion, 390–92, 394. *See also* birth control
academic freedom, 301, 303, 347, 358, 383–85
Academy of Our Lady, 379–80
Action Mass, 278–79, 282
AFL, 15, 115, 217
AFL-CIO, 393
African-Americans: activism among, 198, 215, 218, 334, 378; cemeteries for, 181; children of, 71, 78–79; Church and, 186, 288, 333, 376, 378–80, 395–96, 401; discrimination against, 171–72, 196, 219; education for, 147, 179, 187, 189, 195; Hispanics and, 319–20; migration to Washington D.C. by, 166–68; poverty among, 174, 196, 220–21, 337; riots by, 325–26, 330–334, 373; segregation of, 166–72, 177–78, 182, 189, 325; urban, 174, 376. *See also* integration; race relations; racial justice
aged: care of, 43, 159, 398; home for, 229–31
aggiornamento, 256
Agostinelli, Floyd H., 310, 316, 321–23
Aid to Dependent Children, 68, 70
Aldrich, Winthrop, 85, 88, 94, 102, 104–5
Algeria: war relief for, 93–94
Allied Control Commission, 99
Alter, Karl, 201, 202
Amalgamated Association, 9
American Association of Social Workers, 61
American Council of Voluntary Agencies, 86, 111, 113
American Freedom and Catholic Power (Blanchard), 221
American Jewish Committee, 308
American Jewish Joint Distribution Committee, 113
American Relief for France, 102–3
American Relief for Italy, 103, 105
Amiel, Henri, 94, 102
Annin, Joe, 134
anthracite mining, 7, 10

apostolic delegates, 96–97. *See also* Cicognani, Amleto; Vagnozzi, Egidio
Aquinas, The (magazine), 19
Archbishop John Carroll High School, 146–47, 187
archbishop's appeal, 37–41, 80, 88, 119, 144
Archbishop's Committee on Human Relations (Washington, D.C.), 311–12
Archdiocesan Council of Catholic Nurses (Washington, D.C.), 171
Archdiocesan Office of Urban Affairs (Washington, D.C.), 327–28
Arrowsmith, Michael J., 382
Arthur, E. Robert, 125, 134, 138, 169n. 4, 292; birth control controversy and, 342, 344, 352, 368; on Sacred Liturgy Commission, 276; Vatican honors for, 235
Asia: war relief for, 161, 198, 209
Association of Catholic Trade Unionists, 122
Association of Washington Priests, 338–40, 348–50, 376, 381
Augustinian Fathers, 146
Austria: war relief for, 94, 110, 113
authority: of bishops, 298, 342–43, 373, 377, 402; of the Church, 198, 301, 360, 371–74, 378; O'Boyle's respect for, 165, 228, 245, 255, 272–73, 401–3. *See also* discipline, Church
Awalt, William, 201, 233

Baby Doll (film), 250–51
Ball, William, 337
Ballina (Ireland), 4–5
Baltimore, Archdiocese of, 130–32, 142–44, 150; segregation in, 166, 168, 172
Baltimore Catholic Review (newspaper), 164
Baroni, Geno, 310, 399; civil rights and, 318–22, 324–28, 331–33, 376, 378
Bates, Robert, 129
Baum, William Wakefield, 369, 372, 396, 398
Baumiller, Robert C., 384
Bea, Augustin, 266
Beata, Mother, 241

Begin, Floyd L., 280
Bennett, William, 401
Bernadette, Sister, 159–60
Bernardin, Joseph, 361, 364–65, 370, 398
Bernas, Stephen, 129
Bidault, George, 113
Bird, Robert, 101
birth control, 198, 220–21, 298, 300, 334–72, 390. *See also Humanae Vitae* (Paul VI)
bishops: American, 203, 256–58, 260–61, 263–73, 279–81, 374; authority of, 298, 342–43, 373, 377, 402; Canadian, 362; conservative, 256, 258, 263, 266, 269, 274–75, 278; European, 340, 349, 351, 362, 364; Italian, 257; progressive, 257–58, 260, 266, 275, 373; selection of, 284
Bishops' Commission on Ecumenical Affairs, 290–91
Bishops' Emergency War and Relief Committee, 42, 85–87, 93, 103
Bishops' Relief Campaign for Victims of War, 120
Black Catholic Clergy and Religious of Washington, 379
Black Catholic Lay Caucus, 379, 380, 395–96
blacks. *See* African-Americans
Black United Front, 378
Blake, Eugene Carson, 313–14
Blanchard, Paul, 221
Blessed Martin de Porres Hospice, 170
Blessed Sacrament Church, 377
Blessed Virgin. *See* Virgin Mary
blind: school for, 70, 79
boarding homes, 59, 68. *See also* orphanages/orphans
Board of Education, Brown v., 187–88, 194
Bouchard, Andre, 319, 366
Boyle, Joseph A., 16–18, 20
Bradlee, Benjamin, 388, 390
Bradstreet Company, 16
Brendan, Sister, 241
Briefs, Goetz, 66
Brochbank, James, 55
Brooks, James H., 148–49
Brothers of the Christian Schools, 18
Brown v. Board of Education, 187–88, 194
Buckey, Edward L., 138, 159
Bunche, Ralph, 318
Bureau of Child Guidance, 53
burials, 163
Burke, John E., 78, 105
Burke, Vincent, 294
Byrnes, James F., 114–15
Byron, Joseph, 350, 366–67, 370–71, 381
Cabragh (Ireland), 3
Cafritz, Morris, 230

Cahill, Raymond, 287
Calvert County, Maryland, 189
camps, refugee, 95–96, 110, 112–15, 117
Camp St. Florence, 185
canon law, 130, 153, 301, 349, 367–68
Cappagh National School, 3
Cardinal Gibbons Institute, 189
Cardinal's Appeal, 388
Caritas Verband, 112
Carlo, Nicholas de, 202
Carmelite Sisters for the Aged, 159, 231. *See also* Holy Face Carmelite monastery
Carroll, Anne (cousin), 5
Carroll, Howard, 115
Carroll, John: biography of, 292–93
Carroll, Walter S., 97
Carroll Manor, 159–60, 231
Cartwright, John K., 143, 147, 149–50, 163–64, 206, 243, 249; Joseph McCarthy and, 201; as rector of St. Matthew's Cathedral, 128, 132, 134, 138, 153, 186; on Sacred Liturgy Commission, 276; at Vatican II, 260, 265
Cathedral Latin School, 233
Catholic Biblical Quarterly (journal), 292, 294
Catholic Charities, 33, 90; child and youth programs of, 36, 49, 70–72, 79–80; family services of, 215; fund-raising for, 330, 387–88; housing projects by, 375; international organization of, 212; O'Boyle's work for, 38–68, 82, 97, 117–18, 120–27, 136, 204–5, 402; social reforms by, 51; in Washington, D.C., 138, 156, 159, 172, 183, 185, 206, 330. *See also* childcare institutions; orphanages/orphans
Catholic Church, American, 8, 203, 260–61, 386; authority of, 198, 245, 255, 301, 342–43, 360, 371–74, 378; charitable programs of, 58–59, 61, 213–15, 268, 279, 332; child and youth programs of, 49, 70; discrimination against, 13, 33, 44, 51, 53–54, 219, 221, 401; governance of, 272–73, 284–89; immigrants in, 31–33; O'Boyle as leader of, 304; political influence of, 57–58; racial teachings of, 186–87, 193, 196; renewal of, 198, 227, 255–56, 273–303, 338–40; scholarship in, 21–22, 24–26, 259; social teachings of, 40, 50–51, 56, 167, 199, 206, 214–18, 376; social work by, 50–55, 183–85, 205; unions supported by, 10–12; welfare programs of, 43–47, 380; in World War II, 84–116, 203. *See also individual archdioceses, organizations and parishes*
Catholic Committee for Refugees, 94
Catholic Daughters of America, 62, 224
Catholic Evidence Guild, 171
Catholic Guardian Society, 39, 43, 45–47, 59–61, 82

Catholic Interracial Council: integration and, 171–74, 179, 181–82, 186, 192, 219; Selma march and, 321–22; Washington, D.C. march and, 315–16. *See also* race relations

Catholic Relief Services, 156, 212, 263, 268. *See also* War Relief Services

Catholic Standard (newspaper), 164

Catholic University: birth control controversy and, 335–36, 340–42, 347, 357–58, 370; housing projects by, 328; integration of, 167, 170; O'Boyle as chancellor of, 127, 132, 135, 153, 222, 236, 291, 293–303; social work school at, 61–64

Catholic War Relief, 112, 402. *See also* War Relief Services

Catholic Worker House of Hospitality, 170

Catholic Youth Organization (CYO), 181–82, 233

Cavanagh, William, 36

cemetery workers' strike, 122, 126

Center for Christian Renewal, 356, 376–77

ceremonies, 134–35, 154–56, 243–44, 396–97

charities: government partnership with, 42, 44, 56, 60, 207; integration of, 308; private, 119–20, 207, 212–15, 231. *See also* archbishop's appeal; Cardinal's appeal; Catholic Charities; St. Vincent de Paul Society; voluntary agencies

Charles County, Maryland, 189

Chavez, Cesar, 393

Chelsea district (New York City), 31–32, 51

Chidwick, John P., 26–27

childcare institutions, 42–50, 55–61, 68–70, 81, 213–14, 253, 402; integration of, 78–79; in Washington, D.C., 185. *See also individual institutions*

child labor: abolition of, 11

Child Welfare League of America, 61, 80

Child Welfare Services, 68

Christ Child Society, 129

Church in the Modern World, The (Vatican II), 267–68, 271

church-state relations, 198, 203, 227, 252–54; as Vatican II topic, 260, 264, 270–71; war relief and, 87, 93, 104

Church's Unity Octave, 290, 291

Cicognani, Amleto, 202, 210; as apostolic delegate, 99, 202, 210, 235, 238, 244; O'Boyle's archbishop appointment and, 124–27, 135; race relations and, 172–73, 220; as Vatican secretary of state, 257

Cinderblock O'Boyle, 149, 222, 386

CIO. *See* AFL-CIO

civil rights, 183, 196, 198, 304–34, 401–2; union record on, 147, 215. *See also* integration; race relations

Civil Works Service, 60

clergy: O'Boyle's relations with, 136, 149–54, 237, 245–50, 284–85, 373, 380–85; questioning by, 227–28, 273–74; Vatican honors for, 235–36. *See also* priests

Clergy Advisory Council, 284–85

Coady, Leo J., 128–29, 136, 138–39, 145; Catholic Charities and, 156, 159, 387–88

coal mining, 1, 10

Cody, John, 280, 285, 344

Cohalan, Florence, 165

cold war, 198, 207–8, 244

Coleman, John, 105

colleges: Catholic, 291; integration of, 179. *See also* academic freedom; *and individual colleges and universities*

Collins, Thomas, 238, 240, 399

Columbanus, Saint, 19–20

Commission for Mission Work Among Negroes and Indians, 78

Commission on Seminaries, Studies, and Catholic Schools (Vatican II), 261–62

Committee for Freedom in the Church, 355, 376

Committee of Concerned Canon Lawyers, 367–68

Committee of the Laity, 45

Committee on Community Relations, 324, 327

communism, 66, 107, 198, 200–201, 207–12

Community Chest, 144, 156, 214

"Comparison of Five Child Care Institutions, A" (O'Boyle), 53

Confraternity of Christian Doctrine (CCD), 231–33, 262

Confraternity of Christians and Jews, 290

Confraternity of the Blessed Sacrament, 243

Congregation of Rites, 307

Conley, Rory, 169, 176

Connelly, Joseph, 283

Conroy, Mother Cyril, 17

conscience: bishops' statement on, 360, 364; Church's teachings on, 350; freedom of, 340–41, 343–44, 353–54, 357; O'Boyle's statement on, 347, 351; role of, 348, 355, 362, 367–68, 371

Constitution on the Sacred Liturgy, 258, 264, 275–76

consultors: integration and, 173–75, 180; O'Boyle as, 121; to O'Boyle, 138, 143, 145–46, 228–29, 324

contraception. *See* birth control

Coolaney (Ireland), 3

Corbett, D. Joseph, 232, 237, 249, 398, 399

Corimla South (Ireland), 4

Corrigan, Michael, 24–25, 28; birth control controversy and, 338, 341, 345–46, 349–50, 352, 355, 370–71

Cotter, Joseph, 24

Council of Trent, 267

Cowhig, James: as chancellor, 138, 142, 145, 153; integration and, 178; transfer of, 163–64; Vatican honors for, 235

Cox, Oscar S., 100–101

Coyle, David C., 65

Coyne, Joseph, 276, 284, 340

Cronin, John, 204, 206, 219–20

Crowley, Leo T., 98–102

Crusade of Prayer for World Peace, 244

Cuban missile crisis, 261–62

Cunico, John, 366

curia, 256, 258, 272, 283, 348

Curley, Michael, 125, 130–31, 137, 144, 154, 249

Curran, Charles E., 295–303, 340–41, 347

Curran, John, 10–12

Cushing, Richard: Catholic University conflict and, 298; O'Boyle's friendship with, 201–2, 238; relief work and, 210; Shrine of the Immaculate Conception and, 224; at Vatican II, 267

Czechoslovakia: war relief for, 110

Dade, Thomas B., 181–82, 286

Dalgiewicz, Irene, 94

Daughters of Charity, 101–2

Daughters of the American Revolution (DAR), 209

Davis, James, 260, 379–80

Day, Dorothy, 170

deaneries, 381

Dearden, John, 279–80, 282, 287, 298–99, 332–33; birth control controversy and, 360, 362

debt: O'Boyle's fear of, 148, 229–31, 234

Declaration on Non-Christian Religions (Vatican II), 267, 402

Declaration on Religious Liberty (Vatican II), 269–72, 402

Decq, Louise, 101

Defarrari, Roy J., 63

DeHueck, Dorothy, 170

deicide, 266–67

"Democracy at the Cross-roads" (O'Boyle), 66–67

Democratic Party, 33, 58, 252

dependent children, 43, 45, 59–60, 68, 70, 213–14. *See also* orphanages/orphans

De Valera, Eamon, 139

dialogue, 273–74

Dianda, Carl, 319

Diekmann, Godfrey, 294

disabled people, 43, 232

discipline, Church: O'Boyle's respect for, 21–22, 249, 402–3; updating of, 37, 256–57, 259–60

discrimination, 170, 196, 219–20, 377; causes of, 310–11; fight against, 176, 193, 327, 330, 357, 373, 401; as Vatican II topic, 267–68. *See also* segregation

displaced persons, 110, 112–15, 117–20, 208–10

dissenters, 273–74; on birth control, 335, 341–58, 361–62, 364–70, 395; among laity, 373–80; among priests, 380–85

dock workers, 31–33

doctrine, Church, 300–303; updating of, 256–57, 259–60

Dogmatic Constitution on the Church (Vatican II), 269, 341

domestics, employment as, 5, 15

Donnelly, Joseph, 393

Donoghue, John F., 4n. 5; academic freedom and, 385; birth control controversy and, 352, 368; O'Boyle's friendship with, 125, 237, 242, 305, 396, 398, 399; as vice-chancellor, 286, 288

Donoghue, Thomas J., 126, 398

Doody, William, 55

Dorsey, John, 73

Dougherty, Catherine de Hueck, 183

Dougherty, Emmett, 134

Drexel, Katharine, 78

Driscoll, James, 25–26

Drum, Hugh A., 109

Drumgoole, John C., 69–70

due process: academic, 358; for priests, 349, 362–63

Duffy, Francis P., 25–26, 29

Duffy, Thomas M., 233–34, 248, 350, 399

Dufour, Ray, 343–44, 350

Dunbarton College, 179, 387

Dunn, John J., 38, 39

Dunwoodie (seminary), 22–31

Dupre, Louis, 357

Dwan, Ralph, 319

Dyer, Edward, 25

Eastern Europe: war relief for, 110, 209. *See also individual countries*

Ebony (magazine), 177

Ecclesiastical Review (journal), 294

Eckert, Joseph, 128–29

economic justice, 1, 196, 198, 212, 221, 308, 311, 393; as Vatican II topic, 259

Economic Opportunity Act of 1964, 337

ecumenical council. *See* Vatican II

Ecumenical Training Center, 328

ecumenism, 264, 270, 278–79, 290–91, 312, 327. *See also* inter-faith activities

education: Catholic, 221–22, 231–33, 237, 262–65, 291–303, 385, 392; equal, 313, 325

Egan, Eileen, 88, 94, 112–13
Eisenhower, Dwight D., 156, 209, 219, 225, 252; administration of, 211; during World War II, 110, 114
Elliot, John L., 32
Ellis, John Tracy, 128, 161, 249, 275, 278; biography of Cardinal Gibbons by, 153–54, 292; Catholic University conflict and, 291, 293–94, 295, 298, 300; governance issues and, 284; as historian, 24, 125, 130, 196, 206, 398, 403
Elson, Edward, 210
Emergency Unemployment Relief Committee, 56
Emergency Work Bureau (New York City), 56, 60
Empire State Building, 107–11
employment, 65, 310, 312–14, 324–25. *See also* unemployed, assistance to
encyclicals, social, 216–17, 259, 268, 346, 357, 401. *See also specific encyclicals*
Endicott-Johnson Shoe Company, 102
English, Mass in. *See* vernacular
Episcopal Church, 290–91, 317, 328
Episcopal Committee for Displaced Persons, 208
Ethical Culturists, 32, 37
Eucharistic Congress, 398
Europe: war relief for, 102, 112, 161, 198. *See also individual countries*
evolution: as Vatican II topic, 259
experimentation, liturgical, 248, 264, 272–84, 338–39, 384, 403
extraterrestrial life: as Vatican II topic, 259

Fair Employment Practices Committee, 219
families: planning of, 337, 340; strengthening of, 215, 243
Family Life Bureau, 206, 243
Family Life Movement, 336
Family Rosary Crusade, 154–55
famine, Irish, 3–5, 20
Farina, Michael, 233, 387, 397
Farley, James, 58, 129
Farley, John, 25, 44–45
Farrell, Joseph A., 76
Fauntroy, William, 320, 402
Federal Council of Churches, 115
Federal Emergency Relief Administration, 58
Feeney, Leonard, 259
Felici, Pericle, 266
Fenlon, John, 352
Fenton, Joseph C., 292
Fides House, 170, 185, 380–81
Fitzpatrick, Mallick J., 49, 68–69, 71–72
Flugel, J. C., 52
Fogarty, Gerald, 125–26, 203, 266
Ford, John, 342–44, 384

foster care, 42–43, 45–46, 70. *See also* orphanages/orphans
Foulhioux, Andre, 77
Foundation for Religious Action Against Communism, 210
foundlings, 47–48
Fox, Maurice T., 399
France: war relief for, 101–3, 113, 161
Franciscans. *See* Third Order of St. Francis
Friendship Houses, 129, 183–85
frontier: closing of, 66
fundraising, 37–41, 85, 118, 120, 224, 230–31. *See also* archbishop's appeal; Cardinal's appeal
Furfey, Paul H., 129, 170, 293, 345–46, 371

Gaudium et Spes (Vatican II), 267–68, 271
Gawlina, Joseph, 94
General Theological Seminary, 32
Geneva Convention, 92
Georgetown University, 179, 383–85
German-Americans, 31–32
Germany: war relief for, 93, 110–15, 117
ghettos, Catholic, 32–34, 53, 227, 257
Gibbons, James (Cardinal), 130; biography of, 153–54, 292
Gibbons, James P., 374–75, 377
Giblin, Charles, 81n. 27, 118
Gigot, Francis E., 25–26
Gillen, James, 150, 152, 245; birth control controversy and, 350, 370; CCD and, 232; O'Boyle's friendship with, 237–39, 242, 306, 400
Gingras, George L., 185, 236; civil rights work of, 177–78, 319, 324–25, 331; Office of Urban Renewal and, 309–10
Gleason, Andrew, 129
Goedert, Raymond, 368
Goldberg, Arthur, 147, 231, 307
golf, 123, 161, 201–2, 240
Gonzaga High School, 179
government: birth control and, 336–37, 390–92. *See also* charities; church-state relations; relief work; United States; welfare programs
Grabenstein, Henry, 289
gradualism, 173–75, 179–80, 187–88, 195, 316; problems with, 305, 308, 314, 318, 380
Grady, Thomas J., 225
Great Britain, 99, 101
Great Depression, 42, 46, 51, 55–61, 66
Greater New York Fund, 61
Green, Constance, 168
Griffith, James, 264
Grisez, Germaine, 342–44, 354, 362
"Guidelines for the Teaching of Religion" (O'Boyle/Shehan), 337–38, 340, 360

Guilfoyle, George, 123, 201
Gumbleton, Thomas, 363

Hafey, William J., 150
Haislip, Wade, 225
Hallinan, Paul J.: Catholic University conflict and, 297; vernacular use and, 264, 275, 279–80, 282–83
Hannan, Philip M., 249, 252, 254, 309; Archbishop appointment of, 236; birth control controversy and, 370; Catholic University conflict and, 294, 296–97, 299, 302; as chancellor, 164, 387; fundraising by, 230; integration and, 174–75, 177, 179–80, 192–95, 314, 323–24; O'Boyle's archbishop appointment and, 125–26; real estate knowledge of, 145–46, 149, 229, 334; recruitment of priests by, 150; speechwriting by, 206; Vatican honors for, 235; at Vatican II, 257, 260, 266, 271
Hart, Kevin T., 399, 400
Hart, Luke E., 225
Hart, Mrs. Philip A., 355
Haslinger, Joseph, 366
Hayden Foundation, 80
Hayes, Patrick J., 31, 229, 400; Catholic Charities and, 44–45, 49–50, 55–57, 121; death of, 75–76; orphanages and, 69–73; O'Boyle's work for, 38–40, 63
Heintschel, Donald, 368
Henderson, Malcolm C., 299
Henle, Robert J., 383–85
Herrmann, Edward, 249, 286, 291, 382
Heston, Edward L., 258
Hickey, James A., 400
Higgins, Edward J., 36–37
Higgins, George, 122, 147, 245; Catholic University conflict and, 291, 295, 298, 300–301; civil rights and, 186, 326; dress code and, 248; farmworkers and, 393; hospital drive and, 230; at NCWC, 204, 206; O'Boyle's friendship with, 161; at Vatican II, 257, 260, 266, 271–72; vernacular use and, 280–81
Higgins, William (cousin), 128
high schools: construction of, 127, 143, 221, 229–30, 231; integration of, 147, 172–73, 179–80, 183, 187, 195
Hilldring, John H., 100–101
Hispanics, 319
Hoban, James, 112
Hoban, Michael J., 10–12, 20, 22
Hockwalt, Carroll, 302
Hodur, Francis, 8
Holy Comforter parish, 178
Holy Cross parish, 289

Holy Cross Sisters, 179, 387
Holy Face Carmelite monastery, 397
Holy Face parish, 194, 235
Holy Family parish, 387
Holy Innocents Church, 40–41, 49
Holy Name parades, 154, 243
Holy Name parish, 175, 187
Holy Name Society, 171
Holy Redeemer parish, 175, 179–80
Holy Rosary High School, 73
Holy Rosary parish, 202
Holy Spirit parish, 233
Holy Thursday, 284
Holy Year pilgrimage, 161, 241
homeless: care for, 43, 170, 213
Homeless Child, The (magazine), 69, 72, 74
Home Relief Bureau, 56
Homestead Strike of 1892, 9
Hopkins, Harry, 58–60, 99
Hospital Center Act, 230
hospitals: construction of, 229–30; integration of, 308; segregation in, 181. *See also* Providence Hospital
hours of work, 11, 15
housing projects, 213, 215, 309–13, 320–21, 324–27, 332–34, 374–76
Houston, Mary, 183–84, 319
Howard University, 170
Hudson Guild, 32, 37
Hufnagel, Charles A., 254
Humanae Vitae (Paul VI), 335, 340–46, 350, 352, 355, 365–66; American bishops' position on, 362–64; controversy over, 373, 376–77, 381–82, 395, 398, 403; laity's rejection of, 372; O'Boyle's defense of, 357, 360
Humani Generis (Pius XII), 259
Human Life and Natural Family Planning Foundation, 361
"Human Life in Our Day" (NCCB), 363–67, 370
Human Relations Commission, 310
Hungary: Soviet invasion of, 211

Immaculate Conception parish, 170, 176–78, 180
Immaculate Heart of Mary Church, 192
immigrants, 1, 8, 67, 166, 193; children of, 70; discrimination against, 13, 33, 393, 401; heritage of, 244, 246, 260; laws regarding, 209–11; welfare programs for, 43, 94; working conditions of, 10, 19–21. *See also* parishes, national; *and specific immigrant groups*
"Imperative of Peace, The" (NCCB), 383, 393–94
India: hunger in, 212
indifferentism, 290
influenza epidemic (1918), 29

Institutional Commodity Services (New York City), 80–82, 84, 87, 89–90
Institutional Procurement Service (Philadelphia), 386–87
integration, 147, 167, 170–97, 304–5, 308, 313, 325. *See also* civil rights; race relations; racial justice; Washington, D.C., integration in
Inter-American Catholic Social Action Confederation, 204
inter-faith activities, 210, 290–91, 304, 308, 319–21; housing projects as, 327; race relations as, 309, 311–12, 314; as Vatican II topic, 260, 268. *See also* ecumenism
Intergovernmental Committee on Refugees, 113–14
International Commission on English in the Liturgy, 279
Interreligious Committee on Race Relations, 312, 314, 320–21, 327
Ireland, 2–5, 20, 77, 161, 398; O'Boyle's pride in, 244–45; recruitment of priests from, 150
Irish-Americans, 2–5, 8, 31–33, 83, 152, 397
Isaiah Award, 308
Italian-Americans, 31, 97, 101, 103, 105–6
Italy: war relief for, 93, 96–101, 103, 105–7, 209, 212

Jensen, Elliot, 104–5
Jesuits, 179, 189–92, 235, 284–85; birth control controversy and, 356–57
Jews, 60, 290–91, 305; housing projects by, 328; as Vatican II topic, 266–67, 272; war relief and, 113, 129
John Carroll Society, 155, 243, 252, 254
John Paul II, Pope, 396
Johnson, Hugh, 60
Johnson, Lyndon B., 252, 293, 307, 326, 330, 331
John XXIII, Pope, 256, 259, 262–63, 335
Josephites, 285
Joyce, George V., 181–83

Kaiser, Henry J., 105
Kane, Lawrence, 361
Kavanagh, Michael, 190
Keegan, Robert F.: at Catholic Charities, 39, 43, 45, 48–50, 54–58, 121; death of, 123; health of, 117, 120; O'Boyle's work for, 61–66, 71–72, 75–76, 206
Kelly, George A., 26, 370–71, 403
Kemp, Raymond, 319, 366, 370, 383
Kennedy, Eugene F., 224
Kennedy, Jacqueline, 232
Kennedy, John F., 232, 252, 254–55, 312; administration of, 244, 261–62, 314
Kennedy, Robert F., 232, 314, 317, 375

Kennelly, James C., 349
Kenworthy, Marion E., 51–52
Keough, Francis P., 144, 164
Kerby, William J., 45
Kilmoremoy (Ireland), 4
King, Martin Luther, Jr., 167, 313, 316–18, 320–21, 330–32
Kinney, Edward M.: fundraising by, 118, 120, 224; relief work by, 81–82, 84, 89, 92, 97, 109
Kirchwey, George W., 52
Kirk, Harry J., 157–58
Klonowski, Henry T., 22; as bishop, 202; O'Boyle's friendship with, 19, 52, 128–30, 238, 242
Knights of Columbus, 62, 84, 105, 154, 224–25, 244, 315
Knights of Labor, 9
Knights of St. John, 225
Know-Nothings, 33
Krol, John, 202, 280; birth control controversy and, 344, 360, 363; Catholic University conflict and, 296, 298–99, 303
Küng, Hans, 294
Kuppinger, Eldred, 95

L. B. Smith Brothers, 102
Labor (newspaper), 127
laborers, employment as, 5
labor relations, 32–33, 200–201, 212, 307–8; O'Boyle's involvement in, 121–22, 127, 204, 373, 401; reforms in, 11, 20, 51, 55; as Vatican II topic, 259. *See also* unions
Ladies of Charity, 43–44
Laetare Sunday collections, 85, 120
LaFarge, John, 171–72, 174, 176, 189, 191–92
LaFollette, Robert M., 28
LaGuardia, Fiorello, 48, 55, 108
laity: birth control controversy and, 354–55, 357, 362, 365, 372; charitable work of, 213; Church renewal and, 227–28, 273–74, 287–89; educational work of, 232, 265; O'Boyle's relations with, 136, 154–60, 247, 250–56, 284–85, 373–80, 402; spiritual life of, 243. *See also* dissenters
Landi, Andrew P., 99–100, 103, 263
Lastowski, Lotti and Patrick, 238
Latinos, 328
law: immigration, 209–11; labor, 216; O'Boyle's respect for, 21, 249
Laymen's Retreat League, 243
Lay Women's Association, 243
League of the Sacred Heart, 243
Lee, Porter, 51–52
Legion of Decency, 251
Lehman, Herbert H., 97, 103, 111–12, 129

leisure class, 66
Leo XIII, Pope, 11, 259
Levin, Stephen, 267
Lewis, John, 316–17
Lincoln Hall, 80
Lindeman, Eduard C., 52
Lithuanians: war relief for, 110, 113
Little Flower parish, 289
Little Rock High School, 219
Little Sisters of the Poor, 159
Liturgical Week, 283
liturgy: experimentation with, 248, 264, 272–84, 338–39, 384, 403; reform of, 198, 307; vernacular used in, 262, 279–80
Lombardi, Vince, 240
longshoremen, 31–33
Lord, John Wesley, 290
Low Countries: war relief for, 101
Lowry, Charles, 210
Lt. Joseph P. Kennedy Institute, 232
Ludlow, Samuel, 39, 43
Lumen Gentium (Vatican II), 269, 341
Lyons, Thomas, 401

Mackin High School, 179, 187
Maguire, Edward C., 121
Maloney, Andrew, 123
Maloney, John, 238
Maloney, William F., 189
Malta: war relief for, 93
Manhattan. *See* New York City
Mansfield, Mike, 252
Marchisio, Juvenal, 103, 105
March on Washington for Jobs and Freedom, 313–18, 320
Marin, Isabel, 399
marriage(s): mixed, 162; as Vatican II topic, 259
Marshall, Burke, 314
Martha H. Hall Foundation, 77
Mary. *See* Blessed Virgin
Maryland, southern: integration of, 180, 187–97, 325, 352; parishes in, 131, 235; segregation in, 167, 174, 219, 380
Marywood College, 8, 17
Mass: concelebrated, 266, 268, 284; experimentation with, 277–79; in homes, 282–83; on television, 243; vernacular used in, 262, 264, 277–81
Mathis, Johnny, 252
Mayo, County of (Ireland), 4
Mayo Clinic: O'Boyle's trips to, 106, 118, 123, 241, 271
McArdle, Walter, 247, 388, 390, 399; birth control controversy and, 343–44, 350, 354; O'Boyle's

friendship with, 154, 238, 400; Urban Coalition and, 327
McCarran-Walter Act, 209
McCarrick, Theodore, 293
McCarthy, Eugene, 356, 362
McCarthy, Joseph R., 201
McCarthy, Shane, 366
McClafferty, John, 214, 219
McCloy, John J., 98–99
McCormack, John W., 154, 208, 225, 230, 238, 252
McCormick, John P.: at Vatican II, 258, 260
McDonald, William J., 294, 296, 299, 301
McEntegart, Bryan J., 45, 50, 54, 128, 130; Catholic University conflict and, 292, 294; O'Boyle's work with, 47–48, 58, 63, 72, 80; Shrine of the Immaculate Conception and, 223; during World War II, 84, 86–88, 90–91
McGowen, Raymond A., 204
McGuire, John, 201
McHugh, Connel, 16–18, 22–23
McHugh, Thomas J., 16–17, 23
McIntyre, James Francis: birth control controversy and, 344, 358, 363; Catholic University conflict and, 294, 299; as chancellor in New York, 71, 75, 80, 117–18, 120–22; death of, 398, 399; episcopal style of, 136, 202; O'Boyle's friendship with, 28–29, 49, 128, 130, 137, 238, 241, 252; race relations and, 220; Spellman and, 126; at Vatican II, 265–66, 274; vernacular use and, 280; during World War II, 88, 91, 108–9
McKenna, Horace, 189–90, 352–53
McManus, P. J., 13
McNamara, John M., 127–28, 132, 135, 137–38, 143, 173, 186–87
McNicholas, John T., 83, 120, 125, 135; NCWC and, 200–201; during World War II, 91, 203
McShain, John, 224
McShane, John, 231
McShea, Joseph, 125
McSorley, Richard T., 189–90
Meany, George, 147, 217–18, 327
media. *See* press
Meekins, V. Paul, 16
Methodist Church, 290, 317
Mexico: Polish refugees in, 94, 115
Meyer, Agnes, 310
Meyer, Albert Gregory, 270
migrant farmworkers, 392–93
Mikoyan, Anastas, 208
Mikulski, Barbara, 319
Mindszenty, Josef, 207
mines, 1, 7, 10–13, 20, 215, 401
Mission Helpers of the Sacred Heart, 232

Mission of the Immaculate Virgin for the Protec-
tion of Homeless and Destitute Children,
68–82, 84, 87, 130
Mitchel, John Purroy, 44
Mitchell, John, 10–12, 32, 55
Mitty, John, 25
Modernism, 25, 256
Mohler, Bruce, 94
Monaghan, John P., 121–22, 150
Montgomery, James F., 388
Montgomery County, Maryland, 142
Mooney, Edward: in NCWC, 200–201, 203;
O'Boyle's archbishop appointment and,
124–26; race relations and, 219–20; during
World War II, 86, 90–91, 93, 98, 102, 104, 106,
114
Moon is Blue, The (film), 250
Moore, Frank, 52
Moore, Paul, 290
Moosic Lake, 1, 23, 241–42, 308
morality: Church's teachings on, 385; decline of,
250–51, 390; legislating of, 226, 251
Mount St. Mary's Seminary, 8, 16–17
Mt. Loretto, 69–82, 84, 87, 130, 167, 308, 398
Mt. Olivet Cemetery Association, 143
Muldoon, Annie (aunt), 15
Muldoon, Anthony (cousin), 4n. 5, 75, 240–41
Muldoon, Anthony (uncle), 5–6, 7, 15
Muldoon, Barbara (aunt), 15
Muldoon, Ellen (cousin), 6
Muldoon, James (uncle), 5–7, 15, 16, 18–19
Muldoon, John (uncle), 5, 9, 15
Muldoon, Margaret (aunt), 15, 306
Muldoon, Margaret (cousin), 4n. 5
Muldoon, Mary (aunt), 128
Muldoon, Mary Carroll (grandmother), 4–5, 15
Muldoon, Patrick (cousin), 7
Muldoon, Patrick (grandfather), 4–5
Muldoon, Patrick (uncle), 5–6, 8–9, 15, 49
Muldoon, Stephen (uncle), 9, 14, 15, 128
Muldoon, Steve (cousin), 75, 240
Murphy, Charles, 55
Murphy, John, 225
Murray, John Courtney: Catholic University con-
flict and, 291, 294–95; at Vatican II, 260, 263,
269–70, 272
music, sacred, 277–78

National Association for the Advancement of Col-
ored People (NAACP), 185, 330
National Biscuit Company, 32, 37
National Catholic Resettlement Council, 208
National Catholic War Council, 84–85
National Catholic Welfare Conference (NCWC),

56, 82, 114, 132, 200; Community Services
Committee, 199; O'Boyle's involvement in, 161,
257, 259, 261, 263; race relations and, 219–20;
relief work by, 208–12; reorganization of, 269,
279; Shrine of the Immaculate Conception
and, 199, 223; Social Action Department,
203–4, 206, 211, 215–17, 219, 221; during World
War II, 85–88, 90–91, 96, 113, 115. *See also* Na-
tional Conference of Catholic Bishops
National Committee on Segregation in the Na-
tion's Capital, 169, 176
National Conference of Catholic Bishops
(NCCB), 199, 279, 282–83, 393; birth control
controversy and, 360, 367; Catholic University
conflict and, 302; O'Boyle's work for, 305
National Conference of Catholic Charities
(NCCC), 52, 57, 61–67, 70, 80, 132, 204–6
National Conference of Christians and Jews, 330
National Council of Churches, 327
National Federation of Priests Councils, 284, 287,
339, 349, 354, 367
National Home Visit Day, 320
National Liturgical Conference, 275, 281–83
National Medical Association Foundation, 332
National Office for Black Catholics, 379
National Resettlement Conference, 209
National Theatre, 182
National War Fund, 85–88, 91, 93, 96, 102–4, 110,
112, 119
neglected children, 45, 70
Nelligan, Joseph M., 138, 142
Netherlands, the: war relief for, 104
New Deal, 33, 42, 56, 58
Newell, Philip, 319
Newman Centers, 262
New York City, 21, 31–33, 44; Subcommittee for
the Working Boy, 60; welfare programs in, 56,
60–61, 76, 79–80
New York City, Archdiocese of, 21, 23–24, 75;
charitable programs of, 42–45, 54, 156, 290; in-
stitutional buying in, 80–82; O'Boyle's experi-
ence in, 136–37, 145, 151–52, 162, 164–65, 402
New York Foundling Hospital, 47–48, 55
New York Review (magazine), 25
New York School of Social Work, 50–55, 402
New York State: Conference on Social Work, 61;
Temporary Emergency Relief Administration,
60; welfare programs of, 42, 44, 55–56
Nicholas of Myra, 307n. 6
Nixon, Richard M., 334
Nocturnal Adoration Society, 155, 243
Noll, John F., 223
Norris, James, 71, 74, 77, 146, 263, 399
North Africa: war relief for, 93–94

Notre Dame de Namur sisters, 232
nuclear arms: as Vatican II topic, 271–72

O'Boyle, Bernard (cousin), 75, 128
O'Boyle, Margaret (aunt), 3
O'Boyle, Mary (sister), 6
O'Boyle, Mary McHugh (grandmother), 3
O'Boyle, Mary Muldoon (mother), 4–6, 13–17, 31, 34, 49, 128
O'Boyle, Michael (father), 2–6, 8–9, 11, 12n. 22, 15
O'Boyle, Michael (grandfather), 3
O'Boyle, Neil (uncle), 3, 4n. 5
O'Boyle, Patrick (uncle), 3
O'Boyle, Patrick Aloysius: anniversaries of, 369, 395; archbishop appointment of, 123–29, 131, 134–35; awards for, 115–16, 308, 330; birth of, 1; brusque behavior of, 51, 141, 151–52, 236–37, 351–52, 362–63, 398; cardinal elevation of, 304–8; childhood of, 6–16, 20; death of, 400; as debater, 19, 27, 52; education of, 16–41, 50–54; financial ability of, 149, 228–30, 234; friendships of, 201–2, 237–38, 241; health of, 106, 118, 123, 240–41, 396, 400; kindness of, 152–53, 250, 365–66, 372; lifestyle of, 140–41, 152–53, 237–45; loyalty of, 40, 122, 126, 163, 165, 255, 277, 343, 369; management style of, 21–22, 35–36, 38–39, 43, 47–49, 57, 79, 82–83, 136–37, 159, 228–29, 386; monsignor elevation of, 79, 106; motto of, 134, 371; ordination of, 31; pastoral experience of, 132, 136, 336, 370–71, 402; personality of, 245–47, 403; political views of, 28, 33, 58, 91, 252–53; retirement of, 373, 395–400; singing ability of, 27–28, 139, 206; social philosophy of, 1, 21, 259, 272, 401; speaking ability of, 139–40, 206; spirituality of, 1, 13, 26, 151, 222, 226, 242–43; as teacher, 54; theology of, 20–22, 228, 259, 272–73, 275, 353, 373, 401; vocation of, 17, 22; work ethic of, 20–21, 249–50
O'Boyle, Winifred (cousin), 7
O'Connor, Edward M., 89, 112
O'Connor, Martin, 202, 249
O'Donnell, John, 120, 124, 128
O'Donoghue, Joseph, 285
O'Donoghue, T. Joseph, 338–39, 348–51, 355, 370–71
O'Dwyer, William, 97, 100–101, 129
O'Grady, John: fund-raising by, 230–31; at NCCC, 57–65, 123, 143–44, 204–5; O'Boyle's work with, 80, 206; race relations and, 189; urban renewal and, 309; welfare issues and, 213
O'Hara, John, 86
On the Waterfront (film), 31
O'Reilly, James B., 27, 90, 96, 128
orphanages/orphans, 42–45, 47–48, 49, 69–70, 81,

213–14; integration of, 167. *See also individual institutions*
O'Shea, John, 105
Ottaviani, Alfredo, 266, 294
Oussani, Gabriel, 25–27
Oxnam, G. Bromley, 111

Paris (France): O'Boyle's visit to, 161
parishes: black, 167–70, 189, 192–93, 379; councils in, 288–89; establishment of, 143, 145–46, 148–49, 156, 233–34; inner-city, 288; integration of, 173–87, 308; national, 8, 22, 34; O'Boyle's experience in, 132, 136, 336, 370–71, 402; poor, 325; suburban, 288; white, 167–71, 192. *See also individual parishes*
Parks, Katie Muldoon (aunt), 14–15, 19, 75, 128
Parks, Robert (uncle), 128
Parks, Rosa, 304
parochial schools, 392. *See also* education, Catholic
Parsons, Wilfred, 172–73
Pascendi Dominici Gregis (Pius X), 25
pastoral commission (Washington, D.C.), 287–88
Pastoral Constitution on the Church in the Modern World, The (Vatican II), 267–68, 271
Patrick Cardinal O'Boyle As His Friends Knew Him (Abell), 245
Paul VI, Pope, 258, 263–64, 269–70; birth control controversy and, 335–36, 339, 344–45, 367–68, 370, 372; gratitude of, 304–5, 369, 395; Masses concelebrated with, 268, 284, 307; O'Boyle's audiences with, 268, 364; O'Boyle's elevation to cardinal by, 304–5, 307; O'Boyle's support of, 335, 341–43, 347, 351, 372
Pavloff, George, 353–54
peace, 204, 211, 244, 259, 393–94
pensions, 55
People, the, 278–79, 282, 339, 349
Perkins, Frances, 58
Peyton, Patrick, 154
Philadelphia, Archdiocese of, 7–8
Phillip Murray Memorial Foundation, 231
pill, the. *See* birth control
Pius IX, Pope, 7
Pius X, Pope, 25
Pius XI, Pope, 259
Pius XII, Pope, 100, 106, 259; death of, 220; O'Boyle's audiences with, 161; O'Boyle's friendship with, 75; race relations and, 268; vestments of, 128; Washington, D.C. archdiocese and, 124, 131, 259
Poland: communism in, 208; war relief for, 89, 94–95, 102–4, 110, 113, 115
Polish American Council, 94

Polish National Catholic Church, 8
Pontifical Commission of Assistance for Refugees, 97
poor: abortions and, 390–91; care of, 40, 51, 65, 185, 212–13; housing for, 327; O'Boyle's sympathy for, 334, 373, 401, 404; urban renewal and, 309
pornography, 251
Port Tobacco, 396–97
poverty, 32–33, 50, 66–67; abortion as solution to, 390–91; among African-Americans, 174, 196, 220–21, 337; segregation related to, 220–21; war on, 324, 326–27, 330, 332, 334; in Washington, D.C., 141, 168, 215, 319, 331–32, 334, 401
Powderly, Terrence, 9
Presbyterian Church, 328
press: birth control controversy in, 343, 349–50, 354–55, 361, 364, 371; O'Boyle's relations with, 378, 388, 390
priesthood: O'Boyle's respect for, 83, 137, 250, 402–3; O'Boyle's study for, 22–31
priests: assignment of, 285–87, 381–83; black, 379–80; civil rights involvement of, 320–24; dress code for, 152, 247–48, 320, 324, 402; maverick, 8; personnel committee of, 340, 381–82; recruitment of, 149–51, 235; retreats for, 242–43; senate of, 284–88, 330, 339–40, 352, 362, 369, 386. *See also* dissenters
Prince George's County, Maryland, 142
prisoners of war, 87, 92–93, 110, 113
Project Share, 375
Propagation of the Faith, 235
Prosser, Stewart, 56
Protestants, 33, 43, 60, 290–91, 392; civil rights and, 305, 317, 319–20; housing projects of, 327–28; war relief by, 129
Providence Hospital, 143, 181, 229–31
Psychoanalytic Study of the Family (Flugel), 52
public schools, 231–32, 392
Quadragesimo Anno (Pius XI), 216
Quinn, Louis, 139, 277, 289, 350, 352, 377

race relations, 13, 20, 328, 373; inter-faith involvement in, 309, 311–12, 314, 320–21, 327; NCWC paper on, 204, 311; as Vatican II topic, 259, 266–68; in Washington, D.C., 160, 164, 166–97, 311–12. *See also* Catholic Interracial Council; integration
racial justice, 173, 218–21, 304, 317–18, 324, 378; O'Boyle's fight for, 196, 307–11, 366, 401, 404; as Vatican II topic at, 272
Randolph, A. Philip, 313, 317
rationing, 82
Reagan, Ronald, 401

Red Cross, 85–86, 92
Redevelopment Land Agency, 309
Red Mass, 155, 254
Reeb, James, 319
refugees, 87, 89, 92–97, 110–14, 117–20, 203, 209–11
Relief and Construction Act, 59
relief work: government-church partnership in, 85–87, 212; O'Boyle's experience in, 117, 124, 135–36, 198, 210–11. *See also* War Relief Services
religious freedom, 1, 198, 260, 263–64, 292; as Vatican II topic, 269–72
Rendel, Sir George, 113–14
Rerum Novarum (Leo XIII), 11
resettlement, 113–14, 118–19, 209. *See also* displaced persons; refugees
Restorers, the, 396–97
Resurrection City, 330–31
Reuther, Walter, 313
right-to-work laws, 216
riots, racial, 325–26, 330–34, 373
Ritter, Joseph, 181, 270, 294, 324
Roeder, John B., 224, 236–37, 242, 339
Roe v. Wade, 392
Rome: O'Boyle's visits to, 161–62, 241, 344, 398
Roosevelt, Franklin D., 56–59, 99–101
Roosevelt, Theodore, 10–11
Rosenberg, Anna, 60
Rover, Leo A., 154
Rusk, Dean, 260
Russell, John J., 132, 134, 138, 142, 156, 172
Rustin, Bayard, 313, 317
Ryan, Edmond G., 385
Ryan, Edwin J., 23, 25, 29
Ryan, James H., 58, 62–63
Ryken High School, 195

sacraments: vernacular used in, 264
Sacred Congregation for the Clergy, 367
Sacred Heart parish, 179–80
Sacred Hearts of Jesus and Mary parish, 8
Sacred Liturgy Commission, 276
salvation, doctrine of, 259, 267
Sapieha, Adam, 103
Schmitz, Walter: Catholic University conflict and, 294–95, 297, 299, 300; as master of ceremonies, 139, 162, 237, 275, 277; O'Boyle's friendship with, 242
schools: construction of, 145, 231, 233; federal aid for, 326; inner-city, 325; integration of, 167, 172–87, 193–95, 308; parochial, 392; public, 221–22, 392. *See also* colleges; high schools; *and individual schools*

Schwarzman, Harry Patrick, 81–82
Scott, Llewellyn, 170
Scranton, Pennsylvania, 1–2, 6–21, 51, 53, 167, 307–8, 401
Scranton Bolt and Nut Company, 8–9
Scranton Society for the Prevention and Cure of Tuberculosis, 18n.38
seamen: assistance to, 87, 92
Second Vatican Council. *See* Vatican II
secular humanism, 392
segregation, 166–72, 174, 177–78, 182, 189, 219, 325, 377, 380. *See also* discrimination
self-defense, right of, 383, 394
Selma, Alabama: march in, 321–25
seminarians/seminaries, 81, 151, 232–33, 248, 261–62; as Vatican II topic, 268–69
servicemen: assistance to, 84–85
settlement houses, 32, 170
Seymour, Si, 104
Shahan, Thomas, 222
Shannon, James P., 362
Shaw, G. Howard, 172, 176
Sheen, Fulton J., 155, 298
Shehan, Lawrence J., 171–72, 271, 291, 298; birth control controversy and, 337–38, 344, 351, 360; civil rights and, 315, 317
Sheil, Bernard, 111
Shelley, Thomas, 24, 275
Shrier, Philip, 159–60
Shrine of the Immaculate Conception, 149, 199, 222–26
Sicily: war relief for, 97
sick: care of, 43, 213. *See also* hospitals
Singh, Maximus, 273
Sisters of Charity, 47, 230
Sisters of St. Francis of Hastings-on-Hudson, 69, 72, 78
Sisters of the Immaculate Heart of Mary, 7, 17, 128–29, 134
Sligo, County of (Ireland), 3–4
slums, 31, 70, 168
Smith, Al, 33, 39, 54, 55, 58, 207, 251; during World War II, 86, 88, 90
Smyth, Thomas, 143, 146
social justice, 212–18, 307–8, 310–11, 380, 392–94, 401; O'Boyle's fight for, 164; as Vatican II topic, 272. *See also* labor relations; racial justice
Social Security Act, 65, 68
social services, 42, 328, 332. *See also* welfare programs; *and specific organizations*
social work: casework method of, 46, 50–51, 63; O'Boyle's experience with, 50–55, 62–64, 167, 196, 199, 210, 402; profession of, 42–43, 121–22; psychiatric, 50–55

Sodality, 171
Soviet Union, 103, 113, 207, 211, 261–62
Spalding, John Lancaster, 10
Spellman, Francis J., 43, 75–82, 235; Catholic Charities and, 117–18, 120–21; Catholic University conflict and, 298; episcopal style of, 136–37, 165; labor relations and, 122; moral views of, 250–51; NCWC and, 200–201, 205; O'Boyle's archbishop appointment and, 123–26, 128; peace and, 244; race relations and, 220, 323; Shrine of the Immaculate Conception and, 224; at Vatican II, 263–64, 266, 271–72; Vietnam War and, 394; visits from, 238; during World War II, 84, 86, 88–90, 95, 99, 101, 104, 106–7, 109, 114
Spence, John: advice from, 229, 236–37, 286; birth control controversy and, 350, 369; ecumenism and, 291; education and, 138; integration and, 179–80, 187, 191–92, 194; on Sacred Liturgy Commission, 276; Selma march and, 322–23; Vatican honors for, 235
St. Aloysius High School, 73
St. Aloysius parish (Leonardtown, Maryland), 195
St. Aloysius parish (Washington, D.C.), 179
St. Ann's Infant Home, 158–59, 233–34
St. Augustine's parish, 144, 167–68, 170, 177–78, 182
St. Benedict's home, 71, 73, 78
St. Benedict the Moor parish, 175
St. Charles College, 151
St. Columba's parish, 31–40
St. Cyprian's parish, 168, 178
St. Dominic's High School, 187
St. Dominic's parish, 182, 189
St. Gabriel's parish, 186–87
St. George's parish, 235
St. Ignatius parish, 235
St. James' parish, 189–90
St. John's College, 18
St. Joseph Society, 35–36
St. Joseph's parish, 190
St. Joseph's Seminary, 23–31
St. Joseph's Union, 69, 71–72, 74, 77, 79
St. Louis, Missouri: integration in, 181
St. Malachy's Church, 90
St. Martin's parish, 169, 187
St. Mary's County, Maryland, 127, 172, 189–90, 192, 194
St. Mary's High School, 195
St. Mary's parish, 169, 176
St. Matthew's Cathedral, 128, 131–32, 170
St. Michael's parish (Balden, Maryland), 195
St. Michael's parish (Ridge, Maryland), 189–90
St. Nicholas in Prison Church, 307

St. Patrick, 242

St. Patrick's Academy, 169

St. Patrick's Cathedral (New York City), 5

St. Patrick's Cathedral (Washington, D.C.), 131–32, 171–72

St. Paul's Church (Scranton), 7–8

St. Paul's parish (Washington, D.C.), 177–78

St. Peter Claver Center, 183

St. Peter Claver's parish, 189–90, 192, 195

St. Peter's Cathedral (Scranton), 7–8

St. Peter's parish (Waldorf, Maryland), 192

St. Raphael's parish, 233

St. Thomas College, 8, 16–18

St. Vincent de Paul Society, 33, 43, 57, 61; revitalization of, 204–5, 215; in Washington, D.C., 129, 155–58, 178, 185

St. Vincent Home and School, 328

Stassen, Harold E., 113

Statement of Conscience, 335–36, 341–42, 344–45, 347, 349–50, 352, 357, 365–68

steel mills, 7–10, 15, 20, 215, 401

sterilization, 220–21

Stettinius, Edward R., 103

Stritch, Samuel, 125; advice from, 144; NCWC and, 200; Shrine of the Immaculate Conception and, 223–25; during World War II, 86, 88–89, 91, 93, 112, 114–15

Strong Commission, 44, 70

Sts. Paul and Augustine parish, 289, 319

Student Non-Violent Coordinating Committee (SNCC), 316–17

Suhard, Emmanuel Celestin, 101

Sulpicians, 25, 151

Summa Theologiae (Thomas Aquinas), 267

Sursum Corda, 328

Survey of Souls, 231

Swanstrom, Edward E., 128; Catholic Relief Services and, 212, 263; fundraising by, 120; relief work by, 88, 98, 102, 107–11, 117–18

Swiss Catholic Mission, 92

Talley, Alfred J., 77

Tammany Hall, 33, 36, 37, 55, 257

Taylor, Myron C., 99, 103, 129

teenagers. *See* youth

Teletchea, Joseph, 128–29, 139

tenements, 31, 70, 168

Teresa, Mother Angeline, 231

Teresa of the Cross, Mother, 397

textile mills, 7, 15, 20, 215, 401

theology. *See* O'Boyle, Patrick Aloysius, theology of

Third Order of St. Francis, 170–71

Thornton, William A., 34–35, 37–40

Toolen, Thomas J., 321–23

Trinity College, 179

Truman, Harry S., 112, 114–15, 134, 156, 183, 209; administration of, 206

Tully, Grace, 99

Tunisia: war relief for, 93–94

unemployed: assistance to, 56, 59–61

unions, 9–12, 15; O'Boyle's support of, 121–22, 147–48, 215–18, 230–31, 373; poor race relations in, 147, 215. *See also* labor relations

United Farm Workers, 393

United Mine Workers, 10–11, 12n. 22, 15, 127

United National Clothing Collection Committee, 105

United Nations, 115, 211–12; Relief and Rehabilitation Administration (UNRRA), 97–98, 112–14

United States: Army, 98, 100–102, 110, 112, 115; changes in, 255, 362; economy of, 198, 212, 221; government of, 66, 211; Office of Federal Relief and Rehabilitation Operations, 86; State Department, 85, 87, 94, 98, 111–12, 115; Vatican relations with, 200; War Department, 98, 99, 115

United States Catholic Conference, 199, 279, 287

United Textile Workers, 15

United War Work Drive, 85

universities: supervision of, 262. *See also* academic freedom

University of Scranton, 8, 307

Urban Coalition, 327, 332

Urban Rehabilitation Corporation, 327–28, 332, 334, 374, 376

urban renewal, 212, 309, 327–28, 330

Urban Renewal Council, 309

Urban Youth Corps, 310

vacations, 74–75, 161, 162, 241–42, 308

Vagnozzi, Egidio, 278, 305, 369; birth control controversy and, 361; Catholic University conflict and, 294–96, 298, 303; civil rights and, 323; at Vatican II, 263, 266

Vandenberg, Arthur, 114

Vasken I, 291

Vatican: NCWC dealings with, 211; race relations and, 173, 218, 220; U.S. relations with, 200; during World War II, 85, 96. *See also* curia

Vatican Instruction on Church Music, 277–78

Vatican II, 198, 227–28, 241, 256–73, 284, 296; aftermath of, 373, 386–87, 402–4; birth control controversy and, 335, 337, 340–41, 357

Vatican II Study Group, 282, 338. *See also* Association of Washington Priests

vernacular, 262, 264, 277–81

Vietnam War, 330, 334, 393–94

Villa Rosa, 202
Villot, Jean, 367
Virgin Islands, Diocese of, 305
Virgin Mary: O'Boyle's devotion to, 222, 242; pontifical declaration on, 259
voluntary agencies, 85–86, 104, 106, 111–13, 116, 209. *See also* charities
V Street Center, 319–20, 324

Wade, Roe v., 392
wages, fair, 9–11, 15, 31–33, 357
Walk for Freedom, 321–22
Walsh, Mary Elizabeth, 170
Walsh, Mary Margaret, 129
Walton, Clarence C., 302–3
Walton, Mary, 73
war: as Vatican II topic, 259, 271–72
War Relief Control Board, 85–86, 94, 104–5, 110–11
War Relief Services, 42, 84–120, 261, 290. *See also* Catholic Relief Services
Warren, Earl, 187–88
war victims. *See* displaced persons; prisoners of war; refugees
Washington, D.C.: housing projects in, 327–28; integration in, 170–97, 304–5, 308; poverty in, 141, 168, 215, 319, 331–32, 334, 401; riot in, 330–34; segregation in, 166–72, 182, 218, 311; welfare programs in, 311, 313
Washington, D.C., Archdiocese of, 130–32, 142, 274, 304; board of arbitration and conciliation in, 382; charitable programs of, 156; construction projects in, 142–49, 228–34, 255, 276, 332, 375–76, 385–87; as ecclesiastical province, 305; integration of, 170–97, 218, 304–5, 308; O'Boyle's stewardship of, 123–27, 373, 385–86; pastoral commission in, 287–88; reforms in, 338–40, 348, 373–74, 378; relations of, with city, 309–10; segregation in, 166–72, 377; social programs in, 318–21, 325–30, 366, 373–74, 377, 395
Washington, Walter, 253, 327, 331–32, 401
Washington Lay Association, 355, 362, 374, 376–77
Washington Post (newspaper), 388, 390
wealth, distribution of, 66–67
Weber, Francis J., 399
Weigel, George, 371–72
Weigel, Gustav, 294
Weldon, Christopher J., 121, 123

Welfare Council of New York City, 60
welfare programs, 313; federal, 65, 67, 207, 213, 326; government-private partnership in, 57–61, 63, 67–68, 214; state, 55–56. *See also* New York City, welfare programs in; Washington, D.C., welfare programs in
Wendt, William, 319
West Mountain Sanitarium, 18n. 38
Whalen, Charlie, 13
Whalen, John P., 301
White House Conference on Children and Youth, 214
Wilkins, Roy, 313
Wilkinson, James, 194
Williams, Edward Bennett, 240
Wilson, Gladstone, 178
Wolfe, Ann, 399
womb-to-tomb Catholicism, 34, 402. *See also* ghettos, Catholic
women religious, 381; civil rights and, 315–16, 323–24
working class, 66; rights of, 6–12, 19–21, 32–33, 127, 147, 198, 218; urban, 37, 40. *See also* labor relations
workman's compensation, 55
Works Progress Administration (WPA), 60–61
World War I, 29, 105
World War II, 42, 79, 82; aftermath of, 168, 196, 198, 203; relief efforts during, 84–120
Woznicki, Stephen S., 103
Wright, John J., 210, 299, 367–68, 370
Wycislo, Aloysius J., 120, 124, 129, 222, 399; birth control controversy and, 362; Catholic Relief Services and, 212; during World War II, 89, 91, 95–96, 106, 109–10
Wyszynski, Stefan, 208

Xaverian Brothers, 18

Yalta agreement, 113
Yannone, Henry, 305, 307n. 6
YMCA, 92
youth: charitable work of, 213; employment for, 59–61; integration of, 308; O'Boyle's work with, 35–36. *See also* Catholic Youth Organization (CYO)
Yugoslavia: war relief for, 113

Ziminiski, Victor, 105

 Steadfast in the Faith: The Life of Patrick Cardinal O'Boyle was designed and composed in Bulmer by Kachergis Book Design of Pittsboro, North Carolina. It was printed on 60-pound Natural Smooth and bound by Sheridan Books, Inc., of Chelsea, Michigan.